International Management

Managing Across Borders and Cultures

TEXT AND CASES

NINTH EDITION

Helen Deresky

Professor Emerita, State University of New York-Plattsburgh

PEARSON

Boston   Columbus   Indianapolis   New York   San Francisco   Amsterdam
Cape Town   Dubai   London   Madrid   Milan   Munich   Paris   Montréal   Toronto
Delhi   Mexico City   São Paulo   Sydney   Hong Kong   Seoul   Singapore   Taipei   Tokyo

Vice President, Business Publishing: Donna Batista
Editor in Chief: Stephanie Wall
Acquisitions Editor: Kris Ellis-Levy/Emily Tamburri
Program Management Lead: Ashley Santora
Program Manager: Sarah Holle/Denise Weiss
Editorial Assistant: Lauren Russell
Director of Marketing: Maggie Moylan
Senior Marketing Manager: Lenny Ann Raper
Project Management Team Lead: Jeff Holcomb
Project Manager: Meghan DeMaio
Procurement Specialist: Carol Melville

Creative Art Director: Blair Brown
Creative Director: Blair Brown
Interior and Cover Designer: Integra Software
   Services Pvt. Ltd.
Cover Photo: Rawpixel/Shutterstock
Digital Editor: Brian Surette
Composition/Full-Service Project Management:
   Chakira Lane, Integra Software Services Pvt. Ltd.
Printer/Binder: RR Donnelley/Kendallville
Cover Printer: Phoenix Color/Hagerstown
Text Font: Times LT Std 10/12

Credits and acknowledgments borrowed from other sources and reproduced, with permission, in this textbook appear on the appropriate page within text.

Microsoft® and Windows® are registered trademarks of the Microsoft Corporation in the U.S.A. and other countries. Screen shots and icons reprinted with permission from Microsoft and/or its respective suppliers make no representations about the suitability of the information contained in the documents and related graphics published as part of the services for any purpose. All such documents and related graphics are provided as-is, without warranty of any kind. Microsoft and/or its respective suppliers hereby disclaim all warranties and conditions with regard to this information, including all warranties and conditions of merchantability, whether express, implied, or statutory; fitness for a particular purpose; title; and non-infringement. In no event shall Microsoft and/or its respective suppliers be liable for any special, indirect, or consequential damages or any damages whatsoever resulting from loss of use, data, or profits, whether in an action of contract, negligence, or other tortious action, arising out of or in connection with the use or performance of information available from the services.

The documents and related graphics contained herein could include technical inaccuracies or typographical errors. Changes are periodically added to the information herein. Microsoft and/or its respective suppliers may make improvements and/or changes in the product(s) and/or the program(s) described herein at any time. Partial screen shots may be viewed in full within the software version specified.

Microsoft® Windows®, and Microsoft Office® are registered trademarks of the Microsoft Corporation in the United States and other countries. This book is not sponsored or endorsed by or affiliated with the Microsoft Corporation.

Many of the designations by manufacturers and sellers to distinguish their products are claimed as trademarks. Where those designations appear in this book, and the publisher was aware of a trademark claim, the designations have been printed in initial caps or all caps.

Library of Congress Cataloging-in-Publication Data

Names: Deresky, Helen, author.
Title: International management : managing across borders and cultures : text and cases / Helen Deresky.
Description: Ninth edition. | Hoboken : Pearson Higher Education, [2017]
Identifiers: LCCN 2015036084 | ISBN 9780134376042 | ISBN 0134376048
Subjects: LCSH: International business enterprises—Management. | International business enterprises—
   Management—Case studies. | Industrial management.
Classification: LCC HD62.4 .D47 2017 | DDC 658/.049—dc23
LC record available at http://lccn.loc.gov/2015036084

10 9 8 7 6 5 4 3 2 1

ISBN 10:   0-13-437604-8
ISBN 13: 978-0-13-437604-2

To my husband, John, for his love and support, and to my family members, who always inspire me:
John J. and his wife Alyssa: John Rock, Helena, Max
Mark and his wife Sherry: Jacob, Sarah, Rachel
Lara and her husband Thomas: Thomas (TJ), Luke.

Brief Contents

Contents

Preface

NINTH EDITION CHANGES

- Comprehensive cases: Ten of the 11 comprehensive cases are new and current; one is a popular one from the eighth edition. Three of the new cases have won awards: Vodafone in Egypt; Leading Across Cultures at Michelin; Ethical Leadership: Ratan Tata and India's Tata Group. The case selection provides increased coverage of emerging markets and high-technology companies. A range of topics and geographic locations is included as well as the interactive "Ethics Role-Playing" case.

- Integrative section: The new comprehensive case in the Integrative section—"IKEA in Russia: Emerging Market Strategies and Ethical Dilemmas"—is especially informative and challenging because it covers a range of topics from throughout the book. In addition, the popular Integrative Term Project has been retained.

- The feature box called "Under the Lens" has been expanded with a total of 19 boxes. This feature gives an in-depth look at important aspects of the chapter subjects, including, for example, "Nestlé Company Creates Shared Value," "The Global Role of Information Technology (IT)," "Doing Business in Brazil—Language, Culture, Customs, and Etiquette," "Modern Mexico: Reshoring—Location and Young Workforce Prove Attractive," "Communicating Italian Style," "Breaking Down Barriers for Small-Business Exports," "Amazon of India Uses Curry-Carrying Dabawallas to Spice up Parcel Delivery," "Tales from Trailing Husbands," "Women in Business Leadership," and "Interview: Yoshiaki Fujimori: Lixil Builds a New Style of Japanese Multinational."

- Maps added throughout.

- Chapter-opening profiles: There are seven new opening profiles, such as "BMG Signs Distribution Deal with Alibaba," "Social Media Bring Changes to Saudi Arabian Culture," and "TAG Hueur in Smartwatch Alliance with Google and Intel." The rest are updated favorites.

- Chapter-ending cases: There are seven new chapter-ending cases (keeping four favorites, such as, "Kelly's Assignment in Japan"). New examples are, "Foreign Companies in China Under Attack," "Foreign Businesses Tread Carefully as Cuba Opens Up," and "An Australian Manager in an American Company."

- All of the "Comparative Management in Focus" sections have been revised and updated. These provide in-depth comparative applications of chapter topics in a broad range of specific countries or regions.

- All of the "Management in Action" boxes have been replaced or updated; examples consider global cybertheft, Infosys, Target, and emerging markets.

- New coverage of geopolitical developments, such as in Ukraine, and their effects on strategy have been added throughout the ninth edition.

- Updated coverage of developments in globalization and its growing nationalist backlash.

- Expanded coverage on sustainability and creating shared value.

- Expanded and updated coverage of management issues regarding emerging market economies—in particular China, India, Brazil, Africa, and Russia.

- Expanded section on strategies for emerging markets.

- Added and expanded sections on small businesses and strategies for SMEs.

- Expanded sections on e-businesses, on born-global companies, and on strategy models.
- Expanded sections on the role of technology on business planning and operations.
- New sections throughout the chapters on global management teams and virtual teams.
- New research data and examples added throughout.

The ninth edition of *International Management: Managing Across Borders and Cultures* prepares students and practicing managers around the world for careers in a dynamic global environment wherein they will be responsible for effective strategic, organizational, and interpersonal management with a focus on sustainability. Although managing within international and cross-cultural contexts has been the focus of this text since the first edition, the ninth edition portrays the burgeoning level, scope, and complexity of international business facing managers in the twenty-first century. The ninth edition explores how recent developments and trends within a hypercompetitive global arena present managers with challenging situations; it guides the reader in what actions to take and how to develop the skills necessary to design and implement global strategies, to conduct effective cross-national interactions, and to manage daily operations in and with foreign subsidiaries and with global allies and partners. Emphasis is also placed on the considerable cross-border management that takes place among teams—often virtually. Companies of all sizes wishing to operate overseas are faced with varied and dynamic environments in which they must accurately assess the political, legal, technological, competitive, and cultural factors that shape their strategies and operations. The fate of overseas operations depends greatly on the international manager's cultural skills and sensitivity as well as on the ability to carry out the company's strategy within the context of the host country's business practices. Although much of the research has originated in the United States and Europe, we stress that there is no one best way to manage and no cultural behaviors that are viewed as preferred. We take the perspective of managers around the world so that they can learn about and from one another, how to work effectively in cross-national teams, and how to combine best practices for the local environment in which the firm is operating.

In the ninth edition, cross-cultural management and competitive strategy are evaluated in the context of global changes—the pervasive influence of technology, e-business, and social media on business strategy and operations, including on born globals; the eurozone crisis; the increasing trade between the two Americas; the emerging markets and rapidly growing economies in Asia and Africa—that require new management applications; and the challenges posed by the global war for talent. These developments take place in the context and influence of continuing political and economic problems in the eurozone, in ongoing geopolitical and security crises around the world, and in an era of cybertheft—all of which provide threats and opportunities for businesses, their supply chains, and their personnel. Importantly, the ninth edition includes increased emphasis on small- and medium-sized businesses and their strategies. Throughout, the text emphasizes how the variable of culture interacts with other national and international factors to affect managerial processes and behaviors. Concerns about corporate social responsibility (CSR), sustainability, and ethics while operating in global locations are addressed at length.

This textbook is designed for undergraduate and graduate students majoring in international business or general management. Graduate students might be asked to focus more heavily on the comprehensive cases that conclude each part of the book and to complete the term project in greater detail. It is assumed, though not essential, that most students using *International Management: Managing Across Borders and Cultures,* Ninth Edition, will have taken a basic principles of management course. Although this text is primarily intended for business students, it is also useful for practicing managers and for students majoring in other areas, such as political science or international relations, who would benefit from a background in international management.

NINTH EDITION FEATURES

This edition has streamlined text in 11 chapters, with particular focus on global strategic positioning, entry strategies and alliances, effective cross-cultural understanding and management, and developing and retaining an effective global management cadre. It has been revised to reflect current research, current events, and global developments and includes examples of companies around the world from the popular business press. The following section summarizes specific features and changes.

NEW COMPREHENSIVE CASES IN NINTH EDITION

1. Facebook's Internet.org Initiative: Serving the Bottom of the Pyramid? (several countries)
2. An Ethics Role-Playing Case: Stockholders versus Stakeholders (Global/Sri Lanka) (requested favorite from 8ed)
3. Vodafone in Egypt: National Crises and Their Implications for Multinational Corporations (Egypt)
4. Hailing a New Era: Haier in Japan (China/Japan)
5. Alibaba versus Tencent: The Battle for China's M-Commerce Space (China/Global)
6. Business Model and Competitive Strategy of IKEA in India (India)
7. Wal-Mart in Africa (Africa)
8. Fiat Chrysler Automobiles N.V. (2015): From an Alliance to a Cross-Border Merger (Global)
9. Leading Across Cultures at Michelin (France/US)
10. Ethical Leadership: Ratan Tata and India's Tata (India/Global)
11. IKEA in Russia: Emerging Market Strategies and Ethical Dilemmas (Russia)

COVERAGE AND FEATURES BY PART AND CHAPTER

PART I: The Global Manager's Environment

CHAPTER I: ASSESSING THE ENVIRONMENT: POLITICAL, ECONOMIC, LEGAL, TECHNOLOGICAL

New Opening Profile: Western Businesses Scramble to Assess Their Risks in Russia as Geopolitical Tensions Escalate

New Management in Action (MA): "Global Cybertheft of Corporate Secrets an Increasing Risk"

Revised Comparative Management in Focus (CMF): China Loses Its Allure

Updated Box Feature—Under the Lens: The Global Role of Information Technology (IT)

Updated Case: Apple's iPhones—Not "Made in America"

Chapter 1 has been revised and updated to reflect developments and events in global business, in particular as it is affected by political developments. In Chapter 1, we introduce trends and developments facing international managers and then expand those topics in the context of the subsequent chapters. For example, we discuss the status of attitudes that suggest a retreat from globalization toward protectionism resulting from economic problems, in particular in the eurozone, as well as from political crises, cybertheft, terrorism, and trade barriers. In addition, we have reorganized the chapter to focus specifically on various aspects of globalization, including some retrenching in the globalization of human capital toward regionalization and nearshoring or reshoring as well as the globalization of information technology. We discuss the effects on global business of the rapidly growing economies of China and India and other developing economies such as Brazil, Russia, Mexico, and those in Africa; the increasing number of maturing and now global companies from those areas; the escalating role of information technology and social media; and the global spread of e-business. In addition, we have added material and focus on small and medium-sized companies here and throughout the book. We follow these trends and their effects on the role of the international manager throughout the book.

CHAPTER 2: MANAGING INTERDEPENDENCE: SOCIAL RESPONSIBILITY, ETHICS, SUSTAINABILITY

New Opening Profile: The Bangladesh Disaster: Can Companies Outsource Responsibility for Workers in Its Supply Chain?

New Under the Lens: Nestlé Company Creates Shared Value Globally

Revised CMF: Doing Business in China: CSR and the Human Rights Challenge

New Under the Lens: Rolls-Royce Accused of Bribery to Obtain $100m Petrobras Contract

Under the Lens: BP's Sustainability Systems Under Fire

MA: TerraCycle—Social Entrepreneurship Goes Global

New End Case: Levi Looks to Cut Its Cloth Differently by Rewarding Responsible Suppliers

Chapter 2, as indicated by the title, takes a long-term view of the company's global stakeholders and its strategy. It includes an expanded section on sustainability strategies, including a new model and feature on Nestlé's leadership in sustainability by creating shared value. The chapter is updated throughout, with new examples, and has a new section on ethics in uses of technology as well as coverage of China's clampdown on social media. In addition, the Corruption Perception Index has been updated and its results discussed.

PART 2: The Cultural Context of Global Management

CHAPTER 3: UNDERSTANDING THE ROLE OF CULTURE

New Opening Profile: Social Media Bring Changes to Saudi Arabian Culture

Under the Lens: Religion and the Workplace

New MA: Google's Street View Makes Friends in Japan but Clashes with European Culture

CMF: Expanded Profiles in Culture: Japan, Germany, Latin America

Under the Lens: Doing Business in Brazil—Language, Customs, Culture, and Etiquette

New End Case: An Australian Manager in an American Company

Chapter 3 examines the pervasive effect of culture on the manager's role. It includes a new section, "Consequence or Cause?"; expanded coverage of culture's effects on management; increased emphasis on CQ (cultural quotient); and new coverage of the connection between social media and culture. In particular, this chapter presents ways for managers around the world to anticipate, understand, and therefore adjust to working with people in other countries; those ways include understanding the variables of culture through research and recognizing how to develop a descriptive basis for a cultural profile. Several countries are represented, including an in-depth look at Brazil.

CHAPTER 4: COMMUNICATING ACROSS CULTURES

Updated Opening Profile: The Impact of Social Media on Global Business

Under the Lens: Communicating in India—Language, Culture, Customs, and Etiquette

New Under the Lens: Communicating Italian Style

Under the Lens: How Feng Shui Affects Business

MA: Oriental Poker Face: Eastern Deception or Western Inscrutability?

CMF: Communicating with Arabs

End Case: Miscommunications with a Brazilian Auto Parts Manufacturer

Chapter 4 links culture and communication in its various forms and focuses on how that affects business transactions and how managers should act in other cultural settings. In particular, the section on nonverbal communication has been expanded in the ninth edition, along with the addition of three illustrative "Under the Lens" sections and an in-depth look at communicating with Arabs.

CHAPTER 5: CROSS-CULTURAL NEGOTIATION AND DECISION MAKING

New Opening Profile: Facebook's Continued Negotiations in China

Updated and Expanded CMF—Negotiating with the Chinese

Updated Under the Lens: Negotiations and Decisions to Save the Eurozone System

MA: Target: Frozen Out

CMF: Decision Making in Japanese Companies

New End Case: Search Engines Aid Decision Making and Negotiation

Chapter 5 continues the link among the variables of culture, communication, negotiation, and decision making—they are all intertwined. New examples, features, and cases are introduced to explain and illustrate the effects on the manager's role. A new section focuses on negotiating teams, and the feature on "Negotiating with the Chinese" has been updated and expanded.

PART 3: Formulating and Implementing Strategy for International and Global Operations

CHAPTER 6: FORMULATING STRATEGY

New Opening Profile: Amazon, eBay, and Flipkart Bet Big on India

New CMF: Global Companies Take Advantage of Growth Opportunities in South Africa

New Under the Lens: McDonald's in Russia: A Political Pawn?

New Under the Lens: Modern Mexico: Reshoring—Location and Young Workforce Prove Attractive

Updated and Revised MA: Strategic Planning for Emerging Markets

New End Case: Foreign Businesses Tread Carefully as Cuba Opens Up

Chapter 6 explains the reasons that firms choose to do business abroad and the various means for them to do so. The steps in developing those strategies, for firms of all sizes, are examined along with the explanatory models and the pros and cons of those options, including the move toward reshoring and nearshoring. The ninth edition expands on e-business and born globals and includes an expanded, revised section on strategic planning for emerging markets, including an extensive discussion of a study of 247 executives by Deloitte Review regarding their strategies in emerging markets. Data and charts on global Internet usage and global services are updated. Discussion of cultural distance relative to strategic planning has been added. Throughout, there are new features and updated examples focusing, among others, on Cuba, South Africa, Mexico, and the political effects on McDonald's in Russia.

CHAPTER 7: IMPLEMENTING STRATEGY: STRATEGIC ALLIANCES, SMALL BUSINESSES, EMERGING ECONOMY FIRMS

New Opening Profile: TAG Hueur in Smartwatch Alliance with Google and Intel

Updated and Revised CMF: Joint Ventures in the Russian Federation

Under the Lens: Breaking Down Barriers for Small-Business Exports

Under the Lens: Global Supply Chain Risks—The Japanese Disaster

New MA: Infosys' Path From Emerging Start-up to EMNE

New End Case: Foreign Companies in China Under Attack

Chapter 7, as indicated by the new title and the new features noted here, includes new sections regarding implementing strategies for small businesses and emerging economy firms as well as expanded coverage of implementing alliances, including those among high-tech firms. New examples and discussion of alliances around the world are included. The revised CMF on IJVs in the Russian Federation reflects the effects of recent geopolitical events. In addition, we discuss new trends regarding labor and supply chain sourcing, which provide further updates on issues facing managers. We expand the discussion on challenges in implementing strategies in emerging markets.

CHAPTER 8: ORGANIZATION STRUCTURE AND CONTROL SYSTEMS

New Opening Profile: BMG Signs Distribution Deal with Alibaba

New Under the Lens: Amazon of India Uses Curry-Carrying Dabbawallas to Spice Up Parcel Delivery

Updated MA: Procter & Gamble's Think Globally–Act Locally Structure

CMF: Changing Organizational Structures of Emerging Market Companies

Updated Under the Lens: FIFA—Restructuring for Governance Oversight of Ethics

New End Case: HSBC in 2015: Complex Global Operations and Downsizing

Chapter 8 further examines how to implement strategy effectively by setting up appropriate structural and control systems. The ninth edition gives updated text and organizational examples and includes a new section, "Teams as a Global–Local Structure." Included are new features and cases to explain why and how the way the firm organizes must change to reflect strategic change, which in turn responds to competitive and other environmental factors affecting the industry and the firm. Features include e-businesses such as Alibaba and Flipkart. Issues of monitoring, controlling, and evaluating the firm's ongoing performance are discussed. The end case details the radical changes HSBC is undergoing in 2015.

PART 4 : Global Human Resources Management

CHAPTER 9: STAFFING, TRAINING, AND COMPENSATION FOR GLOBAL OPERATIONS

Opening Profile: Staffing Company Operations in Emerging Markets

Under the Lens: Tata's Staffing Challenges in the United States

New Under the Lens: Tales from Trailing Husbands

CMF: Expatriate Performance Management Practices: Samples from Five Countries

Updated MA: Success! Starbucks' Java Style Helps to Recruit, Train, and Retain Local Managers in Beijing

End Case: Kelly's Assignment in Japan

Chapter 9 continues strategy implementation by focusing on the IHRM issues of preparing and placing managers in overseas locations as well as hiring, training, and compensating local managers. The ninth edition includes updated research information and focuses on the "war for talent" around the world, in particular the competition for talent in emerging markets. We have expanded the coverage in the sections under "Managing Expatriates" and about their performance management, and there is a new section, "Global Team Performance Management."

CHAPTER 10: DEVELOPING A GLOBAL MANAGEMENT CADRE

Updated Opening Profile: The Expat Life

Under the Lens: Expatriates' Careers Add to Knowledge Transfer

Expanded and Updated MA: Women in Management Around the World

New Under the Lens: Ford's Bitter Struggle to Close a Plant in Belgium

Under the Lens: Vietnam: The Union Role in Achieving Manufacturing Sustainability and Global Competitiveness

Updated CMF: Labor Relations in Germany

End Case: Expatriate Management at AstraZeneca Plc

Chapter 10 focuses on ways to maximize the long-term value to the firm of its expatriates, maximize the opportunities of its women in management, and effectively manage its knowledge transfer and global management teams and virtual teams. The "Global Management Teams" and "The Role of Women in International Management" sections have been expanded and updated. In addition, this chapter brings new focus to understanding the role of organized labor around the world and its impact on strategy and human resources management. New survey results regarding expatriate retention and the roles of their families are examined, and a new feature examining the role of expatriates' careers in knowledge transfer to the firm is included.

CHAPTER 11: MOTIVATING AND LEADING

Updated Opening Profile: The EU Business Leader—Myth or Reality?

Updated CMF: Motivation in Mexico

Updated Under the Lens: Managing in Russia—Motivation and Leadership Challenges

New Under the Lens: Interview, Yoshiaki Fujimori: Lixil Builds a New Style of Japanese Multinational

New Under the Lens: Women in Business Leadership

Updated MA: Leadership in a Digital World

New End Case: Interview: Carlo D'Asaro Biondo, Google's Europe Strategy Chief in Charm Offensive

Chapter 11 of the ninth edition has been updated with new examples and research. We have updated and expanded the research on motivation and added new sections, "Women in Business Leadership," "Global Team Leadership," and "The Role of Technology in Leadership," as well as a new end case. The chapter focuses on both classical and modern research on motivation and leadership in the global arena; specific attention is paid to global mindset characteristics and behaviors that are typical of successful cross-cultural leaders. Finally, an integrative model is presented that illustrates the complexities of the leader's role in various contextual, stakeholder, and cross-border environments.

Additional Ninth Edition Features

- **Experiential exercises** at the end of each chapter, challenging students on topics such as ethics in decision making, cross-cultural negotiations, and strategic planning.

- **Integrative section** A new case (case 11) incorporates a range of topics and locations covered in the text. The case challenges students to consider the relationships among the topics and steps in this text and to use a systems approach to problem solving for the global manager's role; it also illustrates the complexity of that role.

- **An integrative term project** outlined at the end of the text provides a vehicle for research and application of the course content.

INSTRUCTOR RESOURCES

At the Instructor Resource Center, www.pearsonhighered.com/irc, instructors can easily register to gain access to a variety of instructor resources available with this text in downloadable format. If assistance is needed, our dedicated technical support team is ready to help with the media supplements that accompany this text. Visit http://247.pearsoned.com for answers to frequently asked questions and toll-free user-support phone numbers.

The following supplements are available with this text:

- **Instructor's Resource Manual**
- **Test Bank**
- **TestGen® Computerized Test Bank**
- **PowerPoint Presentation**

ACKNOWLEDGMENTS

The author would like to acknowledge, with thanks, the individuals who made this text possible. For the ninth edition, these people include John Capella, who updated both the Instructor's Manual and the Test Bank, and Susan Leshnower, who updated the PowerPoint slides.

The author would also like to thank the following reviewers from previous editions:

Gary Falcone, Rider University Lawrenceville, NJ
William Wardrope, University of Central Oklahoma, Edmond, OK
Eric Rodriguez, Everest College, Los Angeles, CA
Paul Melendez, University of Arizona, Tucson, AZ
Kathy Wood, University of Tennessee, Knoxville, TN
Daniel Zisk, James Madison University, Harrisonburg, VA
Dinah Payne, University of New Orleans, New Orleans, LA
Marion White, James Madison University, Harrisonburg, VA
Gary Tucker, Northwestern Oklahoma State University, Alva, OK
David Turnspeed, University of South Alabama, Mobile, AL
Lauren Migenes, University of Central Florida, Orlando, FL
Steven Jenner, California State University, Dominguez Hills, CA
Arthur De George, University of Central Florida, Orlando, FL

—*Helen Deresky*

PART

1 The Global Manager's Environment

PART OUTLINE

1 Assessing the Environment
Political, Economic, Legal, Technological

OUTLINE

OBJECTIVES

1-1. To understand the global business environment and how it affects the strategic and operational decisions that managers must make

1-2. To develop an appreciation for the ways in which political and economic factors and changes influence the opportunities that companies face

1-3. To recognize the role of the legal environment in international business

1-4. To review the technological environment around the world and how it affects the international manager's decisions and operations.

Opening Profile: Western Businesses Scramble to Assess Their Risks in Russia as Geopolitical Tensions Escalate[1]

> *You don't want to be a dedicated Russia guy anymore ... I am trying to learn Turkey.*
>
> AMERICAN BANKER WHO LOST HIS JOB IN MOSCOW
> quoted in the *New York Times*, November 6, 2014

> *GM says it will shut Russian plant; wind down Opel brand.*
>
> WWW.NYTIMES.COM
> March 18, 2015

Starting in spring 2014 and through 2015, it was clear that doing business in or with Russia had become unpredictable for most Western businesses and perilous for many. How did it get to this point for companies that had placed large bets and considerable resources on their future in Russia? In March 2014, Russian President Vladimir Putin annexed Crimea—the southern province of Ukraine—after Ukraine's then President Yanukovych rejected the free trade agreement with the EU in November 2013 under pressure from Putin. This led to the pro-Western protests in Ukraine and caused Yanukovych's downfall and escape to Russia. The move was so swift and unexpected that managers around the world who had business in or with Russia and Ukraine scrambled to assess the potential risks to their operations in those areas. Their concern was magnified as increasing sanctions were imposed on Russia by President Obama and Europe. In particular, managers of Western businesses in Russia were afraid that the turmoil would escalate and that their operations there would be subject to retaliatory measures. In Moscow, offices at the American Chamber of Commerce and at the Association of European Businesses were inundated with calls to try to assess their exposure to risks under different scenarios. In addition, for Western multinationals in Russia, in particular European companies such as Renault and Carlsberg, the fear was that sanctions would adversely affect an already weak economy there and so drive down their businesses.

Europe is Russia's largest trading partner, and Germany has great ties to Russia and so was reluctant to go along with sanctions that would backfire on its businesses. About a third of the exports to Russia from the EU come from Germany, in particular from the auto industry. More than 6,000 German companies, employing about 300,000 people in Germany, have business interests in Russia. In addition, Germany gets about a third of its oil and gas from Russia. There seemed to be a rift between businesspeople and the German Chancellor, Angela Merkl, about the approach toward sanctions.

A number of U.S. companies that manufacture in Russia, such as John Deere, were concerned about the risk to their employees and enacted security measures to protect them. Pepsi and McDonald's are among many that have a sizeable presence in Russia and were keeping a careful watch on developments.

Russian firms, too, especially those with joint ventures with European or U.S. companies, were wondering how events might affect them. Some Russian banks, in particular, soon became vulnerable as President Obama passed measures to freeze their assets abroad; these measures also affected any banks in the world that do business with those Russian banks, resulting in the flight of capital out of Russia due to the suspension of assets and travel privileges of people close to President Putin.

As the weeks passed and tensions escalated over sporadic fighting in eastern Ukraine, the United States and the EU stepped up sanctions against select Russian businesspeople and politicians and widened the program to freeze their assets held abroad. As a result, a number of Western companies expressed concern about their sales in Russia and their rising costs of importing supplies for their businesses there. In addition, a threat was growing about a possible backlash in Russia against Western products. Caterpillar, for example, which has been in Russia for longer than 100 years, and McDonald's, with more than 400 restaurants in Russia, both regard Russia as a key market and wondered about the general instability spreading in the region. Putin, meanwhile, was hinting at retaliatory action against Western firms in Russia, in particular energy companies. The general feeling was that it was perilous to do business with or in Russia.

Many of the sanctions were against the energy and technology industries in Russia. The largest source of investment in Russia comes from U.S. firms, in particular technology and financial companies. Those companies felt that further sanctions would result in losing business to firms from other countries who were not being restricted in doing business in Russia. They felt also that business relationships with customers in Russia would be severed for the future, that export sales would decline, and that deals involving transfer of technology would be jeopardized.

Among the European countries, firms in the U.K, for example, were concerned about financial services, and those in France were mostly worried about losing military sales. However, in spite of an estimated $60 billion of capital outflow from Russia in the first quarter of 2014, the conflict continued; the Ukrainian government maintained that Russia continued to support the rebels in Ukraine by sending tanks and other military supplies.

The standoff continued as Ukraine's President Petro Poroshenko signed a trade and political policies pact with the EU on June 27, along with Georgia and Moldova, and extended a cease-fire with Russian separatists. Meanwhile, the EU, with the support of the United States, announced that Russia had 72 hours to settle conflicts in Ukraine or face further sanctions.

In late July 2014, U.S. and European leaders agreed to escalate sanctions dramatically on Russia's financial, energy, and defense sectors, crippling the state banking sector and curbing the ability for Russia to develop new oil resources. These moves followed a global outcry after a civilian airplane, Malaysia Airlines Flight 17, was shot down over Ukraine by suspected pro-Kremlin separatists, killing all 298 people on board. Now there was an abrupt change in attitude from European leaders and company heads. Total, for example, France's oil giant, severely curtailed its stake in its Russian partner Novatek after the air disaster. Quick to retaliate, on August 7, Putin ordered a ban on imports of all beef, pork, fruit, vegetable, and dairy products from the European Union, the United States, Canada, Australia, and Norway. Clearly, the escalating economic warfare and geopolitical tensions were having drastic effects. Firms and farmers in countries such as the Netherlands, Poland, and Lithuania, heavily dependent on agricultural exports to Russia, were severely hurt; many were scrambling to diversify their exports to other regions such as Asia. It was difficult for farmers to understand that geopolitical conflict far removed from them could put them out of business. EU food exports to Russia amount to about $10 billion euro ($13 billion) a year.

In meetings, German Chancellor Angela Merkel made it clear that Russia was no longer considered a reliable partner and that Germany would continue to impose strict sanctions even though they would hurt German businesses, which had spent decades developing ties and opportunities in Russia, but that trust was now lost. Although the German people supported the sanctions, those with small businesses that exported to Russia were hit especially hard, losing more than 20 percent of business in the first half of 2014, and feared losing future opportunities to firms in Asia. Meanwhile, as the lack of Western foods in the stores drove up food prices for the Russian people and the ruble was hit hard, many Russians were questioning Putin's decisions.

As the fighting escalated, the EU announced broader financial penalties on Russia's banks, arms manufacturers, and its biggest oil company, Rosneft, 19.75 percent of which is owned by Britain's BP. Included were increased restrictions to Europe's capital markets, further restricting the ability to raise capital for major oil and defense companies. The Russian economy and the ruble were considerably pressured at this point; in addition, oil prices were falling, inflation was rising, and Western capital markets were estimating that more than $100 billion of capital would flee Russia in the near future. It was apparent that Putin was scaring away both foreign and Russian businesses. Russian Finance Minister Anton Siluanov estimated that Russia was losing $40 billion a year because of the geopolitical sanctions. By March 2015, even Putin's inner circle was showing considerable concern; the ruble had lost about 60 percent of its value against the dollar since the annexation of Crimea. Tourist businesses in London were upset because they were not getting the usual flood of Russian tourists, who could no longer afford to travel abroad. Foreign companies in Russia such as IKEA and Apple raised their prices to make up for the ruble's drop in value, making them unaffordable for the Russians to purchase. In addition, President Putin was trying to bail out the banks by using government reserves, which was perceived as a desperate move. Added to this, the drastic drop in oil prices—a major revenue source—was hitting the Russian economy hard.

In spite of several failed peace agreements, the fighting continued as of March 2015, with the death toll estimated at 6,000, the Russian-controlled zone in the Ukraine continuing to grow, and President Putin pursuing his apparent endgame to gain autonomy for the eastern regions and so deter Ukraine from aligning further with Europe.

Meanwhile, it is the European and U.S. companies that are held hostage in this geopolitical battle. Many firms, such as Carlsberg and Adidas, were blaming Russia for considerable losses in global revenue. Others such as Schlumberger simply withdrew their American and European employees from Russia. All industries seem to have been affected either by the sanctions or by retaliation from Russia. As of March 2015, the 500 firms researched by the consultant firm A. T. Kearney noted that Russia is simply not a viable investment choice due to the continued uncertainty about whether and when the situation in Ukraine would be resolved and the sanctions lifted; however, most planned to increase investments if it is resolved. As of this writing, this appeared doubtful because the Russian economy was predicted to shrink by 6 percent in 2015. Moreover, in

March 2015, GM announced that it is shutting down its plant in St. Petersburg, anticipating a further decline of 24 to 35 percent in sales because the severely depressed value of the ruble meant that people were not buying cars.

How can firms that operate around the world protect themselves against this kind of geopolitical fallout on their businesses? How can they respond in this type of situation? What has happened since this writing?

As evidenced in the opening profile, managers in the twenty-first century are being challenged to operate in an increasingly complex, interdependent, networked, and changing global environment in which such developments can have repercussions around the world almost instantaneously. Clearly, those involved in international and global business have to adjust their strategies and management styles to those kinds of global developments as well as to those regions of the world in which they want to operate, whether directly or through some form of alliance.

Typical challenges that managers face involve politics, cultural differences, global competition, terrorism, technology, and sustainability. In addition, the opportunities and risks of the global marketplace increasingly bring with them the societal obligations of operating in a global community. An example is the dilemma Western drug manufacturers face of how to fulfill their responsibilities to stockholders, acquire capital for research and development (R&D), and protect their patents while also being good global citizens by responding to the cry for free or low-cost drugs for AIDS in poor countries. Managers in those companies are struggling to find ways to balance their social responsibilities, their images, and their competitive strategies.

To compete aggressively, firms must make considerable investments overseas—not only capital investment but also investment in well-trained managers with the skills essential to working effectively in a multicultural environment. In any foreign environment, managers need to handle a set of dynamic and fast-changing variables, including the pervasive variable of culture that affects every facet of daily life. Added to that behavioral "software" are the challenges of the burgeoning use of technological software and the borderless Internet, which are rapidly changing the dynamics of competition and operations.

International management, then, is the process of developing strategies, designing and operating systems, and working with people around the world to ensure sustained competitive advantage. Those management functions are shaped by the prevailing conditions and ongoing developments in the world, as outlined in the following sections.

THE GLOBAL BUSINESS ENVIRONMENT

Following is a summary of some of the global situations and trends that managers need to monitor and incorporate in their strategic and operational planning. We discuss the status of globalization and the debates about its effects on countries, on corporations, on human capital, and on the relationship with information technology (IT). We look briefly at some of the areas in the world in which you might find yourself doing business, with a particular focus on China (see World Map 1 after the chapter, for reference throughout this book).

Globalization

Regionalization and localization are replacing unfettered globalization.

RANA FOROOHAR
TIME, APRIL 7, 2014[2]

.... [W]e've entered a different phase, which I call 'guarded globalization.'

IAN BREMMER, *HARVARD BUSINESS REVIEW*
JANUARY–FEBRUARY 2014[3]

The types of events described in the opening profile illustrate the interdependence of business, politics, trade, and financial links around the world. That interdependence has come to be known as **globalization**—global competition characterized by networks of international linkages comprising economic, financial, political, and social markets that in turn bind countries, institutions, and people in an interdependent global economy; these linkages have resulted in the free movement of goods, people, money, and information across borders. Economic integration results from the lessening of trade barriers and the increased flow of goods and services, capital, labor, and technology around the world. The invisible hand of global competition has been propelled by the phenomenon of an increasingly borderless world, by technological advancements, and by the rise of emerging markets such as China and India—a process that Thomas Friedman called "leveling the playing field" among countries—or the "flattening of the world."[4] That was then, but this is now—and some are now arguing that the world is no longer so flat and that it is reverting more to **deglobalization**. This retreat, or inversion, is resulting from political crises, cybertheft, protectionism, and increasing trade barriers, which, in turn, have resulted from the global trade slowdown.[5] As Bremmer notes in the *Harvard Business Review*, the governments of many developing nations have become increasingly nationalistic in protecting their own industries rather than opening them to foreign companies, in particular multinational corporations (MNCs).[6]

On a strategic level, Ghemawat argues that the business world is in a state of "semi-globalization"—that various metrics show that only 10 to 25 percent of economic activity is truly global. He bases this conviction on his analysis that "most types of economic activity that can be conducted either within or across borders are still quite localized by country."[7] Ghemawat poses that we are in an "unevenly globalized world" and that business opportunities and threats depend on the individual perspective of country, company, and industry.[8] He observes that, as emerging market countries have gained in wealth and power and increasingly call their own shots, a reverse trend of globalization is taking place—evolving fragmentation—which he says is, ironically, a ripple effect of globalization.[9]

Global Trends

Nevertheless, globalization is still here; it is a matter of degree and direction in the future. The rapid development of globalization over the past decades is attributable to many factors, including the burgeoning use of technology and its accompanying uses in international business; political developments that enable cross-border trade agreements; and global competition for the growing numbers of consumers around the world. From studies by Bisson et al. and others, we can also identify five key global trends that provide both challenges and opportunities for companies to incorporate into their strategic planning:[10]

- The changing balance of growth toward emerging markets compared with developed ones, along with the growing number of middle-class consumers in those areas
- The need for increased productivity and consumption in developed countries to stimulate their economies
- The increasing global interconnectivity—technologically and otherwise, as previously discussed—and in particular the phenomenon of an "electronically flattened earth" that gives rise to increased opportunity and fast-developing competition
- The increasing gap between demand and supply of natural resources, in particular to supply developing economies, along with the push for environmental protection
- The challenge facing governments to develop policies for economic growth and financial stability[11]

Globality and Emerging Markets

Half of the global growth now comes from emerging markets.

ROBERT ZOELLICK, PRESIDENT, WORLD BANK
SEPTEMBER 19, 2011[12]

It is clear that globalization—in the broader sense—has led to the narrowing of differences in regional output growth rates, driven largely by increases led by China, India, Brazil, Russia, and South Africa. There is no doubt that the global economic turmoil has curtailed investment, and company executives remained wary of investment in 2015. However, global trade is increasingly including those developing nations judged to have significant growth potential (see Map 1.1, Emerging Economies). In fact, some are saying that MINT is the new BRIC (Brazil, Russia, India, and China),

MAP 1.1 **Emerging Economies**

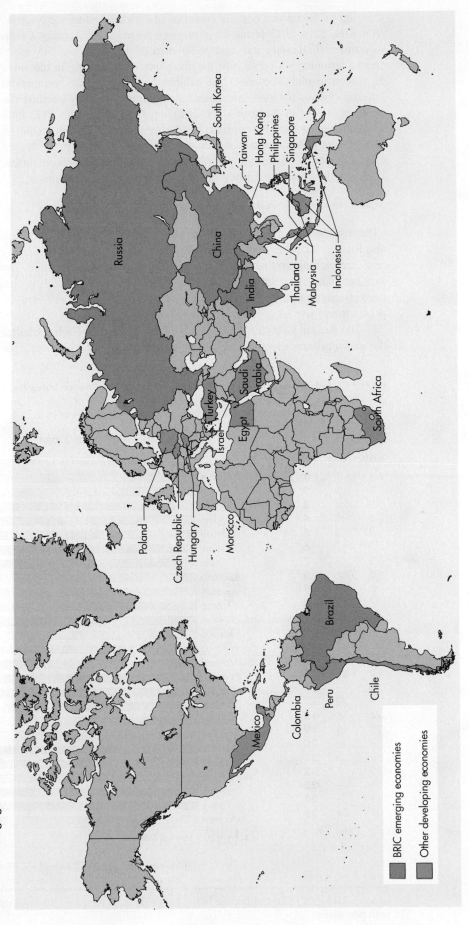

South Korea

Taiwan

Hong Kong

Philippines

Singapore

Russia

China

India

Thailand

Malaysia

Indonesia

Saudi Arabia

Turkey

Israel

Egypt

South Africa

Poland

Czech Republic

Hungary

Morocco

Brazil

Mexico

Colombia

Peru

Chile

■ BRIC emerging economies

■ Other developing economies

referring to the up and coming countries of Mexico, Indonesia, Nigeria, and Turkey. Exhibit 1-1 shows the 2014–2015 results from research by the A. T. Kearney Company of the foreign direct investment (FDI) intentions and preferences of the leaders of 300 top companies in 17 industry sectors spanning six continents; the companies participating in the survey account for more than $2 trillion in global revenue. The exhibit shows the top 25 countries in which those executives have confidence for their investment opportunities. Kearney's results show that the United States continues to be in the lead since 2013, up from fourth in 2012, followed by China, Canada, United Kingdom, and Brazil; India has dropped to seventh from second in two years.[13] Overall, the results show renewed confidence in the economic recovery in the United States and Europe. It is clear also that the phenomenon of rapidly developing economies continues, says Fareed Zakaria, and is something much broader than the much-ballyhooed rise of China or even Asia. Rather, he says:

It is the rise of the rest—the rest of the world.[14]

"The rest," he says, includes countries such as Brazil, Mexico, South Korea, Taiwan, India, China, and Russia. He states that, as traditional industries in the United States continue to decline, "the rest" are picking up those opportunities. Even so, the United States remains dominant in many new age industries such as nanotechnology and biotechnology. It is clear, also, that as emerging markets continue to grow their countries' economies, they will provide growth markets for the products and services of developed economies.

The Boston Consulting Group's (BCG) 2014 list of Global Challengers shows evidence of the growing number of companies from emerging markets: companies that are growing faster

EXHIBIT 1-1 **2014–2015 Foreign Direct Investment Confidence Index Top 25 Targets for FDI**
The main types of FDI are acquisition of a subsidiary or production facility, joint ventures, licensing, and investing in new facilities or expansion of existing facilities.

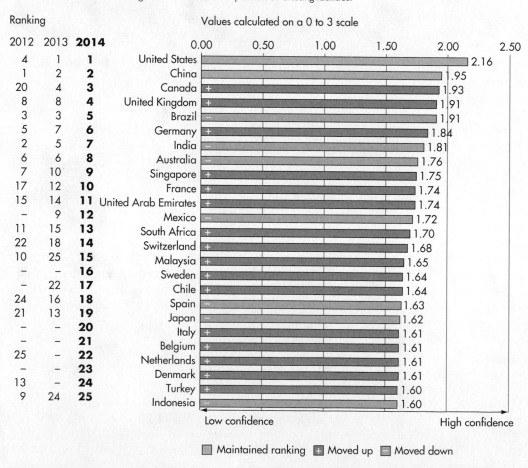

Ranking			Country	Value
2012	**2013**	**2014**		
4	1	**1**	United States	2.16
1	2	**2**	China	1.95
20	4	**3**	Canada	1.93
8	8	**4**	United Kingdom	1.91
3	3	**5**	Brazil	1.91
5	7	**6**	Germany	1.84
2	5	**7**	India	1.81
6	6	**8**	Australia	1.76
7	10	**9**	Singapore	1.75
17	12	**10**	France	1.74
15	14	**11**	United Arab Emirates	1.74
–	9	**12**	Mexico	1.72
11	15	**13**	South Africa	1.70
22	18	**14**	Switzerland	1.68
10	25	**15**	Malaysia	1.65
–	–	**16**	Sweden	1.64
–	22	**17**	Chile	1.64
24	16	**18**	Spain	1.63
21	13	**19**	Japan	1.62
–	–	**20**	Italy	1.61
–	–	**21**	Belgium	1.61
25	–	**22**	Netherlands	1.61
–	–	**23**	Denmark	1.61
13	–	**24**	Turkey	1.60
9	24	**25**	Indonesia	1.60

Values calculated on a 0 to 3 scale

Low confidence — High confidence

■ Maintained ranking ➕ Moved up ⊟ Moved down

than comparable companies are. Although there are relatively fewer from China and India than in previous years, there are more from smaller countries, including five from Thailand, four from Turkey, and three from Chile, which are at all-time highs.[15] Examples of the now more mature emerging giants are, from China, Huwei Technologies, Lenovo Group, and Baosteel; from India, Infosys Technologies, Tata Group, and Bharti Airtel; from Brazil, Embraer and Votorantim Group; from Mexico, Group Bimbo; Gazprom from Russia; and Bumi Resources from Indonesia—to name a few.

> *Simply put: If you're doing business with the biggest companies in the world, you're not just spending time in New York, London, and Hong Kong.*[16]

FORTUNE
JULY 25, 2011

Further evidence that *globalization* is no longer just another word for *Americanization* is the increase in the number of emerging-market companies acquiring established large businesses and brands from the so-called developed countries. For example, in 2008, InBev, a Belgian-Brazilian conglomerate, bought the Budweiser brand, America's favorite beer. Clearly, companies in emerging markets are providing many tangible business opportunities for investment and alliances around the world and establishing themselves as competitors to reckon with. One example of a company enjoying rapid global growth through technology is Alibaba, with Jack Ma, founder and leader.

> *We operate leading online and mobile marketplaces in retail and wholesale trade as well as cloud computing and other services. We provide technology and services to enable consumers, merchants, and other participants to conduct commerce in our ecosystem.*

WWW.ALIBABAGROUP.COM
ACCESSED MARCH 14, 2015

Backlash against Globalization

As we consider the many facets of globalization and how they intertwine, we observe how economic power and shifting opinions and ideals about politics and religion, for example, result in an increasing backlash against globalization and a rekindling of nationalism. Capitalism and open markets, most notably by Western companies, has propelled globalization. Now "economic power is shifting fast to the emerging nations. China and India are replacing the U.S. as the engines of world economic growth."[17]

The rising nationalist tendencies are evident as emerging and developing nations—wielding their economic power in attempted takeovers and inroads around the world—encounter protectionism. There is hostility toward takeovers such as the Indian company Mittal Steel's bid for Europe's largest steel company, Arcelor. In particular, as the demand for energy resources burgeons, we see increased protectionism of those resources around the world as Russia, Venezuela, and Bolivia have privatized their energy resources.

The backlash against globalization comes from those who feel that it benefits advanced industrial nations at the expense of many other countries and the people within them who are not sharing in those benefits. Joseph Stiglitz, a Nobel laureate, for example, argues that such an economic system has been pressed upon many developing countries at the expense of their sovereignty, their well-being, and their environment. Critics point to the growing numbers of people around the world living in poverty.[18] Income inequality has become a major risk factor in the world because so many have limited access to affordable natural resources, services, and products. There is continuing debate about the extent to which globalization has caused income inequality—or at least the realization of it among indigenous people where MNCs operate—or to what extent globalization has furthered the opportunities to people and local areas to improve their lot. This debate is discussed further in Chapter 2. Recently, globalization has also become increasingly unpopular with many in the United States as growth in emerging markets raises prices for energy and commodities and as their jobs are lost overseas, driving down wages.[19]

Although the debate about the effects of globalization continues, it is clear that economic globalization will be advanced by corporations looking to maximize their profits with global efficiencies, by politicians and leaders wishing to advance their countries' economies, and by technological and transportation advances that make firms' production and supply networks more efficient. However, pressure by parties against those trends, as well as the resurgence in nationalism and protectionism, may serve to pull back those advances to a more regional scope in some areas or limit them to bilateral pacts.[20]

In addition, although competition to provide the best and cheapest products to consumers exerts pressure on corporations to maximize efficiencies around the world, there is also increasing pressure and publicity for them to consider the social responsibility of their activities (discussed further in Chapter 2).

Effects of Institutions on Global Trade[21]

Two major groups of institutions (supranational and national) play differing roles in globalization. Supranational institutions such as the World Trade Organization (WTO) and the International Labor Organization (ILO) promote the convergence of how international activities should be conducted. For example, the WTO promotes the lowering of tariffs and a common set of trade rules among its member countries. Similarly, the ILO promotes common standards of how workers should be treated. Although many supranational institutions frequently promote rules or laws favorable to foreign firms (e.g., requiring intellectual property rights protections in China), others have been criticized for infringing on national sovereignty (e.g., challenges to certain environmental laws in the United States).

National institutions, in contrast, play a role in creating favorable conditions for domestic firms and may make it more difficult for foreign firms to compete in those countries. For example, the stringent drug testing rules the U.S. Food and Drug Administration (FDA) require and the anti-dumping rules the U.S. Department of Commerce's International Trade Administration (ITA) enforce act as entry barriers for foreign firms (see Chapter 6 for a more detailed discussion of these entry barriers).

Some supranational institutions represent the interests of a smaller group of countries. For example, the European Commission acts in the interest of the 28 EU members as a whole rather than in the interest of individual member countries. The European Commission is the executive arm of the EU and is responsible for implementing the decisions of the European Parliament and the European Council. Of relevance to international business, the European Commission speaks for the EU at the World Trade Organization and is responsible for negotiating trade agreements on behalf of the EU.[22]

Effects of Globalization on Corporations

In returning to our discussion at the corporate level, we can see that almost all firms around the world are affected to some extent by globalization and, in turn, cause globalization by their activities abroad. Firms that have investment, operations, or marketing activities in several countries are called multinational corporations (MNCs) or multinational enterprises (MNEs). Firms from any country now compete with companies at home and abroad, and domestic competitors are competing on price by outsourcing or offshoring resources and services anywhere in the world. Often it is difficult to tell which competing products or services are of domestic or foreign origin. Examples abound—for example, do you really drive an American car?

> *Look at your vehicle identification number (VIN): If it starts with 1 it is made in America; 2, Canada; 3, Mexico; 4, anywhere else in the world. The only cars allowed to park in a UAW plant are those with VIN numbers beginning with 1 and 2.[23]*

Hondas are made in Ohio; Buicks are made in Germany. In contrast, Japan's Toyota Sienna model is far more American, with 90 percent local components being assembled in Indiana.[24] This didn't happen overnight. Toyota has been investing in North America for 20 years in plants, suppliers, and dealerships as well as in design, testing, and research centers. Toyota became the largest auto manufacturer in the world in sales in 2009.

It would seem that competition has no borders, with most global companies producing and selling more of their global brands and services abroad than domestically. Cisco Systems gets 55 percent of its revenues from overseas, and CEO John Chambers predicted that 70 percent of the firm's growth will come from overseas.[25] Avon, for example, estimates that it employs 5 million sales representatives globally; Nestlé has 50 percent of its sales outside of its home market; Coca-Cola has 80 percent; and Procter & Gamble has 65 percent. The Tata Group, a conglomerate originating in India, has operations in 85 countries and has acquired a number of large firms around the world.

Investment by global companies around the world means that this aspect of globalization benefits developing economies—through the transfer of financial, technological, and managerial resources as well as through the development of local allies that later become self-sufficient and have other operations. Global companies are becoming less tied to specific locations, and their operations and allies are spread around the world as they source and coordinate resources and activities in the most suitable areas and as technology facilitates faster and more flexible interactions and greater efficiencies. In fact, as noted in discussions in the 2012 World Economic Forum, "[I]t is that the world's largest companies are moving beyond governments and countries that they perceive to be inept and anemic. They are operating in a space that is increasingly supranational—disconnected from local concerns and the problems of their home markets."[26]

It is essential, therefore, for managers to look beyond their domestic market. If they do not, they will be even further behind the majority of managers who have already recognized that they must have a global vision for their firms, beginning with preparing themselves with the skills and tools of managing in a global environment. Companies that desire to remain globally competitive and to expand their operations to other countries will have to develop a cadre of top management with experience operating abroad and an understanding of what it takes to do business in other countries and work with people of other cultures. Many large firms around the world are getting to the stage of evolution known as the stateless multinational, when work is sourced wherever it is most efficient; the result of this stage of development is that

[F]or business leaders, building a firm that is seamlessly integrated across time zones and cultures presents daunting obstacles.[27]

Already it is clear that top managers are locating anywhere in the world the firm has operations or is looking for opportunities rather than trying to run the show from a headquarters building in the home country. Jeff Immelt, for example, who is Chairman and CEO of General Electric (GE), calls himself a globalist. GE is clearly a global company—half of GE's 300,000 employees are overseas, and 60 percent of its revenues come from overseas. Petropolis, for example, GE's company town plant in Brazil, has 8,000 employees and is growing at a rate of 35 percent a year compared to one percent in the United States. When Leslie Stahl, in an interview on October 9, 2011, for the CBS program *60 Minutes*, pressured Mr. Immelt about GE's many jobs overseas that could be in the United States, he responded that those plants order components from GE's U.S. plants, and he defended the company's global strategy as being responsible to the shareholders and to grow the company's revenues.

Small and Medium-Sized Enterprises (SMEs)

SMEs are also affected by and, in turn, affect globalization. They play a vital role in contributing to their national economies—through employment, new job creation, development of new products and services, and international operations, typically exporting. The vast majority (about 98 percent) of businesses in developed economies are small and medium-sized enterprises, which are typically referred to as those companies having fewer than 500 employees. Small businesses are rapidly discovering foreign markets. Although many small businesses are affected by globalism only to the extent that they face competing products from abroad, an increasing number of entrepreneurs are being approached by potential offshore customers, thanks to the burgeoning number of trade shows, federal and state export initiatives, and the growing use of websites that ease making contact and placing orders online.[28]

There has never been a better time for SMEs to go global; the Internet is as valid a tool for small companies to find customers and suppliers around the world as it is for large companies. By using the Internet, email, and web-conferencing, small companies can inexpensively contact customers and set up their global businesses.

The Globalization of Human Capital

… [C]ompanies are bringing production closer to home markets ("nearshoring") and sometimes "reshoring" production all the way back home to high-labor-rate countries.

THE BOSTON CONSULTING GROUP
JANUARY 27, 2015[29]

Firms around the world have been offshoring manufacturing jobs to low-cost countries for decades. Firms of all sizes have been and are continuing to produce or assemble parts of their products in many countries, that is, outsourcing by contracting to a local firm and then integrating it into their global supply chains. However, an increasing number of firms are realizing that their cost advantage of producing abroad is disappearing because wages and other manufacturing costs in countries such as China are going up, transportation costs are increasing, the risks involved in complex supply chains are becoming more apparent, and there is continuing pressure to supply jobs at home. In a study by the Boston Consulting Group, 21 percent of U.S. manufacturing firms with more than $1 billion in sales reported that they are actively **reshoring**, and 54 percent said they are considering doing so.[30] Paul Fichter, owner of Taphandles, for example, made a decision in October 2011 to bring back some of its manufacturing to the United States because of the narrowing advantage of producing in China. Taphandles (which manufactures beer taps for breweries) was employing 33 people in Seattle and 450 in China.[31] GE invested $1 billion to move some of its appliance production back to the United States from Mexico and China; and Apple and Google moved some of their electronics production back to the United States from Asia.[32] In addition, hundreds of textile manufacturers, for example, have been diversifying their business to countries such as Cambodia, Vietnam, and Indonesia, where wages are lower than those in China.[33]

But shipping costs do not affect nonmanufacturing jobs, and more and more firms are outsourcing white-collar jobs to India, China, Mexico, and the Philippines. Customer support, medical analysis, technical work, computer programming, form filling, and claims processing—all these jobs can now move around the globe in the same way that farming and factory jobs could move a century ago.[34] We have all experienced talking to someone in India when we call the airlines or a technology support service; now increasingly sophisticated jobs are being outsourced, leaving many people in developed economies worried about job retention. India is experiencing considerable demand for its mobile-app development shops such as for Apple's iPhone and iPad and devices for running Google's Android software.[35]

In Bangalore, India, MNCs such as Intel, Dell, IBM, Yahoo!, and AOL employ workers in chip design, software, call centers, and tax processing. Dell has four call centers in India, where the bulk of its 10,000 employees work, as well as software development and product testing centers. Recently, however, large Indian IT outsourcing companies such as Infosys Limited and the Tata Group were hiring their staff in the United States.

In China—long the world's low-cost manufacturing hub—jobs are on the upswing for back-office support for financial services, telecom, and retail companies in Asia. Such employees communicate with people in Hong Kong and Taiwan in local languages. Whereas backlash from some European and U.S. firms' clients has resulted in repatriating high-end jobs, white-collar job migration is still on the rise for firms around the world, bringing with it a new phase in economic globalization and competition. For global firms, winning the war for talent is one of the most pressing issues, especially because hot labor markets in emerging markets are causing extremely high turnover rates.[36] However, the shift in economic power to the East presents considerable opportunity for companies and economies in the West because of the rising buying power of the 2.5 billion or so people in those developing countries. In addition, firms from China and India, for example, are expanding overseas, bringing their investment and providing jobs, so that

You might just find, for example, that your biggest customers are in Chengdu, not Chicago, or that your boss sits in New Delhi, not New York City. Your paycheck could come in renminbi or rupees instead of in euro or dollars.

TIME
MARCH 28, 2011[37]

FIGURE 1-1 IT allows service jobs to be performed anywhere in the world.

texelart/123RF GB Ltd

The Globalization of Information Technology

Of all the developments propelling global business today, the one that is transforming the international manager's agenda more than any other is the rapid advance in IT. The explosive growth of IT is both a cause and an effect of globalization. The role of IT in international management is discussed later in this chapter, in the section titled "The Technological Environment." Here, the accompanying Management in Action features one of the downsides of technology that some firms are experiencing: global cybertheft.

MANAGEMENT IN ACTION

Global Cybertheft of Corporate Secrets an Increasing Risk [38]

Added to the many risks that businesses have encountered while operating in the global environment is the modern form of industrial espionage through cybertheft, which has become frighteningly common, often hard to detect, and difficult to combat. In May 2014, the U.S. Department of Justice (DOJ) charged five Chinese military personnel of cybertheft. The indictment was accompanied by FBI Wanted photos of those charged with stealing trade secrets and identity theft from U.S. Steel, Alcoa, Westinghouse Electrical, Solar World AG, and United Steelworkers. It was apparent that those companies were targeted because they had been contesting China's trade policies through the World Trade Organization and the Commerce Department. Such digital reprisal has become an increasing risk but a rather surprising one for some of the executives concerned. Foreign companies operating in China almost expect such spying; in fact, protection of intellectual property (IP) is the primary risk of operating there. The Chinese government has been quite transparent about its goal of achieving technological superiority by importing and adapting technologies to its needs. However, this is the first time there have been formal allegations of cybercrimes committed against American companies in the United States, although informal accusations have been made through the press. The Chinese government vehemently denied any such activities.

As examples of the extent of the recent hacking charges, the DOJ accused one of the Chinese hackers of stealing thousands of emails and other files from three senior Solar World executives in 2012. Nuclear power technology was alleged stolen from Westinghouse, which would allow China to take advantage of trade secrets and be more competitive during negotiations. About 3,000 emails were stolen from Alcoa executives, and email messages, which contained sensitive information about attempts to slow down unfairly traded Chinese imports, were stolen from the United Steelworkers labor union. U.S.

(Continued)

Steel had accused China of unfairly dumping below–market priced steel in the United States, which is anticompetitive. During the litigation, one of the hackers allegedly installed malware on the company employees' computers to get inside information about their legal strategy. Consultants said that these are just a few examples of stolen intellectual property and that most large companies have been hacked but either do not know that or do not want that information to be made public. This knowledge is threatening to company executives who try to level the playing field and, certainly, to those who would otherwise likely report such activity.

As the fight over high-tech industrial espionage continues between the United States and China, the DOJ prepared more indictments against Chinese cyberspies. Further allegations were formalized against hackers located in Russia. Although company executives have been aware of such hacking for some time, they are now willing to publicize that information to expose the economic cyberespionage in an attempt to control future damage to their companies.

Although then Attorney General Eric Holder acknowledged that those accused would unlikely be brought to trial because there is no extradition treaty with China, he made it clear that there are costs to pay for stealing trade secrets and harming the interests of U.S. companies.

Regional Trading Blocs

Much of today's world trade takes place within three regional free-trade blocs (Western Europe, Asia, and the Americas). These trade blocs are continually expanding their borders to include neighboring countries, either directly or with separate agreements.

THE EUROPEAN UNION

The European Union (EU) comprises a 28-nation, unified, borderless market of approximately 500 million people, as shown in Map 1.2. Countries around the world trade with the EU countries. Although trade continued to grow in 2010 despite the 2008 global financial crisis, the EU GDP growth was only at 1.8 percent that year, and economic problems in some member states continuing into 2015 were adversely affecting the EU as a whole, resulting in global financial repercussions.

The importance of Germany to the eurozone is clear, but it is also a two-way street. "Germany's prosperity is inextricably linked with the success and survival of the single currency, with more than 38 percent of German exports going to its eurozone partners, and almost 58 percent to the 28 members of the European Union."[39] The strength of the German manufacturing model is evidenced by the fact that, although Germany has about a quarter of the population of the United States, and a quarter of the U.S. GDP (gross domestic product), it exports more than the United States.[40] Germans were concerned, however, that the need to help prop up weaker economies in the eurozone, such as Greece, would dilute their economic strength.

In spite of those problems, the World Economic Forum's 2014–2015 Global Competitiveness Index (GCI) shows that six out of the top ten countries are in Europe (see Table 1–1).[41] The United States' rank rose to third from seventh in two years; interestingly, that corresponds to its rise from fourth to first in two years in the FDI Confidence Index results from the A. T. Kearney research. The GCI is based on 12 pillars of competitiveness that provide attractive conditions and incentives for both local and foreign companies to do business there.[42] However, the elimination of internal tariffs and customs, as well as financial and commercial barriers, has not eliminated national pride. Although most people in Europe are thought of simply as Europeans, they still think of themselves first as British, French, Danish, Italian, and so on, and are wary of giving too much power to centralized institutions or of giving up their national culture. The continuing enlargement of the EU to include many less prosperous countries, such as Croatia in 2013, has also promoted divisions among the older members.[43] In addition, continuing eurozone problems has prompted skepticism of any further enlargement.

Global managers face two major tasks. One is strategic: how firms outside of Europe can deal with the implications of the EU and of what some have called a Fortress Europe—that is, a market giving preference to insiders. Although firms must have a pan-European business

MAP 1.2 European Union

EU members using the euro
EU members using own national currency
Countries not members of the EU
Cities over 1 million
Capitals over 1 million

strategy, they must realize that suitable market entry strategies must be considered on a country-by-country basis.

> *While the European Union continues to move in the direction of a Single Market, the reality today is that U.S. exporters in some sectors continue to face barriers to entry in the EU market. In the world of the Internet and e-commerce, some of these barriers are still pronounced.*[44]

The other task is cultural: how to deal effectively with multiple sets of national cultures, traditions, and customs within Europe such as differing attitudes about how much time should be spent on work versus leisure activities.

TABLE 1-1 2014–2015 Global Competitiveness Index

2014–2015 Rank	Country	2012–2013 Rank
1	Switzerland	1
2	Singapore	2
3	United States	7
4	Finland	3
5	Germany	6
6	Japan	10
7	Hong Kong (SAR)	9
8	Netherlands	5
9	United Kingdom	8
10	Sweden	4

Source: Based on selected data from www.worldeconomicforum.org, accessed March 8, 2015.

ASIA

It would be difficult to overstate the power of the fundamental drivers of Asian growth. First, Asian economies have been enjoying a remarkable period of "productivity catch-up," adopting modern technologies, industrial practices, and ways of organizing—in some cases leapfrogging Western competitors.[45]

Manufacturing, in particular, has propelled Asia's emerging markets, helping to fuel the demand for materials and supplies from the developed world and lending hope for a quick global economic recovery.[46] Japan and the Four Tigers—Singapore, Hong Kong, Taiwan, and South Korea—have provided most of the capital and expertise for Asia's developing countries. Now the focus is on China's role in driving closer integration in the region through its rapidly growing exports. Japan continues to negotiate trade agreements with its neighbors; China is negotiating with the entire thirteen-member Association of Southeast Asian Nations (ASEAN), whereas ASEAN is negotiating for earlier development of its own free trade area, ASEAN Free Trade Area (AFTA).

The Chinese market offers big opportunities for foreign investment, but you must learn to tolerate ambiguity and find a godfather to look after your political connections.[47]

China has enjoyed success as an export powerhouse, a status built on its strengths of low costs and a constant flow of capital. Its tremendous growth, although now slowing, is further discussed in the following feature, "Comparative Management in Focus—China Loses Its Allure."

INDIA

As the world's largest democracy and the third-largest economy, it is clear that there is much opportunity for foreign businesses in India with its population of 1.3 billion and great potential for continued growth. However, with its slow pace of reform and continuing corruption cases, India is losing opportunities to other emerging markets that are more investor friendly. India ranked seventh on the A. T. Kearney 2014–2015 FDI Confidence Index, as shown in Exhibit 1-1; this was down from second in the 2012–2013 Index. Nevertheless, growth for 2015 was estimated at 6.4 percent.[48] In February 2015, India's Prime Minister Narendra Modi laid out a budget to accelerate growth, including a cut in corporate taxes and a pledge of $11.3 billion a year for infrastructure projects.[49]

Whereas China is known as the world's factory, India has become known as the world's services supplier, providing highly skilled and educated workers to foreign companies. India is the world's leader for outsourced back-office services and, increasingly, for high-tech services, with outsourcing firms such as Infosys becoming global giants themselves. India is the fastest-growing free-market democracy, yet its biggest hindrance to growth, in particular for the manufacturing sector, remains its poor infrastructure, with both local and foreign companies

Comparative Management in Focus
China Loses Its Allure[50]

A Slowing China Is Still Seen Leading Global Growth in 2015.

BLOOMBERG BUSINESSWEEK
FEBRUARY 25, 2015[51]

Life is getting tougher for foreign companies. Those that want to stay will have to adjust.

THE ECONOMIST
JANUARY 25, 2014

China's target growth of 7 percent for 2015 was referred to by Premier Li Keqiang as "a new normal."[52] But many doubted that target as China's slowdown hit global companies and markets in late 2015. For China, which, until 2010, had an average growth rate of 10 percent for 30 years, declining since then to 7.3 percent in 2014, this is what is meant by a new normal (compared with an estimated 3.2 percent in 2015 for the United States and United Kingdom). Li admitted that many problems needed to be worked on and declared that "a fixation on growth at all costs has been accompanied by shocking levels of industrial pollution, rampant corruption and disintegration of many social services while exacerbating imbalances in the existing model."[53] However, China is still the fastest growing G20 nation comprising 38 percent of global growth for 2014.[54] It should be noted, however, that there is considerable skepticism about the "official" growth estimates of both China and India, which puts theirs at a similar goal.[55]

China is the second-largest trading partner with the United States, after Canada, and it is the world's second largest recipient of FDI after the United States—investment largely coming from MNCs. China is now a hybrid market-driven economy—driven by competition, capital, and entrepreneurship. As such, it is still attractive to companies wanting a piece of the action in this rapidly growing economy. In fact, more than 400 of the Fortune Global 500 companies are operating there.[56]

SMEs are also active and gaining ground in this complex country; but all companies should do their homework first, as advised by the Foreign Commercial Service (FCS):

> *FCS counsels American companies that to be a success in China, they must thoroughly investigate the market, take heed of product standards, pre-qualify potential business partners and craft contracts that assure payment and minimize misunderstandings between the parties.*[57]

With more than 1.3 billion people, China benefits greatly from its large and rapidly growing foreign and domestic market size, which provides significant economies of scale. Innovation is becoming another competitive advantage with rising company spending on R&D coupled with strong university–industry research collaboration and an increasing rate of patenting. In addition, China has the world's largest foreign-exchange reserves.[58] Not to be overlooked is the fact that the Chinese government often subsidizes and supports its manufacturing base and favors its local industries and companies. Those factors, along with rising costs of labor and shipping, mean that foreign firms are finding it increasingly difficult to do well there.

China's vast population of low-wage workers, with continued large numbers moving to the cities to work, as well as its massive consumer market potential, have long attracted offshoring of manufacturing from companies around the world. It is this low-cost manufacturing base that has contributed greatly to its exports and growth, a major factor in China's uniqueness, making it the world's largest manufacturer, second-largest consumer, largest saver, and probably the second-largest military spender. China has the world's largest shipped goods port capacity. For these reasons, China would seem well positioned to expand globally as long as global demand for its products and manufacturing continues. In all, China is still a developing country, with considerable differences between urban and rural areas making for quite varied markets. The great diversity is indicated by China's eight major languages, several dialects, and several other minority languages. Mandarin is the main language in the north, Cantonese in the south, in particular in Hong Kong. Each language reflects its own history and culture and, therefore, markets and economies. However, the fact remains that, in virtually all industrial sectors, state firms play a significant or dominant role. Sixteen state-owned enterprises (SOEs) make up about half of GDP. In addition, central, regional, and local political influences create

(Continued)

unpredictability for businesses, as do the arbitrary legal systems, suspect data, and underdeveloped infrastructure.[59] The FCS cautions investors to beware of the following factors:

- China's legal and regulatory system is arbitrary. Protection of intellectual property rights is critical.
- In spite of its progress toward a market economy, China still leans toward protecting its local firms, especially the state-owned ones, from imports, and promotes their exports.
- Political goals and agendas often take precedence over commercially based decisions.
- Discrepancies of business practices make it difficult for SMEs with limited budgets to get started. The FCS advises those firms to start with fostering a sales network through regional agents or distributors who can assist in keeping track of policy and regulation updates and who have local contacts.[60]

How to negotiate with the Chinese is the subject of a further feature in Chapter 5. Presented here are ten basic tips for doing business in China, published by Mia Doucet in CanadExport.

TEN TIPS FOR DOING BUSINESS IN CHINA

When doing business in China, the ability to navigate cross-cultural issues is just as important as the goods and services you bring to the marketplace. This is true whether your company is just now considering the China market, recently gained its first sale, or maintains an in-country presence.

Tip #1 Never underestimate the importance of existing connections. You need to be dealing with a Chinese person of influence. If that person feels you are trustworthy enough, and if they can get their network of contacts to trust you, there is a chance you will succeed. Asians want to do business with people they trust. But there is no real trust unless a person is in their circle. At first, they don't know if you will be a good partner. Show respect by keeping some distance. Focus on building the relationship before talking business. Do not go for big profit on your first contract.

Tip #2 To protect your intellectual property, use the same due diligence you would in the West.

Tip #3 Never pressure your Asian colleagues for a decision. To speed up the decision process, slow down. Start from the beginning and work through to a solution in a logical, step-by-step fashion. Then stand your ground.

Tip #4 The negotiation process will be anything but smooth. Your best strategy is a walk away mentality. You have to go in trying not to make the deal. Explain your position in clear, concise words. State your terms clearly. Respectfully. Then be prepared to walk away if your terms are not met.

Tip #5 Respect face. Never argue or voice a difference of opinion with anyone—even a member of your own team. Never make the other person wrong. Never say "no" directly, as that is considered rude and arrogant.

Tip #6 Account for the fact that most Asians understand less spoken English than we think they do. The easiest thing in the world is for a Chinese to say yes. Their smiles and nods have more to do with saving face than getting your meaning. Talk in short sentences. Listen more than you speak. Pause between sentences. Find four or five easy ways to say the same thing. Never ask a question that can be answered with a simple yes. Avoid all slang. Skip humor altogether.

Tip #7 Manage the way you present written information. Document everything in writing and in precise detail. Present your ideas in stages. Write clearly, using plain English text. In order to appeal to Asian visual bias, use sketches, charts, and diagrams.

Tip #8 Prepare for every interaction. Do not count on your ability to wing it. A lack of preparedness can cause loss of face and trust. Do not give or expect to receive partial answers from your Chinese colleagues, as that is considered offensive.

Tip #9 Make sure your facts are 100% accurate in every detail, or you will lose credibility. Do not present an idea or theory that has not been fully researched, proven, or studied beforehand. If you make a mistake, you are not to be trusted.

Tip #10 Everyone on your team needs to know how to avoid costly gaffes.

Most of us are not by nature sensitive to the differences in culture—we have to be taught. Time-honoured passive resistance could bring your company to its knees. It makes sense to teach people the cross-cultural factors that have a direct impact on your profits.

Source: Mia Doucet, author of the award-winning book *China in Motion*, prepared these tips for *CanadExport*, "Ten Tips for Doing Business in China," February 5, 2009. Used with permission of *CanadExport*, Foreign Affairs and International Trade Canada, September 15, 2011.

experiencing traffic gridlocks and power outages. However, much of India's growth has been in technology industries that have not been affected by poor roads, compared with China's manufacturing-based growth. Nevertheless, optimism abounds in India about the country's prospects. The expanding middle class of more than 300 million is fueling demand-led growth. Increasing deregulation is enabling whole sectors to be competitive. Here, too, there is considerable diversity in markets, incomes, and economies; there are 15 major languages and more than 1,600 dialects. Yet India's rise is largely fueled by family firms that often maintain pyramid structures and grow vertically out of convenience because of problems with red tape, erratic supply chains, and infrastructure.

> *Adaptable, ingenious and combustible, the family firm remains the backbone of India's private sector, not an anachronism.... The oldest, such as Aditya Birla, Tata and Bajaj, stretch back over three or more generations and are wily survivors.*[61]

Even so, approximately 40 percent of the profits of India's 100 biggest listed firms come from state-controlled firms; an estimated two-thirds of production from India's finance, energy, and natural resources firms is state controlled, despite India's moves toward further privatization.[62]

A common comparison between China and India notes that China's economy grows because of its government, whereas India's economy grows in spite of it. However, with its 1.3 billion people, many are still mired in poverty, although the poverty rate is half that of 20 years ago. Although India's large upcoming youth bulge—compared with China—will bring a wave of workers for the economy, it will also bring many more mouths to feed. (India has the largest working-age population in the world, with about one-third under age 25 and one-third under age 15, whereas China is experiencing the results of its one-child policy.)

In many areas in India, the economic transformation is startling, with growth fed by firms like the Tata Group—a global conglomerate producing everything from cars and steel to software and consulting systems. Further discussion of doing business in India is included in Chapter 4.

SOUTH ASIA

In South Asia, an agreement was signed to form the South Asia Association of Regional Cooperation (SAARC), a free trade pact among seven South Asian nations: Bangladesh, Bhutan, India, the Maldives, Nepal, Pakistan, and Sri Lanka, effective January 1, 2006. (Afghanistan has since been added.) The agreement was to lower tariffs to 25 percent within three to five years and to eliminate them within seven years. The member nations comprise more than 1.5 billion people, with an estimated one-third of them living in poverty. Officials in those countries hope to follow the success of the other Asian regional bloc, the ASEAN.

AUSTRALIA

Although not regarded as part of Southeast Asia but, rather, of the region called Oceania, which also includes New Zealand and neighboring islands in the Pacific Ocean, Australia did sign an ASEAN friendship treaty with Southeast Asia. Australia is one of the richest countries in the world, with the mining industry responsible for attracting about a third of its investment inflows. More than 50 percent of her exports go to East Asia, with more transported through the region to markets around the world. Australia ranked eighth in the 2014–2015 FDI Confidence Index shown in Exhibit 1-1.

THE AMERICAS

NAFTA

The goal of the North American Free Trade Agreement (NAFTA) (which turned 20 in January 2014) between the United States, Canada, and Mexico was to bring faster growth, more jobs, better working conditions, and a cleaner environment for all as a result of increased exports and trade. This trading bloc—one America—has 470 million consumers. The Canada–United States trade is the largest bilateral flow between two countries. In addition, the vast majority—around 84 percent—of both Canadian and Mexican exports goes to the United States. Mexico is the United States' third largest trade partner (after Canada and China) and second largest export market for U.S. products.

From Mexico's perspective, the country's exports have exploded under NAFTA; U.S–Mexico bilateral trade increased from $88 billion in 1993, the year prior to the implementation of NAFTA, to $383 billion (estimated) in 2010, an increase of 335 percent.[63] However, Mexico's dependence on the United States for its exports—NAFTA's greatest success—was shown to be a liability in the global economic downturn as Mexico felt the full brunt of declining consumption in the United States. The auto industry, for example, which has flourished under NAFTA, ground to a virtual standstill early in 2009.[64] However, with the U.S. economy rebounding, the 2014–2015 FDI Confidence Index showed Canada at third place, and Mexico at twelfth after being kicked off the 2012 index.[65]

Mexican trade policy is among the most open in the world, and the country has become an important exporting and importing power. Although the Mexican economic cycles depend on the American economy, it has signed 12 trade agreements with 43 nations, putting 90 percent of its trade under free trade regulations. In addition, it is estimated that 40 percent of the content of products from Mexico reimported to the United States originated in the United States as well as 25 percent from Canada.[66] However, recent increase in violence among drug gangs, especially in border areas, has created insecurity for businesspeople.

MERCOSUR

This is the fourth largest trading bloc after the EU, NAFTA, and ASEAN. Established in 1991, it comprises the original parties—Brazil, Argentina, Paraguay, Uruguay, and now Venezuela. The EU is Mercosur's first trading partner, accounting for 20 percent of Mercosur's total trade in 2013. EU–Mercosur trade in that year was €110 billion.[67]

BRAZIL

Foreign companies are turning to Brazil not just for the size of its booming domestic market, but also as a platform to its Spanish-speaking neighbors. Fiat's factory in Brazil, for example, is the second biggest in the world.[68]

The Federal Republic of Brazil is Latin America's biggest economy and the fifth largest country in the world in terms of land mass and population, with about 193 million people. According to the U.S. Department of Commerce, Brazil is the seventh largest economy in the world. Bolstered by demand from China and elsewhere for its raw materials, by strong domestic demand, and by a growing middle class, Brazil ranked fifth in the 2014–2015 FDI Confidence Index (see Exhibit 1-1).

Whereas most of the developed world has been mired in debt and stunted growth prospects, Brazil's economy is stable, and growth prospects are bright. Yet poor infrastructure remains an obstacle (less than 10 percent of roads are paved), and drastic inequality among Brazil's people hampers domestic growth. However, there were considerable investment and export opportunities because Brazil spent billions in infrastructure development in preparation for the World Cup in 2014 and the Olympics in 2016. Further discussion regarding doing business in Brazil is included in Chapter 3.

CAFTA-DR

The Dominican Republic-Central America FTA (CAFTA-DR) is the first free-trade agreement between the United States and Costa Rica, El Salvador, Guatemala, Honduras, Nicaragua, and the Dominican Republic. Central America and the Dominican Republic represent the third-largest U.S. export market in Latin America, behind Mexico and Brazil. Trade between the United States and the six CAFTA-DR partners has increased more than 71 percent since inception, from $35 billion in 2005 to $60 billion in 2013. In 2013, U.S. exports to the CAFTA-DR countries totaled $30 billion; imports totaled $30 billion.[69]

Other recent agreements include three trade agreements, between the United States and South Korea, Colombia, and Panama, all passed on October 12, 2011, bringing to 20 the total number of free-trade agreements with the United States.[70]

Other Regions in the World

Sweeping political, economic, and social changes around the world present new challenges to global managers. The move toward privatization has had an enormous influence on the world economy. Economic freedom is a critical factor in the relative wealth of nations.

One of the most striking changes today is that most nations have suddenly begun to develop decentralized, free-market systems to manage a global economy of intense competition, the complexity of high-tech industrialization, and an awakening hunger for freedom.

THE RUSSIAN FEDERATION

Foreign investment in Russia, as well as its consumers' climbing confidence and affluence, did bode well for the economy—until the situation with Ukraine, described in the opening profile, which caused a considerable downturn in confidence and in the economy. The rate of inflation soared to 11.4 percent as the ruble lost nearly half its value over the 2014–2015 period. Forecasts for GDP for 2015 were cut, ranging from zero growth to a contraction of 0.7 percent.[71] Membership in the WTO in 2011 promised additional trade liberalization. Until recently, Russia was regarded as more politically stable. New land, legal, and labor codes have encouraged foreign firms to take advantage of opportunities in that immense area, in particular the vast natural resources and the well-educated population of 145 million. Moscow, in particular, is teeming with new construction sites, high-end cars, and new restaurants. Export opportunities abound in Russia, with a growing middle class and vast infrastructure needs. However, corruption and government interference persist, along with excessive regulations, lack of the rule of law, and infrastructure problems. Further discussion of the business environment in Russia is in Chapter 7.

THE MIDDLE EAST

"You start to differentiate in a post-Arab spring world and you look at the different markets that were affected," says Mustafa Abdel-Wadood, chief executive at Abraaj.[72]

FINANCIAL TIMES U.K.
SEPTEMBER 22, 2011

The changing geopolitical landscape due to the revolutions across the region, which toppled leaders in Tunisia and Egypt and ousted the regime of Colonel Muammer Gaddafi in Libya, have made investors wary but looking for opportunities. Egypt, where the political landscape has been redrawn in recent months, is beginning to attract interest from Gulf, Western, and Asian international investors. "I think the main theme when considering whether to enter these markets is the potential for long-term growth that will ultimately lead to a more positive outcome."[73]

According to Arab World Competitiveness Report by the World Economic Forum, the United Arab Emirates is the most competitive economy in the Arab world among the countries at the third and most advanced stage of development. It is followed by Qatar and Kuwait. Among countries at the second stage of development, Tunisia and Oman are the best performing Arab economies, whereas Egypt is the regional best performer in the third group of countries. The Forum predicted there will be prosperity with challenges for the Middle East.[74]

DEVELOPING ECONOMIES

Developing economies are characterized by change that has come about more slowly as they struggle with low gross national product (GNP) and low per capita income as well as the burdens of large, relatively unskilled populations and high international debt. Their economic situation and the often unacceptable level of government intervention discourage the foreign investment they need. Many countries in Central and South America, the Middle East, and Africa desperately hope to attract foreign investment to stimulate economic growth.

THE AFRICAN UNION (AU)

The AU comprises the 53 African countries and was formed from the original Organization of African Unity (OAU) primarily to deal with political issues. According to the International Monetary Fund (IMF), seven of the world's ten fastest growing economies are in Africa. However, there continue to be many major problems in the region. Unfortunately, Africa has received little interest from most of the world's investors, although it receives increasing investment from companies in South Africa, which has the region's biggest economy. On the bright side, however, trade between China and Africa has risen from $10 billion in 2000 to well over $100 billion today. In fact, China's appetite for commodities led to a $12 billion FDI in 2011.[75] At a projected growth rate of over 5.4 percent in 2015, more than double that predicted for the United States or Europe, prospects for Africa are improving. For example, Coca-Cola's chief executive has targeted the African continent as one of the company's top investment priorities.[76] In addition, Procter & Gamble planned a $250 million factory in 2016 in Lagos, Nigeria, to produce diapers and baby products.[77] However, widespread unemployment and extreme poverty prevail on the continent and remind businesspeople of the tremendous challenges that remain.

SOUTH AFRICA

The South African economy has been growing continuously since 1998 amid a more stable political environment since the defeat of apartheid. Its annual average GNP growth has been 2.2 percent from 2008 through 2014.[78] This is the longest economic upswing in the country's history, although unemployment remains very high.[79] South Africa is a country of 48.7 million people that is rich in diverse cultures, people, and natural resources. "Enjoying remarkable macroeconomic stability and a pro-business environment, South Africa is a logical and attractive choice for U.S. companies to enter the African continent."[80] In fact, the 2014–2015 FDI Confidence Index by A. T. Kearney ranked South Africa thirteenth, up from fifteenth the previous year.[81] The rapid growth of consumer demand, along with increasing tourism and foreign business investment, has made the country's outlook very positive.[82]

For firms willing to take the economic and political risks, developing economies offer considerable potential for international business. Assessing the risk–return trade-offs and keeping up with political developments in these developing countries are two of the many demands on international managers.

The Global Manager's Role

Whatever your level of involvement, it is important to understand the global business environment and its influence on the manager's role. This complex role demands a contingency approach to dynamic environments, each of which has its own unique requirements. Within the larger context of global trends and competition, the rules of the game for the global manager are set by each country (see Exhibit 1-2): its political and economic agenda, its technological status and level of development, its regulatory environment, its comparative and competitive advantages, and its cultural norms. The astute manager will analyze the new environment, anticipate how it may affect the future of the company, and then develop appropriate strategies and operating styles. She or he will need to take into account the business practices and expectations of varying sets of suppliers, partners, customers, and local managers. These factors in the manager's role are the subjects of the rest of this book.

THE POLITICAL AND ECONOMIC ENVIRONMENT

Proactive, globally oriented firms maintain an up-to-date profile of the political and economic environment of the countries in which they maintain operations (or have plans for future investment). Surveys of top executives around the world show that **sustainability**—economic, political, social, and environmental—has become a significant worldwide issue. Executives who recognize that fact are leading their companies to develop new policies and to invest in sustainability projects with the purpose of benefiting the environment as well as profitability.[83] The opening profile provides a recent example of how political developments can suddenly affect the global risk environment. Among the strategic and operational risks global companies report, the top four were government regulation, country financial risks, currency risk, and political and social disturbances; these were followed by a poor legal system; problems with suppliers, customers or partners; terrorist attacks; and theft of intellectual property.[84] Clearly, the drastic fall in oil prices as of 2015 also posed considerable risks to certain industries and to some nations dependent on oil revenue.

EXHIBIT 1-2 **An Open Systems Model**

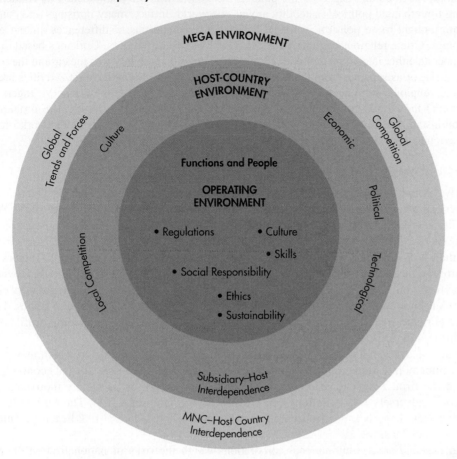

From a separate survey by the Aon Risk Solutions Company, we can see the top ten risks as reported by 960 companies from 58 countries, giving us an overview of how concerns can change over time. The risk of economic slowdown was the number one risk in 17 out of 27 industries surveyed and across all countries reporting.

Those risks have different relative levels of priority and concern, depending on the region. The risk of economic slowdown is the first concern across all regions, whereas subsequent risks vary across those regions. For example, "failure to attract/retain top talent" is far higher on the list for the Asia Pacific region than for the others. In addition, the Aon report noted that "Senior management's intuition and experience remains the primary method used by survey respondents to identify and assess major risks facing their organizations."[85] That led the researchers to conclude that formal risk management using business analytical tools would be more useful than experience in identifying new risks. The top ten risks overall were:

- Economic slowdown.
- Regulatory/legislative changes.
- Increasing competition.
- Damage to reputation/brand.
- Business interruption.
- Failure to innovate/meet customer needs.
- Failure to attract or retain top talent.
- Commodity price risk.
- Technology failure/system failure.
- Cash flow/liquidity risk.[86]

An additional important aspect of the political environment is the phenomenon of ethnicity—a driving force behind political instability around the world. In fact, many uprisings and conflicts that are thought to be political in nature are actually expressions of differences among ethnic groupings. Often, religious disputes lie at the heart of those differences. Uprisings based on religion operate either in conjunction with ethnic differences (as probably was the case in the former Yugoslavia) or as separate from them (as in Northern Ireland). Many terrorist activities are also based on religious differences, as in the Middle East and other parts of the world. Managers must understand the ethnic and religious composition of the host country to anticipate problems of general instability as well as those of an operational nature, such as effects on the workforce, on production and access to raw materials, and on the market.

Political Risk

Clearly, as evidenced by the 2011 Arab Spring uprisings in Egypt and elsewhere, major political changes can affect the business environment and risk level almost overnight. As far as political risk is concerned, a survey—based on 211 countries and territories—by Aon Risk Solutions (the firm discussed earlier) found that the political risk level is rising in more countries than it is declining. That conclusion was based on the level of exposure to factors such as currency inconvertibility and transfer; strikes, riots, and civil commotion; war; sovereign nonpayment; political interference; supply chain interruption; and legal and regulatory risk.[87] It is clear from the past that firms operating in some countries are exposed to political risks that can drastically affect them with little warning, as illustrated by the opening profile on the Ukraine situation.

The managers of a global firm need to investigate the political risks to which they expose their company in certain countries—and the implications of those risks for the economic success of the firm. **Political risks** are any governmental action or politically motivated event that could adversely affect the long-run profitability or value of a firm. The Middle East, as we have seen, has traditionally been an unstable area where political risk heavily influences business decisions.

In unstable areas, multinational corporations weigh the risks of nationalization or expropriation. In April 2012, Argentina, under President Cristina Fernandez de Kerchner, announced plans to nationalize Repsol YPF, the Spanish oil company, taking a 51 percent stake in YPF, which accounts for a third of Argentina's oil production.[88] In retaliation, Spain announced that it would restrict imports of biodiesel from Argentina. **Nationalization** refers to the forced sale of an MNC's assets to local buyers, with some compensation to the firm, perhaps leaving a minority ownership with the MNC.[89]

Expropriation occurs when a local government seizes and provides inadequate compensation for the foreign-owned assets of an MNC; when no compensation is provided, it is confiscation. In countries that have a proven history of stability and consistency, the risk of expropriation is relatively low; it is highest in countries that experience continuous political upheaval, violence, and change. An event that affects all foreign firms doing business in a country or region is called a **macropolitical risk event**. In many regions, **terrorism** poses a severe and random political risk to company personnel and assets and can, obviously, interrupt the conduct of business. According to Micklous, terrorism is "the use, or threat of use, of anxiety-inducing... violence for ideological or political purposes."[90] The increasing incidence of terrorism around the world concerns MNCs. In particular, the kidnapping of business executives has become quite common. In addition, the random acts of violence around the world have a downward effect on global expansion, not the least because of the difficulty in attracting and retaining good managers in high-risk areas as well as the expense of maintaining security to protect people and assets and the cost of insurance to cover them. Companies that go ahead and invest in those high-risk areas do so with the expectation of a higher profit premium to offset risk.

An event that affects one industry or company or only a few companies is called a **micropolitical risk event**. Such events have become more common than macropolitical risk events. Such micropolitical action is often called *creeping expropriation*, indicating a government's gradual and subtle action against foreign firms. This situation occurs when a firm hasn't been expropriated, but it takes ten times longer to do anything. Typically, such continuing problems with an investment present more difficulty for foreign firms than do major events that are insurable by political-risk insurers. The following list describes seven typical political risk events.

- Expropriation of corporate assets without prompt and adequate compensation
- Forced sale of equity to host-country nationals, usually at or below depreciated book value
- Discriminatory treatment against foreign firms in the application of regulations or laws
- Barriers to **repatriation** of funds (profits or equity)
- Loss of technology or other intellectual property (such as patents, trademarks, or trade names)
- Interference in managerial decision making
- Dishonesty by government officials, including canceling or altering contractual agreements, extortion demands, and so forth[91]

Political Risk Assessment

International companies must conduct some form of political risk assessment to manage their exposure to risk and minimize financial losses. Dow Chemical, for example, has a program in which it uses line managers trained in political and economic analysis, as well as executives in foreign subsidiaries, to provide risk analyses of each country.

Risk assessment by MNCs usually takes two forms. One uses experts or consultants familiar with the country or region under consideration. to monitor important trends and make recommendations. A second and increasingly common means of political risk assessment MNCs use is the development of internal staff and in-house capabilities: by having staff assigned to foreign subsidiaries, by having affiliates monitor local political activities, or by hiring people with expertise in the political and economic conditions in regions critical to the firm's operations. Frequently, all means are used, but, nothing can replace timely information from people on the front line. For an autonomous international subsidiary, most of the impact from political risks (nationalization, terrorism) will be at the level of the ownership and control of the firm because its acquisition by the host country would provide the state with a fully operational business. For global firms, the primary risks are likely to be from restrictions (on imports, exports, currency, and so forth), with the impact at the level of the firm's transfers (or exchanges) of money, products, or component parts.

Managing Political Risk

After assessing the potential political risk of investing or maintaining current operations in a specific country, managers face perplexing decisions on how to manage that risk. On one level, they can decide to suspend their firm's dealings with a certain country at a given point—by the avoidance of investment or by the withdrawal of current investment (by selling or abandoning plants and assets). On another level, if they decide that the risk is relatively low in a particular country or that a high-risk environment is worth the potential returns, they may choose to start (or maintain) operations there and to accommodate that risk through adaptation to the political regulatory environment. That adaptation can take many forms, each designed to respond to the concerns of a particular local area. Some means of adaptation that Taoka and Beeman suggest are as follows:

- Equity sharing includes the initiation of joint ventures with nationals (individuals or those in firms, labor unions, or government) to reduce political risks.
- Participative management requires the firm to involve nationals actively, including those in labor organizations or government, in the management of the subsidiary.
- Localization of the operation includes the modification of the subsidiary's name, management style, and so forth, to suit local tastes. Localization seeks to transform the subsidiary from a foreign firm to a national firm.
- Development assistance includes the firm's active involvement in infrastructure development (foreign-exchange generation, local sourcing of materials or parts, management training, technology transfer, securing external debt, and so forth).[92]

In addition to avoidance and adaptation, two other means of risk reduction available to managers are dependency and hedging. Some means that managers might use to maintain **dependency**—keeping both the subsidiary and the host nation dependent on the parent corporation—include, for example, maintaining control over key inputs or technology or control over distribution; other means are through expatriate control in key positions.[93] Firms can also minimize loss through **hedging**, which includes, for example, political risk insurance and local debt financing.

Multinational corporations also manage political risk through their global strategic choices. Many large companies diversify their operations both by investing in many countries and by operating through joint ventures with a local firm or government or through local licensees. By involving local people, companies, and agencies, firms minimize the risk of negative outcomes due to political events. (See Chapters 6 and 7 for further discussion of these and other global strategies.)

Managing Terrorism Risk

No longer is the risk of terrorism for global businesses focused only on certain areas such as South America or the Middle East. That risk now has to be considered in countries such as France, England, and the United States, which had previously been regarded as safe. Eighty countries lost citizens in the World Trade Center attack on September 11, 2001. Many companies from Asia and Europe had office branches in the towers of the World Trade Center.

As incidents of terrorism accelerate around the world, many companies are increasingly aware of the need to manage the risk of terrorism. In high-risk countries, both IBM and Exxon Mobil try to develop a benevolent image through charitable contributions to the local community. They also try to maintain low profiles and minimize publicity in the host countries by using, for example, discreet corporate signs at company sites.[94] Some companies have put together teams to monitor the patterns of terrorism around the world. Almost all MNCs have stepped up their security measures abroad, hiring consultants in counterterrorism (to train employees to cope with the threat of terrorism) and advising their employees to avoid U.S. airlines when flying overseas. For many firms, however, the opportunities outweigh the threats, even in high-risk areas.

Economic Risk

Closely connected to a country's political stability is its economic environment—and the relative risk that it may pose to foreign companies. A country's level of economic development generally determines its economic stability and, therefore, its relative risk to a foreign firm. Historically, most industrialized nations have posed little risk of economic instability; less-developed nations pose more risk. However, recently, the level of economic risk in Europe, for example, was a great concern around the world, in particular regarding concerns in the eurozone brought about by debt problems in Greece.

In 2014, the Heritage Foundation published its annual Index of Economic Freedom (excerpted in Table 1–2), which covers 183 countries and is based on ten specific freedoms such as trade freedom, business freedom, investment freedom, and property rights—all of which reduce economic risk. Interestingly, the much-discussed emerging BRICs—Brazil, Russia, India, and China—are way down on the list, indicating that there is quite a risk–return trade-off for investment in those markets. (Further details of each country on the index are available at www.heritage.org.)

> In economically free societies, governments allow labor, capital, and goods to move freely, and refrain from coercion or constraint of liberty beyond the extent necessary to protect and maintain liberty itself.[95]

A country's ability or intention to meet its financial obligations determines its economic risk. The economic risk incurred by a foreign corporation usually falls into one of two main categories. Its subsidiary (or other investment) in a specific country may become unprofitable if (1) the government abruptly changes its domestic monetary or fiscal policies, or (2) the government decides to modify its foreign-investment policies. The latter situation would threaten the company's ability

TABLE 1–2 2014 Index of Economic Freedom

Rank: FREE	Country	Score
1	Hong Kong	89.6
2	Singapore	89.4
3	New Zealand	82.1
4	Australia	81.4
5	Switzerland	80.5
Mostly Free		
6	Canada	79.1
7	Chile	78.5
8	Ireland	78.7
9	Denmark	78.6
10	Bahrain	77.7
11	United States	76.2
16	Germany	73.9
Moderately Free		
72	S. Africa	62.6
118	Brazil	56.6
128	India	54.6
139	China	52.7
143	Russia	52.1

Source: Based on selected data from the Heritage Foundation, 2014, http://www.heritage.org.

to repatriate its earnings and would create a financial or interest-rate risk. Furthermore, the risk of exchange-rate volatility results in currency translation exposure to the firm when the balance sheet of the entire corporation is consolidated and may cause a negative cash flow from the foreign subsidiary. Currency translation exposure occurs when the value of one country's currency changes relative to that of another. In 2015, for example, the U.S. dollar was so strong against other denominations that developing countries, in particular, were negatively affected because it cost them more to import from the United States, and their exports would bring less revenue. When exchange-rate changes are radical, repercussions are felt around the world.

Because every MNC operating overseas exposes itself to some level of economic risk, often affecting its everyday operational profitability, managers constantly reassess the level of risk that their companies may face in any specific country or region of the world by carefully tracking economic indicators which they have found relevant to the company.[96]

THE LEGAL ENVIRONMENT

The prudent global manager consults with legal services, both locally and at headquarters, to comply with host-country regulations and maintain cooperative long-term relationships in the local area. If the manager waits until a problem arises, little legal recourse may be available outside of local interpretation and enforcement. Indeed, this has been the experience of many foreign managers in China, where financial and legal systems remain limited in spite of attempts to show the world a capitalist face. Local managers there often simply ignore their debts to foreign companies as they did under the old socialist system. The lesson for many foreign companies in China is that they are losing millions because Beijing often does not stand behind the commitments of its state-owned enterprises.

Although no guarantee is possible, the risk of massive losses may be minimized, among other ways, by making sure you get approval from related government offices (national, provincial, and local), by showing that you are not going to run riot over long-term government goals, and by getting loan guarantees from the headquarters of one of Beijing's main banks. Some of the contributing factors in cases that go against foreign companies are often the personal connections—*guanxi*—involved and the fact that some courts offer their services to the business community for profit. In addition, many judges get their jobs through nepotism rather than by virtue of a law degree.

Although the regulatory environment for international managers consists of the many local laws and the court systems in those countries in which they operate, certain other legal issues are covered by international law, which governs relationships between sovereign countries, the basic units in the world political system. One such agreement, which regulates international business by spelling out the rights and obligations of the seller and the buyer, is the United Nations Convention on Contracts for the International Sale of Goods (CISG). This applies to contracts for the sale of goods between countries that have adopted the convention.

Generally speaking, the manager of the foreign subsidiary or foreign operating division will comply with the host country's legal system. Such systems, derived from common law, civil law, or Islamic law (Sharia law), are a reflection of the country's culture, religion, and traditions. Under **common law**, used in the United States and 26 other countries of English origin or influence, past court decisions act as precedents to the interpretation of the law and to common custom. **Civil law** is based on a comprehensive set of laws organized into a code. Interpretation of these laws is based on reference to codes and statutes. About 70 countries, predominantly in Europe (e.g., France and Germany), are ruled by civil law, as is Japan. In Islamic countries, such as Saudi Arabia, the dominant legal system is **Islamic law**; based on religious beliefs, it dominates all aspects of life. Islamic law is followed in approximately 27 countries and combines, in varying degrees, civil, common, and indigenous law.

Contract Law

A **contract** is an agreement by the parties concerned to establish a set of rules to govern a business transaction. Contract law plays a major role in international business transactions because of the complexities arising from the differences in the legal systems of participating countries and because the host government in many developing and state-controlled countries is often a third party in the contract. Both common law and civil law countries enforce contracts, although their means of resolving disputes differ. Under civil law, it is assumed that a contract reflects promises that will be enforced without specifying the details in the contract; under common law, the details of promises must be written into the contract to be enforced. Astute international managers recognize that they will have to draft contracts in legal contexts different from their own, and they prepare themselves accordingly by consulting with experts in international law before going overseas. Whereas Western companies want to spell out every detail in a contract, in some countries the contract may be ignored or changed, and in Asia, "there is no shortcut for managing the relationship."[97] In other words, the contract is in the relationship, not on the paper, and the way to ensure the reliability of the agreement is to nurture the relationship.

Neglect regarding contract law may leave a firm burdened with an agent who does not perform the expected functions, or a firm may be faced with laws that prevent management from laying off employees (which, for example, is often the case in some countries in Europe).

Other Regulatory Issues

Differences in laws and regulations from country to country are numerous and complex. These and other issues in the regulatory environment that concern multinational firms are briefly discussed here.

Countries often impose protectionist policies, such as tariffs and non-tariff barriers, quotas, and other import and trade restrictions, to give preference to their own companies and industries. The Japanese have come under much criticism for protectionism, which they use to limit imports of foreign goods while they continue exporting consumer goods (e.g., cars and electronics) on a large scale.

A country's tax system influences the attractiveness of investing in that country and affects the relative level of profitability for an MNC. Foreign tax credits, holidays, exemptions, depreciation allowances, and taxation of corporate profits are additional considerations the foreign investor must examine before acting. Many countries have signed tax treaties (or conventions) that define such terms as "income," "source," and "residency" and spell out what constitutes taxable activities.

The level of government involvement in the economic and regulatory environment varies a great deal among countries and has a varying impact on management practices. In Canada, for example, the government has a significant involvement in the economy. It has a powerful role in many industries, including transportation, petrochemicals, fishing, steel, textiles, and building materials—forming partly owned or wholly owned enterprises. Wholly owned businesses are called Crown Corporations (Petro Canada, Ontario Hydro, Saskatchewan Telecommunications, and so forth), many of which are as large as major private companies. The government's role in the Canadian economy, then, is one of both control and competition. Government policies, subsidies, and regulations directly affect the manager's planning process, as do other major factors in the Canadian legal environment, such as the high proportion of unionized workers. In Quebec, the law requiring official bilingualism imposes considerable operating constraints and expenses. For a foreign subsidiary, this regulation forces managers to speak both French and English and to incur the costs of language training for employees, translators, the administration of bilingual paperwork, and so on.

THE TECHNOLOGICAL ENVIRONMENT

Cloud computing, data analytics, mobility and socially enabled business processes are reshaping corporate IT, while the emergence of machine-to-machine communications ushers in the "internet of everything." John Chambers, chief executive of Cisco, the supplier of networking equipment, predicted in his keynote speech at the Consumer Electronics Show in Las Vegas (in January 2014) that the internet of everything—connecting people, devices and machines— would drive the next wave of global innovation and deliver $19 trillion in profits and cost savings to the private and public sectors over the next 10 years.... "This transformation will change the way people live, work and play."

FINANCIAL TIMES
JANUARY 29, 2014[98]

From Mr. Chambers's predictions, it is clear that the rapid development of corporate IT innovation will bring in a whole new level of global competition. The effects of technology around the world are pervasive—both in business and in private lives. In many parts of the world, whole

FIGURE 1-2 Cloud computing imagined.

alphaspirit/123RF GB Ltd

generations of technological development are being skipped over and, no doubt, will skip in leaps and bounds in the future.

Advances in information technology are bringing about increased productivity—for employees, for companies, and for countries. As noted by Thomas Friedman, technology, as well as other factors that are opening up borders—"the opening of the Berlin Wall, Netscape, work flow, outsourcing, offshoring, open-sourcing, insourcing, supply-chaining, in-forming"—have converged to create a more level playing field. The result of this convergence was

> *The creation of a global, web-enabled playing field that allows for multiple forms of collaboration—the sharing of knowledge and work—in real time, without regard to geography, distance, or, in the near future, even language.*[99]

Now that we are in a global information society, it is clear that corporations must incorporate into their strategic planning and their everyday operations the accelerating macro-environmental phenomenon of *technoglobalism*, in which the rapid developments in information and communication technologies (ICTs) are propelling globalization and vice versa. Investment-led globalization is leading to global production networks, which result in global diffusion of technology to link parts of the value-added chain in different countries. That chain may comprise parts of the same firm, or it may comprise suppliers and customers or technology-partnering alliances among two or more firms. Either way, technological developments are facilitating, indeed necessitating, the firm network structure that allows flexibility and rapid response to local needs. An additional variable is how networked the countries are in which the firm wants to do business, as described in the accompanying "Under the Lens" section.

Clearly, the effects of technology on global trade and business transactions cannot be ignored; in addition, the Internet is propelling electronic commerce around the world. The ease of use and pervasiveness of the Internet raise difficult questions about ownership of intellectual property, consumer protection, residence location, taxation, and other issues.

New technology specific to a firm's products represents a key competitive advantage to firms and challenges international businesses to manage the transfer and diffusion of proprietary technology, with its attendant risks. Whether it is a product, a process, or a management technology, an MNC's major concern is the **appropriability of technology**—that is, the ability of the innovating firm to profit from its own technology by protecting it from competitors.

An MNC can enjoy many technological benefits from its global operations. Advances resulting from cooperative R&D can be transferred among affiliates around the world, and specialized management knowledge can be integrated and shared. However, the risks of technology transfer and pirating are considerable and costly. Although firms face few restrictions on the creation and dissemination of technology in developed countries, less-developed countries often impose restrictions on licensing agreements, royalties, and so forth, as well as on patent protection.

In most countries, governments use their laws to some extent to control the flow of technology. These controls may be in place for reasons of national security. Other countries in earlier stages of development use their investment laws to acquire needed technology (usually labor-intensive technology to create jobs), increase exports, use local technology, and train local people.

The most common methods of protecting proprietary technology are the use of patents, trademarks, trade names, copyrights, and trade secrets. Various international conventions afford some protection in participating countries; more than 80 countries adhere to the International Convention for the Protection of Industrial Property (often referred to as the Paris Union) for the protection of patents. However, restrictions and differences in the rules in some countries not signatory to the Paris Union, as well as industrial espionage, pose continuing problems for firms trying to protect their technology.

One risk to a firm's intellectual property is the inappropriate use of the technology by joint-venture partners, franchisees, licensees, and employees (especially those who move to other companies). Some countries rigorously enforce employee secrecy agreements.

Another major consideration for global managers is the need to evaluate the **appropriateness of technology** for the local environment—especially in less-developed countries.

UNDER THE LENS
The Global Role of Information Technology (IT)

The rapid advancement in IT and its applications around the world has had, and will continue to have, a transformative effect on global business for businesses of all sizes. The speed and accuracy of information transmission are changing the nature of the global manager's job by making geographic barriers less relevant. Indeed, managers and families around the world recognize the necessity of being able to access IT and are giving priority to that access over other lifestyle accoutrements.

Governments can no longer control information completely; political, economic, market, and competitive information is available almost instantaneously to anyone around the world, permitting informed and accurate decision making. Even cultural barriers are being lowered gradually by the role of information in educating societies about one another. Indeed, as consumers around the world become more aware, through various media, of how people in other countries live, their tastes and preferences begin to converge, as the Arab Spring illustrated.

The explosive growth of information technology is both a cause and an effect of globalism. The information revolution is boosting productivity around the world. Finland is the most networked economy in the world, followed by Singapore, Sweden, the Netherlands, and Norway, according to the 2014 edition of the World Economic Forum *Global Information Technology Report*. The report assessed 138 economies and ranked their ICT readiness levels to use and benefit from ICT for increased growth and development. (Table 1–3 shows the top ten as well as the ranks of selected other countries.) The report stresses the key role of ICT as an enabler of a more economically, environmentally, and socially sustainable world. Among the top ten, Hong Kong and the United Kingdom posted notable improvements; those whose ranking fell back considerably were India and China.[100]

Indeed, the city of Seoul—where nine of every ten residents subscribe to a high-speed wireless Internet connection—is already one gigantic hot spot. "By 2015, when 80 percent of the residents are expected to carry smartphones or tablet PCs, wireless connectivity will be almost as free as it is ubiquitous: the municipal authorities are installing free Wi-Fi wireless hot spots in all the city's public spaces, including 360 parks; 3,200 intersections; and 2,200 streets around shopping centers."[101] Every subway car, motel room, and street corner has high-speed Internet connectivity.

Making cities such as Seoul smart is intended to improve productivity and attract businesses there. In addition, use of the Internet is propelling electronic commerce around the world (as discussed later in this chapter). Companies around the world are linked electronically to their employees, customers, distributors, suppliers, and alliance partners in many countries, resulting in increased communication and efficiency, as is described in the Procter & Gamble website: "P&G has more than

TABLE 1–3   The Network Readiness Index 2014

Top Ten Rank by Country		Selected Other Ranks	
1	Finland	Germany	12
2	Singapore	Japan	16
3	Sweden	Canada	17
4	Netherlands	Australia	18
5	Norway	France	25
6	Switzerland	Russia	50
7	United States	China	62
8	Hong Kong	Brazil	69
9	United Kingdom	Mexico	79
10	Republic of Korea	India	83

Source: Based on selected data from the Global Information Technology
Report 2014, World Economic Forum, www.weforum.org/
global-information-technology-report-2014.

(Continued)

80 video collaboration studios globally. The immersive environment created by video studios allows employees to connect face to face from any part of the world—as if they were in the same room. These studios greatly reduce the need for travel—saving money, time, and reducing P&G's carbon footprint."[102]

Technology, in all its forms, is dispersed around the world by **multinational enterprises (MNEs)** and their alliance partners in many countries. However, some of the information intended for electronic transmission is currently subject to export controls by an EU directive intended to protect private information about its citizens. In addition, some countries, such as China, monitor and limit electronic information flows. So, perhaps IT is not yet borderless but rather is subject to the same norms, preferences, and regulations as human cross-border interactions.

By studying the possible cultural consequences of the transfer of technology, managers must assess whether the local people are ready and willing to change their values, expectations, and behaviors on the job to use new technological methods, whether applied to production, research, marketing, finance, or some other aspect of the business. Often, a decision regarding the level of technology transfer is dominated by the host government's regulations or requirements. In some instances, the host country may require foreign investors to import only their most modern machinery and methods so that the local area may benefit from new technology. In other cases, the host country may insist that foreign companies use only labor-intensive processes, which can help to reduce high unemployment in an area.

When the choice is left to international managers, experts in economic development recommend that managers make informed choices about appropriate technology. The choice of technology may be capital intensive, labor intensive, or intermediate, but the key is that it should suit the level of development in the area and the needs and expectations of the people who will use it.

Global E-Business

Without doubt, the Internet has had a considerable impact on how companies buy and sell goods around the world—mostly raw materials and services going to manufacturers. Internet-based electronic trading and data exchange are changing the way companies do business while breaking down global barriers of time, space, logistics, and culture. However, the Internet is not totally open; governments still make sure that their laws are obeyed in cyberspace. This was made apparent early on when France forced Yahoo! to stop displaying Nazi trinkets for sale where French people could view them.[103] The reality is that

> *Different nations, and different peoples, may want a different kind of Internet—one whose language, content, and norms conform more closely to their own.[104]*

There is no doubt, however, that the Internet has introduced a new level of global competition by providing efficiencies through reducing the number of suppliers and slashing administration costs throughout the value chain. **E-business** is "the integration of systems, processes, organizations, value chains, and entire markets by using Internet-based and related technologies and concepts."[105] **E-commerce** refers directly to the marketing and sales process through the Internet. Firms use e-business to help build new relationships between businesses and customers.[106] The Internet and e-business provide a number of uses and advantages in global business, including the following:

- Convenience in conducting business worldwide; facilitating communication across borders, which contributes to the shift toward globalization and a global market
- An electronic meeting and trading place, which adds efficiency in conducting business sales
- A corporate intranet service, merging internal and external information for enterprises worldwide
- Power to consumers as they gain access to limitless options and price differentials
- A link and efficiency in distribution[107]

Although most early attention was on e-commerce, experts now believe the real opportunities are in business-to-business (B2B) transactions. Alibaba (China), for example, is the largest B2B site in the world. (See the Part 3 comprehensive case on Alibaba.) In addition, although the scope, complexity, and sheer speed of the B2B phenomenon, including e-marketplaces, have global executives scrambling to assess the impact and their own competitive roles, estimates for growth in the e-business marketplace may have been overzealous because of the global economic slowdown and its resultant dampening of corporate IT spending. Although we hear mostly about large companies embracing B2B, it is noteworthy that a large proportion of current and projected B2B use is by small and medium-sized firms for three common purposes: supply chain, procurement, and distribution channel.

A successful Internet strategy—especially on a global scale—is, of course, not easy to develop. Problems include internal obstacles and politics, difficulties in regional coordination and in balancing global versus local e-commerce, languages and cultural differences, and local laws.[108] Barriers to the adoption and progression of e-business around the world include lack of readiness of partners in the value chain, such as suppliers. If companies want to have an effective marketplace, they usually must invest in increasing their trading partners' readiness and their customers' capabilities. Other barriers are cultural. In Europe, for example, "Europe's e-commerce excursion has been hindered by a laundry list of cultural and regulatory obstacles, like widely varying tax systems, language hurdles, and currency issues."[109]

In other areas of the world, barriers to creating global e-businesses include differences in physical, information, and payment infrastructure systems. In such countries, innovation is required to use local systems for implementing a web strategy. In Japan, for example, very few transactions are conducted using credit cards. Typically, bank transfers and COD are used to pay for purchases. In addition, some Japanese use convenience stores, such as 7-Eleven Japan, to pay for their online purchases by choosing that option online.[110]

For these reasons, B2B e-business is likely to expand globally faster than B2C (business-to-consumer) transactions such as those by Amazon.com. In addition, consumer e-commerce depends on each country's level of access to computers and the Internet as well as the relative efficiency of home delivery. Clearly, companies who want to go global through e-commerce must localize to globalize, which means much more than just presenting online content in local languages.

> *Localizing ... also means recognizing and conforming to the nuances, subtleties, and tastes of multiple local cultures, as well as supporting transactions based on each country's currency, local connection speeds, payment preferences, laws, taxes, and tariffs.[111]*

It is clear that e-business is not only a new website on the Internet but also a source of significant strategic advantage. Hoping to capture this strategic advantage, the European Airbus venture—a public and private sector combination—joined a global aerospace B2B exchange for aircraft parts. The exchange illustrates two major trends in global competition: (1) those of cooperative global alliances, even among competitors, to achieve synergies, and (2) the use of technology to enable those connections and synergies. Indeed, "leading B2B firms, including Accenture, DuPont, GE, and IBM, spend significant amounts of money and effort building and managing their brands, and those brands account for a significant portion of their market capitalization."[112] In addition, many small businesses exist almost completely online as B2Bs, purchasing, marketing, and selling their products and services in the ether without ever having to build a physical storefront. Their B2B services can even help small businesses look and feel like a large business. An example of services for small businesses is www.microsoftsmallbusiness.com.[113]

CONCLUSION

A skillful global manager cannot develop a suitable strategic plan or consider an investment abroad without first assessing the environment—political, economic, legal, and technological—in which the company will operate. This assessment should result not so much in a comparison of countries as in a comparison of (1) the relative risk and (2) the projected return on investments among these countries for that particular investment. Similarly, for ongoing operations, both the subsidiary manager and headquarters management must continually monitor the environment for potentially unsettling events or undesirable changes that may require the redirection of

EXHIBIT 1-3 The Environment of the Global Manager

Political Environment	**Economic Environment**
• Form of government	• Economic system
• Political stability	• State of development
• Foreign policy	• Economic stability
• State companies	• GNP
• Role of military	• International financial standing
• Level of terrorism	• Monetary/fiscal policies
• Restrictions on imports/exports	• Foreign investment
Regulatory Environment	**Technological Environment**
• Legal system	• Level of technology
• Prevailing international laws	• Availability of local technical skills
• Protectionist laws	• Technical requirements of country
• Tax laws	• Appropriability
• Role of contracts	• Transfer of technology
• Protection for proprietary property	• Infrastructure
• Environmental protection	
Cultural Environment (see Part 2)	

certain subsidiaries or the entire company. Some of the critical factors affecting the global manager's environment (and therefore requiring monitoring) are listed in Exhibit 1-3.

Risk in the global environment, as discussed in this chapter, has become the new frontier in global business. The skills of companies and the measures taken to manage their exposure to risk on a world scale will soon largely replace their ability to develop, produce, and market global brands as the key element in global competitive advantage.

The pervasive role of culture in international management will be discussed fully in Part 2, with a focus on how the managerial functions and the daily operations of a firm are also affected by a subtle, but powerful, environmental factor in the host country—that of societal culture.

Chapter 2 presents some increasingly critical, and scrutinized, factors in the global environment—those of sustainability, corporate social responsibility (CSR), and ethical behavior. We will consider a variety of questions: What is the role of the firm in the future of other societies and their people? What stakeholders must managers consider in their strategic and operational decisions in other countries? How do the expectations of firm behavior vary around the world, and should those expectations influence the international manager's decisions? What role does long-term global economic interdependence and sustainability play in the firm's actions in other countries?

Summary of Key Points

■ Competing in the twenty-first century requires firms to invest in the increasingly refined managerial skills needed to perform effectively in a multicultural environment. Managers need a global orientation to meet the challenges of world markets and rapid, fundamental changes in a world of increasing economic interdependence.

■ International management is the process of developing strategies, designing and operating systems, and working with people around the world to ensure sustained competitive advantage.

■ One major direction in world trade is the rise of rapidly developing economies such as China, India, Brazil, Russia (often called the BRIC countries), and South Africa. Other emerging markets include Mexico, Indonesia, and Turkey.

■ Drastic worldwide changes in technology, political and economic trends, and terrorism, present dynamic challenges to global managers. Global managers must be aware of political risks around the world that can adversely affect the long-run profitability or value of a firm. Managers must evaluate various means to either avoid or minimize the effects of political risk.

- The risk of terrorist activity represents an increasing risk around the world. Managers have to decide how to incorporate that risk factor in their strategic and operational plans.
- Economic risk refers to a country's ability to meet its financial obligations. The risk is that the government may change its economic policies, thereby making a foreign company unprofitable or unable to repatriate its foreign earnings.

- The regulatory environment comprises the many laws and courts of those nations in which a company operates. Most legal systems derive from common law, civil law, or Islamic law.
- Use of the Internet in e-commerce—in particular, in business-to-business (B2B) transactions—and for intracompany efficiencies, has become a critical factor in global competitiveness.
- The appropriability of technology is the ability of the innovating firm to protect its technology from competitors and obtain economic benefits from that technology.

Discussion Questions

1-1. Poll your classmates about their attitudes toward globalization. What are the trends and opinions around the world that underlie those attitudes?

1-2. How has the economic downturn affected trends in protectionism and nationalization?

1-3. Discuss examples of recent macropolitical risk events and the effect they have or might have on a foreign subsidiary. What are micropolitical risk events? Give some examples and explain how they affect international business.

1-4. What means can managers use to assess political risk? What do you think is the relative effectiveness of these different methods? At the time you are reading this, what countries or areas do you feel pose political risk sufficient to discourage you from doing business there?

1-5. Can political risk be managed? If so, what methods can be used to manage such risk, and how effective are they? Discuss

the lengths to which you would go to manage political risk relative to the kinds of returns you would expect to gain.

1-6. Discuss the importance of contracts in international management and how contracts are viewed in other countries. What steps must a manager take to ensure a valid and enforceable contract?

1-7. Discuss the effects of various forms of technology on international business. What role does the Internet play? Where is all this leading? Explain the meaning of the appropriability of technology. What role does this play in international competitiveness? How can managers protect the proprietary technology of their firms?

1-8. Discuss the risk of terrorism. What means can managers use to reduce the risk or the effects of terrorism? Where in the world, and from what likely sources, would you anticipate terrorism?

Application Exercises

1-9. Do some further research on the technological environment. What are the recent developments affecting businesses and propelling globalization? What problems have arisen regarding use of the Internet for global business transactions, and how are they being resolved?

1-10. Consider recent events and the prevailing political and economic conditions in the Russian Federation. As a manager who has been considering investment there, how do you assess the political and economic risks at this time? What should be your company's response to this environment?

Experiential Exercise

In groups of three, represent a consulting firm. You have been hired by a diversified multinational corporation to advise on the political and economic environment in different countries. The company wants to open one or two manufacturing facilities in Asia. Choose a specific type of company and two specific countries in Asia and present them to the class, including the types of risks that would be involved and what steps the firm could take to manage those risks.

CASE STUDY

Apple's iPhones—Not "Made in America"[1]

Apple has become one of the best-known, most admired and most imitated companies on earth, in part through an unrelenting mastery of global operations.[2]

There are risks and rewards for all in a global economy. The globalization of human capital results in a range of winners and losers around the world: companies and their stockholders, consumers, contractors, firms up and down the supply chain, employed people, and unemployed people, as well as their economies. In February 2011, President Obama asked Apple's Steve Jobs (now deceased) why Apple could not bring back all the jobs it used to provide in the United States. The jobs related to most high-tech products made by companies such as Dell, HP, and Apple have now migrated overseas, including those for Apple's 700 million iPhones (as of March 2015) as well as millions of iPads and now Apple Watches. *Time* broke down a retail price of $500 for Apple's iPhone, for example, and estimated that $61 worth of value comes from Japan, with its high-end technology manufacturing; $30 of value is added from Germany; $23 from South Korea; $7 from Chinese assembly lines; $48 from unspecified sources; and $11 from the United States. Those inputs total $179 for parts and assembly abroad, leaving Apple, the inventor in the United States, a profit of $321.[3] For the first quarter of 2012, Apple made $13 billion in profit.

Although Apple directly employs an estimated 43,000 in the United States and 20,000 overseas, an additional 700,000 people engineer, build, and assemble iPads, iPhones, and Apple's other products in Asia and Europe. Sophisticated component parts outsourced in various countries are assembled in China. Some of those are contracted to the Taiwanese-headquartered company Foxconn's Longhua factory campus in Shenzhen, for example, where more than 300,000 employees live in dorms, eat on site, and churn out iPhones, Sony PlayStations, and Dell computers. Foxconn Technology, with 1.2 million employees in plants throughout the country, is China's largest exporter and assembles an estimated 40 percent of the world's consumer electronics, including for customers such as Amazon, Dell, Hewlett-Packard, Nintendo, Nokia, and Samsung. No other factories in the world have the manufacturing scale of Foxconn.

The answer to President Obama's question is not as simple as the ability to acquire cheaper labor overseas; Apple's executives and those at other high-tech firms claim that "Made in the U.S.A" is not a competitive strategy for them because America does not compare favorably with the industrial skills, hard work, and flexibility that can be found in companies such as Foxconn. Questions about what corporate America owes to Americans are met with the example of thousands of Chinese workers being roused in the night to accommodate a redesigned iPhone screen and, within a few days, being able to produce 10,000 iPhones a day—a feat not possible in U.S. factories. Although the cost of labor is a small percentage of an iPhone's cost, the major advantage and cost saving in China is in the management of supply chains and rapid access to component parts and manufacturing supplies from various factories in close proximity. In addition, Apple maintains that the large number of engineers and other skilled workers who could be accessed on short notice in China simply are not readily available in the United States; nor are the factories with the scale, speed, and flexibility that such a high-tech company needs. Apple executives give the example of visiting a factory to consider whether it could do the necessary work to cut the glass for the iPhone's touchscreen. Upon their arrival, a new wing of the plant was already being built "in case you give us the contract."[4] Fareed Zakaria, in *Time*, maintains that this competitive edge is gained largely through Chinese government subsidies and streamlined regulations to boost domestic manufacturing. In the end, however, Apple maintains that:

We don't have an obligation to solve America's problems. Our only obligation is making the best product possible.[5]

However, after a number of suicides at Foxconn in 2010, reportedly attributable to the poor working conditions and excessive hours for very low pay, Apple was under some pressure from negative publicity; subsequently, Foxconn raised wages, retained counselors, and literally strung nets from its highest buildings (to catch people). Apple does have a supplier code of conduct. In January 2012, Apple joined the Fair Labor Association (FLA), the first technology company to do so, and asked the group to do an independent assessment of conditions at its major factories. This move followed the company's own report that documented numerous labor violations, including employees working 60-hour workweeks and not being paid proper overtime. A few days after the FLA started its investigation, Foxconn said that it would increase salaries for some workers by 16 percent to 20 percent—to about $400 a month before overtime—and that it would reduce overtime. Although this is encouraging news for workers' rights, it should be noted that Apple and other contractors are known to allow only the slimmest of profits to its suppliers, which encourages the suppliers to try anything to reduce their costs, such as using cheaper and more toxic chemicals or making their employees work faster and longer.

> *"The only way you make money working for Apple is figuring out how to do things more efficiently or cheaper," said an executive at one company that helped bring the iPad to market. "And then they'll come back the next year and force a 10 percent price cut."*[6]

China is being forced to take notice of such problems, and labor is gaining some ground; the issue then is that firms have already started to move jobs to other countries with lower wages.

Notes

1. www.apple.com, accessed March 11, 2015; Robin Harding, Kathrin Hille, Song Jung-a, Robin Kwong, "Apple, HP and Dell Probe Foxconn," *Financial Times*, London (UK), May 27, 2010; Charles Duhigg and Keith Bradsher, "How U.S. Lost Out on iPhone Work," www.nytimes.com, January 21, 2012; Jason Dean, "Corporate News: China Worker Suicides Draw Scrutiny," *Wall Street Journal*, May 15, 2010, p. B.5; Frederik Balfour and Tim Culpan, "The Man Who Makes Your iPhone," *Bloomberg Business Week*, September 9, 2010; Andrew Morse and Nick Wingfield, "Apple Audits Labor Practices—Company Says Suppliers Hired Underage Workers, Violated Other Core Policies," *Wall Street Journal*, March 1, 2010, p. B.3; Duncan Hewitt, "Labor's Day in China: Still, there's a risk for China: As labor's lot improves, employers may move where wages are lower and workers more pliable," *Newsweek*, June 21, 2010; Ton Dokoupil, "The Last Company Town: There was a time when employers provided everything: houses, hospitals, bars. Such a place still exists—but not for long. Welcome to Scotia, Calif.," *Newsweek*, February 21, 2011; Charles Duhigg and David Barboza, "In China, Human Costs Are Built into an iPad," www.nytimes.com, January 25, 2012; Fareed Zakaria, "The Case for Making It in the U.S.A.," *Time*, February 6, 2012; Nick Wingfield, "Apple Announces Independent Factory Inspections," www.nytimes.com, February 13, 2012; David Barboza, "Foxconn Plans to Lift Pay Sharply at Factories in China," *New York Times*, February 18, 2012.
2. Duhigg and Bradsher, 2012.
3. M. Schuman, "Adding Up the iPhone: How an American Invention Makes Money for the World," *Time*, May 16, 2011.
4. Ibid.
5. Duhigg and Bradsher, 2012.
6. Duhigg and Barboza, January 25, 2012.

Case Questions

1-11. What is meant by the globalization of human capital? Is this inevitable as firms increase their global operations?

1-12. How does this case illustrate the threats and opportunities facing global companies in developing their strategies?

1-13. Comment on the Apple executive's assertion that the company's only obligation is making the best product possible. "We don't have an obligation to solve America's problems."

1-14. Who are the stakeholders in this situation and what, if any, obligations do they have?

1-15. How much extra are you prepared to pay for an iPhone if assembled in the United States?

1-16. How much extra are you prepared to pay for an iPhone assembled in China but under better labor conditions or pay? What kind of trade-off would you make?

1-17. To what extent do you think the negative media coverage has affected Apple's recent decision to ask the FLA to do an independent assessment and the subsequent decision by Foxconn to raise some salaries?

Endnotes

1. Yuri Bender, "Russia Still Regarded as a Viable Investment," *Financial Times*, March 1, 2015, www.atkearney.com, accessed March 4, 2015; Liz Alderman, "Western Businesses in Russia: Watchful and Wary," *New York Times*, March 7, 2014; "Lovers, Not Fighters: German Firms in Russia," *Economist*, vol. 410, issue 8878, March 15, 2014; Anton Troianovski, Jan Hromadko, "Corporate News: German Firms Fear Fallout If Russia Is Hit with Sanctions," *Wall Street Journal*, Eastern ed., March 17, 2014; "Putin's New 'Cool War' with the West," *The Week*, March 28, 2014; Carol Matlack, Stephen Morris, Robert LaFranco, Alex Sazonov, "Political Turmoil Is Bad for Business in Russia," *Bloomberg Businessweek*, 00077135, March 24, 2014, issue 4372; Michael R. Crittenden, "World News: U.S. Expands Sanctions against Moscow," *Wall Street Journal*, Eastern ed., March 28, 2014, p. A.8; Julie Jargon, "Corporate News: Hold the Fries: McDonald's Closes Its Three Restaurants in Crimea," *Wall Street Journal*, Eastern ed. April 5, 2014, p. B; "BP Says It Can Act as Bridge between Russia and the West," *Reuters*, April 10, 2014; Lewis Krauskopf, "Some U.S. Companies Starting to Feel Pain from Ukraine Crisis," *Reuters*, Wednesday, April 30, 2014; "Putin's Ukrainian U-Turn: Russia and Ukraine," *Economist* 411.8886 (May 10, 2014), p. 12. Mike Dorning, "Business at Odds with Obama over Russia Sanctions Threat," *Bloomberg*, Wednesday, June 25, 13:00:00 UTC 2014; Laurence Norman, Lukas I Alpert, Naftali Bendavid,"New Deadline Set for Ukraine Action: Kiev Extends Cease-Fire After Europe, Backed by U.S., Sets Steps for Moscow to Take in 72 Hours to Avoid New Sanctions," *Wall Street Journal*, Eastern ed. June 28, 2014, p. A.6.; Nataliya Vasilyeva, "Putin: U.S. Sanctions Hurt Bilateral Ties, U.S. Firms," www.time.com, July 17, 2014; *PBS Newshour*, and various news sources, July 29, 2014; Stanley Reed, "Energy Companies Rethinking Russia after a New Round of Sanctions," www.nytimes.com, July 30, 2014; Vladimir Isachenkov, "Russia Hits Back on Sanctions; Bans Food from the West," Associated Press, Thursday, August 7, 2014; Alison Smale, "Ukraine Crisis Hardens Germany against Russia: An Old Partner, "www.nytimes.com, August 13, 2014; Juergen Baetz, "EU Ministers Call for New Sanctions against Russia," Associated Press, Friday, August 29, 2014; Juergen Baetz, "EU Sanctions Hit Russian Oil Companies, Lawmakers," Associated Press, Friday, September 12, 2014; Jeffrey Kluger, Noah Rayman, and Simon Shuster, "Putin Drives Ukraine into a Corner as the West Holds Back," *Time*, September 22, 2014, p.14; Joe Nocera, "Putin Shows His Hand," www.nytimes.com, October 10, 2014; Andrew E. Kramer, "In Ukraine Crisis, U.S. Businesses Face Tit-for-Tat Response to Sanctions," *New York Times*, November 6, 2014; Rob Taylor and Daniel Stacey, "Ukraine Crisis Dominates Agenda at G-20: Russian President Departs Summit Early amid Rebuke from Fellow Leaders; U.S., Europe Force Talks on Climate Change," *Wall Street Journal*, Eastern ed., November 17, 2014, p. A.14; Simon Shuster, "Putin's State of the Nation Speech Unnerves Russian Elites," www.time.com, December 4, 2014; "GM Says It Will Shut Russian Plant, Wind Down Opel Brand," www.nytimes.com, March 18, 2015.
2. Rana Foroohar, "Globalization in Reverse," *Time*, April 7, 2014.
3. Ian Bremmer, "The New Rules of Globalization," *Harvard Business Review*, January–February 2014.
4. Thomas L. Friedman, *The World Is Flat* (New York: Farrar, Strauss and Giroux, 2005), p. 5.
5. Rana Foroohar, "Globalization in Reverse," *Time*, April 7, 2014.
6. Bremmer, 2014.
7. Pankaj Ghemawat, *Redefining Global Strategy* (Boston: Harvard Business School Publishing Corporation, 2007).
8. Pankaj Ghemawat, "Remapping Your Strategic Mindset," *McKinsey Quarterly*, August 2011.
9. Rana Foroohar, "Why the World Isn't Getting Smaller," *Time*, June 27, 2011, p. 20.
10. Peter Bisson, Elizabeth Stephenson, and S. Patrick Viguerie, "Global Forces: An Introduction," *McKinsey Quarterly*, June 2010.
11. Ibid.
12. "Half of the global growth now comes from emerging markets," Robert Zoellick, President World Bank, September 19, 2011, interviewed on *PBS Newshour*.
13. www.atkearney.com, accessed March 7, 2015.
14. Fareed Zakaria, *The Post-American World* (New York: Norton, 2008).
15. Marcos Aguiar et al., "Meet the 2014 BCG Global Challengers," www.bcgperspectives.com, accessed March 8, 2015.
16. "The World's Largest Corporations," *Fortune International (Europe)*, 07385587, July 25, 2011, vol. 164, issue 2.
17. P. Stephens, "A Perilous Collision between Nationalism and Globalisation," *Financial Times*, March 3, 2006.
18. Joseph E. Stiglitz, *Making Globalization Work* (New York: Norton, 2006).
19. Daniel Gross, "Is America Losing at Globalization?" *Newsweek*, September 8, 2008, p. 66.
20. Peter Coy, *BusinessWeek*, July 31, 2008.
21. Section contributed by Charles M. Byles, Virginia Commonwealth University, April 3, 2009.
22. Europa: European Union institutions and other bodies, "The European Commission," accessed March 30, 2009, http://europa.eu/institutions/inst/comm/index_en.htm.
23. Matthew de Paula, "Do You Really Drive an American Car?" *MSN Autos*, January 5, 2011.
24. J. Sapsford and Norihiko Shirouzu, "Mom, Apple Pie and ... Toyota?" *The Wall Street Journal*, May 11, 2006.
25. Charlie Rose, "Charlie Rose Talks to Cisco's John Chambers," *Bloomberg Businessweek*, 00077135, April 23, 2012, issue 4276.
26. Rana Foroohar, "Companies Are the New Countries," *Time*, February 13, 2012.
27. *Economist*, September 20, 2008.
28. J. L. Levere, "A Small Company, a Global Approach," www.nytimes.com, January 1, 2004.
29. Libor Kotlik, Christian Greiser, and Michele Brocca, "Making Big Data Work: Supply Chain Management," www.bcgperspectives.com, January 27, 2015.
30. Ibid.
31. Adriana Gardella, "A Company Grows, and Builds a Plant Back in the U.S.A.," *New York Times*, October 12, 2011.
32. Robert Wright, "'Few' Jobs Come Back to the U.S. via Reshoring," *Financial Times*, September 8, 2014.
33. Dexter Roberts, "Where Made-in-China Textiles Are Emigrating," www.bloombergbusinessweek.com, January 12, 2012.

34. Friedman, p. 6.

35. "Technology," *Bloomberg BusinessWeek*, September 5–11, 2011.

36. *Economist*, September 20, 2008.

37. M. Schuman, "Your New Job: Made in India or China," *Time*, March 28, 2011.

38. Barrett Devlin, Siobhan Gorman, "Chinese Charged in U.S. Hacks: Justice Department Indicts Military Officers, Escalating Fight over Spying," *Wall Street Journal*, Eastern ed., May 20, 2014, p. A.1.; Keith Bradsher, "For U.S. Companies That Challenge China, the Risk of Digital Reprisal," *New York Times*, Tuesday, May 20, 2014; Sam Frizell, "Here's What Chinese Hackers Actually Stole from U.S. Companies," www.time.com, May 20, 2014; and various news organizations; Andreas Schotter and Mary Teagarden, "Protecting Intellectual Property in China," *MIT Sloan Management Review*, June 17, 2014.

39. Financial Times reporters, "Across the Zone: Member States' Finances Dissected," *Financial Times*, September 22, 2011.

40. Excerpts from interviews on the *PBS Newshour*, February 8, 2012.

41. *Global Competitiveness Report 2014–2015*, www.worldeconomic forum.org, accessed March 8, 2015.

42. Ibid.

43. George Parker and Quentin Peel, "A Fractured Europe," *Financial Times*, September 17, 2003, p. 15.

44. U.S. Department of Commerce, www.export.gov, accessed September 16, 2011.

45. Eric Beinhocker, Ian Davis, and Lenny Mendonca, "The Ten Trends You Have to Watch," *Harvard Business Review* 87, No. 7/8 (2009), pp. 55–60.

46. *James C. Cooper*, "A Resurgent Asia Will Lead the Global Recovery," *BusinessWeek*, 4140, (2009), p. 16.

47. FT Summer School, "China: Rough But Ready for Outsiders," *Financial Times*, August 26, 2003.

48. www.imf.org, accessed March 9, 2015.

49. *Time*, March 16, 2015.

50. Title from "China Loses Its Allure," *Economist*, January 25, 2014.

51. Joshua Robinson, "A Slowing China Is Still Seen Leading Global Growth in 2015," *Bloomberg Businessweek*, February 25, 2015.

52. Tom Mitchell and Gabrielle Wildau, "China Lowers GDP Target to around 7 percent," *Financial Times*, March 5, 2015.

53. Ibid.

54. Robinson.

55. Ruchir Sharma, "China and India Need to Make Their Growth Numbers Add Up," FT.com, March 5, 2015.

56. Sources for this section include: Karabell, 2011; U.S. Department of Commerce, "Doing Business in China—2011 Country Commercial Guide for U.S. Companies," www.export .gov, accessed September 20, 2011; Keith Bradsher, "China Plans to Bolster Its Slowing Economy," www.nytimes.com, October 21, 2008; Jim Yardley and Keith Bradsher, "China, an Engine of Growth, Faces a Global Slump," www.nytimes.com, October 23, 2008; Arthur Kroeber and Rosealea Yao, "Large and in Charge," CEQ on FT.com, July 14, 2008; Fareed Zakaria, *The Post American World* (New York: Norton, 2008); www .worldeconomicforum.gov, accessed October 20, 2008; Thomas Friedman, *The World Is Flat* (New York: Farrar, Straus and Giroux, 2005); Tony Fang, Verner Worm, Rosalie L. Tung, "Changing Success and Failure Factors in Business Negotiations with the PRC," *International Business Review* 17, no. 2 (2008).

57. U.S. Department of Commerce: *Doing Business in China—2011 Country Commercial Guide for U.S. Companies*, www.export .gov, accessed September 20, 2011.

58. Simon Rabinovitch in Beijing, "Chinese Foreign Exchange Reserves Shrink," www.ft.com/asia, January 13, 2012.

59. C. Xu, "The Fundamental Institutions of China's Reforms and Development," *Journal of Economic Literature* 49, No. 4 (2011), pp. 1076–1151.

60. U.S. Department of Commerce, September 20, 2011.

61. "Family Firms: The Bollygarchs' Magic Mix," *Economist*, 401. 8756 (October 22, 2011).

62. "State-Controlled Firms: The Power and the Glory," *Economist*, 401. 8756 (October. 22, 2011), p. 17.

63. U.S. Department of Commerce: "Doing Business in Mexico," www.export.gov, accessed September 26, 2011.

64. "World Briefing," *Time*, July 2, 2012.

65. A. T. Kearney 2014–2015 Confidence Index.

66. Mary Anastasia O'Grady, "NAFTA at 20: A Model for Trade Policy," *Wall Street Journal*, January 6, 2014.

67. http://ec.europa.eu/trade/policy/countries-and-regions/regions/ mercosur/, accessed March 9, 2015.

68. John Paul Rathbone, "South America's Giant Comes of Age," www.FT.com, June 28, 2010.

69. https://ustr.gov/trade-agreements/free-trade-agreements/cafta- dr-dominican-republic-central-america-fta, accessed March 9, 2015.

70. B. Appelbaum and J. Steinhauer, "Congress Ends 5-year Standoff on Trade Deals in Rare Accord," www.nytimes, October 12, 2011.

71. Luis Enriquez, Ina Kota, and Sven Smith, "The Outlook for Global Growth in 2015," *McKinsey and Company*, March 2015.

72. Camilla Hall, "Signs of Recovery in M&A," *Financial Times*, London (UK), September 22, 2011, p. 11.

73. Ibid.

74. Khalid Abdulla-Janahi, Chairman of Ithmaar Bank and Co-Chair of the World Economic Forum on the Middle East.

75. Dambisa Moyo, "Beijing, a Boon for Africa," www.nytimes .com, June 27, 2012.

76. Roger Cohen, "The Age of Possibility," *International Herald Tribune,* January 6, 2011.

77. Vivienne Walt, "Is Africa's Rise for Real This Time?" Fortune .com, accessed March 17, 2015.

78. "IMF World Economic Outlook," April 2014, www.imf.org, accessed March 17, 2015.

79. www.statisticssa.gov.za, accessed February 1, 2009.

80. U.S. Department of Commerce, "Doing Business in South Africa," www.export.gov, accessed September 30, 2011.

81. A. T. Kearney, 2014–2015 FDI Confidence Index.

82. N. Itano, "South African Companies Fill a Void," www.nytimes .com, November 4, 2003.

83. www.atkearney.com, accessed September 12, 2008.

84. Ibid.

85. "2011 Aon Global Risk Management Survey," www.aon.com, accessed October 4, 2011.

86. Ibid.

87. Aon Risk Solutions, 2011.

88. Raphael Minder and Simon Romero, "Spain Weighs Response to Nationalization of YPF," www.nytimes.com, April 17, 2012.

89. Clifford J. Levy, "In Hard Times, Russia Tries to Reclaim Industries," www.nytimes.com, December 8, 2008.

90. E. F. Micklous, "Tracking the Growth and Prevalence of International Terrorism," in *Managing Terrorism: Strategies for the Corporate Executive*, P. J. Montana and G. S. Roukis, eds. (Westport, CT: Quorum Books, 1983), p. 3.

91. W. Shreeve, "Be Prepared for Political Changes Abroad," *Harvard Business Review*, (July–August 1984), pp. 111–118.

92. G. M. Taoka and D. R. Beeman, *International Business* (New York: HarperCollins, 1991) p. 112.

93. Ibid.

94. B. O'Reilly, "Business Copes with Terrorism," *Fortune*, January 6, 2004, p. 48.

95. Heritage Foundation, http/www.heritage.org, accessed August 8, 2011.

96. F. John Mathis, "International Risk Analysis," in *Global Business Management in the 1990s*, R. T. Moran, ed. (Washington, DC: Beacham, 1990), pp. 33–44.

97. Rahul Jacob, "Asian Infrastructure: The Biggest Bet on Earth," *Fortune*, October 31, 1994, 139–146.

98. Paul Taylor, "The Connected Business, Corporate IT: Analytics and Mobility among Big 2014 Trends," *Financial Times*, January 29, 2014.

99. Friedman, 2005.

100. World Economic Forum, "2014 Global Information Technology Report," www.weforum.org/.../global-information-technology-report-2014.

101. Choe Sang Hun, "I. H. T. Special Report: Smart Cities—No Rest for the Wired," http://global.nytimes.com/?iht, October 1, 2011.

102. Press release, www.pg.com, accessed October 21, 2011.

103. Jack Goldsmith and Tim Wu, *Who Controls the Internet? Illusions of a Borderless World* (London: Oxford UP, 2006).

104. Ibid.

105. Hans Dieter Zimmerman, "E-Business," www.businessmedia.org, June 13, 2000.

106. J. Rajesh, "Five E-Business Trends," Net. Columns, www.indialine.com, February 18, 1999.

107. "Europe's Borderless Market: The Net," www.businessweek.com, May 17, 2003.

108. "E-Management," *Economist,* November 11, 2000, pp. 32–34.

109. "E-Commerce Report," *New York Times*, March 26, 2001, pp. 7–8

110. S. Mohanbir and M. Sumant, "Go Global," *Business 2.0*, May 2000, pp. 178–213.

111. A. Chen and M. Hicks, "Going Global? Avoid Culture Clashes," *PC Week*, April 3, 2000, pp. 9–10.

112. Steve Muylle, Niraj Dawar, Deva Rangarajan, "B2B Brand Architecture," *California Management Review* 54, No. 2 (Winter 2012).

113. B2B Directory, www.Forbes.com, accessed March 29, 2012.

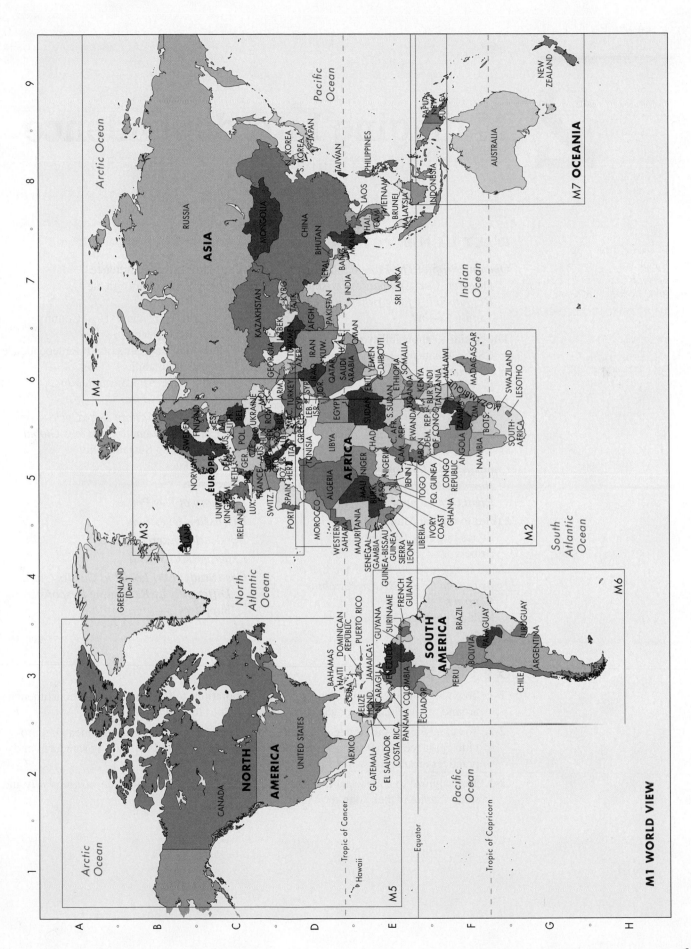

M1 WORLD VIEW

2 Managing Interdependence
Social Responsibility, Ethics, Sustainability

OUTLINE

OBJECTIVES

2-1. To understand the social responsibility of corporations toward their various constituencies around the world, in particular their responsibilities toward human rights

2-2. To acknowledge the strategic role that ethics must play in global management and provide guidance to managers to maintain ethical behavior amid the varying standards and practices around the world

2-3. To recognize the importance of managing interdependence and include *sustainability* and *shared value* in their long-term plans

Opening Profile: The Bangladesh Disaster: Can Companies Outsource Responsibility for Workers in Its Supply Chain?[1]

To what extent was it ignorance or negligence on behalf of the key players in the global apparel industry that led to the fire in the Tazreen Fashions Factory in Bangladesh that killed 1,127 workers in November 2012? Accusations abound of locked doors and too few fire exits. The Bangladesh government inquiry put the blame on the Tazreen factory owner for negligence and unsafe working conditions, and Sears and Walmart said they did not know their clothing was being produced there. Has the apparel industry's global supply chain become so complex that those retailers outsourcing production in Bangladesh can claim ignorance for this terrible failure of its responsibilities? In fact, this was not the first fire in Bangladesh factories used for low-wage production by companies such as Sears, Gap, Walmart, and Hennes and Mauritz AB. Subsequently, in April 2013, the collapse of a factory complex in Dhaka killed more than 1,200 people and brought the problems of oversight to the forefront. In June 2013, the Obama administration suspended Bangladesh from a preferential trade program (although that program did not include garment exports) to pressure the government to improve working conditions and allow unions to form.

These tragedies, in addition to increasing political unrest there, have caused Western companies to scramble in dealing with such a devastating situation and the negative public outcry that resulted. Most started to look for other overseas locations for their production outsourcing; but concern remained for the increased impoverishment that would result from their withdrawal. Walt Disney Company halted its production of branded merchandise in Bangladesh but said the company would reconsider if better labor standards and worker protections were put in place. The strategic problem for large retailers continues to be one of finding low-wage countries that can handle the complexities of producing, labeling, and shipping very large quantities of merchandise in a timely fashion.

As wages in China have risen, more business has gone to Bangladesh, now the world's second largest exporter of apparel, with wages at about $37 a month, far less than that in China. In addition, only about 1 percent of textile workers in Bangladesh is unionized. The 4,500 garment factories there employ more than four million workers, and there is minimal union activity. With such low wages and terrible working conditions, to what extent does the problem of factory conditions belong to those multinationals and to what extent to the local government to oversee conditions? Most of the factories in the region are structurally unsafe, and there are very few local inspectors; in addition, a high level of corruption and pressure from local officials confound the problem.

Is it possible to chase after lower and lower labor costs and still maintain control over the supply chain? If companies insist on the lowest cost basis, is there pressure on the suppliers and local factories contracted for the work to cut corners on safety? What is the responsibility of the global firms to workers in the supply chain for its products? Can they pass that responsibility on to the local factory managers? Can those multinationals really publish their codes of conduct and inspection practices and yet not know what goes on in those factories? What responsibility have those firms taken after these tragedies? A year after the Tazreen fire, many retailers whose clothing had been produced in those factories have declined to add to a compensation fund for the families of the 1,200 plus workers who died in the fire or to the 1,800 who were injured.

For its part, Walmart, for example, says it has 100,000 suppliers, employs independent inspection firms, and cancels contracts with suppliers found deficient in safety.

Since the 2013 fire, about 90 European firms have signed on to a pledge to oversee improvements in factories in Bangladesh, and some U.S. retailers have signed a similar agreement. The group of 17 North American retailers, including Gap, Target, J. C. Penney, Kohls, and Macy's, pledged $42 million for worker safety programs and $100 million in loans to factory owners to correct problems. In addition, the plan called for the retailers to inspect the more than 500 factories they use in Bangladesh for production and work with them to correct any safety problems; but if those factory owners and managers do not bring the situation up to standards, the U.S. retailers say that they will not contract to them.

However, criticism toward U.S. retailers came from the European-led group, the Accord on Fire and Building Safety in Bangladesh, which includes around 100 companies such as Carrefour and H&M. The group has made binding commitments to improve safety at the factories but charged the U.S. group with only committing loans. The U.S. retailers expressed concern about legal liability if they were involved in such decisions regarding worker safety and there is a breakdown in the supply chain oversight; but the European retailers involved in the plan were not concerned about liability. However, both groups have been working together to develop worker safety standards. The problem, according to industry watchers, is that the suppliers often subcontract the manufacturing contracts, thereby further removing the actual oversight of the production from the control of inspectors.

How should retailers balance their profitability against their responsibilities and reputation in overseas contracting? Is the answer to move production to other countries? Would that solve the supply chain oversight problem? Moreover, how would that affect the 3.6 million workers in the garment industry in Bangladesh? Who are the parties who should be held accountable for these disasters? Who are the stakeholders in this kind of situation? Are you one of them?

Global interdependence is a compelling factor in the global business environment, creating demands on international managers to take a positive stance on issues of social responsibility and ethical behavior, economic development in host countries, and ecological protection around the world.

Managers today are usually quite sensitive to issues of social responsibility and ethical behavior because of pressures from the public, from interest groups, from legal and governmental concerns, and from media coverage (as illustrated in the opening profile). The United Nations published guidelines for the responsibilities of transnational corporations and called for companies to be subject to monitoring, verification, and censure. Although many companies agree with the guidelines, they resist the notion that corporate responsibility should be regulated and question where to draw the line between socially responsible behavior and the concerns of the corporation's other stakeholders.[2] In the domestic arena, managers are faced with numerous ethical complexities. In the international arena, such concerns are compounded by the larger numbers of stakeholders involved, including customers, communities, allies, and owners in various countries. However complex, it is clear that for the most part corporations have accepted, acknowledged, and incorporated into their planning process their responsibility toward ethical behavior, human rights issues, and the environment. Unfortunately, what we hear most about is those incidents and examples of poor implementation of those lofty plans, especially in developing countries, and it is those incidents, emphasized in the media, that overshadow the otherwise responsible position of the leaders of those corporations.

This chapter's discussion focuses separately on issues of social responsibility and ethical behavior, though considerable overlap is apparent. The difference between the two is a matter of scope and degree. Whereas ethics deals with decisions and interactions mostly on an individual level, decisions about social responsibility are broader in scope, tend to be made at a higher level, affect more people, and reflect a general stance a company or a number of decision makers takes. Also discussed separately is the topic of sustainability—although it, too, falls under the umbrella of **corporate social responsibility (CSR)** and—for more proactive firms—the direction of creating shared value (CSV).

THE SOCIAL RESPONSIBILITY OF MNCs

… advocates of corporate social responsibility consider it a wealth-creating opportunity that will attract new consumers, idealistic employees, and the potential for reduced capital cost; … critics claim corporate social responsibility is a form of taxation that reduces the value-creation process of capital.[3]

HARVARD BUSINESS REVIEW
JUNE 2011

IKEA is investing €125 million, or $163 million, in social programs to help women and children in India and elsewhere in South Asia…. We're not on the stock exchange, so we can be very long term.

MIKAEL OHLSSON, IKEA CEO,
WWW.NYTIMES.COM SEPTEMBER 20, 2010[4]

Multinational corporations (MNCs) and multinational enterprises (MNEs) have been—and to less extent continue to be—at the center of debate regarding corporate social responsibility (CSR), particularly concerning the benefits versus harm wrought by their operations around the world, especially in developing countries. The criticisms of MNCs have been lessened in recent years by the decreasing economic differences among countries, by the emergence of developing countries' own multinationals, and by the greater emphasis on social responsibility by MNCs.

Issues of social responsibility continue to center on poverty and lack of equal opportunity around the world, the environment, consumer concerns, and employee safety and welfare. Many argue that, because MNCs operate in a global context, they should use their capital, skills, and power to play proactive roles in handling worldwide social and economic problems and that, at the least, they should be concerned with host-country welfare. Others argue that MNCs already have a positive impact on developing economies by providing managerial training, investment capital, and new technology as well as by creating jobs and improving infrastructure. Certainly, multinational corporations constitute a powerful presence in the world economy and often have a greater capacity than local governments to induce change. The sales, debts, and resources of some of the largest multinationals exceed the gross national product, the public and private debt, and the resources, respectively, of some nations.

The concept of **international social responsibility** includes the expectation that MNCs concern themselves with the social and economic effects of their decisions. The issue is how far that concern should go and what level of planning and control that concern should take. Opinions on the level of social responsibility that a domestic firm should demonstrate range from one extreme—the only responsibility of a business is to make a profit, within the confines of the law; to produce goods and services; and serve its shareholders' interests[5]—to another extreme—companies should anticipate and try to solve problems in society. Between these extremes are varying positions described as socially reactive, in which companies respond to some degree of currently prevailing social expectations and to the environmental and social costs of their actions, as illustrated in the opening profile. Although most firms comply with national and local laws and regulations, they also might actually locate some operations where those legal requirements are less restrictive or not imposed at all. As an additional layer of responsibility, most firms will formalize programs for ethical compliance—it's hoped for the right reasons—but also to avoid problems. Usually, those organizations will provide guidelines and programs to avoid problems such as sexual harassment cases and the thorny issue of the expectations of bribery when operating abroad. Beyond those rather minimal approaches, firms that take social responsibility seriously attempt to view the perspectives of all stakeholders involved when taking a long-term approach to the firm's ability to continue operations in any location, as discussed below.

The stance toward social responsibility that a firm should take in its international operations, however, is much more complex—ranging perhaps from assuming some responsibility for economic development in a subsidiary's host country to taking an active role in identifying and solving world problems. The increased complexity regarding the social responsibility and ethical behavior of firms across borders is caused by the additional stakeholders in the firm's activities through operating overseas as well as the legal and regulatory requirements and expectations prevailing where the firm is operating. As illustrated in Exhibit 2-1, managers are faced not only with considering stakeholders in the host country but also with weighing their rights against the rights of their domestic stakeholders. Most managerial decisions will have a trade-off of the rights of these stakeholders—at least in the short term. For example, a decision to discontinue using children in Pakistan to sew soccer balls means the company will pay more for adult employees and will, therefore, reduce the profitability to its owners. That same decision—while taking a stand for human rights according to the social and ethical expectations in the home country and bowing to consumers' demands—may mean that those children and their families go hungry or are forced into worse working situations. Another decision to keep jobs at home to satisfy local employees and unions will mean higher prices for consumers and less profit for shareholders. In addition, if competitors take their jobs to cheaper overseas factories, a company may go out of business, which will mean no jobs at all for the domestic employees and a loss for the owners.

Paul Krugman contends that opposing industrialization based on low wages "means that you are willing to deny desperately poor people the best chance they have of progress for the sake of what amounts to an aesthetic standard—that is, the fact that you don't like the idea of workers being paid a pittance to supply rich Westerners with fashion items."[6]

EXHIBIT 2-1 MNC Stakeholders

MNC Stakeholders

Home Country
Owners
Customers
Employees
Unions
Suppliers
Distributors
Strategic allies
Community
Economy
Government

MNC

Host Country
Economy
Employees
Community
Host government
Consumers
Strategic allies
Suppliers
Distributors

Society in General
(global interdependence/
standard of living)
Global environment and ecology
Sustainable resources
Population's standard of living

Clearly, foreign investment in China, for example, has driven spectacular growth, increased wages, and radically lowered the poverty rate. This compares with Bangladesh, with minimal foreign investment and a population continuing in abject poverty.[7] Nevertheless, the campaigns of anti-sweatshop activists have resulted in some improvements in workers' lives in other countries, in particular regarding health and safety issues.

In spite of conflicting agendas, there is some consensus about what CSR means at a basic level—that "corporate activity should be motivated in part by a concern for the welfare of some non-owners, and by an underlying commitment to basic principles such as integrity, fairness and respect for persons."[8]

In addition, it is clear that long-term competitive benefits derive from CSR, many of which result from the goodwill, attractiveness, and loyalty of the various stakeholders connected with the company. These may be in the local area, such as government, suppliers, employees, brand reputation, and so on, or far-flung, such as consumers. IKEA, quoted previously, is an example of a long-term attitude to CSR. IKEA, the Swedish home retailer with 317 stores worldwide, gave up its plans to open dozens of stores in India after the Indian government would not lift limits on foreign investment in the retail sector. Even so, IKEA plans to double the number of goods it buys in India and is investing 125 million euro (about $163 million) in social programs to help women and children in India and elsewhere in South Asia. These investments made IKEA the largest corporate partner in the world to aid agencies, including UNICEF and Save the Children.[9] Subsequently, IKEA announced in June 2012 that the company had been granted permission to open 25 stores in India under a policy change that allows some retailers to own 100 percent of their units there.[10] It would seem, from this development, that the company's benevolence did pay off.

Manuela Weber suggests that the impact of CSR on business benefits, listed below, can increase the firm's competitiveness and thus economic success.

Business benefits from CSR[11]

- Improved access to capital
- Secured license to operate
- Revenue increases
- Cost decreases
- Risk reduction
- Increase in brand value
- Improved customer attraction and retention
- Improved reputation
- Improved employee recruitment, motivation, and retention

CSR: Global Consensus or Regional Variation?

With the growing awareness of the world's socioeconomic interdependence, global organizations are beginning to recognize the need to reach a consensus on what should constitute moral and ethical behavior. Some think that such a consensus is emerging because of the development of a **global corporate culture**—an integration of the business environments in which firms currently operate. This integration results from the gradual dissolution of traditional boundaries and from the many intricate interconnections among MNCs, internationally linked securities markets, and communication networks. Nevertheless, there are commonly acknowledged regional variations in how companies respond to CSR:

> *The U.S. and Europe adopt strikingly different positions that can be traced largely to history and culture. In the U.S., CSR is weighted more towards "doing business right" by following basic business obligations; ... in Europe, CSR is weighted more towards serving—or at least not conflicting with—broader social aims, such as environmental sustainability.*[12]
>
> FINANCIAL TIMES

While making good faith efforts to implement CSR, companies operating abroad face confusion about the cross-cultural dilemmas it creates, especially concerning how to behave in host countries, which have their own differing expectations and agendas. Recommendations about how to deal with such dilemmas include:

- Engaging stakeholders (and sometimes nongovernmental organizations, or NGOs) in a dialogue.
- Establishing principles and procedures for addressing difficult issues such as labor standards for suppliers, environmental reporting, and human rights.
- Adjusting reward systems to reflect the company's commitment to CSR.[13]

Although it is very difficult to implement a generalized code of morality and ethics in individual countries, such guidelines do provide a basis of judgment regarding specific situations. Bowie uses the term **moral universalism** to address the need for a moral standard that all cultures accept.[14] Although, in practice, it seems unlikely that a universal code of ethics will ever be a reality, Bowie says that this approach to doing business across cultures is far preferable to other approaches such as ethnocentrism or ethical relativism. With an **ethnocentric approach**, a company applies the morality used in its home country—regardless of the host country's system of ethics.

A company subscribing to **ethical relativism**, on the other hand, simply adopts the local moral code of whatever country in which it is operating. With this approach, companies run into value conflicts, such as continuing to do business in China despite home-country objections to China's continued violation of human rights. In addition, public pressure in the home country often forces the MNC to act in accordance with ethnocentric value systems anyway, such as not exporting products that are considered harmful in the home country. In addition, in 2011, "facing pressure from universities and student groups, Nike announced an agreement on Monday in which it pledged to pay $1.54 million to help 1,800 workers in Honduras who lost their jobs when two subcontractors closed their factories."[15]

The difficulty, even in adopting a stance of moral universalism, is in deciding where to draw the line. Individual managers must decide, at some point, based on their own morality, when they feel a situation is simply not right and withdraw their involvement.

One fact, however, is inescapable: in a globalized market economy, CSR has to be part of modern business.

From CSR to Shared Value?

According to Porter and Kramer, the concept of social responsibility in which corporations regard societal issues as legal or image concerns outside of the main business is a short-sighted approach to value creation and therefore to competitiveness.[16] Rather, that Creating Shared Value (CSV) expands the pool of economic and social value and so "leverages the unique resources and expertise of the company to create economic value by creating social value."[17] By viewing the growth, profitability, and sustainability of the corporation as intermeshed with societal and economic progress in the markets in which it operates, companies such as Nestlé (featured in the accompanying "Under the Lens" box), Google, and Intel are creating shared value by "reconceiving products and markets; redefining productivity in the value chain; and enabling local cluster development"[18] (clusters of related business in a local area in which the company operates). Walmart, for example, has reduced its environmental footprint by revamping the plastic used in its stores and by reducing its packaging; it also has cut 100 million miles from its delivery routes, saving $200 million even as it shipped more products.

Google announced its plan to go all out to establish the company in Europe "as more of a local player that is investing in jobs, in facilities, our physical presence, and all the ancillary things that come with that."[19] Google clearly has developed this new approach in response to challenges on issues including privacy, copyright disputes, antitrust actions, and taxation. "The company is spending hundreds of millions of euro to try to demonstrate that it is a responsible corporate citizen and a valuable contributor to the local economy."[20] In this case, one questions whether this is truly creating shared value or simply practicing CSR in response to Google's negative image and lost opportunities. Even now, in 2015, Google is still being charged with violating privacy rules in Europe.

UNDER THE LENS

Nestlé Company Creates Shared Value Globally [21]

Among the increasing number of companies that are transitioning from corporate social responsibility (CSR) to a more strategic perspective known as creating shared value (CSV), Nestlé Corporation stands out for its focus and breadth of action within this realm.

Nestlé, with its head office in Vevey, Switzerland, is the largest food company in the world, with 330,000 employees; 165,000 contractual suppliers; and 456 factories in 86 countries.

In its model, which follows, Nestlé shows how it has advanced the company strategy and resources beyond that of social responsibility to that of creating shared value with its stakeholders in a long-term agenda. As you compare the approach in the model for CSV with those typical of CSR, it is

EXHIBIT 2-2 Nestlé Creates Shared Value

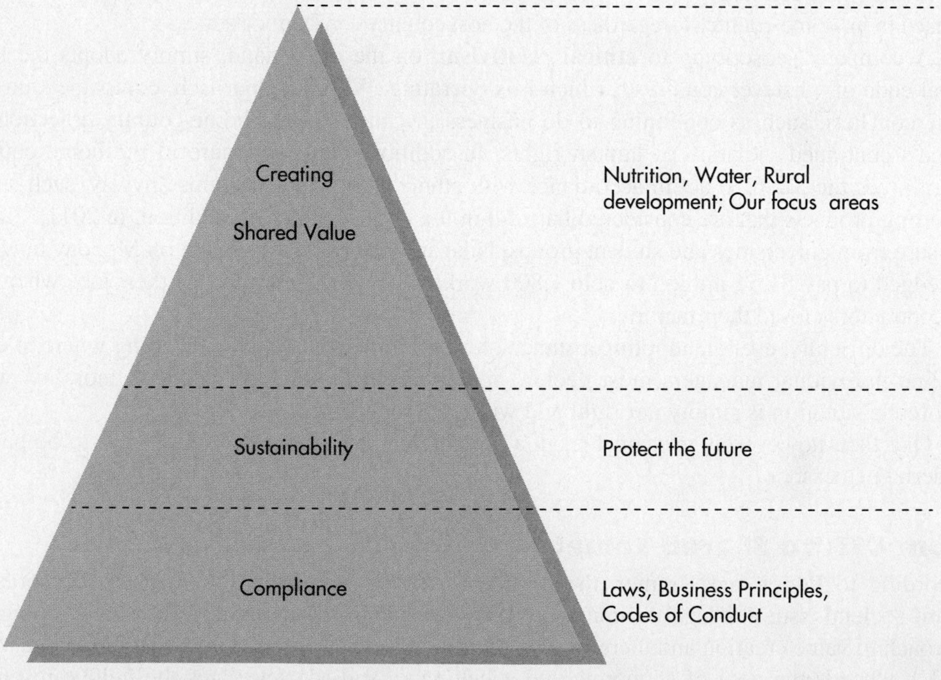

Creating
Shared Value — Nutrition, Water, Rural development; Our focus areas

Sustainability — Protect the future

Compliance — Laws, Business Principles, Codes of Conduct

Source: http://www.nestle.com/csv/what-is-csv/

clear that Nestlé has evolved from a perspective of responding to outside conditions and pressures to that of internal and community initiatives and integration throughout the company's operations, along with the community.

Nestlé's SAI (sustainable agriculture initiative) has become the gold standard within the global food industry for sustainable sourcing and agriculture, promoting rural development. In fact, recognizing that other global food companies faced the same issues, Nestlé joined forces with companies such as Danone and Unilever in 2003 to consult on how to deal with problems such as scarce resources, quality issues, contaminants, and pollution. Today, Nestlé's focus on sustainable water resources, nutrition, and rural development uses consultation with its stakeholders around the world and incorporates that feedback into strategic development. That focus is incorporated into the firm's strategy and operations through its employees at all levels of the company rather than a directive from a compliance officer. The company website explains its CSV philosophy as follows:

> To create value for our shareholders and our company, we must create value for people in the countries where we are present. This includes the farmers who supply us, the employees who work for us, our consumers and the communities where we work.

As an example, Nestlé Bangladesh sources raw materials from local suppliers and farmers to ensure that the farmers get fair prices for their produce and to promote the company's sustainability by reducing dependence on imports. In addition, under the Nestlé Clean Drinking Water project, the company provides water tanks for schools in Gazipur, benefiting more than 43,000 students.

MNC Responsibility toward Human Rights

> With almost all tech products now made by contract manufacturers in low-wage nations where sweatshops are common, … Hewlett Packard, Dell, IBM, Intel, and twelve other tech companies decided to unite to create the Electronic Industry Code of Conduct (EICC).
>
> BUSINESSWEEK[22]

Whereas many situations regarding the morality of the MNC's presence or activities in a country are quite clear, other situations are not, especially when dealing with human rights. So loud has been the cry about products coming from so-called sweatshops around the world that former President Bill Clinton established an Anti-Sweatshop Code of Conduct, which includes a ban on forced labor, abuse, and discrimination and requires companies to provide a healthy and safe work environment and to pay at least the prevailing local minimum wage, among other requirements. Nike's efforts to address its problems include publishing its entire list of contract manufacturers on the Internet to gain transparency. The company admits that it is difficult to keep track of what goes on at its 800-plus contracted factories around the world.[23]

What constitutes human rights is clouded by the perceptions and priorities of people in different countries. Although the United States often takes the lead in the charge against what it considers human rights violations around the world, other countries point to the homelessness and high crime statistics in the United States. Often the discussion of human rights centers on Asia because many of the products sold in the West are imported from Asia by Western companies using manufacturing facilities located there (see, for example, the accompanying "Comparative Management in Focus" section, which focuses on China). It is commonly held in the West that the best chance to gain some ground on human rights issues is for large MNCs and governments around the world to take a unified stance; many global players now question the morality of trading for goods that have been produced by forced labor or child labor. Although laws in the United States ban prison imports, shady deals between the manufacturers and companies acting as intermediaries make it difficult to determine the origin of many products—and make it easy for companies wanting access to cheap products or materials to ignore the law. However, under pressure from their labor unions (and perhaps their consciences), a number of large, image-conscious companies, such as Reebok and Levi Strauss, have established corporate codes of conduct for their buyers, suppliers, and contractors and have instituted strict procedures for auditing

Comparative Management in Focus
Doing Business in China—CSR and the Human Rights Challenge

Apart from cracking down on media and academia, the party has also started tightening internet censorship, adding more layers to the "Great Firewall" which already blocks sites such as Google, Facebook, Twitter, and YouTube.

FINANCIAL TIMES
January 31, 2015[24]

China ranks 100th in the Transparency International 2014 Corruption Perceptions Index—down from 78th in 2010.[25]

WWW.TRANSPARENCYINTERNATIONAL.ORG
February 11, 2015

China's growth engine continued to drive the global economy in 2015 (albeit more slowly), ... propelled by China's $586 billion economic stimulus plan enacted during the global economic downturn. However, although this growth has lifted millions of Chinese out of poverty, many people and their basic rights remain largely behind, and there has been a heavy cost to the environment as energy usage increases and causes pollution. "China has tightened controls over all aspects of public life and clamped down hard on freedom of expression since President Xi Jinping took over in 2012."[26]

Although growth in higher-skilled jobs and in services is now well under way, there is continuing concern among MNCs about the pitfalls of operating in China. These include the uncertain legal climate; the difficulty of protecting intellectual property there; the repression of free speech; and the difficulty of monitoring, let alone correcting, human rights violations in factories. MNCs face considerable pressure in their home markets to address human rights issues in China and elsewhere. Consumers boycott their products, and trade unions in the United States, for example, complain that repression of workers' rights has enabled Chinese companies to push down labor costs, causing considerable loss of manufacturing jobs at home. In addition, whereas the culture of profit has resulted in a market economy in regions of China, reducing the number of state-owned enterprises while

MAP 2.1 **China**

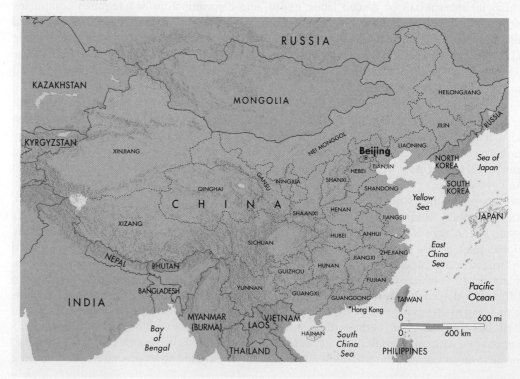

increasing joint ventures and private ownership, that culture seems to have led to shortcuts in manu-facturing, leading to problems with products and poor treatment of workers.

Freedom of information took a particularly hard hit, as the Financial Times reported in January 2015, when "China's education minister has vowed that 'western values' will never be allowed in the country's classrooms as the Communist Party steps up efforts to consolidate autocratic rule and stave off demands for democracy and universal human rights."[27]

This included curbs on Twitter–style microblogs, which had been critical of the government, and severe limits on television programs.

Previously, as is now well known, Google had agreed to China's demands to apply censors' blacklists to its search engine there. In spite of Google's founding principle, "Don't be evil," its business interests apparently clashed with its principles, leading many to conclude that Google is putting its own freedoms at risk in China; however, that is also occurring with Microsoft and Yahoo! in China.[28]

Although Internet and technology executives were called to Capitol Hill in February 2006 to defend their companies' practices in China, it was clear that American corporations and their foreign policy interests would prevail.[29] Rather, the debate continues over how Internet companies can engage more effectively with Beijing on human rights issues. However, in a blow to the industry, Amnesty International accused Yahoo!, Microsoft, and Google of overlook-ing their human rights obligations to tap into China's dynamic online market, stating that "all three companies have in different ways facilitated or participated in the practice of government censorship in China."[30]

The latest censorship moves come as a disappointment because it had seemed that China was becoming more conscious of the need to improve its image regarding CSR as it takes a larger economic role on the world stage; indeed, its membership in the WTO obliges the country to act in concert with the policies and values of a free market.[31] Recognition of the UN Social

FIGURE 2-1 Women in Garment Factory in China   Garment factory of an unnamed company in China, where women work very long hours.

xy/Fotolia

(Continued)

Accountability Code (8000), adopted by more than 200 companies worldwide, has helped establish some norms regarding workers' rights in some provinces and cities in China. Although, as noted by Po Keung Ip, many companies adopted the code because they were forced to do so by their MNC buyers, which were under constant pressure themselves from consumers, investors, NGOs, and governments in their home countries. "Major MNCs, like Walmart, Nike, Adidas, Avon, Motorola, Gap, and Carrefour, have been instrumental in transforming the business behaviors of their Chinese contractors through their ethical supply chain management which selects and audits contractors according to ethical codes."[32]

their imports. In addition, some companies are uniting with others in their industry to form their own code for responsible action.[33]

A considerable number of organizations have developed their own codes of conduct; some have gone further to join others around the world to establish standards to improve the quality of life for workers around the world. Companies such as Avon, Sainsbury Plc., Toys "R" Us, and Otto Versand have joined with the Council on Economic Priorities (CEP) to establish SA8000 (Social Accountability 8000, on the lines of the ISO9000 manufacturing quality standard). Their proposed global labor standards would be monitored by outside organizations to certify whether plants are meeting those standards, among which are the following:

- Do not use child or forced labor.
- Provide a safe working environment.
- Respect workers' rights to unionize.
- Do not regularly require more than 48-hour workweeks.
- Pay wages sufficient to meet workers' basic needs.[34]

In addition, four **international codes of conduct** provide some consistent guidelines for multinational enterprises (MNEs). These codes were developed by several institutions and integrated by Getz into their common underlying principles, thereby establishing MNE behavior toward governments, publics, and people, as shown in Exhibit 2-3. (The originating institutions are in parentheses.) Getz concludes, "As international organizations and institutions (including MNEs themselves) continue to refine the codes, the underlying moral issues will be better identified, and appropriate MNE behavior will be more readily apparent."[35] The examples shown in Exhibit 2-3 are excerpted from the codes and show how companies can provide a cooperative, long-term relationship with the local people and governments where they operate.

ETHICS IN GLOBAL MANAGEMENT

National, as well as corporate, cultures need to be taken into account if multinationals are to enforce their codes across different regions.

FINANCIAL TIMES[36]

Globalization has multiplied the ethical problems facing organizations. However, business ethics have not yet been globalized. Attitudes toward ethics are rooted in culture and business practices. Swee Hoon Ang found, for example, that although east Asians seemed to be less ethical than their expatriate counterparts from the United States and Britain, it was because they considered deception as amoral and acceptable if it has a positive effect on larger issues such as the company, the extended family, or the state.[37] For an MNC, it is difficult to reconcile consistent and acceptable behavior around the world with home-country standards. One question, in fact, is whether it should be reconciled. It seems that, although the United States has been the driving force to legislate moral business conduct overseas, perhaps more scrutiny should have been applied to those global MNCs headquartered in the United States, such as Enron and WorldCom, that so greatly defrauded their investors, employees, and all who had business with them.

The term **international business ethics** refers to the business conduct or morals of MNCs in their relationships with individuals and entities. Such behavior is based largely on the cultural value system and the generally accepted ways of doing business in each country or society, as we have discussed throughout this book. Those norms, in turn, are based on broadly accepted guidelines from religion, philosophy, professional organizations, and the legal system. The complexity of the combination of various national and cultural factors in a particular host

EXHIBIT 2-3 International Codes of Conduct for MNEs

MNE and Host Governments

Economic and Developmental Policies

- MNEs should consult with governmental authorities and national employers' and workers' organizations to ensure that their investments conform to the economic and social development policies of the host country. (ICC; OECD; ILO; UN/CTC)
- MNEs should not adversely disturb the balance-of-payments or currency exchange rates of the countries in which they operate. They should try, in consultation with the government, to resolve balance-of-payments and exchange rate difficulties when possible. (ICC; OECD; UN/CTC)
- MNEs should cooperate with governmental policies regarding local equity participation. (ICC; UN/CTC)
- MNEs should not dominate the capital markets of the countries in which they operate. (ICC; UN/CTC)
- MNEs should provide the information necessary for correctly assessing taxes to be paid to host government authorities. (ICC; OECD)
- MNEs should not engage in transfer pricing policies that modify the tax base on which their entities are assessed. (OECD; UN/CTC)
- MNEs should give preference to local sources for components and raw materials if prices and quality are competitive. (ICC; ILO)
- MNEs should reinvest some profits in the countries in which they operate. (ICC)

Laws and Regulations

- MNEs are subject to the laws, regulations, and jurisdiction of the countries in which they operate. (ICC; OECD; UN/CTC)
- MNEs should respect the right of every country to exercise control over its natural resources, and to regulate the activities of entities operating within its territory. (ICC; OECD; UN/CTC)
- MNEs should use appropriate international dispute settlement mechanisms, including arbitration, to resolve conflicts with the governments of the countries in which they operate. (ICC; OECD)
- MNEs should resolve disputes arising from expropriation by host governments under the domestic law of the host country. (UN/CTC)

Political Involvement

- MNEs should refrain from improper or illegal involvement in local political activities. (OECD; UN/CTC)
- MNEs should not pay bribes or render improper benefits to any public servant. (OECD; UN/CTC)
- MNEs should not interfere in intergovernmental relations. (UN/CTC)

MNEs and the Public

Technology Transfer

- MNEs should cooperate with governmental authorities in assessing the impact of transfers of technology to developing countries and should enhance the technological capacities of developing countries. (OECD; UN/CTC)
- MNEs should develop and adapt technologies to the needs and characteristics of the countries in which they operate. (ICC; OECD; ILO)
- MNEs should conduct research and development activities in developing countries, using local resources and personnel to the greatest extent possible. (ICC; UN/CTC)

Environmental Protection

- MNEs should respect the laws and regulations concerning environmental protection of the countries in which they operate. (OECD; UN/CTC)
- MNEs should cooperate with host governments and with international organizations in the development of national and international environmental protection standards. (ICC; UN/CTC)
- MNEs should supply to appropriate host governmental authorities information concerning the environmental impact of the products and processes of their entities. (ICC; UN/CTC)

MNEs and Persons

Consumer Protection

- MNEs should respect the laws and regulations of the countries in which they operate with regard to consumer protection. (OECD; UN/CTC)
- MNEs should preserve the safety and health of consumers by disclosure of appropriate information, proper labeling, and accurate advertising. (UN/CTC)

(Continued)

EXHIBIT 2-3 Continued

Employment Practices (excerpts)

- MNEs should cooperate with host governments' efforts to create employment opportunities in particular localities. (ICC)
- MNEs should try to increase employment opportunities and standards in the countries in which they operate. (ILO)
- MNEs should give advance notice of plant closures and mitigate the resultant adverse effects. (ICC; OECD; ILO)
- MNEs should provide standards of employment equal to or better than those of comparable employers in the countries in which they operate. (ICC; OECD; ILO)
- MNEs should pay, at minimum, basic living wages. (ILO)
- MNEs should maintain the highest standards of safety and health, and should provide adequate information about work-related health hazards. (ILO)

Human Rights

- MNEs should respect human rights and fundamental freedoms in the countries in which they operate. (UN/CTC)
- MNEs should not discriminate on the basis of race, color, sex, religion, language, social, national and ethnic origin, or political or other opinion. (UN/CTC)
- MNEs should respect the social and cultural objectives, values, and traditions of the countries in which they operate. (UN/CTC)

Sources: OECD: The Organization for Economic Cooperation and Development Guidelines for Multinational Enterprises; ILO: The International Labor Office Tripartite Declarations of Principles Concerning Multinational Enterprises and Social Policy; ICC: The International Chamber of Commerce Guidelines for International Investment; UN/CTC: The United Nations Universal Declaration of Human Rights, UN Code of Conduct on Transnational Corporations.

environment that combine to determine ethical or unethical societal norms is illustrated in Exhibit 2-4. The authors, Robertson and Crittenden, note,

Varying legal and cultural constraints across borders have made integrating an ethical component into international strategic decisions quite challenging.[38]

Should, then, managers of MNC subsidiaries base their ethical standards on those of the host country or those of the home country—or can the two be reconciled? What is the moral responsibility of expatriates regarding ethical behavior, and how do these issues affect business objectives? How do expatriates simultaneously balance their responsibility to various stakeholders—to owners, creditors, consumers, employees, suppliers, governments, and societies? The often conflicting objectives of host and home governments and societies also must be balanced.

The approach to these dilemmas varies among MNCs from different countries. Whereas the American approach is to treat everyone the same by making moral judgments based on general rules, managers in Japan and Europe tend to make such decisions based on shared values, social ties, and their perceptions of their obligations. According to many U.S. executives, there is little difference in ethical practices among the United States, Canada, and Northern Europe. According to Bruce Smart, former U.S. Undersecretary of Commerce for International Trade, the highest ethical standards seem to be practiced by the Canadians, British, Australians, and Germans. As he says, "a kind of noblesse oblige still exists among the business classes in those countries"—compared with the prevailing attitude among many U.S. managers that condones "making it" whatever way one can.[39] Another who experienced few problems with ethical practices in Europe is Donald Petersen, former CEO of Ford Motor Company. However, he warns us about underdeveloped countries, in particular those under a dictatorship where bribery is a generally accepted practice.[40]

Petersen's experience has been borne out by research by Transparency International, a German nongovernmental organization (NGO) that fights corruption. It draws on data from 14 polls and surveys from 13 independent institutions around the world to rank 180 countries, based on results from 63,199 respondents. The organization's year 2014 Global Corruption Barometer (selections are shown in Exhibit 2-5) shows the results of research into the extent that business and other sectors of their society are affected by corruption, as perceived by businesspeople, academics, and risk analysts in 69 countries. A primary focus of the research was the relative prevalence of bribery in various spheres of people's lives, including political and business practices.

EXHIBIT 2-4 **A Moral Philosophy of Cross-Cultural Societal Ethics**

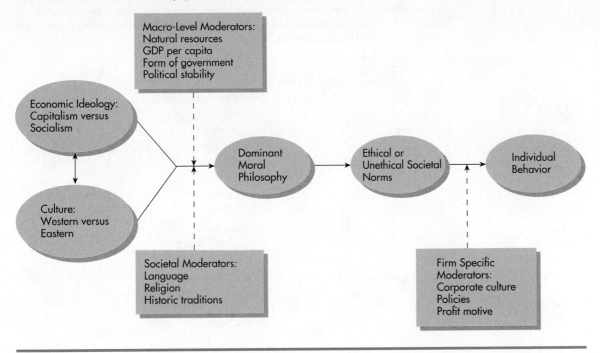

Source: C. J. Robertson and W. F. Crittenden, "Mapping Moral Philosophies: Strategic Implications for Multinational Firms," *Strategic Management Journal* 24 (2003), pp. 385–392, © John Wiley & Sons, Inc. Reproduced with permission.

The 2014 Corruption Perceptions Index shows that more than two thirds of the 178 countries in the index score below fifty on a scale from 100 (highly clean) to 0 (highly corrupt). These results indicate a serious corruption problem.

Overall, the data show that those countries in Western Europe, Singapore, New Zealand, Canada, and Australia were the least corrupt, closely followed by Hong Kong and Japan; the United Kingdom ranked 14th (rising from 20th in 2010); and the United States ranked 17th, for example, compared with Denmark at 1st. France ranked about the same at 26th, South Korea slipped to 43rd; China dropped from 78th to 100th in just four years, with Russia coming 136th, slightly better than previously.[41]

Countries at the bottom need to adopt radical anti-corruption measures in favor of their people. Countries at the top of the index should make sure they don't export corrupt practices to underdeveloped countries.

JOSÉ UGAZ, CHAIR, TRANSPARENCY INTERNATIONAL[42]

The biggest single problem for MNCs in their attempt to define a corporate-wide ethical posture is the great variation of ethical standards around the world. Many practices considered unethical or even illegal in some countries are accepted ways of doing business in others.

Ethics in Uses of Technology

European citizens care deeply about protecting their privacy and data protection rights, … Any company operating in the E.U. market or any online product that is targeted at E.U. consumers should comply with E.U. rules.

VIVIENNE REDING, EUROPEAN JUSTICE COMMISSIONER
MAY 4, 2011[43]

Facebook has been accused of violating EU data protection rules as the social network became the latest U.S. technology company to be criticised by a European regulator.

FINANCIAL TIMES
FEBRUARY 24, 2015[44]

EXHIBIT 2-5 2014 Corruption Perceptions Index—Selected Ranks   Each country's ranking is based on its score as it relates to perceptions of the degree of corruption as seen by business people and country analysts and ranges between 100 (very clean) and 0 (highly corrupt). Denmark's score, for example, was 92, and Russia's score was 27.

Rank	Country
1	Denmark
2	New Zealand
3	Finland
7	Singapore
10	Canada
11	Australia
12	Germany
14	UK
15	Japan
17	Hong Kong
17	U.S.A.
26	France
43	South Korea
67	South Africa
69	Greece
69	Brazil
85	India
100	China
103	Mexico
107	Indonesia
136	Russia

Source: Based on selected data from the TI Corruption Perceptions Index, 2014, www.transparencyinternational.org, accessed February 11, 2015.

The ethical use of technology around the world poses a considerable challenge to have consistent practices because of the varied expectations about the use of technological devices and programs as they intersect with people's private lives. The electronic data privacy laws in Europe illustrate this conflict. The EU Directive on Data Protection guarantees European citizens absolute control over data concerning them. A U.S. company wanting personal information must get permission from that person and explain what the information will be used for; the company must also guarantee that the information won't be used for anything else without the person's consent. It appears that Europe is setting the rules. Regulators in France, Germany, and Italy, for example, were focusing on whether Apple's iPhone and iPad violated privacy rules by tracking the location of users. Google, also, had previously started a firestorm in Germany when it was discovered to have been gathering information for its street mapping service from people's unsecured wireless networks. Later, Sony acknowledged a breach of data of 77 million users of its PlayStation network. Because of such breaches of privacy, Ms. Reding, the European Justice Commissioner, has proposed extending privacy rules to social media and online banking, shopping, and video games, among others.[45] The United States has no agency dedicated to monitoring issues of data privacy as Europe does. In fact, Google is in a fight with the European regulators, which are pressing for the so-called right to be forgotten rule to be imposed outside of Europe.[46]

Bribery

There are few other areas where a single employee can, with one instance of misjudgment, create huge embarrassment [for the company].

FINANCIAL TIMES[47]

The computer is on the dock, it's raining, and you have to pay $100 [bribe] to get it picked up.[48]

WILLIAM C. NORRIS CONTROL DATA CORPORATION

MNCs are often caught between being placed at a disadvantage either by refusing to go along with a country's accepted practices, such as bribery, or being subject to criticism at home for using unethical tactics to get the job done. Large companies that have refused to participate have led the way in taking a moral stand because of their visibility; their potential impact on the local economy; and, after all, their ability to afford such a stance. Some other large companies, however, have not always taken a moral stand. Such was the case in April 2011 when a Justice Department complaint against a Johnson & Johnson subsidiary found internal company emails stating that . . .

> *"[C]ash incentives to surgeons is common knowledge in Greece," and that, were the company to stop paying bribes, "we'd lose 95% of our business by the end of the year."*

WWW.NYTIMES.COM
APRIL 8, 2011[49]

Whereas the upper limits of ethical standards for international activities are set by the individual standards of certain leading companies—or, more realistically, by the moral values of their top managers—it is more difficult to set the lower limits of those standards; that limit is set in each situation by whether the laws are actually enforced in that location.

The bribery of officials is prohibited by law in all countries, but it still goes on as an accepted practice; often, it is the only way to get anything done. In such cases, the MNC managers have to decide which standard of behavior they will follow. What about the $100 bribe to get the computer off the rainy dock? William Norris says he told his managers to pay the $100 because to refuse would be taking things too far. Generally, Control Data did not yield to such pressure, though it said sales were lost as a result.[50]

A specific ethical issue for managers in the international arena is that of **questionable payments**. These are business payments that raise significant questions of appropriate moral behavior either in the host nation or in other nations. Such questions arise out of differences in laws, customs, and ethics in various countries and whether the payments in question are political payments, extortion, bribes, sales commissions, or grease money—payments to expedite routine transactions. Other common types of payments are made to speed the clearance of goods at ports of entry and obtain required certifications. They are called different names in different countries: tokens of appreciation, *la mordida* ("the bite," in Mexico), *bastarella* ("little envelope" in Italy), and *pot-de-vin* ("jug of wine" in France). For the sake of simplicity, all these types of questionable payments are categorized in this text as some form of bribery. In Mexico, for example, companies make monthly payments to the mail carriers, or their mail gets lost.

Most managers perceive bribery as "endemic in business and government in parts of Africa and south and east Asia. Corruption and bribery are considered to be part of the culture and environment of certain markets, and will not simply go away."[51] In some parts of Latin America, for example, customs officers are paid poorly and so are encouraged to take bribes to supplement their incomes. However, developed countries are not immune to bribery—as demonstrated in 2015 when the FIFA president of World Cup Soccer was under criminal investigation for bribery.

The dilemma for Americans operating abroad is how much to adhere to their own ethical standards in the face of foreign customs or how much to follow local ways to be competitive. Certainly, in some societies, gift giving is common to building social and familial ties, and such gifts incur obligation. Nevertheless, a bribe is different from a gift or other reciprocation, and those involved know that by whether it has a covert nature. In his book on bribes, Noonan takes the following position:

> *Bribery is universally shameful. There is not a country in the world that does not treat bribery as criminal on its books.... In no country do bribetakers speak publicly of their bribes, nor do bribegivers announce the bribes they pay. No newspaper lists them. No one advertises that he can arrange a bribe. No one is honored precisely because he is a big briber or bribee. No*

one writes an autobiography in which he recalls the bribes he has taken or paid. . . . Not merely the criminal law—for the transaction could have happened long ago and prosecution be barred by time—but an innate fear of being considered disgusting restrains briber and bribee from parading their exchange. Significantly, it is often the Westerner with ethnocentric prejudice who supposes that a modern Asian or African society does not regard the act of bribery as shameful in the way Westerners regard it.[52]

However, Americans must be able to distinguish between harmless practices and actual bribery, between genuine relationships and those used as a cover-up. To help them distinguish, the **Foreign Corrupt Practices Act (FCPA)** of 1977 was established, which prohibits U.S. companies from making illegal payments, other gifts, or political contributions to foreign government officials for the purpose of influencing them in business transactions. The goal was to stop MNCs from contributing to corruption in foreign governments and to upgrade the image of the United States and its companies operating overseas. Unfortunately, graft is still pervasive in global business today, and in 2012, the U.S. Justice Department was investigating 78 well-known companies for violation of the FCPA. Those included Walmart, investigated for paying $24 million in bribes to Mexican officials to acquire zoning permits for its Mexican subsidiary.[53] Sadly, it is clear that firms around the world have not learned from those experiences, as shown in 2015 by the growing bribery scandal over the U.K.'s Rolls-Royce and Brazil's Petrobras; investigations are threatening to bring down other global companies, politicians in Brazil, and the stability of the government, as detailed in the following "Under the Lens" section.

UNDER THE LENS
Rolls-Royce Accused of Bribery to Obtain $100m Petrobras Contract

Samantha Pearson and Joe Leahy, FT.com, February 17, 2015

UK group named by informant as one of the contractors involved in Brazil scandal. Rolls-Royce has been accused of involvement in a multibillion-dollar bribery and kickback scheme at Petrobras, Brazil's state-controlled oil producer, as more foreign companies are dragged into the corruption scandal.

The British engineering company, which makes gas turbines for Petrobras oil platforms, allegedly paid bribes via an agent in exchange for a $100m contract as part of a scheme in operation during much of the past decade, according to testimony from a former Petrobras executive. It is the one of the biggest international groups so far to be implicated in the Petrobras scandal.

Pedro Barusco, a Petrobras veteran, told police that he personally received at least $200,000 from Rolls-Royce—only part of the bribes he alleged were paid to a ring of politicians and other executives at the oil company. The admission was buried in more than 600 pages of documents released by Brazil's federal court system this month, detailing the testimonies of Mr Barusco who struck a plea bargain in November.

In response, Rolls-Royce said: "We want to make it crystal clear that we will not tolerate improper business conduct of any sort and will take all necessary action to ensure compliance."

The accusations come as Rolls-Royce faces a Serious Fraud Office investigation in the UK over allegations of corruption in China and Indonesia.

Rolls-Royce is the latest foreign company alleged to be involved in the scandal, which threatens the government of President Dilma Rousseff and could push Petrobras into technical default.

Brazil's authorities are already investigating allegations that Petrobras officials accepted bribes from SBM Offshore, a Netherlands-based supplier of offshore oil vessels. SBM has said that it is co-operating with the investigation.

Units of two Singaporean companies, Keppel Corporation and Sembcorp Marine, and three Brazilian shipbuilders with Japanese shareholders, have also been accused of involvement. Keppel and Sembcorp deny participating.

The scandal emerged when the former head of Petrobras's refining unit, Paulo Roberto Costa, struck a plea bargain after being arrested for money laundering in March. According to testimony from Mr. Costa, Mr. Barusco and others, Petrobras contractors paid bribes to executives and politicians from the ruling coalition led by Ms. Rousseff's PT party. Analysts estimate the scheme has cost Petrobras more than $20bn. The PT said the allegations are without proof and has promised to sue the "accusers".

Mr. Barusco alleged that his friend Luiz Eduardo Barbosa, a former executive of Swiss engineering group ABB, was responsible for organising bribes from Rolls-Royce, SBM and Alusa, a Brazilian construction company. Alusa, which has changed its name to Alumini, denied the accusations. Mr. Barbosa could not be reached for comment.

© 2015 The Financial Times Limited

Making the Right Decision

How is a manager operating abroad to know what is the right decision when faced with questionable or unfamiliar circumstances of doing business? Usually, the manager or salesperson is faced with wanting to make certain decisions that will benefit her company, her career, or both. That decision, or set of actions, is likely to be profitable for the company and secure new market opportunities. However, there are many other considerations that make it less clear whether to continue to pursue that avenue, in particular in countries or settings that provide less transparency, and often certain pressures, about what to do. If the manager is faced with such a situation, a number of steps can help her clarify the way to proceed.

Steps to an Ethical Decision

- Consult the laws of both the home and the host countries—such as the FCPA. If any of those laws would be violated, then you, the manager, must find some other way to complete the business transaction or withdraw altogether.

- Consult the International Codes of Conduct for MNEs (see Exhibit 2-3). These are broad and cover various areas of social responsibility and ethical behavior; even so, many issues are subject to interpretation. If there is no apparent conflict on these legal grounds, then proceed with further consultation.

- Consult the company's code of ethics (if there is one) and established norms. Note that it is the responsibility of the company to provide guidelines for the actions and decisions its employees make. What kinds of decisions do your colleagues typically make in these kinds of circumstances? If your intended action runs contrary to the norms or the formal code, discontinue that plan. Consult your superiors if you still need clarification. Unfortunately, often the situation is not that clear-cut, or your boss will tell you to use your own judgment. Sometimes your superiors in the home office just want you to complete the transaction to the benefit of the company and don't want to be involved in what you have to do to consummate the deal. Failing clear guidance:

- Weigh stakeholders' rights (see Exhibit 2-1). To whom are you responsible? What are the priorities of responsibilities to those stakeholders? What is the potential benefit versus harm involved in your decision or set of actions? (For example, does the proposed action [rigged contract bid, bribe, etc.] harm anyone? What are the likely consequences of your decision in both the short run and long run? Who would benefit from your contemplated action? Who might be harmed? In the case of a rigged contract bid through bribery, for example, people are put at a disadvantage, especially over the long term, with a pattern of this behavior.)

- Follow your own conscience and moral code. Ask yourself whether you can live with the potential decision and what would be the next step for you if you continue along that path.

It is important to decide where to draw the line in the sand to operate with integrity; otherwise, the line moves further and further away with each transgression. In addition, what can start here with a small bribe or cover-up—a matter of personal ethics—can, over time, and taken together with many people covering up, result in a situation of a truly negligent, and perhaps criminal, stance toward social responsibility to society, like that revealed by investigations of the tobacco industry in the United States. Indeed, executives are increasingly being held personally

FIGURE 2-2 **Man Refusing Bribe from a Woman**

Source: fuzzbones/Fotolia, LLC

and criminally accountable for their decisions; this is true even for people operating on the board of directors of a company. Criminal charges were brought against 15 executives of WorldCom in 2003, for example; and the noose was thrown around the world after the Enron convictions in 2006 as international banks such as Citigroup and JP Morgan Chase were charged with taking part in sham deals to disguise Enron's financial problems. In 2015, a number of executives of banks and financial institutions were still being investigated in the wake of the financial crisis precipitated by the housing mortgage debacle.

MANAGING INTERDEPENDENCE

Because multinational firms (or other organizations, such as the Red Cross) represent global interdependency, their managers at all levels must recognize that what they do, in the aggregate, has long-term implications for the socioeconomic interdependence of nations. Simply to describe ethical issues as part of the general environment does not address the fact that managers must control their activities at all levels—from simple, daily business transactions involving local workers, intermediaries, or consumers to global concerns of ecological responsibility—for the future benefit of all concerned. Whatever the situation, the powerful long-term effects of MNC and MNE action (or inaction) should be planned for and controlled, not haphazardly considered part of the side effects of business. The profitability of individual companies depends on a cooperative and constructive attitude toward global interdependence.

Foreign Subsidiaries in the United States

Much of the preceding discussion has related to U.S. subsidiaries around the world. However, to highlight the growing interdependence and changing balance of business power globally, foreign subsidiaries in the United States should also be considered. Since much criticism about a lack of responsibility has been directed toward MNCs with headquarters in the United States, we must think of these criticisms from an outsider's perspective. The number of foreign subsidiaries in the United States has grown and continues to grow dramatically; FDI in the United States by other countries is, in a number of industries, far more than U.S. investment outward. Americans are thus becoming more sensitive to what they perceive as a lack of control over their own country's business.

Things look very different from the perspective of Americans employed at a subsidiary of an overseas MNC. Interdependence takes on a new meaning when people over there are calling the shots regarding strategy, expectations, products, and personnel. Often, Americans' resentment about different ways of doing business by foreign companies in the United States inhibits the cooperation that gave rise to the companies' presence in the first place.

Today, managers from all countries must learn new ways, and most MNCs are trying to adapt. In Japan, corporate social responsibility has traditionally meant that companies take care of their employees, whereas in the United States both the public and private sectors are expected to share responsibility for the community. Part of the explanation for this difference is that U.S. corporations get tax deductions for corporate philanthropy, whereas Japanese firms do not; nor are Japanese managers usually familiar with community needs. For these and other reasons, Japanese subsidiaries in the United States have not been active in U.S. philanthropy.

Managing Subsidiary–Host Country Interdependence

Nike believes that we are at the beginning of a shift from a service- or knowledge-based economy to a sustainability-based economy, as environmental constraints increasingly influence business choices.

ORGANIZATIONAL DYNAMICS 39
2010[54]

When **managing interdependence**, international managers must go beyond general issues of social responsibility and deal with the specific concerns of the MNC subsidiary–host country relationship. Outdated attitudes that focus only on profitability and autonomy are shortsighted and usually result in only short-term realization of those goals. Managers in those companies must learn to accommodate the needs of other organizations and countries:

Interdependence rather than independence, and cooperation rather than confrontation are at the heart of that accommodation … the journey from independence to interdependence managed badly leads to dependence, and that is an unacceptable destination.[55]

Most of the past criticism levied at MNCs has focused on their activities in less-developed countries (LDCs). Their real or perceived lack of responsibility centers on the transfer in of inappropriate technology, causing unemployment, and the transfer out of scarce financial and other resources, reducing the capital available for internal development. In their defense, those corporations and NGOs help developing countries by contributing new technology and managerial skills, improving the infrastructure, creating jobs, and bringing in investment capital from other countries by exporting products. The infusion of outside capital provides foreign-exchange earnings that can be used for further development. The host government's attitude is often referred to as a love–hate relationship. It wants the economic growth that foreign investment provides, but it does not want the incursions on national sovereignty or the technological dependence that may result. Most criticisms of MNC subsidiary activities, whether in less-developed or more-developed countries, are along the following lines:

- MNCs locally raise their needed capital, contributing to a rise in interest rates in host countries. The majority (sometimes even 100 percent) of the stock of most subsidiaries is owned by the parent company. Consequently, host-country people do not have much control over the operations of corporations within their borders.

- MNCs usually reserve the key managerial and technical positions for expatriates. As a result, they do not contribute to the development of host-country personnel.

- MNCs do not adapt their technology to the conditions that exist in host countries.

- MNCs concentrate their research and development activities at home, restricting the transfer of modern technology and know-how to host countries.

- MNCs give rise to the demand for luxury goods in host countries at the expense of essential consumer goods.

- MNCs start their foreign operations by purchasing existing firms rather than by developing new productive facilities in host countries.

- MNCs dominate major industrial sectors, thus contributing to inflation by stimulating demand for scarce resources and earning excessively high profits and fees.

- MNCs are not accountable to their host nations but only respond to home-country governments; they are not concerned with host-country plans for development.[56]

Specific MNCs have been charged with tax evasion, union busting, and interference in host-country politics. Of course, corporations have both positive and negative effects on different economics. For every complaint about MNC activities (whether about capital markets, technology transfer, or employment practices), we can identify potential benefits (see Exhibit 2-6).

EXHIBIT 2-6 Potential Benefits and Costs to Host Countries of MNC Operations There

Benefits	Costs
Capital Market Effects	
• Broader access to outside capital • Economic growth • Foreign-exchange earnings • Import substitution effects allow governments to save foreign exchange for priority projects	• Risk sharing • Increased competition for local scarce capital • Increased interest rates as supply of local capital decreases • Capital service effects of balance of payments
Technology and Production Effects	
• Access to new technology and R&D developments • Employee training in new technology • Infrastructure development and support • Export diversification • Introduction of new management techniques	• Technology is not always appropriate • Plants are often for assembly only and can be dismantled • Government infrastructure investment is higher than expected benefits • Increased pollution
Employment Effects	
• Direct creation of new jobs • Introduction of more humane employment standards • Opportunities for indigenous management development • Income multiplier effects on local community business	• Limited skill development and creation • Competition for scarce skills • Low percentage of managerial jobs for local people • Employment instability because of ability to move production operations freely to other countries

Source: Based on R. H. Mason and R. S. Spich, *Management: An International Perspective* (Homewood, IL: Irwin, 1987), p. 202.

Numerous conflicts arise between MNC companies or subsidiaries and host countries, including conflicting goals (both economic and noneconomic) and conflicting concerns, such as the security of proprietary technology, patents, or information. Overall, the resulting trade-offs create an interdependent relationship between the subsidiary and the host government, based on relative bargaining power. The power of large corporations is based on their large-scale, worldwide economies, their strategic flexibility, and their control over technology and production location. The bargaining chips of the host governments include their control of raw materials and market access and their ability to set the rules regarding the role of private enterprise, the operation of state-owned firms, and the specific regulations regarding taxes, permissions, and so forth.

MNCs run the risk of their assets becoming hostage to host control, which may take the form of nationalism, protectionism, or governmentalism. Under **nationalism**, for example, public opinion is rallied in favor of national goals and against foreign influences. Under **protectionism**, the host institutes a partial or complete closing of borders to withstand competitive foreign products, using tariff and nontariff barriers such as those Japan uses. Under **governmentalism**, the government uses its policy-setting role to favor national interests rather than relying on market forces.[57] This was illustrated by the actions of governments around the world to support their banking systems in 2008 and 2009.

The intricacies of the relationship and the relative power of an MNC subsidiary and a host-country government are situation specific. Clearly, such a relationship should be managed for mutual benefit; a long-term, constructive relationship based on the corporation's socially responsive stance should result in progressive strategic success for the company and economic progress for the host country. The effective management of subsidiary–host country interdependence must have a long-term perspective. Although temporary strategies to reduce interdependence through controls on the transnational flows by firms (for example, transfer-pricing tactics) or by governments (such as new residency requirements for skilled workers) are often successful in the short run, they result in inefficiencies that must be absorbed by one or both parties, with negative long-term results. In setting up and maintaining subsidiaries, managers are wise to consider the long-term trade-offs between strategic plans and operational management. By finding out for themselves the pressing local concerns and understanding the sources of past conflicts, they can learn from mistakes and recognize the consequences of the failure to manage problems. Furthermore, managers should implement policies that reflect corporate social responsibility regarding local economic issues, employee welfare, or natural resources. At the least, the failure to manage interdependence effectively results in constraints on strategy. In the worst case, it results in disastrous consequences for the local area, for the subsidiary, and for the global reputation of the company.

The interdependent nature of developing economies and the foreign companies operating there is of particular concern when discussing social responsibility because of the tentative and fragile nature of the economic progression in those countries. Corporations (and nongovernmental organizations [NGOs]) must set a high moral standard and lay the groundwork for future economic development. At the minimum, they should ensure that their actions will do no harm. Some recommendations for MNEs operating in and doing business with developing countries are as follows:

- Do no intentional harm. This includes respect for the integrity of the ecosystem and consumer safety.
- Produce more good than harm for the host country.
- Contribute by their activity to the host country's development.
- Respect the human rights of their employees.
- To the extent that local culture does not violate ethical norms, respect the local culture and work with and not against it.
- Pay their fair share of taxes.
- Cooperate with the local government in developing and enforcing just background (infrastructure) institutions (i.e., laws, governmental regulations, unions, and consumer groups, which serve as a means of social control).[58]

Managing Environmental Interdependence and Sustainability

Sustainability lies at the intersection of financial, social and environmental health—described sometimes as the "triple bottom line."[59]

International managers can no longer afford to ignore the impact of their activities on the environment and their stakeholders. The demand for corporations to consider **sustainability** in their CSR plans comes from various stakeholders around the world. A generally accepted definition of **sustainable development** for business enterprises is that of

adopting business strategies and activities that meet the needs of the enterprise and its stakeholders today, while protecting, sustaining and enhancing the human and natural resources that will be needed in the future.[60]

JOURNAL OF SOCIO-ECONOMICS

Existing literature generally agrees on three dimensions of sustainability: (1) economic, (2) social, and (3) environmental. A sustainable business has to take into account "the interests of future generations, biodiversity, animal protection, human rights, life cycle impacts, and principles like equity, accountability, transparency, openness, education and learning, and local action and scale."[61]

A study by Mirvis et al. found that, although most executives agree that sustainability is important to the financial success of their companies, fewer than half of them are making serious commitments to integrate the necessary steps with their business systems. Reasons include a lack of clear view on what comprises sustainability and the difficulty in allocating responsibility in the company for the vast and overlapping concerns of environmental, social, and governance issues. As a result, sustainability often is not internalized in the culture or systems of the company, and competing priorities such as short-term profits intervene.[62] However, companies such as GE, Nike, Nestlé, and Gap are among the world's prominent sustainable organizations and are providing leadership in their transparent models for other organizations to resolve the complex issues involved in implementing sustainability. Nike, Inc., for example, believes that business success will increasingly depend on contributing to a sustainable world; and GE's chairman and CEO, Jeff Immelt, believes that the next decades will be about technologies and economies to address issues of scarcity.

A more positive report in 2011 from a survey by McKinsey consultants of 3,203 executives representing the full range of industries and geographic regions shows that many companies are actively integrating sustainability principles with their businesses, and they are doing so by pursuing goals that go far beyond earlier concern for reputation management. The McKinsey report noted a more mature attitude toward sustainability and its expected benefits than in prior surveys, saying that, "More companies are managing sustainability to improve processes, pursue growth, and add value to their companies rather than focusing on reputation alone."[63] In addition, 57 percent said their companies have integrated sustainability with their strategic planning. Of the 2,956 executives who responded, the areas that the companies were taking action on included reducing energy use in operations (63 percent), reducing waste from operations (61 percent), and managing corporate reputation for sustainability (51 percent).[64]

Leaders in the research noted that barriers that prevent further value-capture from sustainability initiatives include the pressure of realizing short-term profitability compared with the long-term value aspects of sustainability initiatives, and the lack of performance incentives tied to sustainability results.[65]

The dilemma for corporations is that they believe they are faced with trying to meet two often contradictory requirements: (1) selling at low prices and (2) being environmentally and socially conscious. However, competitive pressures limit the company's ability to raise prices to cover the cost of socially responsible policies. This is obviously contradictory to the well-being of societies.[66] However, a long-term view is that sustainability is good for business, and many companies, such as BP and Nike, have learned this the hard way.

One example of the turnaround in a company's sustainability efforts is the Coca-Cola company in India. The company is struggling to accommodate the rising concerns and protests from local farmers about the company's depletion of water resources. As reported on the *PBS Newshour*,[67] farmers are particularly angry in Kala Dera, in the drought-stricken state of Rajasthan. The Coca-Cola factory there is one of 49 across India. The company has invested over $1 billion, building a market for its products in this country. The plant used about 900,000 liters of water in 2007, about a third of it for the soft drinks, the rest to clean bottles and machinery. It is drawn from wells at the plant but also from aquifers Coca-Cola shares with neighboring farmers. The water is virtually free to all users. The farmers say their problems began after the Coca-Cola factory arrived in 1999. According to the farmers:

> *Before, the water level was descending by about one foot per year. Now it's 10 feet every year. We have a 3.5-horsepower motor. We cannot cope. They (Coca-Cola) have a 50-horsepower pump.*
>
> PBS NEWSHOUR WITH JIM LEHRER
> NOVEMBER 17, 2008[68]

Coca-Cola agreed to an independent third-party assessment of some of its operations in India, which confirmed that the Rajasthan plant is contributing to a worsening water situation. It recommended that the company bring water in from outside the area or shut the factory down. Coca-Cola rejected that recommendation. For his part, Coca-Cola's India head, Atul Singh, says it would be irresponsible to leave, saying that "walking away is the easiest thing we can do. That's not going to help that community build sustainability."[69] So Coca-Cola, while insisting its impact on the water supply was minimal, said it would stay and help. The company has agreed to subsidize one-third of the cost of water-efficient drip irrigation systems for 15 neighboring farmers. The government pays most of the rest; growers themselves must chip in 10 percent. Coca-Cola has also set up concrete collection systems for rainwater. The farmers remain skeptical. They also are critical of the government locally for attracting Coca-Cola to a water-scarce region and nationally for ignoring water policy in a rush to attract industry and foreign investment.[70]

The Coca-Cola example makes clear to global managers that effectively managing environmental interdependence and sustainability includes considering ecological interdependence as well as the economic and social implications of MNC activities. There is an ever-increasing awareness of, and a mounting concern worldwide about, the effects of global industrialization on the natural environment. Clearly, the disastrous effects of the BP oil spill in the Gulf of Mexico in 2010 has exacerbated that concern—as discussed in the accompanying "Under the Lens: BP's Sustainability Systems Under Fire" section. Government regulations and powerful interest groups are demanding ecological responsibility regarding the use of scarce natural resources and production processes that threaten permanent damage to the planet. MNCs have to deal with each country's different policies and techniques for environmental and health protection. Such variations in approach reflect different levels of industrialization, living standards, government–business relations, philosophies of collective intervention, patterns of industrial competition, and degrees of sophistication in public policy.

In recent years, the export of hazardous wastes from developed countries to less-developed ones has increased considerably. E-waste—from electronic components, computers, and cell phones, for example, all of which are full of hazardous materials—has become a major problem for developing economies, producing sickness and death for its handlers there; this continues in spite of laws against such dumping by U.S. companies and others. Often, companies choose to dispose of hazardous waste in less-developed countries to take advantage of weaker regulations and lower costs. Until we have strict international regulation of trade in hazardous wastes, companies should take it upon themselves to monitor their activities, as Singh and Lakhan demand:

> To export these wastes to countries which do not benefit from waste-generating industrial processes or whose citizens do not have lifestyles that generate such wastes is unethical. It is especially unjust to send hazardous wastes to lesser-developed countries which lack the technology to minimize the deleterious effects of these substances.[71]

 ## UNDER THE LENS
BP's Sustainability Systems Under Fire

BP had a compelling vision of going "beyond petroleum." What it lacked was the institutional will and managerial acumen to translate its commitments into responsible operations...."[72]

British Petroleum (BP) has been blamed and extensively criticized for the worst environmental disaster in U.S. history, caused by the explosion of the Deepwater Horizon drilling rig in the Gulf of Mexico on April 20, 2010. The explosion killed 11 workers and injured 17 and resulted in a massive oil spill—an estimated five million barrels of oil—that despoiled the southern U.S. coastline, created lasting ecological damage and health concerns, and threatened industries and livelihoods reliant upon the Gulf waters. BP's record and intentions regarding sustainability came under intensive scrutiny because of its apparent lack of willingness or preparation to take responsibility and to respond effectively—in particular as it became apparent that the company had inadequate control systems in place to prevent such disasters. As the press then reminded the public of previous BP disasters (such as the Prudhoe Bay oil spill in Alaska in March 2006, resulting in more than 212,000 gallons of oil being spilled), the company's environmental record brought into question whether the company was serious in integrating sustainability with its corporate goals, organizational culture, and systems.[73] In fact, many accused BP of negligence and greed after the presidential oil spill commission issued its report in February 2011, laying considerable blame on BP for the disaster in the Gulf of Mexico. The report also highlighted flaws in Halliburton's work and errors by rig owner Transocean. BP was accused of being aware of problems with lab tests of Halliburton's cement for three years, and that "BP decided not to set a lockdown sleeve, an installation deep in the well, during its preparations for temporary abandonment in order to save 5½ days and $2 million in costs."[74]

BP has incurred considerable costs for the cleanup of the beaches and waters in the gulf, for the fund to compensate homeowners and workers in the fishing and tourism industries, for penalties for violating the Clean Water Act, and for the loss of value for the shareholders. In July 2015, BP agreed in a settlement case to pay $18.7 billion to settle claims, which brought its total costs to about $54 billion.[75] In addition, BP's image has suffered a terrible blow; the company had long promoted its sunburst logo and its Be Green campaigns, but after the oil spill, its reputation was based on what the company did or did not do—not what it said—and as a result, BP lost firm value of over $100 billion.[76] Apart from the moral argument for responsibility to its many stakeholders, and for sustainability of the environment, the consequences to BP clearly make the business case for corporate social responsibility.

The BP disaster has raised deeper concerns about the usefulness of voluntary CSR policies and reports.[77] Clearly, many corporations need to focus carefully on the implementation of their sustainability strategies—a subject discussed throughout in this chapter.

The exportation of pesticides poses a similar problem, with the United States and Germany being the main culprits. The United States exports about 200 million pounds of pesticides each year that are prohibited, restricted, or not registered for use in the United States. These are only two of the environmental problems facing countries and large corporations today.

It is clear, then, that MNEs must take the lead in dealing with ecological interdependence by integrating goals of sustainability with strategic planning. Along with an investment appraisal, a project feasibility study, and operational plans, such planning should include an environmental impact assessment. At the least, managers must deal with the increasing scarcity of natural resources in the next few decades by (1) looking for alternative raw materials, (2) developing new methods of recycling or disposing of used materials, and (3) expanding the use of by-products.[78] One company that is doing its part in minimizing waste is TerraCycle, featured in the accompanying Management in Action box.

MANAGEMENT IN ACTION
TerraCycle—Social Entrepreneurship Goes Global[79]

In his book 'Revolution in a Bottle,' TerraCycle CEO Tom Szaky boldly claims the company is out to render waste a thing of the past—be it through recycling, downcycling or upcycling. "Our goal over the next ten years is to be operating in every country...."

BUSINESS WORLD
MAY 31, 2011[80]

TerraCycle—a company that owes its start to worm poop—is the story of Tom Szaky, a Hungarian immigrant and college dropout who became CEO of a company that is now solving global waste problems. Tom Szaky a, 20-year-old Princeton University freshman at the time, founded TerraCycle in 2001 by producing organic fertilizer consisting of liquid worm poop packaged in used soda bottles. Now TerraCycle has 50,000 collecting organizations, including schools, churches, and retail outlets, that run numerous collection programs. Through various alliances, TerraCycle now works with more than 100 million brands in 22 countries[81]. Some of those recycled goods are then turned into other products. In Mexico, Walmart collects toothbrushes and toothpaste tubes, a program Colgate sponsors. In Sweden, pen-maker Bic runs an in-store program in Staples. TerraCycle's designers and scientists "manipulate waste streams into new raw materials and products."[82] The TerraCycle logo is on 20 billion packages around the world.

Szaky's idea for a class assignment at Princeton drew upon his high-school experience of trying to grow marijuana, which only did well when he tried the previously mentioned special fertilizer. That fertilizer resulted from feeding people's garbage to the worms.

After some hard times approaching businesses and other institutions, the idea of upcycling—recycling waste into usable products with added value—took hold with a number of companies such as Walmart and Home Depot; partnerships came next with companies such as Whole Foods, Target, and Kraft, who were happy to get the publicity for being green. It is clear that "From cost savings to goodwill, being green is a marketable benchmark."[83] Nonprofits were happy to be involved with a donation from TerraCycle. Other alliances are with Solo Cups, for example, in which their cups will be re-created into playgrounds. The position of Kim Frankovich, Solo vice president of sustainability, is that "Sustainability is becoming a part of everyday life and making sure our cups can be recycled as part of that ongoing activity is a priority for Solo."[84]

Szaky maintains that people feel good about doing something useful for society. In addition, he says that TerraCycle is fulfilling several needs for society: that corporations have a chance for positive action with the waste created by their processes and that consumers can have a positive feeling about buying eco-friendly products. He maintains that "it is not enough to just offer a green choice at a premium price; the goal is to make green products at a competitive price."[85]

TerraCycle is an example of what Nick et al. call a "social purpose venture." Each exists because of a social, specifically environmental mission, but seeks to achieve profitability and growth.[86] Regardless of the terminology, it is clear that social entrepreneurs such as Skazy provide "the engine of positive, systemic change that will alter what we do, how we do it, and why it matters."[87] In addition, by partnering with companies and institutions around the world, TerraCycle is providing a stimulus and outlet for the CSR of those entities and a direct source of initiatives for environmental sustainability.

Implementing Sustainability Strategies

Effective implementation of sustainability strategies, according to Epstein and Buhovac, requires companies to have both formal and informal systems in place: "Companies need the processes, performance measurement, and reward systems (formal systems) to measure success and to provide internal and external accountability. But they also need the leadership, culture, and people (informal systems) to support sustainability implementation. An alignment among the formal and informal systems along with the organizational structure is critical for success."[88]

Epstein's model (Exhibit 2-7) provides a system for examining, measuring, and managing the drivers of corporate sustainability. Essential to success is the commitment of top leadership and the recognition of sustainability as a process that will benefit the company—i.e., that it is a good business idea. Key to understanding the role of corporate sustainability is the relationship between managers' decisions, their impact on the society and its environment, and financial performance. In Epstein's model, the inputs include the external context in which the company operates that are specific to the locations; the internal context of the company's systems and structure; the business context, such as the industry sector, customers, and products; and the human and financial resources available to the corporation for sustainability purposes.[89] Output measures of the success of the corporation's sustainability would include, for example, reduction in energy use or hazardous waste, positive change in human rights complaints, and so on. These could result, among other factors, in cost savings and in increased sales from improved reputation (as was the case, for example, when Nike turned around its human rights reputation after a student embargo on its products).

Multinational corporations already have had a tremendous impact on foreign countries, and this impact will continue to grow and bring about long-lasting changes. Because of interdependence at both the local and global level, it is not only moral but also in the best interest of MNCs to establish a single clear posture toward social and ethical responsibilities worldwide and to ensure that it is implemented. In a real sense, foreign firms enter as guests in host countries and must respect the local laws, policies, traditions, and culture as well as those countries' economic and developmental needs.

EXHIBIT 2-7 Corporate Sustainability Model

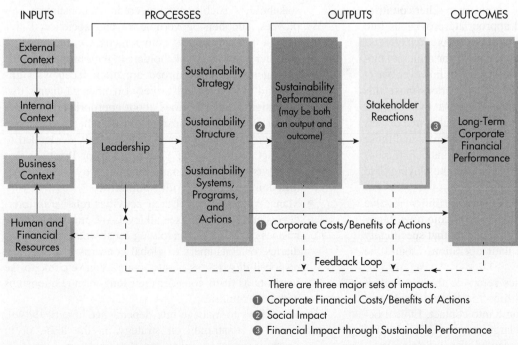

Source: Marc J. Epstein, "Implementing Corporate Sustainability: Measuring and Managing Social and Environmental Impacts," *Strategic Finance*, January 2008. Copyright 2008 by IMA, Montvale, NJ, www.imanet.org, used with permission.

CONCLUSION

When research findings and corporate actions indicate differential attitudes toward ethical behavior and social responsibility across cultures, MNCs must take certain steps. For example, they must be careful when placing a foreign manager in a country whose values are incongruent with his or her own because this could lead to conflicts with local managers, governmental bodies, customers, and suppliers. As discussed earlier, expatriates, as well as local employees, should be oriented to the legal and ethical ramifications of questionable foreign payments, the differences in environmental regulations, and the local expectations of personal integrity. They should also be supported as they attempt to integrate host-country behaviors with the expectations of the company's headquarters.

Social responsibility, ethical behavior, interdependence, and sustainability are important concerns to be built into management control—not as afterthoughts but as part of the ongoing process of planning and controlling international operations for the long-term benefit of all. The perspective of CSV—creating shared value—encompasses a positive and proactive role in including those concerns in the strategic planning of the organization. Part 2 focuses on the pervasive and powerful influence of culture in the host-country environment in which the international manager operates. Chapter 3 examines the nature of culture. What are its various dimensions and roots? How does culture affect the behavior and expectations of employees, and what are the implications for how managers operating in other countries should behave?

Summary of Key Points

- The concept of international social responsibility (known in business circles as CSR—corporate social responsibility) includes the expectation that MNCs should be concerned about the social and economic effects of their decisions on activities in other countries and that they should build appropriate provisions into their strategic plans to deal with those potential effects.

- Moral universalism refers to the need for a moral standard that is accepted around the world; however, varying cultural attitudes and business practices make this goal unattainable at this time. A number of groups of corporations within industries have collaborated on sets of policies for CSR for both their companies and those in their supply chains. Such collaborations help to raise the standard in host countries and level the playing field for managers within those industries.

- Concerns about MNC social responsibility revolve around issues of human rights in other countries. Many organizations develop codes of conduct that specifically deal with human rights in their operations around the world.

- International business ethics refers to the conduct of managers in their relationships to all individuals and entities with whom they come into contact. Ethical behavior is judged and based largely on the cultural value system and the generally accepted ways of doing business in each country or society. Managers must decide

whether to base their ethical standards on those of the host country or those of the home country and whether these different standards can be reconciled.

- MNCs must balance their responsibility to various stakeholders, such as owners, creditors, consumers, employees, suppliers, governments, and societies. Firms with a long-term perspective recognize the need to consider all of their stakeholders in their business plans.

- Managers operating abroad are often faced with differing attitudes toward bribery or other payments that raise significant questions about appropriate moral behavior in either the host nation or other nations, yet bribery or other payments are frequently demanded to conduct business. The Foreign Corrupt Practices Act prohibits most questionable payments by U.S. companies doing business in other countries.

- Managers must control their activities relative to interdependent relationships at all levels—from simple, daily business transactions involving local workers, intermediaries, or consumers to global concerns of ecological responsibility. Issues of sustainability have come to the forefront as firms consider their long-term relationships with host countries.

- The failure to manage interdependence effectively will result in constraints on strategy, in the least, or in disastrous consequences for the local area, the subsidiary, and the global reputation of the company. The perspective of CSV—creating shared value—provides a proactive model to guide companies to incorporate these concerns into their strategic planning.

■ Managing environmental interdependence includes the need to consider ecological interdependence as well as the economic and social implications of MNC activities.

■ Implementation of sustainability strategies requires the company to have both formal and informal systems to support the goals. Essential to success is the commitment of top leadership and the recognition of sustainability as a process that will benefit the company—that it is a good business idea.

Discussion Questions

2-1. Discuss the concept of CSR. What role does it play in the relationship between a company and its host country? How does CSV move beyond CSR?

2-2. Discuss the criticisms that have been leveled against MNCs in the past regarding their activities in less-developed countries. What counterarguments are there to those criticisms?

2-3. What does moral universalism mean? Discuss your perspective on this concept. Do you think the goal of moral universalism is possible? Is it advisable?

2-4. What do you think should be the role of MNCs toward human rights issues in other countries? What are the major human rights concerns at this time? What ideas do you have for dealing with these problems? What is the role of corporate codes of conduct in dealing with these concerns?

2-5. What is meant by international business ethics? Should the local culture affect ethical practices? What are the

implications of local norms for ethical decisions by MNC managers?

2-6. As a manager in a foreign subsidiary, how can you reconcile local expectations of questionable payments with the Foreign Corrupt Practices Act? What is your stance on the problem of payoffs? How does the degree of law enforcement in a particular country affect ethical behavior in business?

2-7. What do you think are the responsibilities of MNCs toward the global environment? Give some examples of MNC activities that run counter to the concepts of ecological interdependence and sustainability.

2-8. Discuss the ethical issues that have developed regarding the use of IT in cross-border transactions. What new conflicts have developed since the printing of this book? What solutions can you suggest?

Application Exercise

2-9. Do some research to determine the codes of conduct of two familiar companies. Compare the issues that they cover and share your findings with the class. After several students have

presented their findings, prepare a chart showing the commonalities and differences of content in the codes presented. How do you account for the differences?

Experiential Exercise

Consider the ethical dilemmas in the following situation and decide what you would do. Then meet in small groups of students and come to a group consensus. Discuss your decisions with the class.

You are the VP for global sales of a telecommunications equipment company. The accounting manager of your company recently brought to your attention an unusual charge of a 3 percent commission to a purchasing manager in Russia with whom your company had recently started doing business. One state-owned manufacturing company in Russia (for privacy's sake, we will call the company "R") submitted a bid for a large order of your equipment. You remember being surprised to get the contract with "R" because your company had never been able to do business with it since it started there many years ago. As it turned out, your new sales manager for the region had a relative in "R" who promised to supply him with all of your competitors' bids if he paid him a 3 percent commission on all of the sales to his company. The area manager accepted this arrangement. He got the competing bids and secured the deal with your company.

What would you do, given the following: (1) If you refuse to accept the business without any legitimate reasons (presently, there are none), your company will be blacklisted in that country—which amounts to about 20 percent of gross yearly profit. (2) If you accept the business and do not pay the 3 percent commission, the purchasing manager will make much trouble when he receives your shipment. No doubt he will not release the 5 percent bank guarantee letter about the quality and quantity of the material. (3) If you accept the business and pay the 3 percent commission, you feel that it would malign your company's reputation and your beliefs.

You have three ethical problems here: First, your company has won a rigged bid. Second, you must pay the person who rigged it or he will make life miserable for you. Third, you have to decide what to do with the area manager who accepted this arrangement.

Source: Based on Delaney and D. Sockell, "Ethics in the Trenches," *Across the Board* (October 1990), p 17.

CASE STUDY

Levi Looks to Cut Its Cloth Differently by Rewarding Responsible Suppliers

Shawn Donnan, *Financial Times* [London (UK)] November 5, 2014, p. 1

Calling all hipsters: you may just have a new reason to feel better about your skinny jeans.

In a bid to bolster its ethical credentials and meet the demands of increasingly fussy millennial consumers, Levi Strauss & Co is offering a new financial incentive to suppliers as far away as Bangladesh and China to meet environmental, labor, and safety standards.

The San Francisco–based jeans maker said yesterday that it would begin providing lower-cost working capital to those of its 550 suppliers that do best on those measures.

The financing, which is being arranged with the World Bank's private sector arm, the International Finance Corporation, will operate on a sliding scale. As suppliers improve their environmental performance and conditions for workers, they will be rewarded with lower interest rates on working capital provided through a special IFC facility.

The project sprang out of conversations started at the IFC following the 2013 Rana Plaza factory collapse in Bangladesh, which left more than 1,100 people dead and prompted new scrutiny of fashion brands' supply chains.

Through the IFC, Levi Strauss suppliers will have access to cheaper capital than they would otherwise in their home countries. However, Olaf Schmidt, who heads the IFC's global retail practice, said that those suppliers that did best on labor and other standards would receive a further discount of up to 50 basis points on the interest charged.

The initiative comes at a time when consumers are becoming increasingly interested in the conditions in which their clothes are made. Multinational companies are responding by tightening their bonds with suppliers and using new tools to manage them.

Michael Kobori, Levi Strauss's vice president of sustainability, said that the company told contractors about the scheme last week and had already received expressions of interest. If the pilot with the IFC worked, Mr. Kobori said, Levi Strauss was committed to helping expand it to the rest of the garment industry as part of a global race to the top in standards.

Rachel Wilshaw, ethical trade manager for Oxfam, said that offering incentives to suppliers to improve their practices was a good idea, but whether the scheme worked would depend on how Levi Strauss and the IFC monitored suppliers. "The devil will be in the process rather than in the incentive," she said.

© 2015 The Financial Times Limited

Case Questions

2-10. Consider what happened in Bangladesh (see the opening profile). To what extent do you think the efforts by Levi Strauss can resolve the kinds of problems that led to that disaster?

2-11. What other people and factors are involved? Who are the stakeholders, and how are they affected? Consider the process and what steps are necessary to make this good idea happen.

2-12. How do these types of incentives relate to the overall goal of sustainability for the company?

Endnotes

1. Miguel Bustillo, Tom Wright, Shelly Banjo, "Tough Questions in Fire's Ashes: Blaze in Bangladesh Reveals Troubles Wal-Mart, Others Face in Policing Factories," *Wall Street Journal*, Eastern ed., [New York, N.Y] November 30, 2012, p. B.1.

Barney Jopson, Amy Kazmin, Richard Milne, "Cheap Clothes Come at a Price in the Factories of Bangladesh," *Financial Times* [London (UK)] December 19, 2012, p. 8.

Julfikar Ali Manik and Jim Yardley, "Bangladesh Finds Gross Negligence in Factory Fire," *New York Times*, December 17, 2012; Steven Greenhouse, "Some Retailers Rethink Role in Bangladesh," *New York Times*, May 1, 2012; Keith Bradsher, "After Bangladesh, Seeking New Sources," *New York Times*, May 15, 2013; Steven Greenhouse, "U.S. Retailers See Big Risk in Safety Plan for Factories in Bangladesh," *New York Times*,

May 22, 2013; The editorial board, "Obama Gets Tough on Bangladesh," *New York Times*, June 27, 2013.

Syed Zain Al-Mahmood; Shelly Banjo, "World News: Plant Fire Shows Challenges—Bangladesh Factory Blaze Comes as Industry Safety Still Vexes Foreign Companies," *Wall Street Journal*, Eastern ed. [New York, N.Y] October 10, 2013, p. A.18.; Steven Greenhouse and Stephanie Clifford, "U.S. Retailers Offer Plan for Safety at Factories," *New York Times*, July 10, 2013.

Steven Greenhouse, "*U.S. Retailers Decline to Aid Factory Victims in Bangladesh*," Reuters, November 22, 2013; Steven Greenhouse, "Europeans Fault American Safety Effort in Bangladesh," *New York Times*, November 12, 2013.

2. A. Maitland, "No Hiding Place for the Irresponsible Business," *Financial Times Special Report*, September 29, 2003, p. 4.

3. Theo Vermaelen, "An Innovative Approach to Funding CSR Projects," *Harvard Business Review* 89, No. 6 (June 2011), pp. 28–29.

4. Heather Timmons, "For Now, IKEA Gives More than It Gets from India," www. nytimes.com, September 10, 2010.

5. Milton Friedman, *Capitalism and Freedom* (Chicago: University of Chicago Press, 1962).

6. Eduardo Porter, "Dividends Emerge in Pressing Apple over Working Conditions in China," www.nytimes.com, March 6, 2012.

7. Ibid.

8. T. Donaldson, "Defining the Value of Doing Good Business," *Financial Times*, June 3, 2005.

9. Heather Timmons, "IKEA Expects to Double Buying of Goods from India," www.nytimes.com, September 21, 2010.

10. Amol Sharma and Jens Hansegard, "IKEA Says It Is Ready to Give India a Try," *Wall Street Journal*, June 25, 2012, p. B.1.

11. Based on Manuela Weber, "The Business Case for Corporate Social Responsibility: A Company-Level Measurement Approach for CSR," *European-Management Journal* 26, No. 4 (2008), pp. 247–261.

12. *Financial Times*, June 3, 2005.

13. Weber, 2008.

14. N. Bowie, "The Moral Obligations of Multinational Corporations," in *Problems of International Justice*, Steven Luper-Foy, ed. (New York: Westview Press: 1987), pp. 97–113.

15. Steven Greenhouse, "Nike Agrees to Help Laid-Off Workers in Honduras," www.nytimes.com, July 26, 2011.

16. Michael E. Porter and Mark R. Kramer, "Creating Shared Value," *Harvard Business Review*, 00178012, 89, No. 1/2 (January–February 2011).

17. Ibid.

18. Ibid.

19. Eric Pfanner, "Google Turns on Charms to Win over Europeans," www.nytimes.com, May 15, 2011.

20. Ibid.

21. www.nestle.com/csv, July 3, 2014; Hans Joehr (Nestlé), interviewed by Nina Kruschwitz, "Creating Shared Value at Nestlé," *MIT Sloan Management Review*, September 2013; "Creating Shared Value Cared for Nestlé," *Financial Express*, Dhaka, May 6, 2014; Stephen Graham Saunders, "Ethical Performance Evaluation: An Extension and Illustration," *European Business Review* 23, No. 6 (2011), pp. 561–571; Daniel S. Fogel, Janet Elizabeth Palmer, "Water as a Corporate Resource," *Journal of Global Responsibility* 5, No. 1 (2014), p. 104–1.

22. Peter Burrows, "Stalking High-Tech Sweatshops," *BusinessWeek*, June 19, 2006, p. 63.

23. Jem Bendell, "Nike Says Time to Team Up," *The Journal of Corporate-Citizenship*, Autumn 2005, No. 19, p. 10(3).

24. Jamil Anderlini, "Communist Clampdown: Beijing Blocks 'Western Values' in Classrooms," *Financial Times*, January 31, 2015.

25. www.transparencyinternational.org, accessed February 11, 2015.

26. Anderlini, January 31, 2015.

27. Ibid.

28. John Gapper, "Google Is Putting Its Own Freedoms at Risk in China," *Financial Times*, January 20, 2006.

29. R. Waters, M. Dickie, and S. Kirchgaessner, "Evildoers? How the West's Net Vanguard Toils behind the Great Firewall of China," *Financial Times*, February 15, 2006.

30. M. Dickie, "Amnesty Accuses Web Groups over Human Rights in China," *Financial Times*, July 20, 2006.

31. Po Keung Ip, "The Challenge of Developing a Business Ethics in China," *Journal of Business Ethics* 88 (2009), pp. 211–224.

32. Ibid.

33. *BusinessWeek*, June 19, 2006, p. 63.

34. "Sweatshop Police," *BusinessWeek*, October 20, 1997, pp. 30–32.

35. Kathleen A. Getz, "International Codes of Conduct: An Analysis of Ethical Reasoning," *Journal of Business Ethics* 9 (1990), pp. 567–577.

36. Alison Maitland, "How Ethics Codes Can Be Made to Work," *Financial Times*, March 7, 2005.

37. Swee Hoon Ang, "The Power of Money: A Cross-Cultural Analysis of Business-Related Beliefs," *Journal of World Business* 35, No. 1 (2000), p. 43.

38. C. J. Robertson and W. F. Crittenden, "Mapping Moral Philosophies: Strategic Implications for Multinational Firms," *Strategic Management Journal* 24 (2003), pp. 385–392.

39. A. Singer, "Ethics—Are Standards Lower Overseas?" *Across the Board* (September 1991), pp. 31–34.

40. Ibid.

41. www.transparencyinternational.org, accessed February 11, 2015.

42. Ibid.

43. James Kanter, "Europe Leads in Pushing for Privacy of User Data," *New York Times*, May 3, 2011.

44. Duncan Robinson, Hannah Kuchler, "Facebook Accused over Privacy Rules," *Financial Times*, February 25, 2015.

45. Kanter, 2011.

46. Robinson and Kuchler, 2015.

47. Reena SenGupta, "Trouble at Home for Overseas Bribes," *Financial Times*, February 2, 2006.

48. Ibid.

49. Gardiner Harris, "Johnson and Johnson Settles Bribery Complaint," www. nytimes.com, April 8, 2011.

50. G. R. Laczniak and J. Naor, "Global Ethics: Wrestling with the Corporate Conscience," *Business*, July–August–September 1985, p. 152.

51. "How to Respond When Only Bribe Money Talks," *Financial Times*, July 11, 2005.

52. J. T. Noonan, Jr., *Bribes* (New York: Macmillan, 1984), p. ii.

53. "Wal-Mart's Woes: Investigators Should Leave No Stone Unturned," *Financial Times*, April 25, 2012, p. 8.

54. Marc J. Epstein, A. R. Buhovac, and K. Yuthas, "Why Nike Kicks Butt in Sustainability," *Organizational Dynamics* 39, pp. 353–356.

55. P. W. Beamish et al., *International Management* (Homewood, IL: Irwin, 1991).

56. Based on Asheghian and Ebrahimi, *International Business* (NY: Harper and Row, 1990).

57. R. H. Mason and R. S. Spich, *Management: An International Perspective* (Homewood, IL: Irwin, 1987).

58. R. T. De George, *Competing with Integrity in International Business* (New York: Oxford University Press, 1993), pp. 3–4.

59. Hilary Bradbury-Huang, "Sustainability by Collaboration: The SEER Case," *Organizational Dynamics* 39, No 4, October–December 2010, pp. 335–344.

60. György Málovics, Noémi Nagypál Csigéné, and Sascha Kraus, "The Role of Corporate Social Responsibility in Strong Sustainability," *Journal of Socio-Economics* 37, No. 3 (2008), pp. 907–918.

61. J. A. G. van Kleef and N. J. Roome, "Developing Capabilities and Competence for Sustainable Business Management as Innovation: A Research Agenda," *Journal of Cleaner Production* 15 (2007), pp. 38–51.

62. Philip Mirvis, Bradley Googins, and Sylvia Kinnicutt, "Vision, Mission, Values: Guideposts to Sustainability," *Organizational Dynamics* 39, No. 4 (October–December 2010), pp. 316–324.

63. "The Business of Sustainability: McKinsey Global Survey Results," *McKinsey Quarterly*, October 2011.

64. Ibid.

65. Ibid.

66. B. Atkins, "Corporate Social Responsibility: Is It 'Irresponsibility'?" *Corporate Governance Advisor* 14 (2006), pp. 28–29.

67. *Newshour with Jim Lehrer,* PBS news report, November 17, 2008.

68. Ibid.

69. Ibid.

70. Ibid.

71. Jang B. Singh and V. C. Lakhan, "Business Ethics and the International Trade in Hazardous Wastes," *Journal of Business Ethics* 8 (1989), pp. 889–899.

72. Philip Mirvis, Bradley Googins, and Sylvia Kinnicutt, "Vision, Mission, Values: Guideposts to Sustainability," *Organizational Dynamics* 39, No. 4, (October–December 2010), pp. 316–324.

73. Ibid.

74. Steven Mufson, "Federal Report Lays Bulk of Fault for Gulf Oil Spill on BP," *Washington Post* (Washington, DC) February 18, 2011, p. 18.

75. Daniel Gilbert and Sarah Kent, "BP Agrees to Pay 418.7 billion to Settle Deepwater Horizon Oil Spill Claims," *Wall Street Journal*, July 2, 2015.

76. D. Minor, J. Morgan, "CSR as Reputation Insurance: Primum Non Nocere," *California Management Review* 53, No. 3 (Spring 2011).

77. Jem Bendell, "World Review: July–September 2010," *Journal of Corporate Citizenship* (Winter 2010), p. 40.

78. P. Asheghian and B. Ebrahimi, *International Business* (New York: Harper and Row, 1990), pp. 640–641.

79. Linda M. Castellito, "TerraCycle Founder's Journey Started with Worm Poop: Even the Book about the Company Is Green," *USA Today*, July 27, 2009, p. 5; Blair Koch, "The Business of Being Green," *McClatchy-Tribune Business News* (Washington), April 22, 2011; Victoria Vizcarra, "Special Feature: Leed-Certified Properties," *BusinessWorld* (Philippines) May 31, 2011; "TerraCycle Inc., Garbage In, Products Out," *Retail-Merchandiser.com*, November–December, 2011; Heidi Neck, Candida Brush, and Elaine Allen, "The Landscape of Social Entrepreneurship," *Business Horizons*, 2009, 52: 13.9.

80. *Business World*, 2011.

81. http://www.terracycle.com/en-US/pages/about-us.html, accessed August 6, 2015.

82. *Retail-Merchandiser.com*, 2011.

83. *Tribune Business News*, 2011.

84. Ibid.

85. *Business World*, 2011.

86. *Business Horizons*.

87. *Business Horizons*.

88. Marc J. Epstein and Adriana Rejc Buhovac, "Solving the Sustainability Implementation Challenge," *Organizational Dynamics* 39 (2010), pp. 306–315.

89. Marc J. Epstein, "Implementing Corporate Sustainability: Measuring and Managing Social and Environmental Impacts," *Strategic Finance*, January 2008.

AMITY
RESEARCH CENTERS
HEADQUARTER
BANGALORE

Case I Facebook's Internet.org Initiative: Serving the Bottom of the Pyramid?

Abstract: Crusading to bring every single human being online, Facebook's founder Mark Zuckerberg had partnered with leading technological companies and launched Internet.org in August 2013. With active support from local governments, the Internet.org initiative had brought basic Internet facilities to the countries of Zambia, Paraguay, Indonesia, Kenya, Rwanda and Philippines. Championing the cause of Internet connectivity for economic betterment, Zuckerberg understood the crucial market presented by India and other developing countries presented for its future growth opportunity. Mixing business with philanthropy, Facebook's Internet.org initiative was lauded as well as criticized by many. Critics had termed this initiative as "venture humanitarianism" and "Facebook's gateway drug." Moreover, scathing remarks were also made for creating a monopoly portal and ignoring the principle of net neutrality. The initiative was considered as a ploy to get more users to boost the company's bottom line for future growth prospects. Amid this backdrop, it would be interesting to watch whether the initiative would altruistically deliver on the promise of a connected world with assured economic prosperity or work only in favor of the organization to mine the fortunes at the bottom of the pyramid.

Case Study

Universal Internet access will be the next great industrial revolution.[1]

STEPHEN ELOP
Nokia's President and CEO

Connectivity cannot just be a privilege of the rich and powerful. It is a human right.[2]

MARK ZUCKERBERG
Facebook CEO

This case was written by Punithavathi Srikant, Amity Research Centers Headquarters, Bangalore. It is intended to be used as the basis for class discussion rather than to illustrate either effective or ineffective handling of a management situation. The case was compiled from published sources.
© 2015, Amity Research Centers Headquarter, Bangalore.

[1] Bora Kukil, "Internet.org: A Facebook Initiative to Connect the Unconnected," http://www.ibtimes.com/Internetorg-facebook-initiative-connect-unconnected-1393301, August 21, 2013.

[2] Singh Vikas, "When One Billion Are Offline, the World Is Robbed of Ideas, Facebook CEO Mark Zuckerberg Says," http://timesofindia.indiatimes.com/tech/tech-news/When-one-billion-are-offline-the-world-is-robbed-of-ideas-Facebook-CEO-Mark-Zuckerberg-says/articleshow/44765195.cms, October 10, 2014.

I do have to question Zuckerberg's motives though. Users are offered limited Internet access before being asked to pay for more. Is this a philanthropic project or money making exercise for Facebook?[3]

–BRENDON PETSCH
IT Director, Gritit

Moments in history were made memorable due to the invention of new technologies that completely rewired the way society functioned. One such invention was the Internet, which revolutionized the way people connected and improved their economic well-being. Social networking site Facebook redrew the map of the connected world and scouted for future growth from developing countries. By spearheading the nonprofit initiative called Internet.org in collaboration with other technology partners, Facebook had promised to bring low-cost Internet access to emerging economies of the world. This initiative took effect in Philippines, Zambia, Rwanda, Paraguay, and Tanzania with a pay-as-you-app model that charged different rates for data consumed by different apps. In that process, Facebook emerged as an intermediary and offered services ranging from education to banking and health with its profit-driven motives. Also, this initiative would make access to content through Facebook networks alone, thereby influencing its users. India too had joined the bandwagon, and Internet.org was launched in India in 2014. Facebook's founder Mark Zuckerberg (Zuckerberg) had acknowledged the initiative as the organization's long-term project that would eventually turn profitable. Praised and criticized by many, the case study looks into the motives behind the launch of nonprofit initiative Internet.org and how it served Facebook's business interests. While doing so, the case study also analyzes whether Internet.org was a canny business move dressed up to sound like charity.

Internet.org: A Facebook Initiative

"The goal of Internet.org is to make Internet access available to the two thirds of the world who are not yet connected, and to bring the same opportunities to everyone that the connected third of the world has today,"[4] stated Internet.org in a press release. Internet.org was an initiative of a global partnership among technology leaders, nonprofit organisations, local communities, and experts who were working together to bring

[3] Donnelly Caroline, "Facebook CEO Mark Zuckerberg Sets Out Vision to Grant World Internet Access," http://www.itpro.co.uk/strategy/21695/facebook-ceo-mark-zuckerberg-sets-out-vision-to-grant-world-Internet-access, February 24, 2014," © 2015, Amity Research Centers HQ, Bangalore. All rights reserved.

[4] "Internet.org," https://Internet.org/.

Internet access to the two thirds of global population who do not have net connectivity.[5] The partners were working toward exploring solutions in areas of affordability, efficiency, and business models by sharing their tools and resources and by adopting best practices. Internet.org had also planned to invest in tools and software to transmit data efficiently by compressing the data. Through innovative business models, Internet.org would work with developers, device manufacturers, and mobile operators to bring more people online.[6]

Apart from Facebook, the other founding partners of Internet.org had believed in the power of a connected world and had come together to achieve the lofty goal of making the Internet available to everyone on Earth (see Exhibit I).

A study by Deloitte revealed that Internet connectivity was a major driver for economic growth in developing countries. It would become a powerful tool of social change capable of creating nearly 140 million jobs and uplifting 160 million from absolute poverty besides providing critical information for leading a healthy life. But the major challenge encountered in becoming a knowledge economy was the slow growth of Internet connectivity. Only a third of the world population, around 2.7 billion people, were connected.

Even though more than 85 percent of the global population lived under cellular companies' coverage area, only 30 percent were accessing the Internet. To increase affordability and awareness, the key challenges for Internet adoption, Internet.org introduced the Internet.org app, which gave free basic services to the users. Through this application, people could access information regarding health, employment, and local news. This was made available initially in Zambia through Bharti Airtel and extended to other parts of the world as well[7] (see Exhibit II).

In the Philippines, where the Internet.org initiative was adopted in collaboration with the mobile operator Globe, promising results were seen. More people got free access to apps, and through loans, they registered for its various data plans. Within a few months of starting this initiative, the mobile user subscriber base on Globe network increased by 25 percent. In Paraguay, in collaboration with TIGO,[8] this initiative increased the user base by 50 percent. Nearly 3 million people had access to the Internet, and their daily data usage increased by 50 percent.[9]

Also, in Indonesia, Internet.org improved the country's network and enhanced its app performance, thereby closing the connectivity gap.[10] Tanzania also joined this initiative in October 2014.[11] In Kenya, along with Airtel, Internet.org started offering

EXHIBIT I   Internet.org's Founding Partners

Ericsson	-	Ericsson is a world-leading provider of communications technology and services.
MediaTek	-	MediaTek Inc. is a leading fabless semiconductor company for wireless communications and digital multimedia solutions.
Opera Software	-	Opera products enable more than 350 million Internet consumers to discover and connect with the content and services that matter most to them.
Samsung	-	Samsung is a global leader in technology, opening new possibilities for people everywhere through relentless innovation and discovery.
Facebook	-	Facebook's mission is to give people the power to share and make the world more open and connected.
Nokia	-	Nokia is a global leader in mobile communications whose products have become an integral part of the lives of people around the world.
Qualcomm	-	Qualcomm is a world leader in 3G, 4G, and next-generation wireless technologies.

Source: "About—Internet.org," https://Internet.org/about.

EXHIBIT II   Internet.org's Services in Zambia

- AccuWeather
- Airtel
- eZeLibrary
- Facebook
- Facts for Life
- Google Search
- Go Zambia Jobs
- Kokoliko
- MAMA (Mobile Alliance for Maternal Action)
- Messenger
- Wikipedia
- WRAPP (Women's Rights App)
- Zambia uReport
- SuperSport
- Zambia Reports
- Ebola FAQ by UNICEF

Source: Guy Rosen, "Introducing the Internet.org App," https://Internet.org/press/introducing-the-Internet-dot-org-app, July 31, 2014.

[7]Guy Rosen, "Introducing the Internet.org App," https://Internet.org/press/introducing-the-Internet-dot-org-app, July 31, 2014.
[8]Tigo is the first cellular network in Tanzania. It started operations in 1994 and is Tanzania's most affordable and innovative mobile phone operator.
[9]"Connecting the World from the Sky," https://fbcdn-dragon-a.akamaihd.net/hphotos-ak-ash3/t39.2365-6/851574_611544752265540_1262758947_n.pdf.
[10]"Improving App and Network Performance in Indonesia," http://www.Internet.org/press/improving-app-and-network-performance-in-indonesia, October 12, 2014.
[11]"Internet.org App Launches in Tanzania," https://Internet.org/press/Internet-dot-org-app-launches-in-tanzania, October 29, 2014.

[5]"About—Internet.org," https://Internet.org/about.
[6]Ibid.

basic Internet services free of cost in November 2014. The people of Kenya would have access to features such as AccuWeather, BBC News, BBC Swahili, BabyCenter & MAMA, Brighter Monday, Daily Nation, Ebola Information, Facebook, Facts for Life, Girl Effect, Jamii Forums, Messenger, OLX, Scholars4Dev, Super Sport, Toto Health, Wattpad, and Wikipedia.[12]

Another pilot initiative of Internet.org was the introduction of Social EDU, which provided Rwandan students with free access to online education in collaboration with the government of Rwanda, together with Nokia subsidizing its smartphones for the initiative.[13]

In India, Internet.org collaborated with Unilever to expand net connectivity in rural areas and evaluate educational and cultural factors that limited the usage of Internet in India. Unilever's Chief Marketing and Communications Officer, Keith Weed, asserted, "Access to the Internet is improving in countries like India but there is still a very high proportion of people that would love the opportunity to connect and engage but who cannot enjoy what many of us take for granted. Having no Internet access naturally removes all associated opportunities that it brings which, in turn, can be a barrier to learning and ultimately hinder economic development. Through our long history of serving the Indian market we bring an in-depth understanding of rural Indian communities. We hope, together with Internet.org, we can use this know-how to understand better how a vital modern resource can benefit many more millions."[14]

Internet.org was planning to partner with other countries to expand its operations in other markets as well. Other than partnerships, the initiative needed new technologies to solve the barriers for connectivity, and Facebook was investing in technology to deliver the necessary solution. Because different communities required different technologies, Facebook was focusing on developing different platforms to serve different population densities. Facebook's connectivity lab would develop technologies in the forms of drones, satellites, mesh networks, radios, and free space optics, employing leading experts from reputed organizations such as NASA.[15]

Also, Facebook, in collaboration with Ericsson, set up the Internet.org innovation lab at Facebook's Menlo Park headquarters. This lab would give developers an opportunity to test their apps in simulated network conditions that existed in new growth markets so as to optimize their applications for use in diverse markets of the world.[16]

Globally, 4.4 billion people were without access to Internet as of September 2014; bringing them into a connected world required a major collaborative effort from governments, civil society, and companies[17] (Annexure I). Johan Wibergh, executive vice president and Ericsson's head of Business Unit Networks, while elaborating on its collaboration with Facebook for the innovation lab said, "The goals of Internet .org are very much aligned with our long-standing ideal that communications is a basic human need. The creation of the lab will provide a unique environment for testing and ultimately optimizing applications regardless of network, device, or operating system. The collaboration with app developers will provide Ericsson with invaluable understanding of their requirements on our networks, which we can apply to ensure the continued development of the best performing networks globally."[18] But Jen Schradie, a PhD student at the University of California, felt that the initiative was a Trojan horse and was intended to expand Facebook's potential market.[19] He opined, "The Internet as a human right is more than just freedom of speech; it is also freedom to access all of the tools of that speech. Access to Facebook and participating in its black box algorithms that generate profits for the company are not human rights."[20]

A Solace for Emerging Economies or a Canny Business Move?

Zuckerberg felt that the Internet.org initiative would generate a positive impact on the global population. "They're going to use it to decide what kind of government they want. Get access to health care for the first time ever. Connect with family hundreds of miles away. Getting access to the Internet is a really big deal." But barriers to Internet connectivity were many, and Internet.org was geared to break the barriers (Exhibit III).

Also, compelling findings were revealed in the study conducted on the impact of Internet access in the developing world.[21] (See Exhibit IV.)

EXHIBIT III   Barriers to Internet Connectivity

- Devices are too expensive.
- Service plans are too expensive.
- There's no mobile network to connect to.
- Content isn't available in the local language.
- Awareness of the value of the Internet is limited.
- Availability of power sources is limited.
- Networks can't support large amounts of data.

Source: "Internet.org," https://Internet.org/.

[12]Batambuze III Ephraim, "Free Internet access to Kenyans Thanks to Airtel and Facebook," http://pctechmag.com/2014/12/free-Internet-access-to-kenyans-thanks-to-airtel-and-facebook/, December 2014.

[13]"Introducing SocialEDU," http://www.Internet.org/press/introducing-socialedu, February 23, 2014.

[14]"Unilever and Internet.org Partner on Internet Study for Communities across India," http://www.unilever.com/mediacentre/pressreleases/2014/unileverandInternetorgpartneronInternetstudyforcommunitiesacrossindia.aspx, February 24, 2014.

[15]"Connecting the World from the Sky," op. cit.

[16]"Internet.org Innovation Lab," https://Internet.org/press/Internet-dot-org-innovation-lab, February 23, 2014.

[17]"Offline and Falling Behind," https://Internet.org/press/offline-and-falling-behind, September 30, 2014.

[18]"Ericsson and Facebook Create Innovation Lab for Internet.org," http://www.ericsson.com/us/thecompany/press/releases/2014/02/1763215, February 24, 2014.

[19]"Facebook's Universal Access 'Trojan Horse' attacked," http://www.scidev.net/global/communication/news/facebook-universal-web-access-trojan-horse-attacked.html, November 27, 2014.

[20]Ibid.

[21]"Value of Connectivity: Economic and Social Benefits of Expanding Internet Access," op. cit.

EXHIBIT IV   Impact of Internet Connectivity Across the Globe

Summary of health impacts of extending internet penetration by region				
	Africa	Latin America	Indian	South and East Asia
General health (Lives saved)	Nearly 1M	160,000	775,000	460,000
Child Mortality (Infants saved)	130,000	6,000	85,000	25,000
HIV/AIDS (Patients live longer)	2.2M	130,000	200,000	160,000

Summary of economic impacts of extending internet penetration by region				
	Africa	Latin America	Indian	South and East Asia
Increase in the rate of growth of GDP	92%	37%	110%	75%
Increase in annual GDP per capita	$450	$630	$500	$630
Additional jobs	44M	5M	65M	27M
Decrease in extreme poverty	–30%	–13%	–28%	–16%

Source: "Value of Connectivity," https://Internet.org/press/value-of-connectivity, February 23, 2014.

More so, Facebook focused its approach toward India because it was blocked in China. However, in India, the low penetration of the Internet and low average revenue per user (ARPU) did pose a challenge to Facebook. Zuckerberg made efforts to explore his options in India. Ultimately, he wanted to improve Facebook's revenue and increase the number of Facebook users, which would increase its ARPU from the Asian region.[22] Internet and Mobile Association of India (IAMAI) and IMRB[23] International found that availability of regional language content in India would boost Internet growth by 24 percent in rural areas; Facebook executives claimed that India was a "brutally localized"[24] country.[25]

Zuckerberg always framed his Internet.org initiative as a non-profit and humanitarian aid type of mission, but scathing remarks and criticisms were raised against his statement that connectivity was a basic human right.[26] Critics called his initiative venture humanitarianism and Facebook's gateway drug. Even Bill Gates, Zuckerberg's mentor, commented on this initiative, "Hmm, which is more important, connectivity or malaria vaccine? If you think connectivity is the key thing, that's great. I don't."[27]

All along, Zuckerberg had reiterated that Internet.org was not meant to make money immediately. "Traditional businesses would view people using your service that you don't make money from as a cost."[28] But he had wanted this initiative to become profitable in the long run. He himself acknowledged, "There are good examples of companies—Coca-Cola is one—that invested before there was a huge market in countries, and I think that ended up playing out to their benefit for decades to come. I do think something like

[22]Khan Aarzu, "Mark Zuckerberg's Visit to India Has a Hidden Agenda for Facebook Inc. (FB)!" http://www.dazeinfo.com/2014/10/10/mark-zuckerbergs-visit-india-hidden-agenda-facebook-inc-fb/, October 10, 2014.
[23]IMRB International is one of the premier sources for market research and consultancy services throughout South Asia, the Middle East, and North Africa.
[24]Lev Grossman, "The Man Who Wired the World," http://time.com/facebook-world-plan/, December 15, 2014.
[25]Prasant Naidu, "Not Just for Facebook but Internet.org Makes Business Sense for India Too," http://lighthouseinsights.in/not-just-for-facebook-but-Internet-org-makes-business-sense-for-india-too.html/, October 10, 2014.

[26]"The Man Who Wired the World," op. cit.
[27]Ibid.
[28]Ibid.

that is likely to be true here. So even though there's no clear path that we can see to where this is going to be a very profitable thing for us, I generally think if you do good things for people in the world, that that comes back and you benefit from it over time."[29]

Tim Worstall, a contributor in *Fortune* and a supporter of Facebook's Internet.org initiative, said that connectivity had brought economic growth and cited the success story of sardine fishermen of Kerala, India, referring to the article by Robert Jensen, a development economist at Harvard University[30] (Exhibit V).

On the contrary, many view Internet.org as a pseudohumanitarian effort and questioned its motives.[31] But defending the criticism, Guy Rosen, Internet.org Product Manager said that the initiative was meant to be benevolent and made a positive impact on career and educational opportunities for people

EXHIBIT V Network Connectivity Supported Kerala Fishermen's Law of One Price

- As phone coverage spread between 1997 and 2000, fishermen started to buy phones and use them to call coastal markets while still at sea. (The area of coverage reaches 20 to 25 km off the coast.) Instead of selling their fish at beach auctions, the fishermen would call around to find the best price. By dividing the coast into three regions, Mr. Jensen found that the proportion of fishermen who ventured beyond their home markets to sell their catches jumped from zero to around 35 percent as soon as coverage became available in each region. At that point, no fish were wasted and the variation in prices fell dramatically. By the end of the study, coverage was available in all three regions. Waste had been eliminated, and the law of one price—the idea that in efficient markets identical goods should cost the same—had come into effect in the form of a single rate for sardines along the coast.
- This more efficient market benefited everyone. Fishermen's profits rose by 8 percent on average, and consumer prices fell by 4 percent on average. Higher profits meant the phones typically paid for themselves within two months, and the benefits are enduring rather than one-off. All of this, says Mr. Jensen, shows the importance of the free flow of information to ensure that markets work efficiently. "Information makes markets work, and markets improve welfare," he concludes.

Source: Robert Jensen, "To Do with the Price of Fish," http://www.economist.com/node/9149142, May 10, 2007.

who were not previously connected in developing countries. He reiterated, "We're here to build a program that covers more than Facebook so we can accelerate the pace at which people are connecting to the Internet which is 9% a year. We really want to make that happen faster."[32]

The technological companies based in Silicon Valley that were earlier content with dominating the tech world had now ventured into operations outside their area of interests. They had promised promotion of international development through their app-fuelled disruption activities. Called by critics venture humanitarianism in action, these companies made people believe that the tech industry would solve the problems of the developing world, and Internet.org was intended to give a few useful applications to its users with Facebook acting as its middleman. Another under-discussed strategy of Internet.org was its pay-as-you-app model that was followed in the Philippines, Paraguay, and Tanzania. In that model, different charges were levied for various apps.[33]

Despite critics terming the initiative more profit driven than a beneficial one, Zuckerberg himself stated, "One of its goals is to show people why it's rational and good for them to spend the limited money they have on the Internet."[34] He defended the initiative, saying that the initiative was an "on-ramp to the Internet" and not a gateway drug as alleged by critics.[35]

Internet.org's on-ramp would bring in contents through Facebook alone and would influence the users in their access to entertainment and news. Also, it influenced them in their education, health, and banking activities. Zuckerberg also stated that the goal of the Internet.org initiative was to offer credit and identity infrastructure in developing countries "that is still nascent in many developing countries."[36] It should be noted that Lenddo[37] was a lender operating in developing countries and would give credits to the users of social media sites by assessing the users' activity and finding their credit worthiness. However, analysts warned that with limitations of their own, the social media sites would in turn increase the anxiety level of the site users. Also, Facebook was not the only entity to provide these services to developing countries. Users should bear in mind that Facebook was a for-profit organization whose interests were much different from those of an ordinary citizen.[38]

Criticisms were also raised about the plans put in place in developing countries by organizations such as Facebook to promote their business interests. They lobbied and manipulated to bring in reforms such as privatization and liberalization to further their commercial interests in those countries. With long-term growth expected to come from the developing countries, Facebook played its cards well through Internet.org initiative. It emerged as a monopoly and obtained data to increase its revenue from advertisements. "Internet connectivity to all"

[29]Ibid.

[30]Tim Worstall, "Facebook and Internet.org: Evgeny Morozov's Absurd Misunderstanding of the Profit Motive," http://www.forbes.com/sites/timworstall/2014/08/03/facebook-and-Internet-org-evgeny-morozovs-absurd-misunderstanding-of-the-profit-motive/, March 8, 2014.

[31]Morozov Evgeny, "Facebook's Gateway Drug", http://www.nytimes.com/2014/08/03/opinion/sunday/evgeny-morozov-facebooks-gateway-drug.html?ref=opinion&_r=0, August 2nd 2014

[32]"Facebook's Gateway Drug", op. cit.

[33]Ibid.

[34]"Facebook's Gateway Drug", op. cit.

[35]Ibid.

[36]Ibid.

[37]Lenddo is a startup company that allows the emerging middle class to use their online social connections to build their creditworthiness and access local financial services.

[38]"Facebook's Gateway Drug", op. cit.

had become a commodity for the technological companies and was disguised as a humanitarian activity.[39]

Critics of Internet.org initiative also questioned Zuckerberg's lofty vision of "connectivity is a human right" because it provided free access for some basic contents while holding the robust content for a price. It was following the well-trodden path of technological companies that offered the bait of limited free usage to use to their advantage later. It was demonstrated by the World Bank that in the name of development many technological companies made money through people who were at the bottom of the pyramid and, invariably, they became the losers.[40] As Adam Smith[41] pointed out, it was not the benevolence of the butcher or the baker to give supper to the needy; it was done to perpetuate their own self-interest. Also, it became disadvantageous to the people at the bottom of the pyramid, for it was that they lacked the opportunity and freedom to pursue their own interests that caused losses to the society at large.[42]

Journalist and author Evgeny Morozov (Morozov) made scathing remarks about Zuckerberg's positioning of Internet.org as a humanitarian mission of Facebook and not as a for-profit business expansion plan. Morozov was worried that it would expand Facebook's reach, sell more of its advertisements, and squeeze other app developers. In addition, others not in the Facebook ecosystem would be pressured to join the rest to use its apps.[43]

Apart from that, in a price-sensitive developing market such as India, Internet.org tilted the scale in favor of free services that brought distortion in the neutral access space. The initiative forced the competitors to enter into revenue-sharing arrangements and gave excessive power to people who selected services for the Internet.org initiative. Net neutrality was forgotten; Internet.org made business sense for Facebook and not for India.[44]

The altruistic propaganda of Internet.org had its own catch because it affected net neutrality and Internet freedom. People got access to limited sites and acted as a gatekeeper to their offered choice. In that process, poor people became hostage to freedom of accessing sites. They were also forced not to access other sites and networks[45] thereby creating a monopoly portal, ignoring net neutrality and controlled people in both the developing world and the developed ones.[46] Gigaom's[47] David

Meyer warned, "Zero-rating entrenches powerful monopolies, hurts competition and potentially slows down innovation."[48] Critics voiced [the opinion] that any universal good would have its own drawbacks; hence, it was better to look for solutions to avoid any control imposed on what people could see and access.[49]

Zuckerberg championed the cause of Internet connectivity for economic betterment, understanding the crucial market India presented for Facebook's future growth opportunity. "A lot of people can afford to be on the Internet but they don't understand why it would be valuable,"[50] opined Zuckerberg, and they needed to be given a free sample before they wanted to spend money online. However, India had its own challenges to be met, said a McKinsey report. "For India's Internet user growth to be more inclusive, significant challenges—including the lack of basic infrastructure, low quality of coverage, uneven distribution of wealth, and lagging human capital development—will need to be overcome."[51] To overcome the obstacles, solar-powered drones were to be deployed. Zuckerberg stated that it not only helped his business to grow but, in the process, gave millions of Indians access to the Internet and contributed to the country's growth. He said, "India is just at the beginning. The benefits of connectivity here are going to be profound."[52]

That echoed the statement proclaimed management guru C. K. Prahalad (Prahalad) made about how access to Internet connectivity would help mine the "fortune at the bottom of the pyramid." Many organizations tend to overlook this aspect because these markets offered low revenue potential while their operating expenses cost more. Prahalad wanted an entrepreneurial approach rather than a charity to elevate the poor and needy. He felt that, "If we stop thinking of the poor as victims or as a burden, and start recognizing them as resilient and creative entrepreneurs and value-conscious consumers, a whole new world of opportunity will open up."[53] He also wanted multinational organizations to pursue partnerships with them to innovate and sustain growth.[54]

Alibaba was successful in rural regions of China through its e-tailing approach, and a McKinsey study stated that, "E-tailing's impact is more pronounced in China's underdeveloped small and midsize cities. We found that while incomes in these urban areas are lower, their online shoppers spend almost as much money online as do people in some larger, more prosperous cities—and also spend a larger portion of their

[39]Ibid.

[40]Ibid.

[41]Adam Smith was often touted as the world's first free-market capitalist.

[42]"Facebook and Internet.org: Evgeny Morozov's Absurd Misunderstanding of the Profit Motive," op. cit.

[43]Julie Bort, "The *New York Times* Published a Scathing Column Ripping Apart Mark Zuckerberg's Internet.org," http://www.businessinsider.in/The-New-York-Times-Published-A-Scathing-Column-Ripping-Apart-Mark-Zuckerbergs-Internet-Org/articleshow/39578455.cms, August 4, 2014.

[44]Nikhil Pawa, "Zuckerberg's Sucker Punch: Would You Want Free Internet If It Wasn't Really Free?" http://blogs.timesofindia.indiatimes.com/toi-edit-page/zuckerbergs-sucker-punch-would-you-want-free-Internet-if-it- wasnt-really-free/, October 13, 2014.

[45]Hal Eric Schwartz, "What Facebook's Free Internet Offer in Zambia Means for Net Neutrality," http://inthecapital.streetwise.co/2014/07/31/facebook-free-Internet-zambia-net-neutrality/, July 31, 2014.

[46]Dan Gillmor, "Thank You, Facebook Inc, But What Developing Nations Need Is Net Freedom," http://www.theguardian.com/commentisfree/2013/aug/21/facebook-developing-nations-Internet, August 21, 2013.

[47]Gigaom is a blog-related media company delivering news, in-depth analysis, and opinions on technology-related topics.

[48]Peter Judge, "Zambia Gets Free Basic Internet with Internet.org's Facebook App," http://www.techweekeurope.co.uk/workspace/facebook-zambia-Internet-org-airtel-150080, August 1, 2014.

[49]"What Facebook's Free Internet Offer in Zambia Means for Net Neutrality," op. cit.

[50]Eric Bellman, "Zuckerberg Champions World-Wide Spread of Internet," http://www.wsj.com/articles/zuckerberg-champions-world-wide-spread-of-Internet-1412865610, October 9, 2014.

[51]"Zuckerberg Champions World-Wide Spread of Internet," op. cit.

[52]Ibid.

[53]Panos Mourdoukoutas, "How Facebook and Alibaba Are Turning the World's Poor into Entrepreneurs," http://www.forbes.com/sites/panosmourdoukoutas/2014/10/05/how-facebook-and-alibaba-are-turning-the-worlds-poor-into-entrepreneurs/, October 5, 2014.

[54]Ibid.

disposable income online. For these shoppers, the utility of online purchasing may be higher, since they now have access to products and brands previously not available to them, in locations where many retailers have yet to establish beachheads."[55] That clued organizations to mine the bottom of the pyramid for their fortunes from future growth and revenue.[56]

As Prahalad reaffirmed, "Cases certainly can be found of large firms and multinational corporations (MNCs) that may have undermined the efforts of the poor to build their livelihoods, [but] the greatest harm they might have done to the poor is to ignore them altogether. When the poor at the BOP are treated as consumers, they can reap the benefits of respect, choice, and self-esteem and have an opportunity to climb out of the poverty trap. The problem of poverty must force us to innovate, not claim "rights to impose our solutions."[57]

Visualising the path ahead, Zuckerberg observed, "The mission is to make this world more open and connected. In terms of connected, we want to go from one billion connected to the next five billion connected. I don't know how long that will take, and it might be a lot harder than the first billion, but that's what we are focused on. That's what Internet.org is all about.…We are also focused on making the economy work better. We built our business on ad products. When we are building product for businesses, we are not thinking only about making money, we are thinking about how can we help aspiring entrepreneurs create their companies, create jobs, how can we help e-commerce companies sell more."[58]

Ben Popper (Popper), business editor at The Verge, an online website, commented on the Internet.org initiative, "You could be generous and call this enlightened self-interest, but more likely, Internet.org is a canny business move dressed up to sound like charity.…" A number of articles mistakenly referred to Internet.org as a nonprofit. It's easy to see how they were confused. In the opening lines of his essay about the new project, Zuckerberg writes, "It may not actually be profitable for us to serve the next few billion people for a very long time, if ever."[59] Popper also highlighted Zuckerberg's clarification on this initiative, "We believe it's possible to sustainably provide free access to basic Internet services in a way that enables everyone with a phone to get on the Internet and join the knowledge economy while also enabling the industry to continue growing profits."[60] Popper summed up by saying, "Bringing Internet access to everyone is a noble goal for sure, but that's not why Zuckerberg, as CEO of a public company, is pursuing it. He wants to make sure that when people in emerging markets like Africa, India, and Asia get their first smartphones and connect to the Internet, Facebook will be the one to greet them."[61]

Bolstering Facebook users and thus obtaining data from the users to serve ads was the implication of Facebook's Internet.org initiative. Chris Smith[62] wrote in the article, "The Hidden Cost of Facebook's Internet.org Project," "Developers and online services will have to make sure they have apps ready to run inside Facebook to reach as many users as possible, especially users who may not want to pay for additional access outside of what Facebook will offer for free."[63] Elaborating more, he said, "Imagine your water meter giving you free quick showers but charging you for a bath.… And this is the profit-driven assumption behind Internet.org's alleged beneficence: Once it gets enough people to take its free digital showers, more users will reach into their pockets to take a digital bath."[64] He cautioned, "Whenever Mark Zuckerberg says that 'connectivity is a human right,' as he put it in his Internet.org essay, you should think twice before agreeing. There is, after all, little joy in obtaining free access to an empty library, or browsing a bookstore with empty pockets—which is, in effect, what Internet.org offers, while holding out the promise of robust content, if users will pay, a few cents at a time, for the privilege."[65] Not to be left behind, Google was also planning to connect the unconnected to the Internet.[66]

Sheryl Sandberg (Sandberg), COO of Facebook, explained, on the future of Facebook, "If the first decade was starting the process of connecting the world, the next decade is helping connect the people who are not yet connected and watching what happens."[67] She added, "When we've been accused of doing this for our own profit, the joke we have is, God, if we were trying to maximize profits, we have a long list of ad products to build! We'd have to work our way pretty far down that list before we got to this."[68] Allaying the criticisms heaped on the initiative, Sandberg stated that people were missing the big picture and said, "No one is saying that getting the next group of people online doesn't one day also help Facebook's business. But if you were actually prioritizing helping Facebook's business, boy do I have a lot of ad products that these engineers can build that we need in the market."[69]

Critics of Internet.org also warned that the initiative was a campaign of self-serving techno-colonialism and a zombie plague: World War Z(uckerberg) which was meant to enrich himself and others by expanding and consolidating Facebook's dominance. It had empowered people by providing Internet access and disempowering them by making them into consumers and its marketing targets.[70]

[55]Ibid.

[56]Ibid.

[57]"Fortune at the Bottom of the Pyramid Quotes," https://www.goodreads.com/work/quotes/62368-the-fortune-at-the-bottom-of-the-pyramid-eradicating-poverty-through-pr.

[58]Pankaj Mishra, "Mark Zuckerberg: Why We Need Internet.org," http://www.livemint.com/Industry/dxOWXbsl0qn0v6lyiQNAxN/Mark-Zuckerberg-Why-we-need-Internetorg.html, August 26, 2013.

[59]Ben Popper, "Zuckerberg's Big Idea Is No Charity," http://edition.cnn.com/2013/08/22/opinion/popper-zuckerberg-facebook/, August 22, 2013.

[60]"Zuckerberg's Big Idea Is No Charity," op. cit.

[61]Ibid.

[62]Chris Smith writes about Gadgets in BGR, a leading online destination for news and commentary focused on the mobile and consumer electronics markets.

[63]Chris Smith, "The Hidden Cost of Facebook's Internet.org Project," http://bgr.com/2014/08/04/facebook-Internet-org-Internet-expansion/, August 4, 2014.

[64]Ibid.

[65]Ibid.

[66]Ibid.

[67]"The Man Who Wired the World," op. cit.

[68]Ibid.

[69]Caroline Fairchild, "For Facebook, Access to Women's Rights Information Is a Basic One," http://fortune.com/2014/08/14/for-facebook-access-to-womens-rights-information-is-a-basic-one/, August 14, 2014.

[70]"The Man Who Wired the World," op. cit.

Nevertheless, the kids who were the likely beneficiaries of the initiative at a computer center in Chandauli, India, where Zuckerberg had made a visit, would have thought, "The global knowledge economy is leaving the station, and we want to get on board, and you're sitting there wringing your hands because we have to look at a few ads? Come on, man. That's some zeroth-world bull, right there"[71] opined Lev Grossman in the article, "The Man Who Wired the World," which appeared in *Time* magazine. But so-called cyberimperialist Zuckerberg had made Facebook's users pay through their attention and personal information. Apple's CEO Tim Cook stated, "When an online service is free, you're not the customer. You're the product."[72]

However, some analysts felt that the initiative would be a win–win situation for both Facebook and its consumers in the developing countries because it would help the company improve its network penetration as well as the quality of life of its consumers. Internet.org would be self-sustaining because of the founders' self-interest and their competitive nature and focus. Mixing up business and social cause is considered normal, and organizations such as Facebook, with its experience and expertise, would crack down on tough problems to offer solutions to developing countries in net connectivity. The only solution offered by the critics of the initiative was that the public should to be ever vigilant and check their activities to see to that the beneficiaries were not trampled upon in perpetuating the self-interest of the companies involved in the initiative.[73] Margaret Coady,[74] nevertheless, accused the initiative of being "business dressed up like charity" and posed the question, "Does the proportion of selflessness to self-interest matter in the end?"[75]

Case Questions

1. Give a brief outline of Facebook's Internet.org's initiative.
2. Discuss the impact of Internet.org on emerging economies.
3. Was the Internet.org initiative really about serving the bottom of the pyramid or was it more about Facebook trying to expand its reach? Analyze.

---

[71]"The Man WhoWwired the World," op. cit.
[72]Ibid.

[73]Margaret Coady, "Internet.org: A Wolf in Sheep's Clothing? Not So Fast," http://www.huffingtonpost.com/margaret-coady/Internetorg-a-wolf-in-she_b_3844995.html, September 30, 2013.
[74]Margaret Coady, the Director of the Committee Encouraging Corporate Philanthropy.
[75]"Internet.org: A Wolf in Sheep's Clothing? Not So Fast," op. cit.

ANNEXURE I Global Internet Adoption: Major Findings

1. **Over the past decade, the global online population grew to just over 2.7 billion people, driven by five trends.**
   Some 1.8 billion people have come online since 2004, with this growth fuelled by five trends: the expansion of mobile-network coverage and increasing mobile-Internet adoption, urbanization, shrinking device and data-plan prices, a growing middle class, and the increasing utility of the Internet.

2. **At the current trajectory, an additional 500 million to 900 million people are forecast to join the online population by 2017.**
   However, these gains will still leave up to 4.2 billion people offline. The rate of growth of worldwide Internet users slowed from a three-year compound annual growth rate (CAGR) of 15.1 percent from 2005 to 2008 to 10.4 percent from 2009 to 2013. Without a significant change in technology, in income growth, or in the economics of access, or policies to spur Internet adoption, the rate of growth will continue to slow. The demographic profile and context of the offline population makes it unlikely that these individuals will come online solely as a result of the trends that have driven adoption over the past decade. Estimates from multiple sources suggest that 500 million to 900 million people will join the online ranks by 2017, expanding the online population to 3.2 billion to 3.6 billion users. By these projections, between 3.8 billion and 4.2 billion people—more than half of the forecasted global population – will remain offline in 2017.

3. **About 75 percent of the offline population is concentrated in 20 countries and is disproportionately rural, low income, elderly, illiterate, and female.**
   We estimate that approximately 64 percent of these offline individuals live in rural areas, whereas 24 percent of today's Internet users are considered rural. As much as 50 percent of offline individuals have an income below the average of their respective country's poverty line and median income. Furthermore, we estimate that 18 percent of non-Internet users are seniors (aged 55 or older), while about 7 percent of the online population are in that age bracket. Approximately 28 percent of the offline population is illiterate, while we estimate that close to 100 percent of the online population can read and write. Lastly, we estimate that 52 percent of the offline population is female, while women make up 42 percent of the online population.

4. **The offline population faces barriers to Internet adoption spanning four categories.**
   Incentives Despite the increasing utility of the Internet in providing access to information, opportunities, and resources to improve quality of life, there remain large segments of the offline population that lack a compelling reason to go online. Barriers in this category include a lack of awareness of the Internet or use cases that create value for the offline user, a lack of relevant (that is, local or localized) content and services, and a lack of cultural or social acceptance. The root causes of these consumer barriers include the high costs that content and service providers face in developing and localizing relevant content and services and their associated business model constraints, low awareness or interest from brands and advertisers in reaching certain audiences, a lack of trusted logistics and payment systems (thereby limiting Internet use cases such as e-commerce and online banking), low ease of doing business in specific regions (thereby impeding development of local or localized content and services), and limited Internet freedom and information security.

   Low Incomes and Affordability In this area, the predominant barrier is the low income of individuals in the offline population. This barrier is exacerbated by the high costs associated with providing access to the Internet for these populations, which are disproportionately rural. The low incomes reflect the poor economic circumstances of large segments of the offline population, often including unemployment and the need for economic development, employment, and income growth opportunities in their regions. At the same time, there is often a lack of adjacent infrastructure (such as roads and electricity), thereby increasing the costs faced by network operators in extending coverage. Several other factors can contribute to high costs of service for device manufacturers and network operators, including taxes and fees, and, in the case of some countries, an unfavorable market structure.

   User Capability This category includes barriers such as a lack of digital literacy (that is, unfamiliarity with or discomfort in using digital technologies to access and use information) and a lack of language literacy (that is, the inability to read and write). The root cause of such literacy barriers is often an under resourced education system.

   Infrastructure Barriers in this area include a lack of mobile Internet coverage or network access in addition to a lack of adjacent infrastructure such as grid electricity. The root causes of these consumer barriers include limited access to international bandwidth; an underdeveloped national core network, backhaul, and access infrastructure; limited spectrum availability; a national information and communications technology (ICT) strategy that doesn't effectively address the issue of broadband access; and under resourced infrastructure development.

5. **These issues cannot be considered in isolation—we found a systematically positive and, in some cases large, correlation between barrier categories and with Internet penetration rates.**
   We measured the performance of 25 countries against a basket of metrics relating to each category of barriers to develop the Internet Barriers Index. We found that all factors correlate strongly and separately with Internet penetration, and all regressions indicate an elastic effect on Internet penetration—that is, improvements on each individual pillar of the Internet Barriers Index will have a disproportionately positive impact on Internet penetration. In addition, we found a systematically positive and, in some cases, large correlation between barrier categories. This implies that the factors are not totally independent and

that countries with low Internet penetration tend to have multidimensional bottlenecks when it comes to increasing their Internet adoption. Further, it means that meaningfully addressing these barriers and boosting Internet penetration will require coordination across Internet ecosystem participants.

6. **Approximately 2 billion people—or nearly half the offline population—reside in ten countries that face significant challenges across all four barrier categories. An additional 1.1 billion people live in countries in which a single barrier category dominates.**

   Based on the combination and severity of the barriers they face (as indicated by the Internet Barriers Index), countries fall into one of five groups. These groupings provide insight into each set's common challenges, which could stem from similar root causes.

   Group One   High barriers across the board. This group consists of five countries in Africa and Asia—Bangladesh, Ethiopia, Nigeria, Pakistan, and Tanzania—that are home to just over 550 million offline individuals and face entrenched obstacles to expanding Internet adoption. Each of the countries in this group performed poorly across all four barrier categories of the Internet Barriers Index; their scores in individual pillars fall primarily in the lowest quartile. The offline populations in these countries are predominantly young and rural and have low literacy rates. The aggregate Internet penetration rate across the group was 15 percent in 2013.

   Group Two   Medium to high barriers. Countries in this group include Egypt, India, Indonesia, the Philippines, and Thailand, each of which faces medium to high barriers to Internet adoption. The countries in this group rank in the lowest two quartiles in several categories in the Internet Barriers Index, with their greatest challenges lying in the incentives and infrastructure barrier categories. Home to an offline population of more than 1.4 billion individuals, this group had an aggregate Internet penetration rate of 19 percent in 2013.

   Group Three   Medium barriers, greatest challenges in incentives. Comprising China, Sri Lanka, and Vietnam, this group is home to approximately 800 million offline individuals. The offline population in each country is largely rural and literate. With the exception of the incentives category, where both China and Vietnam scored in the bottom quartile, the countries in this group rank in the middle (second or third) quartiles across each pillar of the Internet Barriers Index. In aggregate, this group has an Internet penetration rate of 45 percent.

   Group Four   Medium barriers, greatest challenges in low incomes and affordability. This group consists of Brazil, Colombia, Mexico, South Africa, and Turkey and accounts for an offline population of just under 260 million individuals. With an aggregate Internet penetration rate of 49 percent, these countries are characterized by offline populations that are predominantly urban, literate, and low income. All of the countries in this group score in the middle (second or third) quartiles in the user capability and infrastructure categories of the Internet Barriers Index, and a couple countries rank in the first quartile in the incentives category. However, in contrast with those bright spots, low incomes and affordability remains a significant challenge; each of the countries in this group faces some combination of low GDP per capita, large proportions of their population with low incomes, and a high poverty rate.

   Group Five   Low barriers across the board. This group is composed of countries that face relatively low barriers compared with the other four groups, resulting in an aggregate Internet penetration rate of 79 percent. Countries in this group include Germany, Italy, Japan, Korea, Russia, and the United States. Despite the low barriers, these six countries are still home to aggregate offline population of approximately 180 million people. Interestingly, given the high Internet penetration rates in this group, the offline populations are disproportionately low income and female.

7. **Current initiatives, forthcoming innovations, and lessons from countries that have made headway are cause for optimism.**

   Nations around the world have recognized the transformational impact of bringing more of their population online and are moving aggressively on several fronts to do just that. Governments are setting ambitious goals for mobile-Internet coverage and investing to extend fixed-broadband infrastructure and increase public Wi-Fi access. At the same time, network operators and device manufacturers are exploring ways to further reduce the cost of access and provide service to underserved populations. In addition, content and service providers are innovating on services that could improve the economic prospects and quality of life of Internet users.

   Going forward, sustained, inclusive Internet user growth will require a multipronged strategy—one that will depend on close collaboration among players across the ecosystem, including governments, policy makers, nongovernmental organizations, network operators, device manufacturers, content and service providers, and brands.

Source: "Offline and Falling Behind: Barriers to Internet Adoption," http://www.mckinsey.com/insights/high_tech_telecoms_Internet/offline_and_falling_behind_barriers_to_internet_adoption, September 2014.

Case 2 An Ethics Role-Playing Case: Stockholders versus Stakeholders

–TIM MANUEL[1]
University of Montana, USA

Instructions to Students:
Please read the background information (Handout I) and be prepared to discuss it on the assigned class day. Then **read Handout II and write out your Decision 1 and answer the questions.** After these discussions your instructor will provide you with further handouts requiring sequential decisions resulting from your Decision 1.

Handout I. Introduction and Background[2]

You are a United States citizen employed by HotFeet, a Seattle- based and U.S.-owned shoe company that manufactures many of its shoes overseas. You live in Sri Lanka and work at the wholly-owned subsidiary located there, Asian HotFeet (AHF). You have been employed by HotFeet for twenty years. For fifteen of those years you have lived in Sri Lanka, and for the last five years you have been AHF's Chief Operating Officer. You were hired by George Landon, who is now the president of the company. The two of you continue to have a good relationship, and you play tennis together whenever he visits. Landon's personal loyalty to you has positively affected your career at several critical points, and you know you owe him a lot. You are married to a local who has extensive family, many of whom are directly or indirectly employed by your company. You have three beautiful children. You are quite proud of your family and enjoy your lifestyle very much. A major part of your satisfaction is derived from the knowledge that your company's presence has greatly benefited the local populace. This is, in no small part, because of your efforts to ensure fair treatment of local workers and maintain a high level of reinvestment in the country whenever possible. Because of this, and because of your local connections through your spouse, you are a highly esteemed individual in Sri Lankan society. Although you are still a U.S. citizen, you have begun to notice that you really don't think of yourself as an American anymore. You know that the home office gossip

is that you have "gone native," but that's OK with you, because you have no aspirations to move back to the U.S., or live anywhere else for that matter.

Asian HotFeet is owned and officially run out of the parent company's Seattle headquarters (USHF), but in reality you have significant leeway in running local operations as long as you meet the company's profit expectations. AHF comprises about 15% of the total operations of USHF, and so this subsidiary is a very important strategic investment for the parent company. The subsidiary is evaluated as a profit center; about 60% of output is sold directly by AHF in the Asian markets, but the remainder is "sold" to the parent at a transfer price set by the parent company. Traditionally, the transfer price has been set fairly high to keep the profits in Sri Lanka, which has a lower tax rate than the United States. USHF then directs how the profits are reinvested around the world and in Sri Lanka, with your consultation on local projects. Long-term financing and foreign exchange management are, however, centralized functions managed directly by USHF. You have little experience with either large scale financing or measuring and managing foreign exchange risk, although you have lobbied many times for more responsibilities in these areas. AHF's profit growth was very high for many years, until the Asian crisis and the continuing weakness in Japan generated several years of losses. More recently, AHF has had acceptable levels of profits, but is now once again having difficulty meeting the profit goals set by USHF. The parent company finance group has asked you to fly to the U.S. and discuss some changes. At that meeting, your bosses indicate that due to a combination of factors, USHF is considering either closing the AHF facility or relocating it to another country. They explain to you that the firm's cost of capital has risen, making AHF's return on investment inadequate to satisfy their goal of maximizing USHF's shareholder wealth. In addition, the firm was surprised by the recent weakening of the dollar, resulting in speculative foreign exchange losses that have exacerbated the parent firm's profit problems. More to the point, newer production technology with higher productivity and automation has recently become available, and the parent is rethinking its strategy about locating in low-cost labor areas that are far from the major markets. In addition, Sri Lankan wage rates are beginning to rise, and the cost advantages of that location are not as great as they once were, particularly considering the added costs and inconveniences of operating in a lesser developed country. Landon tells you that you would most likely be the manager of the new facility, and you would work with the finance and operations groups in determining where the new facility would be located.

A license has been granted to Pearson Education Inc., for Print Permission for publication in International Management 9th Edition, pp. PC1-11–PC1-12 Publication date 1/1/2016. Apart from these licensed copies, none of the material protected by the copyright notice can be reproduced or used in any form either electronic or mechanical, including photocopying, recording or by any other information recording or retrieval system, without prior written permission from the owner(s) of the copyright. © NeilsonJournals Publishing 2012.

[1]This project was funded by a Department of Education Northwest International Business Educators Network grant and by a University of Montana School of Business Summer Research Grant.
[2]All students should receive Handouts I and II. They should receive the appropriate versions of Handouts III, IV, and V depending on their decisions. Detailed instructions appear in the Instructor's Resources.

You argue that AHF should not be closed or relocated, pointing out the strong, mutually beneficial relationships that have been built between the local populace, the Sri Lankan government, and the AHF—relationships that, though perhaps not measurable in dollars, are very valuable and time consuming to build. These would be forfeited by a move or a closure and would be costly to develop elsewhere. You argue that capital costs and exchange rates are subject to frequent changes and that it is naïve to make long-term operating decisions according to what may be short-lived unfavorable interest rates and exchange rates. You indicate that "your people" can certainly be taught to use any new technology, that they are good at their jobs, and culturally they have a history of taking pride in craftsmanship that would be hard to find elsewhere. That is why AHF has a lower rejection rate and less waste than any other plant owned by USHF. You argue that the rising wage rates in Sri Lanka indicate the success of AHF and other multinationals at improving the quality of life of the local people, and you remind the home office that we are also building potential customers for our product as local incomes rise. Finally, you tell them that they do not understand the differences that businesses like AHF have made in the lives of many of the indigenous people. Education levels are starting to rise, and the use of child labor, a common practice, is dropping. The selling of children by impoverished families with no hope of feeding them has dropped dramatically in the last ten years. But all these gains are precarious, and yes, the Asian economy as a whole is still weak compared to the high-growth years, but you are convinced that better times are ahead as the Japanese and Chinese markets improve. Still, the local economy is very dependent on a few large employers, and if AHF and even one or two others leave the human cost could be high, very high indeed. How do you weigh this potential cost against the shareholder wealth goal?

Handout II. Decision 1

Landon is impressed by your passion and your arguments. He indicates that they may allow AHF to continue if you can cut costs sufficiently. The finance people are not happy with this, however, and they indicate that allowing AHF to continue at its current profit rate is tantamount to running AHF as a charitable operation, and that USHF's substantial contributions to U.S. charities such as the American Red Cross, United Way, and so forth, will likely have to be eliminated to at least partially offset the drain on profits caused by continuing AHF. Landon is a big supporter of the Red Cross and he does not like that alternative at all.

To wrap it up, Landon lays it on the line for you. He tells you up front that he would prefer to close AHF and start over in another country with the new technology. He explains why: USHF's stockholders are upset at the recent poor stock performance. Shutting down and selling AHF's assets would provide some ready cash and allow the parent firm to pay a bonus dividend to the shareholders, while still providing a sizeable down payment on the capital investment required for the new technology. Given the current economic situation and the skill level of Sri Lankans, it just doesn't make sense to locate the new facilities in Sri Lanka. He obviously thinks this is the best thing for the company, and it would avoid a potentially serious row with the stockholders. Landon indicates, though, that if you can prove that AHF can meet the necessary profit targets, he might reconsider. If you are willing to try, you will have to figure out how to cut costs or otherwise improve profits to keep AHF running. Can you do it? He tells you he will give you six months and then reevaluate if they still want to continue. Landon makes sure you understand that this will mean reducing the work force, cutting wage rates, and trying to find lower-cost supplies without sacrificing quality.

You have looked at the finance group's numbers and profit targets. You also know that, politically, it will be very difficult to fire or lay off people in Sri Lanka, which means that extensive wage cuts of 50% or more will be necessary. This will reduce many families to just enough income to survive. Worse, you will have to act very quickly, and your employees will have no warning of what's coming. Even that may not be enough. Plus, you know that your reputation with Landon and the company is on the line with this decision. If you try and you can't make this go, your career with this company will suffer and you will not only lose your shot at managing the new facility, but will probably lose your job.

Decision 1

Part A: Does this decision involve ethics or is it a business decision? Please explain. Should the shareholder wealth goal be paramount in this situation? Why or why not?

Part B: The decision is up to you. What do you do? Please circle (a) or (b).

(a) Continue operations and try to cut costs within six months.

(b) Decide to shut down now.

Please tell why you made the decision you did.

PART

2 The Cultural Context of Global Management

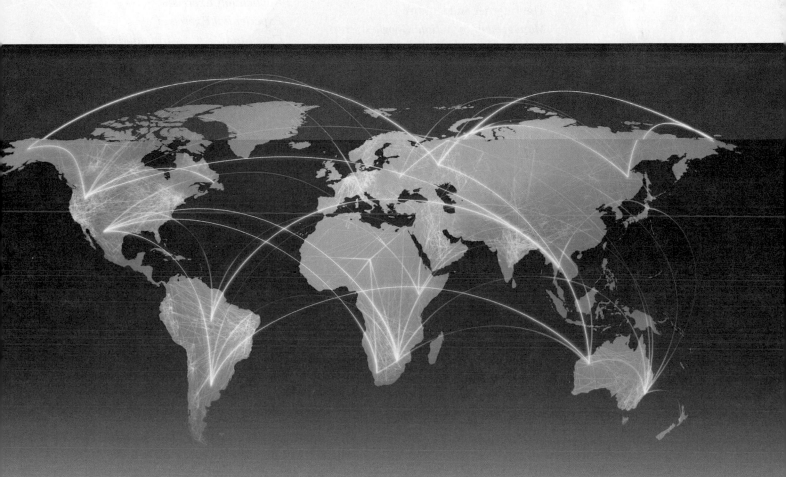

3 Understanding the Role of Culture

OUTLINE

OBJECTIVES

3-1. To understand how culture affects all aspects of international management

3-2. To be able to distinguish the major value dimensions that define cultural differences among societies or groups

3-3. To understand the interaction between culture and the use of the Internet

3-4. To be able to develop a working cultural profile typical of many people within a certain society as an aid to anticipating attitudes toward work, negotiations, and so on

3-5. To gain some insight into different management styles around the world

Opening Profile: Social Media Bring Changes to Saudi Arabian Culture[1]

Why is Arabic the fastest growing language of all time on Twitter and Riyadh ranked #10 globally of the cities with the most tweets? What is behind such a rapid growth of this increasingly tech-savvy population?

As of mid-2014, the social media penetration in Saudi Arabia included 88 percent on Facebook, 81 percent on Twitter, and 78 percent on Google+. Each day, more than 90 million videos are viewed on YouTube, more than 3 million people are on Twitter, and more than 840,000 are on LinkedIn, with email usage becoming passé. It is clear that not only do these platforms present important avenues for international businesses to communicate and engage with customers, but also that cultural and lifestyle factors are involved. Because 70 percent of the Saudi population is under 30 and most own smartphones, many are turning to Twitter and YouTube out of boredom with the severe lack of entertainment; there are no cinemas, theaters, or bars and little to interest them in the newspapers or television. In addition, social interaction is closely monitored and restricted by patrolling religious police. For most young people, then, Twitter represents an avenue of escape from the lack

FIGURE 3-1 Islamic Woman Using a Smartphone

michaeljung/Fotolia

of social freedom and legal restrictions on freedom of assembly or association, especially for women. Gender separation is enforced, and women cannot interact with men, go to an appointment, travel, and so on without permission from a male guardian, often accompanied by him. However, by using Facebook, Twitter, and other outlets, women and men can at least step around the morality police to have conversations with one another and, perhaps, get to know each other for a future relationship. In addition, more open dialog between men and women has changed the power structure and created opportunities for everyone to participate in a broad array of roles. Nevertheless, although most people consider the use of social media a positive and legitimate means of communication for everyone, some women still feel they are betraying the morals they have observed all their lives and are embarrassed to admit to virtual conversations with men.

However, the young people are not the only ones using Twitter; the use of such media is spreading to all sectors of society—government officials, the royalty, sheikhs, and those in industry. In addition, the Saudi government, which is an absolute monarchy with no parliament or political parties, does review online activity to gather intelligence and monitor public opinion. As such, there are lines that cannot be crossed, such as criticizing religion or allowing accounts that promote adultery and homosexuality. On the other hand, it has become apparent that government authorities can conceal little because information is now rapidly disseminated through social media, so now those authorities are more likely to use the media to give their version of events or updates to get ahead of the rumors and, in particular, quell political dissent.

Clearly, social media have presented a virtual world as a force for modernity in Saudi Arabia and cause powerful interactions with cultural mores; it is a matter of personal judgment whether those changes are viewed as progressive, but it is also clear that there is no turning back.

Questions

1. Discuss the role of social media in societal culture. Is this virtual world, with no geographic boundaries, presenting a normalizing effect across those boundaries? Is that a positive or a negative effect?
2. Is societal culture and lifestyle as intricately intertwined with religion in your country as it is in Saudi Arabia?
3. Discuss other countries where social media are having a radical effect on cultural expectations.

> *In the era of globalization, however, our companies, managers, partners, colleagues and constituents are spread out all over the world.*
>
> INTERNATIONAL NEW YORK TIMES[2]

This chapter's opening profile describes the interaction between social media and culture. It is clear that the widespread use of social media both helps people become familiar with other cultures and ways of life and, perhaps, smooth out the differences. In this chapter, we discuss how an understanding of the local culture and business environment can give managers an advantage in competitive industries. Foreign companies—no matter what their size—ignore those aspects to their peril. Such differences in culture and the way of life in other countries necessitate that managers develop international expertise to manage on a contingency basis according to the host-country environment. Powerful, interdependent factors in that environment—political, economic, legal, technological, and cultural—influence management strategy, functions, and processes.

> *Cultural Intelligence: an outsider's seemingly natural ability to interpret someone's unfamiliar and ambiguous gestures in just the way that person's compatriots and colleagues would.*
>
> HARVARD BUSINESS REVIEW[3]

Managing people and processes in other countries requires a working knowledge of the cultural variables affecting management decisions and how to use that knowledge to adapt behaviors and expectations accordingly. This skill has become known as **cultural intelligence**, or **cultural quotient (CQ)**—a measure of how well a person can adapt and manage effectively in culturally diverse settings.[4] There is further discussion of how to adapt to different cultures in Chapter 4. First, we need to gain an understanding of what culture is, what the variables are that will enable us to adapt, and how those variables affect the manager's job. Clearly, it is important for anyone wishing to be successful when working with people in other countries to be able to plan how to relate to and adapt to people from different cultures.

Managers have often seriously underestimated the significance of cultural factors. According to numerous accounts, many blunders made in international operations can be attributed to a lack of cultural sensitivity.[5] Examples abound. Scott Russell, senior vice president for human resources at Cendant Mobility in Danbury, Connecticut, recounts the following:

> *An American company in Japan charged its Japanese HR manager with reducing the work-force. The Japanese manager studied the issue but couldn't find a solution within cultural Japanese parameters; so when he came back to the Americans, he reduced the workforce by resigning—which was not what they wanted.*[6]

Cultural sensitivity, or **cultural empathy**, is the awareness of and an honest caring about another individual's culture. Such sensitivity requires the ability to understand the perspective of those living in other (and very different) societies and the willingness to put oneself in another's shoes.

International managers can benefit greatly from understanding the nature, dimensions, and variables of a specific culture and how these affect work and organizational processes. This cultural awareness enables them to develop appropriate policies and determine how to plan, organize, lead, and control in a specific international setting. Such a process of adaptation to the environment is necessary to implement strategy successfully. It also leads to effective interaction in a workforce of increasing cultural diversity, in both the United States and other countries.

Company reports and management studies make it clear that a lack of cultural sensitivity costs businesses money and opportunities. One study of U.S. multinational corporations found that poor intercultural communication skills still constitute a major management problem. Managers' knowledge of other cultures lags far behind their understanding of other organizational processes.[7] In a synthesis of the research on cross-cultural training, Black and Mendenhall found that up to 40 percent of expatriate managers leave their assignments early because of poor performance or poor adjustment to the local environment. About half of those who remain are considered only marginally effective. Furthermore, they found that cross-cultural differences are the cause of failed negotiations and interactions, resulting in losses to U.S. firms of more than $2 billion a year for failed expatriate assignments alone.[8]

Other evidence indicates, however, that cross-cultural training is effective in developing skills and enhancing adjustment and performance. In spite of such evidence, U.S. firms do little to take advantage of such important research and incorporate it into their ongoing training programs, whose purpose is ostensibly to prepare managers before sending them overseas. Too often, the importance of such training in developing cultural sensitivity is realized much too late.

This chapter provides a conceptual framework with which companies and managers can assess relevant cultural variables and develop cultural profiles of various countries. This framework is then used to consider the probable effects of cultural differences on an organization and their implications for management. To do this, the powerful environmental factor of cultural context is examined. The nature of culture and its variables and dimensions are first explored, and then specific differences in cultural values and their implications for the on-the-job behavior of individuals and groups are considered. Cultural variables, in general, are discussed in this chapter. The impact of culture on specific management functions and processes is discussed in later chapters as appropriate. We emphasize throughout this book that no one style or management practice or culture is deemed overall to be better than others; rather, any manager from any region or society needs to find the most effective way to achieve objectives that works in that particular situation or locale.

CULTURE AND ITS EFFECTS ON ORGANIZATIONS

We know that cultural values can predict employee outcomes with similar or even more strength than more traditional factors such as demographics, personality traits, and cognitive ability.

V. TARAS ET AL., *ORGANIZATIONAL DYNAMICS*
APRIL 6, 2011[9]

Societal Culture

As generally understood, the **culture** of a society comprises the shared values, understandings, assumptions, and goals that are learned from earlier generations, imposed by present members of a society, and passed on to succeeding generations. This shared outlook results, in large part, in common attitudes, codes of conduct, and expectations that subconsciously guide and control certain norms of behavior.[10] One is born into, not with, a given culture and gradually internalizes its subtle effects through the socialization process. Culture results in a basis for living grounded in shared communication, standards, codes of conduct, and expectations.[11] Over time, cultures evolve as societies adapt—by choice or otherwise—to transitions in their external and internal environments and relationships. In 2011, for example, people in Egypt brought about political and cultural changes because of economic conditions, oppression, and increasing exposure through social media to what they perceived to be a better way to live within systems in democratic societies. Globalization, in all its forms of personal and business contacts and information crossing borders, brings about changes that result in **cultural diffusion**. When immigrants adopt some aspects of the local culture while keeping aspects of their culture of origin, this process is called **creolization**. Some countries, such as France, fiercely protect their culture against outside influences and insist that immigrants assimilate into their society and respect their values.[12]

A manager assigned to a foreign subsidiary must expect to find large and small differences in the behavior of individuals and groups within that organization. As depicted in Exhibit 3-1, these differences result from the societal, or sociocultural, variables of the culture, such as religion and language, as well as from prevailing national variables such as economic, legal, and political factors. National and sociocultural variables, thus, provide the context for the development and perpetuation of cultural variables. These cultural variables, in turn, determine basic attitudes toward work, time, materialism, individualism, and change. Such attitudes affect an individual's motivation and expectations regarding work and group relations, and they ultimately affect the outcomes that can be expected from that individual.

Organizational Culture

Compared to societal culture, which is often widely held within a region or nation, **organizational culture** varies a great deal from one organization, company, institution, or group to another. Organizational culture represents those expectations, norms, and goals held in common

EXHIBIT 3-1 Environmental Variables Affecting Management Functions

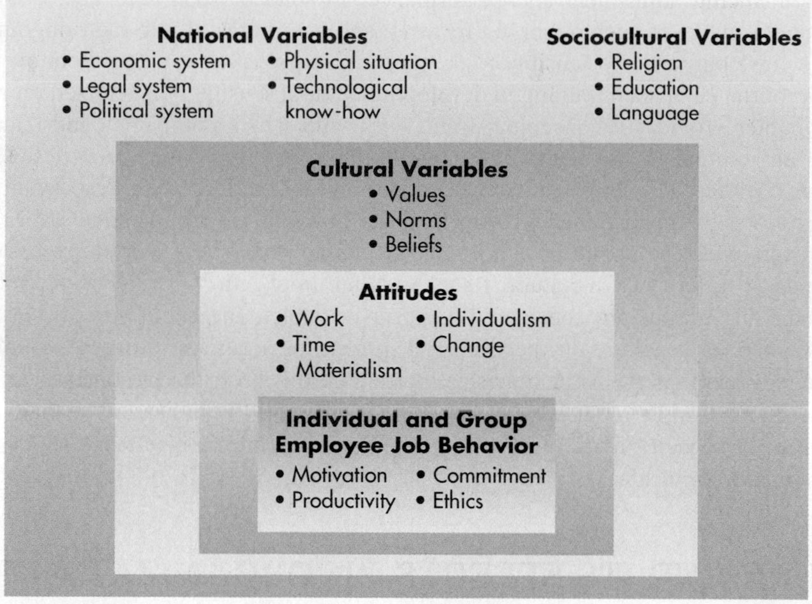

National Variables
- Economic system
- Legal system
- Political system
- Physical situation
- Technological know-how

Sociocultural Variables
- Religion
- Education
- Language

Cultural Variables
- Values
- Norms
- Beliefs

Attitudes
- Work
- Time
- Materialism
- Individualism
- Change

Individual and Group Employee Job Behavior
- Motivation
- Productivity
- Commitment
- Ethics

by members of that group. For a business example, consider the oft-quoted comparison between IBM, considered traditionally to be very formal, hierarchical, and rules-bound, with its employees usually in suits, and Apple Computer, whose organizational culture is very organic, or loose and informal, with its employees typically wearing casual clothes and interacting informally.

Research shows that societal culture tends to be stronger than organizational culture, so that employees working with or for a foreign company may not easily fall into the new organizational culture.[13] Clearly, there is a relationship between organizational culture and societal (national) culture, both of which can cause disputes in the workplace at all levels, including the management of cross-border alliances. Such was the case with the DaimlerChrysler AG alliance—largely contributing to the downfall of the alliance in 2007. As Syed Anwar observed:

> In the auto industry, Daimler-Benz was viewed as a conservative and rigid company regarding its corporate bureaucracy, product development, and quality standards—a corporate culture reflective of Germany's national culture. On the other hand, Chrysler's corporate culture was typical American—informal, outward oriented, and somewhat less rigid in its operations and more risk-taking. Daimler-Benz lacked exposure to the American way of management and business practices. The cultural mismatch eventually created problems in the areas of future planning, supervisory board, research and development, expatriate management, executive salaries, and labor relations.[14]

Culture's Effects on Management

Clearly, societal culture affects organizational culture, and there are often interaction effects, as illustrated by the comments by Kenichi Watanabe, CEO of Japan's Nomura Group, when asked how he would characterize his company's corporate culture:

> The positives: trust, loyalty, teamwork, long-term commitment. The negatives: resistance to change and an overly domestic focus. That's why I tell my people to embrace change and be world class.[15]

FINANCIAL TIMES UK
SEPTEMBER 23, 2011

Which organizational processes—technical and otherwise—are most affected by cultural differences, and how they are affected, is the subject of ongoing cross-cultural management research and debate.[16] Oded Shenkar suggests that we should:

[C]onsider cultural differences as having the potential for both synergy and disruption, [and that] this point cannot be overstated as it lies at the intersection of strategic logic and operational challenges that underline the FDI, expatriate adjustment, auditing and other international business issues.[17]

ODED SHENKAR JOURNAL OF INTERNATIONAL BUSINESS STUDIES
JANUARY 2012

Further, Shenkar poses that, rather than focusing on how *different* two cultures are—that is, cultural distance (CD)—in reality, it is the *interaction* between them that is the working issue in international management; this is because cultural distance has little effect on management until the two cultures come in contact with each other. He proposes that we focus on the concept of friction instead of distance by considering how the relevant people and organizational processes would interact and what the effects would be on the relative success of the international business venture.[18] Moreover, each situation is unique and may involve people from several cultures meeting in a location relative to one of them, creating a specific, multidimensional arena for understanding and communicating. Throw in the local business practices and the corporate cultures of each, and you have a complex scenario to navigate. An example might be an American preparing to meet in Russia with the German subsidiary manager there. As Nardon and Steers point out, several combinations of factors might complicate each specific global encounter, such as:

The broad cultural and institutional context based on local geography or the firm's industry, for example.

The organizational culture, as discussed earlier, which may or may not conflict with the culture and business practices in the specific locale of interaction.

The situational context, which includes factors such as the physical setting, the types of positions members have in their firms, each person's individual characteristics and cross-cultural preparation, and the method of interactions at the time.[19]

Many researchers have acknowledged the need to recognize and adapt to the overall situational context.[20] Many companies, such as Walmart, have found that their success in some countries was definitely not transferrable to others. As Tarun Khanna notes, for managers to be successful around the world, there is no doubt that:

*[I]t requires **contextual intelligence**: the ability to understand the limits of our knowledge and to adapt that knowledge to an environment different from the one in which it was developed.*

HARVARD BUSINESS REVIEW
SEPTEMBER 2014[21]

Some argue that the effects of culture are more evident at the individual level of personal behavior than at the organizational level because of convergence. **Convergence** describes the phenomenon of shifting individual management styles to become more similar to one another. The convergence argument is based on the belief that the demands of industrialization, worldwide coordination, and competition tend to factor out differences in organizational-level processes such as choice of technology and structure. In a study of Japanese and Korean firms, Lee, Roehl, and Choe found that globalization and firm size were sources of convergence of management styles.[22] At the individual level, the research we will discuss in this chapter and throughout the book clearly shows that whereas an assertive, take-charge management style typically works best in the West, people across Asia usually respond better to a more subtle leadership style in which the manager works behind the scenes to accomplish goals; then again, Latino cultures tend to prefer a paternal management style and look up to leaders who command respect by virtue of their position in society.[23] These factors are discussed in more detail later in this chapter.

The effects of culture on specific management functions are particularly noticeable when we attempt to impose our own values and systems on another society. Exhibit 3-2 gives some examples of the values typical of U.S. culture, compares some common perspectives held by people in other countries, and shows which management functions might be affected, clearly implying the need for the differential management of organizational processes. For example, American

EXHIBIT 3-2 **The Role of Cultural Variables in Enacting Management Functions: A Comparison of Some Typical Views of People in the United States with Other Commonly Held Perspectives Around the World**

Management Function	Aspects of U.S. Culture*	Other Perspectives
Strategic planning, scheduling events and operations	People can affect what happens in the future.	What happens in the future is determined by the will of God (fatalistic attitude).
Sustainability management; productivity	It is acceptable for people to interfere with nature and make changes to their environment.	People should live within the given environment and adjust to it without interference.
Leadership and motivation	Leadership is shared and participative.	Leadership is often paternal and/or authoritative.
Planning, social responsibility, human resource management.	Employees' goals should be realistic.	Idealism is valued regardless of what is "reasonable."
Motivation and reward system	Hard work is valued and will accomplish our objectives (Puritan ethic).	The will of God, good fortune, play an important part in success as well as hard work.
Negotiating and bargaining	People should follow up on their commitments and their word.	A commitment only indicates an intention to perform, but may be changed as developments occur.
Long-and short-range planning	It is important to effectively use one's time (time is money that can be saved or wasted).	Relationships and personal concerns can take priority over meetings and schedules.
Loyalty, commitment, and motivation	A primary obligation of an employee is to the organization.	The individual employee has a primary obligation to his or her family and friends.
Motivation and commitment to the company	People know that their jobs are impermanent and that they or their employers may end that commitment at any time.	Employment is for a lifetime.
Employment, promotions, and reward	The best-qualified people should be hired.	Nepotism is practiced. Family, friendship, and other considerations take precedence in employment.

*Aspect here refers to a belief, value, attitude, or assumption that is part of a culture in that a large number of people in that culture share it.

Source: Based on *Managing Cultural Differences* by Philip R. Harris and Robert T. Moran, 5th ed. Copyright © 2000 by Gulf Publishing Company, Houston, TX. Used with permission. All rights reserved.

managers plan activities, schedule them, and judge their timely completion based on the belief that people influence and control the future rather than assuming that events will occur only at the will of Allah, as managers in an Islamic nation might believe.

Many people in the world understand and relate to others only in terms of their own culture. This unconscious reference point of one's own cultural values is called a **self-reference criterion**. The result of such an attitude is illustrated in the following story.

Once upon a time there was a great flood, and involved in this flood were two creatures, a monkey and a fish. The monkey, being agile and experienced, was lucky enough to scramble up a tree and escape the raging waters. As he looked down from his safe perch, he saw the poor fish struggling against the swift current. With the very best of intentions, he reached down and lifted the fish from the water. The result was inevitable.[24]

The monkey assumed that its frame of reference applied to the fish and acted accordingly. Thus, international managers from all countries must understand and adjust to unfamiliar social and commercial practices—especially the practices of that mysterious and unique nation, the United States. Japanese workers at a U.S. manufacturing plant learned to put courtesy aside and interrupt conversations with Americans when there were problems. Europeans, however, are often confused by Americans' apparent informality, which then backfires when the Europeans do not get work done as the Americans expect.

As a first step toward cultural sensitivity, international managers should understand their own cultures. This awareness helps guard against adopting either a parochial or an ethnocentric attitude. **Parochialism** occurs, for example, when a Frenchman expects those from or in another country to fall automatically into patterns of behavior common in France. **Ethnocentrism** describes the attitude of those who operate from the assumption that their ways of doing things are best—no matter where or under what conditions they are applied. Companies both large and small have demonstrated this lack of cultural sensitivity in countless subtle (and not so subtle) ways with varying disastrous effects.

Procter & Gamble (P&G) was one such company. In an early Japanese television commercial for Camay soap, a Japanese woman is bathing when her husband walks into the bathroom. She starts telling him about her new beauty soap. Her husband, stroking her shoulder, hints that he has more on his mind than suds. The commercial, which had been popular in Europe, was a disaster in Japan. For the man to intrude on his wife "was considered bad manners," says Edwin L. Artzt, P&G's vice chairman and international chief. "And the Japanese didn't think it was very funny." P&G has learned from its mistakes and now generates about half of its revenue from foreign sales.[25]

After studying his or her own culture, the manager's next step toward establishing effective cross-cultural relations is to develop cultural sensitivity. Managers not only must be aware of cultural variables and their effects on behavior in the workplace, but also must appreciate cultural diversity and understand how to build constructive working relationships anywhere in the world. The following sections explore cultural variables and dimensions. Later chapters suggest specific ways in which managers can address these variables and dimensions to help build constructive relationships.

Given the great variety of cultures and subcultures around the world, how can a student of cross-cultural management, or a manager wishing to be culturally savvy, develop an understanding of the specific nature of a certain people? With such an understanding, how can a manager anticipate the probable effects of an unfamiliar culture within an organizational setting and thereby manage human resources productively and control outcomes?

One approach is to develop a cultural profile for each country or region with which the company does or is considering doing business. Developing a cultural profile requires some familiarity with the cultural variables universal to most cultures. From these universal variables, managers can identify the specific differences found in each country or people—and, hence, anticipate their implications for the workplace.

Managers should never assume that they can successfully transplant American, or Japanese, or any other country's styles, practices, expectations, and processes. Instead, they should practice a basic tenet of good management—**contingency management**. Contingency management requires managers to adapt to the local environment and people and manage accordingly. That adaptation can be complex because the manager may confront differences not only in culture but also in business practices. The need for managers to adapt to local conditions, particularly within a joint venture, was illustrated by Baruch Shimoni in his research of Thai and Israeli managers of two MNCs headquartered in Sweden and the United States. He found that the firms' local management cultures ran into each other and produced new hybrid forms of management cultures.[26] Shimoni found that the managers developed a hybrid management style that was between their own and the corporation's management practices. Whereas the Thai culture focuses on harmonious personal relationships and avoidance of confrontation, in the Israeli office practices focused on informal relationships, performance, work processes, and supervision.[27]

Over time, the Thai managers (Chindakohrn and Hansa) and the Israeli managers (Tamir and Shuki) came to adapt their feelings and management style to create a hybrid style suited to the situation. As Hansa said, "I try to compromise. Working together, get your opinion, what you want, what you think, then I make decisions...you [I] have to be very quick and execute immediately.... I try to change myself, to be adopting to this [the MNC's] kind of character, culture."[28]

Influences on National Culture

Managers should recognize, of course, that generalizations in cultural profiles will produce only an approximation, or stereotype, of national character. Many countries comprise diverse **subcultures** whose constituents conform only in varying degrees to the national character. In Canada, distinct subcultures include Anglophones and Francophones (English-speaking and French-speaking people, respectively) and indigenous Canadians.

Above all, good managers treat people as individuals, and they consciously avoid any form of **stereotyping**. However, a cultural profile is a good starting point to help managers develop some tentative expectations—some cultural context—as a backdrop to managing in a specific international setting. It is useful, then, to look at what cultural variables have been studied and what implications can be drawn from the results.

Before we can understand the culture of a society, we need to recognize that there are subsystems in a society that are a function of where people live; these subsystems influence, and are influenced by, people's cultural values and dimensions and thus affect their behaviors, both on and off the job. Harris and Moran identified eight categories that form the subsystems in any society.[29] This system's approach to understanding cultural and national variables—and their effects on work behavior—is consistent with the model shown in Exhibit 3-1 that shows those categories as a broad set of influences on societal culture. Those categories are the *kinship* system of relationships among families; the *education system*; the *economic* and *political systems*; the *associations* that make up formal and informal groups; the *health system*; attitudes toward *recreation* and leisure; and—perhaps most important—*religion* (further discussed in the accompanying Under the Lens feature).

UNDER THE LENS
Religion and the Workplace

Since the basis of a religion is shared beliefs, values, and institutions, it is closely aligned with the accepted underpinnings of societal culture; thus, religion and culture are inextricably linked. As such, religion underlies both moral and economic norms and influences everyday business transactions and on-the-job behaviors. The connections between culture and work behavior for employees and managers in various countries are discussed throughout this book. Here we note specifically that managers in the home country or abroad must recognize both the legal religious rights in the workplace and the value of such diversity in the workplace. Days off for religious holidays, accommodation for prayers, dietary requirements, and so on, are the more obvious considerations. In addition, foreign managers abroad must be particularly sensitive to the local religious context and the expectations and workplace norms of employees and others because those managers will be immersed in that context in dealing with employees, clients, suppliers, and others. Failure to do so will minimize or negate the goals of the firm in that location.

Most readers of this book are familiar with the major religions of the world (see Map 3-1), and an in-depth discussion of religions is beyond the focus here. (The four religions with the largest number of followers are Christianity, with 33.1% of world population; Islam, with 20.4%; Hinduism, with 13.5%; and Buddhism, with 6%. These figures are approximate because, of course, they are changing every day.)[30] What we do focus on as we progress through the chapters are the ways in which religion intersects with culture and affects business interactions, expectations, operations, motivations, and leadership, including attitudes toward work, time, ethics, and decision-making.

Hinduism is over 5,000 years old and typically involves worship of many gods. Prayer is usually a private matter in one's own home. The traditional caste system, now illegal, still tends to affect the labor markets. As another example of the effects of religion in the workplace, a Western manager operating in some areas or enterprises in India might note the employees' lack of sensitivity to time. As noted by Agam Nag, that attitude is attributed to the religious belief and the philosophical background. "It has been variously traced to the concept of immortality of soul and reincarnation in Hinduism that gives a sense of infiniteness to life and hence time."[31] Nag explains that the lack of sensitivity to time cuts across all religions in India, including the endless variations of Hinduism as well as many other religions such as Islam, Christianity, and Sikhism.[32] Clearly, religious belief is only one dimension of Indian culture to explain the way they view time. However, we can also observe the influence and competitiveness of foreign companies operating in the cities in India, such as the many companies in the

MAP 3.1 Major World Religions

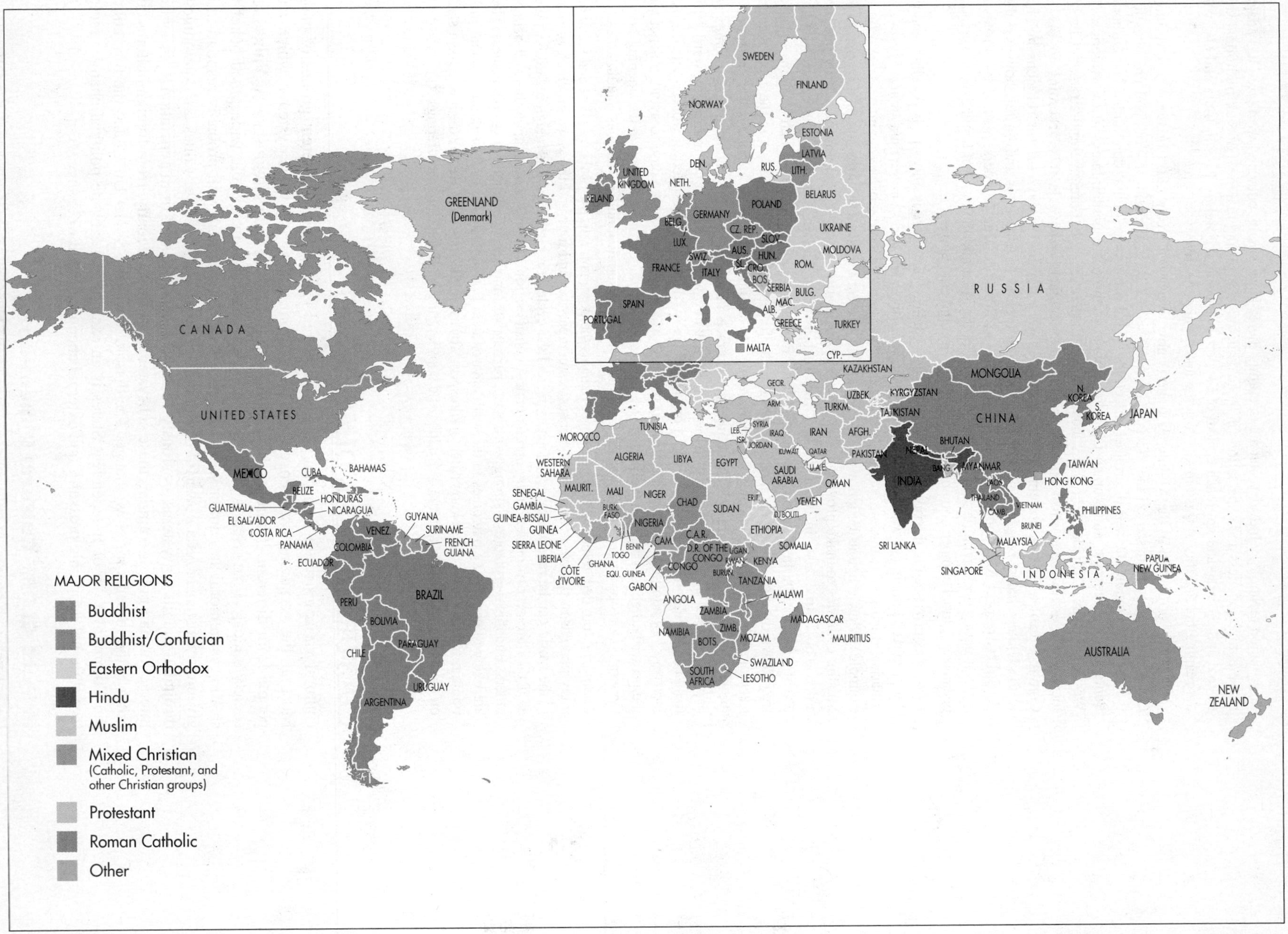

MAJOR RELIGIONS

Buddhist

Buddhist/Confucian

Eastern Orthodox

Hindu

Muslim

Mixed Christian
(Catholic, Protestant, and
other Christian groups)

Protestant

Roman Catholic

Other

Source: Data from various sources, including the U.S. Bureau of the Census international database, U.S. State Department Reports, UN Human development report.

information technology industry that are operating there. Their young, educated workforce has adapted to the competitiveness and expectations in those companies, resulting in a meld of their traditional value system and the practical approach typical of Western companies. Foreign firms in India and elsewhere are reaping the benefits of this rapidly growing and highly effective workforce.[33]

Christianity originated in the Middle East and is now over 2,000 years old. Christians believe in one God. Christianity is based on the life and death of Jesus Christ, the son of God, and preaches love, the value of human life, self-discipline, and ethics. There are four principal denominations: Orthodox, Pentecostal, Protestant, and Roman Catholic. Roman Catholicism predominates in the Americas and Western Europe. Orthodox Christians mostly live in Eastern Europe. Foreign corporations in Christian locales can assume that most employees and other contacts behave largely according to the Ten Commandments. In Europe, employees typically have a number of days off for religious holidays. In the United States, religious holidays are typically limited to Christmas and Easter; however, there should be respect for people not wanting to work on Sundays. One wonders, also, if the Protestant ethic of hard work, saving, and efficiency, common in the West and the basis of capitalism, is spreading because of global competition and the influence of foreign companies.

Islam was discussed in the opening profile. Muslims believe that there is only one god, Allah, and that the prophet Muhammad was his final messenger. Their lives are based on the Qur'an and Muslim law (Sharia). Businesses can be affected by the Sharia law against receiving or paying interest. As a further example of how religious beliefs affect the workplace, respect for Islam requires companies operating in Muslim countries to make provisions—in time and space allocation—for employees to pray five times a day. This is true, also, in countries and cities such as in the United Kingdom where there is a large Muslim population. In addition, out of respect for Ramadan, a month during which Muslims must fast from dawn till dusk, managers must expect and plan for productivity to go down in the event that contractual obligations are scheduled. Businesspeople not familiar with Islam might become frustrated by the lack of precision regarding scheduling and contracts attributable to the perspective that things will happen in good time as Allah wills. However, the Islamic work ethic is a commitment toward fulfillment and the individual's obligation to society, so there is considerable respect for workers and business motives.[34] In addition, managers operating in Muslim countries must take care to avoid conflict with the prescribed gender roles in their hiring and placement practices, as described in the opening profile. Generally, job opportunities for women are limited in strict Islamic countries such as Saudi Arabia.

Buddhism, founded in India 2,500 years ago, remains the dominant religion of the Far East and is increasingly popular in the West. Buddhism emphasizes compassion and love and the ways in which suffering in the world can be relieved by righteous living and the cycle of rebirth. There is a high regard for others as if they are all part of the family and an ethical consideration of one's actions upon the well-being of others. Buddhism promotes a strong work ethic, persistence, and hard work and frowns on laziness. There are likely to be positive outcomes in the work environment by emphasizing teamwork and responsibility. Foreign managers should acknowledge and respect, for example, that employees expect to have a shrine on the wall or floor with a statue of Buddha and cups holding food and drink as offerings.[35]

CULTURAL VALUE DIMENSIONS

Cultural variables result from unique sets of shared values among different groups of people. Most of the variations between cultures stem from underlying value systems, which cause people from different cultures to behave differently under similar circumstances. **Values** are a society's ideas about what is good or bad, right or wrong—such as the widespread belief that stealing is immoral and unfair. Values determine how individuals will probably respond in any given circumstance. As a powerful component of a society's culture, values are communicated through the eight subsystems previously described and are passed from generation to generation. Interaction and pressure among these subsystems (or more recently, from foreign cultures) may provide the impetus for slow change. The dissolution of the Soviet Union and the formation of the Commonwealth of Independent States is an example of extreme political change resulting from internal economic pressures and external encouragement to change.

Project GLOBE Cultural Dimensions

Recent research results on cultural dimensions have been made available by the GLOBE (Global Leadership and Organizational Behavior Effectiveness) Project team. The team comprises 170 researchers who have collected data over seven years on cultural values and practices and leadership attributes from 18,000 managers in 62 countries. Those managers were from a wide variety of industries and sizes of organizations from every corner of the globe. The team identified nine cultural dimensions that distinguish one society from another and have important managerial implications: assertiveness, future orientation, performance orientation, humane orientation, gender differentiation, uncertainty avoidance, power distance, institutional collectivism versus individualism, and in-group collectivism. Only the first four are discussed here; this avoids confusion for readers because the other five dimensions are similar to those researched by Hofstede, which are presented in the next section. (Other research results from the GLOBE Project are presented in subsequent chapters where applicable, such as in the Leadership section in Chapter 11.) The descriptions are as follows, along with selected rankings based on the GLOBE results shown in the accompanying bar charts.[36]

ASSERTIVENESS

This dimension refers to how much people in a society are expected to be tough, confrontational, and competitive versus modest and tender. Austria and Germany, for example, are highly assertive societies that value competition and have a can-do attitude. This compares with Sweden and Japan, less assertive societies, which tend to prefer warm and cooperative relations and harmony. The GLOBE team concluded that those countries have sympathy for the weak and emphasize loyalty and solidarity.

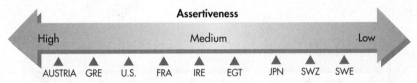

*Not to scale—indicates relative magnitude.

Source: Based on results from the GLOBE project.

FUTURE ORIENTATION

This dimension refers to the level of importance a society attaches to future-oriented behaviors such as planning and investing in the future. Switzerland and Singapore, high on this dimension, are inclined to save for the future and have a longer time horizon for decisions. This perspective compares with societies such as Russia and Argentina, which tend to plan more in the shorter term and place more emphasis on instant gratification.

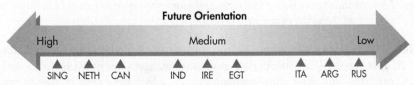

*Not to scale—indicates relative magnitude.

Source: Based on results from the GLOBE project.

PERFORMANCE ORIENTATION

This dimension measures the importance of performance improvement and excellence in society and refers to whether people are encouraged to strive for continued improvement. Singapore, Hong Kong, and the United States score high on this dimension; typically, this means that people tend to take initiative and have a sense of urgency and the confidence to get things done. Countries such as Russia and Italy have low scores on this dimension; they hold other priorities ahead of performance, such as tradition, loyalty, family, and background, and they associate competition with defeat.

*Not to scale—indicates relative magnitude.

Source: Based on results from the GLOBE project.

HUMANE ORIENTATION

This dimension measures the extent to which a society encourages and rewards people for being fair, altruistic, generous, caring, and kind. Highest on this dimension are the Philippines, Ireland, Malaysia, and Egypt, indicating a focus on sympathy and support for the weak. In those societies, paternalism and patronage are important, and people are usually friendly and tolerant and value harmony. This compares with Spain, France, and the former West Germany, which scored low on this dimension; people in these countries give more importance to power and material possessions as well as self-enhancement.

Clearly, research results such as these are helpful to managers seeking to be successful in cross-cultural interactions. Anticipating cultural similarities and differences allows managers to develop the behaviors and skills necessary to act and decide in a manner appropriate to the local societal norms and expectations.

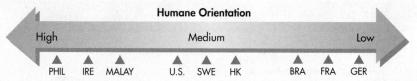

*Not to scale—indicates relative magnitude.

Source: Based on results from the GLOBE project.

Cultural Clusters

Gupta et al., from the GLOBE research team, also analyzed their data on the nine cultural dimensions to determine where similarities cluster geographically. Their results support the existence of ten cultural clusters: South Asia, Anglo, Arab, Germanic Europe, Latin Europe, Eastern Europe, Confucian Asia, Latin America, sub-Saharan Africa, and Nordic Europe. They point out the usefulness to managers of these clusters:

> *Multinational corporations may find it less risky and more profitable to expand into more similar cultures rather than those which are drastically different.*[37]

These clusters are shown in Exhibit 3-3. To compare two of their cluster findings, for example, Gupta et al. describe the Germanic cluster as masculine, assertive, individualistic, and result-oriented. This compares with the Latin American cluster, which they characterize as practicing high power distance, low performance orientation, uncertainty avoidance, and collectivism.

> *Latin American societies tend to enact life as it comes, taking its unpredictability as a fact of life, and not overly worrying about results.*[38]

Most researchers feel that there is a relationship between geographic cultural clusters and their similar economic systems, histories, or environmental characteristics.[39]

Hofstede's Value Dimensions

Earlier research resulted in a groundbreaking framework for understanding how basic values underlie organizational behavior; Geert Hofstede developed this framework based on his research on more than 116,000 people in 50 countries. He proposed four value dimensions: power

EXHIBIT 3-3 Geographic Culture Clusters

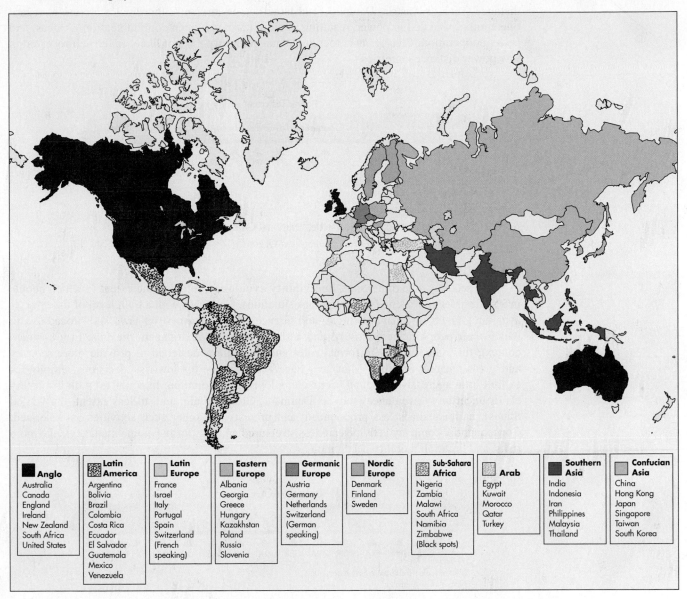

Anglo	**Latin America**	**Latin Europe**	**Eastern Europe**	**Germanic Europe**	**Nordic Europe**	**Sub-Sahara Africa**	**Arab**	**Southern Asia**	**Confucian Asia**
Australia	Argentina	France	Albania	Austria	Denmark	Nigeria	Egypt	India	China
Canada	Bolivia	Israel	Georgia	Germany	Finland	Zambia	Kuwait	Indonesia	Hong Kong
England	Brazil	Italy	Greece	Netherlands	Sweden	Malawi	Morocco	Iran	Japan
Ireland	Colombia	Portugal	Hungary	Switzerland		South Africa	Qatar	Philippines	Singapore
New Zealand	Costa Rica	Spain	Kazakhstan	(German		Namibia	Turkey	Malaysia	Taiwan
South Africa	Ecuador	Switzerland	Poland	speaking)		Zimbabwe		Thailand	South Korea
United States	El Salvador	(French	Russia			(Black spots)			
	Guatemala	speaking)	Slovenia						
	Mexico								
	Venezuela								

Source: Data from V. Gupta, P. J. Hanes, and P. Dorfman, *Journal of World Business* 37, No. 1 (2002), p. 13.

distance, uncertainty avoidance, individualism, and masculinity.[40] We should be cautious when interpreting these results, however, because his research findings are based on a sample drawn from one multinational firm, IBM, and because he does not account for within-country differences in multicultural countries. Although we introduce these value dimensions here to aid in the understanding of different cultures, their relevance and application to management functions will be discussed further in later chapters.

The first of Hofstede's value dimensions, **power distance**, is the level of acceptance by a society of the unequal distribution of power in institutions. What are the attitudes toward hierarchy and the level of respect for authority? How reluctant are employees to express disagreement with their managers? In the workplace, inequalities in power are normal, as evidenced in hierarchical boss–subordinate relationships. However, the extent to which subordinates accept unequal power is societally determined. In countries in which people display high power distance (such as Malaysia, the Philippines, and Mexico), employees acknowledge the boss's authority simply by respecting that individual's formal position in the hierarchy, and they seldom bypass the chain of command. This respectful response results, predictably, in a centralized structure and autocratic leadership. In countries where people display low power distance (such as Austria, Denmark, and Israel), superiors and subordinates are apt to regard one another as equal in power, resulting in more harmony, open communication of ideas, and better cooperation. Clearly, an autocratic management style is not likely to be well received in low power distance countries.

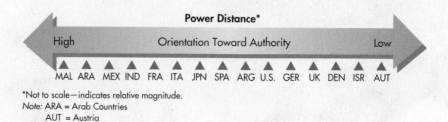

*Not to scale—indicates relative magnitude.
Note: ARA = Arab Countries
          AUT = Austria

Source: Data based on G. Hofstede, "National Cultures in Four Dimensions," *International Studies of Management and Organization* (Spring-Summer, 1983).

The second value dimension, **uncertainty avoidance**, refers to the extent to which people in a society feel threatened by ambiguous situations. Countries with a high level of uncertainty avoidance (such as Japan, Portugal, and Greece) tend to have strict laws and procedures to which their people adhere closely, and a strong sense of nationalism prevails. In a business context, this value results in formal rules and procedures designed to provide more security and greater career stability. Managers have a propensity for low-risk decisions, employees exhibit little aggressiveness, and lifetime employment is common. In countries with lower levels of uncertainty avoidance (such as Denmark, Great Britain, and, to less extent, the United States), nationalism is less pronounced, and protests and other such activities are tolerated. Consequently, company activities are less structured and less formal, some managers take more risks, and high job mobility is common.

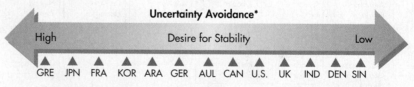

*Not to scale—indicates relative magnitude.
Note: AUL = Australia

Source: Data based on G. Hofstede, 1983.

The third of Hofstede's value dimensions, **individualism**, refers to the tendency of people to look after themselves and their immediate families with less emphasis on the needs of society; the primary focus is on the individual or the nuclear family. In countries that prize individualism (such as the United States, Great Britain, and Australia), democracy, individual initiative, and achievement are highly valued; the relationship of the individual to organizations is one of independence on an emotional level, if not on an economic level.

In countries such as Pakistan and Panama, where low individualism prevails—that is, where **collectivism** predominates—there is more emphasis on group achievements and harmony and the importance of the extended family or group. In such societies, there are tight social frameworks, emotional dependence on belonging to the organization, and a strong belief in group decisions. People from a collectivist country, such as Japan, believe in the will of the group rather than that of the individual, and their pervasive collectivism exerts control over individual members through social pressure and the fear of humiliation. The society valorizes harmony and saving face, whereas individualistic cultures generally emphasize self-respect, autonomy, and independence. Hiring and promotion practices in collectivist societies are based on paternalism rather than achievement or personal capabilities, which are valued in individualistic societies. Other management practices (such as the use of quality circles in Japanese factories) reflect the emphasis on group decision-making processes in collectivist societies. The individualism–collectivism dimension, then, relates to the manner in which members of a group relate to one another and work together.[41]

Hofstede's findings indicate that most countries scoring high on individualism have both a higher gross national product and a freer political system than those countries scoring low on individualism—that is, there is a strong relationship among individualism, wealth, and a political system with balanced power. Other studies have found that the output of individuals working in a group setting differs between individualistic and collectivist societies. In the United States, a highly individualistic culture, social loafing is common—that is, people tend to perform less when working as part of a group than when working alone.[42] In a comparative study of the United States and the People's Republic of China (a highly collectivist society), Earley found that the Chinese did not exhibit as much social loafing as the Americans.[43] This result can be attributed to Chinese cultural values, which subordinate personal interests to the greater goal of helping the group succeed. However, more recently, one sees the younger generation in the cities adopting more of a capitalist and individualistic attitude toward their jobs as global competition increases. and as more western companies operate there and hire locals.

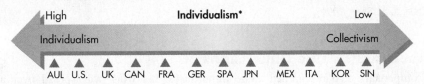

*Not to scale—indicates relative magnitude.

Source: Data based on G. Hofstede, 1983.

The fourth value dimension, **masculinity**, refers to the degree of traditionally masculine values—assertiveness, materialism, and a lack of concern for others—that prevail in a society. In comparison, femininity emphasizes feminine values—a concern for others, for relationships, and for the quality of life. In highly masculine societies (Japan and Austria, for example), women are generally expected to stay home and raise a family. In organizations, one finds considerable job stress, and organizational interests generally encroach on employees' private lives. In countries with low masculinity (such as Switzerland and New Zealand), one finds less conflict and job stress, more women in high-level jobs, and a reduced need for assertiveness. The United States lies somewhat in the middle, according to Hofstede's research. American women typically are encouraged to work, and families often are able to get some support for child care (through day-care centers and maternity leaves).

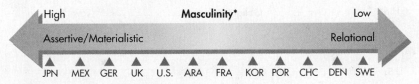

*Not to scale—indicates relative magnitude.

Source: Data based on G. Hofstede, 1983.

The four cultural value dimensions Hofstede proposed do not operate in isolation; rather, they are interdependent and interactive—and thus complex—in their effects on work attitudes and behaviors.

LONG-TERM/SHORT-TERM ORIENTATION

Later research in 23 countries, using a survey developed by Bond and colleagues called the Chinese Value Survey, led Hofstede to develop a fifth dimension—called the Confucian work dynamism—which he labeled a long-term/short-term dimension. He defined long-term orientation as "the extent to which a culture programs its members to accept delayed gratification of their material, social, and emotional needs."[44] In other words, managers in most Asian countries are more future-oriented, so they strive toward long-term goals; they value investment in the future and are prepared to sacrifice short-term profits. However, managers in countries such as Great Britain, Canada, and the United States place a higher value on short-term results and profitability and evaluate their employees accordingly.

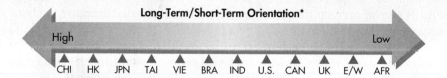

*Not to scale—indicates relative magnitude.

Source: Databased on G. Hofstede, *Culture's Consequences: Comparing Values, Behaviors, Institutions, and Organizations across Nations,* 2nd ed. (Thousand Oaks, CA: Sage, 2001).

Trompenaars's Value Dimensions

Fons Trompenaars also researched value dimensions; his work was spread over a ten-year period, with 15,000 managers from 28 countries representing 47 national cultures. Some of those dimensions, such as individualism, people's attitude toward time, and relative inner- versus outer-directedness, are similar to those discussed elsewhere in this chapter and others, and so are not presented here. Other selected findings from Trompenaars's research that affect daily business activities are explained next, along with the placement of some of the countries along those dimensions, in approximate relative order.[45] If we view the placement of these countries along a range from personal to societal, based on each dimension, some interesting patterns emerge.[46] One can see that the same countries tend to be at similar positions on all dimensions with the exception of the emotional orientation.

In Trompenaars's dimension of **universalism versus particularism**, we find that the universalistic approach applies rules and systems objectively without consideration for individual circumstances, whereas the particularistic approach—more common in Asia and Spain, for example—puts the first obligation on relationships and is more subjective. Trompenaars found, for example, that people in particularistic societies are more likely to pass on insider information to a friend than those in universalistic societies.

*Not to scale—indicates relative magnitude.

Source: Data based on F. Trompenaars, 1993.

In the **neutral versus affective** dimension, the focus is on the emotional orientation of relationships. The Italians, Mexicans, and Chinese, for example, would openly express emotions, even in a business situation, whereas the British and Japanese would consider such displays unprofessional; they, in turn, would be regarded as hard to read.

*Not to scale—Indicates relative magnitude.

Source: Data based on F. Trompenaars, 1993.

As far as involvement in relationships goes, people tend to be either *specific or diffuse* (or somewhere along that dimension). Managers in specific-oriented cultures—the United States, United Kingdom, France—separate work and personal issues and relationships; they compartmentalize their work and private lives, and they are more open and direct. In diffuse-oriented cultures—Sweden, China—work spills over into personal relationships and vice versa.

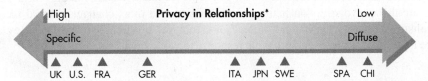

*Not to scale—indicates relative magnitude.

Source: Data based on F. Trompenaars, 1993.

In the **achievement versus ascription** dimension, the question that arises is, "What is the source of power and status in society?" In an achievement society, the source of status and influence is based on individual achievement—how well one performs the job and what level of education and experience one has to offer. Therefore, women, minorities, and young people usually have equal opportunity to attain position based on their achievements. In an ascription-oriented society, people ascribe status based on class, age, gender, and so on; one is more likely to be born into a position of influence. Hiring in Indonesia, for example, is more likely to be based on who you are than is the case in Germany or Australia.

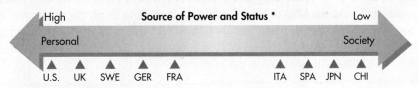

*Not to scale—indicates relative magnitude.

Source: Data based on F. Trompenaars, 1993.

It is clear, then, that a lot of what goes on at work can be explained by differences in people's innate value systems as described by Hofstede, Trompenaars, and the GLOBE researchers. Awareness of such differences and how they influence work behavior can be very useful to you as a future international manager.

Consequence or Cause?

At this point, it is worth considering the results of a study by Steel and Taras, published in 2010, in which they challenge the view held by Hofstede and others of culture as the cause, and not the effect, of variations in cultural values. Steel and Taras argue that the opposite can be true, that "culture is a consequence of certain individual and national-level factors."[47] They conclude that the research results provide a basis for explaining variations in cultural values within and between countries and that "cultures are determined by a set of individual and country level factors and are likely to change in response to a change in the culture-determining factors."[48] Examples of the factors they considered are macrofactors such as wealth and freedom and microfactors such as age, gender, education, and socioeconomic status. Steel and Taras stress, therefore, that we should not rely on national averages to draw conclusions about individuals.[49] Other researchers also hold this broader concept of the origins of cultural behavior; Meuthel and Hoegl, for example, state that "we extend the traditional view of culture as an exclusive country-level determinant to a more comprehensive view that integrates social institutions such as the education system, economic freedom, and civil liberties."[50]

Clearly, the origins, causes, and effects of cultural variables are complex, but the fact remains that culture plays a key role in the workplace, and international managers must be aware of that role and manage accordingly.

Critical Operational Value Differences

After studying various research results about cultural variables, it helps to identify some specific culturally based variables that cause frequent problems for managers around the world. Important variables are those involving conflicting orientations toward time, change, material factors, and individualism. We try to understand these operational value differences because they strongly influence a person's attitudes and probable response to work situations.

TIME

Americans often experience much conflict and frustration because of differences in the concept of time around the world—that is, differences in temporal values. To Americans, time is a valuable and limited resource; it is to be saved, scheduled, and spent with precision, lest we waste it. The clock is always running—time is money. Therefore, deadlines and schedules have to be met. When others are not on time for meetings, Americans may feel insulted; when meetings digress from their purpose, Americans tend to become impatient. Similar attitudes toward time occur in Western Europe and elsewhere.

In many parts of the world, however, people view time from different and longer perspectives, often based on religious beliefs (such as reincarnation, in which time does not end at death), on a belief in destiny, or on pervasive social attitudes. In Latin America, for example, a common attitude toward time is *mañana*, a word that literally means "tomorrow." A Latin American person using this word, however, usually means an indefinite time in the near future. Similarly, the word *bukra* in Arabic can mean "tomorrow" or "some time in the future." Although Americans usually regard a deadline as a firm commitment, Arabs often regard a deadline imposed on them as an insult. They feel that important things take a long time and therefore cannot be rushed. To ask an Arab to rush something, then, is to imply that you have not given him an important task or that he would not treat that task with respect. International managers have to be careful not to offend people—or lose contracts or employee cooperation—because they misunderstand the local language of time.

CHANGE

Because they are based largely on long-standing religious beliefs, values regarding the acceptance of change and the pace of change can vary immensely among cultures. Western people generally believe that an individual can exert some control over the future and can manipulate events, particularly in a business context—that is, individuals feel they have some internal control. In many non-Western societies, however, control is considered external; people generally believe in destiny or the will of their God and, therefore, adopt a passive attitude or even feel hostility toward those introducing the evil of change. In societies that place great importance on tradition (such as Japan), one small area of change may threaten an entire way of life. However, the younger generations are becoming more exposed to change through globalization, technology, and media exposure. International firms are agents of change throughout the world. Some changes are more popular than others are.

MATERIAL FACTORS

In large part, Americans consume resources at a far greater rate than most of the rest of the world. Their attitude toward nature—that it is there to be used for their benefit—differs from the attitudes of Indians and Koreans, for example, whose worship of nature is part of their religious

EXHIBIT 3-4 Fundamental Differences between Japanese and Mexican Culture That Affect Business Organizations

Dimension	Japanese Culture	Mexican Culture
Hierarchical nature	Rigid in rank and most communication; blurred in authority and responsibility	Rigid in all aspects
Individualism vs. collectivism	Highly collective culture; loyalty to work group dominates; group harmony very important	Collective relative to family group; doesn't transfer loyalty to work group; individualistic outside family
Attitudes toward work	Work is sacred duty; acquiring skills, working hard, thriftiness, patience, and perseverance are virtues	Work is means to support self and family; leisure more important than work
Time orientation	Balanced perspective; future oriented; monochronic in dealings with outside world	Present oriented; time is imprecise; time commitments become desirable objectives
Approach to problem solving	Holistic, reliance on intuition, pragmatic, consensus important	Reliance on intuition and emotion, individual approach
Fatalism	Fatalism leads to preparation	Fatalism makes planning, disciplined routine unnatural
View of human nature	Intrinsically good	Mixture of good and evil

Source: J. J. Lawrence and Ryh-song Yeh, "The Influence of Mexican Culture on the Use of Japanese Manufacturing Techniques in Mexico," *Management International Review* 34, No. 1 (1994), pp. 49–66, used with permission.

beliefs. Whereas Americans often value physical goods and status symbols, many non-Westerners find these things unimportant; they value the aesthetic and the spiritual realm. Such differences in attitude have implications for management functions such as motivation and reward systems because the proverbial carrot must be appropriate to the employee's value system.

INDIVIDUALISM

In general, Americans tend to work and conduct their private lives independently, valuing individual achievement, accomplishments, promotions, and wealth above any group goals. In many other countries, individualism is not valued (as discussed previously in the context of Hofstede's work). In China, for example, much more of a "we" consciousness prevails, and the group is the basic building block of social life and work. For the Chinese, conformity and cooperation take precedence over individual achievement, and the emphasis is on the strength of the family or community—the predominant attitude being, "We all rise or fall together."

International managers often face conflicts in the workplace because of differences in these four basic values of time, change, materialism, and individualism. If these operational value differences and their likely consequences are anticipated, managers can adjust expectations, communications, work organization, schedules, incentive systems, and so forth to provide for more-constructive outcomes for the company and its employees. Some of these operational differences are shown in Exhibit 3-4, using Japan and Mexico as examples. Note in particular the factors of time, individualism, change (fatalism), and materialism (attitudes toward work) expressed in the exhibit.

THE INTERNET AND CULTURE

> *As of June 30, 2014, South Korea had 92.4% of its population who were internet users—compared with 86.9% for the United States for the internet population penetration.*
>
> WWW.INTERNETWORLDSTATS.COM.[51]

We would be remiss if we did not acknowledge the contemporary phenomenon of the increasingly pervasive use of the Internet in society, for it seems to be encroaching on many of the social variables discussed earlier—in particular, associations, education, and the economy, as well as politics, as evidenced in the 2011 Arab Spring, discussed in Chapter 1. In South Korea, for example, there is an obsession for anything digital. Over 92 percent of homes are connected to a high-speed Internet service. That compares with an average of 70 percent for the European countries, 87 percent in the United States, and 47 percent for China. Seoul is the most technologically advanced city in the world. This phenomenon seems to be changing the lives of many Koreans. Teenagers, once used to hanging out at the mall, now do so at the country's thousands of personal computer (PC) parlors to watch movies, check email, and surf the Net.

At the same time that the Internet is affecting culture, culture is also affecting how the Internet is used. One of the pervasive ways that culture is determining how the Internet may be used in various countries is through the local attitude to **information privacy**—the right to control information about oneself, as observed in the following quote.

> *You Americans just don't seem to care about privacy, do you?*
>
> SWEDISH EXECUTIVE[52]

Although Americans collect data about consumers' backgrounds and what they buy, often trading that information with other internal or external contacts, the Swedes, for example, are astounded that this is done, especially without governmental oversight.[53] The Swedes are required to register all databases of personal information with the Data Inspection Board (DIB), their federal regulatory agency for privacy, and to get permission from that board before that data can be used. Indeed, the Swedish system is typical of most countries in Europe in their societal approaches to privacy.[54] Generally, in Europe, each person must be informed, and given the chance to object, if the information about that person will be used for direct marketing purposes or released to another party. That data cannot be used for secondary purposes if the consumer objects.

> *In Italy, data cannot be sent outside—even to other EU countries—without the explicit consent of the data subject....*
>
> *In Spain, all direct mail has to include the name and address of the data owner so that the data subject is able to exercise his rights of access, correction, and removal.*[55]

The manner in which Europe views information privacy has its roots in culture and history, leading to a different value set regarding privacy. The preservation of privacy is considered a human right, perhaps partially because of an internalized fear about how personal records were used in war times in Europe. In addition, research by Smith on the relationship between levels of concern about privacy and Hofstede's cultural dimensions revealed that high levels of uncertainty avoidance were associated with the European approach to privacy, whereas higher levels of individualism, masculinity, and power distance were associated with the U.S. approach.[56]

It seems, then, that societal culture and the resultant effects on business models can render the assumptions about the global nature of information technology incorrect. U.S. businesspeople, brought up on a strong diet of the market economy, need to realize that they will often need to localize their use of IT to different value sets about its use. This advice applies in particular to the many e-commerce companies doing business overseas. With 75 percent of the world's Internet market living outside the United States, multinational e-businesses are learning the hard way that their websites must reflect local markets, customs, languages, and currencies to be successful in foreign markets. Different legal systems, financial structures, tastes, and experiences necessitate attention to every detail to achieve global appeal. In other words, e-businesses must localize to globalize, which means much more than translating online content to local languages. Lycos Europe, for example, based its privacy policies upon German law because it is the most stringent.

One problem area often beyond the control of e-business is the cost of connecting to the Internet for people in other countries. Other practical problems in Asia, as well as in Germany, the Netherlands, and Sweden, include the method of payment, which in most of these places still involves cash or letters of credit and written receipts. Dell tackled this problem by offering debit payments from consumers' checking accounts. Some companies have learned the hard way that they need to do their homework before launching sites aimed at overseas consumers. Dell, for example, committed a faux pas when it launched an e-commerce site in Japan with black borders on its website; black is considered negative in the Japanese culture, so many consumers took one look and didn't want anything else to do with it. Dell executives learned that the complexity of language translation into Japanese was only one area in which they needed to localize.

As much as cultural and societal factors can affect the use of the Internet for business, it is also clear that IT can impose dramatic changes on culture and society; in addition, cultural preferences and legal expectations can impose restrictions on the use of IT, as illustrated by the accompanying Management in Action feature about Google's experiences in Japan and in Europe.

MANAGEMENT IN ACTION

Google's Street View Makes Friends in Japan but Clashes with European Culture[57]

After the 9.0 earthquake in Japan in March 2011, which was followed by a devastating tsunami, Google used its assembly of nine cameras creating 360-degree panoramic digital images of the disaster zone to archive damage. Its Street View mapping service was welcomed after the disaster, as observed by the major of Kesennuma.

"I'd like them to record Kesennuma's streets now," Mr. Sugawara said. "Then I'd like them to come back, when the city is like new again, and show the world the new Kesennuma."[58]

In addition, Google went live with its online Person Finder service less than two hours after the quake. The site helped people find out about the status of family and friends in the aftermath of the disaster. Although many did not have Internet access after the disaster and simply posted signs about missing people, others took photos of the signs and uploaded them to Google for use in the Person Finder service. Even the National Police posted information, and soon Person Finder had collected 616,300 records, Japan's largest database of missing people from the disaster. After Google's many blunders in Japan and privacy concerns about the company's services, it now seems that its technology was able to help the Japanese people and resulted in raising its brand and social networking identity there.[59]

However, Google has been less well received in Europe. The company has been expanding into European markets for years and now has a headquarters in Dublin, large offices in Zurich and London, and smaller centers in countries such as Denmark, Russia, and Poland. However, the company has been caught in a cultural web of privacy laws that threaten its growth and the positive image it has cultivated.

"The framework in Europe is of privacy as a human-dignity right," said Nicole Wong, a lawyer with the [Google] company. "As enforced in the U.S., it's a consumer-protection right."[60]

Google's plan to introduce Street View, a mapping service that provides a vivid, 360-degree, ground-level photographic panorama from any address, met with considerable resistance. Data protection officials in Switzerland pressured Google to cancel those plans because Street View would violate strict Swiss privacy laws that prohibit the unauthorized use of personal images or property. In Germany, where Street View is also not available, simply taking photographs for the service violates privacy laws. After pressure from a German data protection official, Google had to show what its Street View cars had been collecting: "Snippets of e-mails, photographs, passwords, chat messages, postings on websites and social networks—all sorts of private Internet communications."[61] This was a blatant violation of Europe's data protection laws, and European antitrust regulators gave the company an ultimatum to change its search business or face legal consequences. This conflict was continuing to play out in summer 2014 and had spread to the United States and other countries, seemingly all having difficulty in holding Google accountable. At the same time, the EU's Article 29 Data Protection Working Group, which is a collaboration among all the information and data protection watchdogs within the European Union, is also contesting Google's practices. The EU

FIGURE 3-2 Google street view car in Toledo, Spain.

philipus /Alamy

(Continued)

Justice Commissioner, Franco Frattini, was backing the investigation. Google, the world's largest search engine, also provoked a debate about Internet privacy in May 2008, when it announced it would institute changes to its policies on holding personal information about its customers. The policy change related to Google's server logs (the information a browser sends back to Google when somebody visits a site). At present, the search engine retains a log of every search indefinitely, including information—such as the unique computer address, browser type, and language—that could be traced back to a particular computer. The policy change was to reduce how long that information was retained to 18 to 24 months.

Peter Schaar, chair of Article 29 and Germany's federal commissioner for freedom of information, developed a report on the relationship between search-engine business models and European privacy laws. The draft report concluded that Internet Protocol (IP) addresses are personal information because they can help identify a person. Europeans fiercely protect their privacy and trust that the government enforces it in law. Mr. Schaar has challenged Peter Fleischer of Google's global privacy law team to explain why such a long storage period was chosen and to give a legal justification for the storage of server logs in general. Google's response so far, from founders Sergei Brin and Larry Page, is to identify others as the greater threat to Internet users' privacy. They stated that information posted on social networking sites, such as photographs of young people at drunken parties, are a greater privacy concern. They defended the value of users' information for refining search results and blamed the way some companies have used that information for privacy problems in the industry. The outcome of this cross-cultural Internet communication clash remains to be seen. One thing that is clear is that the European Union (EU) has fired a warning shot across the bows of the search-engine companies.

DEVELOPING CULTURAL PROFILES

Managers can gather considerable information about cultural variables from current research, personal observation, and discussions with people. From these sources, managers can develop cultural profiles of various countries—composite pictures of working environments, people's attitudes, and norms of behavior. As we have previously discussed, these profiles are often highly generalized; many subcultures, of course, may exist within a country. However, managers can use these profiles to anticipate drastic variances in motivation, communication, ethics, loyalty, and individual and group productivity that may be encountered in a given country. More such homework may have helped Walmart's expansion efforts into Germany and South Korea, from which it withdrew in 2006. Walmart's executives simply did not do enough research about the culture and shopping habits of people in those countries; for example:

> In Germany, Walmart's stopped requiring sales clerks to smile at customers—a practice that some male shoppers interpreted as flirting—and scrapped the morning Wal-Mart chant by staff members. "People found these things strange; Germans just don't behave that way," said Hans-Martin Poschmann, the secretary of the Verdi union.[62]

It is relatively simple for Americans to pull together a descriptive profile of U.S. culture, even though regional and individual differences exist, because Americans know themselves and because researchers have thoroughly studied U.S. culture. The results of one such study by Harris and Moran are shown in Exhibit 3-5, which provides a basis of comparison with other cultures and, thus, suggests the likely differences in workplace behaviors.

It is not so easy, however, to pull together descriptive cultural profiles of peoples in other countries unless one has lived there and been intricately involved with those people. Still, managers can make a start by using what comparative research and literature are available. The accompanying Comparative Management in Focus feature provides brief, generalized country profiles based on a synthesis of research, primarily from Hofstede[63] and England,[64] as well as from numerous other sources.[65] These profiles illustrate how to synthesize information and gain a sense of the character of a society—from which implications may be drawn about how to adapt to and learn from that society to manage more effectively. More extensive implications and applications related to managerial functions are drawn in later chapters.

Recent evidence in Japan points to some convergence with Western business culture resulting from Japan's economic contraction and subsequent bankruptcies. Focus on the group, lifetime employment, and a pension has given way to a more competitive business environment with job security no longer guaranteed and an emphasis on performance-based pay. This has led Japan's

EXHIBIT 3-5 **Americans at a Glance**

1. *Goal and achievement oriented*—Americans think they can accomplish anything, given enough time, money, and technology.
2. *Highly organized and institutionally minded*
3. *Freedom-loving and self-reliant*—a belief that all persons are equal; they admire self-made people.
4. *Work-oriented and efficient*—a strong work ethic; conscious of time and efficient in doing things.
5. *Friendly and informal*—informal in greeting and dress; a noncontact culture (avoid embracing in public).
6. *Competitive and aggressive*—driven to achieve and succeed in play and business.
7. *Values in transition*—traditional family values are undergoing transition.
8. *Generosity*—Americans are a sharing people.

Source: Based on excerpts from *Managing Cultural Differences* by Philip R. Harris and Robert T. Moran, 5th ed. Copyright © 2000 by Gulf Publishing Company, Houston, TX.

salarymen to recognize the need for personal responsibility on the job and in their lives. Although only a few years ago emphasis was on the group, Japan's long economic slump seems to have caused some cultural restructuring of the individual. Corporate Japan is changing from a culture of consensus and groupthink to one touting the need for an "era of personal responsibility" as a solution to revitalize its competitive position in the global marketplace.[66]

> *To tell you the truth, it's hard to think for yourself, says Mr. Kuzuoka...[but, if you don't]...in this age of cutthroat competition, you'll just end up drowning.[67]*

Comparative Management in Focus

Profiles in Culture—Japan, Germany, Latin America

JAPAN

The traditional Japanese business characteristics of politeness and deference have left companies without the thrusting culture needed to succeed internationally.[68]

With intense global competition, many Japanese companies are recognizing the need for more assertiveness and clarity in their business culture to expand abroad. As a result, Japanese employees are recognizing the need to manage their own careers as companies move away from lifetime employment to be more competitive. Only a handful of large businesses, such as Toyota, Komatsu, and Canon, have managed to become indisputable global leaders by maintaining relationships as a foundation for their operations around the world.[69] For the majority of Japanese, the underlying cultural values still predominate—at least for now.

Japanese culture is strong, formal, and largely homogeneous and inculcated to the young through the teachings and expectations conveyed by the extended family. Much of Japanese culture—and the basis of working relationships—can be explained by the principle of *wa*, "peace and harmony." This principle, embedded in the value the Japanese attribute to *amae* ("indulgent love"), probably originated in the Shinto religion, which focuses on spiritual and physical harmony. *Amae* results in *shinyo*, which refers to the mutual confidence, faith, and honor necessary for successful business relationships. Japan ranks high on pragmatism, masculinity, and uncertainty avoidance and fairly high on power distance. At the same time, much importance is attached to loyalty, empathy, and the guidance of subordinates. The result is a mix of authoritarianism and humanism in the workplace, similar to a family system. These cultural roots are evident in a homogeneous managerial value system, with strong middle management, strong working relationships, strong seniority systems that stress rank, and an emphasis on looking after employees. The principle of *wa* carries forth into the work group—the building block of Japanese business. The Japanese strongly identify with their work groups and seek to cooperate with them. The emphasis is on participative management, consensus problem solving, and decision making

(Continued)

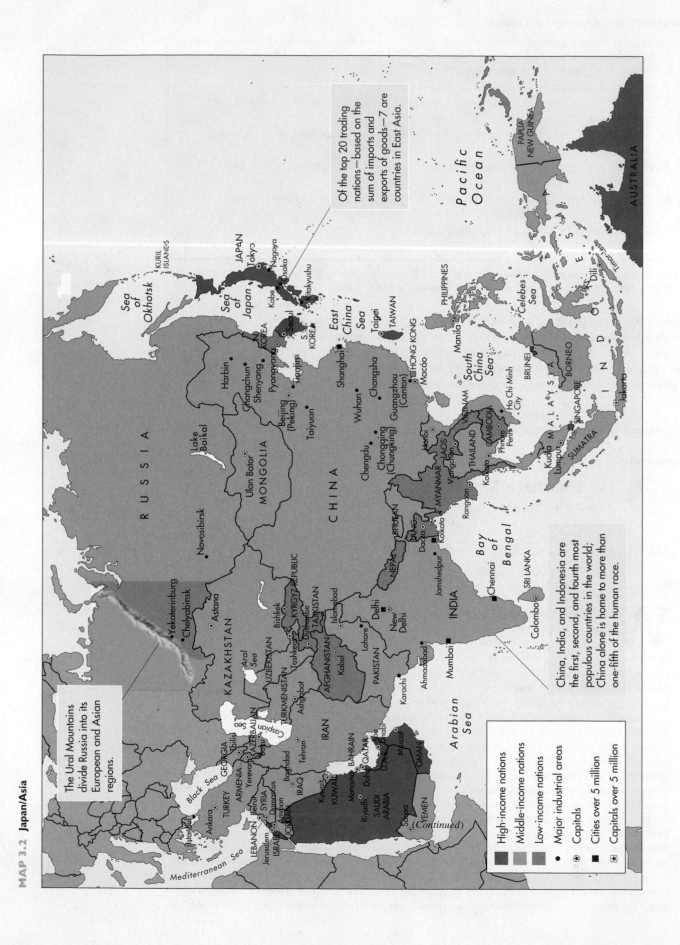

MAP 3.2 Japan/Asia

The Ural Mountains divide Russia into its European and Asian regions.

Of the top 20 trading nations—based on the sum of imports and exports of goods—7 are countries in East Asia.

China, India, and Indonesia are the first, second, and fourth most populous countries in the world; China alone is home to more than one-fifth of the human race.

High-income nations
Middle-income nations
Low-income nations
Major industrial areas
Capitals
Cities over 5 million
Capitals over 5 million

with a patient, long-term perspective. Open expression and conflict are discouraged, and it is of paramount importance to avoid the shame of not fulfilling one's duty. These elements of work culture result in a devotion to work, collective responsibility, and a high degree of employee productivity. In meetings, punctuality is essential; the meeting should start with a bow or handshake, then an exchange of business cards (*meishi*) using both hands, and then reading the card before you put it in your pocket. Titles and last names should be used, and some small talk should take place before business.[70] Do not invade the personal space of the Japanese, and avoid any confrontation or nonverbal excess. In addition, it is important to avoid singling out any one Japanese person, because it is a group process.

Professor Nonaka, a specialist in how companies tap the collective intelligence of their workers, discusses a similar Japanese concept of *ba*: an interaction among colleagues on the job that leads to knowledge-sharing. He says that

> *Ba can occur in a work group, a project team, an ad hoc meeting, a virtual e-mail list, or at the frontline point of contact with customers. It serves as a petri dish in which shared insights are cultivated and grown.[71]*

The message is clear that, in Japan, companies that give their employees freedom to interact informally are likely to benefit from new ideas and collaboration.

If we extend this cultural profile to its implications for specific behaviors in the workplace, we can draw a comparison with common American behaviors. Most of those American behaviors seem to be opposite to those of their Japanese counterparts; it is no wonder that many misunderstandings and conflicts in the workplace arise between Americans and Japanese (see Exhibit 3-6). For example, a majority of the attitudes and behaviors of many Japanese stems from a high level of collectivism, compared with a high level of

EXHIBIT 3–6 The American-Japanese Cultural Divide

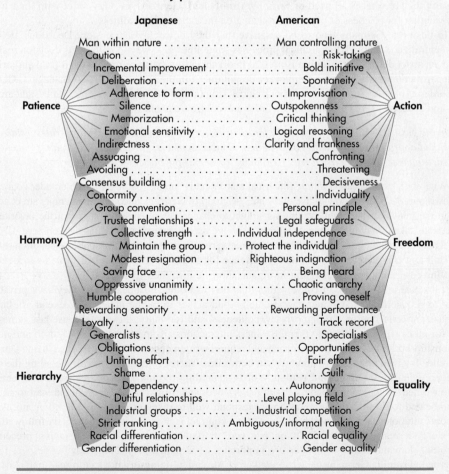

Japanese	American
Man within nature	Man controlling nature
Caution	Risk-taking
Incremental improvement	Bold initiative
Deliberation	Spontaneity
Adherence to form	Improvisation
Silence	Outspokenness
Memorization	Critical thinking
Emotional sensitivity	Logical reasoning
Indirectness	Clarity and frankness
Assuaging	Confronting
Avoiding	Threatening
Consensus building	Decisiveness
Conformity	Individuality
Group convention	Personal principle
Trusted relationships	Legal safeguards
Collective strength	Individual independence
Maintain the group	Protect the individual
Modest resignation	Righteous indignation
Saving face	Being heard
Oppressive unanimity	Chaotic anarchy
Humble cooperation	Proving oneself
Rewarding seniority	Rewarding performance
Loyalty	Track record
Generalists	Specialists
Obligations	Opportunities
Untiring effort	Fair effort
Shame	Guilt
Dependency	Autonomy
Dutiful relationships	Level playing field
Industrial groups	Industrial competition
Strict ranking	Ambiguous/informal ranking
Racial differentiation	Racial equality
Gender differentiation	Gender equality

(Clusters: Patience, Harmony, Hierarchy / Action, Freedom, Equality)

Source: R. G. Linowes, "The Japanese Manager's Traumatic Entry into the United States: Understanding the American–Japanese Cultural Divide," *Academy of Management Executive* 7, No. 4 (1993), p. 24.

(Continued)

individualism common to Americans. This contrast is highlighted in the center of Exhibit 3-6—"Maintain the group" compared with "Protect the individual." In addition, the strict social order of the Japanese permeates the workplace in adherence to organizational hierarchy and seniority and in loyalty to the firm. This contrasts markedly with the typical American responses to organizational relationships and duties based on equality. In addition, the often blunt, outspoken American businessperson offends the indirectness and sensitivity of the Japanese, for whom the virtue of patience is paramount, causing the silence and avoidance that so frustrates Americans. As a result, Japanese businesspeople tend to think of American organizations as having no spiritual quality and little loyalty to employees, and they think of Americans as assertive, frank, and egotistic. Their American counterparts, in turn, respond with the impression that Japanese businesspeople have little experience and are secretive, arrogant, and cautious.[72] Westerners doing business in Japan need to be aware of the importance of *giri*—the expectations of reciprocity in relationships and how to behave. Managers should inform themselves in particular about the practice of gift-giving and the relationship of the type of gift suitable for the relative status of the parties involved; gift giving is accepted practice, but make sure it is not too big or it will be an embarrassment and may be considered an attempt to bribe.

Germany The reunited Germany is somewhat culturally diverse inasmuch as the country borders several nations. Generally, Germans rank quite high on Hofstede's dimension of individualism, although their behaviors seem less individualistic than those of Americans. They score fairly high on uncertainty avoidance and masculinity and have a relatively small need for power distance. These cultural norms show up in the Germans' preference for being around familiar people and situations; they are also reflected in their propensity to do a detailed evaluation of business deals before committing themselves.

Christianity underlies much of German culture—more than 96 percent of Germans are Catholics or Protestants. This may be why Germans tend to like rule and order in their lives and why there is a clear public expectation of acceptable and unacceptable ways to act. Public signs everywhere in Germany dictate what is allowed or *verboten* (forbidden). Germans are very strict with their use of time, whether for business or pleasure, frowning on inefficiency or tardiness.

In business, Germans tend to be assertive, but they downplay aggression. Decisions are typically centralized, although hierarchical processes sometimes give way to consensus decision making. However, strict departmentalization is present in organizations, with centralized and final authority at the departmental manager level. Employees do not question the authority of their managers. German companies typically have a vertical hierarchical structure with detailed planning and standardized rules and procedures; the emphasis is on order and control to avoid risk.

> *In the business setting, Germans look for security, well-defined work procedures, rules, established approaches, and clearly defined individual assignments. In short, the German business environment is highly structured. "Ordnung" (order) is the backbone of company life.*[73]

What the Germans call *Ordnung* (the usual translation is "order," but it is a much broader concept) is the unwritten road map of how to live one's life. "A group of Germans lined up on an empty street corner, even in the middle of the night, waiting for a light to change before crossing, is one of the favorite first impressions taken away by visiting Americans, who are usually jaywalking past as they observe it."[74] For self-reliant Americans, the German adherence to precise rules and regulations is impressive but often stifling.

Hall and Hall describe the German preference for closed doors and private space as evidence of the affinity for compartmentalization in organizations and in their own lives. They also prefer more physical space around them in conversation than do most other Europeans, and they seek privacy so as not to be overheard.[75] German law prohibits loud noises in public areas on weekend afternoons. Germans are conservative, valuing privacy, politeness, and formality; they usually use last names and titles for all except those close to them. Business interactions are specifically task-focused and not for relationship-building. Meetings are formal and require written documents in both English and German. Deference is given to people of authority on both sides. There is a strict protocol, including the order of people entering the room and getting seated—according to rank and age, and with men entering before women! It all requires patience with the protocol and formality, and you should wait to sit until it is indicated to do so. The Germans do not respond well to displays of emotions and promises, and any confrontational behavior will backfire. Once a contract is in place, it will be strictly followed.[76]

Most Germans prefer to focus on one task or issue at a time, that task taking precedence over other demands; strict schedules are important, as is punctuality, both showing respect for all concerned. Overall, Germany is what Walker et al. call a doing-oriented culture—that is, a task and achievement orientation of work first, pleasure second.[77] Such cultures include Switzerland, Germany, Austria, the Netherlands, and the Scandinavian countries. (This compares with being-oriented cultures—such as those of Belgium, France, Greece, Ireland, and most Latin American countries—where the general predisposition is more toward work to live, rather than live to work. Priority is given to affiliation and personal qualities in being-oriented cultures.)

In negotiations, Germans want detailed information before and during discussions, which can become lengthy. They give factors such as voice and speech control much weight. However, since Germany is a low-context society, communication is explicit, and Americans find negotiations easy to understand.[78] On the other hand, Germans communicating with businesspeople from a high-context culture such as that in Japan will be perceived as abrupt, insensitive, and indifferent. (Low-context refers to a direct communication style, compared with a high-context, indirect style. This variable is further explained in Chapter 4.) Whereas most Asians, for example, will be implicit and indirect, always aware of the need to save face for everyone concerned, most Germans are very direct and straightforward; tact and diplomacy takes second place to voicing their opinions.

Latin America Latin America is not one homogeneous area, of course; rather, it comprises many diverse, independent nations (most commonly referred to as those territories in the Americas where the Spanish or Portuguese languages prevail: Mexico; most of Central and South America; and Cuba, the Dominican Republic, and Puerto Rico in the Caribbean). Businesspeople are most likely to go to the rapidly developing economies of Chile and Brazil and, of course, to Mexico. (Portuguese is the language in Brazil.) Christianity—predominantly Roman Catholicism—prevails throughout Latin America. Latin America is the second most important emerging area economically, after Southeast Asia, with a GDP about half of China's and three times that of India.[79]

For our purposes here, although we acknowledge some regional cultural differences, we can draw upon the similarities of Latin American culture and business practices as a starting point in developing a helpful profile. Indeed, Latin America is relatively homogeneous culturally. Some of these generalities are discussed in the following paragraphs.

Using Hofstede's dimensions, we can generalize that most people are high on power distance and uncertainty avoidance, fairly high on masculinity, low on individualism, and tend to have a comparatively short-term orientation toward planning.

Latin Americans are typically being-oriented—with a primary focus on relationships and enjoying life in the present—as compared with the doing-oriented German (and mostly Western) culture discussed earlier. For Latin Americans, work lives and private lives are much more closely integrated than that of Westerners, so they emphasize enjoying life and have a more relaxed attitude toward work; because of that, Westerners often stereotype them as lazy rather than realizing that it is simply a different attitude toward the role of work in life. Connected with that attitude is the tendency to be rather fatalistic—that is, a feeling that events will be determined by God—rather than a feeling of their own control or responsibility for the future.

Most people in those countries have a fluid orientation toward time and tend to be multifocused, as discussed earlier in this chapter. Planning, negotiations, and scheduling take place in a relaxed and loose time framework; those processes take second place to building a trusting relationship and reaching a satisfactory agreement.[80] Communication is based on their high-context culture (this concept is discussed further in Chapter 4). This means that communication tends to be indirect and implicit, based largely on nonverbal interactions and the expectation that the listener draws inference from understanding the people and the circumstances without the need to be blunt or critical. Westerners need to take time, to be subtle and tactful, and to be incremental in discussing business to avoid being viewed as pushy and thus cutting off the relationship. Maintaining harmony and saving face is very important, as is the need to avoid embarrassing the other people involved. Managers must avoid any public criticism of employees, and any reprimand should be by way of suggestion.

Communication is also very expressive and demonstrative; courtesy, formality, and good manners are respected and lead to very complimentary and hospitable expressions to guests. Latin Americans tend to stand closer and touch more often than most Westerners, exuding the warmth and hospitality that is typical in the region.

Hierarchy prevails in all areas of life, from family to institutions such as government and the workplace. Each level and relationship is expected to show deference, honor, and respect to the next person or level. Status is conveyed by one's position and title and the formality of dress and etiquette. Traditional managers have the respect of their position and are typically autocratic and paternal. Loyalty is to the superior as a person. Employees expect to be assigned tasks with little participation involved, although younger managers who have been educated in Europe or the United States are starting to delegate. However, although most Latin Americans can show some flexibility in structure, Chile is probably the most order-oriented country; managers there are very high on uncertainty avoidance and try hard to minimize risk and strictly adhere to social and business norms.[81]

(Continued)

Relationships have priority whether among family, friends, or business contacts. Loyalty among family and friends leads to obligations, and often nepotism, which can lead to varying levels of quality in the work performance and less initiative than a Western businessperson might expect. Business is conducted through social contacts and referrals—that is, success does not depend as much on what you know as on whom you know. Latin Americans do business with people with whom they develop a trusting relationship, so it behooves businesspeople, here as in much of the world, to take time to develop a friendly, trusting relationship before getting down to business.

Western managers need to develop a warm attitude toward employees and business contacts and cultivate a sense of family at work; they should communicate individually with employees and colleagues and develop a trusting relationship.

Further discussion about the Mexican culture in particular is in the Comparative Management in Focus section in Chapter 11.

CULTURE AND MANAGEMENT STYLES AROUND THE WORLD

As an international manager, after you have researched the culture of a country in which you may be going to work or do business, and after you have developed a cultural profile, it is useful then to apply that information to develop an understanding of the expected management styles and ways of doing business that predominate in that region or in that type of business setting. The nearby feature, "Under the Lens: Doing Business in Brazil—Language, Culture, Customs, and Etiquette," illustrates the relationship between culture and management. Two further examples then follow in the sections titled "Saudi Arabia" and "Chinese Small Family Businesses."

UNDER THE LENS
Doing Business in Brazil—Language, Culture, Customs, and Etiquette

MAP 3.3 **Brazil**

Source: Olinchuk/Shutterstock

FIGURE 3-3 Brazilian Flag

Source: © CPJ Photography/Fotolia LLC

FIGURE 3-4 Rio De Janeiro Photo

Source: Mark Schwettmann/Shutterstock

FACTS AND STATISTICS

Location Eastern South America bordering Argentina, 1,224 km; Bolivia, 3,400 km; Colombia, 1,643 km; French Guiana, 673 km; Guyana, 1,119 km; Paraguay, 1,290 km; Peru, 1,560 km; Suriname, 597 km; Uruguay, 985 km; and Venezuela, 2,200 km

Capital Brazilia

Climate Mostly tropical but temperate in south

Population 184,101,109

Ethnic Make-up White (includes Portuguese, German, Italian, Spanish, and Polish) 55%; mixed white and black, 38%; black, 6%; other (includes Japanese, Arab, Amerindian), 1%

(Continued)

Religions Roman Catholic (nominal) 80%

Government Federative republic

LANGUAGE IN BRAZIL

Language is one of the strongest elements of Brazil's national unity. Nearly 100 percent of the population speaks Portuguese. The only exceptions are some members of Amerindian groups and pockets of immigrants, primarily from Japan and South Korea, who have not yet learned Portuguese. The principal families of Indian languages are Tupí, Arawak, Carib, and Gê.

There is about as much difference between the Portuguese spoken in Brazil and that spoken in Portugal as between the English spoken in the United States and that spoken in the United Kingdom. Within Brazil, there are no dialects of Portuguese, only moderate regional variation in accent, vocabulary, and use of personal nouns, pronouns, and verb conjugations. Variations tend to diminish because of mass media, especially national television networks the majority of Brazilians view.

BRAZILIAN SOCIETY AND CULTURE

Brazilian Diversity

- Brazil is a mixture of races and ethnicities, resulting in rich diversity.
- Many original Portuguese settlers married native women, which created a new race called "mestizos."
- "Mulattoes" are descendants of the Portuguese and African slaves.
- Slavery was abolished in 1888, creating, over time, a further blurring of racial lines.
- Unlike many other Latin American countries that have a distinct Indian population, Brazilians have intermarried to the point that it sometimes seems that almost everyone has a combination of European, African, and indigenous ancestry.

BRAZILIAN FAMILY VALUES

- The family is the foundation of the social structure and forms the basis of stability for most people.
- Families tend to be large (although family size has been diminishing in recent years), and the extended family is quite close.
- The individual derives a social network and assistance in times of need from the family.
- Nepotism is considered a positive thing because it implies that employing people one knows and trusts is of primary importance.

THE BRAZILIAN CLASS SYSTEM

- Despite the mixing of ethnicities, there is a class system in Brazil.
- Few Brazilians could be described as racist, although social discrimination based on skin color is a daily occurrence.
- The middle and upper classes often have only brief interaction with the lower classes—usually maids, drivers, and so on.
- Class is determined by economic status.
- There is a great disparity in wages—and therefore lifestyle and social aspirations—among the different classes.
- Although women make up 40% of the Brazilian workforce, they are typically found in lower-paid jobs such as teaching, administrative support, and nursing.
- The 1988 constitution prohibits discrimination against women, but inequities still exist. The one place where women are achieving equality is in the government.

ETIQUETTE AND CUSTOMS IN BRAZIL

Meeting Etiquette

- Men shake hands while maintaining steady eye contact when greeting one another.
- Women generally kiss each other, starting with the left and alternating cheeks.
- Hugging and backslapping are common greetings among Brazilian friends.
- If a woman wishes to shake hands with a man, she should extend her hand first.

Gift-Giving Etiquette

- If invited to a Brazilian's house, bring the hostess flowers or a small gift.
- Orchids are considered a very nice gift, but avoid purple ones.
- Avoid giving anything purple or black, because these are mourning colors.
- Handkerchiefs are also associated with funerals, so they do not make good gifts.
- Gifts are opened when received.

Dining Etiquette

If you are invited to a Brazilian's house:

- Arrive at least 30 minutes late if the invitation is for dinner.
- Arrive up to an hour late for a party or large gathering.
- Brazilians dress with a flair and judge others on their appearance. Casual dress is more formal than in many other countries. Always dress elegantly and err on the side of over-dressing rather than underdressing.
- If you did not bring a gift to the hostess, flowers the next day are always appreciated.

BUSINESS ETIQUETTE AND PROTOCOL IN BRAZIL

Relationships and Communication

Brazilians need to know whom they are doing business with before they can work effectively.

- Brazilians prefer face-to-face meetings to written communication because it allows them to know the person with whom they are doing business.
- The individual they deal with is more important than the company.
- Because this is a group culture, it is important not to do anything to embarrass a Brazilian.
- Criticizing an individual causes that person to lose face with the others in the meeting.
- The person making the criticism also loses face because he or she has disobeyed the unwritten rule.
- Communication is often informal and does not rely on strict rules of protocol. Those who feel they have something to say will generally add their opinion.
- It is considered acceptable to interrupt someone who is speaking.
- Face-to-face, oral communication is preferred over written communication. At the same time, when it comes to business agreements, Brazilians insist on drawing up detailed legal contracts.

BUSINESS NEGOTIATIONS

- Expect questions about your company because Brazilians are more comfortable doing business with people and companies they know.
- Wait for your Brazilian colleagues to raise the business subject. Never rush the relationship-building time.
- Brazilians take time when negotiating. Do not rush them or appear impatient.
- Expect a great deal of time to be spent reviewing details.
- Often, the people you negotiate with will not have decision-making authority.
- It is advisable to hire a translator if your Portuguese is not fluent.
- Use local lawyers and accountants for negotiations. Brazilians resent an outside legal presence.
- Brazilian business is hierarchical. Decisions are made by the highest-ranking person.
- Brazilians negotiate with people, not companies. Do not change your negotiating team or you may have to start over from the beginning.

BUSINESS MEETING ETIQUETTE

- Business appointments are required and can often be scheduled on short notice; however, it is best to make them 2 to 3 weeks in advance.
- Confirm the meeting in writing. It is not uncommon for appointments to be canceled or changed at the last minute.

(Continued)

- In Sao Paulo and Brasilia, it is important to arrive on time for meetings. In Rio de Janeiro and other cities, it is acceptable to arrive a few minutes late for a meeting.
- Do not appear impatient if you are kept waiting. Brazilians see time as something outside their control, and the demands of relationships take precedence over adhering to a strict schedule.
- Meetings are generally rather informal.
- Expect to be interrupted while you are speaking or making a presentation.
- Avoid confrontations. Do not appear frustrated with your Brazilian colleagues.

DRESS ETIQUETTE

- Brazilians pride themselves on dressing well.
- Men should wear conservative, dark-colored business suits. Three-piece suits typically indicate that someone is an executive.
- Women should wear suits or dresses that are elegant and feminine with good-quality accessories. Manicures are expected.

BUSINESS CARDS

- Business cards are exchanged during introductions with everyone at a meeting.
- It is advisable, although not required, to have the other side of your business card translated into Portuguese.
- Present your business card with the Portuguese side facing the recipient.

Source: http://www.kwintessential.co.uk/resources/global-etiquette/brazil-country-profile.html, September 5, 2011. Used with permission of www.kwintessential.co.uk.

Saudi Arabia

Understanding how business is conducted in the modern Middle East requires an understanding of the Arab culture because the Arab peoples are the majority there, and most of them are Muslim. As discussed in the opening profile, the Arab culture is intertwined with the pervasive influence of Islam. Even though not all Middle Easterners are Arab, Arab culture and management style predominate in the Arabian Gulf region. Shared culture, religion, and language underlie behavioral similarities throughout the Arab world. Islam permeates Saudi life—Allah is always present, controls everything, and is frequently referred to in conversation.[82] Employees may spend more than two hours a day in prayer as part of the life pattern that intertwines work with religion, politics, and social life.

Arab history and culture are based on tribalism, with its norms of reciprocity of favors, support, obligation, and identity passed on to the family unit, which is the primary structural model. Family life is based on closer personal ties than in the West. Arabs value personal relationships, honor, and saving face for all concerned; these values take precedence over the work at hand or verbal accuracy. Outsiders must realize that establishing a trusting relationship and respect for Arab social norms has to precede any attempts at business discussions. Honor, pride, and dignity are at the core of shame societies such as the Arabs. As such, shame and honor provide the basis for social control and motivation.[83] Circumstances dictate what is right or wrong and what constitutes acceptable behavior.

Arabs avoid open admission of error at all costs because weakness (*muruwwa*) is a failure to be manly. It is sometimes difficult for Westerners to get at the truth because of the Arab need to avoid showing weakness; instead, Arabs present a desired or idealized situation. Shame is also brought on someone who declines to fulfill a request or a favor; therefore, a business arrangement is left open if something has yet to be completed.

The communication style of Middle Eastern societies is high context (that is, implicit and indirect), and their use of time is polychronic; many activities can be taking place at the same time, with constant interruptions commonplace. The imposition of deadlines is considered rude, and business schedules take a backseat to the perspective that events will occur sometime when Allah wills (*bukra insha Allah*). Arabs give primary importance to hospitality; they are

EXHIBIT 3-7 Behavior That Will Likely Cause Offense in Saudi Arabia

- Introducing business subjects too soon.
- Commenting on a man's wife or female children over 12 years of age.
- Raising colloquial questions that may be considered as an invasion of privacy.
- Using disparaging or swear words and off-color or obscene attempts at humor.
- Talking about religion, politics, or Israel.
- Bringing gifts of alcohol or using alcohol, which is prohibited in Saudi Arabia.
- Requesting favors from those in authority or esteem, for it is considered impolite for Arabs to say no.
- Pointing your finger at someone or showing the soles of your feet when seated.

Source: Based on excerpts from P. R. Harris and R. T. Moran, *Managing Cultural Differences*, 5th ed. (Houston: Gulf Publishing, 2000).

cordial to business associates and lavish in their entertainment, constantly offering strong black coffee (which you should not refuse) and banquets before considering business transactions. Westerners must realize the importance of personal contacts and networking, socializing and building close relationships and trust, practicing patience regarding schedules, and doing business in person. Exhibit 3-7 gives some selected actions and nonverbal behaviors that may offend Arabs. The relationship between cultural values and norms in Saudi Arabia and managerial behaviors is illustrated in Exhibit 3-8.

EXHIBIT 3-8 The Relationship between Culture and Managerial Behaviors in Saudi Arabia

Cultural Values	Managerial Behaviors
Tribal and family loyalty	Work group loyalty
	Paternal sociability
	Careful selection of employees
	Nepotism
Arabic language	Business as an intellectual activity
	Access to employees and peers
	Management by walking around
	Conversation as recreation
Close and warm friendships	People orientation
	Theory Y management
	Avoidance of judgment
Islam	Sensitivity to Islamic virtues
	Observance of the Qur'an and Sharia
	Work as personal or spiritual growth
	Adherence to norms
Honor and shame	Conflict avoidance
	Positive reinforcement
	Private correction of mistakes
	Avoidance of competition
	Responsibility
Polychronic use of time	Right- and left-brain facility
	Action oriented
	Patience and flexibility
Male domination	Separation of sexes
	Open work life; closed family life

Source: Based on excerpts from P. R. Harris and R. T. Moran, *Managing Cultural Differences,* 5th ed. (Houston: Gulf Publishing, 2000).

Chinese Family Small Businesses

The predominance of small businesses in China and the region highlights the need for managers from around the world to gain an understanding of how such businesses operate. Many small businesses—most of which are family or extended-family businesses—become part of the value chain (suppliers, buyers, retailers, etc.) within industries in which foreign firms may compete.

Some specifics of Chinese management style and practices in particular are presented here as they apply to small businesses. (Further discussion of the Chinese culture continues in Chapter 5 in the context of negotiation.) It is important to note that no matter the size of a Chinese company, but especially in small businesses, it is the all-pervasive presence and use of *guanxi* that provides the little red engine of business transactions in China. *Guanxi* means "connections"—the network of relationships the Chinese cultivate through friendship and affection; it entails the exchange of favors and gifts to provide an obligation to reciprocate favors. Those who share a *guanxi* network share an unwritten code.[84] The philosophy and structure of Chinese businesses comprise paternalism, mutual obligation, responsibility, hierarchy, familialism, personalism, and connections. Autocratic leadership is the norm, with the owner using his or her power—but with a caring about other people that may predominate over efficiency.

According to Lee, the major differences between Chinese management styles and those of their Western counterparts are human-centeredness, family-centeredness, centralization of power, and small size.[85] Their human-centered management style puts people ahead of a business relationship and focuses on friendship, loyalty, and trustworthiness.[86] The family is extremely important in Chinese culture, and any small business tends to be run like a family.

Globalization has resulted in ethnic Chinese businesses (in China or other Asian countries) adapting to more competitive management styles. They are moving away from the traditional centralized power structure in Chinese organizations that comprised the boss and a few family members at the top and the employees at the bottom, with no ranking among the workers. In fact, family members no longer manage many Chinese businesses. Frequently, the managers are those sons and daughters who have studied and worked overseas before returning to the family company—or even foreign expatriates. Examples of Chinese capitalism responding to change and working to globalize through growth are Eu Yan Sang Holdings Ltd., the Hiap Moh Printing businesses, and the Pacific International Line.[87]

As Chinese firms in many modern regions in the Pacific Rim seek to modernize and compete locally and globally, a tug of war has begun between the old and the new: the traditional Chinese management practices and the increasingly imported Western management styles. As Lee discusses, this struggle is encapsulated in the different management perspectives of the old and young generations. A two-generational study of Chinese managers by Ralston et al. also found generational shifts in work values in China. They concluded that the new generation manager is more individualistic, more independent, and less risk averse in the pursuit of profits. However, they also found the new generation holding on to their Confucian values, concluding that the new generation may be viewed as "crossverging their Eastern and Western influences, while on the road of modernization."[88]

CONCLUSION

This chapter has explored various cultural values and how managers can be prepared to understand them with the help of some general cultural profiles. The following chapters focus on application of this cultural knowledge to management in an international environment (or, alternatively in a domestic multicultural environment)—especially as relevant to cross-cultural communication (Chapter 4), negotiation and decision making (Chapter 5), and motivating and leading (Chapter 11). Culture and communication are essentially synonymous. What happens when people from different cultures communicate, and how can international managers understand the underlying process and adapt their styles and expectations accordingly? For the answers, read the next chapter.

Summary of Key Points

- The culture of a society comprises the shared values, understandings, assumptions, and goals that are passed down through generations and imposed by members of the society. These unique sets of cultural and national differences strongly influence the attitudes and expectations—and therefore the on-the-job behavior—of individuals and groups.

- Managers must develop cultural sensitivity to anticipate and accommodate behavioral differences in various societies. As part of that sensitivity, they must avoid parochialism—an attitude that assumes one's own management techniques are best in any situation or location and that other people should follow one's patterns of behavior.

- From his research in 50 countries, Hofstede proposed four underlying value dimensions that help identify and describe the cultural profile of a country and affect organizational processes: power distance, uncertainty avoidance, individualism, and masculinity. In his later research, Hofstede explored the concept of long-term versus short-term orientation

  to explain the cultural variation of the types of decisions people make.

- Through his research, Fons Trompenaars confirmed some similar dimensions and found other unique dimensions: obligation, emotional orientation, privacy, and source of power and status.

- The GLOBE project team of 170 researchers in 62 countries concluded the presence of a number of other dimensions and ranked countries on those dimensions, including assertiveness, performance orientation, future orientation, and humane orientation. Gupta et al. from that team found geographical clusters on nine of the GLOBE project cultural dimensions.

- On-the-job conflicts in international management frequently arise out of conflicting values and orientations regarding time, change, material factors, and individualism.

- Managers can use research results and personal observations to develop a character sketch, or cultural profile, of a country. This profile can help managers anticipate how to motivate people and coordinate work processes in a particular international context.

Discussion Questions

3-1. What is meant by the culture of a society, and why is it important for international managers to understand it? Do you notice cultural differences among your classmates? How do those differences affect the class environment? How do they affect your group projects?

3-2. Discuss the types of operational conflicts that could occur in an international context because of different attitudes toward time, change, material factors, and individualism. Give examples relative to specific countries.

3-3. Discuss how the Internet and culture interact. Which most affects the other, and how? Give some examples.

3-4. Discuss collectivism as it applies to the Japanese workplace. What managerial functions does it affect?

3-5. Discuss the role of Islam in cross-cultural relations and business operations.

Application Exercises

3-6. Develop a cultural profile for one of the countries in the following list. Form small groups of students and compare your findings in class with those of another group preparing a profile for another country. Be sure to compare specific findings regarding religion, kinship, recreation, and other subsystems. What are the prevailing attitudes toward time, change, material factors, and individualism?

Any African country
People's Republic of China
Mexico
France
India

3-7. In small groups of students, research Hofstede's findings regarding the four dimensions of power distance, uncertainty avoidance, masculinity, and individualism for one of the following countries in comparison to the United States. (Your instructor can assign the countries to avoid duplication.) Present your findings to the class. Assume you are a U.S. manager of a subsidiary in the foreign country and explain how differences on these dimensions are likely to affect your management tasks. What suggestions do you have for dealing with these differences in the workplace?

Brazil
Italy
People's Republic of China
Russia

Experiential Exercises

3-8. A large Baltimore manufacturer of cabinet hardware had been working for months to locate a suitable distributor for its products in Europe. Finally invited to present a demonstration to a reputable distributing company in Frankfurt, it sent one of its most promising young executives, Fred Wagner, to make the presentation. Fred not only spoke fluent German but also felt a special interest in this assignment because his paternal grandparents had immigrated to the United States from the Frankfurt area during the 1920s. When Fred arrived at the conference room where he would be making his presentation, he shook hands firmly, greeted everyone with a friendly *guten tag*, and even remembered to bow the head slightly as is the German custom. Fred, an effective speaker and past president of the Baltimore Toastmasters Club, prefaced his presentation with a few humorous anecdotes to set a relaxed and receptive atmosphere. However, he felt that his presentation was not well received by the company executives. In fact, his instincts were correct, for the German company chose not to distribute Fred's hardware products. What went wrong?

3-9. Bill Nugent, an international real estate developer from Dallas, had made a 2:30 P.M. appointment with Mr. Abdullah, a high-ranking government official in Riyadh, Saudi Arabia. From the beginning, things did not go well for Bill. First, he was kept waiting until nearly 3:45 P.M. before he was ushered into Mr. Abdullah's office. When he finally did get in, several other men were also in the room. Even though Bill felt that he wanted to get down to business with Mr. Abdullah, he was reluctant to get too specific because he considered much of what they needed to discuss sensitive and private. To add to Bill's sense of frustration, Mr. Abdullah seemed more interested in engaging in meaningless small talk than in dealing with the substantive issues concerning their business. How might you help Bill deal with his frustration?

3-10. Tom Forrest, an up-and-coming executive for a U.S. electronics company, was sent to Japan to work out the details of a joint venture with a Japanese electronics firm. During the first several weeks, Tom felt that the negotiations were proceeding better than he had expected. He found that he had very cordial working relationships with the team of Japanese executives, and in fact, they had agreed on the major policies and strategies governing the new joint venture. During the third week of negotiations, Tom was present at a meeting held to review their progress. The meeting was chaired by the president of the Japanese firm, Mr. Hayakawa, a man in his mid-forties, who had recently taken over the presidency from his 82-year-old grandfather. The new president, who had been involved in most of the negotiations during the preceding weeks, seemed to Tom to be one of the strongest advocates of the plan that had been developed to date. Hayakawa's grandfather, the recently retired president, also was present at the meeting. After the plans had been discussed in some detail, the octogenarian past president proceeded to give a long soliloquy about how some of the features of this plan violated the traditional practices on which the company had been founded. Much to Tom's amazement, Mr. Hayakawa did nothing to explain or defend the policies and strategies that they had taken weeks to develop. Feeling extremely frustrated, Tom then gave a fairly strong argument in defense of the plan. To Tom's further amazement, no one else in the meeting spoke up in defense of the plan. The tension in the air was quite heavy, and the meeting adjourned shortly thereafter. Within days, the Japanese firm completely terminated the negotiations on the joint venture. How could you help Tom understand better this bewildering situation?

Source: Gary P. Ferraro, *The Cultural Dimensions of International Business*, 2nd ed. (Upper Saddle River, NJ: Prentice Hall, 1994).

CASE STUDY

Case Study: An Australian Manager in an American Company

"Qantas Flight 23 to Sydney is now boarding. Please have your boarding passes and passports ready for the attendant at the gate."

Les Collins picked up his briefcase and started toward the jet way. He paused to look around the waiting area and, as had been the case so often here in Houston, he saw nothing to indicate that he was in a foreign country. Certainly the accents were different from in Sydney, but the language was English and readily understandable. This superficial familiarity, he concluded, must help explain why he had had difficulties adjusting to his role at the Global Oil Company office in Houston.

Global Oil Company, or GOC, was headquartered in Houston, Texas, with partners and subsidiaries in countries around the world. Les had worked at GOC's Sydney office for eight years before being offered the chance to work at Houston headquarters for two years. His boss, Jim Branson, had encouraged Les to apply for the job in Houston because he knew it would enhance Les's chances for promotion within GOC-Australia. Although Les's family—his wife and two middle school–age children—was not very enthusiastic about the move, he reluctantly applied for the job because he knew it was critical to his success at GOC.

As he settled back in his seat on the flight to Sydney, Les thought back to the day he arrived in Houston over a year ago. Les had left Sydney on a hot, humid day in January and arrived 30 hours later to find Houston almost closed down due to a sleet and ice storm. That juxtaposition of seasons probably should have alerted him that there would be many differences between Australia and the United States. When he hailed a taxi outside the terminal at IAH, the driver looked at him in amazement when Les opened the door to the front seat and sat down next to the driver.

During his first few weeks at the Houston office, everything seemed to go well. He met with his staff to introduce himself and his goals for his two-year assignment. Everyone seemed friendly enough, although he didn't get much feedback at that meeting or in subsequent meetings on his request for their ideas and input on how he could fit in and be effective. Thinking that maybe he needed to get to know the staff in a more informal setting, he invited them to join him after work one day at a local pub. Several staff members begged off, citing personal commitments, and the three senior managers who did come were clearly uncomfortable and left after about 30 minutes of awkward conversation.

Over the next six months, Les stayed busy learning operations for his area at GOC headquarters. He met often with his Houston boss, Tom Sanchez, to discuss the changes Tom wanted Les to help him realize during his tenure there.

"I'm counting on you, Les, to help me bring the staff around on the changes we've discussed. Your group hasn't moved nearly as fast as I think they could and that's partly due to the staff's reluctance to change the ways they've always done things. I'm confident that a new leader, especially someone from a completely different country, will convince them of the soundness of what I'm proposing.

"Keep me posted on your progress," Tom concluded, as he walked Les to the reception area outside his office.

One of the things Les noticed soon after arriving in Houston was how many more management levels the U.S. operation had than comparable offices in Australia. The hierarchy seemed excessive to Les, and he sought to break down some of the communication barriers he perceived by meeting with all staff members in one large meeting.

At one of these meetings, Les brought up the proposed changes in procedures that he had discussed with Sanchez. "I know that some of you may not be in favor of the changes we're proposing and I'd like to know your reasons for this. Let's have an open discussion of the changes in general and see where our major disagreement lies."

After a few minutes of silence, one of the senior managers explained his reasons for resisting a change in their reporting procedures for expenses. "I'm not sure that the new method will capture a true picture of expenses and outlay if we change what we're doing now. I'm not opposed to making changes that improve our work—I just am not convinced that the new method will be better."

"Okay, I'd like to hear from others on that specific change. Let's table this discussion," Les said.

The managers and staff at the table looked at each other in confusion at that point. No one said anything for several minutes and Les concluded that no one else had an objection or concern on this particular point. The meeting continued for another hour as Les moved through the list of changes he was charged with making and when no one offered much objection or proposed any alternatives, he concluded that his predecessor and Sanchez had misinterpreted the staff's resistance to the changes.

A week later, in a meeting with Bill Crosby, one of the senior managers in his department, Les decided to get his manager's views on how to involve junior managers in decisions and how to encourage their ideas on various topics.

"I notice that in most meetings only the senior managers seem to participate in discussions," Les began. "I'm eager to have more input on some ideas I have for a new marketing plan, and I'm wondering how I can get junior managers and staff to contribute in our meetings."

Bill hesitated before saying, "Sometimes staff are reluctant to put forward ideas when their bosses are in the same meeting. Perhaps you should have some of the senior managers solicit ideas in their own staff meetings and then bring these to the meeting with you."

"But what about the synergy we can create if we have people from different levels discussing an idea together? Especially if the idea will affect the work staff are expected to do. I think there's too much separation of people by level in our department. I'd like to eliminate some of the impediments to collaboration that hierarchy creates," Les said. "What are your thoughts on how to do that?"

"I'll need to take some time to think about that," Bill said. "Maybe we can talk about it in our next one-on-one."

Later that day, during lunch with one of his peers in the company cafeteria, Bill brought up his discussion with Les. "He wants to eliminate some of the barriers that the hierarchy puts in the way of collaboration," Bill began. "What exactly do you think he means by collaboration? We all get along just fine as far as I can see. We cooperate when we need to. And I really don't know how to get staff to speak their minds if they don't want to. I don't feel comfortable forcing anybody to be part of a discussion in a meeting if they prefer to just listen."

At the next all-staff meeting, Les began by handing out a sheet with five topics on it. "Rather than following one of our regular agendas today, I thought we might do a little brainstorming on the topics I've outlined here. As you can see, these topics all relate to marketing, and what we come up with in our discussion can go a long way toward finalizing that plan.

"And here's a twist on our usual meeting protocol: instead of my leading the discussion, I'm going to assign one of these topics to five people and let you take over the discussion."

In thinking about the meeting afterward, Les decided that although it hadn't been a complete success, he thought he had made some progress in getting increased participation. When one of the senior managers requested a meeting a couple of days later, Les was surprised at the manager's comments about the meeting.

"I'm sure you were sincere in your request for ideas from everybody but I need to tell you that you made a lot of people very uncomfortable. Staff are not used to leading a discussion with senior managers present. When that staff member is leading a brainstorming session and has to tell a manager that he's out of order because he's criticizing someone's idea, you're putting the staff member in a really awkward position."

"I guess I don't understand," Les said. "The whole point of doing what I did was to break down the barriers that make people feel uncomfortable. I think everybody has good ideas, and I'm trying to figure out how I can get them to share those ideas. I thought putting people in different roles would be helpful."

At his next meeting with Tom Sanchez, Les expressed his frustration with achieving as much as he hoped for when he started.

"It just seems as though I'm being stonewalled at every turn. In fact, I've heard that several people are thinking of transferring to another department," Les said. "What am I missing? I've done things just like I do at GOC-Sydney, but the results are not the same.

"Maybe I can make some progress when I get back after vacation. Sometimes three weeks away helps give a different perspective on things."

"Yes, Les," Tom began, "we'll need to talk about this when you get back from vacation. Three weeks is a pretty long time for a senior manager to be gone, but I know you and your family have plans to visit a lot of the national parks in the west, so I reluctantly approved your request. Have a good trip and I'll talk with you when you get back."

When Les returned from vacation, Tom Sanchez was out of the office for a week and they didn't have a chance to meet before Les got word that his mother had passed away suddenly and that he needed to return to Sydney for the funeral. As he headed for Sydney, Les wondered how he could explain to his former boss in Sydney the problems he was having at GOC headquarters.

Discussion Questions

3-11. Using Geert Hofstede's cultural characteristics, compare Australia and the United States on various measures. As you'll see, the two countries are fairly similar, but there are some differences that may help explain Les Collins's apparent lack of success in the American setting. Which of these do you think is the most significant and why?

3-12. What could GOC have done to prepare Collins for his assignment in the United States? Outline an action plan for companies to use in preparing executives—and their families—for international assignments.

3-13. Articulate and evaluate your own opinion about the degree of distance prevalent in U.S. companies between managers and their direct reports. Who is protected by this management style? What adverse organizational impacts might result from this style?

Source: Linda Catlin. Ms Catlin is an organizational anthropologist and the co-author of *International Business: Cultural Sourcebook and Case Studies*. She consults with clients on projects related to crosscultural business communications, organizational culture, and organizational change dynamics. Her clients include the Mayo Clinic, the Kellogg Foundation, General Motors, Ascension Health, and BASF. Linda Catlin, Claymore Associates. Used with permission.

Endnotes

1. Ian Black, "Saudi Digital Generation Takes on Twitter, YouTube,…and the Authorities," *Guardian,* Tuesday, December 17, 2013; Helen Gaskell, "Saudi Arabia Reviews Social Media Laws," ArabianBusiness.com, June 3, 2014, http://www.socialmedia-series.com/saudi/, accessed October 1, 2014; "A Virtual Revolution; Social Media in Saudi Arabia," *Economist*, 412, 8904, 57, September 13, 2014; Statista, http://www.statista.com/statistics/284451/saudi-arabia-social-network-penetration/, accessed October 1, 2014; Saudi Social Media Summit, http://www.socialmedia-series.com/saudi/, accessed October 1, 2014; "Social Media Plays Matchmaking Role in Saudi Arabia," February 11, 2014, http://www.al-monitor.com/pulse/culture/2014/03/social-media-saudi-breaking-barriers.html##fixzz3FCdKXc5r, accessed October 3, 2014.

2. A. Levit, "Seeing the World as Your Stage," *International New York Times*, June 8, 2013.

3. P. Christopher Earley and Elaine Mosakowski, "Cultural Intelligence," *Harvard Business Review* 82, No. 10 (October 2004), pp. 139–146.

4. P. C. Earley and S. Ang, *Cultural Intelligence: Individual Interactions across Cultures.* (Palo Alto, CA: Stanford University Press, 2003).

5. David A. Ricks, *Big Business Blunders: Mistakes in Multinational Marketing* (Homewood, IL: Dow Jones–Irwin, 1983).

6. Carla Joinson, "Why HR Managers Need to Think Globally," *HR Magazine* (April, 1998), pp. 2–7.

7. Ibid.

8. J. Stewart Black and Mark Mendenhall, "Cross-Cultural Training Effectiveness: A Review and a Theoretical Framework for Future Research," *Academy of Management Review* 15, No. 1 (1990), pp. 113–136.

9. V. Taras et al., "Three Decades of Research on National Culture in the Workplace, *Organizational Dynamics* (2011), doi:10.1016/j.orgdyn.2011.04.006.

10. Geert Hofstede, *Culture's Consequences: International Differences in Work-Related Values* (Beverly Hills, CA: Sage Publications, 1980), P. 25; E. T. Hall, *The Silent Language* (Greenwich, CT: Fawcett, 1959). For a more detailed definition of the culture of a society, see A. L. Kroeber and C. Kluckholhn, "A Critical Review of Concepts and Definitions," in *Peabody Museum Papers* 47, No. 1 (Cambridge, MA: Harvard University Press, 1952), p. 181.

11. David Dressler and Donald Carns, *Sociology: The Study of Human Interaction* (New York: Knopf, 1969), pp. 56–57.

12. Maia de la Baume and Steven Erlanger, "Social and Economic Ills Feed Rise of a Far-Right Party in France," www.nytimes.com, March 27, 2011.

13. Hofstede, 1980.

14. Syed Anwar, "DaimlerChrysler AG: A Decade of Global Strategic Challenges Leads to Divorce in 2007," case study in Helen Deresky, *Managing across Borders and Cultures*, 6th ed. (Upper Saddle River, NJ: Prentice Hall), pp. 325–337.

15. Emma Jacobs, "20 Questions: Kenichi Watanabe, Nomura: 'I don't like to analyse myself,'" *Financial Times*, London (UK), September 23, 2011, p. 12.

16. Lane Kelley, Arthur Whatley, and Reginald Worthley, "Assessing the Effects of Culture on Managerial Attitudes: A Three-Culture Test," *Journal of International Business Studies* (Summer 1987), pp. 17–31.

17. Oded Shenkar, "Cultural Distance Revisited: Towards a More Rigorous Conceptualization and Measurement of Cultural Differences," *Journal of International Business* 43, No. 1 (January 2012), pp. 1–11.

18. Ibid.

19. Luciardo Nardon and Richard M. Steers, "Managing Cross-Cultural Encounters: Putting Things in Context," *Organizational Dynamics* 43 (2014), pp. 138–145.

20. Tarun Khanna, "Contextual Intelligence," *Harvard Business Review*, 59 (September 2014).

21. Ibid.

22. Jangho Lee, T. W. Roehl, and Soonkyoo Choe, "What Makes Management Style Similar and Distinct across Borders? Growth Experience and Culture in Korean and Japanese Firms," *Journal of International Business Studies* 31, No. 4 (2000), pp. 631–652.

23. C. Sanchez-Runde et al., "Looking beyond Western Leadership Models," *Organizational Dynamics* (2011), doi:10.1016/j.orgdyn.2011.04.008, in press.

24. E. T. Hall, "The Silent Language in Overseas Business," *Harvard Business Review* (May–June 1960).

25. "One Big Market," *Wall Street Journal*, February 6, 1989, p. 16.

26. Baruch Shimoni, "The Representation of Cultures in International and Cross Cultural Management: Hybridizations of Management Cultures in Thailand and Israel," *Journal of International Management* 17 (2011), pp. 30–41.

27. Ibid.

28. Ibid.

29. Philip R. Harris and Robert T. Moran, *Managing Cultural Differences* (Houston: Gulf Publishing, 1987).

30. Data from various sources, including the U.S. Bureau of the Census international database, U.S. State Department Reports, U.N. Human Development Report.

31. Agam Nag, "Cross Cultural Management: An Indian Perspective," *Business Review, Cambridge* 17.2 (Summer 2011), pp. 255–260.

32. Ibid.

33. Ibid.

34. A. Ali, "The Islamic Work Ethic in Arabia," *Journal of Psychology* 126 (1992), pp. 507–519.

35. "Buddhism in the Thai Workplace," www.businesstrendsasia.com, accessed February 10, 2012.

36. Mansour Javidan and Robert J. House, "Cultural Acumen for the Global Manager: Lessons from Project GLOBE," *Organizational Dynamics* (Spring 2001), pp. 289–305.

37. V. Gupta, P. J. Hanges, and P. Dorfman, "Cultural Clusters: Methodology and Findings," *Journal of World Business* 37 (2002), pp. 11–15.

38. Ibid.

39. Taras et al., 2011.

40. Geert Hofstede, *Cultures and Organizations: Software of the Mind* (New York: McGraw-Hill, 1997), pp. 79–108.

41. K. Roth, T. Kostova, and M. Dakhli, "Exploring Cultural Misfit: Causes and Consequences," *International Business Review* 20 (2011), pp. 15–26.

42. Elizabeth Weldon and Elisa L. Mustari, "Felt Dispensability in Groups of Coactors: The Effects of Shared Responsibility on Cognitive Effort" (unpublished manuscript, Kellogg Graduate School of Management, Northwestern University).

43. P. Christopher Earley, "Social Loafing and Collectivism: A Comparison of the United States and the People's Republic of China," *Administrative Science Quarterly* 34 (1989), pp. 565–581.

44. G. Hofstede, *Culture's Consequences: Comparing Values, Behaviors, Institutions, and Organizations across Nations*, 2nd ed. (Thousand Oaks, CA: Sage, 2001), 500–502.

45. F. Trompenaars, *Riding the Waves of Culture* (London: Nicholas Brealey, 1993).

46. L. Hoeklin, *Managing Cultural Differences: Strategies for Competitive Advantage* (New York: The Economist Intelligence Unit/Addison-Wesley, 1995).

47. P. Steel and V. Taras, "Culture as a Consequence: A Multilevel Multivariate Meta-analysis of the Effects of Individual and Country Characteristics on Work-related Cultural Values," *Journal of International Management*, 16 (2010), pp. 211–233.

48. Ibid.

49. Ibid.

50. M. Muethel and M. Hoegl, "Cultural and Societal Influences on Shared Leadership in Globally Dispersed Teams," *Journal of International Management* 16 (2010), pp. 234–246.

51. www.internetworldstats.com, accessed February 19, 2014.

52. H. Jeff Smith, "Information Privacy and Marketing: What the U.S. Should (and Shouldn't) Learn from Europe," *California Management Review* 43, No. 2 (2001), pp. 30–34.

53. Ibid.

54. Ibid.

55. R. Howells, "Update on Safe Harbor for International Data Transfer," *Direct Marketing* 63, No. 4 (2000), p. 40.

56. Smith, pp. 30–34.

57. Hiroko Tabuchi, "Quick Action Helps Google Win Friends in Japan," *New York Times Online*, July 10, 2011; Kevin J. O'Brien, "Privacy Laws Trip Up Google's Expansion in Parts of Europe," www.nytimes.com, November 18, 2008; Scott Bradner, "Telling Google and Others to Do Less Evil," *Network World*, 25, No. 16 (2008), p. 25; "EU Panel Queries Google on Privacy Concerns," *Wall Street Journal*, May 26, 2007; Laura Smith, "Spotlight on the Spy in the Surf," *Information World Review*, Oxford, U.K., November 2007, i.240; Andrew Edgecliffe-Johnson, "Google Founders in Web Privacy Warning," www.ft.com, May 19, 2008.

58. Hiroko Tabuchi, "Quick Action Helps Google Win Friends in Japan," *New York Times Online*, July 10, 2011.

59. Ibid.

60. Adam Liptak, "When American and European Ideas of Privacy Collide," www.nytimes.com, February 26, 2010.

61. www.nytimes.com, May 22, 2012.

62. Mark Landler and Michael Barbaro, "Wal-Mart Finds That Its Formula Doesn't Fit Every Culture," *New York Times*, August 2, 2006.

63. Geert Hofstede, *Culture's Consequences: International Differences in Work-Related Values* (Beverly Hills, CA: Sage, 1980).

64. George W. England, "Managers and Their Value Systems: A Five-Country Comparative Study," *Columbia Journal of World Business* (Summer 1978), pp. 35–44.

65. Philip R. Harris and Robert T. Moran, *Managing Cultural Differences* (Houston: Gulf Publishing, 2004); Lennie Copeland and Lewis Griggs, *Going International* (New York: Random House, 1985); Boye De Mente, *Japanese Etiquette and Ethics in Business* (Lincolnwood, IL: NTC Business Books, 1989); R. L. Tung, *Business Negotiations with the Japanese* (Lexington, MA: Lexington Books, 1984); W. G. Ouchi and A. M. Jaeger, "Theory Z Organization: Stability in the Midst of Mobility," *Academy of Management Review* 3, No. 2 (1978), pp. 305–314; Fernando Quezada and James E. Boyce, "Latin America," in *Comparative Management*, Raghu Nath, ed. (Cambridge, MA: Ballinger Publishing, 1988), pp. 245–270; Simcha Ronen, *Comparative and Multinational Management* (New York: John Wiley and Sons, 1986); and V. Terpstra and K. David, *The Cultural Environment of International Business*, 3rd ed. (Cincinnati, OH: South-Western, 1991).

66. Akio Kuzuoka, a forty-year employee at a Japanese company, quoted in the *Wall Street Journal*, December 29, 2000.

67. Ibid.

68. FT Business School, "Go West for a New Mind-Set," *Financial Times*, October 10, 2004.

69. Ibid.

70. "Doing Business in Japan—Japanese Social and Business Culture," www.communicaid.com, accessed April 20, 2012.

71. www.ft.com, November 26, 2008.

72. Yumiko Ono and William Spindle, "Japan's Long Decline Makes One Thing Rise—Individualism," *Wall Street Journal*, December 29, 2000, p. 5.

73. D. Walker, T. Walker, and J. Schmitz, *Doing Business Internationally*, 2nd ed. (New York: McGraw-Hill, 2003), pp. 188–189.

74. Nicholas Kulish, "The Lines a German Won't Cross," www.nytimes.com, April 4, 2009.

75. E. T. Hall and M. R. Hall, *Understanding Cultural Differences* (Yarmouth, ME: Intercultural Press, 1990), p. 4.

76. "Germany: Language, Culture, Customs and Business Etiquette," www.kwintessential.co.uk, accessed April 21, 2012.

77. Walker et al., 2003.

78. E. T. Hall and M. R. Hall, *Understanding Cultural Differences* (Yarmouth, ME: Intercultural Press, 1990), 4.

79. Roberto S. Vassolo, Julio O. De Castro, and Luis R. Gomez-Mejia, "Managing in Latin America: Common Issues and a Research Agenda," *Academy of Management Perspectives*, November 2011.

80. Walker et al., 2003, p. 188.

81. Ibid., p. 195.

82. P. R. Harris and R. T. Moran, *Managing Cultural Differences*, 4th ed. (Houston, TX: Gulf Publishing Co., 1996).

83. Ibid.

84. John A. Pearce II and Richard B. Robinson Jr, "Cultivating *Guanxi* as a Foreign Investor Strategy," *Business Horizons* 43, No. 1 (2000), p. 31.

85. J. Lee, "Culture and Management: A Study of Small Chinese Family Business in Singapore," *Journal of Small Business Management* (July 1996), pp. 17–24.

86. R. Sheng, "Outsiders' Perception of the Chinese," *Columbia Journal of World Business* 14, No. 2 (Summer 2000), pp. 16–22.

87. Henry Yeung Wai-chung, "Debunking the Myths of Chinese Capitalism," May 11, 2005, www.nus.edu.sg/cororate/research/gallery/research30.htm.

88. D. A. Ralston, Yu-Kai-Ceng, Xun Wang, R. H. Terpstra, and He Wei, "An Analysis of Managerial Work Values across the Six Regions of China," paper presented at the Academy of International Business, Boston, November 1994.

4 Communicating Across Cultures

OUTLINE

OBJECTIVES

4-1. To recognize the communication process and how cultural differences can cause noise in that process.

4-2. To appreciate the cultural variables that affect communication for both the sender and the listener.

4-3. To be aware of the impact of IT on cross-border communications.

4-4. To learn how to manage cross-cultural business communications successfully.

Opening Profile: The Impact of Social Media on Global Business

[I]t's becoming more and more evident to enterprises that the social web actually does make sense for businesses.[1]

K. Ananth Krishnan (Tata Consultancy Services)
April 27, 2011

BNP Paribas, the French bank, launched its Facebook and Twitter sites in 2010 and has one of the largest followings, with about 120,000 Facebook "fans."[2]

Financial Times
January 10, 2011

Managers in international businesses or nonprofit enterprises around the world are grappling with the question of how to benefit from the burgeoning use of social media networks—through the Internet, video, audio, and phone—both external and internal to the organization. The networks, such as Facebook, are directly and indirectly linking people and business around the world. (Facebook, for example, had 1.44 billion monthly users around the world as of April 2015.) The power of such linkages for political and social motives was made clear during the Arab Spring in 2011, started by one person in Egypt protesting the government by using YouTube, iPhones, and other media.

Global business managers are realizing that these social media are potential sources of rich information, outside the normal chain of communication, that their companies could use to find out more about what customers want, how new ideas might be received, what competitors are doing, what problems might be lurking and how to deal with them, and so on. As an example, K. Ananth Krishnan, the chief technology officer (CTO) of Tata Consultancy Services, observed in an interview that, "Increasingly, data is coming at businesses in *unstructured ways*. It's coming from outside of companies, in the kinds of networking and SMS messaging habits that customers have. And it's coming from unstructured sources *inside* companies, from in-house blogs to internal knowledge markets."[3] (Tata Consultancy Services, based in India, has 198,000 IT consultants in 42 countries.) Krishnan notes, however, that concerns about privacy of information gathered through such sources must be taken into account.

Another challenge to the effective use of social media is how to measure the effectiveness of each source as a benefit to the company, given the considerable investment their use would require. Firms such as Target, Dell, and Burger King are trying to find what works best for them as social media applications such as Google+, Facebook, LinkedIn, YouTube, blogs, microblogs such as Twitter, and so on, have changed the way consumers interact with companies and friends about brands and services—with both positive and negative feedback.[4]

39 percent of companies we've surveyed already use social-media services as their primary digital tool to reach customers, and that percentage is expected to rise to 47 percent within the next four years.

McKinsey Quarterly
April 2012[5]

FIGURE 4-1 Social Media

Source: arrow/Fotolia

(Continued)

Although many companies are trying out social media to market their products or services and get feedback, others feel that the audience is too general and does not work as well as being able to target their message to specific demographic markets.[6]

Regardless of how companies interact with and use social media networks, it is clear that they are here to stay, that they can have considerable impact on global businesses, and that they are affecting political and social trends as well. In China, for example, more than 300 million people use social media, which is very popular because it is less likely to be monitored by the government. Years ahead of the West, with social media such as Renren and Sina Weibo, China's online users spend more than 40 percent of their time online on social media, a figure that continues to rise rapidly, according to McKinsey and Company consultants.[7] There is no Facebook, YouTube, or Twitter. However, in spite of the complexities and challenges, the sheer numbers of users present considerable opportunity for marketing.

Cultural communications are deeper and more complex than spoken or written messages. The essence of effective cross-cultural communication has more to do with releasing the right responses than with sending the "right" messages.

HALL AND HALL[8]

Multi-local online strategy…is about meeting global business objectives by tuning in to the cultural dynamics of their local markets.

"THINK GLOBALLY, INTERACT LOCALLY," *NEW MEDIA AGE*[9]

As the opening profile suggests, communication in all its forms is a critical factor in the cross-cultural management issues discussed in this book, particularly those of an interpersonal nature, involving motivation, leadership, group interactions, and negotiation. Culture is conveyed and perpetuated through communication in one form or another. Culture and communication are so intricately intertwined that they are, essentially, synonymous.[10] By understanding this relationship, managers can move toward constructive intercultural management. Nardon et al. point out that although global managers cite multicultural communication as a serious challenge, at the same time, it can open up important sources of business opportunity. "It is through communication that relationships are formed, conflicts are resolved, and innovative ideas are created and shared."[11]

Managers doing business around the world invariably complain that cross-cultural communication challenges have led to lost business, unintended offenses, and embarrassment—in particular in countries where it is crucial to develop relationships and trust. Communication, whether in the form of writing, talking, listening, or through the Internet, is an inherent part of a manager's role and takes up the majority of a manager's time on the job. Studies by Mintzberg demonstrate the importance of oral communication; he found that most managers spend between 50 and 90 percent of their time talking to people.[12] The ability of a manager to communicate effectively across cultural boundaries will largely determine the success of international business transactions or the output of a culturally diverse workforce. It is useful, then, to break down the elements involved in the communication process, both to understand the cross-cultural issues at stake and to maximize the opportunities to establish common meaning among the parties communicating.

THE COMMUNICATION PROCESS

The term **communication** describes the process of sharing meaning by transmitting messages through media such as words, behavior, or material artifacts. Managers communicate to coordinate activities, to disseminate information, to motivate people, and to negotiate future plans. It is of vital importance, then, for a receiver to interpret the meaning of a particular communication in the way the sender intended. Unfortunately, the communication process (see Exhibit 4-1) involves stages during which meaning can be distorted. Anything that undermines the communication of the intended meaning is typically referred to as **noise**.

The primary cause of noise is that the sender and the receiver each exists in a unique, private world thought of as her or his life space. The context of that private world, largely based on culture, experience, relations, values, and so forth, determines the interpretation of

EXHIBIT 4-1 The Communication Process

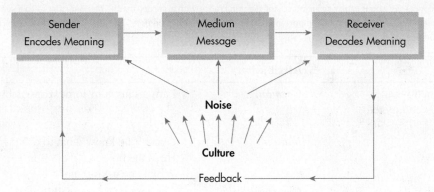

meaning in communication. People filter, or selectively understand, messages consistent with their own expectations and perceptions of reality and their values and norms of behavior. The more dissimilar the cultures of those involved, the greater the likelihood of misinterpretation. In this way, as Samovar, Porter, and Jain state in their book, *Understanding Intercultural Communication*, cultural factors pervade the communication process:

> *Culture not only dictates who talks with whom, about what, and how the communication proceeds, it also helps to determine how people encode messages, the meanings they have for messages, and the conditions and circumstances under which various messages may or may not be sent, noticed, or interpreted. In fact, our entire repertory of communicative behaviors is dependent largely on the culture in which we have been raised. Culture, consequently, is the foundation of communication. And, when cultures vary, communication practices also vary.*[13]

Communication, therefore, is a complex process of linking up or sharing the perceptual fields of sender and receiver; the perceptive sender builds a bridge to the life space of the receiver.[14] After the receiver interprets the message and draws a conclusion about what the sender meant, he or she will, in most cases, encode and send back a response, making communication a circular process.

The communication process is rapidly changing, however, as a result of technological developments; therefore it is propelling global business forward at a phenomenal growth rate. These changes are discussed later in this chapter.

Cultural Noise in the Communication Process

In Japanese there are several words for "I" and several words for "you" but their use depends on the relationship between the speaker and the other person. In short, there is no "I" by itself; the "I" depends on the relationship.[15]

Because the focus in this text is on effective cross-cultural communication, it is important to understand what cultural variables cause noise in the communication process. This knowledge of **cultural noise**—the cultural variables that undermine the communication of intended meaning—will enable us to take steps to minimize that noise and so improve communication.

When a member of one culture sends a message to a member of another culture, **intercultural communication** takes place. The message contains the meaning the encoder intends. When it reaches the receiver, however, it undergoes a transformation in which the influence of the decoder's culture becomes part of the meaning.[16] Exhibit 4-2 provides an example of intercultural communication in which the meaning got all mixed up. Note how the attribution of behavior differs for each participant. **Attribution** is the process by which people look for an explanation of another person's behavior. When they realize that they do not understand another person, they tend, say Hall and Hall, to blame their confusion on the other's "stupidity, deceit, or craziness."[17]

In the situation depicted in Exhibit 4-2, the Indian employee becomes frustrated and resigns after experiencing communication problems with his German boss. How could this outcome have been avoided? We do not have much information about the people or the context of the situation, but we can look at some of the variables that might have been involved and use them as a basis for analysis.

EXHIBIT 4-2 Cultural Noise in International Communication[18] The vice president for operations of a German manufacturing company headquartered in Munich became concerned about satisfying an important client in France with an order that he had outsourced to a subsidiary in India. He decided to visit the local manager and confirm the importance of delivering the order on time. The following is what transpired in his interaction with the local production manager.

Behavior		Attribution	
German:	"What can be done to make sure this project is completed on time?"	*German:*	I am giving him some responsibility.
		Indian:	Doesn't he know what to do? He is the boss. Why is he asking me?
Indian:	"I don't know. What do you suggest?"	*German:*	Can't he take responsibility?
		Indian:	I asked him for instructions.
German:	"You know the scheduling and staffing situation here better than me."	*German:*	I want to train him to make some decisions.
		Indian:	What kind of manager is he? Well, he expects me to say something.
Indian:	"I'll hire another worker, then we should be ready in two weeks."	*German:*	One more worker is totally insufficient; he doesn't know how to schedule properly. I need a definite deadline commitment—not "should be ready."
German:	"Hire three workers and give them a deadline of three weeks. Are we agreed on that deadline?"	*German:*	I offer a contract.
		Indian:	These are my orders: three weeks.

The German returned to his office in Munich, confident that the project would be completed on time and the order delivered on schedule, which he conveyed to the client. After four weeks, the customer called to complain that he had not received the order. The German VP immediately called the Indian manager:

German:	"Why hasn't the order been sent out as we agreed?"	*German*:	I am holding him responsible for our agreement.
		Indian:	He wants to know why it is not ready.
Indian:	"It will be completed next week."	(Both attribute that it is not ready.)	
German:	"But you told me it would be sent out in three weeks."	*German*:	I must teach him to take responsibility for deadlines.
		Indian:	This person does not know how to manage; it was not possible to complete the project in three weeks. I am going to get another job where the boss knows how to manage!

THE CULTURE–COMMUNICATION LINK

The following sections examine underlying elements of culture that affect communication. The degree to which one is able to communicate effectively largely depends on how similar the other person's cultural expectations are to our own. However, cultural gaps can be overcome by prior learning and understanding of those variables and how to adjust to them.

Trust in Communication

The key ingredient in a successful alliance is trust.

JAMES R. HOUGHTON, FORMER CHAIRMAN, CORNING, INC.[19]

Effective communication, and therefore effective collaboration in alliances across national boundaries, depends on the informal understandings among the parties that are based on the trust that has developed between them. However, the meaning of trust, and how it is developed and communicated, varies across societies. In China and Japan, for example, business transactions are based on networks of long-standing relationships based on trust rather than on the formal contracts and arm's-length relationships typical of the United States. When there is trust between parties, implicit understanding arises within communications. This understanding has numerous benefits in business, including encouraging communicators to overlook cultural differences and minimize problems. It allows communicators to adjust to unforeseen circumstances with less conflict than would be the case with formal contracts, and it facilitates open communication in exchanging ideas and information.[20] From his research on trust in global collaboration, John Child suggests the following guidelines for cultivating trust:

- Create a clear and calculated basis for mutual benefit. There must be realistic commitments and good intentions to honor them.

- Improve predictability: Strive to resolve conflicts and keep communication open.

- Develop mutual bonding through regular socializing and friendly contact.[21]

What can managers anticipate with regard to the level of trust in communications with people in other countries? If trust is based on how trustworthy we consider a person to be, then it must vary according to that society's expectations about whether that culture supports the norms and values that predispose people to behave credibly and benevolently. Are there differences across societies in those expectations of trust? Research on 90,000 people in 45 societies by the World Values Study Group provides some insight on cultural values regarding predisposition to trust. When we examine the percentage of respondents in each society who responded that "most people can be trusted," we can see that the Nordic countries and China had the highest predisposition to trust, followed by Canada, the United States, and Britain, whereas Brazil, Turkey, Romania, Slovenia, and Latvia had the lowest level of trust in people.[22]

The GLOBE Project

Results from the GLOBE research on culture, discussed in Chapter 3, provide some insight into culturally appropriate communication styles and expectations for the manager to use abroad. GLOBE researchers Javidan and House make the following observations:[23] For people in societies that ranked high on performance orientation—for example, the United States—presenting objective information in a direct and explicit way is an important and expected manner of communication; this contrasts with people in Russia or Greece—societies that ranked low on performance orientation—for whom hard facts and figures are not readily available or taken seriously. In those cases, a more indirect approach is preferred. People from countries ranking low on assertiveness, such as Sweden, also recoil from explicitness; their preference is for much two-way discourse and friendly relationships.

People ranking high in the humane dimension, such as those from Ireland and the Philippines, make avoiding conflict a priority and tend to communicate with the goal of being supportive of people rather than of achieving objective results. This contrasts with people from France and Spain, whose agenda is achievement of goals.

The foregoing provides examples of how to draw implications for appropriate communication styles from the research findings on cultural differences across societies. Astute global managers have learned that culture and communication are inextricably linked and that they should prepare themselves accordingly. Most will also suggest that you carefully watch and listen to how your hosts are communicating and then follow their lead.

Cultural Variables in the Communication Process

On a different level, it is also useful to be aware of cultural variables that can affect the communication process by influencing a person's perceptions; some of these variables have been identified by Samovar and Porter and discussed by Harris and Moran and others.[24] These variables are as follows: attitudes; social organization; thought patterns; roles; language (spoken or written); nonverbal communication (including kinesic behavior, proxemics, paralanguage, and object language); and time. Although these variables are discussed separately in this text, their effects are interdependent and inseparable—or, as Hecht, Andersen, and Ribeau put it, "Encoders and decoders process nonverbal cues as a conceptual, multichanneled gestalt."[25] As you read the explanations of these variables in the discussion that follows, consider how they apply in the context of communicating and managing in India, as outlined in the nearby feature, "Under the Lens: Communicating in India—Language, Culture, Customs, and Etiquette."

UNDER THE LENS

Communicating in India—Language, Culture, Customs, and Etiquette

FACTS AND STATISTICS

Location   Southern Asia, bordering Bangladesh, 4,053 km; Bhutan, 605 km; Burma, 1,463 km; China, 3,380 km; Nepal, 1,690 km; and Pakistan, 2,912 km

Capital   New Delhi

Climate   Varies from tropical monsoon in south to temperate in north

Population   1.28 billion (as of August 12, 2015.)

FIGURE 4-2 Map of India

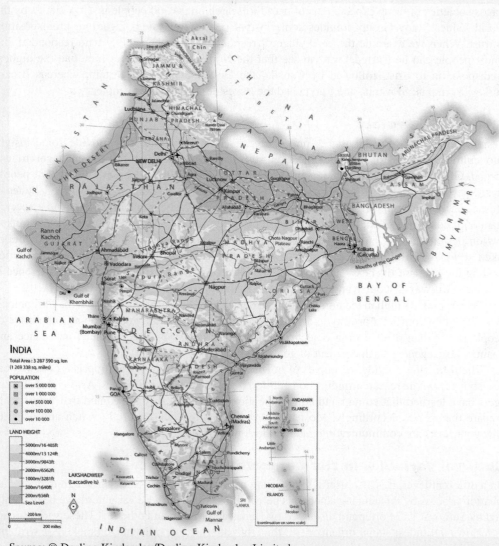

Source: © Dorling Kindersley/Dorling Kindersley Limited

FIGURE 4-3 Indian Flag

Source: Malgorzata Kistryn/Fotolia LLC

Ethnic Make-up   Indo-Aryan, 72%; Dravidian, 25%; Mongoloid and other, 3% (2000)

Religions   Hindu, 81.3%; Muslim, 12%; Christian, 2.3%; Sikh, 1.9%; other groups, including Buddhist, Jain, and Parsi, 2.5% (2000)

Government   Federal republic

LANGUAGES IN INDIA

The different states of India have different official languages, some of them not recognized by the central government. Some states have more than one official language. Bihar in east India has three official languages—Hindi, Urdu, and Bengali—that are all recognized by the central government. But Sikkim, also in east India, has four official languages, of which only Nepali is recognized by the central government. Besides the languages officially recognized by central or state governments are other languages that don't have this recognition, and their speakers are waging political struggles to obtain this recognition. The central government decided that Hindi was to be the official language of India, and therefore, it also has the status of official language in the states.

You can learn some useful Hindi phrases by visiting http://www.kwintessential.co.uk/resources/language/hindi-phrases.html.

INDIAN SOCIETY AND CULTURE

Hierarchy

- The influences of Hinduism and the tradition of the caste system have created a culture that emphasizes established hierarchical relationships.

- Indians are always conscious of social order and their status relative to other people, whether family, friends, or strangers.

- All relationships involve hierarchies. In schools, teachers are called *gurus* and are viewed as the source of all knowledge. The patriarch, usually the father, is considered the leader of the family. The boss is seen as the source of ultimate responsibility in business. Every relationship has a clear-cut hierarchy that must be observed for the social order to be maintained.

(Continued)

FIGURE 4-4 **The Taj Mahal**

Source: olgagomenyuk/Fotolia LLC

The Role of the Family

- People typically define themselves by the groups to which they belong rather than by their status as individuals. Someone is deemed to be affiliated to a specific state, region, city, family, career path, religion, and so on.
- This group orientation stems from the close personal ties Indians maintain with their family, including the extended family.
- The extended family creates a myriad of interrelationships, rules, and structures. Along with these mutual obligations comes a deep-rooted trust among relatives.

Just Can't Say No

- Indians do not like to express "no," whether verbally or nonverbally.
- Rather than disappoint you, for example, by saying something isn't available, Indians will offer you the response that they think you want to hear.
- This behavior should not be considered dishonest. An Indian would be considered terribly rude if he did not attempt to give a person what had been asked.
- Because they do not like to give negative answers, Indians may give an affirmative answer but be deliberately vague about any specific details. This will require you to look for nonverbal cues, such as a reluctance to commit to an actual time for a meeting or an enthusiastic response.

Etiquette and Customs in India

Meeting Etiquette

- Religion, education, and social class all influence greetings in India.
- This is a hierarchical culture, so greet the eldest or most senior person first.
- When leaving a group, each person must be bade farewell individually.
- Shaking hands is common, especially in the large cities among the more educated who are accustomed to dealing with Westerners.
- Men may shake hands with other men, and women may shake hands with other women; however, there are seldom handshakes between men and women because of religious beliefs. If you are uncertain, wait for him or her to extend his or her hand.

Naming Conventions

Indian names vary based on religion, social class, and region of the country. The following are some basic guidelines to understanding the naming conventions.

Hindus

- In the north, many people have both a given name and a surname.
- In the south, surnames are less common, and a person generally uses the initial of his or her father's name in front of their own name.
- The man's formal name is their name s/o (son of) and the father's name. Women use d/o to refer to themselves as the daughter of their father.
- At marriage, women drop their father's name and use their first name with their husband's first name as a sort of surname.

Muslims

- Many Muslims do not have surnames. Instead, men add the father's name to their own name with the connector "bin," so "Abdullah bin Ahmed" is "Abdullah, the son of Ahmed."
- Women use the connector binti.
- The title Hajji (m) or Hajjah (f) before the name indicates that the person has made his or her pilgrimage to Mecca.

Sikhs

- Sikhs all use the "Singh" name. It is either adopted as a surname or as a connector name to the surname.

Gift-Giving Etiquette

- Indians believe that giving gifts eases the transition into the next life.
- Gifts of cash are given to friends and members of the extended family to celebrate life events such as birth, death, and marriage.
- It is not the value of the gift, but the sincerity with which it is given, that is important to the recipient.
- If invited to an Indian's home for a meal, it is not necessary to bring a gift, although one will not be turned down.
- Do not give frangipani or white flowers because they are used at funerals.
- Yellow, green, and red are lucky colors, so try to use them to wrap gifts.
- A gift from a man should be said to come from both him and his wife, mother, sister, or some other female relative.
- Hindus should not be given gifts made of leather.
- Muslims should not be given gifts made of pigskin or alcoholic products.
- Gifts are not opened when received.

Dining Etiquette

- Indians entertain in their homes, restaurants, private clubs, or other public venues, depending on the occasion and circumstances.
- Although Indians are not always punctual themselves, they expect foreigners to arrive close to the appointed time.
- Take off your shoes before entering the house.
- Dress modestly and conservatively.
- Politely turn down the first offer of tea, coffee, or snacks. You will be asked again and again. Saying no to the first invitation is part of the protocol.

There are diverse dietary restrictions in India, and these may affect the foods that are served:

- Hindus do not eat beef, and many are vegetarians.
- Muslims do not eat pork or drink alcohol.
- Sikhs do not eat beef.
- Lamb, chicken, and fish are the most commonly served main courses for nonvegetarian meals because they avoid the meat restrictions of the religious groups.

(Continued)

Table manners are somewhat formal, but this formality is tempered by the religious beliefs of the various groups.

- Much Indian food is eaten with the fingers.
- Wait to be told where to sit.
- If utensils are used, they are generally a tablespoon and a fork.
- Guests are often served in a particular order; the guest of honor is served first, followed by the men, and the children are served last. Women typically serve the men and eat later.
- You may be asked to wash your hands before and after sitting down to a meal.
- Always use your right hand to eat, whether you are using utensils or your fingers.
- In some situations, food may be put on your plate for you, whereas in other situations, you may be allowed to serve yourself from a communal bowl.
- Leaving a small amount of food on your plate indicates that you are satisfied. Finishing all your food means that you are still hungry.

Business Etiquette and Protocol in India

Relationships and Communication

- Indians prefer to do business with those they know.
- Relationships are built on mutual trust and respect.
- In general, Indians prefer to have long-standing personal relationships prior to doing business.
- It may be a good idea to go through a third-party introduction. This gives you immediate credibility.

Business Meeting Etiquette

- If you will be traveling to India from abroad, it is advisable to make appointments by letter at least one month and, preferably, two months in advance.
- It is a good idea to confirm your appointment because they can be cancelled at short notice.
- The best time for a meeting is late morning or early afternoon. Reconfirm your meeting the week before and call again that morning; it is common for meetings to be cancelled at the last minute.
- Keep your schedule flexible so that it can be adjusted for last-minute rescheduling of meetings.
- You should arrive at meetings on time because Indians are impressed with punctuality.
- Meetings will start with a great deal of getting-to-know-you talk. In fact, it is quite possible that no business will be discussed at the first meeting.
- Always send a detailed agenda in advance. Send back-up materials, charts, and other data as well. This allows everyone to review and become comfortable with the material prior to the meeting.
- Follow up a meeting with an overview of what was discussed and the next steps.

Business Negotiating

- Indians are nonconfrontational. It is rare for them to disagree overtly, although this is beginning to change in the managerial ranks.
- Decisions are reached by the person with the most authority.
- Decision making is a slow process.
- If you lose your temper, you lose face and prove you are unworthy of respect and trust.
- Delays are to be expected, especially when dealing with the government.
- Most Indians expect concessions in both price and terms. It is acceptable to expect concessions in return for those you grant.
- Never appear overly legalistic during negotiations. In general, Indians do not trust the legal system, and someone's word is sufficient to reach an agreement.
- Do not disagree publicly with members of your negotiating team.
- Successful negotiations are often celebrated by a meal.

Dress Etiquette

- Business attire is conservative.
- Men should wear dark-colored, conservative business suits.
- Women should dress conservatively in suits or dresses.
- The weather often determines clothing. In the hotter parts of the country, dress is less formal, although dressing as previously suggested for the first meeting will indicate respect.

Titles

- Indians revere titles such as Professor, Doctor, and Engineer.
- Status is determined by age, university degree, caste, and profession.
- If someone does not have a professional title, use the honorific title "Sir" or "Madam."
- Titles are used with the person's name or the surname, depending on the person's name. (See Social Etiquette for more information on Indian naming conventions.)
- Wait to be invited before using someone's first name without the title.

Business Cards

- Business cards are exchanged after the initial handshake and greeting.
- If you have a university degree or any honor, put it on your business card.
- Use the right hand to give and receive business cards.
- Business cards need not be translated into Hindi.
- Always present your business card so the recipient may read the card as it is handed to him or her.

Source: http://www.kwintessential.co.uk/resources/global-etiquette/India-country-profile.html, September 5, 2011. Used with permission of www.kwintessential.co.uk.

ATTITUDES

We all know that our attitudes underlie the way we behave and communicate and the way we interpret messages from others. Ethnocentric attitudes are a particular source of noise in cross-cultural communication. In the incident described in Exhibit 4-2, both the Indian and the German are clearly attempting to interpret and convey meaning based on their own experiences of that kind of transaction. The German is probably guilty of stereotyping the Indian employee by quickly jumping to the conclusion that he is unwilling to take responsibility for the task and the scheduling.

This problem, **stereotyping**, occurs when a person assumes that every member of a society or subculture has the same characteristics or traits. Stereotyping is a common cause of misunderstanding in intercultural communication. It is an arbitrary, lazy, and often destructive way to find out about people. Astute managers are aware of the dangers of cultural stereotyping and deal with each person as an individual with whom they may form a unique relationship.

SOCIAL ORGANIZATIONS

Our perceptions can be influenced by differences in values, approach, or priorities relative to the kind of social organizations to which we belong. These organizations may be based on one's nation, tribe, or religious sect, or they may consist of the members of a certain profession. Examples of such organizations include the Academy of Management or the United Auto Workers (UAW).[26]

THOUGHT PATTERNS

The logical progression of reasoning varies widely around the world and greatly affects the communication process. Managers cannot assume that others use the same reasoning processes, as illustrated by the experience of a Canadian expatriate in Thailand, related in a book by Harris and Moran.

While in Thailand a Canadian expatriate's car was hit by a Thai motorist who had crossed over the double line while passing another vehicle. After failing to establish that the fault lay with the Thai driver, the Canadian flagged down a policeman. After several minutes of seemingly futile discussion, the Canadian pointed out the double line in the middle of the road and asked the policeman directly, "What do these lines signify?" The policeman replied, "They indicate the center of the road and are there so I can establish just how far the accident is from that point." The Canadian was silent. It had never occurred to him that the double line might not mean "no passing allowed."[27]

In the Exhibit 4-2 scenario, perhaps the German did not realize that the Indian employee had a different rationale for his time estimate for the job. Because the Indian was not used to having to estimate schedules, he just took a guess, which he felt he had been forced to do.

ROLES

Societies differ considerably in their perceptions of a manager's role. Much of the difference is attributable to their perceptions of who should make the decisions and who has responsibility for what. In the Exhibit 4-2 example, the German assumes that his role as manager is to delegate responsibility, to foster autonomy, and to practice participative management. He prescribes the role of the employee without any consideration of whether the employee will understand that role. The Indian's frame of reference leads him to think that the manager is the boss and should give the order about when to have the job completed. He interprets the German's behavior as breaking that frame of reference, and therefore he feels that the boss is "stupid and incompetent" for giving him the wrong order and for not recognizing and appreciating his accomplishments. The manager should have considered what behaviors Indian workers would expect of him and then either should have played that role or discussed the situation carefully, in a training mode.

LANGUAGE

Spoken or written language, of course, is a frequent cause of miscommunication, stemming from a person's inability to speak the local language, a poor or too-literal translation, a speaker's failure to explain idioms, or a person missing the meaning conveyed through body language or certain symbols. Even among countries that share the same language, problems can arise from the subtleties and nuances inherent in the use of the language, as noted by George Bernard Shaw: "Britain and America are two nations separated by a common language." This problem can exist even within the same country among different subcultures or subgroups.[28]

Many international executives tell stories about lost business deals or lost sales because of communication blunders.

When Pepsi Cola's slogan "Come Alive with Pepsi" was introduced in Germany, the company learned that the literal German translation of "come alive" is "come out of the grave."

A U.S. airline found a lack of demand for its "rendezvous lounges" on its Boeing 747s. They later learned that "rendezvous" in Portuguese refers to a room that is rented for prostitution.[29]

More than just conveying objective information, language also conveys cultural and social understandings from one generation to the next. Examples of how language reflects what is important in a society include the 6,000 Arabic words that describe camels and their parts and the 50 or more classifications of snow the Inuit, the Eskimo people of Canada, use.

In as much as language conveys culture, technology, and priorities, it also serves to separate and perpetuate subcultures. In India, 14 official and many unofficial languages are used, and more than 800 languages are spoken on the African continent.

Because of increasing workforce diversity around the world, the international business manager will have to deal with a medley of languages. For example, assembly-line workers at the Ford plant in Cologne, Germany, speak Turkish and Spanish as well as German.

In Malaysia, Indonesia, and Thailand, many of the buyers and traders are Chinese. Not all Arabs speak Arabic; in Tunisia and Lebanon, for example, French is the language of commerce.

International managers need either a good command of the local language or competent interpreters. The task of accurate translation to bridge cultural gaps is fraught with difficulties: Joe Romano, a partner of High Ground, an emerging technology-marketing company in Boston, found out on a business trip to Taiwan how close a one-syllable slip of the tongue can come to torpedoing a deal. He noted that one is supposed to say to the chief executive "Au-ban," meaning "Hello, No. 1. Boss." Instead, he accidentally said "Lau-ban ya," which means "Hello, wife of the boss." Essentially, Mr. Romano called him a woman in front of 20 senior Taiwanese executives, who all laughed; but the boss was very embarrassed because men in Asia have a very macho attitude.[30]

Even the direct translation of specific words does not guarantee the congruence of their meaning, as with the word "yes" used by Asians, which usually means only that they have heard you, and, often, that they are too polite to disagree. The Chinese, for example, through years of political control, have built into their communication culture a cautionary stance to avoid persecution by professing agreement with whatever opinion was held by the person questioning them.[31]

Sometimes even a direct statement can be misinterpreted instead as an indirect expression, as when a German businessman said to his Algerian counterpart, "My wife would love something like that beautiful necklace your wife was wearing last night. It was beautiful." The next day the Algerian gave him a box with the necklace in it as a gift to his wife. The Algerian had interpreted the compliment as an indirect way of expressing a wish to possess a similar necklace. The German was embarrassed, but had to accept the necklace. He realized he needed to be careful how he expressed such things in the future—such as asking where that kind of jewelry is sold.[32]

In much of the world, politeness and a desire to say only what the listener wants to hear create noise in the communication process. Often, even a clear translation does not help a person understand what is meant because the encoding process has obscured the true message. With the poetic Arab language—replete with exaggeration, elaboration, and repetition—meaning is attributed more to how something is said than to what is actually said.

For the German supervisor and Indian employee cited in Exhibit 4-2, it is highly likely that the German could have picked up some cues from the employee's body language that probably implied problems with the interpretation of meaning. How might body language have created noise in this case?

Nonverbal Communication

Clearly, as explained by Roger Axtel in his book, *Essential Do's and Taboos*,[33] the nonverbal signal that, in the U.S., is interpreted as "okay" is absolutely not "okay" in many countries. Axtel gives the example of when Vice President Richard Nixon flew to Brazil in an attempt to improve relations between the two countries. As reported in the newspapers, when Nixon stepped off the plane in Sao Paulo, he gave the "A-okay" sign—with both hands! The crowd at the airport booed—of course—given the meaning in Brazil (a private part of a woman's body); not surprisingly, photos of this incident were in the paper the next day!

Behavior that communicates without words (although it often is accompanied by words) is called **nonverbal communication**. People will usually believe what they see over what they hear—hence the expression, "A picture is worth a thousand words." Studies show that these subtle messages account for between 65 and 93 percent of interpreted communication.[34] Even minor variations in body language, speech rhythms, and punctuality, for example, often cause mistrust and misperception of the situation among cross-national parties.[35] The media for such nonverbal communication can be categorized into four types: (1) kinesic behavior, (2) proxemics, (3) paralanguage, and (4) object language.

The term **kinesic behavior** refers to communication through body movements—posture, gestures, facial expressions, and eye contact, as illustrated in the accompanying "Under the Lens: Communicating Italian Style" feature. Although such actions may be universal, often

UNDER THE LENS

Communicating Italian Style[36]

When travelling around Europe, you will probably notice that Italians use the most body language when communicating; they seem to be walking down the street mumbling while their hands are going all over wildly, typically while on their *telefonini*. In fact, it is difficult for the person listening on the phone to interpret sometimes because the speaker's hand gestures and other nonverbal signals are invisible. Their hands convey much meaning, and Italians commonly make about 250 gestures when talking and doing other things simultaneously such as conversing on the cell phone. Examples are that of wagging the hands downward, meaning "come here"; slowly drawing a circle with the hand, meaning "whatever"; pressing a finger into the cheek, meaning that something tastes good; and brushing the back of the hand outward across the chin meaning "I don't give a damn." Gestures can convey that the person feels pride, or shame, or desperation, or fear, giving more meaning than the words alone. Of course, gestures are culture-specific (varying also according to the area within Italy, those in the south tending to be louder and more effusive than those in the north) so you should be careful to be aware that their meanings may differ significantly around the world and may cause offense. Women should realize that flirtatious behavior from Italian men is common and part of their culture. This behavior, along with the close-talking nature of Italians, including sitting close and perhaps lightly touching the arm of the other person, can make it uncomfortable for women who are used to more personal space in communicating.

Italians tend to be gregarious and loud but interrupt one another anyway. They are uncomfortable with silence but do not seem to lack interesting subjects to discuss, such as their architecture and art, Italian history and football, and especially their families.

Italians' dress is conservative and chic and formal for business meetings. One is expected to use formal titles and last names until requested to do otherwise; and women use their maiden names in business. Present your business cards face up, and be sure to read theirs before putting them away.

One is expected to shake hands with everyone present when arriving and when leaving, and it is customary to kiss friends on both cheeks, left first. Eye contact is essential when talking to an Italian; otherwise, you would be viewed as unfriendly and perhaps untrustworthy. Italians do not observe personal space when conversing, so one should expect close contact and much hand movement even with business contacts. People from reserved cultures such as the British will likely be perceived as disinterested by Italians since they tend to be very emotionally engaged with the conversation.

their meaning is not. Because kinesic systems of meaning are culturally specific and learned, they cannot be generalized across cultures. Most people in the West would not correctly interpret many Chinese facial expressions; for example, sticking out the tongue expresses surprise, a widening of the eyes shows anger, and scratching the ears and cheeks indicates happiness.[37] Research has shown for some time, however, that most people worldwide can recognize displays of the basic emotions of anger, disgust, fear, happiness, sadness, surprise, and contempt.[38]

As illustrated previously, visitors to other countries must be careful about their gestures and how they might be interpreted. For example, people in Japan may point with their middle finger, which is considered an obscene gesture to others. To Arabs, showing the soles of one's feet is an insult; recall the reporter who threw his shoe at President Bush in late 2008 during his visit to Iraq. This was, to Arabs, the ultimate insult.

Many businesspeople and visitors react negatively to what they feel are inappropriate facial expressions, without understanding the cultural meaning behind them. In his studies of cross-cultural negotiations, Graham observed that the Japanese feel uncomfortable when faced with the Americans' eye-to-eye posture. They are taught since childhood to bow their heads out of humility, whereas the automatic response of Americans is, "look at me when I'm talking to you!"[39]

Subtle differences in eye behavior (called *oculesics*) can throw off a communication badly if they are not understood. Eye behavior includes differences not only in eye contact but also in the use of eyes to convey other messages, whether or not that involves mutual gaze. For example, during speech, Americans will look straight at you, but the British keep your attention by looking away. The British will look at you when they have finished speaking, which signals that it is your turn to talk. The implicit rationale for this is that you can't interrupt people when they are not looking at you.[40]

It is helpful for U.S. managers to be aware of the many cultural expectations regarding posture and how they may be interpreted. In Europe or Asia, a relaxed posture in business meetings may be taken as bad manners or the result of poor upbringing. In Korea, you are expected to sit upright, with feet squarely on the floor, and to speak slowly, showing a blending of body and spirit.

Proxemics deals with the influence of proximity and space on communication—both personal space and office space or layout. Americans expect office layouts to provide private space for each person and, usually, a larger and more private space as one goes up the hierarchy. In much of Asia, the custom is open office space with people at all levels working and talking in close proximity to one another. Space communicates power in both Germany and the United States, evidenced by the desire for a corner office or one on the top floor. The importance of French officials, however, is made clear by a position in the middle of subordinates, communicating that they have a central position in an information network, where they can stay informed and in control.[41] The following "Under the Lens" feature illustrates the connections between beliefs about the variables of proxemics and business decisions.

Do you ever feel vaguely uncomfortable and start moving backward slowly when someone is speaking to you? This is because that person is invading your bubble—your personal space. Personal space is culturally patterned, and foreign spatial cues are a common source of misinterpretation. When someone seems aloof or pushy, it often means that she or he is operating under subtly different spatial rules.

Hall and Hall suggest that cultural differences affect the programming of the senses and that space, perceived by all the senses, is regarded as a form of territory to be

UNDER THE LENS
How Feng Shui Affects Business

Feng Shui (pronounced "fung shway") is an ancient Chinese system of aesthetics believed to use the laws of both heaven and earth to help one improve life by receiving positive *qi*. Feng shui translates into English as "wind-water."[42] Qi (pronounced "chee" in English) is "a movable positive or negative life force which plays an essential role in feng shui."[43]

Throughout history, Asian experts have read these energy patterns and discerned how to benefit by facing their buildings and offices in a particular direction, by designing gardens and entrances in a positive way, and by using Qi in rooms to influence aspects in an individual's life. "The quality of Qi is expressed through form, shape, color, direction, time, and the feeling it generates within us."[44] Various methods to establish beneficial settings have included compass directions, dowsing (commonly known as using a rod to move over the earth to find underground water, buried metals, and so on), and geomancy (loosely referred to as attempting to interpret meanings from patterns or markings in the soil or sand).

Westerners also use Feng shui, often in the process of building or decorating offices and homes—although not always following expert advice. When Donald Trump lost some important Asian clients due to his properties' apparently bad feng shui, he hired a feng shui master to analyze the auspiciousness of Trump Towers. In fact, feng shui and other beliefs from Chinese culture can drastically influence business deals. Michael Rudder, a real-estate broker in New York, found this out the hard way and now integrates feng shui in his planning—especially because most of his recent sales of office buildings and condominiums have been to Asians.[45] Also, as found by many others involved in real-estate, certain numbers have specific meanings in different cultures. In Chinese, Japanese, and Korean, for example, the pronunciation of the number four sounds the same as the word for death. No wonder many buildings in Asia do not have a fourth floor. In Chinese, the number eight is a homophone for the word for getting rich. The eighth floor, and building numbers with eights in them, often sell at a premium.[46]

protected.[47] South Americans, southern and eastern Europeans, Indonesians, and Arabs have **high-contact cultures**, preferring to stand close, touch a great deal, and experience a close sensory involvement. Latin Americans, for example, have a highly physical greeting such as putting their arms around a colleague's back and grabbing him by the arm. On the other hand, North Americans, Asians, and northern Europeans have **low-contact cultures** and prefer much less sensory involvement, standing farther apart and touching far less. They have a distant style of body language. In France, a relationship-oriented culture, good friends greet members of the opposite sex with a peck on each cheek; a handshake is a way to make a personal connection.

Interestingly, high-contact cultures are mostly located in warmer climates, and low-contact cultures in cooler climates. Americans are relatively nontouching, automatically standing at a distance so that an outstretched arm will touch the other person's ear. Standing any closer than that is regarded as invading intimate space. However, Americans and Canadians certainly expect a warm handshake and maybe a pat on the back from closer friends, though not the very warm double handshake of the Spaniards (clasping the forearm with the left hand). The Japanese, considerably less **haptic** (touching), do not shake hands; an initial greeting between a Japanese businessperson and a Spanish businessperson would be uncomfortable for both parties if they were untrained in cultural haptics. The Japanese bow to one another—the depth of the bow revealing their relative social standing.

> *Imagine the smartphone app that would ask your identity, the identity of the other greeter, where you both are and how many times you have greeted each other. It would then propose a compromise—a namaste followed by a handshake, perhaps, or a bow punctuated by a slap on the back.*[48]

When considering high- and low-contact cultures, we can trace a correlation between Hofstede's cultural variables of individualism and collectivism and the types of kinesic and proxemic behaviors people display. Generally, people from individualistic cultures are more remote and distant, whereas those from collectivist cultures are interdependent; they tend to work, play, live, and sleep in close proximity.[49]

The term **paralanguage** refers to how something is said rather than the content—that is, the rate of speech, the tone and inflection of voice, other noises, laughing, or yawning. The culturally aware manager learns how to interpret subtle differences in paralanguage, including silence. Silence is a powerful communicator. It may be a way of saying "no," of being offended, or of waiting for more information to make a decision. There is considerable variation in the use of silence in meetings. Whereas Americans become uncomfortable after 10 or 15 seconds of silence, Chinese prefer to think the situation over for 30 seconds before speaking. The typical scenario between Americans and Chinese, then, is that the American gets impatient, says something to break the silence, and offends the Chinese by interrupting his or her chain of thought and comfort level with the subject.[50]

The term **object language**, or **material culture**, refers to how we communicate through material artifacts, whether architecture, office design and furniture, clothing, cars, or cosmetics. Material culture communicates what people hold as important. In the United States, for example, someone wishing to convey his important status and wealth would show guests his penthouse office or expensive car. In Japan and China, a businessman presents his business card to a new contact and expects the receiver to study it and appreciate his position. The cards are called name cards in China and are an essential aspect of doing business—a way to build networks. The exchange of cards occurs as soon as you meet, and visitors should be careful to get an appropriate translation for their cards.[51] In Mexico, a visiting international executive or salesperson is advised to take time out, before negotiating business, to show appreciation for the surrounding architecture, which Mexicans prize. The importance of family to people in Spain and much of Latin America would be conveyed by family photographs around the office and, therefore, an expectation that the visitor would enquire about the family.

TIME

Another variable that communicates culture is the way people regard and use time (see also Chapter 3). To Brazilians, relative punctuality communicates the level of importance of those involved. To Middle Easterners, time is something controlled by the will of Allah.

To initiate effective cross-cultural business interactions, managers should know the difference between *monochronic time systems* and *polychronic time systems* and how they affect

EXHIBIT 4-3 **Forms of Nonverbal Communication**

- Facial expressions
- Body posture
- Gestures with hands, arms, head, etc.
- Interpersonal distance (proxemics)
- Touching, body contact
- Eye contact
- Clothing, cosmetics, hairstyles, jewelry
- Paralanguage (voice pitch and inflections, rate of speech, and silence)
- Color symbolism
- Attitude toward time and the use of time in business and social interactions
- Food symbolism and social use of meals

communications. Hall and Hall explain that in **monochronic cultures** (Switzerland, Germany, and the United States), time is experienced in a linear way, with a past, a present, and a future, and time is treated as something to be spent, saved, made up, or wasted. Classified and compartmentalized, time serves to order life. This attitude is a learned part of Western culture, probably starting with the Industrial Revolution. Monochronic people, found in individualistic cultures, generally concentrate on one thing at a time, adhere to time commitments, and are accustomed to short-term relationships.

In contrast, **polychronic cultures** tolerate many things occurring simultaneously and emphasize involvement with people. Two Latin friends, for example, will put an important conversation ahead of being on time for a business meeting, thus communicating the priority of relationships over material systems. Polychronic people—Latin Americans, Arabs, and those from other collectivist cultures—may focus on several things at once, be highly distractible, and change plans often.[52]

The relationship between time and space also affects communication. Polychronic people, for example, are likely to hold open meetings, moving around and conducting transactions with one party and then another, rather than compartmentalizing meeting topics, as do monochronic people.

The nuances and distinctions regarding cultural differences in nonverbal communication are endless. The various forms are listed in Exhibit 4-3; wise intercultural managers will take careful account of the role that such differences might play.

What aspects of nonverbal communication might have created noise in the interactions between the German supervisor and the Indian employee in Exhibit 4-2? Undoubtedly, some cues could have been picked up from the kinesic behavior of each person. It was the responsibility of the manager, in particular, to notice any indications from the Indian that could have prompted him to change his communication pattern or assumptions. Face-to-face communication permits the sender of the message to get immediate feedback, both verbal and nonverbal, and thus to have some idea as to how that message is being received and whether additional information is needed. What aspects of the Indian employee's kinesic behavior or paralanguage might have been evident to a more culturally sensitive manager? Did both parties' sense of time affect the communication process?

Context

> *East Asians live in relatively complex social networks with prescribed role relations; attention to context is, therefore, important for their effective functioning. In contrast, westerners live in less constraining social worlds that stress independence and allow them to pay less attention to context.*
>
> RICHARD E. NISBETT[53]

A major differentiating factor that is a primary cause of noise in the communication process is that of context—which actually incorporates many of the variables discussed earlier. The **context** in which the communication takes place affects the meaning and interpretation of the interaction. Cultures are known to be high- or low-context cultures, with a relative range in between.[54] In **high-context cultures** (Asia, the Middle East, Africa, and the Mediterranean), feelings and thoughts are not explicitly expressed; instead, one has to read between the lines and interpret meaning from one's general understanding. Two such high-context cultures are the South Korea and Arab cultures. In such cultures, key information is embedded in the context rather than made explicit. People make assumptions about what the message means through their knowledge of the person or the surroundings. In these cultures, most communication takes place within a context of extensive information networks resulting from close personal relationships. See the following "Management in Action" feature for further explanation of the Asian communication style.

In **low-context cultures** (Germany, Switzerland, Scandinavia, and North America), where personal and business relationships are more compartmentalized, communication media have to be more explicit. Feelings and thoughts are expressed in words, and information is more readily available. Westerners focus more on the individual and therefore tend to view events as the result of specific agents, whereas Easterners view events in a broader and longer-term context.[55]

In cross-cultural communication between high- and low-context people, a lack of understanding may preclude reaching a solution, and conflict can arise. Germans, for example, will expect considerable detailed information before making a business decision, whereas Arabs will base their decisions more on knowledge of the people involved—the information is present, but it is implicit. People in low-context cultures, such as those in Germany, Switzerland, Austria, and the United States, convey their thoughts and plans in a direct, straightforward communication style, saying something like, "We have to make a decision on this today." People in high-context cultures, such as in Asia and, to less extent in England, convey their thoughts in a more indirect, implicit manner; this means that someone from Germany needs to have more patience and tact and be willing to listen and watch for clues—verbal and nonverbal—about his or her colleagues' wishes.

People in high-context cultures expect others to understand unarticulated moods, subtle gestures, and environmental clues that people from low-context cultures simply do not process. Misinterpretation and misunderstanding often result.[56] People from high-context cultures perceive those from low-context cultures as too talkative, obvious, and redundant. Those from low-context cultures perceive high-context people as secretive, sneaky, and mysterious. Research indicates, for example, that Americans find talkative people more attractive, whereas the Koreans—a high-context people—perceive less-verbal people as more attractive. (These conflicts are illustrated in the accompanying "Management in Action" feature). Finding the right balance between low- and high-context communications can be tricky, as Hall and Hall point out: "Too much information leads people to feel they are being talked down to; too little information can mystify them or make them feel left out."[57] Exhibit 4-4 shows the relative level of context in various countries.

The importance of understanding the role of context and nonverbal language to avoid misinterpretation is illustrated in the accompanying feature, *Comparative Management in Focus: Communicating with Arabs.*

EXHIBIT 4-4 Cultural Context and Its Effects on Communication

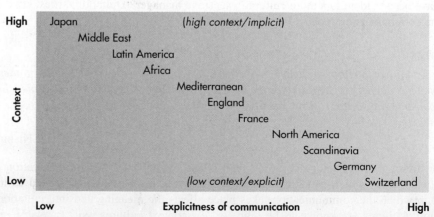

Source: Based on information drawn from E. T. Hall and M. R. Hall, *Understanding Cultural Differences* (Yarmouth, ME: Intercultural Press, 1990); and Martin Rosch, "Communications: Focal Point of Culture," *Management International Review* 27, No. 4 (1987).

MANAGEMENT IN ACTION
Oriental Poker Face: Eastern Deception or Western Inscrutability?

Among many English expressions that are likely to offend those of us whose ancestry may be traced to the Far East, two stand out quite menacingly for me: "Oriental poker face" and "idiotic Asian smile." The former refers to the supposedly inscrutable nature of a facial expression that apparently reflects no particular state of mind, while the latter pokes fun at a face fixed with a perpetually friendly smile. Westerners' perplexity, when faced with either, arises from the impression that these two diametrically opposed masquerading strategies prevent them from extracting useful information—at least the type of information that at least they could process with a reasonable measure of confidence—about the feelings of the person before them. An Asian face that projects no signs of emotion, then, seems to most Westerners nothing but a facade. It does not matter whether that face wears an unsightly scowl or a shining ray; a facial expression they cannot interpret poses a genuine threat.

Compassionate and sympathetic to their perplexity as I may be, I am also insulted by the Western insensitivity to the significant roles that subtle signs play in Asian cultures. Every culture has its unique modus operandi for communication. Western culture, for example, apparently emphasizes the importance of direct communication. Not only are the communicators taught to look directly at each other when they convey a message, but they also are encouraged to come right to the point of the message. Making bold statements or asking frank questions in a less than diplomatic manner (i.e., "That was really a very stupid thing to do!" or "Are you interested in me?") is rarely construed as rude or indiscreet. Even embarrassingly blunt questions such as "President Clinton, did you have sexual intercourse with Monica Lewinsky?" are tolerated most of the time. Asians, on the other hand, find this direct communicative communication style quite unnerving. In many social interactions, they avoid direct eye contact. They "see" each other without necessarily looking directly at each other, and they gather information about inner states of mind without asking even the most discreet or understated questions. Many times they talk around the main topic, and, yet, they succeed remarkably well in understanding one another's position. (At least they believe they have developed a reasonably clear understanding.)

To a great extent, Asian communication is listening-centered; the ability to listen (and a special talent for detecting various communicative cues) is treated as equally important as, if not more important than, the ability to speak. This contrasts clearly with the American style of communication that puts the utmost emphasis on verbal expression; the speaker carries most of the burden for ensuring that everyone understands his or her message. An Asian listener, however, is prone to blame himself or herself for failing to reach a comprehensive understanding from the few words and gestures performed by the speaker. With this heavier burden placed on the listener, an Asian speaker does not feel obliged to send clearly discernible message cues (at least not nearly so much as he or she is obliged to do in American cultural contexts). Not obligated to express themselves without interruption, Asians use silence as a tool in communication. Silence, by most Western conventions, represents discontinuity of communication and creates a feeling of discomfort and anxiety. In the Orient, however, silence is not only comfortably tolerated but is considered a desirable form of expression. Far from being a sign of displeasure or animosity, it serves as an integral part of the communication process, used for reflecting on messages previously exchanged and for carefully crafting thoughts before uttering them.

It is not outlandish at all, then, for Asians to view Americans as unnecessarily talkative and lacking in the ability to listen. For the Asian, it is the American who projects a mask of confidence by being overly expressive both verbally and nonverbally. Since the American style of communication places less emphasis on the act of listening than on speaking, Asians suspect that their American counterparts fail to pick up subtle and astute communicative signs in conversation. To one with a cultural outlook untrained in reading those signs, an inscrutable face represents no more than a menacing or amusing mask.

Source: Dr. Jin Kim, State University of New York–Plattsburgh. Copyright © 2003 by Dr. Jin Kim. Used with permission of Dr. Kim.

Comparative Management In Focus
Communicating with Arabs

In the Middle East, the meaning of a communication is implicit and interwoven and, consequently, much harder for Americans, accustomed to explicit and specific meanings, to understand.

Arabs are warm, emotional, and quick to explode: sounding off is regarded as a safety valve. In fact, the Arabic language aptly communicates the Arabic culture, one of emotional extremes. The language contains the means for overexpression, many adjectives, words that allow for exaggeration, and metaphors to emphasize a position. What is said is often not as important as *how* it is said. Eloquence and flowery speech are admired for their own sake, regardless of the content. Loud speech is used for dramatic effect.

At the core of Middle Eastern culture are friendship, honor, religion, and traditional hospitality. Family, friends, and connections are very important on all levels in the Middle East and will take precedence over business transactions. Arabs do business with people, not companies, and they make commitments to people, not contracts. A phone call to the right person can help to get around seemingly insurmountable obstacles. An Arab expects loyalty from friends, and it is understood that giving and receiving favors is an inherent part of the relationship; no one says no to a request for a favor. A lack of follow-through is assumed to be beyond the friend's control.[58]

Because hospitality is a way of life and highly symbolic, a visitor must be careful not to reject it by declining refreshment or rushing into business discussions. Part of that hospitality is the elaborate system of greetings and the long period of getting acquainted, perhaps taking up the entire first meeting. Although the handshake may seem limp, the rest of the greeting is not. Kissing on the cheeks is common among men, as is handholding between male friends. However, the Arab social code strictly forbids any public display of intimacy between men and women.

Women play little or no role in business or entertainment; the Middle East is a male-dominated society, and it is impolite to inquire about women. Other nonverbal taboos include showing the soles of one's feet and using the left (unclean) hand to eat or pass something. In discussions, slouching in a seat or leaning against a wall communicates a lack of respect.

The Arab society also values honor. Harris and Moran explain, "Honor, social prestige, and a secure place in society are brought about when conformity is achieved. When one fails to conform, this is considered to be damning and leads to a degree of shame."[59] Shame results not just from doing something wrong but from others finding out about that wrongdoing. Establishing a climate of honesty and trust is part of the sense of honor. Therefore, considerable tact is needed to avoid

MAP 4.1 **Saudi Arabia and the Arabian Peninsula**

FIGURE 4-5 Westerner Meeting with Arab Businessman

Source: Hi Brow Arabia/Alamy

conveying any concern or doubt. Arabs tend to be quite introverted until a mutual trust is built, which takes a long time.[60]

In their nonverbal communication, most Arab countries are high-contact cultures. Arabs stand and sit closer and touch people of the same sex more than Westerners. They do not have the same concept of public and private space or, as Hall puts it, "Not only is the sheer noise level much higher, but the piercing look of the eyes, the touch of the hands, and the mutual bathing in the warm moist breath during conversation represent stepped-up sensory inputs to a level which many Europeans find unbearably intense. On the other hand, the distance preferred by North Americans may leave an Arab suspicious of intentions because of the lack of olfactory contact."[61]

The Muslim expression *Bukra insha Allah*—"Tomorrow if Allah wills"—explains much about the Arab culture and its approach to business transactions. A cultural clash typically occurs when an American tries to give an Arab a deadline. "'I am going to Damascus tomorrow morning and will have to have my car tonight,' is a sure way to get the mechanic to stop work," explains Hall, "because to give another person a deadline in this part of the world is to be rude, pushy, and demanding."[62] In such instances, the attitude toward time communicates as loudly as words.

In verbal interactions, managers must be aware of different patterns of Arab thought and communication. Compared to the direct, linear fashion of American communication, Arabs tend to meander. They start with social talk, discuss business for a while, loop around to social and general issues, then back to business, and so on.[63] American impatience and insistence on sticking to the subject will cut off their loops, triggering confusion and dysfunction. Instead, Westerners should accept that considerable time will be spent on small talk and socializing, with frequent interruptions, before getting down to business.

Exhibit 4-5 illustrates some of the sources of noise that are likely to interfere in the communication process between Americans and Arabs, thereby causing miscommunications and misunderstandings.

For people doing business in the Middle East, the following are some useful guidelines for effective communication.

- Be patient. Recognize the Arab attitude toward time and hospitality—take time to develop friendship and trust because these are prerequisites for any social or business transactions.

- Recognize that people and relationships matter more to Arabs than the job, company, or contract—conduct business personally, not by correspondence or telephone.

EXHIBIT 4-5 Miscommunication between Americans and Arabs Caused by Cross-Cultural Noise

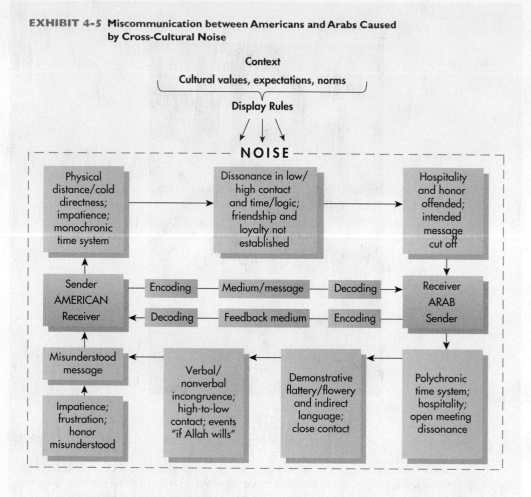

- Avoid expressing doubts or criticism when others are present—recognize the importance of honor and dignity to Arabs.
- Adapt to the norms of body language, flowery speech, and circuitous verbal patterns in the Middle East and don't be impatient to get to the point.
- Expect many interruptions in meetings, delays in schedules, and changes in plans.[64]

Communication Channels

In addition to the variables related to the sender and receiver of a message, the variables linked to the channel itself and the context of the message must be taken into consideration. These variables include fast or slow messages and information flows as well as different types of media.

INFORMATION SYSTEMS

Communication in organizations varies according to where and how it originates, the channels and the speed at which it flows, whether it is formal or informal, and so forth. The type of organizational structure, the staffing policies, and the leadership style will affect the nature of an organization's information system.

As an international manager, it is useful to know where and how information originates and the speed at which it flows, both internally and externally. In centralized organizational structures, as in South America, most information originates from top managers. Workers take less responsibility for keeping managers informed in a South American company than in a typical company in the United States, where delegation results in information flowing from the staff to the managers. In a decision-making system in which many people are involved, such as the **ringi system** of consensus decision making in Japan, the expatriate needs to understand that there is a systematic pattern for information flow.

Context also affects information flow. In high-context cultures (such as in the Middle East), information spreads rapidly and freely because of the constant close contact and the implicit ties among people and organizations. Information flow is often informal. In low-context cultures (such as Germany or the United States), information is controlled and focused and thus does not flow so freely.[65] Compartmentalized roles and office layouts stifle information channels; information sources tend to be more formal.

It is crucial for an expatriate manager to find out how to tap into a firm's informal sources of information. In Japan, employees usually have a drink together on the way home from work, and this becomes an essential source of information. However, such communication networks are based on long-term relationships in Japan (and in other high-context cultures). The same information may not be readily available to outsiders. A considerable barrier in Japan separates strangers from familiar friends, a situation that discourages communication.

Americans are more open and talk freely about almost anything, whereas Japanese will disclose little about their inner thoughts or private issues. Americans are willing to have a wide public self, disclosing their inner reactions verbally and physically. In contrast, the Japanese prefer to keep their responses largely to their private self. The Japanese expose only a small portion of their thoughts; they reduce, according to Barnlund, "the unpredictability and emotional intensity of personal encounters."[66] In intercultural communication between Americans and Japanese, cultural clashes between the public and private selves result when each party forces its cultural norms of communication on the other. In the American style, the American's cultural norms of explicit communication impose on the Japanese by invading the person's private self. The Japanese style of implicit communication causes a negative reaction from the American because of what is perceived as too much formality and ambiguity, which wastes time.[67]

Cultural variables in information systems and context underlie the many differences in communication style between Japanese and Americans. Exhibit 4-6 shows some specific differences. The Japanese *ningensei* (human beingness) style of communication refers to the preference for humanity, reciprocity, a receiver orientation, and an underlying distrust of words and analytic logic.[68] The Japanese believe that true intentions are not readily revealed in words or contracts but are, in fact, masked by them. In contrast to the typical American's verbal agility and explicitness, Japanese behaviors and communications are directed to defend and give face for everyone concerned; to do so, they avoid public disagreements at all costs. In cross-cultural negotiations, this last point is essential.

The speed with which we try to use information systems is another key variable that needs attention to avoid misinterpretation and conflict. Americans expect to give and receive information very quickly and clearly, moving through details and stages in a linear fashion to the conclusion. They usually use various media for fast messages—IMs, emails, Skype, faxes, social media, and familiar relationships—to give all the facts up front. In contrast, the French use the slower message channels of deep relationships, culture, and sometimes mediators to exchange information. A French written communication will be tentative, with subsequent letters slowly building up to a new proposal. The French preference for written communication, even for informal interactions, echoes the formality of their relationships—and results in slowing a message transmission down that often seems unnecessary to Americans.[69]

In short, it behooves Americans to realize that, because much of the world exchanges business information through slower message media, it is wise to schedule more time for transactions, develop patience, and learn to get at needed information in more subtle ways—after building rapport and taking time to observe the local system for exchanging information.

We have seen that cross-cultural misinterpretation can result from noise in the actual transmission of the message—the choice or speed of media. Interpreting the meaning of a message can thus be as much a function of examining the transmission channel (or medium) as it is of examining the message itself.

EXHIBIT 4-6 Differences between Japanese and American Communication Styles

Japanese Ningensei Style of Communication	U.S. Adversarial Style of Communication
1. Indirect verbal and nonverbal communication	1. More direct verbal and nonverbal communication
2. Relationship communication	2. More task communication
3. Discourages confrontational strategies	3. Confrontational strategies more acceptable
4. Strategically ambiguous communication	4. Prefers more to-the-point communication
5. Delayed feedback	5. More immediate feedback
6. Patient, longer-term negotiators	6. Shorter-term negotiators
7. Uses fewer words	7. Favors verbosity
8. Distrustful of skillful verbal communicators	8. Exalts verbal eloquence
9. Group orientation	9. More individualistic orientation
10. Cautious, tentative	10. More assertive, self-assured
11. Complementary communicators	11. More publicly critical communication
12. Softer, heart-like logic	12. Harder, analytic logic preferred
13. Sympathetic, empathetic, complex use of pathos	13. Favors logos, reason
14. Expresses and decodes complex relational strategies and nuances	14. Expresses and decodes complex logos, cognitive nuances
15. Avoids decision making in public	15. Frequent decision making in public
16. Makes decisions in private venues, away from public eye	16. Frequent decision in public at negotiating tables
17. Decisions via *ringi* and *nemawashi* (complete consensus process)	17. Decisions by majority rule and public compromise is more commonplace
18. Uses go-betweens for decision making	18. More extensive use of direct person-to-person, player-to-player interaction for decisions
19. Understatement and hesitation in verbal and nonverbal communication	19. May publicly speak in superlatives, exaggerations, nonverbal projection
20. Uses qualifiers, tentativeness, humility as communicator	20. Favors fewer qualifiers, more ego-centered
21. Receiver/listening–centered	21. More speaker- and message-centered
22. Inferred meanings, looks beyond words to nuances, nonverbal communication	22. More face-value meaning, more denotative
23. Shy, reserved communicators	23. More publicly self-assertive
24. Distaste for purely business transactions	24. Prefers to "get down to business" or "nitty gritty"
25. Mixes business and social communication	25. Tends to keep business negotiating more separated from social communication
26. Utilizes *matomari* or "hints" for achieving group adjustment and saving face in negotiating	26. More directly verbalizes management's preference at negotiating tables
27. Practices *haragei* or "belly logic" and communication	27. Practices more linear, discursive, analytical logic; greater reverence for cognitive than for affective

Source: A. Goldman, "The Centrality of 'Ningensei' to Japanese Negotiating and Interpersonal Relationships: Implications for U.S.–Japanese Communication," *International Journal of Intercultural Relations* 18, No. 1 (1994), with permission from the *International Journal of Intercultural Relations*, 2011.

INFORMATION TECHNOLOGY:
GOING GLOBAL AND ACTING LOCAL

Microsoft has struck a deal with the biggest Chinese search engine, Baidu.com, to offer Web search services in English.

WWW.NYTIMES.COM
JULY 4, 2011[70]

All information is local; IT systems can connect every corner of the globe, but IT managers are learning they have to pay attention to regional differences.

COMPUTERWORLD[71]

Using the Internet as a global medium for communication has enabled companies of all sizes to develop a presence quickly in many markets around the world—and, in fact, has enabled them to go global. However, their global reach cannot alone translate into global business. Those companies are learning that they have to adapt their e-commerce and their enterprise resource planning (ERP) applications to regional idiosyncrasies beyond translation or content management issues; for example, even asking for a name or an email address can incur resistance in many countries where people do not like to give out personal information.[72] Although communication over the Internet is clearly not as personal as face-to-face, cross-cultural communication, those transactions must still be regionalized and personalized to adjust to differences in language, culture, local laws, and business models as well as differences in the level of development in the local telecommunications infrastructure. Yet, if the Internet is a global medium for communication, why do so many U.S. companies treat the web as a U.S.-centric phenomenon? Giving preference to some geographic regions, languages, and cultures is "a short-sighted business decision that will result in diminished brand equity, market share, profits and global leadership."[73]

When Baidu.com—China's leading search engine—made a business decision in July 2011 to partner with Microsoft to offer web search services in English, it had clearly realized that it needed to go beyond Chinese because of the 10 million per day searches for English terms on its site.

"More and more people here are searching for English terms," Kaiser Kuo, the company's spokesman, said Monday. "But Baidu hasn't done a good job. So here's a way for us to do it."[74]

For its part, Microsoft's expansion of Bing in China gave it access to the world's largest Internet population of more than 470 million users. Both companies realized that the English-language search results would be censored (as happened to Google, which pulled out of the mainland and went to Hong Kong), and it is reported that Microsoft is cooperating with China's government on censorship rules regarding the content that can be accessed.[75] Beijing requires Internet companies operating on the mainland to censor results the government considers threatening, including references to human rights issues and dissidents.[76] Clearly, both going global and acting local can be fraught with difficulties.

It seems essential, then, for a global online strategy also to be multilocal. The impersonal nature of the web must somehow be adapted to local cultures to establish relationships and create customer loyalty. Effective technological communication requires even more cultural sensitivity than face-to-face communication because of the inability to assess reactions and get feedback or, in many cases, even retain contact. It is still people, after all, who respond to and interact with other people through the medium of the Internet, and those people interpret and respond according to their own languages and cultures as well as their local business practices and expectations. In Europe, for example, significant differences in business cultures and e-business technology have slowed e-business progress there. However, some companies are making progress in pan-European integration services, such as leEurope, which aims to cross language, currency, and cultural barriers. Specifically, leEurope is building a set of services "to help companies tie their back-end e-business systems together across European boundaries through a series of mergers involving regional e-business integrators in more than a dozen countries."[77]

MANAGING CROSS-CULTURAL COMMUNICATION

Steps toward effective intercultural communication include the development of cultural sensitivity, careful encoding, selective transmission, careful decoding, and appropriate follow-up actions.

Developing Cultural Sensitivity

When acting as a sender, a manager must make it a point to know the receiver and encode the message in a form that will most likely be understood as intended. On the manager's part, this requires an awareness of his or her own cultural baggage and how it affects the communication process. In other words, what kinds of behaviors does the message imply, and how will they be perceived by the receiver? The way to anticipate the most likely meaning that the receiver will attach to the message is to internalize honest cultural empathy with that person. What is the cultural background—the societal, economic, and organizational context—in which this communication is taking place? What are this person's expectations regarding the situation, what are the two parties' relative positions, and what might develop from this communication? What kinds of transactions and behaviors is this person used to? Cultural sensitivity (discussed in Chapter 3) is really just a matter of understanding the other person, the context, and how the person will respond to the context. Americans, unfortunately, have a rather negative reputation overseas of not being culturally sensitive. One not-for-profit group, called Business for Diplomatic Action, has the following advice for Americans when doing business abroad, in its attempts to counteract the stereotypical American traits such as boastfulness, loudness, and speed.

- **Read a map** Familiarize yourself with the local geography to avoid making insulting mistakes.
- **Dress up** In some countries, casual dress is a sign of disrespect.
- **Talk small** Talking about wealth, power, or status—corporate or personal—can create resentment.
- **No slang** Even casual profanity is unacceptable.
- **Slow down** Americans talk fast, eat fast, move fast, live fast. Many cultures do not.
- **Listen as much as you talk** Ask people you're visiting about themselves and their way of life.
- **Speak lower and slower** A loud voice is often perceived as bragging.
- **Religious restraint** In many countries, religion is not a subject for public discussion.
- **Political restraint** Steer clear of this subject. If someone is attacking U.S. politicians or policies, agree to disagree.[78]

Careful Encoding

In translating his or her intended meaning into symbols for cross-cultural communication, the sender must use words, pictures, or gestures that are appropriate to the receiver's frame of reference. Of course, language training is invaluable, but senders should also avoid idioms and regional sayings (such as "Go fly a kite" or "Foot the bill") in a translation, or even in English when speaking to a non-American who knows little English.

Literal translation, then, is a limited answer to language differences. Even for people in English-speaking countries, words can have different meanings. Ways to avoid problems are to speak slowly and clearly, avoid long sentences and colloquial expressions, and explain things in several ways and through several media if possible. However, even though English is in common use around the world for business transactions, the manager's efforts to speak the local language will greatly improve the climate. Sometimes people from other cultures resent the assumption by English-speaking executives that everyone else will speak English.

Language translation is only part of the encoding process; the message also is expressed in nonverbal language. In the encoding process, the sender must ensure congruence between the nonverbal and the verbal message. In encoding a message, therefore, it is useful to be as objective as possible and not to rely on personal interpretations. To clarify their messages further, managers can hand out written summaries of verbal presentations and use visual aids such as graphs or pictures. A good general guide is to move slowly, wait, and take cues from the receivers.

Selective Transmission

The type of medium chosen for the message depends on the nature of the message, its level of importance, the context and expectations of the receiver, the timing involved, and the need for personal interaction, among other factors. Typical media include instant messaging (IM), email, letters or memos, reports, meetings, telephone calls, teleconferences, videoconferences, or face-to-face conversations. The secret is to find out how communication is transmitted in the local organization—how much is downward versus upward or vertical versus horizontal, how the grapevine works, and so on. In addition, the cultural variables discussed earlier need to be considered: whether the receiver is from a high- or low-context culture, whether he or she is used to explicit or implicit communication, and what speed and routing of messages will be most effective.

For the most part, it is best to use face-to-face interaction for relationship building or for other important transactions, particularly in intercultural communications, because of the lack of familiarity between parties. Personal interactions give the manager the opportunity to get immediate verbal and visual feedback and make rapid adjustments in the communication process.

International dealings are often long-distance, of course, limiting the opportunity for face-to-face communication. However, personal rapport can be established or enhanced through telephone calls or videoconferencing and through trusted contacts. Modern electronic media and social networks can be used to break down communication barriers by reducing waiting periods for information, clarifying issues, and allowing instant consultation, such as through Skype, for one-on-one or group video-chat. Ford Europe uses videoconferencing for engineers in Britain and Germany to consult about quality problems. Through the video monitors, they examine one another's engineering diagrams and usually find a solution that gets the factory moving again in a short time.

Careful Decoding of Feedback

Timely and effective feedback channels can also be set up to assess a firm's general communication about the progression of its business and its general management principles. The best means for getting accurate feedback is through face-to-face interaction because this allows the manager to hear, see, and immediately sense how a message is being interpreted. When visual feedback on important issues is not possible or appropriate, it is a good idea to use several means of attaining feedback, in particular by employing third parties.

Decoding is the process of translating the received symbols into the interpreted message. The main causes of incongruence are because (1) the receiver misinterprets the message, (2) the receiver encodes his or her return message incorrectly, or (3) the sender misinterprets the feedback. Two-way communication is thus essential for important issues so that successive efforts can be made until an understanding has been achieved. Asking other colleagues to help interpret what is going on is often a good way to break a cycle of miscommunication.

Perhaps the most important means for avoiding miscommunication is to practice careful decoding by improving one's listening and observation skills. A good listener practices projective listening, or empathic listening—listening, without interruption or evaluation, to the full message of the speaker; attempting to recognize the feelings behind the words and nonverbal cues; and understanding the speaker's perspective.

At the multinational corporation (MNC) level, avenues of communication and feedback among parent companies and subsidiaries can be kept open through telephone calls, regular meetings and visits, reports, and plans, all of which facilitate cooperation, performance control, and the smooth running of the company. Communication among far-flung operations can be managed best by setting up feedback systems and liaison people. The headquarters people should maintain considerable flexibility in cooperating with local managers and allowing them to deal with the local context as they see fit.

Follow-up Actions

Managers communicate through both action and inaction. Therefore, to keep open the lines of communication, feedback, and trust, managers must follow through with action on what has been discussed and then agreed upon—typically a contract, which is probably the most important formal business communication. Unfortunately, the issue of contract follow-through is a particularly sensitive one across cultures because of the different interpretations regarding what constitutes a contract (perhaps a handshake, perhaps a full legal document) and what actions should result. Trust, future communications, and future business are based on such interpretations, and it is up to managers to understand them and follow through on them.

The management of cross-cultural communication depends largely on a manager's personal abilities and behavior. Behaviors that researchers indicate to be most important to intercultural communication effectiveness (ICE) are listed here, as reviewed by Ruben.

- Respect (conveyed through eye contact, body posture, voice tone, and pitch)
- Interaction posture (the ability to respond to others in a descriptive, nonevaluative, and nonjudgmental way)
- Orientation to knowledge (recognizing that one's knowledge, perception, and beliefs are valid only for oneself and not for everyone else)
- Empathy
- Interaction management
- Tolerance for ambiguity
- Other-oriented role behavior (one's capacity to be flexible and adopt different roles for the sake of greater group cohesion and group communication)[79]

Researchers have established a relationship between personality traits and behaviors and the ability to adapt to the host-country's cultural environment.[80] What is seldom pointed out, however, is that communication is the mediating factor between those behaviors and the relative level of adaptation the expatriate achieves. The communication process facilitates cross-cultural adaptation, and, through this process, expatriates learn the dominant communication patterns of the host society. Therefore, we can link personality factors shown by research to ease adaptation with those necessary for effective intercultural communication.

Kim has consolidated the research findings of these characteristics into two categories: (1) **openness**—traits such as open-mindedness, tolerance for ambiguity, and extrovertedness—and (2) **resilience**—traits such as having an internal locus of control, persistence, a tolerance of ambiguity, and resourcefulness.[81] These personality factors, along with the expatriate's cultural and racial identity and the level of preparedness for change, comprise that person's potential for adaptation. The level of preparedness can be improved by the manager before his or her assignment by gathering information about the host country's verbal and nonverbal communication patterns and norms of behavior. However, we must remember the practicalities of situational factors that can affect the communication process—variables such as the physical environment, time constraints, the degree of structure, and feelings of irritability or overwork, among others.

CONCLUSION

Effective intercultural communication is a vital skill for international managers and domestic managers of multicultural workforces. Because miscommunication is much more likely to occur among people from different countries or racial backgrounds than among those from similar backgrounds, it is important to be alert to how culture is reflected in communication—in particular through the development of cultural sensitivity and an awareness of potential sources of cultural noise in the communication process. A successful international manager is thus attuned to these variables and is flexible enough to adjust his or her communication style to address the intended receivers best—that is, to do it their way.

Cultural variables and the manner in which culture is communicated underlie the processes of negotiation and decision making. How do people around the world negotiate? What are their expectations and their approach to negotiations? What is the importance of understanding negotiation and decision-making processes in other countries? Chapter 5 addresses these questions and makes suggestions to help the international manager handle these important tasks.

Summary of Key Points

- Communication is an inherent part of a manager's role, taking up the majority of the manager's time on the job. Effective intercultural communication largely determines the success of international transactions or the output of a culturally diverse workforce.
- Culture is the foundation of communication, and communication transmits culture. Cultural variables that can affect the communication process by influencing a person's perceptions include attitudes, social organizations, thought patterns, roles, language, nonverbal language, and time.
- Language conveys cultural understandings and social norms from one generation to the next. Body language, or nonverbal communication, is behavior that communicates without words. It accounts for 65 to 93 percent of interpreted communication.
- Types of nonverbal communication around the world are kinesic behavior, proxemics, paralanguage, and object language.
- Effective cross-cultural communication must take into account whether the receiver is from a country with a monochronic or a polychronic time system.

- Variables related to channels of communication include high- and low-context cultures, fast or slow messages and information flows, and various types of media.
- In high-context cultures, feelings and messages are implicit and must be accessed through an understanding of the person and the system. In low-context cultures, feelings and thoughts are expressed, and information is more readily available.
- The effective management of intercultural communication necessitates the development of cultural sensitivity, careful encoding, selective transmission, careful decoding, and follow-up actions.
- Certain personal abilities and behaviors facilitate adaptation to the host country through skilled intercultural communication.
- Communication through the Internet must still be localized to adjust to differences in language, culture, local laws, and business models.

Discussion Questions

4-1. How does culture affect the process of attribution in communication? Can you relate this to some experiences you have had with your classmates?

4-2. What is stereotyping? Give some examples. How might people stereotype you?

4-3. What is the relationship between language and culture? How is it that people from different countries who speak the same language may still miscommunicate?

4-4. Give some examples of cultural differences in the interpretation of body language. What is the role of such nonverbal communication in business relationships?

4-5. Explain the differences between high- and low-context cultures, giving some examples. What are the differential effects on the communication process?

4-6. Discuss the role of information systems in a company, how and why they vary from country to country, and the effects of these variations.

Application Exercises

4-7. Form groups in your class—multicultural groups, if possible. Have each person make notes about his or her perceptions of (1) Mexican-Americans, (2) Native Americans, (3) African Americans, and (4) Americans of European descent. Discuss your notes and draw conclusions about common stereotypes. Discuss any differences and why stereotyping occurs.

4-8. Invite some students who are from other countries to your class. Ask them to bring photographs, slides, and so forth of people and events in their native countries. Have them explain the meanings of various nonverbal cues such as

gestures, dress, voice inflections, architecture, and events. Discuss with them any differences between their explanations and the attributions you assigned to those cues.

4-9. Interview a faculty member or a businessperson who has worked abroad. Ask him or her to identify factors that facilitated or inhibited adaptation to the host environment. Ask whether more preparation could have eased the transition and what, if anything, that person would do differently before another trip.

Experiential Exercise

4-10. Form two or three pairs to enact skits—separately—in front of the class and then ask your class for feedback and to guess where you are from.

Each person in each pair decides on a different cultural profile to enact—for example, act as if one of you is, say, Japanese or Arab, and the other is, say, German or Mexican. Set up a five-to-

ten minute skit, presumably for an intended business transaction. Research and practice with your partner the typical communication style, both verbal and nonverbal (use English for everyone).

Both you and your class will see how difficult it is to put yourself in the persona of someone from a different cultural background.

CASE STUDY

Miscommunications with a Brazilian Auto Parts Manufacturer

The Brazilian sun beat down steadily on the tarmac outside as Alessandro Silva and Agosto Ventura stood inside the São Paulo-Guarulhos International Airport. They were awaiting the arrival of two representatives from Lucky Auto Parts Company, a regional wholesaler and retailer based in Ames, Iowa.

Mr. Silva, the president of a mid-sized auto parts manufacturer in São Paulo, and Mr. Ventura, the company's sales manager, were looking forward to a new business relationship with Henry Williams, president of Lucky Auto Parts Company. A few weeks previously, in an initial phone call, President Silva invited President Williams to visit the Brazilian manufacturing facility, a potential source of after-market auto parts for Lucky. This would be the American company's first venture into buying parts directly from a foreign manufacturer. Williams planned to take his new vice president of purchasing, Wally Astor, who also happened to be his son-in-law, on this first trip. Mr. Williams thought this exploratory buying trip would be a good introduction to the auto parts business for Wally; although Wally had experience as a new car salesman, he had no experience in the auto parts field.

Unfortunately, a few days before the trip, Williams had to cancel his trip to be available for a deposition on a court case pending against his company. It had taken a long time to get the appointment with Mr. Silva, and Williams did not think it wise to cancel the trip. Because Wally was eager to prove himself in his new role, Williams decided to let him handle this mission without the old man looking over his shoulder. In the rush to review the legal documents for the deposition, Williams forgot to notify his Brazilian counterpart that he would not be coming on this visit.

As he was preparing for the trip, Wally Astor realized that it was summer in Brazil and that it was a long flight to Brazil from Ames through Miami. Based on this, he decided to dress as informally and comfortably as possible.

At the airport, both Mr. Silva and Mr. Agosto were dressed as usual when conducting business or in the public eye for social occasions, that is, in suits and ties. As they stood outside the door of the international arrivals area, Agosto held a neatly printed sign with Wally Astor's name on it. Soon a young man in his late twenties approached them and announced that he was Wally Astor; both Mr. Silva and Mr. Ventura were visibly surprised, especially because the young man was dressed in faded blue jeans, sneakers, and a checked shirt with the sleeves rolled up.

"Hey, thanks for picking me up," Wally said as the three shook hands. "You must be Alexander and Agosto? My father-in-law said you were going to meet us at the airport."

"I am President Alessandro Silva, and this is my Marketing Director, Mr. Ventura," Mr. Silva said icily. "We expected to see President Williams. Will he be coming on a later flight?"

"No, he had something important come up, so he sent me to take care of the visit to Brazil," Wally replied. "Oh, here, let me give you my business card so you'll know I really am who I say I am."

President Silva read the card carefully and turned to Agosto with a frown. The card had the U.S. flag emblazoned on it with an italicized inscription under it: "An American-owned business."

Agosto turned to Wally and said politely, "I'm certain you are tired from your long journey. Shall we drop you at your hotel and then pick you up for dinner about nine o'clock?"

"Nine o'clock! Isn't that a little late for dinner?" Wally exclaimed. "No, let's just go to your office and get right to it, shall we? I have a contract drawn up by the lawyer-types in my department. I think you'll find it covers all the details and is more than fair."

President Silva spoke up more forcefully than he intended, "Mr. Astor ..."

"Please call me Wally."

"No, Mr. Astor. I don't know you or your company well enough to call you by your first name and certainly not well enough to look at an important contract with you today. I was impressed with the phone conversation I had with President Williams, but *he* is not here today, so let's drop you at your hotel and begin our discussion over dinner later this evening."

Wally was surprised and uncomfortable to see Mr. Silva standing very close to him, staring intently into his eyes and gesticulating to emphasize his words. Wally took a step back, but Mr. Silva took a step toward him to close the gap between them.

"OK, Mr. Silva. Maybe I sounded like I was trying to rush things a bit. But you see, I booked my flight out for tomorrow evening so I can spend a couple days in Rio to see what that's about."

There was an uncomfortable silence during which no one spoke. Finally, Wally said, "I guess I would like to go to my hotel and rest up. Then we can have dinner at 9:00. OK?"

Ventura knew that President Silva was not warming to Wally, so he decided to see whether he could get the relationship back on track. Because he and Wally were about the same age and held the same status within their respective organizations, he felt comfortable doing this.

"That sounds very good, Wally," Ventura said. "We will pick you up at 9:00. And please, call me Agosto."

Once he was settled in his hotel room, Wally phoned Henry Williams to check in as instructed.

"Yeah, Dad," Wally said. "I met with them at the airport. They drove me to the hotel and we're going to dinner tonight to get acquainted. Can you believe they want to eat at 9 P.M.?"

"That's good," Williams replied. "Did you see their facility yet?"

"No. The president, Mr. Silva, is kinda stiff. He said he wants to get to know us better before he talks business. I think he's doing the Latin American thing about *mañana*. I tried to get the ball rolling this afternoon, but he wouldn't hear of it."

"Well, he's just being cautious, like I am. I like to know a man personally before I enter into a long-term contract with him, too. Wally, this isn't like selling cars. It's building relationships that have to work day after day. I'm sorry I threw you into this situation alone."

"You know," Wally said, "I think he's upset that you aren't here."

"I hope you conveyed my apology to him," Williams replied, "and explained that this deposition came up at the last minute."

"I sure did."

"OK. Call me tomorrow afternoon to let me know how the dinner conversation went. How long do you think you'll be out there?"

"Well, I made reservations to leave for Rio tomorrow evening for a couple days," Wally said.

"Why are you going to Rio? Who is out there?" Williams asked.

"I promised Mindy I'd check out Rio as a possible vacation spot for later this year."

"Wally, you don't work for Mindy. You work for me. If Mr. Silva wants to talk with you for the next few days, that's exactly what you're going to do. Forget about going to Rio!"

That evening at the restaurant, Mr. Silva insisted that Wally sit across the table from him and Mr. Agosto.

"Mr. Astor, I want to thank you for joining us for a Brazilian business dinner this evening," said Mr. Silva. "We always start with cafezinho, a very strong espresso. We think it helps the conversation to flow."

For the next hour, Wally found himself talking freely about his wife, their relationship, his in-laws, his childhood and parents, and many other topics that would never find their way into a business discussion in the U.S. To encourage Wally, Mr. Silva and Agosto shared humorous stories about themselves and shared their favorite sports, movies, pastimes, wines, and vacation areas.

Their free exchange about themselves continued throughout the dinner, and as the three men were served cafezinho after the meal, they began to talk business for the first time that evening. President Silva introduced the topic.

"Wally, I think tomorrow morning you should join us to see the plant. I want you to meet with our purchasing and quality assurance managers. We pride ourselves on using the best materials and maintaining the strictest tolerance standards. After you are more familiar with how we do things, we will meet again for dinner before your flight to Rio and discuss when Mr. Williams can visit us to resume exploring our potential business partnership."

"Sir," Wally began, "I cancelled my trip to Rio so I can learn more about your operation, your products, and where our mutual interests may lie. Perhaps we can have dinner again tomorrow night and decide what our next steps should be for the following few days."

"I'm very happy to hear you say that. And please, call me Alessandro."

Case Questions

4-11. What are three of the cultural missteps that Wally Astor and his father-in-law, Henry Williams, made in this scenario? Why do you think this happened?

4-12. If you were a native of Brazil and advising American business representatives about what to do when talking with Brazilian business partners, what would you tell the Americans about Brazilian culture?

4-13. Imagine that the situation in this case study was reversed, that is, the Brazilian businessmen were coming to the United States to look for a supplier. What would you tell the Brazilians about American business culture to prepare them for success?

Source: Linda Catlin. Ms. Catlin is an organizational anthropologist and the co-author of *International Business: Cultural Sourcebook and Case Studies.* She consults with clients on projects related to cross-cultural business communications, organizational culture, and organizational change dynamics. Her clients include the Mayo Clinic, the Kellogg Foundation, General Motors, Ascension Health, and BASF.

Linda Catlin, Claymore Associates. Used with permission.

Endnotes

1. K. Ananth Krishnan (Tata Consultancy Services), interviewed by Michael S. Hopkins, "The 'Unstructured Information' Most Businesses Miss Out On," *MIT Sloan Management Review: The Magazine*, April 27, 2011.

2. Sharlene Goff, "Lenders Eye Social Media Angles," *Financial Times*, London (UK), January 10, 2011, p. 18.

3. Krishnan.

4. Donna L. Hoffman and Marek Fodor, "Can You Measure the ROI of Your Social Media Marketing?" *MIT Sloan Management Review* 52 (Fall 2010), p. 1.

5. Roxane Divol, David Edelman, and Hugo Sarrazin, "Demystifying Social Media," *McKinsey Quarterly*, April 2012; "What Marketers Say about Working Online: McKinsey Global Survey Results," mckinseyquarterly.com, November 2011.

6. "Facebook Takes a Dive: Why Social Networks Are Bad Businesses," http://www.time.com/time/business/article/0,8599, 1888796,00.html#ixzz1RosHjXUq, accessed July 10, 2011.

7. Cindy Chiu, Chris Ip, and Ari Silverman, "Understanding Social Media in China," *McKinsey Quarterly*, April 2012.

8. E. T. Hall and M. R. Hall, *Understanding Cultural Differences* (Yarmouth, ME: Intercultural Press, 1990), p. 4.

9. E. Wilmott, "New Media Vision," *New Media Age*, September 9, 1999, p. 8.

10. Hall and Hall; K. Wolfson and W. B. Pearce, "A Cross-Cultural Comparison of the Implications of Self-discovery on Conversation Logics," *Communication Quarterly* 31 (1983), pp. 249–256.

11. L. Nardon, R. M. Steers, and C. J. Sanchez-Runde, "Seeking Common Ground: Strategies for Enhancing Multicultural Communication," *Organizational Dynamics*, 2011, in press, http://dx.doi.org/10.1016/j.orgdyn.2011.01.002.

12. H. Mintzberg, *The Nature of Managerial Work* (New York: Harper and Row, 1973).

13. L. A. Samovar, R. E. Porter, and N. C. Jain, *Understanding Intercultural Communication* (Belmont, CA: Wadsworth Publishing, 1981).

14. P. R. Harris and R. T. Moran, *Managing Cultural Differences*, 3rd ed. (Houston: Gulf Publishing, 1991).

15. H. C. Triandis, quoted in *The Blackwell Handbook of Cross-Cultural Management*, M. Gannon and K. Newman, eds. (Oxford, UK: Blackwell Publishers, 2002).

16. Samovar, Porter, and Jain.

17. Hall and Hall, p. 15.

18. Based on H. C. Triandis, *Interpersonal Behavior* (Monterey, CA: Brooks/Cole, 1997), p. 248.

19. James R. Houghton, former chairman of Corning, Inc., quoted in *Organizational Dynamics* 29, No. 4 (2001).

20. J. Child, "Trust: The Fundamental Bond in Global Collaboration," *Organizational Dynamics* 29, No. 4 (2001), pp. 274–288.

21. Ibid.

22. World Values Study Group, *World Values Survey, ICPSR Version* (Ann Arbor, MI: Institute for Social Research, 1994); R. Inglehart, M. Basanez, and A. Moreno, *Human Values and Beliefs: A Cross-Cultural Sourcebook* (Ann Arbor: University of Michigan Press, 1998).

23. Mansour Javidan and Robert J. House, "Cultural Acumen for the Global Manager," *Organizational Dynamics* 29, No. 4 (2001), 289–305.

24. Samovar and Porter; Harris and Moran.

25. M. L. Hecht, P. A. Andersen, and S. A. Ribeau, "The Cultural Dimensions of Nonverbal Communication, in *Handbook of International and Intercultural Communication*, M. K. Asante and W. B. Gudykunst, eds. (Newbury Park, CA: Sage Publications, 1989), pp. 163–185.

26. H. C. Triandis, *Interpersonal Behavior* (Monterey, CA: Brooks/Cole, 1977).

27. Harris and Moran.

28. Adapted from N. Adler, *International Dimensions of Organizational Behavior*, 2nd ed. (Boston: PWS-Kent, 1991).

29. D. A. Ricks, *Big Business Blunders: Mistakes in Multinational Marketing* (Homewood, IL: Dow Jones–Irwin, 1983).

30. P. Garfinkel, "On Keeping Your Foot Safely Out of Your Mouth," www.nytimes.com, July 13, 2004.

31. Jiatao Li, Katherine R. Xin, Anne Tsui, and Donald C. Hambrick, "Building Effective International Joint Venture Leadership Teams in China," *Journal of World Business* 34, No. 1 (1999), pp. 52–68.

32. D. Walker, T. Walker, and J. Schmitz, *Doing Business Internationally* (New York: McGraw-Hill, 2003).

33. Roger E. Axtell, *Essential Do's and Taboos,"* (Hoboken, NJ: John Wiley and Sons, Inc., 2007).

34. R. L. Daft, *Organizational Theory and Design*, 3rd ed. (St. Paul, MN: West Publishing, 1989).

35. Li et al., 1999.

36. Rachel Donadio, "When Italians Chat, Hands and Fingers Do the Talking," www.nytimes.com, *Rome Journal*, June 30, 2013, www.ediplomat.com, accessed July 8, 2014; http://www.theguardian.com/world/shortcuts/2013/jul/02/how-speak-italian-with-hand-gestures; http://acad.depauw.edu/mkfinney_web/teaching/Com227/culturalPortfolios/ITALY/Italy%20Nonverbal.html, accessed July 8, 2014; http://www.goinglobal.com/articles/1112/, accessed July 8, 2014.

37. O. Klineberg, "Emotional Expression in Chinese Literature," *Journal of Abnormal and Social Psychology* 33 (1983), pp. 517–530.

38. P. Ekman and W. V. Friesen, "Constants Across Cultures in the Face and Emotion," *Journal of Personality and Social Psychology* 17 (1971), pp. 124–129.

39. J. Pfeiffer, "How Not to Lose the Trade Wars by Cultural Gaffes," *Smithsonian* 18, No. 10 (January 1988).

40. E. T. Hall, *The Silent Language* (New York: Doubleday, 1959).

41. Hall and Hall.

42. Random House, American Heritage, Merriam Webster; *fengshui*, Oxford English Dictionary, 2nd ed. (Oxford University Press, 1989); Tina Marie, *"Feng Shui Diaries, Esoteric Feng Shui* (2007–2009); "Baidu Baike," *Huai Nan Zi*; Stephen L. Field, *The Zangshu, or Book of Burial*.

43. http://www.instituteoffengshui.com/fengshui.html, accessed June 24, 2011.

44. Ibid.

45. Jonathan Vatner, "When Feng Shui Helps Determine a Deal's Fate," www.nytimes.com, August 24, 2010.

46. Ibid.

47. Hall and Hall.

48. Anand Giridharadas, "How to Greet in a Global Microcosm," New York Times Online, October 15, 2010.

49. Hecht, Andersen, and Ribeau.

50. Li et al., 1999.

51. "The Name Game: Business Cards an Essential Part of Operating in China," *The International Herald Tribune*, January 10, 2011.

52. Hall and Hall.

53. Robert Matthews, "Where East Can Never Meet West," *Financial Times*, October 21, 2005.

54. Hall and Hall.

55. Matthews, 2005.

56. Hecht, Andersen, and Ribeau.

57. Hall and Hall.

58. M. K. Nydell, *Understanding Arabs* (Yarmouth, ME: Intercultural Press, 1987).

59. Harris and Moran.

60. E. T. Hall, *The Hidden Dimension* (New York: Doubleday, 1966), p. 15.

61. Hall and Hall.

62. Ibid.

63. Based largely on the work of Nydell; and R. T. Moran and P. R. Harris, *Managing Cultural Synergy* (Houston: Gulf Publishing, 1982), pp. 81–82.

64. Ibid.

65. Hall and Hall.

66. D. C. Barnlund, "Public and Private Self in Communicating with Japan," *Business Horizons* (March–April 1989), pp. 32–40.

67. Hall and Hall.

68. A. Goldman, "The Centrality of 'Ningensei' to Japanese Negotiating and Interpersonal Relationships: Implications for U.S.–Japanese Communication," *International Journal of Intercultural Relations* 18, No. 1 (1994).

69. Jean-Louis Barsoux and Peter Lawrence, "The Making of a French Manager," *Harvard Business Review* (July–August 1991), pp. 58–67.

70. D. Barboza, "Microsoft Forms Partnership with China's Leading Search Engine," www.nytimes.com, July 4, 2011.

71. D. Shand, "All Information Is Local: IT Systems Can Connect Every Corner of the Globe, But IT Managers Are Learning They Have to Pay Attention to Regional Differences," *Computerworld* 88 No. 1 (2000).

72. Shand.

73. Wilmott.

74. Barboza, July 4, 2011.

75. Doug Tsuruoka, "Hudong to Help Microsoft's Bing in Chinese Search," *Investor's Business Daily*," June 6, 2012.

76. Barboza, July 4, 2011.

77. T. Wilson, "B2B Links, European Style: Integrator Helps Applications Cross Language, Currency and Cultural Barriers," *InternetWeek*, October 9, 2000, p. 27.

78. Based on www.Businessfordiplomaticaction.org, accessed August 19, 2006.

79. R. B. Ruben, "Human Communication and Cross-Cultural Effectiveness," in *Intercultural Communication: A Reader*, L. Samovar and R. Porter, eds. (Belmont, CA: Wadsworth, 1985), p. 339.

80. D. Ruben and B. D. Ruben, "Cross-Cultural Personnel Selection Criteria, Issues and Methods," in *Handbook of Intercultural Training*, vol. 1, *Issues in Theory and Design*, D. Landis and R. W. Brislin, eds. (New York: Pergamon, 1983), pp. 155–175.

81. Young Yun Kim, *Communication and Cross-Cultural Adaptation: An Integrative Theory* (Clevedon, UK; Multilingual Matters, 1988).

5 Cross-Cultural Negotiation and Decision Making

OUTLINE

OBJECTIVES

5-1. To become familiar with the role of negotiation in implementing a firm's strategy, and the various stakeholders who must be considered.

5-2. To learn the stages of the negotiation process and how to prepare for cross-cultural business negotiations.

5-3. To gain insight into the various types of negotiating styles around the world.

5-4. To recognize that managing negotiation requires learning about the culturally based behavioral differences, values, and agendas of the negotiating parties and how to build trust for successful negotiations.

5-5. To learn the complexities of negotiating with the Chinese.

5-6. To appreciate the variables in the decision-making process and understand the influence of culture on decision making.

Opening Profile: Facebook's Continued Negotiations in China[1]

We continue to evaluate entering China…. However, this market has substantial legal and regulatory complexities that have prevented our entry into China to date.

DEAL JOURNAL, 2012, *quoting from Facebook's IPO Filing*[2]

In 2014, Facebook signed a three-year lease for office space in Beijing's central business district. And the real estate negotiation may only be the first move from Facebook to retake the world's biggest population.

WWW.IBTIMES.COM
May 13, 2014

As Facebook filed for its IPO (initial public offering—symbol FB) on the stock market in February 2012, investors questioned the company's ability to negotiate further expansion overseas to justify its goal of a $100 billion market value. As of that time, Facebook had 845 million users, making it the largest institution of all time (more than 1.4 billion active users worldwide as of 2015); if it were a country, it would be the world's third most populous country. Of Facebook's users, 80 percent are overseas; however, because six out of ten Internet users in the United States and Canada are Facebook friends, most of the company's growth must come from other countries. To date, the company's progress overseas has been impressive, although those markets are far less profitable than the home market.

However, negotiations have been thwarted in accessing some important large markets such as China. (Facebook has been officially banned there for six years (as of 2015), although many there find ways around the restrictions.) This has led observers to comment that, as indicated in the company's IPO filing, Facebook's Asia strategy is India, Japan, and South Korea because Internet censorship in China has left the company with near zero penetration. The Chinese government bars its citizens from direct access to Facebook; instead, people are steered toward censored, home-grown social networks such as Renren and Sina.

Government agencies in China would probably want not only to censor postings but to have access to personal data that Chinese citizens posted. Much of the population can't afford the products and services needed for Facebook, including broadband Internet access, a personal computer, or a smartphone, Agrawal said.[3]

It's clear that Facebook's founder, Mark Zuckerberg, who is learning Mandarin and has made trips to China, intends to continue negotiations to pursue the Chinese market, saying, "We continue to evaluate entering China…. However, this market has substantial legal and regulatory complexities that have prevented our entry into China to date. If we fail to deploy or manage our operations in international markets successfully, our business may suffer."[4] The company fears losing out to domestic Internet companies such as Alibaba and Tencent; other local competitors in China are Weibo, WeChat, Renren Inc., and Sina Corp.

Although other Internet companies such as Google have tried to negotiate a compromise with the Chinese government, Facebook executives are clearly concerned about the prospect of citizens giving up their personal details to the government authorities, not knowing how that information might be used.

Some progress has been made. In April 2011, after several meetings between Facebook Chief Executive Officer (CEO) Mark Zuckerberg and Baidu CEO Robin Li, Facebook signed an agreement with Baidu; however, the China website won't be integrated with Facebook's international service, and the start date was not confirmed. Facebook executives have had a number of meetings to negotiate agreements with various partners in China to enter the market, stating, "We are currently studying and learning about China, as part of evaluating any possible approaches that could benefit our users, developers and advertisers."[5]

In 2010, Google withdrew its search engine from China amid protests in the West about allowing content censoring. Websites such as Facebook, Twitter Inc., and Google's YouTube are blocked in China because they don't follow the government's self-censorship rules. China bans anything critical of the government and any pornography or gambling.

Clearly, Zuckerberg is planning to continue negotiations in China, but, as acknowledged in the IPO filing, "We do not know if we will be able to find an approach to managing content and information that will be acceptable to us and to the Chinese government."[6] Meanwhile, Facebook opened a sales office in Hong Kong to give the company ready access to the 1 billion person–strong market if that ever changes; and in 2015, the company leased office space in Beijing; the primary activity is advertising. Facebook is finding ways to profit by advertising for Chinese businesses in spite of the blockage of its primary activity.

We've got 1.3 billion people on Facebook, and it turns out that marketing to those people from China works really well.

FACEBOOK VICE PRESIDENT VAUGHAN SMITH

WWW.BLOOMBERGBUSINESSWEEK
JANUARY 26, 2015

As illustrated in the opening profile, global managers negotiate with parties in other countries to make specific plans for strategies (exporting, joint ventures, acquisitions, etc.) as well as for continuing operations. Although the complexities of cross-cultural negotiations among firms around the world present challenge enough, managers may also be faced with negotiating with government-owned companies.

Managers must prepare for strategic negotiations. Next, the operational details must be negotiated—staffing key positions, sourcing raw materials or component parts, and repatriating profits, to name a few. As globalism burgeons, the ability to conduct successful cross-cultural negotiations cannot be overemphasized. Failure to negotiate productively will result at best in confusion and delays and at worst in lost potential alliances and lost business.

During the process of negotiation—whether before, during, or after negotiating sessions—all kinds of decisions are made, both explicitly and implicitly. A consideration of cross-cultural negotiations must therefore include the various decision-making processes that occur around the world. Negotiations cannot be conducted without making decisions.

This chapter examines the processes of negotiation and decision making as they apply to international and domestic cross-cultural contexts. The objective is a better understanding of successful management.

NEGOTIATION

Implementing strategy depends on management's ability to negotiate productively—a skill widely considered one of the most important in international business. In the global arena, cultural differences produce great difficulties in the negotiation process. Ignorance of native bargaining rituals, more than any other single factor, accounts for unimpressive sales efforts.[7] Important differences in the negotiation process from country to country include (1) the amount and type of preparation for a negotiation, (2) the relative emphasis on tasks versus interpersonal relationships, (3) the reliance on general principles rather than specific issues, and (4) the number of people present and the extent of their influence.[8] In every instance, managers must familiarize themselves with the cultural background and underlying motivations of the negotiators—and the tactics and procedures they use—to control the process, make progress, and therefore maximize company goals.

The term **negotiation** describes the process of discussion by which two or more parties aim to reach a mutually acceptable agreement. For long-term positive relations, the goal should be to set up a win–win situation—that is, to bring about a settlement beneficial to all parties concerned. This process, difficult enough when it takes place among people of similar backgrounds, is even more complex in international negotiations because of differences in cultural values, lifestyles, expectations, verbal and nonverbal language, approaches to formal procedures, and problem-solving techniques. The complexity is heightened when negotiating across borders because of the greater number of stakeholders involved. These stakeholders are illustrated in Exhibit 5-1. In preparing for negotiations, it is critical to avoid projective

EXHIBIT 5-1 Stakeholders in Cross-Cultural Negotiations

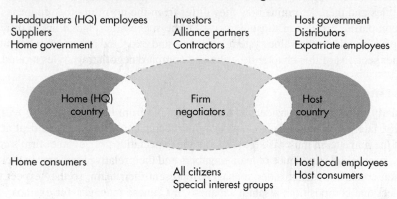

Headquarters (HQ) employees
Suppliers
Home government

Investors
Alliance partners
Contractors

Host government
Distributors
Expatriate employees

Home (HQ) country   Firm negotiators   Host country

Home consumers

All citizens
Special interest groups

Host local employees
Host consumers

cognitive similarity—that is, the assumption that others perceive, judge, think, and reason in the same way when, in fact, they do not because of differential cultural and practical influences. Instead, astute negotiators empathically enter the private world or cultural space of their counterparts while willingly sharing their own view of the situation.[9]

THE NEGOTIATION PROCESS

The negotiation process comprises five stages, the ordering of which may vary according to the cultural norms (in any event, for most people, relationship building is part of a continuous process): (1) preparation, (2) relationship building, (3) the exchange of task-related information, (4) persuasion, and (5) concessions and agreement.[10] Of course, in reality, these are seldom distinct stages but rather tend to overlap; negotiators may also temporarily revert to an earlier stage. With that in mind, it is useful to break down the negotiation process into stages to discuss the issues relevant to each stage and what international managers might expect so that they might manage this process more successfully. These stages are shown in Exhibit 5-2 and discussed in the following sections.

Stage One: Preparation

The importance of careful preparation for cross-cultural negotiations cannot be overstated. To the extent that time permits, a distinct advantage can be gained if negotiators familiarize themselves with the entire context and background of their counterparts (no matter where the meetings will take place) in addition to the specific subjects to be negotiated. Because most negotiation problems are caused by differences in culture, language, and environment, hours or days of tactical preparation for negotiation can be wasted if these factors are not carefully considered.[11]

EXHIBIT 5-2 The Negotiation Process

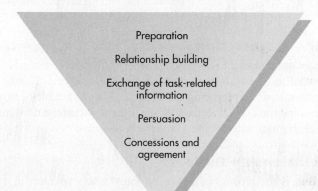

Preparation

Relationship building

Exchange of task-related information

Persuasion

Concessions and agreement

To understand cultural differences in negotiating styles, managers first must understand their own styles and then determine how they differ from the norm in other countries. They can do this by comparing profiles of those perceived to be successful negotiators in different countries. Such profiles reflect the value system, attitudes, and expected behaviors inherent in a given society. Other sections of this chapter describe and compare negotiating styles around the world.

Negotiating Teams

It is particularly important to consider the teams of people from both parties who will be negotiating. Clearly, lack of thought or planning regarding teams can jeopardize the deal at any point. Selection of the home team must take into account the expectations of the other firm's counterparts as far as the number and experience of team members and their relative hierarchy in their positions. In most Asian countries, senior, older, managers represent their team, so they expect the foreign team to reflect that composition; a senior Japanese or Chinese manager, for example, is likely to be insulted if one of the lead team members from your firm is young and lower on the career ladders, rendering all other preparations a waste of time and money. Another recommendation is to have managers on the team who have already established relationships with counterparts; given the extreme focus that is placed on trust in many countries, existing relationships give the negotiating process a head start, some information about the motivations of the counterparts, and who has the power to seal the deal.

After developing thoughtful profiles of the other party or parties, managers can plan for the actual negotiation meetings, at the same time remaining open to realizing that specific people may not fit the assumed cultural prototype. Prior to the meetings, they should find out as much as possible about the kinds of demands that might be made and whether conflicts might occur. After this, the managers can gear their negotiation strategy specifically to the other side's firm, allocate roles to different team members, decide on concessions, and prepare an alternative action plan in case a negotiated solution cannot be found.[12]

Following the preparation and planning stage, which is usually done at the home office, the core of the actual negotiation takes place on-site in the foreign location (or at the manager's home office if the other team has decided to travel there). In some cases, a compromise on the location for negotiations can signal a cooperative strategy, which Weiss calls "Improvise an Approach: Effect Symphony"—a strategy available to negotiators familiar with each other's culture and willing to put negotiation on an equal footing. Weiss gives the following example of this negotiation strategy:

> *For their negotiations over construction of the tunnel under the English Channel, British and French representatives agreed to partition talks and alternate the site between Paris and London. At each site, the negotiators were to use established, local ways, including the language ... thus punctuating approaches by time and space.*[13]

In this way, each side was put into the context and the script of the other culture about half the time.

The next stage of negotiation—often given short shrift by Westerners—is that of relationship building. In most parts of the world, this stage usually has already taken place or is concurrent with other preparations.

Variables in the Negotiation Process

Adept negotiators conduct research to develop a profile of their counterparts so that they know, in most situations, what to expect, how to prepare, and how to react. Exhibit 5-3 shows some of the variables to consider when preparing to negotiate. These variables can, to a great degree, help managers understand the deep-rooted cultural and national motivations and traditional processes underlying negotiations with people from other countries.

Stage Two: Relationship Building

Relationship building is the process of getting to know one's contacts in a host country and building mutual trust before embarking on business discussions and transactions. This process is regarded with much more significance in most parts of the world than it is in the United States.

EXHIBIT 5-3 **Variables in the Negotiation Process**

1. *Approach to negotiation process:* Competitive or problem-solving
2. *Composition of negotiating team:* Number and experience of team members. Relative hierarchy in position. Relationships with counterparts. Decision-making power of team members. Motivated by individual, company, or community goals.
3. *Method of reaching decisions:* By individual determination, by majority opinion, or by group consensus.
4. *Purpose of negotiations:* One-time contract. Joint venture or other alliance. Long-term relationship-building.
5. *Negotiation process:* Behavioral expectations, typical procedures.
6. *Communication context used by teams:* Low context, explicit; high-context, implicit; nature of surroundings.
7. *Nature of persuasive arguments:* Factual presentations and arguments, accepted tradition, or emotion.
8. *Bases of trust:* Relationships, past experience, intuition, or rules.
9. *Risk-taking propensity:* Level and methods of uncertainty avoidance in trading information or making a contract.
10. *Value and uses of time:* Attitude toward time. Use of time in scheduling and proceeding with negotiations; use of time to pressure for agreement.
11. *Form of satisfactory agreement:* Based on trust (perhaps just a handshake), the credibility of the parties, commitment, or a legally binding contract.

Source: Based on excerpts from S. E. Weiss and W. Stripp, *Negotiation with Foreign Business Persons: An Introduction for Americans with Propositions on Six Cultures* (New York University Faculty of Business Administration, February 1985).

U.S. negotiators are, generally speaking, objective about the specific matter at hand and usually want to waste no time getting down to business and making progress. This approach, well understood in the United States, can be disastrous if the foreign negotiators want to take enough time to build trust and respect as a basis for negotiating contracts. In such cases, American efficiency interferes with the patient development of a mutually trusting relationship—the very cornerstone of an Asian business agreement.[14]

Nontask Sounding

Five minutes of nontask sounding in the United States can translate into five days, weeks, or even months of nontask sounding in Shanghai, Lagos, Rio de Janeiro, or Jeddah. There is no other way because in such countries real business cannot be conducted until a good interpersonal relationship has been established.[15]

In many countries, such as Mexico, Saudi Arabia, and China, personal commitments to individuals, rather than to the legal system, form the basis for the enforcement of contracts. Effective negotiators allow plenty of time in their schedules for such relationship building with bargaining partners. This process usually takes the form of social events, tours, and ceremonies along with much **nontask sounding**—general, polite conversation and informal communication before meetings—while all parties get to know one another. In such cultures, one patiently waits for the other party to start actual business negotiations, aware that relationship building is, in fact, the first phase of negotiations.[16] It is usually recommended that managers new to such scenarios use an intermediary—someone who already has the trust and respect of the foreign managers and who therefore acts as a relationship bridge. Middle Easterners, in particular, prefer to negotiate through a trusted intermediary, and for them as well, initial meetings are only for getting acquainted. Arabs do business with the person, not the company; therefore, mutual trust must be established.

In their best seller on negotiation, *Getting to Yes*, Fisher and Ury point out the dangers of not preparing well for negotiations.

> *In Persian, the word "compromise" does not have the English meaning of a midway solution which both sides can accept, but only the negative meaning of surrendering one's principles. Also, "mediator" means "meddler," someone who is barging in uninvited. In 1980, United Nations Secretary-General Kurt Waldheim flew to Iran to deal with the hostage situation. National Iranian radio and television broadcast in Persian a comment he was said to have made upon his arrival in Tehran: "I have come as a mediator to work out a compromise." Less than an hour later, his car was being stoned by angry Iranians.*[17]

As a bridge to the more formal stages of negotiations, such relationship building is followed by posturing—that is, general discussion that sets the tone for the meetings. This phase should result in a spirit of cooperation. To help ensure this result, negotiators must use words such as *respect* and *mutual benefit* rather than language that would suggest arrogance, superiority, or urgency.

Stage Three: Exchanging Task-Related Information

In the next stage—exchanging task-related information—each side typically makes a presentation and states its position; a question-and-answer session usually ensues, and alternatives are discussed. From an American perspective, this represents a straightforward, objective, efficient, and understandable stage. However, negotiators from other countries continue to take a more indirect approach at this stage. Mexican negotiators are usually suspicious and indirect, presenting little substantive material and more lengthy, evasive conversation. French negotiators enjoy debate and conflict and will often interrupt presentations to argue about an issue even if it has little relevance to the topic being presented. The Chinese also ask many questions of their counterparts and delve specifically and repeatedly into the details at hand; conversely, Chinese presentations contain only vague and ambiguous material. For instance, after about 20 Boeing officials spent six weeks presenting masses of literature and technical demonstrations to the Chinese, the Chinese said, "Thank you for your introduction."[18]

The Russians also enter negotiations well prepared and well versed in the specific details of the matter being presented. To answer their (or any other side's) questions, it is generally a good idea to bring along someone with expertise to answer any grueling technical inquiries. Russians also put a lot of emphasis on protocol and expect to deal only with top executives.

Adler suggests that negotiators should focus not only on presenting their situation and needs but also on showing an understanding of their opponents' viewpoint. Focusing on the entire situation confronting each party encourages the negotiators to assess a wider range of alternatives for resolution rather than limiting themselves to their preconceived, static positions. She suggests that to be most effective, negotiators should prepare for meetings by practicing role reversal.[19]

Stage Four: Persuasion

In the next phase of negotiations—persuasion—the hard bargaining starts. Typically, both parties try to persuade the other to accept more of their position and to give up some of their own. Often, some persuasion has already taken place beforehand in social settings and through mutual contacts. In the Far East, details are likely to be worked out ahead of time through the backdoor approach (*houmani*). However, the majority of the persuasion generally takes place over one or more negotiating sessions. International managers usually find that this process of bargaining and making concessions is fraught with difficulties because of the different uses and interpretations of verbal and nonverbal behaviors. Although variations in such behaviors influence every stage of the negotiation process, they can play a particularly powerful role in persuasion, especially if they are not anticipated.

Studies of negotiating behavior have revealed the use of certain tactics, which skilled negotiators recognize and use, such as promises, threats, and so on. Other, less savory tactics are sometimes used in international negotiations. Often called dirty tricks, these tactics, according to Fisher and Ury, include efforts to mislead "opponents" deliberately.[20] Some negotiators may give wrong or distorted information or use the excuse of ambiguous authority—giving conflicting impressions about who in their party has the power to make a commitment. In the midst of hard bargaining, the prudent international manager will follow up on possibly misleading information before taking action based on trust.

Other rough tactics are designed to put opposing negotiators in a stressful situation physically or psychologically, so that their giving in is made more likely. These include uncomfortable room temperatures, too-bright lighting, rudeness, interruptions, and other irritations. International negotiators must keep in mind, however, that what might seem like dirty tricks to Americans is simply the way other cultures conduct negotiations. In some South American countries, for example, it is common to start negotiations with misleading or false information.

The most subtle behaviors in the negotiation process—and often the most difficult to deal with—are usually the nonverbal messages: the use of voice intonation, facial and body expressions, eye contact, dress, and the timing of the discussions. Nonverbal behaviors, discussed in previous chapters, are ingrained aspects of culture people use in their daily lives; they are not specifically changed for the purposes of negotiation. Among those behaviors affecting negotiations is the direct communication style, such as with Germans, compared with the indirect style, such as with Japanese. Clearly, also, the individualism–collectivism cultural dimension is one that greatly guides negotiation because of the relative motivation of personal self-interest in individualistic societies such as the United States; this compares with the group interest in Asian cultures, so that Asian negotiators will likely give more importance to their social obligations and the needs of the group.[21]

Although persuasion has been discussed as if it were always a distinct stage, it is really the primary purpose underlying all stages of the negotiation process. In particular, persuasion is an integral part of the process of making concessions and arriving at an agreement.

Stage Five: Concessions and Agreement

In the last stage of negotiation—concessions and agreement—tactics vary greatly across cultures. Well-prepared negotiators are aware of various concession strategies and have decided ahead of time what their own concession strategy will be. Familiar with the typical initial positions that various parties are likely to take, they know that Russians and Chinese generally open their bargaining with extreme positions, asking for more than they hope to gain, whereas Swedes usually start with what they are prepared to accept.

Research in the United States indicates that better results are attained by starting with extreme positions. With this approach, the process of reaching an agreement involves careful timing of the disclosure information and of concessions. Most people who have studied negotiations believe that negotiators should disclose only the information that is necessary at a given point and that they should try to obtain information piece by piece to get the whole picture gradually without giving away their goals or concession strategy. These guidelines will not always work in intercultural negotiations because the American process of addressing issues one at a time, in a linear fashion, is not common in other countries or cultures. Negotiators in the Far East, for example, approach issues in a holistic manner, deciding on the whole deal at the end, rather than making incremental concessions.

Again, at the final stage of agreement and contract, local practices determine how these agreements will be honored. Whereas Americans take contracts very seriously, Russians often renege on their contracts. The Japanese, on the other hand, consider a formal contract to be somewhat of an insult and a waste of time and money in legal costs, since they prefer to operate based on understanding and social trust.[22]

UNDERSTANDING NEGOTIATION STYLES

Global managers can benefit from studying differences in negotiating behaviors (and the underlying reasons for them), which can help them recognize what is happening in the negotiating process. Exhibit 5-4 shows some examples of differences among North American, Japanese, and Latin American styles. Brazilians, for example, generally have a spontaneous, passionate, and dynamic style. They are very talkative and particularly use the word *no* extensively—more than 40 times per half-hour, compared with 4.7 times for Americans and only 1.9 times for

EXHIBIT 5-4 Comparison of Negotiation Styles: Japanese, North American, and Latin American

Japanese	North American	Latin American
Emotional sensitivity highly valued	Emotional sensitivity not highly valued	Emotional sensitivity valued
Hiding of emotions	Dealing straightforwardly or impersonally	Emotionally passionate
Subtle power plays; conciliation	Litigation not so much as conciliation	Great power plays; use of weakness
Loyalty to employer; employer takes care of employees	Lack of commitment to employer; breaking of ties by either if necessary	Loyalty to employer (who is often family)
Face-saving crucial; decisions often on basis of saving someone from embarrassment	Decisions made on a cost-benefit basis; face-saving does not always matter	Face-saving crucial in decision making to preserve honor, dignity
Decision makers openly influenced by special interests	Decision makers influenced by special interests but often not considered ethical	Execution of special interests on decision expected, condoned
Not argumentative; quiet when right	Argumentative when right or wrong, but impersonal	Argumentative when right or wrong; passionate
What is down in writing must be accurate, valid	Great importance given to documentation as evidential proof	Impatient with documentation as obstacle to understanding general principles
Step-by-step approach to decision making	Methodically organized decision making	Impulsive, spontaneous decision making
Good of group is the ultimate aim	Profit motive or good of individual is the ultimate aim	What is good for group is good for the individual
Cultivate a good emotional social setting for decision making; get to know decision makers	Decision making impersonal; avoid involvements, conflict of interest	Personalism necessary for good decision making

Source: Pierre Casse, *Training for the Multicultural Manager: A Practical and Cross-cultural Approach to the Management of People* (Washington, D.C.: Society for Intercultural Education, Training, and Research, 1982), used with the permission of the Society for Intercultural Education, Training and Research, 2012.

the Japanese. They also differ markedly from Americans and the Japanese by their use of extensive physical contact.[23]

The Japanese are typically skillful negotiators. They have spent a great deal more time and effort studying U.S. culture and business practices than Americans have spent studying Japanese practices, and many have been to business school in the United States. However, differences in philosophy and style between the two countries reflect past feelings of betrayal in trade negotiations. John Graham, a California professor who has studied international negotiating styles, says that the differences between United States and Japanese styles are well illustrated by their respective proverbs; the Americans believe that "The squeaking wheel gets the grease," and the Japanese say that "The pheasant would not be shot but for its cry."[24] The Japanese are calm, quiet, patient negotiators; they are accustomed to long, detailed negotiating sessions. Whereas Americans often plunge straight to the matter at hand, the Japanese instead prefer to develop long-term, personal relationships. The Japanese want to get to know those on the other side and will spend some time in nontask sounding.

In negotiations, the Japanese culture of politeness and hiding of emotions can be disconcerting to Americans when they are unable to make straightforward eye contact or when the Japanese maintain smiling faces in serious situations. It is important for Americans to understand what is polite and what is offensive to the Japanese—and vice versa. Americans must avoid anything that resembles boasting because the Japanese value humility, and physical contact or touching of any sort must be avoided.[25] Consistent with the culture-based value of maintaining harmony, the Japanese are likely to be evasive or even leave the room rather than give a direct negative answer.[26] Fundamental to Japanese culture is a concern for the welfare of the group; anything that affects one member or part of society affects the others. Thus, the Japanese view decisions carefully in light of long-term consequences; they use objective, analytic thought patterns; and they take time for reflection.[27]

Further insight into negotiating styles around the world can be gained by comparing the North American, Arab, and Russian styles. Basic cultural values often shed light on the way information is presented, whether and how concessions will be made, and the general nature and duration of the relationship. For North Americans, negotiations are businesslike; their factual appeals are based on what they believe is objective information, presented with the assumption that it is understood by the other side on a logical basis. Arabs use affective appeals based on emotions and subjective feelings. Russians employ axiomatic appeals—that is, their appeals are based on the ideals generally accepted in their society. The Russians are tough negotiators; they stall until they unnerve Western negotiators by continually delaying and haggling. Much of this approach is based on the Russians' different attitude toward time. Because Russians traditionally do not subscribe to the Western belief that time is money, they are more patient, more determined, and more dogged negotiators. They try to keep smiles and other expressions of emotion to a minimum to present a calm exterior.[28]

In contrast to the Russians, Arabs are more interested in long-term relationships and are, therefore, more likely to make concessions. Compared with Westerners, Arabs have a casual approach to deadlines, and the negotiators frequently lack the authority to finalize a deal.[29]

Successful Negotiators around the World

Following are selected profiles of what it takes to be a successful negotiator as perceived by people in their home countries. These are profiles of American, Indian, Arab, Swedish, and Italian negotiators, based on selections from the work of Pierre Casse, and give some insight into what to expect from different negotiators and what they expect from others.[30]

AMERICAN NEGOTIATORS
According to Casse, a successful American negotiator acts as follows:

- They are respectful, courteous, and honest in negotiations but operate from a firm stand from the beginning, without revealing the options that are open to negotiation.

- They are generally well-versed in the issues at hand and how to time the interactions and so wait for the other party to make the first move in negotiating.

- They are explicit about their position and will only reveal their compromises when negotiations have come to a stalemate.

INDIAN NEGOTIATORS
Indians have traditionally followed Gandhi's approach to negotiation, which Gandhi called *satyagraha*, "firmness in a good cause." This combines strength with the love of truth. Therefore, successful Indian negotiator acts as follows:

- They are humble and truthful and act in good faith, at the same time trusting that the opponent will act similarly.

- They act with self-control and attempt to come to a win-win outcome for all parties, in the spirit of *satyagraha*, thus putting the negotiation process on a spiritual level.

- They respect the other parties, are very patient in explaining and negotiating, do not insult others, and keep the big picture in mind.

- They will meditate and trust their instincts to consider the opponents' viewpoints, do not keep secrets, and are willing to change their minds.

ARAB NEGOTIATORS

Many Arab negotiators, following Islamic tradition, use mediators to settle disputes. Successful Arab mediators act in the following way:

- They possess a level of respect, trust, and prestige to be able to be a mediator.
- They maintain 'face' for all the parties by respecting their dignity, minimizing conflicts among opponents, and avoiding situations which would make any party feel inferior.
- They use persuasive techniques such as referring to other respected people and what those people would want, and use conferences to mediate issues.
- They retain their impartiality and look for honorable solutions for all parties.

SWEDISH NEGOTIATORS

Swedish negotiators are:

- Polite, punctual, serious, and thoughtful, though tend to be overcautious.
- They run meetings efficiently with little apparent emotion, and like to get straight down to business.
- They can be quite flexible, but are wary of confrontations and take time to react to new ideas from the other parties in negotiations.

ITALIAN NEGOTIATORS

Italians value negotiators who act as follows:

- They are dramatic, do not hide emotions, and use and read nonverbal gestures - typical of the Italian culture.
- They use flattery in negotiation communications and - always mindful of creating a good impression (the *bella figura*) - are helpful and simpatico to keep up their reputation.
- They are tactful in handling confrontations and tend not to be opinionated, but they also are creative in finding ways to come out ahead of the opponents in negotiations.

Comparing Profiles

Comparing such profiles is useful. Indian negotiators, for example, are humble, patient, respectful of the other parties, and very willing to compromise compared with Americans, who are firmer about taking stands. An important difference between Arab negotiators and those from most other countries is that the negotiators are mediators, not the parties themselves; hence, direct confrontation is impossible. Successful Swedish negotiators are conservative and careful, dealing with factual and detailed information. This profile contrasts with Italian negotiators, who are expressive and exuberant but less straightforward than their Swedish counterparts.

MANAGING NEGOTIATION

Skillful global managers must assess many factors when managing negotiations. They must understand the position of the other parties concerning their goals—whether national or corporate—and whether these goals are represented by principles or specific details. They should have the ability to recognize the relative importance attached to completing the task versus developing interpersonal relationships. Managers also must know the composition of the teams involved, the power allotted to the members, and the extent of the teams' preparation. In addition, they must grasp the significance of personal trust in the relationship. As stated earlier, the culture of the parties involved affects their negotiating styles and behavior and thus the overall process of negotiation. However, whatever the culture, research by Tse, Francis, and Walls has found person-related conflicts to "invite negative, more relation-oriented (versus information-oriented) responses," leading them to conclude that "The software of negotiation—that is, the nature and the appearance of the relationship between the people pursuing common goals—needs to be carefully addressed in the negotiation process."[31]

This is particularly true when representatives of individual-focused cultures (such as the Americans) and group-focused cultures (such as the Chinese) are on opposite sides of the table. Many of these culture-based differences in negotiations came to light in Husted's study on Mexican negotiators' perceptions of the reasons for the failure of their negotiations with U.S. teams.[32] The Mexican managers' interpretations were affected by their high-context culture, with the characteristics of an indirect approach, patience in discussing ideas, and maintenance of dignity. Instead, the low-context Americans conveyed an impatient, cold, blunt communicative style. To maintain the outward dignity of their Mexican counterparts, Americans must approach negotiations with Mexicans with patience and tolerance and refrain from attacking ideas because these attacks may be taken personally. The relationships among the factors of cross-cultural negotiation discussed in this chapter are illustrated in Exhibit 5-5.

The successful management of intercultural negotiations requires a manager to go beyond a generalized understanding of the issues and variables involved. As discussed earlier, she or he must find out as much specific information about the counterparts as possible and consider in advance how to use that information to create a positive climate that will result in a win–win situation. Research has shown that a problem-solving approach is essential to successful cross-cultural negotiations, whether abroad or in the home office, although the approach works differently in various countries.[33] This problem-solving approach requires a negotiator to treat everyone with respect, avoid making anyone feel uncomfortable, and refrain from criticizing or blaming the other parties in a personal way that may make someone feel shame—that is, lose face.

Research by the Huthwaite Research Group reveals how successful negotiators, compared to average negotiators, manage the planning process and their face-to-face behavior. The group found that during the planning process, successful negotiators consider a wider range of options and pay greater attention to areas of common ground. Skillful negotiators also tend to make twice as many comments regarding long-term issues and are more likely to set upper and lower limits regarding specific points. In their face-to-face behavior, skillful negotiators make fewer irritating comments—such as, "We're making you a generous offer"—make counterproposals

EXHIBIT 5-5 Cross-Cultural Negotiation Variables

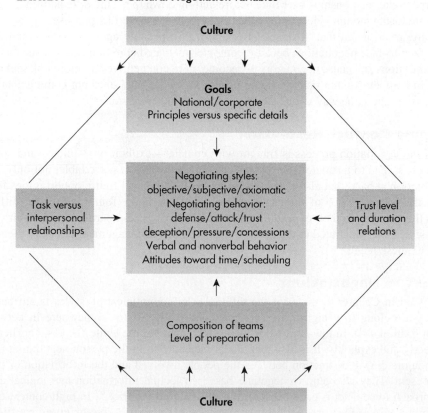

less frequently, and use fewer reasons to back up arguments. In addition, skilled negotiators practice active listening—asking questions, clarifying their understanding of the issues, and summarizing the issues.[34]

Using the Internet to Support Negotiations

Modern technology can provide support for the negotiating process, though it can't take the place of the essential face-to-face ingredient in many instances. A growing component for electronic commerce is the development of applications to support the negotiation of contracts and resolution of disputes. Web applications can provide support for various phases and dimensions, such as "Multiple-issue, multiple-party business transactions of a buy–sell nature; international dispute resolution (business disputes, political disputes); and internal company negotiations and communications, among others."[35]

Negotiation support systems (NSS) can provide support for the negotiation process in the following ways:

- Increasing the likelihood that an agreement is reached when a zone of agreement exists (solutions that both parties would accept)
- Decreasing the direct and indirect costs of negotiations, such as costs caused by time delays (strikes, violence), and attorneys' fees, among others
- Maximizing the chances for optimal outcomes[36]

One Web-based support system—called INSPIRE—developed at Carleton University in Ottawa, Canada, provides applications for preparing and conducting negotiations and for renegotiating options after a settlement. Users can specify preferences and assess offers; the site also has graphical displays of the negotiation process.[37]

E-NEGOTIATIONS

The advantages of electronic communications are well known: speed, less travel, and the ability to lay out much objective information to be considered by the other party over time. The disadvantages, however, might kill a deal before it gets off the ground by the inability to build trust and interpersonal relationships over time before getting down to business. In addition, nonverbal nuances are lost, although videoconferencing is a compromise for that purpose.

Rosette et al. noted that "opening offers may be especially aggressive in e-mail as compared to face-to-face negotiations because computer-mediated communications, such as e-mail, loosen inhibitions and cause negotiators to become more competitive and more risk seeking. The increase in competitive and risky behavior occurs because e-mail does not communicate social context cues in the same way as does the presence of another person."[38]

Managing Conflict Resolution

Much of the negotiation process is fraught with conflict—explicit or implicit—and such conflict can often lead to a standoff, or a lose–lose situation. This is regrettable, not only because of the situation at hand, but also because it probably will shut off future opportunities for deals between the parties. Much of the cause of such conflict can be found in cultural differences between the parties—in their expectations, in their behaviors, and particularly in their communication styles—as illustrated in the following Comparative Management in Focus, Negotiating with the Chinese feature.

Context in Negotiations

As discussed in Chapter 4, much of the difference in communication styles is attributable to whether you belong to a high-context or low-context culture (or somewhere in between, as shown in Exhibit 4-4). In low-context cultures such as that in the United States, conflict is handled directly and explicitly. It is also regarded as separate from the person negotiating—that is, the negotiators draw a distinction between the people involved and the information or opinions they represent. They also tend to negotiate based on factual information and logical analysis. That approach to conflict is called **instrumental-oriented conflict**.[69] In high-context cultures, such as in the Middle East, the approach to conflict is called **expressive-oriented conflict**—that

Comparative Management In Focus
Negotiating with the Chinese

The Chinese way of making decisions begins with socialization and initiation of personal guanxi rather than business discussion. The focus is not market research, statistical analysis, facts, Power-Point presentations, or to-the-point business discussion. My focus must be on fostering guanxi.

SUNNY ZHOU, GENERAL MANAGER OF KUNMING LIDA WOOD AND BAMBOO PRODUCTS[39]

With the increasing business being conducted in China (see Map 5.1) or with Chinese allies or other companies, business practices there are now showing more similarity to those in the West. However, when Westerners initiate business negotiations with representatives from the People's Republic of China, cultural barriers confront both sides. At the same time, we should recognize that there are regional cultural differences as well as regional economic differences that may affect negotiation; some examples of regional differences are noted below as researched by Tung et al. In addition, there are considerable generational differences, in particular with those younger people who have been educated in the West and are more familiar with Western ways and languages, in contrast with the older generation, which holds to more traditional culture and negotiation strategies.[40]

- **Beijing (capital)** "Political, bureaucratic, educated, diversified, high relationship orientation, more direct, high 'face.'"[41]
- **Shanghai (commercial center)** "Business savvy, focus on details, bottom line, career-oriented younger people, materialistic, confident."[42]
- **Guangzhou/Shenzhen (south, near Hong Kong)** "Entrepreneurial, hard-working, manufacturing center, outside the norm, more risk-taking, like Hong Kong, more informal."[43]
- **Western China (Chengdu/Chongqing)** "Traditional 'People's' mentality, less experience with international business/negotiations, socializing importance."[44]

MAP 5.1 China

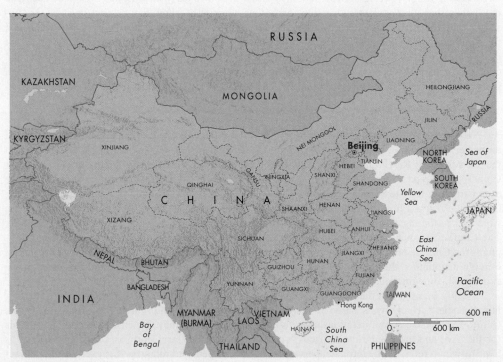

(Continued)

For the most part, the negotiation process the Chinese use is mystifying to most Westerners. For instance, the Chinese put much greater emphasis than Americans and Europeans on respect and friendship, on saving face, and on group goals. Long-term goals are more important to the Chinese than the specific current objectives typical of Western negotiators. Even though market forces now have more influence in China, political and economic agendas are still expected to be considered in negotiations. Economic conditions, political pervasiveness, and the influence that political and state agencies have on the negotiating parties in China are key practical factors that, added to cultural factors, make up the context affecting Chinese negotiations.

Business people report two major areas of conflict in negotiating with the Chinese: (1) the amount of detail the Chinese want about product characteristics, and (2) their apparent insincerity about reaching an agreement. In addition, Chinese negotiators frequently have little authority, frustrating Americans who do have the authority and are ready to conclude a deal.[45] This situation arises because many Chinese companies report to the government trade corporations, which are involved in the negotiations and often have a representative on the team. Often, the goals of Chinese negotiators remain primarily within the framework of state planning and political ideals. Although China has become more profit-oriented, most deals are still negotiated within the confines of the state budget allocation for that project rather than because of a project's profitability or value. It is crucial, then, to find out which officials—national, provincial, or local—have the power to make, and keep, a deal. According to James Broering of Arthur Andersen, who does much business in China, "companies have negotiated with government people for months, only to discover that they were dealing with the wrong people."[46]

Research shows that for the Chinese, three cultural norms greatly affect the negotiation process: their ingrained politeness and emotional restraint, their emphasis on social obligations, and their belief in the interconnection of work, family, and friendship. Because of the Chinese preference for emotional restraint and saving face, aggressive or emotional attempts at persuasion in negotiation are likely to fail. Instead, the Chinese tendency to avoid open conflict will more likely result in negative strategies such as discontinuing or withdrawing from negotiation.[47] The concept of face is at the heart of this kind of response—it is essential for foreigners to recognize the role that face behavior plays in negotiations. There are two components of face—*lien* and *mien-tzu. Lien* refers to a person's moral character; it is the most important thing defining that person, and without it, one cannot function in society. It can only be earned by fulfilling obligations to others. *Mien-tzu* refers to one's reputation or prestige, earned through accomplishments or through bureaucratic or political power.[48] Giving others one's time, gifts, or praise enhances one's own face. In negotiations, it is vital for you not to make it obvious that you have won, because that means that the other party has lost and will lose face. One must, therefore, make token concessions and other attempts to show that respect must be demonstrated, and modesty and control must be maintained; otherwise, anyone who feels he or she has lost face will not want to deal with you again. The Chinese will later ignore any dealings or incidents that caused them to lose face, maintaining the expected polite behavior out of social consciousness and concern for others. When encountering an embarrassing situation, they will typically smile or laugh in an attempt to save face, responses that are confusing to Western negotiators.[49]

It is critical that you give face, save face and show face when doing business in China.[50]

Generally, Westerners tend to feel that the Chinese negotiators are not truthful with them and do not give them straight answers. In turn, the Chinese sense that tension and feel a lack of trust in the Westerners.[51] Research by Chua emphasized the need for Western negotiators to develop their Chinese counterparts' trust in their competence and capability; without that trust, there will not be a constructive long-term relationship.[52] The emphasis on social obligations underlies the strong orientation of the Chinese toward collective goals. Therefore, appeals to individual members of the Chinese negotiating team, rather than appeals to benefit the group as a whole, will probably backfire. The Confucian emphasis on the kinship system and the hierarchy of work, family, and friends explains the Chinese preference for doing business with familiar, trusted people and trusted companies. Foreign negotiators, then, should focus on establishing long-term, trusting relationships, even at the expense of some immediate returns.

Deeply ingrained in the Chinese culture is the importance of harmony for the smooth functioning of society. Harmony is based primarily on personal relationships, trust, and ritual. After the Chinese establish a cordial relationship with foreign negotiators, they use this relationship as a basis for the give-and-take of business discussions. This implicit cultural norm is commonly known as *guanxi*, which refers to the intricate, pervasive network of personal relations that every Chinese carefully cultivates. It is the primary means of getting ahead, in the absence of a proper commercial legal system.[53] In other words, *guanxi* establishes obligations to exchange favors in future business activities.[54] Even within the Chinese bureaucracy, *guanxi* prevails over legal interpretations. Although networking is important anywhere to do business, the difference in China is that "*guanxi* networks are not just commercial, but also social, involving the exchange both of favor and affection."[55] Firms that have special *guanxi* connections and give preferential treatment to one another are known as members of a *guanxihu* network.[56] Sunny Zhou, general manager of Kunming Lida Wood and Bamboo Products, states that when he shops for lumber, "The lumber price varies drastically, depending on whether one has strong *guanxi* with the local administrators."[57] Western managers should thus anticipate extended preliminary visiting (relationship building), in which the Chinese expect to learn more about them and their trustworthiness. The Chinese also use this opportunity to convey their deeply held principles. They attach considerable importance to mutual benefit.[58]

Americans often experience two negotiation stages with the Chinese: the technical and the commercial. During the long technical stage, the Chinese want to hammer out every detail of the proposed product specifications and technology. If there are two teams of negotiators, it actually may be several days before the commercial team is called in to deal with aspects of production, marketing, pricing, and so forth. However, the commercial team should sit in on the first stage to become familiar with the Chinese negotiating style.[59] The Chinese negotiating team is usually about twice as large as the Western team; about a third of the time is spent discussing technical specifications, and another third on price negotiations, with the rest devoted to general negotiations and posturing (see Fig. 5-1).[60]

The Chinese are among the toughest negotiators in the world. American managers must anticipate various tactics, such as their delaying techniques and their avoidance of direct, specific answers; they use both ploys to exploit Americans' known impatience. The Chinese frequently try to put pressure on Americans by shaming them, thereby implying that the Americans are trying to renege on the friendship—the basis of the implicit contract. Whereas Westerners come to negotiations with specific and segmented goals and find it easy to compromise, the Chinese are reluctant to negotiate details. They find it difficult to compromise and trade because they have entered negotiations with a broader vision of achieving development goals for China, and they are offended when Westerners don't internalize those goals.[61] Under these circumstances, the Chinese will adopt a rigid posture, and no agreement or contract is final until the negotiated activities have actually been completed. Successful negotiations with the Chinese depend on many factors. Research by Fang et al. found the top success factors to be sincerity on behalf of the Western team, their team's preparation, technical expertise, patience, knowledge of PRC (People's Republic of China) business practices, and good personal relationships.[62] Generally speaking, patience, respect, and experience are necessary prerequisites for anyone negotiating in China. For the best outcomes, older, more experienced people are more acceptable to the Chinese in cross-cultural negotiations. The Chinese want to deal with the top executive of an American company, under the assumption that the highest officer has attained that position by establishing close personal relationships and trust with colleagues and others outside the organization.[63] During introductions, the Western group should line up according to seniority and greet the most senior Chinese representative first. He or she may be greeted with applause, in which case, he

FIGURE 5-1 Chinese-western negotiation teams

Paylessimages/Fotolia

(Continued)

or she should applaud back.[64] Use full names and titles until invited to do otherwise. "To beckon a Chinese person, face the palm of your hand downward and move your fingers in a scratching motion. Never use your index finger to beckon anyone."[65]

Western delegation practices are unfamiliar to many Chinese, and they are reluctant to come to an agreement without the presence of the Chinese foreign negotiator.[66] From the Western perspective, confusing jurisdictions of government ministries hamper decisions in negotiations. Americans tend to send specific technical personnel with experience in the task at hand; therefore, they have to take care in selecting the most suitable negotiators. In addition, visiting negotiating teams should realize that the Chinese are probably negotiating with other foreign teams, often at the same time, and will use that setup to play one company's offer against the others. On an interpersonal level, Western negotiators must also realize that, although a handshake is polite, physical contact is not acceptable in Chinese social behavior, nor are personal discussion topics such as one's family. However, it is customary to give and take small gifts as tokens of friendship. Keep in mind the following tips.[67]

- Some time before the trip, establish a contact in China who will act as a reference; be your interpreter, and navigate you through the bureaucracy, legal system, and local business networks.

- Be very prepared before doing business in China. The Chinese plan meticulously and will know your business, and possibly you, inside out.

- Send some literature about your company in advance and convey a set agenda before each meeting. Be punctual, or you will insult them before you start; begin with small, polite social talk but avoid politics.

- Expect initial meetings to involve long, convoluted discussions that are really intended to get to know one another, establish trust, and find out the actual goals of your team.

- The Chinese are not confrontational and will not say "no." You will need to be observant and recognize that perhaps those items are not negotiable.

- Practice patience. Introducing delays and obstacles is a Chinese negotiating tactic. They will wait until the deadline has passed and demand another concession, knowing that the Westerners are focused on their deadline for departure, so let them know your schedule is open and keep calm.

- Expect prolonged periods of stalemate; hang loose and don't say anything about the point in question. Try to change the momentum by, say, suggesting going to dinner.

- Refrain from exaggerated expectations and discount Chinese rhetoric about future prospects.

- Remember at all times to save face for everyone and keep in mind the importance of trust and *guanxi* in negotiations.

China's rapidly changing business environment is apparent in more professionalism in the negotiation process. At the same time, research by Fang et al. shows that "one should not underestimate the impact of culture on Chinese business negotiations. Western companies that seek to succeed in China need to demonstrate sincerity and commitment in conducting business in order to gain the Chinese partner's trust as this appears to be the ultimate predictor for success of business relations in China."[68]

is, the situation is handled indirectly and implicitly, without clear delineation of the situation by the person handling it. Such negotiators do not want to get into a confrontational situation because it is regarded as insulting and would cause a loss of face, so they tend to use evasion and avoidance if they cannot reach agreement through emotional appeals. Their avoidance and inaction conflict with the expectations of the low-context negotiators who are looking to move ahead with this matter and arrive at a solution.

The differences between high- and low-context cultures that often lead to conflict situations are summarized in Exhibit 5-6. Most of these variables were discussed previously in this chapter or in Chapter 4. They overlap because the subjects, culture, and communication are inseparable and because negotiation differences and conflict situations arise from variables in culture and communication.

So, how can a manager from France, Japan, or Brazil, for example, manage conflict situations? The solution, as discussed previously, lies mainly in one's ability to know and understand the people and the situation to be faced. Managers must be prepared by developing an understanding of the cultural contexts in which they will be operating. What are the expectations of

EXHIBIT 5-6 Negotiation Conflicts between Low-Context and High-Context Cultures

Low-Context Conflict Area	High-Context Conflict Area
Explicit and direct; verbal; linear presentation of facts, rationale, analysis.	Implicit, indirect discussion and decision-making; non-verbal; may be circular logic.
Individualistic; tend to be short-term-oriented.	Collective; group motivations and decisions by consensus.
Task-oriented. Up-front, impatient, sometimes confrontational; action and solution directive.	Tend to be long-term-oriented. "Face" and relationship-oriented; indirect, non-confrontational, patient.

Source: Based on W. Gudykunst, L. Stewart, and S. Ting-Toomey, *Communication, Culture, and Organizational Processes* (Sage Publications, 1985).

the persons with whom they will be negotiating? What kinds of communication styles and negotiating tactics should they expect, and how will they differ from their own? It is important to bear in mind one's own expectations and negotiating style as well as to be aware of the other parties' expectations. Managers ought to consider in advance what it will take to arrive at a win–win solution. Often it helps to use the services of a host-country adviser or mediator, who may be able to help defuse a conflict situation early.

DECISION MAKING

Negotiation actually represents the outcome of a series of small and large decisions. The decisions include those each party makes before actual negotiations start—for example, in determining the position of the company and what fallback proposals it may suggest or accept. The decisions also include incremental decisions, made during the negotiation process, about how to react and proceed, when to concede, and on what to agree or disagree. Negotiation can thus be seen as a series of explicit and implicit decisions, and the subjects of negotiation and decision making become interdependent.

For instance, sometimes just the way a decision is made during the negotiation process can have a profound influence on the outcome, as this example from a book by Copeland and Griggs shows.

> In his first loan negotiation, a banker new to Japan met with seven top Japanese bankers who were seeking a substantial amount of money. After hearing their presentation, the American agreed on the spot. The seven Japanese then conferred among themselves and told the American they would get back to him in a couple of days regarding whether they would accept his offer or not. The American banker learned a lesson he never forgot.[70]

The Japanese bankers expected the American to negotiate, to take time to think it over, and to consult with colleagues before giving the final decision. His immediate decision made them suspicious, so they decided to reconsider the deal.

There is no doubt that the speed and manner of decision making affect the negotiation process. In addition, how well negotiated agreements are implemented is affected by the speed and manner of decision making. In that regard, it is clear that the effective use of technology is playing an important role, especially when dealing with complex cross-border agreements in which the hundreds of decision makers involved are separated by time and space.

The role of decision making in management, however, goes far beyond the finite occasions of negotiations. It is part of the manager's daily routine—from operational-level, programmed decisions requiring minimal time and effort to those decisions not programmed, of far broader scope and importance, such as the decision to enter into a joint venture in a foreign country.

The Influence of Culture on Decision Making

It is crucial for international managers to understand the influence of culture on decision-making styles and processes. Culture affects decision making both through the broader context of the nation's institutional culture, which produces collective patterns of decision making, and through culturally based value systems that affect each individual decision maker's perception or interpretation of a situation.[71] The ways in which these factors can come together to affect people's negotiations and decisions is illustrated in the following Under the Lens feature.

UNDER THE LENS

Negotiations and Decisions to Save the Eurozone System[72]

> *Within each class, attitudes are hardening against the other. "The birth defect of the euro was to put very different cultures of economic activity in the straitjacket of a single currency."*[73]
>
> *Greece's prime minister joined the May Day demonstration of defiance against the country's international creditors on Friday (May 1, 2015) as talks to end the impasse over bailout money continued.*[74]

In 2012, a major issue at the intersection of politics, economics, and business was how the eurozone crisis would be resolved. The outcome of the negotiations and decisions among representatives of the euro countries would have lasting repercussions for businesses around the world and European businesses in particular. At the heart of the negotiations among the eurozone countries and the International Monetary Fund (IMF) were the potential effects of a massive financial rescue plan for Greece, which was threatened with default. In spite of the passage of radical reforms and austerity cuts in Greece, the European Commission, European Central Bank, and the IMF were demanding further cuts from Greece in order to receive the $170 billion in bailout money that Greece needs to avert default. (As you can see from the preceding quote, this problem continued into 2015 as the headlines blared, "Eurozone Fears Financial Chaos over Greece's Stance on Bailout."[75])

The Italian economy, the seventh largest in the world, was also in a fragile state with massive debt, and Mario Monti, then prime minister, was taking drastic measures to avoid default; there were fears that a default of such a large economy could bring a default of the entire euro system. At stake in the negotiations was the eurozone pact and the continuation of the euro itself.

> *Italy's problems have become the world's problems, and Monti must fix Italy to prevent another global financial crisis.*
>
> *And as Italy goes, so goes the euro. Italy looms as the biggest threat to the embattled currency's survival, because Italy is both too big to fail and too big to save.*[76]

Mario Monti, then an unelected official from academia, had almost uncontested control of such weighty decisions, which would determine both Italy's fate and that of the euro. His negotiation and decision-making capabilities were vital to so many people, but Monti believed his detachment from the politicians was what was needed to do the job; he had a reputation for being very willful in achieving his objectives.[77]

As negotiations continued, cultural, historical, and lifestyle differences among the major countries involved brought out old prejudices that threatened to derail the negotiations. With Germany as the richest and most stable economy in the eurozone, its people were resentful and fearful of the prospect of bailing Greece out. Angela Merkel, the German prime minister, herself very conservative and consultative, was in the difficult position of making decisions to protect both the German economy and its people and, at the same time, needing to play a prominent role in decisions to aid Greece and save the euro system. As such, Ms. Merkel was holding out for Greece and Italy to take on strict reforms. Germany had a much-respected manufacturing and export base, and the fear was that the crisis would undermine its businesses. In fact, in February 2012, Angel Gurría, the OECD's secretary general, in a speech in Berlin, congratulated Germany on a well-managed economy, saying that Germany's "growth model has been so successful in navigating through the stormy waters of the crisis."

Interviews by Margaret Warner of PBS in February 2012 revealed the depth of angst of the German people. At the heart of their culture is a strong desire for security and safety, no doubt partly evolving from the German history. Germans are very conservative and cautious, with a focus on frugality and saving. The economy is based largely on cash, not credit; a home mortgage requires a minimum of a 30 percent down payment, and the banks are very conservative. Hence, Germany did not have the real estate bubble and subsequent meltdown that occurred in the United States, and the German people felt that they should not have to bail out their free-spending southern neighbors. Germany had already endured painful austerity measures a decade before, in absorbing the poorer East Germany. It now had a much-respected and robust manufacturing and export base. In addition, its recent sacrifices, such as raising the retirement age to 67, had resulted in lower unemployment and deficits. An additional bone of contention with the German people was that although they pay high taxes, it was commonly understood that a large proportion of Greeks and Italians don't pay taxes.

In all, the negotiations were undermined by a lack of trust among the EU members. Greeks are very proud of their cultural heritage and felt that negotiations were going to "deprive Greece of the last trace of national sovereignty," according to Georgios Karatzaferis, who headed the right-wing Popular Orthodox Rally; he expressed frustration with German officials, who had taken a hard line in the negotiations. "Greece cannot survive outside the E.U.," he said, "but it can do without a German jackboot."[78]

For their part, Greeks are skilled negotiators and will not be pushed into decisions before they are ready. Business interactions are formal and based on friendship and trust. This became clear at all levels in the eurozone negotiations. Within Greece, as the plan for the austerity measures demanded by the Greek creditors went to parliament, it was clear that there would be a lot of debate over then-Prime Minister Papademos's plan.

> *The [Greek] prime minister's comments kicked off what is expected to be a long and chaotic weekend of brinkmanship, with Greek politicians fighting for their survival in the face of unpopular austerity measures and European leaders demanding more concessions in a climate of growing urgency—and mistrust—between Greece and its foreign lenders.*[79]

The Greek people are fearful of a continued downward spiral in their economy under the austerity measures; they blame the tightknit elite who have run the country for so long. However, they will admit that "The Greek way of life is to spend and then overspend." At the same time, everyone complains that the bureaucracy is a menace. "*Fakelaki* (literally "little envelopes") are a legendary feature of society. If you're starting a business, you need lots of signatures, and handing over the cash-stuffed envelopes has traditionally been part of the process."[80] A quarter of all Greek companies have gone out of business since 2009, and half of all small businesses in the country say they are unable to meet payroll.[81]

Meanwhile, businesses in Italy and elsewhere that depended on clients in Greece, Spain, Portugal, and other hurting countries were suffering because their good customers had no cash and no credit. This was relayed in the PBS interview with Roberto Belloli, CEO of Antonio Aspesi Srl in the fashion industry. As a result, he said the company had to retrench. However, Italy's labor laws made it extremely hard to fire anyone, and laying off an employee costs the company 60 months of salary.

The business style in Italy depends on whether you are dealing with someone from the north or the south:

> *In the north, people are direct, see time as money, and get down to business after only a brief period of social talk.*
>
> *In the south, people take a more leisurely approach to life and want to get to know the people with whom they do business.*[82]

Italians prefer to negotiate with high-ranking people; hierarchy is very important to them. In addition, negotiations are likely to be very protracted. Your image is likely to be just as important to your Italian counterparts as the specific business objectives. Networking is important because they like to do business with people they know and trust; they also like to conduct face-to-face meetings.[83]

As uncertainty took its toll on all sides, it was clear that "[w]ithin each class, attitudes are hardening against the other. 'The birth defect of the euro was to put very different cultures of economic activity in the straitjacket of a single currency.'"[84] As the situation worsened, national identities hardened, further hampering negotiations. As of May 2015, what was a good relationship between Greece and Germany has turned into extreme dislike, with old stereotypes of Germans as domineering and southern Europeans as lazy poisoning European politics.[85] Many were proposing the idea of a Grexit (Greek exit from the eurozone), saying that it would reestablish the rules of the eurozone and encourage countries such as Italy and France to go ahead with their own structural reforms.[86]

Today, many developments have occurred in the eurozone crisis. You could discuss what led up to the crisis; what cultural, economic, historical, and lifestyle differences contributed to the situation; and what part those factors played in the negotiations and decisions by all parties.

The extent to which decision making is influenced by culture varies among countries. For example, Hitt, Tyler, and Park have found a "more culturally homogenizing influence on the Korean executives' cognitive models" than on those of U.S. executives, whose individualistic tendencies lead to different decision patterns.[87] The ways that culture influences an executive's decisions can be studied by looking at the variables involved in each stage of the rational decision-making process. These stages are (1) defining the problem, (2) gathering and analyzing relevant data, (3) considering alternative solutions, (4) deciding on the best solution, and (5) implementing the decision.

One of the major cultural variables affecting decision making is whether a people tend to assume an objective approach or a subjective approach. Whereas the Western approach is based on rationality (managers interpret a situation and consider alternative solutions based on objective information), this approach is not common throughout the world. Latin Americans, among others, tend to be more subjective, basing decisions on emotions.

Another cultural variable that greatly influences the decision-making process is the risk tolerance of those making the decision. Research shows that people from Belgium, Germany, and Austria have a considerably lower tolerance for risk than people from Japan or the Netherlands—whereas American managers have the highest tolerance for risk.[88]

In addition, an often-overlooked but important variable in the decision-making process is the manager's perception of the locus of control over outcomes—whether that locus is internal or external. Some managers feel they can plan on certain outcomes because they are in control of events that will direct the future in the desired way. In contrast, other managers believe that such decisions are of no value because they have little control over the future—which lies in the hands of outside forces, such as fate, God, or nature. American managers believe strongly in self-determination and perceive problem situations as something they can control and should change. However, managers in many other countries, Indonesia and Malaysia among them, tend to be resigned to problem situations and do not feel that they can change them. Obviously, these different value systems will result in a great difference in the stages of consideration of alternative actions and choice of a solution, often because certain situations may or may not be viewed as problems in the first place.

Yet another variable that affects the consideration of alternative solutions is how managers feel about staying with familiar solutions or trying new ones. Many managers, particularly those in Europe, value decisions based on experience and tend to emphasize quality. Americans, on the other hand, are more future oriented and look toward new ideas to get them there. However, sometimes decisions regarding cross-border plans can be rushed, neglecting the thorough decision-making process necessary to evaluate cross-cultural factors and local business practices and constraints—with disastrous results. Coming to that conclusion was hard for Brian Cornell, the new Target CEO, as he "pulled the plug on the discount retailer's ill-fated, poorly executed foray into Canada, its first attempt at international expansion,"[89] as illustrated in the following Management in Action section, "Target: Frozen Out."

MANAGEMENT IN ACTION
Target: Frozen Out

Last year, Target said that rolling out 100-plus stores in Canada in just two years was too ambitious. It turns out that the appropriate number of locations was zero. Yesterday, it abruptly said it would wind down its entire Canadian operation—133 remaining stores and 17,000 workers.

U.S. empire builders, commercial and otherwise, have long struggled to accept that foreign countries are hard to conquer. Like other invaders expecting to be greeted as saviors by the locals, Target failed to appreciate the facts on the ground. Canada is not, as it turns out, a colder, friendlier version of its southern neighbor. Labor and property are more expensive. Managing the supply chain is trickier because pockets of population density are dispersed, and brand recognition can be a curse. Canadians were well aware of Target's reputation for affordable quality, so when the chain did not deliver the shopping experience customers expected, that poor first impression was hard to reverse.

The Canadian catastrophe comes after a tough stretch for the chain. Its reputation was damaged by a customer credit card breach in late 2013, but the company changed its CEO last August, and since November, its shares have rallied nearly 30 percent, including a 2 percent pop yesterday.

In its upcoming fourth-quarter results, Target Canada will show a loss of $5.4 billion stemming from the shutdown, although the cash costs will be just $500 million to $600 million. Fortunately for shareholders, new chief Brian Cornell has shown no attachment to the previous management's vision. The rally in Target shares reflects not just the end of the Canadian losses but also company comments that fourth-quarter sales in the United States will be better than expected.

Yet Canada appeared to be a natural extension of a business that had reached $70 billion in U.S. sales. If Target cannot find growth just over the border, it is fair to ask where it can.

Source: Financial Times [London (UK)], January 16, 2015, p. 12.

Approaches to Decision Making

In addition to affecting different stages of the decision-making process, value systems influence the overall approach of decision makers from various cultures. The relative level of *utilitarianism versus moral idealism* in any society affects its overall approach to problems. Generally speaking, utilitarianism strongly guides behavior in the Western world. Research has shown that Canadian executives are more influenced by a short-term, cost-benefit approach to decision making than their Hong Kong counterparts.

Another important variable in companies' overall approach to decision making is that of *autocratic versus participative leadership*. In other words, who has the authority to make what kinds of decisions? A society's orientation—whether it is individualistic or collectivist (see Chapter 3)—influences the level at which decisions are made. In many countries with hierarchical cultures—Germany, Turkey, and India, among others—authorization for action has to be passed upward through echelons of management before final decisions can be made. Most employees in these countries simply expect the autocrat—the boss—to do most of the decision making and will not be comfortable otherwise. Even in China, which is a highly collectivist society, employees expect autocratic leadership because their value system presupposes the superior to be automatically the most wise. In comparison, decision-making authority in Sweden is very decentralized. Americans talk a lot about the advisability of such participative leadership, but in practice, they are probably near the middle between autocratic and participative management styles.

Arab managers have long traditions of consultative decision making, supported by the Qur'an and the sayings of Muhammad. However, such consultation occurs more on a person-to-person basis than during group meetings and thus diffuses potential opposition.[90] Although business in the Middle East tends to be transacted in a highly personalized manner, the top leaders make the final decisions and feel that they must impose their will for the company to be successful. In comparison, in cultures that emphasize collective harmony, such as Japan, participatory or group decision making predominates, and consensus is important. The best-known example is the bottom-up (rather than top-down) decision-making process used in most Japanese companies, described in more detail in the accompanying Comparative Management in Focus section.

One final area of frequent incongruence concerns the relative speed of decision making. A country's culture affects how fast or slow decisions tend to be made. The relative speed may be closely associated with the level of delegation, as just discussed—but not always. The pace at which decisions are made can be very disconcerting for outsiders. North Americans and Europeans pride themselves on being decisive; managers in the Middle East, with a different sense of temporal urgency, associate the importance of the matter at hand with the length of time needed to make a decision. Without knowing this cultural attitude, a hasty American would insult an Egyptian; a quick decision, to the Egyptian, would reflect a low regard for the relationship and the deal.

Exhibit 5-7 illustrates, in summary form, ways in which the variables just discussed can affect the steps in the decision-making process.

EXHIBIT 5-7 Cultural Variables in the Decision-Making Process

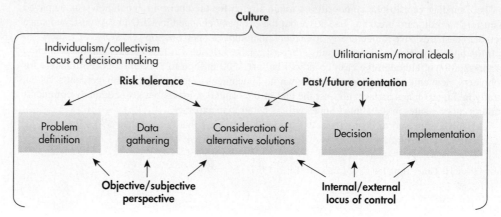

Comparative Management In Focus
Decision Making in Japanese Companies

The length of the decision-making process is one of the most common complaints of anyone who works with or for Japanese organizations.
ROCHELLE KOPP, MANAGING PRINCIPAL, JAPAN INTERCULTURAL CONSULTING[91]

Japanese companies are involved in joint ventures throughout the world, especially with U.S. companies. The GM–Toyota joint venture agreement process, for example, was the result of more than two years of negotiation and decision making; in similar alliances, Americans and Japanese are involved in decision making at all levels on a daily basis. The Japanese decision-making process differs greatly not only from the U.S. process but also from that of many other countries—especially at the higher levels of their organizations.

An understanding of the Japanese decision-making process—and indeed of many Japanese management practices—requires an understanding of Japanese national culture. Much of the Japanese culture and, therefore, the basis of Japanese working relationships, can be explained by the principle of *wa*, meaning "peace and harmony." This principle is one aspect of the value the Japanese attribute to *amae*, meaning "indulgent love," a concept probably originating in the Shinto religion, which focuses on spiritual and physical harmony. *Amae* results in *shinyo*, which refers to the mutual confidence, faith, and honor required for successful business relationships. The principle of *wa* influences the work group, the basic building block of Japanese work and management. The Japanese strongly identify with their work groups, where the emphasis is on cooperation, participative management, consensus problem solving, and decision making based on a patient, long-term perspective. Open expression of conflict is discouraged, and it is of utmost importance to avoid embarrassment or shame—to lose face—because of not fulfilling one's obligations. These elements of work culture generally result in a devotion to work, a collective responsibility for decisions and actions, and a high degree of employee productivity. It is this culture of collectivism and shared responsibility that underlies the Japanese *ringi* system of decision making.

In the *ringi* system, the process works from the bottom up. Americans are used to a centralized system, where major decisions are made by upper-level managers in a top-down approach typical of individualistic societies. The Japanese process, however, is dispersed throughout the organization, relying on group consensus.

The *ringi* process is one of gaining approval on a proposal by circulating documents to those concerned throughout the company. It usually comprises four steps: proposal, circulation, approval, and record.[92] Usually, the person who originates the written proposal, which is called a *ringi-sho*, has already worked for some time to gain informal consensus and support for the proposal within the section and then from the department head.[93] The next step is to attain a consensus in the company from those who would be involved in implementation. To this end, department meetings are held, and, if necessary, expert opinion is sought. If more information is needed, the proposal goes back to the originator, who finds and adds the required data. In this way, much time and effort—and the input of many people—go into the proposal before it becomes formal.[94]

EXHIBIT 5-8 Decision-Making Procedure in Japanese Companies

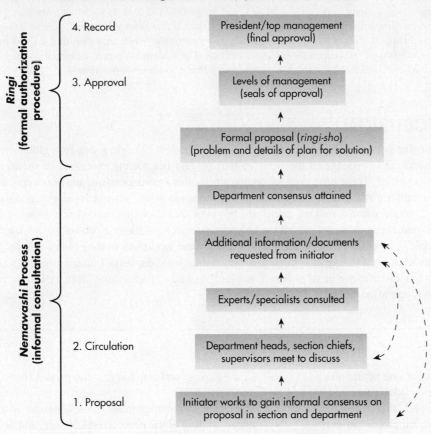

Up to this point, the process has been an informal one to gain consensus; it is called the *nema-washi* process. Then the more formal authorization procedure begins, called the *ringi* process. The *ringi-sho* is passed up through successive layers of management for approval—the approval made official by seals. In the end, many such seals of approval are gathered, thereby ensuring collective agreement and responsibility and giving the proposal a greater chance of final approval by the president. The whole process is depicted in Exhibit 5-8.

The *ringi* system is cumbersome and very time-consuming prior to the implementation stage, although implementation is facilitated because of the widespread awareness of and support for the proposal already gained throughout the organization. However, its slow progress is problematic when decisions are time-sensitive. This process is the opposite of the Americans' top-down decisions, which are made quite rapidly and without consultation, but which then take time to implement because unforeseen practical or support problems often arise.

Another interesting comparison is often made regarding the planning horizon (aimed at short- or long-term goals) in decision making between the American and Japanese systems. The Japanese spend considerable time in the early stages of the process, defining the issue, considering what the issue is all about, and determining whether there is an actual need for a decision. They are more likely than Americans to consider an issue in relation to the overall goals and strategy of the company. In this manner, they prudently look at the big picture and consider alternative solutions instead of rushing into quick decisions for immediate solutions, as Americans tend to do.[95]

The challenge for Japanese companies today is that the quickening rate of technological progress is leading to radically shortened product lifecycles and rapidly emerging opportunities.

ROCHELLE KOPP[96]

(Continued)

Of course, in a rapidly changing environment, quick decisions are often necessary—to respond to competitors' actions, a political uprising, and so forth—and it is in such contexts that the *ringi* system sometimes falls short because of its slow response rate. However, the Japanese culture does not regard time as such a valuable commodity as those in the West; they feel that a good outcome requires a thorough and consensus-building decision. The system is, in fact, designed to manage continuity and avoid uncertainty, which is considered a threat to group cohesiveness.[97]

CONCLUSION

It is clear that competitive positioning and long-term successful operations in a global market require a working knowledge of the decision-making and negotiating processes of managers from different countries. These processes are complex and often interdependent, and are deeply ingrained into their culture. Although managers may make decisions that do not involve negotiating, they cannot negotiate without making decisions, however small, or they would not be negotiating. In addition, managers must understand the behavioral aspects of these processes to work effectively with people in other countries or with a culturally diverse workforce in their own countries.

With an understanding of the environment and cultural context of international management as background, we move next, in Part 3, to planning and implementing strategy for international and global operations.

Summary of Key Points

- The ability to negotiate successfully is one of the most important in international business. Managers must prepare for certain cultural variables that influence negotiations, including the relative emphasis on task versus interpersonal relationships, the use of general principles versus specific details, the number of people present, and the extent of their influence.

- The negotiation process typically progresses through the stages of preparation, relationship building, exchange of task-related information, persuasion, and concessions and agreement. The process of building trusting relationships is a prerequisite to doing business in many parts of the world.

- Culturally based differences in verbal and nonverbal negotiation behavior influence the negotiation process at every stage. Such tactics and actions include promises, threats, initial concessions, silent periods, interruptions, facial gazing, and touching; some parties resort to various dirty tricks.

- The effective management of negotiation requires an understanding of the perspectives, values, and agendas of other parties and the use of a problem-solving approach.

- Decision making is an important part of the negotiation process as well as an integral part of a manager's daily routine. Culture affects the decision-making process both through a society's institutions and through individuals' risk tolerance, their objective versus subjective perspectives, their perceptions of the locus of control, and their past versus future orientations.

- The Internet is used increasingly to support the negotiation of contracts and resolution of disputes. Websites that provide open auctions take away the personal aspects of negotiations, though those aspects are still essential in many instances.

Discussion Questions

5-1. Discuss the stages in the negotiation process and how culturally based value systems influence these stages. Specifically, address the following.
- Explain the role and relative importance of relationship-building in different countries.
- Discuss the various styles and tactics that can be involved in exchanging task-related information.
- Describe differences in culturally based styles of persuasion.
- Discuss the kinds of concession strategies a negotiator might anticipate in various countries.

5-2. Discuss the relative use of nonverbal behaviors, such as silent periods, interruptions, facial gazing, and touching, by people from various cultural backgrounds. How does this behavior affect the negotiation process in a cross-cultural context?

5-3. Describe what you would expect in negotiations with the Chinese and how you would handle various situations.

5-4. What are some of the differences in risk tolerance around the world? What is the role of risk propensity in the decision-making process?

5-5. Explain differences in culturally based value systems relative to the amount of control a person feels he or she has over future outcomes. How does this belief influence the decision-making process?

Experiential Exercises

Exercise: Multicultural Negotiations

Goal

To experience, identify, and appreciate the problems associated with negotiating with people of other cultures.

Instructions (Note: Your professor will give out additional instruction sheets)

1. Eight student volunteers will participate in the role-play. Four represent a Japanese automobile manufacturer, and four represent a U.S. team that has come to sell microchips and other components to the Japanese company. The remainder of the class will observe the negotiations.

2. The eight volunteers will divide into the two groups and then separate into different rooms if possible. At that point, they will be given instruction sheets. Neither team can have access to the other's instructions. After dividing the roles, the teams should meet for 10 to 15 minutes to develop their negotiation strategies based on their instructions.

3. While the teams are preparing, the room will be set up, using a rectangular table with four seats on each side. The Japanese side will have three chairs at the table with one chair set up behind the three. The American side of the table will have four chairs side by side.

4. Following these preparations, the Japanese team will be brought in so they may greet the Americans when they arrive. At this point, the Americans will be brought in, and the role-play begins. Time for the negotiations should be 20 to 30 minutes. The rest of the class will act as observers and will be expected to provide feedback during the discussion phase.

5. When the negotiations are completed, the student participants from both sides and the observers will complete their feedback questionnaires. Class discussion of the feedback questions will follow.

Feedback Questions for the Japanese Team

1. What was your biggest frustration during the negotiations?
2. What would you say the goal of the American team was?
3. What role (e.g., decider, influencer, etc.) did each member of the American team play?

   Mr. Jones
   Mr./Ms. Smith
   Mr./Ms. Nelson
   Mr./Ms. Frost

4. How would you rate the success of each of the American team members in identifying your team's needs and appealing to them?

   Mr./Ms. Jones, Vice President and Team Leader
   Mr./Ms. Smith, Manufacturing Engineer
   Mr./Ms. Nelson, Marketing Analyst
   Mr./Ms. Frost, Account Executive

5. What strategy should the American team have taken?

Feedback Questions for the American Team

1. What was your biggest frustration during the negotiations?
2. What would you say the goal of the Japanese team was?
3. How would you rate the success of each of the American team members?

   Mr. Jones, Vice President and Team Leader
   Mr./Ms. Smith, Manufacturing Engineer
   Mr./Ms. Nelson, Marketing Analyst
   Mr./Ms. Frost, Account Executive

4. What would you say the goal of the American team was?
5. What role (e.g., decider, influencer, etc.) did each member of the Japanese team play?

   Mr. Ozaka
   Mr. Nishimuro
   Mr. Sheno
   Mr. Kawazaka

6. What strategy should the American team have taken?

Feedback Questions for the Observers

1. What was your biggest frustration during the negotiations?
2. What would you say the goal of the Japanese team was?
3. How would you rate the success of each of the American team members?

   Mr./Ms. Jones, Vice President and Team Leader
   Mr./Ms. Smith, Manufacturing Engineer
   Mr./Ms. Nelson, Marketing Analyst
   Mr./Ms. Frost, Account Executive

4. What would you say the goal of the American team was?
5. What role (e.g., decider, influencer, etc.) did each member of the Japanese team play?

   Mr. Ozaka
   Mr. Nishimuro
   Mr. Sheno
   Mr. Kawazaka

6. What strategy should the American team have taken?

Note: Your professor will give the instructions from the Instructor's Manual for this exercise.

Source: E. A. Diodati, in C. Harvey and M. J. Allard, *Understanding Diversity* (New York: HarperCollins Publishers, 1995). Used with permission.

CASE STUDY

Search Engines Aid Decision Making and Negotiation

Search engines help consumers search for and find useful information on the World Wide Web (WWW). In technical terms, the search queries and their results show up in the forms of search engine results pages (SERPs) and related information. This information may encompass web images and other types of useful files. Data mining is also part of this process. Major parts of the global web traffic include computers, networks, the Internet, WWW, browsers, search engines, and content.[1] "Collecting, storing and disseminating Internet-based content" come from search engines, which use processes such as crawling and caching.[2] In today's fast-changing world business and MNCs' domestic and global markets, search engines are highly useful and have been introduced in a multitude of languages. Local cultures and environments matter a lot when designing country-specific search engines.

Within search engines, data is an important part of technology. When retrieving information from search engines, the need for large-scale data is imperative in global business. Chief executive of IBM Virginia Rometty in *The Economist's World in 2014* correctly commented:

> *A new model for the firm is on its way; data constitute a vast new natural resource; our world has become pervasively instrumented and interconnected, with computation infused into things nobody would think of as a computer; … and powerful new computing systems can store and make sense of it nearly instantaneously.[3]*

Search engines come in different forms and types and may include general search engines, P2P search engines, meta-search engines, information-specific search engines, geographically based search engines, business search engines, enterprise search engines, and so on.[4] In 2015, Google (now renamed "Alphabet") was the most popular and powerful search engine in the world, followed by Baidu (China), Bing (United States), Yahoo, AOL Global, Ask.com, and so on.[5] Of course, Google is highly diversified in its products and maintains sites in various languages. This is a perfect example of today's global business with diverse markets and localization strategies. In 2014, Google sales surpassed $66 billion with a market capitalization of $384 billion. This shows the company's immense power, R&D capability, and corporate visibility.[6]

Search engines in global business are mostly affected by local cultures, country-specific regulations, data authenticity, and national ideologies. For example, in 2015, Baidu was the largest search engine in China, with sales of $7.91 billion and market capitalization of $76.15 billion.[7] Yandex was a leading search engine in Russia. In addition, South Korea had Naver and Daum. In the Czech Republic, Seznam is pretty popular. Sohu continues to be a dominant player in the Chinese market. Regardless of their types and forms, search engines in global business are highly differentiated based on their national languages, functions, country image, and usage. Search engines' contents and search results can reveal an interesting array of data and information.[8] Above all, search engines and their commercial identity remain country- and region-specific. No wonder we witness a few search engines that dominate global business. This is also the result of proprietary technologies, unique algorithms, and knowledge capital. In short, search engines are still being refined and will have major implications for MNCs, domestic companies, governments, and consumers alike.[9] Above all, consumers' privacy and national policies are critical issues in the growth of the global search engines industry.

Notes

1. Wikipedia, (2015), Web search engine, http://en.wikipedia.org/wiki/Web_search_engine, accessed April 24, 2015.
2. G. Gürkaynak, I. Yilmaz, and D. Durlu, Understanding Search Engines: A Legal Perspective on Liability, *Computer Law & Security Review* 29, (2013), pp. 40–47.
3. V. Rometty, "The Year of the Smarter Enterprise," *Economist: The World in 2014* (December 2014), p. 117.
4. Wikipedia, List of search engines, http://en.wikipedia.org/wiki/List_of_search_engines, accessed April 26, 2015.
5. NetMarketShare, "Desktop Search Engine Market Share," https://www.netmarketshare.com/search-engine-market-share.aspx?qprid=4&qpcustomd=0, accessed April 26, 2015.
6. YahooFinance, *Google, Inc.*, http://finance.yahoo.com/q/ks?s=GOOG+Key+Statistics, accessed April 26, 2015.

7. YahooFinance, "Baidu, Inc.," http://finance.yahoo.com/q/ks?s=bidu&ql=1 accessed April 26, 2015.

8. K. Jerath, L. Ma, and Y-G. Park, "Consumer Click Behavior at a Search Engine: The Role of Key Word Popularity," *Journal of Marketing Research* 51, (2014), pp. 480–486.

9. For more information, see Y. Chang et al., "Multimedia Search Capabilities of Chinese Language Search Engines," *Information Processing and Management* 46 (2010), pp. 308–319; B. J. Jansen and A. Spink, "How Are We Searching the World Wide Web? A Comparison of Nine Search Engine Transaction Logs. *Information Processing & Management* 42, No. 1 (2006), pp. 248–263; K. Kim and E. T. S. Tse, "Dynamic Search Engine Competition with a Knowledge-Sharing Service," *Decision Support Systems* 52 (2012), pp. 427–437; D. Tjondronegoro, A. Spink, and B. J. Jansen, "A Study and Comparison of Multimedia Web Searching: 1997–2006," *Journal of the American Society for Information Science & Technology* 60, No. 9 (2009), pp. 1756–1768.

Case Questions

5-6 Compare and contrast five search engines in global business. How do they aid in decision-making and negotiation processes?

5-7 Within today's global business, what do you see happening in the next five years regarding search engines' growth and global strategies?

5-8 Search engines carry national identities and cultures. Compare five major search engines from each continent, based on their local markets, strategies, and national characteristics.

Source: Copyright © 2015 by Syed Tariq Anwar, West Texas A&M University, used with permission.

Endnotes

1. KukilBora, SophieXSong, "Facebook's China Strategy Coming into Focus As It Plans to Open Sales Office There," www.ibtimes.com, May 13, 2015; "China Bans Facebook, But Air China Still Likes It," *Bloomberg Businessweek*, January 26, 2015; Hiawatha Bray, "Overseas Growth Challenges Facebook: Culture, Politics Make International Future Uncertain," *Boston Globe*, February 6, 2012, pp. B.8; Jenna Wortham, "Facebook's Filing: The Highlights," *New York Times*, February 1, 2012; Yun-Hee Kim, "Facebook's Asia Strategy? India, Japan, South Korea," *Bloomberg Businessweek Deal Journal*, February 1, 2012; Shira Ovide, "Facebook IPO: The Company Still Has Hopes for China," *Bloomberg News*, February 2, 2012; Alexandra Stevenson, "Facebook in Hong Kong: Closer to China," www.ft.com, February 9, 2011; Mark Lee, "Facebook Reaches Deal for China Site with Baidu, Sohu Reports," *Bloomberg News,* April 11, 2011.

2. *Deal Journal, 2012*, quoting from Facebook's IPO Filing.

3. www.nytimes.com, 2012.

4. www.bostonglobe.com 2012.

5. Lee, 2012.

6. *Bloomberg News*, February 2, 2012.

7. John Pfeiffer, "How Not to Lose the Trade Wars by Cultural Gaffes," *Smithsonian* 18, No. 10 (1988), pp. 145–156.

8. Nancy J. Adler, *International Dimensions of Organizational Behavior*, 4th ed. (Boston: PWS-Kent, 2002), 208–232.

9. Philip R. Harris and Robert T. Moran, *Managing Cultural Differences*, 3rd ed. (Houston: Gulf Publishing, 1991).

10. John L. Graham and Roy A. Herberger, Jr., "Negotiators Abroad—Don't Shoot from the Hip," *Harvard Business Review* (July–August 1983), pp. 160–168; Adler; John L. Graham, "A Hidden Cause of America's Trade Deficit with Japan," *Columbia Journal of World Business* (Fall 1981), pp. 5–15.

11. Phillip D. Grub, "Cultural Keys to Successful Negotiating," in *Global Business Management in the 1990s*, F. Ghader et al., eds. (Washington, DC: Beacham, 1990), pp. 24–32.

12. R. Fisher and W. Ury, *Getting to Yes* (Boston: Houghton Mifflin, 1981).

13. S. Weiss, "Negotiating with 'Romans,'" *Sloan Management Review* (Winter 1994), pp. 51–61.

14. John A. Reeder, "When West Meets East: Cultural Aspects of Doing Business in Asia," *Business Horizons* (January–February 1987), pp. 72.

15. John L. Graham, William Hernandez Requejo, "Managing Face-to-Face International Negotiations," *Organizational Dynamics* 38, No. 2 (2009), pp. 167–177.

16. Adler, 197.

17. Fisher and Ury.

18. Lennie Copeland and Lewis Griggs, *Going International* (New York: Random House, 1985), 85.

19. Adler, 197–98.

20. Fisher and Ury.

21. Jeanne M. Brett, *Negotiating Globally* (San Francisco, CA: John Wiley and Sons, 2001).

22. G. Fisher, *International Negotiation: A Cross-Cultural Perspective* (Chicago: Intercultural Press, 1980).

23. Pfeiffer.

24. John L. Graham, "Brazilian, Japanese, and American Business Negotiations," *Journal of International Business Studies* (Spring–Summer 1983), pp. 47–61.

25. T. Flannigan, "Successful Negotiating with the Japanese," *Small Business Reports* 15, No. 6 (1990), pp. 47–52.

26. Graham, 1983; Boye De Mente, *Japanese Etiquette and Ethics in Business* (Lincolnwood, IL: NTC Business Books, 1989).

27. Robert H. Doktor, "Asian and American CEOs: A Comparative Study," *Organizational Dynamics* (Winter 1990), p. 49.

28. Harris and Moran, 461.

29. Adler, 181.

30. These profiles are based on selections from Pierre Casse, *Managing Intercultural Negotiations: Guidelines for Trainers and Negotiators* (Washington, DC: Society for Intercultural Education, Training, and Research, 1985).

31. D. K. Tse, J. Francis, and J. Walls, "Cultural Differences in Conducting Intra- and Inter-Cultural Negotiations: A Sino-Canadian Comparison," *Journal of International Business Studies* (3rd quarter 1994), pp. 537–555.

32. B. W. Husted, "Bargaining with the Gringos: An Exploratory Study of Negotiations between Mexican and U.S. Firms," *International Executive* 36, No. 5 (1994), pp. 625–644.

33. Nigel Campbell, John L. Graham, Alain Jolibert, and Hans Meissner, "Marketing Negotiations in France, Germany, the United Kingdom, and the United States," *Journal of Marketing* 52 (1988), pp. 49–63.

34. Neil Rackham, *The Behavior of Successful Negotiators* (Reston, VA: Huthwaite Research Group, 1982).

35. J. Teich, H. Wallenius, and J. Wallenius, "World-Wide-Web Technology in Support of Negotiation and Communication," *International Journal of Technology Management* 17, Nos. 1/2 (1999), pp. 223–239.

36. Ibid.

37. Ibid.

38. A. Rosette, Jeanne Brette, Zoe Barsness, Anne Lytle, "When Cultures Clash Electronically: The Impact of E-mail and Culture on Negotiation Behavior," The Dispute Resolution Research Center, Northwestern University, accessed February 9, 2009.

39. J. A. Pearce II and R. B. Robinson Jr., "Cultivating *Guanxi* as a Foreign Investor Strategy," *Business Horizons* 43, No. 1 (January 2000), p. 31.

40. Rosalie L. Tung, Verner Worm, and Tony Fang, "Sino-Western Business Negotiations Revisited—30 Years after China's Open Door Policy," *Organizational Dynamics* 37, No. 1 (2008), pp. 60–74.

41. Tung, 2008.

42. Ibid.

43. Ibid.

44. Ibid.

45. Joan H. Coll, "Sino–American Cultural Differences: The Key to Closing a Business Venture with the Chinese," *Mid-Atlantic Journal of Business* 25, No. 2–3 (December 1988/January 1989), pp. 15–19.

46. M. Loeb, "China: A Time for Caution," *Fortune* (February 20, 1995), pp. 129–130.

47. O. Shenkar and S. Ronen, "The Cultural Context of Negotiations: The Implications of Chinese Interpersonal Norms," *Journal of Applied Behavioral Science* 23, No. 2 (1987), pp. 263–275.

48. Tse et al.

49. J. Brunner, teaching notes, the University of Toledo.

50. http://www.kwintessential.co.uk/etiquette/doing-business-china .html, accessed September 15, 2011.

51. Kam-hon Lee, Guang Yang, and John L. Graham, "Tension and Trust in International Business Negotiations: American Executives Negotiating with Chinese Executives," *Journal of International Business Studies* 37, No. 5 (2006), p. 623.

52. Roy Y. J. Chua, "Building Effective Business Relationships in China," *MIT Sloan Management Review*, Summer 2012.

53. J. M. Banthin and L. Stelzer, "'Opening' China: Negotiation Strategies When East Meets West," *Mid-Atlantic Journal of Business* 25, No. 2–3 (December 1988/January 1989).

54. Brunner.

55. Pearce and Robinson.

56. Ibid.

57. Ibid.

58. C. Blackman, "An Inside Guide to Negotiating," *China Business Review* 27, No. 3 (May 2000), pp. 44–45.

59. Boye De Mente, *Chinese Etiquette and Ethics in Business* (Lincolnwood, IL: NTC Business Books, 1989), pp. 115–123.

60. S. Stewart and C. F. Keown, "Talking with the Dragon: Negotiating in the People's Republic of China," *Columbia Journal of World Business* 24, No. 3 (Fall 1989), pp. 68–72.

61. Banthin and Stelzer, "'Opening' China."

62. Tony Fang, Verner Worm, and Rosalie L. Tung, "Changing Success and Failure Factors in Business Negotiations with the PRC," *International Business Review* 17 (2008).

63. www.ediplomat.com, accessed May 1, 2015.

64. www.ediplomat.com, accessed May 1, 2015.

65. Ibid.

66. Blackman.

67. "Doing Business in China," www.kwintessential.com, accessed October 2, 2011; "Avoiding Pitfalls, and Forging Success, in East-West Contract Negotiations," *International Herald Tribune*, January 24, 2011; Lucian Pye, *Chinese Commercial Negotiating Style* (Cambridge, MA: Oelgeschlager, Gunn, and Hain, 1982).

68. Fang et al., 2008.

69. W. B. Gudykunst and S. Ting Tomey, *Culture and Interpersonal Communication* (Newbury Park, CA: Sage Publications, 1988).

70. L. Copeland and L. Griggs, *Going International* (New York: Random House, 1985), p. 80.

71. M. A. Hitt, B. B. Tyler, and Daewoo Park, "A Cross-Cultural Examination of Strategic Decision Models: Comparison of Korean and U.S. Executives," in *Best Papers Proceedings of the 50th Annual Meeting of the Academy of Management* (San Francisco, CA, August 12–15, 1990), pp. 111–115; G. Fisher, *International Negotiation: A Cross-Cultural Perspective* (Chicago: Intercultural Press, 1980); G. W. England, "Managers and Their Value Systems: A Five-Country Comparative Study," *Columbia Journal of World Business* 13, No. 2 (1978); W. Whitely and G. W. England, "Variability in Common Dimensions of Managerial Values Due to Value Orientation and Country Differences," *Personnel Psychology* 33 (1980), pp. 77–89.

72. *PBS NewsHour*: "Italian Prime Minister on 'Prejudices' in Europe," February 9, 2012; *PBS NewsHour*: "Italy: 'Going the Greece Way' Would Be Disastrous," February 10, 2012; Niki Kitsantonis and Rachel Donadio, "As Europe Seeks More, Divisions Rise in Greece over New Austerity Plan," *New York Times*, February 10, 2012; Mohamed El-Erian, "Sadly This Greek Deal Faces the Sorry Fate of Its Forebears," *Financial Times*, London (UK), February 10, 2012, pp. 9; Russell Shorto, "The Way Greeks Live Now," www.nytimes.com, February 16, 2012; http://www .kwintessential.co.uk/-resources/global-etiquette/italy-country-profile.html, accessed February 15, 2012; Michael Schuman, "The Most Important Man in Europe," *Time* (February 20, 2012); Floyd Norris, "Germany vs. the Rest of Europe," *New York Times*, February 16, 2012.

73. Floyd Norris, February 16, 2012.

74. Kerin Hope, "Greeks Mark May Day with Anti-Austerity Protests," FT.com, May 1, 2015.

75. Anne-Sylvaine Chassan and Peter Spiegel, "Eurozone Fears Financial Chaos over Greece's Stance on Bailout," FT.com, February 2, 2015.

76. *Time*, February 20, 2012.

77. Ibid.

78. *New York Times*, February 10, 2012.

79. Ibid.

80. Russell Shorto, "The Way Greeks Live Now," www.nytimes .com, February 16, 2012.

81. Ibid.

82. www.kwintessential.co.uk.

83. Ibid.

84. Floyd Norris, "Germany vs. the Rest of Europe," *New York Times*, February 16, 2012.

85. Gideon Rachman, "Grexit Might Be the Best End for a Bad Marriage," FT.com, May 5, 2015

86. Ibid.

87. Hitt, Tyler, and Park, p. 114.

88. B. M. Bass and P. C. Burger, *Assessment of Managers: An International Comparison* (New York: Free Press, 1979), p. 91.

89. Phil Wahba, "Why Target Failed in Canada," *Fortune*, January 15, 2015.

90. Copeland and Griggs; M. K. Badawy, "Styles of Mideastern Managers," *California Management Review* 22 (1980), pp. 51–58.

91. Rochelle Kopp, Managing Principal, Japan Intercultural Consulting, "The Decision-Making Process in Japan," www.japanintercultural.com, April 2, 2012.

92. N. Namiki and S. P. Sethi, "Japan," in *Comparative Management—A Regional View*, R. Nath, ed. (Cambridge, MA: Ballinger Publishing, 1988), pp. 74–76.

93. De Mente, *Japanese Etiquette*, 80.

94. S. Naoto, *Management and Industrial Structure in Japan* (New York: Pergamon Press, 1981); Namiki and Sethi.

95. Harris and Moran, 397.

96. Rochelle Kopp, 2012.

97. S. P. Sethi and N. Namiki, "Japanese-Style Consensus Decision-Making in Matrix Management: Problems and Prospects of Adaptation," in *Matrix Management Systems Handbook,* D. I. Cleland, ed. (New York: Van Nostrand, 1984), pp. 431–456.

PART 2: Comprehensive Cases

Case 3 Vodafone in Egypt: National Crises and Their Implications for Multinational Corporations

Urs Müller

Shirish Pandit

Introduction

On Thursday, January 27, 2011, hundreds of thousands of protesters in Egypt were vociferously demanding an end to the 30-year rule of President Hosni Mubarak and to the state of emergency he had let prevail and nurtured during that tenure.[1] The protest movement was expected to gather even greater momentum following the afternoon prayers the next day, a Friday. The communication and connectivity through social media had acted as a key catalyst in enabling the protesters to coordinate their actions. President Mubarak's government decided to strike hard at the lifeline of this virtual medium by exploiting some of the rights that the state of emergency had accorded the government. That afternoon, it ordered the three main voice and data communications providers in Egypt— Vodafone, Mobinil, and Etisalat—to suspend services in selected areas.[2] Among these areas was Tahrir Square (Freedom/ Martyrs' Square) in Cairo, the biggest nucleus where protesters had assembled. Later, the government would also instruct these communications providers to broadcast propaganda text messages to all their subscribers, imploring them to be on the side of the Egyptian Army, which the government said was the true protector of Egypt.

Winner of the 2014 Case Centre case writing award "Hot Topic: crisis as opportunity"

This case study was prepared by Urs Müller and Shirish Pandit of European School of Management and Technology (ESMT). Sole responsibility for the content rests with the author(s). It is intended to be used as the basis for class discussion rather than to illustrate either effective or ineffective handling of a management situation. It was prepared from public sources. The correctness of the information in the case depends on the correctness of the information available from these public sources and could not be ascertained in all instances. The public information sources used are mentioned in the reference sections of the case study and the teaching note.

ESMT cases are distributed through Harvard Business Publishing, http:// hbsp.harvard.edu, and the Case Centre, http://www.thecasecentre.org; please contact them to request permission to reproduce materials.

Source: Copyright 2014 by ESMT European School of Management and Technology, Berlin, Germany, www.esmt.org.

[1] Amnesty International (2011), State of Human Rights in the Middle East and North Africa, January to Mid-April 2011," http://www.amnesty.org/en/ library/asset/POL10/012/2011/en/a31cf35a-0d47-4374-82ff-a4d440398861/ pol100122011en.pdf (accessed, January 24, 2014).

[2] J. Ben-Avie, "Vodafone: Response on Issues Relating to Mobile Network Operations in Egypt," Access Now blogpost, February 22, 2011, https://www .accessnow.org/blog/vodafone-response-on-issues-relating-to-mobile-network- operations-in-egypt (accessed January 24, 2014).

When Hatem Dowidar, CEO of Vodafone Egypt, heard about the government's order, he was about to make a crucial decision. He knew that the situation in Egypt was being observed closely from all over the world. Dowidar also realized that the course of action he opted for would have consequences, not just for Vodafone Egypt but also for the parent Vodafone Group. He contemplated the possible consequences, well aware that any decision he took would invariably evoke strong reactions.

Vodafone Group: Formation and Key Developments

By early 2011, Vodafone was among the leading wireless telecom providers worldwide.[3] It operated globally primarily under the brand name Vodafone, except in the United States, where it operated as Verizon Wireless. Vodafone's product and service offering included providing fixed-line, mobile, data, voice, and messaging services. The company was expanding its services to include integrated mobile and PC communication services. For the financial year 2009–2010 ending March 31, 2010, Vodafone reported having 341 million proportionate customers worldwide,[a] with equity interests in 30 countries and partner markets in 40 countries. In terms of subscribers, it only trailed China Mobile[4] (see Exhibit 1).

The origins of Vodafone dated back to 1982,[5] when Racal Strategic Radio Ltd. was established as a subsidiary of Racal Electronics PLC, the U.K.'s largest maker of military radio technology at the time. The newly formed subsidiary won one of the two U.K. cellular telephone network licenses; British Telecom winning the other. This network was managed by Racal Vodafone, a joint venture (JV) between Racal Strategic Radio Ltd. and Millicom Holding. The name Vodafone stood for voice data fone, reflecting the provision of voice and data services over mobile phones. At the start of 1985, Vodafone was launched with its first office based in the Courtyard, in Newbury, Berkshire.

In 1988, when parent company Racal Electronics floated 20 percent of the stock in its telecom operations—Racal Telecom—on the London Stock Exchange, the telecom stake was valued so high that Racal Electronics came under increasing pressure to demerge the Racal Telecom operations. This happened in 1991, and Racal Telecom was demerged from

[3] Vodafone Group PLC, "Annual Report, Section Operational Highlights" (2010).

[4] Vodafone Group PLC, "Annual Report, Section Global Presence" (2010).

[5] Vodafone, "About us," http://www.vodafone.com/content/index/investors/ about_us/background_history/history_of_the_group.html (accessed January 24, 2014); Vodafone Group PLC, "Annual Report, Section History and Development (2010).

Racal Electronics as the Vodafone Group, with Gerry Whent as its first CEO. During the next five years under Whent, Vodafone acquired either entire or controlling stakes in various phone chain stores, service providers, and so forth in the U.K.

In 1997, Whent retired and was replaced by Sir Christopher Gent as CEO. Gent was responsible for transforming Vodafone from a small, U.K.-based operator into the global giant through some significant international acquisitions.[6] In 1998, Vodafone expanded into Egypt and acquired AirTouch Communications Inc. for about $75 billion. The merged company commenced trading as Vodafone AirTouch PLC. It was through this merger that Vodafone also acquired a 35 percent stake in Mannesmann, which owned Germany's largest mobile network. In the United States, Vodafone merged its wireless assets with Bell Atlantic Corp. to form Verizon Wireless. In 2000, the company dropped AirTouch from its name and became Vodafone Group once again. In 1999, Mannesmann acquired Orange Telecom of the U.K., contravening what was a gentleman's agreement with Vodafone not to compete in each other's territory. Vodafone launched an unsolicited offer for Mannesmann and, when that failed, a fierce struggle for control continued until the Mannesmann Board finally agreed to Vodafone's offer of $185 billion, then the largest corporate merger ever.[7]

In April 2003, the expansionist Sir Chris Gent was replaced at the helm by Arun Sarin for the next five years. Sarin withdrew Vodafone's operations from saturated and/or unprofitable markets like Sweden, Belgium, and Japan.[8] Given the slowing growth in Vodafone's core European markets, he subsequently expanded Vodafone into emerging markets such as India, Turkey, and Romania.[9] He put Vodafone in a leading position in India by acquiring a controlling stake in Hutchison Essar.[10] Sarin also extended Vodafone's product offering to include Internet, data, and broadband services. By the time Sarin resigned in mid-2008, he had steered Vodafone to more than double its customer base, to 260 million globally. He also brought Vodafone Group back to profitability following the £21.9 billion loss in 2006—the largest in European corporate history—partly as a result of massive write-downs following acquisitions during the Gent era.[11]

Sarin was replaced by the then deputy CEO, Vittorio Colao. Colao stated that the company's plans included a continued expansion into Africa, Asia, and the Middle East

through acquisitions and partnerships while exiting noncore markets.[12] The key areas for growth in terms of service segments were identified as mobile data, broadband, and corporate accounts. In 2008, Vodafone raised its stake in the key mobile operators and wireless carriers in South Africa, Ghana, and Australia. In 2010, revenues in most of Vodafone's European strongholds were showing low or even declining growth, whereas those in emerging markets such as India and Egypt were showing strong trends.[13] This development could be confirmed by looking at the prospects for mobile penetration rates across various regions with an average global mobile penetration rate of about 70 percent; Europe was well above 120 percent. Various emerging countries in Asia and Africa, with mobile penetration rates of between 40 and 70 percent, held the real growth potential.[14] Two developments in 2010 reinforced the growing importance of the mobile market in the Arab world, and in Egypt in particular. The first Arabic (that is, non-Latin) Country Code Top-Level Domain (CCTLD) "misr" (in Arabic characters) was added to the Internet root zone, and the National Telecommunication Regulatory Authority (NTRA) of Egypt announced a plan to extend the length of mobile numbers from 10 to 11 digits by adding an extra digit to the code of each mobile operator. The latter decision would allow for the creation of new mobile numbers because the existing system approached full capacity.[15]

Vodafone In Egypt

Market Entry and Development

Vodafone expanded into Egypt in 1998 as the second mobile telecom operator by buying a minority (30%) stake in the MisrFone Group.[b] As part of the liberalization of the Egyptian telecom market that began in 1999, MisrFone Group became the second operator to be awarded a license for GSM operations in Egypt, which it began to run under the name of Click GSM. Initially, these operations were in the form of a consortium among Vodafone International, AirTouch, and local/international partners. In 1999, Vodafone Group acquired the AirTouch share and, in 2002, that of Vivendi of France. In January 2002, Click GSM was rebranded Vodafone Egypt.

In early 2005, in a promising move to establish a level playing field and facilitate competition, the Ministry of Communications and Information Technology (MCIT) and the NTRA of Egypt launched the Universal Service Fund (USF). The USF aimed to finance the expansion of unprofitable services into remote areas of Egypt and subsidize the provision of services in low-income areas through contributions, which all telecom companies in Egypt were obliged to make.[16]

[6]"Gent Influence Felt by Successor," BBC News online, March 13, 2006, http://news.bbc.co.uk/2/hi/business/4801996.stm (accessed January 24, 2014).

[7]"Vodafone Seals Mannesmann Deal," BBC News online, February 11, 2000, http://news.bbc.co.uk/2/hi/business/630293.stm (accessed January 24, 2014).

[8]"Sarin Leaves Vodafone after 5 Turbulent Years," *New York Times* online, May 27, 2008, http://www.nytimes.com/2008/05/27/technology/27iht-voda.4.13254645.html?_r=0 (accessed January 24, 2014).

[9]"Vodafone's Sarin Breaks Feb Jinx with Hutch Essar Win," Reuters, February 11, 2007, http://www.reuters.com/article/2007/02/12/hutchison-india-vodafone-idUSL1182577020070212 (accessed January 24, 2014).

[10]"Sarin leaves Vodafone under His Own Terms," *Guardian* online, May 28, 2008, http://www.theguardian.com/business/2008/may/28/vodafonegroup.telecoms2 (accessed January 24, 2014).

[11]"Sarin Leaves Vodafone after 5 Turbulent Years," *New York Times* online, May 27, 2008. http://www.nytimes.com/2008/05/27/technology/27iht-voda.4.13254645.html?_r=0 (accessed January 24, 2014).

[12]Excerpted from http://www.vodafone.com/content/index/investors/about_us/strategy/archived_ strategystatements.html. (accessed January 24, 2014).

[13]Vodafone Group PLC, "Annual Report, Section Global Presence" (2010).

[14]Vodafone Group PLC, "Annual Report, Section Telecommunications Industry at a Glance (2010).

[15]Arab Republic of Egypt, Ministry of Communications and Information Technology (MCIT) (2010) Yearbook.

[16]EIU Economist Intelligence Unit Egypt Telecoms Update, January 2011.

EXHIBIT I **Vodafone: Global Presence and Key Developments**

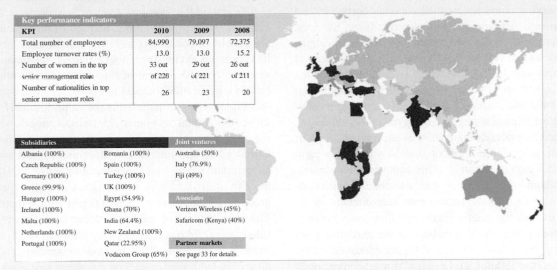

Key performance indicators			
KPI	**2010**	**2009**	**2008**
Total number of employees	84,990	79,097	72,375
Employee turnover rates (%)	13.0	13.0	15.2
Number of women in the top senior management roles	33 out of 228	29 out of 221	26 out of 211
Number of nationalities in top senior management roles	26	23	20

Subsidiaries		Joint ventures
Albania (100%)	Romania (100%)	Australia (50%)
Czech Republic (100%)	Spain (100%)	Italy (76.9%)
Germany (100%)	Turkey (100%)	Fiji (49%)
Greece (99.9%)	UK (100%)	
Hungary (100%)	Egypt (54.9%)	**Associates**
Ireland (100%)	Ghana (70%)	Verizon Wireless (45%)
Malta (100%)	India (64.4%)	Safaricom (Kenya) (40%)
Netherlands (100%)	New Zealand (100%)	
Portugal (100%)	Qatar (22.95%)	**Partner markets**
	Vodacom Group (65%)	See page 33 for details

Revenue growth (%)

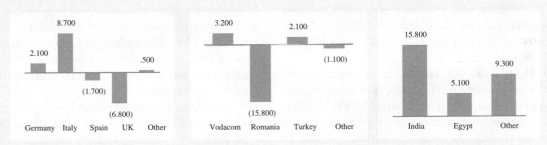

Germany 2.100, Italy 8.700, Spain (1.700), UK (6.800), Other .500

Vodacom 3.200, Romania (15.800), Turkey 2.100, Other (1.100)

India 15.800, Egypt 5.100, Other 9.300

Timeline

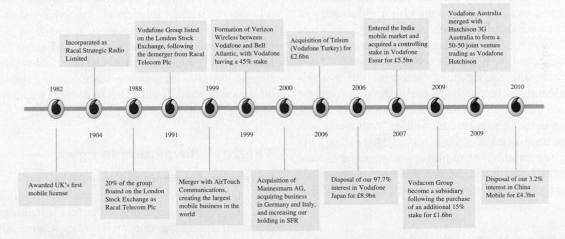

1982 — Incorporated as Racal Strategic Radio Limited

1988 — Vodafone Group listed on the London Stock Exchange, following the demerger from Racal Telecom Plc

1999 — Formation of Verizon Wireless between Vodafone and Bell Atlantic, with Vodafone having a 45% stake

2000 — Acquisition of Telsim (Vodafone Turkey) for £2.6bn

2006 — Entered the India mobile market and acquired a controlling stake in Vodafone Essar for £5.5bn

2010 — Vodafone Australia merged with Hutchison 3G Australia to form a 50-50 joint venture trading as Vodafone Hutchison

1904 — Awarded UK's first mobile license

1991 — 20% of the group floated on the London Stock Exchange as Racal Telecom Plc

1999 — Merger with AirTouch Communications, creating the largest mobile business in the world

2006 — Acquisition of Mannesmann AG, acquiring business in Germany and Italy, and increasing our holding in SFR

2007 — Disposal of our 97.7% interest in Vodafone Japan for £8.9bn

2009 — Vodacom Group become a subsidiary following the purchase of an additional 15% stake for £1.6bn

2009 — Disposal of our 3.2% interest in China Mobile for £4.3bn

Source: Vodafone Group PLC (2010). Group annual report, http://www.vodafone.com/content/dam/vodafone/investors/factsheet/group_presentation.pdf (accessed January 24, 2014).

Vodafone Egypt agreed to pay 0.5 percent of its revenues into the USF.[17]

In 2006, Vodafone Egypt launched off-shore operations under the name of Vodafone International Services. This subsidiary was dedicated to outsourcing business processes and IT services for Vodafone operators and beyond. Both its business-process outsourcing (BPO) and information technology outsourcing units grew successfully in the subsequent years. By 2010,

they employed over 2,200 staff, speaking 10 different languages, to provide customer and technical support for customers in 80 countries. To complement its wide set of voice and mobile Internet services, Vodafone Egypt acquired a 51 percent controlling stake in Egypt's Raya Telecom in October 2006.[18] Raya

[17]Vodafone Group PLC, "Annual Report" (2010), p. 135.

[18]Press Release, "Dr. Tarek Kamel Witnesses a Landmark in the Telecom Industry: Vodafone and Raya Sign Contract for Raya Telecom," http://web.archive.org/web/20100317152514/http://www.rayacorp.com/ShowPage.aspx?PID=559 (accessed January 24, 2014).

was a leading data operator in Egypt, with a modern network infrastructure serving domestic and international, corporate, and consumer segments. To strengthen its Internet-based services, Vodafone Egypt acquired Sarmady Communications in August 2008. Sarmady had grown steadily since its establishment in 2001, to dominate some of the Arab world's most popular Internet content services, such as ContactCars.com, FilBalad.com, FilFan .com, and FilGoal.com.[19] Sarmady became the digital arm delivering the Vodafone Internet experience in Egypt, putting Vodafone Egypt at the forefront of data innovation in the market. In 2007, Hatem Dowidar took over as CEO of Vodafone Egypt. In early 2011, Vodafone Egypt's executive team comprised nine members, two of whom—Marwa El Ayouti, the chief financial officer, and Dalia El Gezery, the human resources director—were women. Tony Dolton, the chief technology officer, was the only non-Arabic director, though all members of the executive team had international experience in terms of higher education and/or work experience (see Exhibit 2). Of the 470 management positions, 82 (17%) were occupied by women, whereas there were 1,450 women (33%) in the total workforce of 4,360.[20] Vodafone Egypt's shareholder structure consisted of Vodafone Group (54.93%), state-owned Telecom Egypt (44.94%), and a minority free float (0.13 %).

Vodafone Egypt was also active in corporate social responsibility (CSR) initiatives. In 2003, it established the Vodafone Egypt Foundation, which supported NGOs and civil society organizations in implementing developmental projects in the areas of health and education for children, community development, the usage of mobile technology for development, and access to communications. The CSR section of Vodafone Egypt's website conveyed the vision and strategy of the foundation (see Exhibit 2). Some of the notable initiatives by early 2011 included the following: medical caravans, various charity events, and initiatives for school children.[21]

Since its entry into the Egyptian market in 1998 as a minority stakeholder in the second GSM license holder, Vodafone Egypt grew over the years to become the leading mobile operator in Egypt in terms of revenues as well as, with the largest customer base. By the end of 2010, it served 24.6 million customers,[22] and employed 6,500 employees. It operated its own network in Egypt, but at the same time was heavily dependent on the government for running some critical elements of this infrastructure.

Egyptian Telecom Market Overview

Since the liberalization of the Egyptian telecom industry in 1999, and the ratification of the Telecommunication Act of 2003, development of the mobile communications sector became a

priority for the Egyptian government.[23] From 2006 onward, rivalry among the three key players[24]—Vodafone, Mobinil, and Etisalat—started intensifying, and led to falling tariff prices, to the benefit of consumers in lower income brackets. With fixed line revenues decreasing, mobile telecommunications revenues made up over 65 percent of total telecommunications revenues by 2011, up from 50 percent in 2006.

Of an overall population of approximately 85 million, there was a total of almost 75 million mobile subscribers at the end of 2010 (see Exhibit 3). Among the addressable population[c] of 55 million for mobile communications, Egypt had an estimated real mobile penetration rate[d] of 95 percent at the end of 2010.[25] This penetration rate was expected to keep growing gradually and reach 100 percent by the end of 2014. The competition was led by Vodafone with almost 30.7 million subscribers, followed closely by Mobinil with 30.3 million. Etisalat, with about 13.8 million subscribers, was a distant third. The competition among the three key players had been dynamic. The former incumbent operator, Mobinil, had been losing market share considerably, dropping from 47.3 percent in 2008 to 40.5 percent in 2010. Etisalat was the main beneficiary from Mobinil's decline, expanding its market share from 11.4 to 18.4 percent over the same period. Vodafone Egypt's market share had been fairly constant at around 41 percent over the 2008–2010 period.

With these high mobile penetration rates, the potential for existing mobile services was reaching saturation. At the same time, the average amount of money earned from each subscriber had been decreasing, as seen in the blended average revenue per user (ARPU)[e] trends for Vodafone and Mobinil. The growth in revenues, as well as subscribers, was projected to come down sharply from the 30 percent levels a couple of years back, to just three percent from 2013 onward (see Exhibit 3). On the one hand, the Egyptian government had been undertaking important steps to liberalize the growing telecommunications industry, but on the other hand, it still exercised enough control over these players to monitor their ICT activities.

The 2011 Revolution In Egypt

Sovereign Egypt until Early 2011

Since acquiring sovereignty from the British officially in July 1952, Egypt as a nation first underwent a high degree of centralization during the rule of President Gamal Abdel Nasser. After Nasser, Anwar Sadat took over as president in 1970, and, following the latter's assassination in 1981, then Vice President Mubarak assumed power. Under those circumstances, Mubarak declared a state of emergency in Egypt. In the years that followed,

[19]Sarmady press release, "Sarmady," July 24, 2009, http://sarmady.net/news .php?id=137 (accessed January 24, 2014).

[20]Figures intrapolated from information for March 31, 2010, and March 31, 2012, "Vodafone Egypt Sustainability Report" (2013), http://www.vodafone .com.eg/SustainabilityReport/EN/index.html (accessed January 24, 2014).

[21]Vodafone Egypt, "Our Initiatives," www.vodafone.com.eg/vodafoneportalWeb/ en/P1900336425135962 0204544 (accessed January 24, 2014).

[22]Vodafone Group PLC, "Annual Report" (2010), p. 11.

[23]Ministry of Communications and Information Technology (MCIT), Egypt, "Telecom Reform Milestones," http://www.mcit.gov.eg/TeleCommunications/ Telecom_Act_Law/Telecom_Reform_Milestones. (accessed January 24, 2014).

[24]National Telecommunication Regulatory Authority (NTRA), "Telecom Market, Indicators," http://www.ntra.gov.eg/english/dpages_dpagesdetails .asp?ID=352&Menu=3 (accessed January 24, 2014).

[25]HC Brokerage, "Egyptian Telecom Sector: A Yield Game," MENA research sector note (2010).

EXHIBIT 2 Vodafone Egypt: Executive Team and CSR Strategy

Hatem Dowidar
Chief Executive Officer

Marwa El Ayouti
Chief Financial Officer

Tony Dolton
Chief Technology Officer

Emad El-Azhary
Strategy Director

Dalia El Gezery
Human Resources Director

Khaled Hegazy
External Affairs & Legal Director

Ashraf Helal
Customer Care Director

Sherif Bakir
International Services Director

Ahmed Yehia
Consumer Sales & Retail Director

Source: Vodafone Egypt, "Executive Team," http://www.vodafone.com.eg/vodafoneportalWeb/ en/P609322281289119392636 (accessed January 24, 2014).

Our mission: to be admired as a diverse ethical company operating responsibly and providing products and services that enable a more sustainable society for our customers and our community by being the leading telecommunications company for:

Demonstrating a responsible, ethical and honest behavior	**Promoting a greener environment and eco-efficiency**	**Contributing to our community development with a focus on children's wellbeing & youth employability**	**Developing sustainable products and services for differently-abled customers**
We are committed to acting responsibly in all our activities to maintain the trust of our customers, our employees and our stakeholders	We aim to reduce the environmental impact of our operations and across our value chain while promoting a greener environment	We are committed to mobilizing our talent, technology and social investments to improve lives and livelihoods of Egypt's children and youth	We are committed to developing products, services and solutions that enable seamless communications for customers with special needs.

Employee giving programs and engagement is key to all our activities.

Source: Vodafone Egypt, "Our Strategy," http://www.vodafone.com.eg/vodafoneportalWeb/en/ P660027791300699032363 (acccsscd January 24, 2014).

he started opening up the Egyptian economy, but he also maintained the state of emergency and refrained from appointing a vice president.[26] Through Mubarak, the Western world saw Egypt as a great political ally, especially because of Mubarak's support for the allied powers in ousting Iraq out of Kuwait during

the 1991 Gulf War, of his diplomatic stance toward Israel, and his suppression of Islamic fundamentalism in Egypt.

Within Egypt however, Mubarak's rule was harsh. Mubarak had remained in power as president on the basis of a one-party rule. For four of his five six-year terms, Mubarak was nominated by parliament as the sole candidate and then confirmed in a popular referendum. Moreover, the continuous state of emergency that prevailed allowed for significant

[26]"The Upheaval in Egypt: An End or a Beginning?" *Economist* (February 2013); "Egypt after Hosni Mubarak (July 2009); A Survey of Egypt: The IMF's Model Pupil" (March 1999).

EXHIBIT 3   **Egyptian Telecoms Market: Key Indicators, Current and Projected**

	2008a	2009a	2010e	2011e	2012e	2013e	2014e
Population (a)	78,066	79,667	81,298	82,929	84,489	86,071	87,607
Market subscribers (b)	42,554	57,020	74,861	84,242	89,206	91,659	93,999
Market subscriber growth	37%	34%	31%	13%	6%	3%	3%
Market net adds (c)	11,503	14,466	17,841	9,381	4,964	2,453	2,340
SIM penetration	54.5%	71.6%	92.1%	101.6%	105.6%	106.5%	107.3%
Population < 9 and > 75 years (d)	17,947	18,064	18,207	18,351	18,424	18,524	18,590
50% of population below poverty line (e)	7,338	7,329	7,398	7,464	7,520	7,574	7,622
Addressable population (a-d-e) = (f)	52,781	54,274	55,693	57,114	58,545	59,973	61,395
Age and poverty adjusted penetration	81%	105%	134%	147%	152%	153%	153%
% of dual SIM	0%	14%	39%	50%	53%	53%	53%
Dual SIMs (g)(1)	–	7,860	21,726	28,405	31,299	32,006	32,764
Market sub. adjusted for dual SIM (b-g) = (h)	42,554	49,160	53,135	55,837	57,907	59,653	61,235
Real penetration = (h/f)	81%	91%	95%	98%	99%	99%	100%

Adjustments made to market subscribers and population to arrive at real human penetration ('000)

	2008a	2009a	2010e	2011e	2012e	2013e	2014e	2015e
Subscribers								
Mobinil	20,115	25,354	30,339	33,298	34,591	35,313	36,027	36,689
VFE	17,600	23,325	30,734	33,742	35,062	35,797	36,522	37,196
Etisalat	4,839	8,341	13,789	17,201	19,553	20,549	21,449	22,343
Net adds								
Mobinil	4,997	5,239	4,985	2,959	1,293	722	714	662
VFE	4,267	5,725	7,409	3,008	1,320	735	725	674
Etisalat	2,239	3,502	5,448	3,412	2,352	996	900	894
Market Share								
Mobinil	47.3%	44.5%	40.5%	39.5%	38.8%	38.5%	38.3%	38.1%
VFE	41.4%	40.9%	41.1%	40.1%	39.3%	39.1%	38.9%	38.7%
Etisalat	11.4%	14.6%	18.4%	20.4%	21.9%	22.4%	22.8%	23.2%

Source: HC Brokerage, "Egyptian Telecom Sector: A Yield Game," MENA research sector note (2010), p. 3.

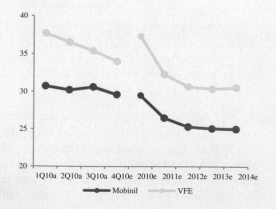

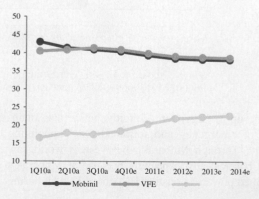

EXHIBIT 3 Continued

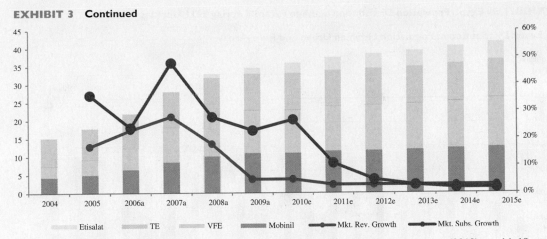

Source: HC Brokerage, "Egyptian Telecom Sector: A Yield Game," MENA research sector note (2010), pp. 14, 18.

EXHIBIT 4 Emergency Law in Egypt: Selected Excerpts in English

Article 1: The state may declare a state of emergency whenever security or public safety in Egypt, or in a specific area of Egypt, is threatened by war or an uprising/rebellion that puts people in danger or threatens public safety.

Article 2: The declaration and termination of a state of emergency is to be declared by the President of the Republic and the following must be included: why the state of emergency is being declared, the area it covers, and when it will be enforced.

Article 3: When the President of the Republic declares a state of emergency the following measures can be taken:

Restrictions will be placed on the freedom to assemble, to move residence, and drive in certain places, or at certain times (a curfew), as well as the arrest (without warrant) of those suspected of disrupting public order, as well as being able to search homes with no warrant.

The security forces have the right to seize or confiscate all types of publications (newspapers, pamphlets, advertisements), as well as screen them before publication.

The state has the right to shut down stores, open others, or close all in a certain area. The state has the right to seize any companies threatening civil order.

The state has the right to seize any unregistered arms, weapons, or weapons depot.

The state has the right to evacuate areas, restrict transportation to areas, search individuals, and request identification.

Article 3B: A person detained under these pretenses may appeal against the detention after six months. If a detainee wants to be released, the President of the Republic must approve a court ordered release.

Article 5: Detainees will be sentenced to hard labor and a fine of 40 thousand Egyptian pounds.

Article 6: After six months a detainee will be brought to court for trial.

Article 13: The President of the Republic has the right to dismiss any rulings by the court or demand the release of a detainee.

Source: Carnegie Endowment for International Peace, "Guide to Egypt's Transition, Emergency Law," http://egyptelections.carnegieendowment .org/2010/09/09/emergency-law (accessed January 24, 2014).

reduction in basic human and civil rights such as prohibition of street demonstrations, limitation of political organization, candidate bans in elections, and right to imprison individuals indefinitely without reason (see Exhibit 4). Police brutality was excessive and widespread, with Amnesty International reporting about 567 documented cases of torture by police, resulting in 167 deaths between 1993 and 2007. The same report also estimated that between 5,000 and 10,000 people were being held in long-term detention without charge or trial as a result of abuse of the emergency law. Some of these detainees were assumed to have been held for more than a decade.[27]

During his last term, Mubarak aggressively pursued economic reforms to attract foreign investment and facilitate GDP growth. Yet despite the relatively high levels of economic growth, huge damage had been done on the economic as well as sociopolitical fronts. Living conditions for the average Egyptian were rather poor, with PPP-adjusted GDP per capita of $6,393 per annum, which was well below the global average of $11,131 per annum.[28] Workers' unions were getting louder in demanding better worker rights and minimum wages. Unemployment in 2010 was around nine percent, which was lower than that in the United States and European Union, though in the case of Egypt, almost 80 percent of the unemployed had received either university or intermediate education. On the sociodemographic front, there was growing dissatisfaction particularly among young and well-educated Egyptians. The significant reduction in child mortality in Mubarak's early years, combined with a rapidly declining absolute population growth since the late 1980s, led to a "youth bulge" (see Exhibit 5). The result was that third and fourth sons no longer found prestigious positions, leading to social unrest, war, and terrorist tendencies. A significant

[27]Amnesty International Public Statement, "Egypt: Keep Promise to Free Detainees by End of June," June 2010, http://www.amnesty.org/en/library/ asset/MDE12/027/2010/en/f46e9f8c-3517-4a03-8184-aefedb9bb9e4/ mde120272010en.pdf (accessed January 24, 2014).

[28]World Bank, "GDP per Capita, PPP," http://data.worldbank.org/indicator/ NY.GDP.PCAP.PP.CD/countries/1W-EG?display=graph (accessed January 24, 2014).

EXHIBIT 5: Egypt: Population Distribution and Age Pyramid during 2011 Uprising

Egypt: Distribution of Population between Urban and Rural Areas

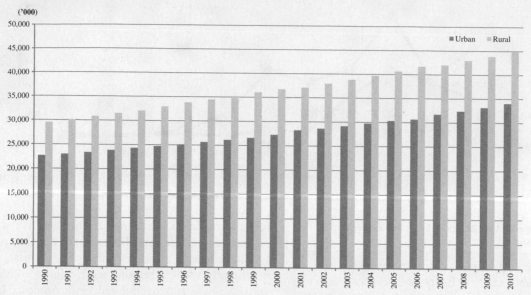

Source: "Statistical Yearbook of Egypt 2012," http://www.capmas.gov.eg/pdf/Electronic%20Static%20Book_eng/
population/untitled1/index.html?pageNumber=10 (accessed January 24, 2014).

Egypt: Age Pyramid of Population in 2010 Showing the "Youth Bulge"

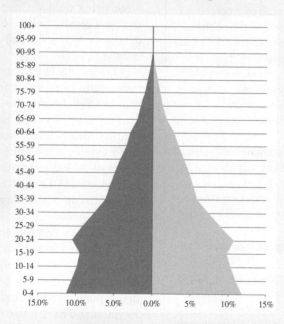

Source: Friducation.com, "Population and Demographic Trends," http://friducation.com/wp-content/
uploads/2012/03/Egypt-Population-Pyramid-2010.jpgLandscapeFormat (accessed January 24, 2014).

proportion of the population (11%) lived in and around Cairo, but the majority of the rest was spread over rural areas.[29]

Egypt and the Arab Spring of 2011

Taking a cue from the uprising that started on January 14, 2011, in Tunisia resulting in the overthrow of Ben Ali's rule,

[29]Central Agency for Public Mobilization & Statistics (CAPMAS), "Statistical Yearbook" (2013), http://www.capmas.gov.eg/pdf/Electronic%20Static%20Book2013/english/population/untitled1/index.html?pageNumber=1 (accessed January 24, 2014).

Egyptians began their popular uprising on Tuesday, January 25, 2011. This day, already known as National Police Day, was marked as the day of revolt and witnessed mainly nonviolent protests throughout Egypt. These protests took the form of demonstrations, marches, labor strikes, nonviolent civil resistance, civil disobedience, and so forth. The protests continued the next day, too, spreading to the Suez regions. Stepping up the momentum further, more massive rallies were planned in Cairo and other cities for Friday, January 28, after the weekly prayers past noon. As the focus of the protests, it was planned to assemble tens of thousands of protesters at Tahrir Square in Cairo. Among the main demands of the protesters were a limitation to the president's term and the termination of the Emergency Law. The law did not only restrict civil rights; it also put pressure on the telecom operators in Egypt, including Vodafone Egypt

Role of Social Media and Mobile Operators

Popular Internet-based social media networks, such as Twitter and Facebook, provided the technological platform that was critical for the protesters' ability to communicate among themselves and with the larger masses to get them organized. Of the 142 nations that were ranked by the World Economic Forum regarding the use of virtual social networks, Egypt was ranked 56 with a score of 5.4 out of 7.0 (7.0 being the best).[30] Mubarak's government perceived the popularity of social networks as posing a potential threat to its power. In June 2010, plainclothes agents in Alexandria had beaten to death a young Internet aficionado, Khaled Said, spawning a Facebook campaign that prompted silent vigils across the country.

In January 2011, the protest movement was initially led mostly by Islamic, anticapitalist, and feminist activists, but as a result of the power of social media, it soon turned into a mass movement that eventually managed to bring up to two million people together around Tahrir Square. The 26-year old blogger Asma Mahfouz became instrumental in mobilizing the masses for the protests on January 25. The freelance Egyptian-American journalist Mona Eltahawy referred to Mahfouz as, "the girl who helped start a revolution." Mahfouz posted a video blog on YouTube a week before the event on January 18, a video that became viral.[31] In it, she said:

> Four Egyptians have set themselves on fire to protest humiliation, and hunger, and poverty, and degradation they had to live with for thirty years. Four Egyptians have set themselves on fire thinking maybe we can have a revolution like Tunisia, maybe we can have freedom, justice, honor, and human dignity. I am making this video to give you one simple message: We want to go down to Tahrir Square on January 25. If we still have honor, and want to live in dignity on this land, we have to go down on January 25.[32]

A Facebook group that was set up particularly for the demonstrations on January 25 attracted 80,000 attendees. Observing the importance of communication channels, such as Twitter and Facebook, the government decided to block access to Twitter on January 25 and to Facebook on January 27.

Orders Issued by the Egyptian Government

On January 27, Vodafone, along with the other two key mobile operators in Egypt, Mobinil and Etisalat, was ordered to shut down the mobile network in specified areas. Later, it was also instructed by the Egyptian authorities to send propaganda SMS messages. The content of the messages was meant to appeal to the patriotism of all Egyptians, imploring them not to side with the protesting forces but, rather, with forces such as the Egyptian Army, which had Egypt's best interests at heart.

It was already being rumored that, during a protest of textile workers previously in April 2008 in the town of El-Mahalla, the Egyptian government authorities had successfully carried out an experiment, "involving the use of provocative elements of SMS and Internet services to spread false rumors, that would eventually lead to chaos."[33]

The Egyptian government could not only monitor ICT activities, but it was also technologically in a position to disconnect the entire system forcibly. In case of such a forced closure, restoration of services would have had to rely on the Egyptian authorities, and it was likely that the restoration would take much longer compared to a disconnection by the mobile operators themselves.

Hatem Dowidar's Decision

Since its formation, the U.K.-based Vodafone Group was one of the few telecom companies that grew, primarily through mergers, acquisitions, and joint ventures, from a local operation with a focused product offering to become a global player offering a broad range of mobile and data telecommunication services. Vodafone's products and services were playing a key role as the backbone of communication in the countries in which it operated.

In January 2011, significant developments were taking place in Egypt and the Arab world, thousands of kilometers away from Vodafone's home base. Hatem Dowidar, the CEO of Vodafone's Egyptian operations, was about to make a difficult decision that could potentially impact the reputation of the Vodafone Group. Dowidar knew that the danger of national crises spreading to other countries, where Vodafone had operations, was very real and that his decision would be watched closely, not only in Egypt but also in similarly affected neighboring countries as well as at the group's U.K. headquarters.

On that day, group CEO Vittorio Colao was among the various dignitaries assembled in Davos, approximately 2,500 kilometers northwest of Cairo, for the 2011 World Economic Forum. Referring to the ongoing developments in Egypt, Ban Ki-moon, the United Nations secretary-general, was reported to have said on that occasion, "I believe that one of the ground principles of democracy should be to protect the freedom of speech of the people."[34] The availability of uninterrupted communications services was an important prerequisite for

[30]S. Dutta and B. Bilbao-Osorio, "The Global Information Technology Report: Living in a Hyperconnected World, INSEAD Inside Report," (2012), http://www3.weforum.org/docs/Global_IT_Report_2012.pdf (accessed January 24, 2014).

[31]Archived website of Asma Mahfouz's website: http://web.archive.org/web/20110707122412/http://asmamahfouz.com/ (accessed January 24, 2014).

[32]Archives of website of Democracy Now, February 8, 2011, "Asmaa Mahfouz and the YouTube Video That Helped Spark the Egyptian Uprising," http://www.democracynow.org/2011/2/8/asmaa_mahfouz_the_youtube_video_that (accessed January 24, 2014).

[33]Egypt's Connections Blackout Was Planned since April 2008," Ahram Online, May 30, 2011.

[34]T. Bradshaw, "Condemnation over Egypt's Internet Shutdown," *Financial Times*, January 28, 2011.

Egyptians to enjoy their freedom of speech and express themselves. Amid these circumstances and developments, what decision should Hatem Dowidar have taken?

Case Questions

1. Compile a list of at least five alternative actions for Vodafone Egypt.
2. Provide reasons to support all identified alternatives.
3. Select the action that you would take if you were in the position of Hatem Dowidar as CEO of Vodafone Egypt.
4. Identify information or perspectives that you are missing. Whom would you like to talk to in order to get the information you are looking for?

Endnotes

a. Proportionate customers represent the number of mobile customers in ventures which the Vodafone Group either controls or in which it invests, based on the Group's ownership in such ventures (Vodafone Group PLC (2010). Annual report, 141).
b. "Misr" is the Romanized Arabic name of Egypt.
c. Addressable population is the portion of the total population after adjusting for age and income.
d. The real penetration rate reflects the proportion of mobile subscribers among the addressable population after adjusting for the number of dual SIM holders.
e. Blended ARPU is the weighted average ARPU from prepaid and postpaid subscribers.

As one of the most valuable brands in China, Haier designs, manufactures, and sells various home appliances, including refrigerators, air conditioners, and washing machines in over 100 countries. Under the leadership of its well-respected and visionary founder and CEO Zhang Ruimin, Haier Group has rapidly grown from a small refrigerator plant in Qingdao, Shandong province, China, to a global leader in home appliances. Haier's 2011 annual sales reached RMB151 billion. As part of its internationalization strategy, Haier entered the Japanese market in 2002 and formed a joint venture with Sanyo in 2007 to produce and sell refrigerators and washing machines in Japan.

In 2012, after five years of collaboration with Sanyo, Haier acquired Sanyo's white goods business in Japan and the related operations in six other Southeast Asian countries. Du Jingguo, president of Haier Asia International, moved from China to live in Japan in 1998 and learned the specificities of the Japanese culture well. Knowing his role in realizing Haier's globalization strategy that aims to turn each localized brand into a mainstream product in its respective market, Du is pondering how he can more effectively lead the team based in Japan. In particular, he needs to instill Haier's culture and innovative management system in its Japanese operation.

Company Background and Its International Expansion

Established in 1984, Haier has experienced four stages of expansion over the past 28 years, each representing the formulation and execution of different strategies: brand building (1984–1991), diversification (1991–1998), internationalization (1998–2005) and developing a global brand (2006–now).

1. Brand Building Period (1984–1991)

When Zhang took control of Haier in 1984 at the age of 35, the company was in financial distress and lacked basic standards and procedures. It was not uncommon for workers to steal

This case was prepared by Professors Carlos Sánchez-Runde, Yih-teen Lee, and Sebastian Reiche, with the assistance of Yen-Tung Chen and Yuki Kotake, researchers, as the basis for class discussion rather than to illustrate either effective or ineffective handling of an administrative situation. November 2012. This case was written with the support of SEAT Chair of Labor Relations. Copyright © 2012 IESE. To order copies, contact IESE Publishing at www. iesep.com. Alternatively, write to iesep@iesep.com, send a fax to +34 932 534 343 or call +34 932 534 200.

Last edited: 2/22/13
Distributed by The Case Centre
North America
Rest of the world
www.thecasecentre.org
t +1 781 239 588; t +44 (0)1234 750903
case centre
All rights reserved   f +1 781 239 5885; f +44 (0)1234 751125
e info.usa@thecasecentre.org

materials from company premises or simply not show up to work. Zhang inherited a workforce that, due to the Cultural Revolution, was largely undereducated. To foster discipline and proper work processes, Zhang began by defining a list of simple rules of conduct (see Exhibit 1) that would later evolve into sophisticated policies. This was particularly important because Haier faced fierce competition from over 300 local refrigerator plants. At that time, demand in home appliance products in China was growing, and customers were willing to pay for second-rate products. Quality was a rare concept. Zhang, however, believed that customers would be willing to pay more for higher quality products and services. Hence, whereas its competitors strived to pursue economies of scale to meet increasing demand and ignore quality control, Haier focused on the manufacturing of refrigerators and strictly emphasized product quality. To demonstrate his commitment to high quality, Zhang once personally pulled 76 refrigerators with minor defects from the production line and smashed them in public. This event marked an inflexion point in Haier's culture and is still the object of commentaries by current employees today, almost 30 years later.

By 1990, Haier had become the leading refrigerator maker in China with an average 9.5 percent growth rate over the past decade. At this early stage, Haier had also already started its international collaborations. In 1984, Haier signed a technology licensing agreement with Liebherr, a German refrigerator maker. Later, Haier imported freezer and air conditioner production lines from Derby (Denmark) and Sanyo (Japan). Joint ventures with Mitsubishi (Japan) and Merloni (Italy) further introduced advanced technology and innovation into Haier's operations and culture.

2. Diversification Period (1991–1998)

In its second phase, Haier adopted a stunned-fish tactic to diversify its product lines. "Stunned fish" referred to those companies that performed poorly due to weak management and yet owned advanced technology and equipment. Haier actively identified and acquired 20 of these companies and turned them around.

Haier also started to demonstrate its capability in management innovation by introducing the OEC (Overall, Every, Control and Clearance) approach, referring to Haier's practice of planning, executing, and clearing every task and performance dimension on a daily basis. This practice proved to be instrumental to Haier's success in changing the mentality of its workers to the pursuit of high quality. Later, Zhang introduced the concept of Miniature Companies within Haier, whereby each employee's tasks and responsibilities would be understood in terms of income and expenses to be recorded in a personal bankbook that served as an individual profit and loss statement and determined a person's salary.

Whereas the various acquisitions provided access to advanced technology and sources of diversification, they also

EXHIBIT 1   The Rules Introduced by Zhang in 1984

Note: The rules in English:

1. No late arrivals, no leaving early, no absenteeism.
2. No signing in for others at work.
3. No playing poker or chess or knitting sweaters during work hours.
4. No visiting friends for personal reasons during work hours.
5. No drinking alcohol during work hours.
6. No sleeping during work hours.
7. No gambling during work hours.
8. No damaging the production facilities of the factory.
9. No stealing equipment from the factory.
10. No defecating and urinating on the work floor.
11. No damaging public goods in the factory.
12. No using cotton yarn and diesel fuel to make fires in the factory.
13. No bringing children or unrelated persons into the factory.

Source: Picture taken by the case authors at the Haier Museum in Qingdao, May 2012.

added a substantial number of workers with different profiles and who used different forms of work organization. Haier had then to align the acquired companies with its increasingly sophisticated management systems. The formalization of Haier's systems helped provide a guiding frame, but it was insufficient by itself to unify the entire workforce. In fact, the pressure to quickly turn around the acquired companies meant that Haier had to socialize the new workforce into Haier's corporate culture and operating systems, often within short periods of time. Haier started to provide formal training, which later led to the creation of Haier University. The company also deployed staff from its Corporate Culture Center to the newly acquired companies to help with the integration.

3. Internationalization Period (1998–2005)

After Haier's refrigerators outperformed Liebherr's in a blind quality test held by a German magazine, Haier decided to develop its own brand globally. Influenced by successful Japanese and Korean companies such as Sony and Samsung, Haier also decided to bear the cost of building up the firm as an independent brand overseas. Haier adopted a strategy to enter more difficult, mature markets first and leave the easier ones for later. Initially, Haier focused on the European and U.S. markets, which contributed to over 3 percent of group sales. In the late 1990s, China joined the WTO, and the government called on enterprises to follow its national policy of expanding operations overseas. In 1999, Haier established the Overseas Promotion Division and aggressively pursued exports and overseas production in Asia (Indonesia, Philippines, Pakistan, India, and Japan), the Americas (South Carolina), Europe (Italy and Germany), and the Middle East (Dubai, Saudi Arabia, Iran, Algeria, Syria, and Jordan).

The internationalization period tested Haier's ability to effectively manage its workforce across an increasingly wide network of foreign operations. Although Haier had successfully integrated a host of different product divisions into its domestic organization and created an overarching management system, moving across borders meant that Haier now faced the challenge of expanding its systems abroad and managing across growing geographic and cultural distances. In contrast to many multinationals that staffed their foreign operations with managers from headquarters, Haier selected experienced local staff to manage its foreign operations from the beginning. Haier was convinced that, to ensure proximity to local customers, the company needed local people to develop the sales and distribution channels and better understand local customer needs. Although many aspects of Haier's systems were successfully transferred to other countries, Haier also adapted specific practices to the local context. For example, after the practice of having low performers publically share their mistakes in front of their peers was deemed a violation of human rights in the United States, it was replaced by having top performers share best practices. The European context required further adaptations of Haier's management practices.

4. Global Brand Period (2006–Present)

Since 2006, Haier has continued to evolve its business models and extend its global reach. During the latest phase, Haier developed a global brand strategy. Unlike its previous internationalization strategy, which saw Haier expand to international markets while maintaining a focus on its home market, the new strategy aims to make each localized brand of Haier a mainstream product in the respective local market with the ultimate goal of leading local market trends.

As the company grew larger throughout the years, Zhang noticed that it was becoming harder for Haier to respond to the market in a speedy and timely fashion. Recognizing the need to adapt to the Internet era with a high level of speed and responsiveness to customers, Zhang introduced a new business strategy called a Win–Win Mode of Individual-Goal Combination to (1) link each employee more closely to the clients he or she serves, and (2) satisfy clients' specific needs by consolidating R&D, manufacturing, and marketing resources through the Internet. To implement this strategy, Zhang proposed a restructuring that would organize employees into self-managed units (called ZZJYT, the abbreviation of zizhu jingyin ti—自主经营体 in Chinese) with an inverted triangle structure. Haier also made a conscious effort to develop the corresponding corporate culture. (The system will be discussed in more detail later.) Haier has been experimenting with this model in China and aims to gradually implement it overseas.

It is in this context that Du was asked to acquire Sanyo's white appliances operations in Japan and Southeast Asia and turn them into an integral part of the Haier Group in building its global brand.

Haier's Innovative Organizational Structure and Culture

Since 1984, Zhang has continuously proposed new strategies, most of which combined Western management concepts and Chinese philosophical thought. Although unable to receive a systematic, formal education due to the Cultural Revolution, Zhang is a diligent autodidact and has educated himself in different ways. He reads extensively, especially on topics related to traditional Chinese philosophy and literature and Western management theories, from which he created the unique Haier management models. In many public interviews, Zhang has consistently maintained that it is the ancient Chinese teachings, such as Confucius' Analects, Lao Tzu's Tao-De Ching, and Sun Tzu's *The Art of War*, that helped him face Haier's various challenges and form its management philosophy and corporate culture.

As a result, Haier adopted Western management theories, infused them with Chinese ancient philosophy, and executed them according to local practice. These concepts emerged gradually and developed by trial and error over time. ZZJYT is a vivid example. ZZJYT refers to a self-operating, self-managing entity that determines goals, recruits members, and formulates rules. The concept was already mentioned by Zhang in 2002, when he witnessed how the Internet changed traditional business models in various industries. To address the essential transformation from manufacturing to services and customer-centric models of operation, Zhang proposed an inverted triangle corporate structure to serve customers in the future. With the aim of leading the company into the Internet era, Haier formally adopted ZZJYTs in 2007.

ZZJYT (Self-Managed Unit) and the Inverted Triangle

Traditional management theory tends to see a company as a triangle that locates senior executives at the top, followed by middle managers in charge of different functional areas, and employees facing the markets and other external stakeholders at the bottom. In such a structure, top executives assume traditional roles as decision makers. Employees then follow managers' instructions and guidance in their daily operations. By contrast, the ZZJYT concept subverts this organizational structure by adopting an inverse triangle. At the company level, Haier differentiates between three vertical levels. Each level consists of specialized ZZJYTs (see Exhibit 2).

The first vertical level consists of ZZJYTs of manufacturing, marketing, and R&D functions that directly face customers. Employees of this level will directly contact customers, assess demand, and formulate and execute projects to efficiently satisfy customer needs. For instance, with the support of marketing and sales colleagues, R&D staff will communicate with customers and identify customers' needs onsite. As a manager of Haier explained: "Employees don't get orders from executives, but rather actively listen to the market. They are their own CEOs." In Zhang's view, the most unique characteristic of ZZJYTs was their ability to shorten the gap between internal and external users. It would be the employees who would closely coordinate with each other to directly create value for their internal and external customers, achieving zero distance between Haier and its end users.

The second level of ZZJYTs comprises a number of platforms that provide support to first-level ZZJYTs, including specific R&D, human resources, and finance support. The third level, the same as the executive level in a traditional triangle

EXHIBIT 2   ZZJYT and the Inverted-Triangle Organizational Structure

Customers · Customers

R&D · Marketing

Tier-1 ZZJYTs: Finding and creating demands

Manufacturing

Tier-2 ZZJYTs: Resource suppliers

Tier-3 ZZJYTs: Coordinated optimization inside, market opportunity innovation outside.

Haier's Inverted-triangular Organizational Structure

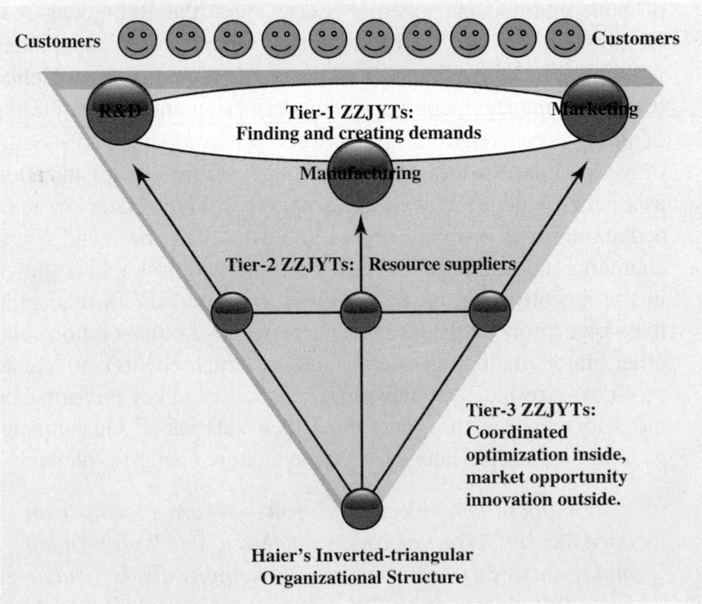

Source: Haier, 2012.

organization, is responsible for identifying and formulating strategic opportunities. It is expected to support the second-level platforms and facilitate resource allocation to the first-level ZZJYTs. In other words, the second-level and third-level ZZJYTs, serving as a resource platform and resource allocators, stand behind the first-level ZZJYTs to integrate ZZJYTs and employees and achieve another zero gap in Haier internally. This also translates into a zero inventory policy that requires specific planning of user resources to avoid any inventory. Manufacturing only produces according to the specific orders that sales units provide—and that is agreed upon in an internal order contract.

According to Zhang, ZZJYTs transform the company from a static organization into a network of units that can offer customized solutions to satisfy the unique, fragmented users of the Internet era. In Haier's jargon, users and hence markets not only represent external customers and stakeholders but also internal customers, that is, other ZZJYTs. The adoption of the ZZJYT concept goes as far as replicating the three-level inverted triangle structure within each ZZJYT. By 2012, Haier had established more than 2,000 ZZJYTs among its 80,000 employees. The ZZJYTs usually comprised between nine and 30 members. Although the majority operates in China, Haier aims to transfer the concept to its foreign operations too, notably to the newly acquired operations in Japan and the rest of Southeast Asia.

As independent and self-governed organizational units, ZZJYTs function in an open-system fashion to motivate employees to reinforce this self-driven mechanism in their respective ZZJYT. Specifically, Haier implements this open system in the following aspects. The degree of autonomy is such that it is basically for tax purposes that each unit does not become a fully independent company by itself.

Win–Win Mode of Individual-Goal Combination (人单合一双赢) It is the founding philosophy of ZZJYTs. Here, "individual" refers to employees; goal refers to customer orders in general but further implies the needs and value of resources of both internal and external users. Thus, the Individual-Goal Combination focuses on the integration of employees' capabilities with the value they create for users and the user resources. Unlike traditional management theory that defines an enterprise in terms of the contract relationships between the company and its employees, Haier uses this new concept to redefine its organization as a network between users and employees. Thus, Haier becomes a dynamic and evolving organization that can meet end users' changing and fragmented needs. The win–win principle is shown in the incentive system that is based on the ZZJYTs managing their own profit and loss statement, in close collaboration with other units (including internal and external clients), to create profit. As a result, each individual has to achieve key performance indicators that, in turn, determine their salaries. Ji Guangqiang, general director of Haier's Corporate Culture Center, explained:

"Haier doesn't provide a job for you—you are working in an open market. As an employee you need to find your own job and resources to meet your ever-changing goals. Of course, you can't always grow, but your targets may continuously change and it is your responsibility to account for these changes. Maybe your customer doesn't want a three-door fridge anymore, but rather prefers four or five doors. It is the customer that demands and you will need to follow suit to succeed."

Catfish Mechanism The team leader is elected through a voting process with each ZZJYT member exercising voting rights. The voting process can be initiated at any time. This results in a dynamic optimization of operations and equal opportunities for all employees. It also actively encourages internal competition for positions. If a ZZJYT member showed higher performance levels than the current leader, he or she could then assume the leadership of the unit. In addition to the actual team leader, ZZJYTs also comprise a leader-in-waiting—a role that Haier, drawing from a Norwegian tale, referred to as the catfish. The team leader is responsible for taking care of and developing the catfish so that the latter may be able to step in and substitute for the leader in the future.

Negative Entropy and Positive Feedback Loops. Negative entropy refers to the constant influx of first-class talent into Haier. For example, ZZJYTs are temporary organizational units in the sense that if they do not perform, they are quickly disbanded. The positive feedback loop emphasizes the positive correlation between Haier employees' capabilities and market objectives. Based on new talent and a positive loop between talents and their market goals, Haier aims to form a self-managed, virtuous cycle in its ZZJYT structure (see Exhibit 3).

ZZJYT in Practice

The ZZJYT and inverted triangle system is continuously evolving. Sometimes even managers at Haier's Qingdao headquarters find it difficult to define how the system works because it is constantly revised. Operationally, Haier uses three forms to assess the performance of a ZZJYT: a Strategic Income Statement, a Clearance Form, and a People-Goal Incentive Form. Different from the traditional balance sheet, income statement, and cash

EXHIBIT 3 Negative Entropy and Positive Feedback Loops

Source: Haier, 2012.

flow statement, Haier designed its Strategic Income Statement to track the performance of each ZZJYT and each individual employee. Based on managerial accounting theory, the Strategic Income Statement emphasizes pre-budget and execution. It contains four quadrants: user value created, human resources, process (forecasting and accounting), and gap-closing optimization. The performance of each individual employee is thus determined by the user value created rather than the completion of tasks or seniority in the organization. The Clearance Form comes from the OEC (Overall, Every, Control and Clearance) approach that was implemented by Haier several years before and referred to Haier's practice of planning, executing, and clearing every task and performance dimension on a daily basis. This form, in support of the Strategic Income Statement, tracks the progress of pre-budget plans and pursues zero discrepancy between plan estimation and actual result. Finally, the People-Goal Incentive Form sets goals for each employee in relation to market factors (rather than internally determined targets). Employees' salaries are calculated based on customer value recorded in this form. Ultimately, this means that the salary is paid by the market, not Haier. As Zhang explained:

> *"The ZZJYT concept completely changes traditional incentive systems. Before, you were paid a salary from the company. Now, however, you are paid by the market, not Haier. There is no glass ceiling for what you can earn. If you want to get paid more, you need to develop your capability to meet more customer needs. People who leave the company often complain about the low salary they received from Haier, but the main problem is that they don't feel comfortable with being their own boss."*

Naturally, income can also go down because of underperforming. For instance, in 2012, a new 24-hour delivery for all home appliances was established by Haier in China. If the goods are not delivered within 24 hours, the customer receives them free of charge, and the responsible employee is made to personally pay for them. During the year, this actually happened just four times, which is still considered a success. Similarly, if a given unit does not perform adequately, the unit is disbanded and its members are left on their own to find a place in another unit that is willing to hire them, or leave the company. This is no different from actually starting a new firm and failing. Nobody will give you any guarantees in case of failing in your new venture.

Although the pressure to perform is relentless, Haier recognizes employee loyalty. Employees who have served the company for a long time are often given less demanding jobs that allow them to still keep pace with the Haier rhythm. A Haier manager explained that "it is a bit like a chair. You don't need four legs to sit on and yet you won't cut off the fourth leg."

In the end, the CEO likes to stress that the key to success is not in doing or not doing something specific, but in being aligned with the major tendencies of the times. In that sense, Haier does not aim at being successful (such success comes and goes too easily) but at being a "company of the times," thus moving in the flow of the overall context, worldwide.

Haier in Japan

Due to a traditional preference for local brands and strong competition among Japanese home appliances makers, Japan is one of the most difficult markets in the world for foreign brands to step into. Haier officially entered Japan in 2002 when it established an alliance with Sanyo Electric Co. In 2007, this alliance was formalized through a joint venture between the two partners, in which Haier owned 60 percent. Under this alliance, Sanyo products were sold under both the Sanyo and Haier brand names in China through Haier's sales-and-service network. The joint venture in Japan was responsible for sales of Haier products in Japan through Sanyo's distribution and service outlet. This was the first time a major Japanese company ever promoted Chinese products. Such an alliance, however, was a smart move for both sides because they were able to take advantage of each other's resources. It helped Haier break into the Japanese market and gradually establish its brand name through unique design and competitive prices.

On July 28, 2011, Haier and Sanyo Electric signed a merger and acquisition (M&A) memorandum of understanding. In October 2011, both sides agreed for Haier to acquire Sanyo's white goods business in Japan, Vietnam, Indonesia, the Philippines, and Malaysia.

The first delivery was made in January and the whole process was completed in March 2012. All remaining parts of Sanyo were acquired by Panasonic. During integration, Haier implemented a system-wide M&A approach to maximize synergy among the various functional teams in different countries and sustain its global brand strategy. Specifically, it rearranged resources in technology, manufacturing, marketing, and sales, and the service network. Ultimately, Haier came to comprise two R&D centers; four manufacturing bases (in Kyoto and Tokyo); four manufacturing bases in Hunan Motor (Japan), Vietnam, Thailand, and Indonesia; and six marketing frameworks for six Asia-Pacific regions. The company adopted a dual brand strategy, with Haier and Aqua brands focusing on different market segments.

The Leader in Japan–Du Jingguo

Du Jingguo, the current president of Haier Asia International (HAI), has served at Haier since 1985. With an engineering background, Du started his career as an engineer on the production line before being promoted to manager and product developer. He was then assigned to introduce the technology transfer from Germany and became involved in operations management in the refrigerator plant. Later, he was in charge of business management, including sales service and advertisement, and was named president of the Haier Sales Company. In 1998, Du left Haier and moved to Japan for three years due to family reasons. During this period, he learned the language, customs, and business practices of Japan. In 2002, at the age of 36, Du rejoined Haier and was responsible for the overall management of Haier's operations in Japan, including sales and R&D. He has also been the key person leading the

Haier-Sanyo joint venture since 2007. In 2011, Du executed the acquisition of Sanyo's white goods business and established HAI.

As the presence of Haier in Japan gradually evolved from a simple import center to a joint venture, and finally to acquiring Sanyo to enter the mainstream market, Du realized that he had to instill the Haier system and culture in its Japanese operation, yet at the same time adapt to the local cultural values and traditions. Although for Western outsiders the Japanese culture may seem close to the Chinese, the invisible divides can be huge. What is more, Haier is implementing an unconventional organizational structure and management system in an attempt to be an "enterprise of its time that can adapt well to the trend," in the words of Zhang. Du needs to introduce this system in the units he leads in Japan and the operations in other Southeast Asian countries.

Challenges in Leading the New Haier in Japan

Du adopted the following guiding principles in leading Haier Japan: respecting Japanese culture, integrating Haier culture, and, finally, shaping a unique local culture of Haier Japan. CEO Zhang commented: "It is very easy to merge and purchase any enterprise with capital, but success can only be achieved with culture and strategy, and culture integration is the most decisive factor." As a keen follower of Zhang's management philosophy, Du paid special attention to cultural differences and made extra efforts to communicate with workers at different levels to ensure a better mutual understanding and a smooth introduction of Haier's system.

In total, Du leads 350 employees in Japan and 6,700 workers in other Southeast Asian countries. In implementing the ZZJYT and inverted triangle system in Japan, Du faces huge challenges, which are intensified by the many cultural differences. How can he lead a Chinese brand to break into a market that has been traditionally dominated by well-known Japanese brands such as Hitachi, Panasonic, Sharp, and Mitsubishi? Also, customers in China and Japan, much like the employees in Haier and Sanyo, hold a different understanding of quality. Although generally Haier enjoys a reputation for its product quality, the quality standard in Japan tends to be higher and customers are much more demanding, not tolerating, for instance, a slight scratch on the packaging materials of an otherwise perfect product.

Internally, a strong collectivistic culture in Japan prevents companies from adopting a more individual-based compensation system, which is the core of the Individual-Goal Combination mechanism in Haier. While leading the joint venture, Du once wanted to distribute individualized incentives and encountered strong objections from Sanyo managers, who insisted on the importance of team spirit and equality.

Moreover, traditional lifelong employment and seniority-based reward and promotion systems, though gradually abandoned by some Japanese companies, still exist in big Japanese firms. This makes merit-based promotions extremely difficult to implement. Finally, Du also faced the ultimate question of whether Sanyo workers would be willing to join Haier,

since they had the choice to stay with Sanyo, now part of the Panasonic Group. When Du first started running the Haier-Sanyo joint venture, a Japanese director came to him with a provoking comment: "Each Chinese individual alone is smart and competent, but when you put two Chinese workers together, they will not be able to perform. The Japanese are different—we play collective games."

Aiming High

One day, Du was reviewing the first post-acquisition annual sales target prepared by the sales team. "JPY7 billion seems a bit low," Du thought. But he didn't want to impose a sales target on the team.

Du had always kept in mind the vision of CEO Zhang of making Haier the number one brand in home appliances in the world, and he decided to move quickly toward this goal. He was determined to revise the first sales target of JPY7 billion and push it higher. As Du remarked:

> *The goal is to one day be number one. Although we cannot reach it overnight, we need to start with number five, then number three, then eventually reach the place of number one. I did a calculation based on the idea of being number five in the market as a baseline for the discussion, but I did not reveal it to the sales team.*

He then called a series of meetings with the sales team and asked them to explain how they derived the JPY7 billion figure. The team pointed to the specific constraints they faced for a higher target. For example, the team emphasized that several negotiations would still be ongoing, leaving uncertainty as to the overall project. It would take three months after the January delivery date to withdraw all old products from the market. Furthermore, more time would be required to prepare the new product launch. Communication and coordination with the marketing team would also take time. In total, it would take another six months to improve the products and develop new designs.

Du then went through the list of constraints and asked the team for alternatives in overcoming them. Du explained, "I wanted them to operate as an inverted triangle. They would make decisions and I would offer support and resources."

The R&D team originally planned to start developing new products for Haier Japan after the initial delivery of the M&A, with a possible launch date around March/April 2012. However, Du came up with a bold strategy; he decided to launch all new products right after the M&A delivery. To achieve this, he would need the R&D team to start working on completely newly designed products even before the Haier R&D office and facility were ready and the employees had been officially transferred from Sanyo to Haier. Du rented an empty building near Kyoto that would be the future R&D Center of Haier washing machines and asked the R&D staff to start designing new products with the objective of launching new products on January 6. For some weeks, the building had no windows, yet the team was already working inside. It was

EXHIBIT 4 Commitment of the Sales Team to the JPY35 Billion Target

In the photo: Du Jingguo, president of Haier Japan.
Source: Picture taken by the case authors at the Haier Japanese headquarters in Osaka, July 2012.

winter and extremely cold. "The team needed to wear heavy coats and worked very long hours in the building without the protection of windows in the cold winter to meet the deadline," Du commented.

Finally, they accomplished the challenging goal and launched 33 new products designed for Japanese customers on January 6 and had them distributed all over Japan within two weeks. This "instant launch" was something never before seen and surprised Japanese competitors.

When Du met with the sales team and they together found solutions to overcome the obstacles one by one, they were able to move the target of JPY7 billion first to JPY27 billion, then to JPY32 billion, and, finally, to JPY35 billion. All members of the sales team expressed their commitment to reaching the target of JPY35 billion in their own way, displayed as an inverted triangle in the office of the sales team in Osaka (Exhibit 4). In July 2012, this target was 100 percent on schedule, with the sale of Haier washing machine and refrigerator brands occupying third and fourth place, respectively, in the Japanese market. Du remarked:

In fact, Japanese workers are very diligent and hardworking. It is only that they could not imagine that reaching such ambitious goal within such a short time was attainable. Once I broke these mental obstacles and set up clear goals for them, they became committed to the goals and did their best to make them happen. When they saw the first results, they knew that it was really possible and gained the confidence to achieve future challenging goals.

Bridging Cultural Differences

Having lived in Japan for years and being married to a Japanese woman, Du had learned about Japanese culture and was able to clearly see the cultural differences. When Du first took charge of the Haier-Sanyo joint venture in 2007, Japanese workers would often not express their feelings openly to Du. To communicate better with the Japanese workers, he divided the 160 employees at that time into 16 teams of 10. Every few nights, he would go out drinking with a team. After two years of drinking, the Japanese workers finally felt comfortable talking and drinking with Du in a more open way. "However," Du said with a wry smile, "I got all kinds of gastric and duodenal ulcers after that." Little by little, in his way, Du gained acceptance from the Japanese workers.

Merit-Based Rewards and Promotions

One of the core concepts of ZZJYT is to connect each worker's performance with the market and reward him or her accordingly (i.e., individual-goal combination and win–win). This means that workers do not receive equal amounts of incentive bonuses but rather receive rewards according to their contribution. For Japanese workers, this practice was hard to accept. While leading the joint venture, Du spent six months communicating with the Japanese team on this issue. Finally, he decided to withhold the part of the bonuses representing Sanyo's share because his Japanese counterpart did not agree with his approach, but insisted on implementing the system in the Haier way and gave out

60 percent of the bonuses that represented Haier's share in the joint venture.

Similarly, Du at one point wanted to promote a 35-year-old worker to the position of director. However, it would go against the Japanese value of seniority if he got promoted sooner than an older colleague. Over the course of a year, Du publicized the performance of this young man in the company and indicated the problem of the current appraisal system that failed to reveal the outstanding performance of the young man. Two years later, Du promoted the young man to director, at the same time assigning the more senior colleagues titles of Responsible Director with clear roles and responsibilities so that they would not feel ignored. Little by little, the merit-based system embedded in Haier's ZZJYT was accepted in Haier's Japanese operation.

After the acquisition, Du talked to former Sanyo salespeople and tried to convince them to sign an Individual-Goal Combination contract, offering them higher incentives for higher performance (win–win). Some of them did not feel comfortable and refused to sign it in the beginning. Rather than pushing them, Du tried to help them understand the underlying logic of the contract.

Retaining Japanese Workers

When Haier was about to acquire Sanyo's home appliances operation, Du and his management team estimated that about 30 percent of employees might quit. Indeed, many workers had joined Sanyo with the idea of staying there until retirement. They were afraid of moving to a Chinese company. At that moment, Sanyo had very limited new product development and resource investment, but Du kept communicating with the employees about the plan, system, and prospects if they stayed with Haier.

Cultural Integration as an Ongoing Process

Haier Japan seemed to be off to a successful start under the leadership of Du, who attributes his achievement to the well-devised strategy and management system defined by Zhang. "What I am doing is simply trying to understand the thinking and strategy of Mr. Zhang, trying to align my operation with it, and continuously adapting it to local realities," said Du. Yet, cultural integration is an ongoing process; challenges may persist and require further effort to handle them. For example, some Japanese workers continue to feel confused about the structure. They see Haier Japan functioning as a star (i.e., the juxtaposition of a normal and an inverted triangle). Du and Haier Japan will need to continuously experiment with the ZZJYT system (still quite new and in a fine-tuning stage back in China) and instill the Haier values into the Japanese operation.

Conversations among Japanese Employees

The day after a regular visit of Du to the washing machine research center near Kyoto, three senior managers and two chief engineers of the center had lunch together.

"We knew Sanyo was not performing at the levels at which it used to perform some years ago," one manager said. "In fact, the company was putting itself in the same position that other companies faced in the final years of the last century, when Sanyo bought them. In the end, it all worked out for the best, for the former independent companies and for Sanyo. So we keep asking ourselves if this is not the same situation."

"Yes, the situation is similar, but there are some differences. Haier is a Chinese company, and when we talk with Mr. Du we feel confident about his capabilities and his intentions. But where will Mr. Du be in 20 years? With Sanyo, we did not have to think about this, because we were confident that Sanyo was going to be there for us always, forever. We used to say that we were Sanyo employees the same way I say I belong to my family. Can we say the same now? Are we going to 'be' Haier employees, or should we say that we are 'now' Haier employees?" added another manager.

"There is little we can do about that," commented one chief engineer. "We will never see ourselves as Haier employees the same way we saw ourselves as Sanyo employees, but Haier provides us with important challenges in developing new technologies, and the market will respond to that. In fact, Haier is being very brave entering the Japanese market, competing head-to-head with the most advanced brands and products. It shows an amazing drive to succeed in the most difficult environment. And this is our environment. If we succeed here, we will succeed anywhere. There was a time when we felt exactly the same with Sanyo, but that was gone well before Haier acquired us. We just might have an interesting combination: a resourceful company, strong market prospects, and the will to face all the technological challenges. What else do we need?"

The other chief engineer responded, "Well, we need to combine those aspects into a new way of organizing ourselves through the inverted triangle, and this does not seem easy. Mr. Du is telling us that we are an inverted triangle but he talks from his top position. I would like to see how that works in practice."

"Actually, Mr. Du says that he is the one who wants to see how it works—that he is here to see (not us) and we are here to act (not he)," explained one senior manager. "Also, I find that the idea of an inverted triangle is promising in helping us move beyond country issues. So far, it makes a difference for us to think in terms of whether our boss is Chinese or Japanese. But if the inverted triangle idea works out the way it should, there is nobody above us, neither Chinese nor Japanese, just our customers. It is just us figuring out the best way to produce something. Haier probably has an advantage here in terms of how to deal with global and local tensions (as long as the idea really works, obviously)."

"Actually, Sanyo had tried some empowerment approaches in the past that somehow remind us of the inverted triangle, but they never really worked. They seemed to be very fashionable in the United States, but not here," echoed one chief engineer.

"Indeed, but we need to be careful. If possible, I would still prefer a Japanese boss," said one manager. "On the other hand, the Chinese seem to behave differently from the Japanese. We prefer someone who is Japanese because we think of how Japanese leaders behave. But these people are not

Japanese; they will behave differently, so it may not be relevant at all whether they are Japanese or not. Mr. Du and most of the Chinese Haier employees in Japan actually speak very decent Japanese. They do not speak like us, but they are closer to fully mastering our language than anyone who has been around here in the past. It may actually be easier for them to adapt to us than the other way around. And yet, this idea of the inverted triangle can be very powerful; it may relativize these differences. We need to see how it really works."

"That is up to us," said a manager. "Remember, we are not here to see it happen, we are here to make it happen. It is for headquarters to see that we, not they, do it."

Yet, another chief engineer commented, "A few days ago I performed a little experiment at home with my two kids. They are 16 and 14 years old. I told them that we at Haier were going to begin to work under a different system, the inverted triangle. I asked them how that would work in their school. They could not understand at all what I was telling them. They were afraid their class would turn into total chaos if the teacher proposed something like that, and that students would not know what to do. My wife nearly suggested that I was a little bit crazy. The question is whether we are prepared for this: to become our own bosses and answer not only for our work and hours, but for our initiative and creativity as well. It is like we have been under a school system, with someone always monitoring our work, and now we have to become the teachers. This is not going to be easy, at least not for the older people, and they are our masters. Should we expect everybody, absolutely everybody, to be able to perform under this new system? I am afraid it may create a division between those who enjoy the system more, especially the younger people, and those who have worked too many years under the Sanyo system. How are Haier and Mr. Du going to deal with this?"

Case Questions

1. How far has Haier come since its creation in 1984?

2. What is special about Haier's current management system? Why did the company create this system?

3. What role has CEO Zhang played in Haier's development? How would you describe him as a leader?

4. What kind of tensions could arise for Haier when implementing its management system in Japan?

5. How did Du manage the tensions during his leadership of Haier Japan? Please assess Du in terms of how he goes about reconciling cultural differences. In which aspects would you agree with him and in which would you not?

6. Should Haier adapt to the Japanese culture and change its management system? Or should Haier impose its system in Japan?

7. What types of cultural challenges might Haier face in other cultures? What would you suggest that Haier improve in order to better manage the cultural complexity of its global footprint?

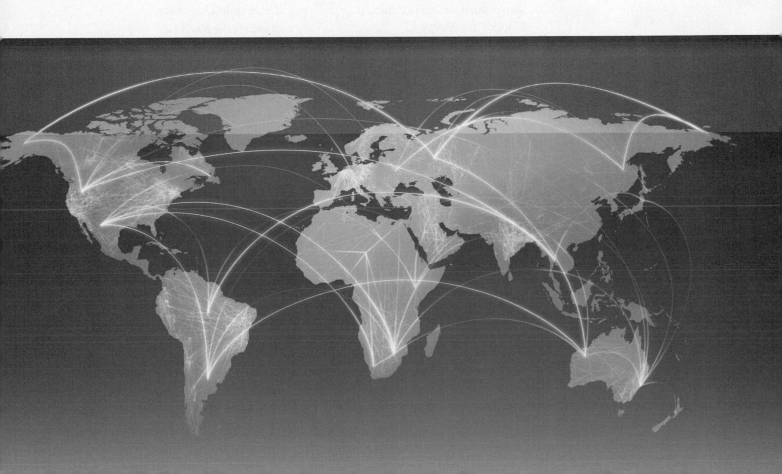

6 Formulating Strategy

OUTLINE

OBJECTIVES

6-1. To understand the reasons companies engage in international business.

6-2. To learn the steps in global strategic planning, including assessing entry strategies for different markets.

6-3. To become familiar with strategic planning for emerging markets.

Opening Profile: Amazon, eBay, and Flipkart Bet Big on India[1]

In July 2014, Amazon, which had been in India since 2013, announced new investment there of $2 billion, and Flipkart, India's biggest e-retailer, announced it was injecting $1 billion of fresh capital there. At that time, Flipkart, the Indian e-commerce pioneer started in 2007 by two former Amazon employees, had 22 million registered users, although it was losing money. Amazon only entered India in 2013 but clearly is on a march to catch up with and dominate the e-retailing marketplace and get a foothold before Walmart expands its e-commerce venture there. Snapdeal, backed by eBay, also has a substantial c-retailing presence in India and is a rival of Flipkart. EBay has been in India since 2005 and has invested large amounts in Snapdeal to grow its market share there, following its model of investing in e-commerce firms in a number of countries to gain a foothold locally. In February 2014, eBay was the primary investor in a $133.7 million funding of Snapdeal. Although e-commerce was still in early stages in India, Amazon managers were expecting it would be the fastest country for the firm to reach $1 billion in sales. Overall, online buyers in India were expected to reach $1 billion in gross sales.

E-retailing goes global

Christos Georghiou/Fotolia

Although the Indian online retail market was only 0.5 percent of the total retail market there of $415 billion in 2013, it has grown at 56 percent annually for the past seven years and is expected to grow to $8.3 billion in 2015. In addition to direct investments, acquisitions and consolidations in e-retailing are increasing in India.

All this has traditional Indian retailers very concerned, further pressuring the Indian government to protect them. Although the government has set up considerable barriers to traditional retail giants such as Walmart and IKEA, foreign e-retailers are finding ways to circumvent the stringent regulations on brick-and-mortar stores designed to protect the small stores, which represent 93 percent of retail sales. The Indian government is very concerned that foreign online retailers will shut out the myriad of small and midsize Indian retailers. As of 2014, India does not allow foreign firms to own majority stakes in any retail companies that deal in more than one brand. This means that although foreign investment in the business-to-consumer (B2C) segment is prohibited, investment is permitted within the business-to-business (B2B) category, known as the marketplace business model.

Therefore, firms such as eBay and Amazon have to operate under strict rules that bar them from warehousing their stocks in India; they are also not allowed to sell directly to consumers. They can have their suppliers store the inventory and deliver the products that they have sold through the e-retailers. Amazon has found a way around these regulations by charging third-party suppliers to use its website to sell their products so that Amazon and other e-retailers are allowed to store and deliver the products that other companies wish to sell. Thus, Amazon uses the marketplace business model in India. It has two warehouses, one each in Bangalore and Mumbai. Flipkart uses the inventory-led model with registered suppliers and warehouses in Bangalore, Mumbai, Delhi, and Kolkata.

Other major challenges to e-retailing companies like Snapdeal, Flipkart, and Amazon include the extremely inefficient infrastructure and transportation systems as well as the antiquated payment system. Only about 12 percent of Indians use credit or debit cards, so those companies have had to deal with cash-on-delivery payment. Consumers also wish to use COD because they too distrust the reliability of the transportation system; it is their practice to inspect the product and then pay. As the e-retailers plan for future expansion to meet growing demand, they have to deal with the delivery logistics by building more warehouses and fulfillment centers.

To alleviate the transportation challenges, Amazon is planning to test drone deliveries of packages up to about 5 pounds in India, where there are fewer regulations on drones. Meanwhile, most business

(Continued)

involves the big cities, where the rate of Internet penetration and income are higher. Even so, given the vast geographical distances in India, much delivery is by air, adding to the delivery costs for the e-retailers. FlipKart, for example, is trying to reduce its transportation costs by setting up a number of regional warehouses and adding to the supplier base.

In spite of growing demand and potential for e-retailers in India, the poor infrastructure has so far kept delivery costs up so that profits are minimal.

More recently, however, the Indian government is wishing to secure more foreign investment, so it is reconsidering the restrictions on foreign companies' e-retailing there.

As with the opening profile illustrating the global digital consumer e-businesses, companies continue to look for opportunities around the world in search of profitable new markets, outsourcing facilities, acquisitions, and alliances—and this search is increasingly directed at emerging markets.

However, the recent economic slowdown caused many companies to retrench rather than expand to conserve cash flow in the economic slowdown. Thus, whereas much of the focus in this chapter is on going international and expansion abroad, we need to keep in mind that retrenchment is also a very real strategy, especially in difficult economic times. However, the long-term trend is clear. After the Boston Consulting Group identified 100 emerging-market companies that it felt have the potential to reach the top rank of global corporations in their industries, *BusinessWeek* challenged that:

> *Multinationals from China, India, Brazil, Russia, and even Egypt are coming on strong. They're hungry—and want your customers. They're changing the global game.*[2]

Management consultant Ram Charan advises that we are now truly in a global game, one that he calls a "seismic change" to the competitive landscape brought about by globalization and the Internet. This first wave of emerging-nation players, he says, are taking advantage of three forces spurred on by the Internet—mobility of talent, mobility of capital, and mobility of knowledge. The strategies of companies such as America Movil of Mexico, Alibaba of China, Petrobras of Brazil, and Mahindra and Mahindra of India (which is penetrating Deere's market on its own U.S. turf) use their bases in their emerging markets as "springboards to build global empires."[3] Add these new challengers to the already hypercompetitive arena of global players, and it is clear that managers need to pay close and constant attention to strategic planning. Most large companies, such as IBM, which we think as American, actually sell the majority of their products abroad, and that is also true of many from emerging markets, such as Mumbai-based Tata Consultancy Services (TCS).

As will be explained in this chapter, corporate strategies must change in response to shifting global economic conditions and other environmental and competitive factors. With continuing economic challenges around the world, TCS must consider how it will respond, but it is strengthened by its geographic diversification. IBM, meanwhile, now making about half its revenues in its services business—in particular in emerging markets—has diversified with a two-track approach. The company is helping clients in the United States cut costs, and in emerging markets, it helps customers develop their technology infrastructure. These are examples of corporate strategies that are being developed to respond to or anticipate current global trends, as noted by Beinhocker et al. of McKinsey & Company and discussed in various chapters throughout this book. They note that:

> *Companies' strategic behavior should be tied closely to ten important trends: strains on natural resources, a damper on globalization, the loss of trust in business, the growing role of government, investment in quantitative decision tools, shifting patterns of global consumption, the economic rise of Asia, industry structure upheaval, technological innovation, and price instability.*[4]

Because international opportunities are far more complex than those in domestic markets, managers must plan carefully—that is, strategically—to benefit from them. Many experienced managers are wary about expanding into politically risky areas or those countries whose government practices they find prohibitive.

The process by which a firm's managers evaluate the future prospects of the firm and decide on appropriate strategies to achieve long-term objectives is called **strategic planning**. The basic means by which the company competes—its choice of business or businesses in which to operate and the ways in which it differentiates itself from its competitors—is its **strategy**. Almost all successful companies engage in long-range strategic planning, and those with a global orientation position themselves to take full advantage of worldwide trends and opportunities. Multinational enterprises (MNEs), in particular, report that strategic planning is essential both to contend with increasing global competition and to coordinate their far-flung operations.

In reality, however, that rational strategic planning is often tempered, or changed at some point, by a more incremental, sometimes messy, process of strategic decision making by some managers. When a new CEO is hired, for example, she or he will often call for a radical change in strategy. That is why new leaders are chosen carefully, based on what they are expected to do. So, although the rational strategic planning process is presented in this text because it is usually the ideal, inclusive, method of determining long-term plans, managers must remember that people are making decisions, and their own personal judgments, experiences, and motivations will shape the ultimate strategic direction.

REASONS FOR GOING INTERNATIONAL

Companies of all sizes go international for different reasons—some reactive (or defensive), and some proactive (or aggressive). The threat of their own decreased competitiveness is the over-riding reason many large companies adopt an aggressive global strategy. To remain competitive, these companies want to move fast to build strong positions in key world markets with products or services tailored to the needs of increasingly global and diverse sets of customers.

Reactive Reasons
GLOBALIZATION OF COMPETITORS

One of the most common reactive reasons that prompts a company to go overseas is global competition. If left unchallenged, competitors who already have overseas operations or investments may get so entrenched in foreign markets that it becomes difficult for other companies to enter later. In addition, the lower costs and market power available to these competitors operating globally may also give them an advantage domestically. Nor is this global perspective limited to industries with tangible products, as a whole range of services have followed suit, including office functions, engineering, publishing, medical, consulting, media, and so on, facilitated by the Internet Following the global expansion of banking, insurance, credit cards, and other financial services, for example, financial exchanges have been going global by buying or forming partnerships with exchanges in other countries, their strategies facilitated by advances in technology.[5]

Strategic moves by competing global giants prompt countermoves by other firms in the industry to solidify and expand their global presence. Such was the case after the Pfizer takeover of Wyeth in January 2009; Pfizer, the world's biggest drug maker, bid $68 billion for Wyeth. Subsequently, Roche, the Swiss pharmaceutical company, paid $46.8 billion to acquire the biotechnology company Genentech, in which it already owned a majority stake. Not to be outdone, Merck, the American pharmaceutical giant, announced in March 2009 that it would pay $41 billion to acquire its rival Schering-Plough—the combined company to keep the Merck name. Clearly, Merck will benefit from the worldwide reach of Schering-Plough, which generates most of its sales outside of the United States, in particular in emerging markets.

TRADE BARRIERS

Although trade barriers have been lessened in recent years by trade agreements that have led to increased exports, some countries' restrictive trade barriers do provide another reactive reason for companies often switching from exporting to overseas manufacturing. Barriers such as tariffs, quotas, buy-local policies, and other restrictive trade practices can make exports to foreign markets too expensive and too impractical to be competitive. Toyota, for example, has manufacturing plants in the United States to circumvent import quotas. In May 2011, ZTE—China's second largest telecom equipment maker and a state-controlled company listed in Hong Kong—moved to Brazil; the purpose was to avoid that country's high import tariffs, even though it is cheaper to manufacture in China.[6]

REGULATIONS AND RESTRICTIONS

Similarly, a firm's home government's regulations and restrictions can become so expensive that companies will seek out less restrictive foreign operating environments. Avoiding such regulations prompted U.S. pharmaceutical maker SmithKline and Britain's Beecham to merge. Both thereby guaranteed that they would avoid licensing and regulatory hassles in their largest markets: Western Europe and the United States. The merged company is now an insider in both Europe and America.

CUSTOMER DEMANDS

Operations in foreign countries frequently start as a response to customer demands or as a solution to logistical problems. Certain foreign customers, for example, may demand their supplying company to operate in their local region so that they have better control over their supplies, forcing the supplier to comply or lose the business. McDonald's is one company that asks its domestic suppliers to follow it to foreign ventures. Meat supplier OSI Industries does just that, with joint ventures in 17 countries, such as Germany, so that it can work with local companies making McDonald's hamburgers.

Proactive Reasons

Many more companies are using their bases in the developing world as springboards to build global empires, such as Mexican cement giant Cemex, Indian drugmaker Ranbaxy, and Russia's Lukoil, which has hundreds of gas stations in New Jersey and Pennsylvania.[7]

Careful, long-term strategic planning encourages firms to go international for proactive reasons, some of which are described below.

ECONOMIES OF SCALE

One pressing reason for many large firms to expand overseas is to seek economies of scale—that is, to achieve world-scale volume to make the fullest use of modern capital-intensive manufacturing equipment and to amortize staggering research and development costs when facing brief product life cycles.[8] The high costs of research and development, such as in the pharmaceutical industry (for example, Merck and Pfizer), along with the cost of keeping up with new technologies, can often be recouped only through global sales.

GROWTH OPPORTUNITIES

According to the Small Business Administration (SBA), 96 percent of the world's customers live outside the United States, and two thirds of the world's purchasing power is in foreign countries.[9]

Clearly, there are vast opportunities for small businesses—those with fewer than 500 workers—to do business overseas. In fact, as of 2011, small businesses accounted for about 30 percent of total export revenue, or about $500 billion in annual sales. "Still, only about 1% of the nation's roughly 30 million small businesses sell overseas, according to U.S. Census data. Those that do usually work with no more than one foreign market—typically Canada, Mexico, the United Kingdom, Germany or China, Census data show."[10] As domestic growth declines because of slow-growth economies, opportunities abroad look more attractive, in particular since the Internet now greatly facilitates the ability to link to contacts in other countries quickly. New start-ups in Europe, for example, feeling the weight of the continent's continuing debt crisis, realize that they must go global from the beginning to establish sufficient market size to be viable. Indeed, most European entrepreneurs and managers are well equipped personally to go global because they are accustomed to moving easily among different languages and customers. This is particularly true of Internet-based companies such as audio-sharing web service SoundCloud, cofounded in Stockholm by Alex Ljung, a multi-lingual entrepreneur, who observed that:

> *It was obvious that our business had to be global from the start. We're more like citizens of the Internet than citizens of a country.*
>
> "COMPANIES BORN IN EUROPE, BUT BASED ON THE PLANET," WWW.NYTIMES.COM
> *JUNE 12, 2012*[11]

Whatever their size, companies in mature markets in developed countries experience a growth imperative to look for new opportunities in emerging markets such as South Africa, as illustrated in the following Comparative Management in Focus feature.

Comparative Management In Focus
Global Companies Take Advantage of Growth Opportunities in South Africa

Global companies with a presence in South Africa all cite numerous advantages for setting up shop in the country, from low labor costs to excellent infrastructure—and a base from which to export products internationally. Jim Myers, president of the American Chamber of Commerce in South Africa, says that nearly 50 percent of the chamber's members are Fortune 500 companies and that more than 90 percent operate beyond South Africa's borders into southern Africa, sub-Saharan Africa, and across the continent. "The sophisticated business environment of South Africa provides a powerful strategic export and manufacturing platform for achieving global competitive advantage, cost reductions and new market access," says Myers.[12]

South Africa (see Maps 6.1 and 6.2) was ranked the leading economy in Africa and 14th out of 26 emerging economies, behind China, India, and Russia, in the Grant Thornton Emerging Markets

MAP 6.1 **South Africa has a population of 51.77 million and consists of 1,221,037 sq. km.**

(Continued)

MAP 6.2 Africa

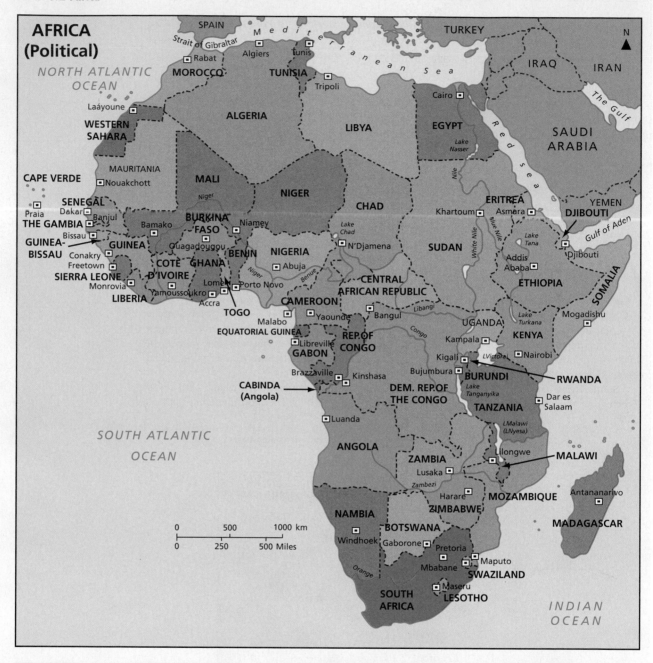

Source for maps: https://www.cia.gov/library/publications/the-world-factbook/maps/maptemplate_sf.html.

Opportunity Index.[13] Among South Africa's success stories is BMW, which has produced more than a million 3-Series sedans from its plant in Rosslyn, Pretoria. The factory remains "a vivid example of a successful market entry through local production," says Harald Krüger, the chief executive of BMW South Africa.[14] In addition, CCI Call Centers has three facilities in South Africa, employing more than 4,000 people. CCI services the mobile, technology, telecommunications, and financial sectors of companies in the United Kingdon.[15] IBM also has a considerable presence in South Africa and has committed a further R700 million (about $54 million) to expand its research lab in Tshimologong Precinct in Braamfontein. The lab will focus on advancing big data, cloud computing, and mobile technologies.[16]

Businesses are taking advantage of opportunities because of the legal protection of property, high labor productivity, low tax rates, reasonable regulation, a low level of corruption, and good access to credit, all of which were seen as factors contributing to the country's investment climate. Threats include the low level of skills and education of workers, labor regulation, exchange rate instability, and crime. In addition, South Africa is closely tied to companies in Europe, making it vulnerable to economic downturns.

Nevertheless, the business environment is favorable. South Africa was rated ninth out of 30 countries to live in—ranked between Germany and Australia—according to a global survey of more than 5,100 expatriates conducted by HSBC Bank International; responses were based on experiences and perceptions of daily life, including accommodation, food, social life, health care, schools, working hours, and family life.[17]

According to the World Economic Forum Global Competitiveness Index, which ranked South Africa 53rd out of 148 countries surveyed, the country rates well regarding the quality of its institutions (41st), including intellectual property protection (18th), property rights (20th), and legal efficiency in challenging and settling disputes (13th and 12th, respectively).[18]

Further examples of companies taking advantage of growth opportunities abound. In an effort to continue its long-term strategy to expand into China—with its 1.3 billion consumers—Nestlé, the Swiss food giant, announced on July 11, 2011, that it had agreed to pay $1.7 billion for a 60 percent stake in Hsu Fu Chi, a big Chinese confectioner, in one of the biggest deals ever made by a foreign company in China. The founding Hsu family eventually retained 40 percent, and Hsu Chen, current CEO, heads the joint venture.[19] In addition, in March 2012, United Parcel Service (UPS) reached an agreement to acquire TNT Express, a Dutch shipping company, for 5.2 billion euro, or $6.8 billion, to increase market share in Europe and provide growth opportunities in China. UPS stated that, "The additional capabilities and broadened global footprint will support the growth and globalization of our customers' businesses."[20] Cemex, the Mexican cement giant, has been one company aggressively taking advantage of growth opportunities through acquisitions. After learning his family's business from the bottom up for 18 years, Lorenzo Zambrano became CEO and started his gutsy expansion into world markets. His strategy has been to acquire foreign companies, allow time to integrate them into Cemex and pay off the debt, and then look for the next acquisition. In 2009, however, environmental factors forced strategic changes; the global economic slowdown caused declining construction demand, the peso declined in value vis à vis the dollar, and Cemex was not able to refinance its debt, causing Mr. Zambrano to reflect on how he has enacted his strategies, stating, "I have to admit it; it was an error.... This time we forgot to ask, 'What is the worst that can happen?'"[21] Subsequently, Cemex had to retrench considerably around the world, but in 2015, was successful with a new niche in supplying building materials and help for do-it-yourselfers.

RESOURCE ACCESS AND COST SAVINGS

Resource access and cost savings entice many companies to operate from overseas bases. The availability of raw materials and other resources offers both greater control over inputs and lower transportation costs. Lower labor costs (for production, service, and technical personnel)—another major consideration—lead to lower unit costs and have proved a vital ingredient to competitiveness for many companies.

Sometimes just the prospect of shifting production overseas improves competitiveness at home. When the Xerox Corporation started moving copier-rebuilding operations to Mexico, the U.S. union agreed to needed changes in work rules and productivity to keep the jobs at home. Lower operational costs in other areas—power, transportation, and financing—frequently prove attractive.

INCENTIVES

Governments in countries such as Poland seeking new infusions of capital, technology, and know-how willingly provide incentives—including tax exemptions, tax holidays, subsidies, loans, and the use of property. Because they both decrease risk and increase profits, these incentives are attractive to foreign companies.

In February 2009, for example, companies were rushing to conclude M&A deals in Brazil while a tax break that allows companies to deduct 34 percent of the premium paid in an acquisition was still guaranteed, amid fears that it would be rescinded. This kind of tax incentive is rare, so it attracts considerable interest from foreign investors. Coupled with the recent devaluation of the Brazilian real—which made acquisitions cheaper for foreign bidders—tax deductions are currently one of the great attractions for acquisition deals in Brazil.[22] Nor are those incentives limited to emerging economies. The state of Alabama in the United States has spent hundreds of millions of dollars in incentives to attract the Honda, Hyundai, and Toyota plants.[23] And, in 2014, Cuba passed a law offering tax breaks for foreign companies planning joint ventures with Cuban companies or the Cuban state.[24]

However, the practice (called inversion) of U.S.-based companies changing their domicile country to those that offer a lower corporate tax rate, such as in Ireland, was coming under considerable fire in 2015 in the United States because of the loss of taxes and jobs. One such tax haven is Luxembourg, a grand duchy country with 550,000 people, most of whom are in or near the city of Luxembourg (a beautiful city and country, situated between Germany, France, and Belgium, that this author has visited many times). The city has attracted many foreign company headquarters seeking to be in the middle of Europe but to gain deep discounts on corporate taxes. In February 2015, *Fortune* carried an article indicating that the reporter had discovered a number of post-office boxes with names of foreign corporations on them, but that was the extent of the companies' presence there.[25]

Luxembourg City, Luxembourg

STRATEGIC FORMULATION PROCESS

Typically, the strategic formulation process is necessary both at the headquarters of the corporation and at each of the subsidiaries. Most organizations operate on planning cycles of five or more years, with intermediate reviews. However, adjustments are frequently necessary to respond to changes in a dynamic global environment, in particular in rapidly changing industries such as those driven by technological developments.

The global strategic formulation process, as part of overall corporate strategic management, parallels the process followed in domestic companies. However, the variables, and therefore the process itself, are far more complex because of the greater difficulty in gaining accurate and timely information; the diversity of geographic locations; and the differences in political, legal, cultural, market, and financial processes. These factors introduce a greater level of risk in strategic decisions. However, for firms that have not yet engaged in international operations (as well as for those that do), an ongoing strategic planning process with a global orientation identifies potential opportunities for (1) appropriate market expansion, (2) increased profitability, and (3) new ventures by which the firm can exploit its strategic advantages. Even in the absence of immediate opportunities, monitoring the global environment for trends and competition is important for domestic planning.

The strategic formulation process is part of the strategic management process in which most firms engage, either formally or informally. The planning modes range from a proactive, long-range format to a reactive, more seat-of-the-pants method, whereby the day-by-day decisions of key

EXHIBIT 6-1 The Strategic Management Process

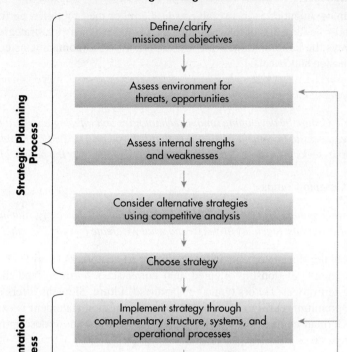

managers, in particular owner-managers, accumulate to what can be discerned retroactively as the new strategic direction.[26] The stages in the strategic management process are shown in Exhibit 6-1. In reality, these stages seldom follow such a linear format. Rather, the process is continuous and intertwined, with data and results from earlier stages providing information for the next stage.

The first phase of the strategic management process—the *planning phase*—starts with the company establishing (or clarifying) its mission and its overall objectives. The next two steps comprise an assessment of the external environment that the firm faces in the future and an analysis of the firm's relative capabilities to deal successfully with that environment. Strategic alternatives are then considered, and plans are made based on the strategic choice. These five steps constitute the planning phase, which will be further explained in this chapter.

The second part of the strategic management process is the *implementation phase*. Successful implementation requires the establishment of the structure, systems, and processes suitable to make the strategy work. These variables, as well as functional-level strategies, are explored in detail in the remaining chapters on strategic implementation, organizing, leading, and staffing. At this point, however, it is important to note that the strategic planning process by itself does not change the posture of the firm until the plans are implemented. In addition, feedback from the interim and long-term results of such implementation, along with continuous environmental monitoring, flows directly back into the planning process.

STEPS IN DEVELOPING INTERNATIONAL AND GLOBAL STRATEGIES

In the planning phase of strategic management—strategic formulation—managers need to evaluate dynamic factors carefully, as described in the stages that follow. However, as discussed earlier, managers seldom consecutively move through these phases; rather, changing events and variables prompt them to combine and reconsider their evaluations on an ongoing basis.

Step 1. Establish Mission and Objectives

The *mission* of an organization is its overall *raison d'être*, or the function it performs in society. This mission charts the direction of the company and provides a basis for strategic decision making. It also conveys the cultural values that are important to the company, as contrasted in the following two mission statements:

SANYO (A Japanese Company, now part of Panasonic)

SANYO Electric Group, by developing unique technologies and offering excellent products and sincere services, seeks to become a corporation that is loved and trusted by people around the world. The Group seeks to become "as indispensable as the Sun" for the people of the world.[27]

SIEMENS (A German Company)

We make real what matters, by setting the benchmark in the way we electrify, automate and digitalize the world around us. Ingenuity drives us and what we create is yours. Together we deliver.[28]

Although both mission statements indicate a focus on customers, Sanyo offers them a more enjoyable life, is more relationship-oriented, and emphasizes harmony and the environment, indicating a long-term focus, factors typical of Japanese culture. Siemens offers efficiency to its customers and a premium return to its shareholders; this mission statement is explicit and decisive, typical of German communication; this compares with the more descriptive and implicit statement by Sanyo gives.[29]

A company's overall *objectives* flow from its mission, and both guide the formulation of international corporate strategy. Because we are focusing on issues of international strategy, we will assume that one of the overall objectives of the corporation is some form of international operation (or expansion). The objectives of the firm's international affiliates should also be part of the global corporate objectives. A firm's global objectives usually fall into the areas of marketing, profitability, finance, production, research and development, and sustainability, among others, as shown in Exhibit 6-2. Goals for market volume and profitability

EXHIBIT 6-2 Global Corporate Objectives

Marketing
Total company market share—worldwide, regional, national
Annual percentage sales growth
Annual percentage market share growth
Coordination of regional markets for economies of scale

Production
Relative foreign versus domestic production volume
Economies of scale through global production integration
Quality and cost control
Introduction of cost-efficient production methods

Finance
Effective financing of overseas subsidiaries or allies
Taxation—globally minimizing tax burden
Optimum capital structure
Foreign-exchange management

Profitability
Long-term profit growth
Return on investment, equity, and assets
Annual rate of profit growth

Research and Development
Develop new products with global patents
Develop proprietary production technologies
Worldwide research and development labs

are usually set higher for international than for domestic operations because of the greater risk involved. In addition, financial objectives on the global level must take into account differing tax regulations in various countries and the methods to minimize overall losses from exchange rate fluctuations.

Step 2. Assess External Environment

After clarifying the corporate mission and objectives, the first major step in weighing international strategic options is the **environmental assessment**. This assessment includes environmental scanning and continuous monitoring to keep abreast of variables around the world that are pertinent to the firm and that have the potential to shape its future by posing new opportunities (or threats). Firms must adapt to their environment to survive. The focus of strategic planning is how to adapt.

The process of gathering information and forecasting relevant trends, competitive actions, and circumstances that will affect operations in geographic areas of potential interest is called **environmental scanning**. This activity should be conducted on three levels—global, regional, and national (discussed in detail later in this chapter). Scanning should focus on the future interests of the firm and cover the major variables such as political and economic risk; major technological, legal, and physical constraints; and the global competitive arena as well as the opportunities available in different countries. Some generalized areas of risk to consider are shown in Exhibit 6-3. As an example of such risks needing to be monitored, see the following Under the Lens feature.

The firm can also choose varying levels of environmental scanning. To reduce risk in investments, many firms take on the role of the follower, meaning that they limit their own investigations. Instead, they simply watch their competitors' moves and go where they go, assuming that the competitors have done their homework. Other firms go to considerable lengths to carefully gather data and examine options in the global arena.

Ideally, the firm should conduct global environmental analysis on three levels: multinational, regional, and national. Analysis on the multinational level provides a broad assessment of significant worldwide trends—through identification, forecasting, and monitoring activities.

EXHIBIT 6-3 Levels of Risk for Strategic Entry Scanning

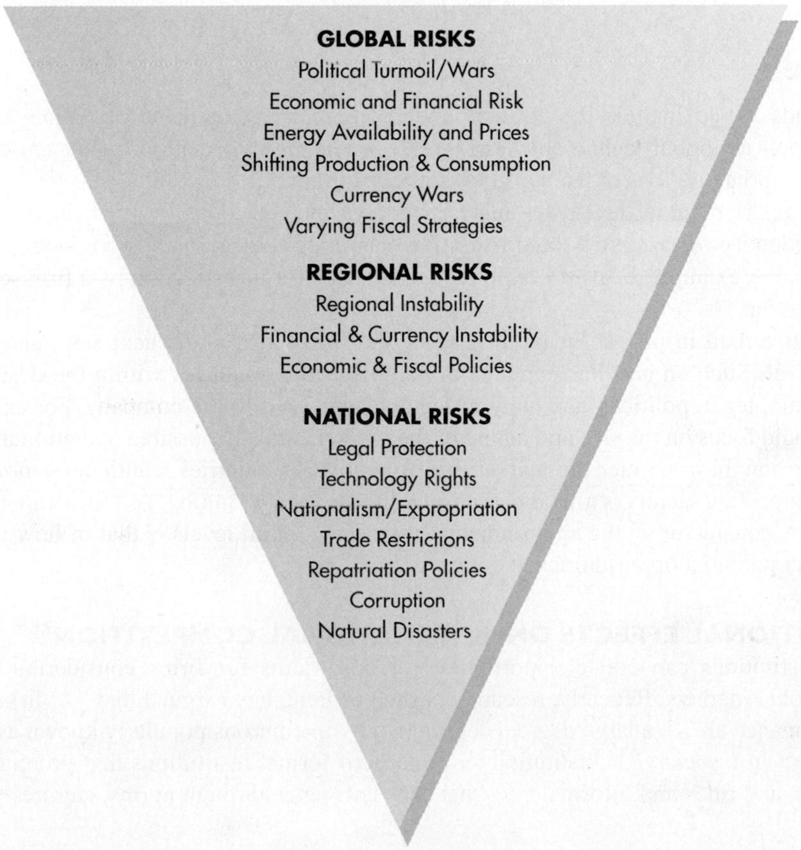

GLOBAL RISKS
Political Turmoil/Wars
Economic and Financial Risk
Energy Availability and Prices
Shifting Production & Consumption
Currency Wars
Varying Fiscal Strategies

REGIONAL RISKS
Regional Instability
Financial & Currency Instability
Economic & Fiscal Policies

NATIONAL RISKS
Legal Protection
Technology Rights
Nationalism/Expropriation
Trade Restrictions
Repatriation Policies
Corruption
Natural Disasters

UNDER THE LENS
McDonald's in Russia: A Political Pawn?[30]

The mounting tensions between Russia and the Ukraine in summer 2014 were described in the Chapter 1 opening profile. After the latest rounds of European and U.S. sanctions against Russian banks and the oil and energy industry, and the subsequent Russian embargo of imports of Western agricultural products, one Western firm in particular experienced unexpected and unusual activity. On August 20, 2014, the Russian government consumer watchdog, Rospotrebnadzor, closed down four McDonald's restaurants in Moscow and were conducting unscheduled checks on other branches throughout the country; the stated reason was that the health authority in Moscow had found unsanitary conditions. The company had previously been in the news, when Russia annexed Crimea, because management had decided to close its outlets in Crimea to protect its employees. Was this latest move to punish the company for that response? Or was it an unstated attack on an American icon, the McDonald's stores? The company was particularly hit when the closings included its outlet in Moscow's Pushkin Square, which does the most business of all its global outlets and opened to much fanfare in 1990, a symbol of improving relations with the West. McDonald's has 37,000 employees in 440 branches in Russia, out of about 35,000 globally. The company is concerned about its future growth prospects in Russia because of these indications of government interference and crackdowns on its business. On August 29, two news items were widely reported in the press, one that the EU ministers were planning a new round of sanctions, following the alleged invasion farther into Ukraine; the other was that the number of McDonald's branches closed in Russia reached 12, with more than 100 inspections of other branches under way. The company reiterated that it was studying the allegations of sanitary violations to find a way to reopen the stores.

The situation was rather curious because most of the stakeholders who would be directly affected were Russian owners and customers and, in particular, the Russian suppliers of food to the restaurants, comprising more than 80 percent of McDonald's supplies. Local sourcing began in the 1990s because it was cheaper; since then, with more than 80 percent sourced from local suppliers, many small businesses have grown to million-dollar companies, including Belaya Dacha, a vegetable supplier, and Wlmm-Bill-Dann, McDonald's dairy supplier. Given that situation, it would seem that Russian businesses also would be hurt by the closings.

Could environmental monitoring have anticipated this situation? What are the root causes?

These trends would include the political and economic developments of nations around the world as well as global technological progress. From this information, managers can choose certain appropriate regions of the world to consider further.

Next, at the regional level, the analysis focuses in more detail on critical environmental factors to identify opportunities (and risks) for marketing the company's products, services, or technology. For example, one such regional location ripe for investigation by a firm seeking new markets is Asia.

Having zeroed in on one or more regions, the firm must, as its next step, analyze at the national level. Such an analysis explores in depth specific countries within the desired region for economic, legal, political, and cultural factors significant to the company. For example, the analysis could focus on the size and nature of the market, and any possible operational problems, to consider how best to enter the market. In many volatile countries, continuous monitoring of such environmental factors is a vital part of ongoing strategic planning. Another important factor that must be considered in the environmental assessment at all levels is that of how institutions might affect potential opportunities to compete.

INSTITUTIONAL EFFECTS ON INTERNATIONAL COMPETITION[31]
Various institutions can create opportunities or constraints for firms considering entry into specific global markets. Recently, researchers such as Peng have argued that "... firm strategies and performance are, to a large degree, determined by institutions popularly known as the 'rules of the game' in a society."[32] Institutions include both formal institutions that promulgate laws, regulations, and rules and informal ones that exert influence through norms, cultures, and ethics

(discussed elsewhere in this book).[33] Specific ways in which formal institutions affect international competition are (1) the attractiveness of overseas markets, (2) entry barriers and industry attractiveness, and (3) antidumping laws.[34]

ATTRACTIVENESS OF OVERSEAS MARKETS

The extent to which countries have institutions to promote the rule of law affects the attractiveness of those economies to outside investors. Specifically, institutions provide a broad framework of liberty and democracy as well as human rights protections. In addition, institutions contribute to a stable environment for firms by creating specific laws such as those protecting property rights. Countries with more developed institutions appear more stable and attractive to foreign firms.[35]

ENTRY BARRIERS AND INDUSTRY ATTRACTIVENESS

Institutions create barriers to entry in certain industries and, hence, make those industries more attractive (profitable) for incumbent firms. For example, in the U.S. pharmaceutical industry, the U.S. Food and Drug Administration creates barriers in the form of stringent drug approval requirements. Because new entrants (with potentially cheaper drugs) are restricted, Americans pay double what Canadians and Europeans pay for the same drugs produced in the United States. Americans spend about $240 billion a year on drugs, more than Britain, Canada, France, Germany, Italy, and Japan combined. In turn, U.S. firms in this industry earn above-average profits because the institutional barriers restrict entrants and reduce rivalry.[36]

ANTIDUMPING LAWS AS AN ENTRY BARRIER

Current U.S. antidumping laws illustrate a second example of an entry barrier. They place a foreign entrant at a disadvantage if accused of dumping (defined as selling a product below the cost of producing that product with the intent to raise prices later) because of the extensive legal forms and evidence that the United States requires.[37]

Clearly, many formal institutions affect international strategy, but what explains successes of companies despite the failure or absence of these formal institutions? China is a common illustration of where domestic firms have built competitive advantages despite poorly developed formal institutions. The answer lies in the extensive use of informal institutions or networks of interpersonal connections known in Chinese as *guanxi*. These networks function as substitutes for the weaknesses of the formal institutions. Research has shown that these informal networks are common in a variety of emerging markets with different cultural traditions and are a response to transitions in many emerging markets where formal institutions are evolving.[38]

SOURCES OF ENVIRONMENTAL INFORMATION

The success of environmental scanning depends on the ability of managers to take a global perspective and ensure that their sources of information and business intelligence are global. A variety of public resources is available to provide information. In the United States alone, more than 2,000 business information services are available on computer databases tailored to specific industries and regions. Other resources include corporate clipping services and information packages. However, internal sources of information are usually preferable—especially alert field personnel who, with firsthand observations, can provide up-to-date and relevant information for the firm. Extensively using its own internal resources, Mitsubishi Trading Company employs worldwide more than 50,000 people in 50 countries, many of whom are market analysts, whose job it is to gather, analyze, and feed market information to the parent company.[39] Internal sources of information help to eliminate unreliable information from secondary sources, particularly in developing countries, where even the official data from such countries can be either misleading or tampered with for propaganda purposes, or it may be restricted.[40]

In summary, this process of environmental scanning, from the broad global level down to the local specifics of entry planning, is illustrated in Exhibit 6-4. The first broad scan of all potential world markets enables the firm to eliminate from its list those markets that are closed or insignificant or do not have reasonable entry conditions. The second scan of remaining regions, and then countries, is done in greater detail—perhaps eliminating some countries based on, for example, political instability. Remaining countries are then assessed for competitor strengths, suitability of products, and so on. This analysis leads to serious entry planning in selected countries; managers start to work on operational plans such as negotiations and legal arrangements.

EXHIBIT 6-4 Global Environmental Scanning and Strategic Decision-Making Process

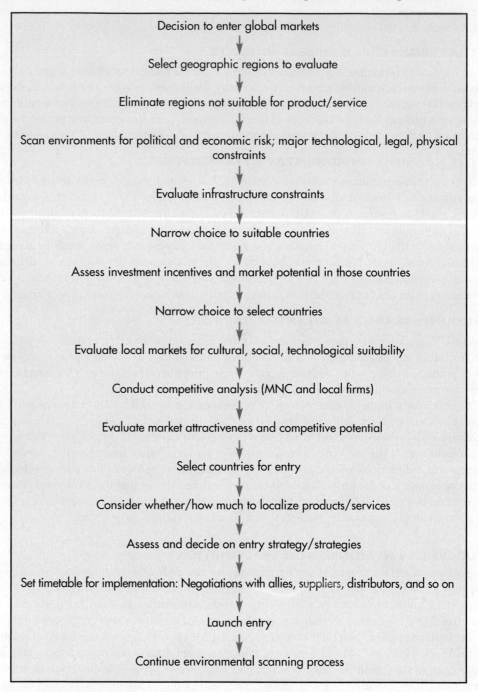

Decision to enter global markets

Select geographic regions to evaluate

Eliminate regions not suitable for product/service

Scan environments for political and economic risk; major technological, legal, physical constraints

Evaluate infrastructure constraints

Narrow choice to suitable countries

Assess investment incentives and market potential in those countries

Narrow choice to select countries

Evaluate local markets for cultural, social, technological suitability

Conduct competitive analysis (MNC and local firms)

Evaluate market attractiveness and competitive potential

Select countries for entry

Consider whether/how much to localize products/services

Assess and decide on entry strategy/strategies

Set timetable for implementation: Negotiations with allies, suppliers, distributors, and so on

Launch entry

Continue environmental scanning process

Step 3. Analyze Internal Factors

After the environmental assessment, the second major step in weighing international strategic options is the **internal analysis**. This analysis determines which areas of the firm's operations represent strengths or weaknesses (currently or potentially) compared to competitors, so that the firm may use that information to its strategic advantage.

The internal analysis focuses on the company's resources and operations and on global synergies. The strengths and weaknesses of the firm's financial and managerial expertise and functional capabilities are evaluated to determine what key success factors (KSFs) the company has and how well they can help the firm exploit foreign opportunities. Those factors increasingly involve superior technological capability (as with Apple and Huawei Technologies) as well as other strategic advantages such as effective distribution channels (Carrefour and Walmart), superior promotion capabilities (Nike and Disney), a low-cost production and sourcing position (Toyota), a superior patent and new product pipeline (Merck), and so on.

All companies have strengths and weaknesses. Management's challenge is to identify both and then take appropriate action. Many diagnostic tools are available for conducting an internal resource audit. Financial ratios, for example, may reveal an inefficient use of assets that is restricting profitability; a sales-force analysis may reveal that the sales force is an area of distinctive competence for the firm. If a company is conducting this audit to determine whether to start international ventures or to improve its ongoing operations abroad, certain operational issues must be considered. These issues include (1) the difficulty of obtaining marketing information in many countries, (2) the often poorly developed financial markets, (3) the complexities of exchange rates and government controls, (4) institutional voids in target countries, and (5) poor infrastructure, whether physical or technological.

Competitive Analysis

At this point, the firm's managers perform a *competitive analysis* to assess the firm's capabilities and key success factors compared to those of its competitors. They must judge the relative current and potential competitive position of firms in that market and location—whether that is a global position or that for a specific country or region. Managers must also specifically assess their current competitors—global and local—for the proposed market. They must ask some important questions: What are our competitors' positions, their goals and strategies, their resources, and their strengths and weaknesses, relative to those of our firm? What are the likely competitor reactions to our strategic moves? Like a chess game, the firm's managers also need to consider the strategic intent of competing firms and what might be their future moves (strategies). This process enables the strategic planners to determine where the firm has distinctive competencies that will give it strategic advantage as well as what direction might lead the firm into a sustainable competitive advantage—that is, one that will not be immediately eroded by emulation. The result of this process will also help to identify potential problems that can be corrected or that may be significant enough to eliminate further consideration of certain strategies.

This stage of strategic formulation is often called a **SWOT analysis** (strengths, weaknesses, opportunities, and threats), in which a firm's capabilities relative to those of its competitors are assessed as pertinent to the opportunities and threats in the environment for those firms. In comparing their company with potential international competitors in host markets, it is useful for managers to draw up a competitive position matrix for each potential location. For example, Exhibit 6-5 analyzes a U.S. specialty seafood firm's competitive profile in Malaysia. The U.S. firm has advantages

EXHIBIT 6-5 Global Competitor Analysis

A. U.S. Firm Compared with Its International Competitors in Malaysian Market

Comparison Criteria	A (U.S. MNC)	B (Korean MNC)	C (Local Malaysian Firm)	D (Japanese MNC)	E (Local Malaysian Firm)
Marketing capability	0	0	0	0	−
Manufacturing capability	0	+	0	0	0
R&D capability	0	0	0	−	0
HRM capability	0	0	0	0	0
Financial capability	+	−	0	0	−
Future growth of resources	+	0	−	0	−
Quickness	−	0	+	−	0
Flexibility/adaptability	0	+	+	0	0
Sustainability	+	0	0	0	−

Key:
+ = Firm is better relative to competition.
0 = Firm is same as competition.
− = Firm is poorer relative to competition.
Source: Diane J. Garsombke, "International Competitor Analysis," *Planning Review* 17, No. 3 (1989), pp. 42–47, used with permission of Emerald Insight.

in financial capability, future growth of resources, and sustainability, but a disadvantage in quickness. It also is at a disadvantage compared to the Korean MNC in important factors such as manufacturing capability and flexibility and adaptability. Because the other firms seem to have little **comparative advantage**, the major competitor is likely to be the Korean firm. At this point, then, the U.S. firm can focus in more detail on assessing the Korean firm's relative strengths and weaknesses.

Most companies develop their strategies around key strengths, or **distinctive competencies**. Distinctive—or core—competencies represent important corporate resources because, as Prahalad and Hamel explain, they are the "collective learning in the organization, especially how to coordinate diverse production skills and integrate multiple streams of technologies."[41] Core competencies are usually difficult for competitors to imitate and represent a major focus for strategic development at the corporate level.[42] Apple, for example, has used its capacity to innovate constantly and apply its technology to new products and services. Firms such as McDonald's, Disney, the Tata Group, and IKEA, which have established their business models domestically, have successfully transferred them to global markets while also adjusting to local tastes.

Managers must also assess their firm's weaknesses. A company already on shaky ground financially, for example, will not be able to consider an acquisition strategy, or perhaps any growth strategy. Of course, the subjective perceptions, motivations, capabilities, and goals of the managers involved in such diagnoses frequently cloud the decision-making process. The result is that because of poor judgment by key players, sometimes firms embark on strategies that objective information contraindicates.

STRATEGIC DECISION-MAKING MODELS

We can further explain and summarize the hierarchy of the strategic decision-making process described here by means of three leading strategic models. Their roles and interactions are conceptualized in Exhibit 6-6. At the broadest level are those global, regional, and country factors and risks previously discussed and in Chapter 1 that are part of those considerations in an **institution-based theory** of existing and potential risks and influences in the host area.[43]

EXHIBIT 6-6 A Hierarchical Model of Strategic Decision Making

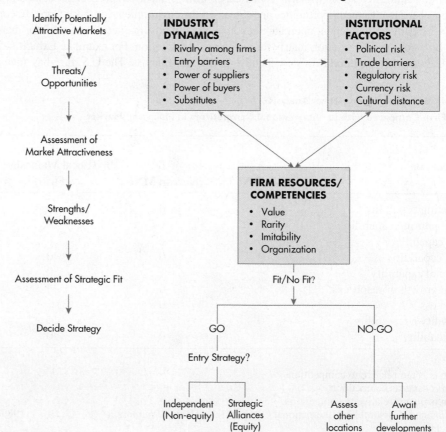

Secondly, or concurrently, the firm's potential competitive position in its industry can be reviewed by using Michael Porter's **industry-based model** of five forces that examines the dynamics within an industry, as follows:

Porter's Five Forces Industry-Based Model

- The relative level of global and local competition already in the industry; for example, in computers, social networking sites, and auto manufacturing. A high level of competition presents barriers to entry; firms may then decide on a different entry strategy or be deterred from that market altogether.

- The relative ease with which new competitors may or may not enter the field, which determines the level of threat of new entrants. In other words, if your firm is already competing in that industry, what level of protection, or barriers to new entrants, do you have? Toyota, for example, presents huge barriers to entry for new car manufacturers: worldwide scale, volume, alliance partners and suppliers, and reputation.

- How much power the buyers have within the industry; that is, what is the level of bargaining power that buyers have to influence competition? Walmart, for example, has a lot of buying power because of the volume of its business and, therefore, has a downward pressure on prices. Potential entrants would therefore have to provide some differentiation or innovation to combat that pressure on prices and thus the profitability of the firm.

- The level of bargaining power of suppliers in the industry. High bargaining power would exert pressure and vulnerability to a potential entrant as well as squeeze profits. Suppliers of raw materials or component parts could disrupt production if alternate sources are not available.

- The level of threat of substitute products or services, including the likelihood of innovations.[44] Kodak, for example, declared bankruptcy in 2012, put out of business by digital photography even though the company invented it. And, as everyone is aware, the Internet is threatening the survival of music CDs, print newspapers, movie rental stores, the U.S. Post Office, and so on.

These strategic models can provide the decision makers with a picture of the kinds of opportunities and threats that the firm would face in a particular region or country within its industry. This assumes, of course, that the locations under consideration have already been pinpointed as attractive and growing markets for the industry. However, that picture would be true for any firm within the particular industry. In other words, all firms within an industry face the same environmental and industrial factors; the difference among firms' performance is because of each firm's own resources, capabilities, and strategic decisions. The factors that determine a firm's unique niche or competitive advantage within that arena are a function of its own capabilities (strengths and weaknesses) relative to the opportunities and threats perceived for that location. This is the **resource-based** view of the firm when considering the unique value of the firm's competencies and that of its products or services.[45]

Although these models may indicate varying choices, this strategic decision-making process should enable the managers to give an overall assessment of the strategic fit between the firm and the opportunities in that location and so result in a go/no go decision for that point in time. Those managers may want to start the process again toward a different location to compare the relative levels of strategic fit. If a good strategic fit is determined and a decision is made to enter that market/location, the next step, as indicated in Exhibit 6-6, is to consider alternative entry strategies. A discussion of these entry strategies follows after we first examine the broader picture of the overall strategic approach that a firm might take toward world markets.

Step 4. Evaluate Global and International Strategic Alternatives

The strategic planning process involves considering the advantages (and disadvantages) of various strategic alternatives in light of the competitive analysis. While weighing alternatives, managers must take into account the goals of their firms and the competitive status of other firms in the industry. Depending on the size of the firm, managers must consider two levels of strategic alternatives. The first level, *global strategic alternatives* (applicable primarily to MNCs), determines what overall approach to the global marketplace a firm wishes to take. The second level, *entry strategy alternatives*, applies to firms of any size; these alternatives determine what specific entry strategy is appropriate for each country in which the firm plans to operate. Entry strategy alternatives are discussed in a later section. The two main global strategic approaches to world markets—global strategy and regional, or local, strategy—are presented in the following subsections.

Approaches to World Markets
GLOBAL STRATEGY

In the past decade, increasing competitive pressures have forced businesses to consider global strategies—to treat the world as an undifferentiated worldwide marketplace. Such strategies are now loosely referred to as **globalization**—a term that refers to the establishment of worldwide operations and the development of standardized products and marketing. Many analysts, such as Porter, have argued that globalization is a competitive imperative for firms in global industries: "In a global industry, a firm must, in some way, integrate its activities on a worldwide basis to capture the linkages among countries. This includes, but requires more than, transferring intangible assets among countries."[46] The rationale behind globalization is to compete by establishing worldwide economies of scale, offshore manufacturing where appropriate, and international cash flows. The term *globalization*, therefore, is as applicable to organizational structure as it is to strategy. (Organizational structure is discussed further in Chapter 8.)

The pressures to globalize include (1) increasing competitive clout resulting from regional trading blocs; (2) declining tariffs, which encourage trading across borders and open up new markets; and (3) the information technology explosion, which makes the coordination of far-flung operations easier and increases the commonality of consumer tastes.[47] Use of websites has allowed entrepreneurs, as well as established companies, to go global almost instantaneously through e-commerce—either B2B or B2C.[48] Examples are eBay, Yahoo!, and Lands' End. In addition, the success of Japanese companies with global strategies has set the competitive standard in many industries—most visibly in the automobile industry. Other companies, such as Caterpillar, ICI, and Sony, have fared well with global strategies. Another company bent on a global strategy is Lenovo, a Chinese computer-maker that became a global brand when it bought IBM's PC business in 2005 for $1.75 billion. Says Mr. Yang, Lenovo's chairman:

> We are proud of our Chinese roots, but we no longer want to be positioned as a Chinese company. We want to be a truly global company.[49]

As a result, Lenovo has no headquarters and its senior managers rotate meetings around the world. The company's global marketing department is in Bangalore, and its development teams comprise people in several centers around the world, often meeting virtually. Mr. Yang himself moved his family to North Carolina to immerse himself in the culture and language of global business.[50]

One of the quickest and cheapest ways to develop a global strategy is through strategic alliances. Many firms are trying to go global faster by forming alliances with rivals, suppliers, and customers. The rapidly developing information technologies are spawning cross-national business alliances from short-term virtual corporations to long-term strategic partnerships. (Strategic alliances are discussed further in Chapter 7.)

A global strategy is inherently more vulnerable to environmental risk, however, than a regionalization (or multi-local) strategy. Global organizations are difficult to manage because doing so requires the coordination of broadly divergent national cultures. It also means that firms must lose some of their original identity—they must "denationalize operations and replace home-country loyalties with a system of common corporate values and loyalties."[51] In other words, the global strategy necessarily treats all countries similarly, regardless of their differences in cultures and systems. Problems often result, such as a lack of local flexibility and responsiveness and a neglect of the need for differentiated products. Many companies, such as Google, now feel that regionalization/localization is a more manageable and less risky approach, one that allows them to capitalize on local competencies as long as the parent organization and each subsidiary retain a flexible approach to each other. Walmart is one global company that has learned the hard way that it should have acted more local in some regions of the world, including Germany and South Korea, where it has had to abandon operations.

REGIONALIZATION/LOCALIZATION

Nokia, Nestlé, Google, and Walmart have failed to adjust to the tastes of South Korean consumers.[52]

For firms in multidomestic industries—industries in which competitiveness is determined on a country-by-country basis rather than on a global basis—regional strategies are more appropriate than globalization. The **regionalization strategy [multidomestic (or multi-local) strategy]** is one in which local markets are linked within a region, allowing more local responsiveness and specialization. Top managers within each region decide on their own investment locations, product mixes, and competitive positioning; in other words, they run their subsidiaries as quasi-independent organizations.

Although there are pressures to globalize—such as the need for economies of scale to compete on cost—there are opposing pressures to regionalize, especially for newly developed economies (NDEs) and developing, or emerging, economies. These localization pressures include unique consumer preferences resulting from cultural or national differences (perhaps something as simple as right-hand-drive cars for Japan), domestic subsidies, and new production technologies that facilitate product variation for less cost than before.[53] By acting local, firms can focus individually in each country or region on the local market needs for product or service characteristics, distribution, customer support, and so on. The British retailer Tesco has enjoyed considerable success with its localizing strategy; in South Korea, for example, Samsung Tesco, which is 89 percent owned by Tesco Ltd., owes much of its acceptance to hiring local managers from Samsung. Their success compares well with those from other well-known companies that did not localize to the South Korean market, including Walmart and Google.[54]

Ghemawat argues that strategy cannot be decided either on a country-by-country basis or on a one-size-fits-all-countries basis but, rather, that both the differences and the similarities between countries must be taken into account. He bases his perspectives on the cultural, administrative, geographic, and economic (CAGE) distances between countries, for example:

Cultural distance: Differences in values, languages, religion, trust.

Administrative distance: Lack of common trading bloc or currency, political hostility, nonmarket or closed economy.

Geographical distance: Remoteness, different time zones, weak transportation or communication links.

Economic distance: Differences in level of development, natural or human resources, infrastructure, information or knowledge.

He concludes:

A semiglobalized perspective helps companies resist a variety of delusions derived from visions of the globalization apocalypse: growth fever, the norm of enormity, statelessness, ubiquity, and one-size-fits-all.

Semi-globalization is what offers room for cross-border strategy to have content distinct from single-country strategy.[55]

As with any management function, the strategic choice of where a company should position itself along the globalization/regionalization continuum is contingent on the nature of the industry, the type of company, the company's goals and strengths (or weaknesses), and the nature of its subsidiaries, among many factors. In addition, each company's strategic approach should be unique in adapting to its own environment. Many firms may try to go global but act local to trade off the best advantages of each strategy. Matsushita, which grew to be Japan's largest electronics firm and renamed itself Panasonic Corporation in October 2008, is one firm with considerable expertise at being a GLOCAL firm (GLObal, LoCAL). Panasonic has operations in 60 countries and employs more than 300,000 people in its 634 domain companies; those companies follow policies to develop local R&D to tailor products to markets, to let plants set their own rules, and to be a good corporate citizen in every country.[56] Google is another company that has had to step back from its ideal of being just global to instead adapting to local markets. Ghemawat explains why the company had problems with a one-size-fits-all-countries strategy by using his CAGE distance framework, as follows:

> *Cultural distance:* Google's biggest problem in Russia seems to have been associated with a relatively difficult language.

> *Administrative distance:* Google's difficulties in dealing with Chinese censorship reflect the difference between Chinese administrative and policy frameworks and those in its home country, the United States.

> *Geographic distance:* Although Google's products can be digitized, it had trouble adapting to Russia from afar and has had to set up offices there.

> *Economic distance:* The underdevelopment of the payment infrastructure in Russia has been another handicap for Google relative to local rivals.[57]

Global Integrative Strategies

Many MNCs have developed their global operations to the point of being fully integrated—often both vertically and horizontally, including suppliers, productive facilities, marketing and distribution outlets, and contractors around the world. Dell, for example, is a globally integrated company, with worldwide sourcing and a fully integrated production and marketing system. It has factories in Ireland, Brazil, China, Malaysia, Tennessee, and Texas, and it has an assembly and delivery system from 47 locations around the world. At the same time, it has extreme flexibility. Because Dell builds each computer to order, it carries very little inventory and, therefore, can change its operations at a moment's notice. Thomas Friedman described the process that his notebook computer went through when he ordered it from Dell:

> *The notebook was co-designed in Austin, Texas, and in Taiwan.... The total supply chain for my computer, including suppliers of suppliers, involved about four hundred companies in North America, Europe, and primarily Asia, but with thirty key players. (It was delivered by UPS 17 days after ordering.)*[58]

Although some companies move very quickly to the stage of global integration—often through mergers or acquisitions—many companies evolve into multinational corporations by going through the entry strategies in stages, taking varying lengths of time between stages. Typically, a company starts with simple exporting, moves to large-scale exporting with sales branches abroad (or perhaps begins licensing), then—for a manufacturing company—proceeds to assembly abroad (either by itself or through contract manufacturing), and eventually evolves to full production abroad with its own subsidiaries. Finally, the company will undertake the global integration of its foreign subsidiaries, setting up cooperative activities among them to achieve economies of scale. By this point, the MNC has usually adopted a geocentric orientation, viewing opportunities and entry strategies in the context of an interrelated global market instead of regional or national markets. In this way, alternative entry strategies are viewed on an overall portfolio basis to take maximum advantage of potential synergies and leverage arising from operations in multicountry markets.[59] Whereas Procter & Gamble, for example, took around 100 years to go fully global, many companies more recently are "**born global**"—that is, they start out with a global reach, typically by using their Internet capabilities and hiring people with international experience and contacts around the world.

> *Born globals globalize some aspects of their business—manufacturing, service delivery, capital sourcing, or talent acquisition, for instance—the moment they start up.*

> *... Standing conventional theory on its head, start-ups now do business in many countries before dominating their home markets.*[60]

Isenberg notes that successful entrepreneurs can establish multinational organizations from the outset by setting up and managing global supply chains and striking alliances from positions of weaknesses. The major challenges for born globals are those of accessing resources and the physical and cultural distances in their markets and operations.[61]

Using E-Business for Global Expansion

Companies of all sizes are increasingly looking to the Internet as a means of expanding their global operations. Clearly, the Internet is available to anyone and levels the playing field for small businesses.

"Just think," said Ms. Sinha, "my little six-person operation is now a global business."

WWW.NYTIMES
SEPTEMBER 10, 2011[62]

Ms. Sinha, a Silicon Valley entrepreneur, has six employees in her software company—two in the United States and four in New Delhi. There are many micro-multinationals such as hers and, just as with large companies, they run their businesses using email, web pages, voice-over-Internet phone services, and other Internet technology to coordinate their far-flung operations.

The globalization of the web is evident, as shown in Table 6–1, which compares the statistics between 2014 and 2012. Out of a total number of Internet users as of 2014, Asia already had 45.7 percent of world usage, up slightly from 2012. The penetration rate of users for Asia, for example, of 34.7 percent, is a considerable increase in people using the Internet. Nevertheless, of particular note is that Africa's penetration rate has doubled, although still low, which indicates a far greater growth capacity than in Europe and North America. In China alone, there are more than 513 million Internet users, including more than 150 million online shoppers. However, there, as in other countries, the logistics of providing customer service is often a barrier to efficient e-commerce. The growth of express delivery over a broad geographic base has lagged behind the growth of the e-commerce market there.[63] Three strategies are recommended to deal with the logistics problems in China and elsewhere.

- Build your own internal logistics network.
- Outsource delivery services to third-party providers.
- Form partnerships with or acquire existing logistics companies.[64]

Many developing nations, in particular, are realizing the opportunities for e-commerce and improving their infrastructure to take advantage of those opportunities. Governments and businesses are experiencing pressure to go online, especially those companies that export goods to countries where a significant amount of business is conducted through the Internet, such as the United States. For example, Everest S.A., a family-run business in San Salvador, sold a 69-kilogram lot (152 pounds) of coffee beans from one of its five farms in an Internet auction for a record price of $14.06 a pound.[65]

As a result, American technology giants and e-retailers such as Amazon are devoting great amounts of money and time to build and develop foreign-language websites and services. "Gone are the days in which you can launch a website in English and assume that readers from around the globe are going to look to you simply because of the content you're providing."[66]

There are many benefits of e-business, including rapid entrance into new geographic markets and lower operational costs, as indicated by respondents to the IDC Internet Executive Advisory

TABLE 6–1 Change in World Internet Usage as of Q2 2014

Regions	Usage % of World		Penetration Rates (%)	
	2012	**2014**	**2012**	**2014**
Africa	6.2	9.8	13.5	26.5
Asia	44.8	45.7	26.2	34.7
Europe	22.1	19.2	61.3	70.5
Middle East	3.4	3.7	35.6	48.3
North America	12.0	10.2	78.6	87.7
Latin America/Caribbean	10.4	10.5	39.5	52.3
Oceana/Australia	1.1	0.9	67.5	72.9

Source: Based on selected data from www.internetworldstats.com, accessed March 18, 2015.

EXHIBIT 6-7 Benefits of B2B

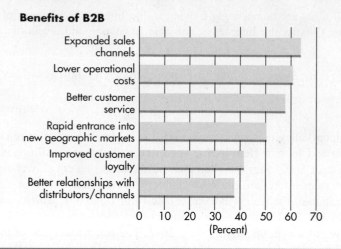

Benefits of B2B

Source: Data from IDC Internet executive Advisory Council Surveys, 2001

Council surveys (see Exhibit 6-7). Less touted, however, are the many challenges inherent in a global B2B or B2C strategy. These include cultural differences and varying business models as well as governmental wrangling and border conflicts—in particular the question over which country has jurisdiction and responsibility over disputes regarding cross-border electronic transactions.[67] Potential problem areas that managers must assess in their global environmental analysis include conflicting consumer protection, intellectual property, and tax laws; increasing isolationism, even among democracies; language barriers; and a lack of tech-savvy legislators worldwide.[68]

Savvy global managers will realize that e-business cannot be regarded as just an extension of current businesses. It is a whole new industry in itself, complete with a different pool of competitors and entirely new sets of environmental issues. A reassessment of the environmental forces in the newly configured industry, using Michael Porter's five forces analytical model, should take account of shifts in the relative bargaining power of buyers and suppliers, the level of threat of new competitors, existing and potential substitutes, and a present and anticipated competitor analysis.[69] The level of e-competition will be determined by how transparent and imitable the company's business model is for its product or service as observed on its website. In addition, competitors may also be other brick-and-mortar stores as well as their own—such as for Staples or JCPenney.

There is no doubt that the global e-business competitive arena is a challenging one, both strategically and technologically, but many companies around the world are plunging in, fearing that they will be left behind in this fast-developing global e-marketplace.

For companies such as eBay, e-business is their business—services are provided over the Internet for end users and for businesses. With a unique business model, eBay embarked on a global e-strategy. The company has positioned itself to be global and giant: part international swap meet, and part clearinghouse for the world's manufacturers and retailers.

E-GLOBAL OR E-LOCAL?

Alibaba has more than 8 million small and midsize companies using its business-to-business online marketplace.... The company has launched local versions of its B2B service in Japan, South Korea, and India.[70]

Although the Internet is a global medium, a company still faces the same set of decisions regarding how much its products or services can be globalized or how much they must be localized to national or regional markets. Local cultural expectations, differences in privacy laws, government regulations, taxes, and payment infrastructure are just a few of the complexities encountered in trying to globalize e-commerce. Further complications arise because the local physical infrastructure must support e-businesses that require the transportation of actual goods for distribution to other businesses in the supply chain or to end users. In those instances, adding e-commerce to an existing old-economy business in those international markets is likely to be more successful than starting an e-business from scratch without the supply and distribution channels already in place. However, many technology consulting firms, such as NextLinx, provide software solutions and tools to penetrate global markets, extend their supply chains, and enable new buyer and seller relationships around the globe.

Going global with e-business, as Yahoo! has done, necessitates a coordinated effort in a number of regions around the world at the same time to gain a foothold and grab new markets before competitors do. Certain conditions dictate the advisability of going e-global:

> The global beachhead strategy makes sense when trade is global in scope; when the business does not involve delivering orders; and when the business model can be hijacked relatively easily by local competitors.[71]

This strategy would work well for global B2B markets in steel, plastics, and electronic components.

The e-local, or regional strategic, approach is suited to consumer retailing and financial services, for example. Amazon and eBay have started their regional approach in Western Europe. Again, certain conditions would make this strategy more advisable.

> [The e-local/regional approach] is preferable under three conditions: when production and consumption are regional rather than global in scope; when customer behavior and market structures differ across regions but are relatively similar within a region; and when supply-chain management is very important to success.[72]

The selection of which region or regions to target depends on the same factors of local market dynamics and industry variables as previously discussed in this chapter. However, for e-businesses, additional variables must also be considered, such as the rate of Internet penetration and the level of development of the local telecommunications infrastructure.

One company that learned the hard way how to localize its e-business is Handango, Inc., of Hurst, Texas—a maker of smartphone and wireless-network software. As Clint Patterson, the company's vice president of marketing, said while reflecting on its move into Asian markets several years ago, "We didn't understand what purchasing methods would be popular or even what kinds of content. We didn't have a local taste. We realized we needed someone on the street to hold our hand."[73] For example, Handango found it needed a local bank account to do business in Japan because Japanese consumers use a method called *konbini* to make online payments. This means that when they place their order online, instead of paying with a credit card, they go to a local convenience store and pay cash to a clerk, who then transfers the payment to the online vendor's account. To adapt to this system, Handango formed an alliance with @irBitway, a local consumer-electronics web portal, which now acts as Handango's agent in the konbini system and has taken over Handango's local marketing and translation.[74] Handango ran into a similar problem in Germany when it discovered that Germans do not like debt and prefer to pay for their online purchases with wire transfers from their bank accounts. To get around this, the company found a local partner to interface with local banks and then adapted its website to the new payment method.[75]

Step 5. Evaluate Entry Strategy Alternatives

For a multinational corporation (or a company considering entry into the international arena), a more specific set of strategic alternatives, often varying by targeted country, focuses on different ways to enter a foreign market. Managers need to consider how potential new markets may be served best by their company in light of the risks and the critical environmental factors associated with their entry strategies. The following sections examine the various entry and ownership strategies available to firms, including exporting, licensing, franchising, contract manufacturing, offshoring, service-sector outsourcing, turnkey operations, management contracts, joint ventures, fully owned subsidiaries set up by the firm, and e-business. These alternatives are not mutually exclusive; several may be employed at the same time. They are addressed in order of ascending risk (typically), although e-business is usually low-risk.

EXPORTING

Exporting is a relatively low-risk way to begin international expansion or to test out an overseas market. Little investment is involved, and fast withdrawal is relatively easy. Small firms seldom go beyond this stage, and large firms use this avenue for many of their products. Because of their comparative lack of capital resources and marketing clout, exporting is the primary entry strategy small businesses use to compete on an international level. Many firms from emerging or developing markets use exporting extensively to compete overseas in a narrow product category; an example is the Hong Kong–based Johnson Electric (Johnson), which exports most of the 3 million tiny electric motors it produces per day.

An experienced firm may want to handle its exporting functions by appointing a manager or establishing an export department. Alternatively, an export management company (EMC) may be retained to take over some or all exporting functions, including dealing with host-country regulations, tariffs, duties, documentation, letters of credit, currency conversion, and so forth. Frequently, it pays to hire a specialist for a given host country.

Certain decisions need special care when managers are setting up an exporting system, particularly the choice of distributor. Many countries have regulations that make it very hard to remove a distributor who proves inefficient. Other critical environmental factors include export–import tariffs and quotas, freight costs, and distance from supplier countries.

LICENSING

An international licensing agreement grants the rights to a firm in the host country to either produce or sell a product or both. This agreement involves the transfer of rights to patents, trademarks, or technology for a specified period in return for a fee the licensee pays. Many food-manufacturing MNCs license their products overseas, often under the names of local firms, and products like those of Nike and Disney appear around the world under various licensing agreements. Like exporting, licensing is also a relatively low-risk strategy because it requires little investment, and it can be a useful option in countries where market entry by other means is constrained by regulations or profit-repatriation restrictions.

Licensing is especially suitable for the mature phase of a product's life cycle when competition is intense, margins decline, and production is relatively standardized. It is also useful for firms with rapidly changing technologies, for those with many diverse product lines, and for small firms with few financial and managerial resources for direct investment abroad. A clear advantage of licensing is that it avoids the tariffs and quotas usually imposed on exports. The most common disadvantage is the licensor's lack of control over the licensee's activities and performance.

Critical environmental factors to consider in licensing are whether sufficient patent and trademark protection is available in the host country, the track record and quality of the licensee, the risk that the licensee may develop its competence to become a direct competitor, the licensee's market territory, and legal limits on the royalty rate structure in the host country.

FRANCHISING

Similar to licensing, **franchising** involves relatively little risk. The franchisor licenses its trademark, products and services, and operating principles to the franchisee for an initial fee and ongoing royalties. Franchises are well known in the domestic fast-food industry; Pizza Hut, for example, operates primarily on this basis. For a large up-front fee and considerable royalty payments, the franchisee gets the benefit of the firm's reputation, existing clientele, marketing clout, and management expertise. Pizza Hut is well recognized internationally, as are many other fast-food and hotel franchises, such as Hampton Hotels, along with, for example, MyGym of Mexico, and other services such as Supercuts and H&R Block. A critical consideration for the franchisor's management is quality control, which becomes more difficult with greater geographic dispersion.

Franchising can be an ideal strategy for small businesses because outlets require little investment in capital or human resources. Through franchising, an entrepreneur can use the resources of franchisees to expand; most of today's large franchises started out with this strategy. An entrepreneur can also use franchisees to enter a new business. Higher costs in entry fees and royalties are offset by the lower risk of an established product, trademark, and customer base as well as the benefit of the franchisor's experience and techniques.

Franchising in some countries can be complicated. In China, for example, franchising is a rather new concept. Almost all firms that franchise in China "either manage the operations themselves with Chinese partners (typically establishing a different partner in each major city or region), or sell to a master franchisee, which then leases out and oversees several franchise areas within a territory."[76] There are considerable problems, including finding suitable franchisees and collecting royalty payments.

CONTRACT MANUFACTURING

A common means of outsourcing cheaper labor overseas is contract manufacturing (also commonly called outsourcing), which involves contracting for the production of finished goods or component parts. These goods or components are then imported to the home country, or to other countries, for assembly or sale. Alternatively, they may be sold in the host country. If managers can ensure the reliability and quality of the local contractor and work out adequate means of capital repatriation, this strategy can be a desirable means of quick entry into a country with a low capital investment and none of the problems of local ownership. Firms such as Nike use contract manufacturing around the world. However, in 2011, the Boston Consulting Group warned about assuming that this strategy would continue to deliver big cost reductions by itself and that it should be considered just one part of a global sourcing strategy.[77]

OFFSHORING

Offshoring is when a company moves one or all of its factories from the home country to another country, as is the case with some of Nissan's factories in the United States. In fact, more than 40 percent of cars built in the United States are made by Japanese and other foreign companies.[78] Offshoring provides the company with access to foreign markets while avoiding trade barriers as well as, frequently, achieving an overall lower cost of production. According to the U.S. Commerce Department, approximately 90 percent of the output from U.S.-owned offshore factories is sold to foreign consumers.[79]

However, some companies attribute their global success to their local connections for part or all of their manufacturing. An example is the BAG shoe company in Italy. Just over half the upper shoe parts are made in low-cost countries such as Serbia and Tunisia. The rest of the uppers and the soles are made locally. Having such a large part of its shoes made by local suppliers enables BAG's CEO, Mr. Bracalente, to emphasize the "Made in Italy" label as a big marketing advantage. Moreover, having suppliers close by means production problems are quickly solved. "Our technicians can go and visit the suppliers, often in just half an hour," says Mr. Bracalente. He feels that splitting the assembly functions between BAG and many outside companies is a strength, not a weakness.[80] He argues that this mix of production locations gives the company a vital source of flexibility and the capacity to make rapid changes in shoe style.[81]

One means of gaining increased efficiencies and therefore lower costs is through **clustering**, used when contract manufacturing, offshoring, or service-sector outsourcing (explained below). Sirkin et al. note that many companies from emerging market economies—companies that they call challengers—have gained rapid success by clustering:

> *Challengers are particularly expert at keeping their costs low by clustering—operating in concentrations of related, interdependent companies within an industry that use the same suppliers, specialized labor, and distribution channels.*[82]

Examples of industry clusters are an appliance cluster in Monterey, Mexico, serving the North American market and firms both global and local, and including around two hundred local suppliers; the many manufacturing clusters in China; and service center clusters in India, as discussed elsewhere in this chapter.

RESHORING/NEARSHORING

More recently, a number of companies in developed economies have begun reconsidering some or all of their outsourcing strategies and started to relocate some productive facilities to newly preferred locations, or to home—a process called **reshoring**—or at least closer to home and to major markets, called **nearshoring**. Reasons for this include the increasing costs of labor as emerging countries enter a new phase of development and rising consumer classes, currency fluctuations, the costs of transportation and length of time to market, the risks of long supply chains with multiple stages and parties involved and the difficulty to retain complete control over the production and supply chains from a long distance, the pressure to consider the social responsibility and sustainability in distant and low-economic venues, and the pressure to bring jobs back home. Add to these the scarcity of skilled labor, the risks of natural disasters and terrorism, and moves by local governments to protect their own interests, and the result seems to have turned the tables somewhat on the advantages of distant outsourcing. In their research of 319 companies in various industries, Tate et al. found that 40 percent of those companies had evinced a trend toward reshoring.[83]

Mexico has provided favorable nearshoring opportunities for some U.S. companies because of its proximity and industrial clusters, as discussed in the following Under the Lens feature.

UNDER THE LENS

Modern Mexico: Reshoring—Location and Young Workforce Prove Attractive

Jude Webber, FT.com, March 4, 2015

The country is attracting companies from the US but needs better infrastructure, writes Jude Webber.

Axiom, a New York-based fishing rod manufacturer, used to have its products made under contract in China. Low costs were attractive; less so was having to wait for a container to be filled with 15,000 fishing rods, then a month or more for them to be shipped to the US, and then a further three or four weeks in a truck en route to its facility.

The company, which had begun to consider moving out of China because of concerns over quality and its contractor's transparency, looked around, considering Vietnam and Thailand as potential Asian manufacturing locations. Eventually, the company decided to stop contracting out and to set up shop in Mexico.

Logistics won out. It was "just too cumbersome" for Axiom to keep its manufacturing base so far away, says Bob Penicka, president of Axiom Industries. Slightly higher Mexican costs were offset by faster transport.

After suffering an exodus of manufacturing companies to China from 2000-2010, Mexico's star has been rising again as a destination for US companies "reshoring" into the Americas, as Chinese labour costs have increased.

However, as Axiom discovered, wages are only part of the picture. "Being able to service the US faster and cheaper is one heck of an advantage," says Hal Sirkin, senior partner and manufacturing expert at the Boston Consulting Group in Chicago.

In some industries, such as car production, aerospace and manufacturing, Mr Sirkin estimates that China's wages overtook Mexico's in 2012-13. Mexico is now Latin America's top car producer and the country makes an attractive base from which manufacturers can serve the US as well as Latin America.

"A lot of what is going on in terms of expansion in Mexico has nothing to do with cost, it has to do with regionalism," says Doug Donahue, vice-president of business development for Entrada Group, a US-based company that helps foreign manufacturers - including Axiom - set up and run their own production in Mexico.

Mexico has a host of reshoring advantages besides location: a young and increasingly skilled workforce; the right timezone for US companies; and successful industrial clusters that have enabled the car and aerospace industries, for example, to thrive.

But Cidac, a Mexican think-tank, warned in a study last year that the country could be squandering its advantages because the government is failing to promote Mexico as a strategic relocation destination, tax rises that hit labour-intensive industries hard and infrastructure bottlenecks.

In 2011, Mexico was rated by 70 per cent of companies selling into the US market as the top place to relocate, but by 2014 that had shrunk to 28 per cent, says Miguel Toro, a Cidac researcher, citing data from AlixPartners, a consultancy. The US, by contrast, has overtaken Mexico: now 42 per cent of companies say they would choose the US, the survey found.

The US may be more costly, adds Mr Toro, but it can be more productive while opening operations in Mexico can be fraught with bureaucracy. He also fears that "terrible" security conditions in some border areas are a drag on what could be huge investment. By some estimates, North America could see a $120bn influx from reshoring by 2020.

Mexico faces further challenges, including building a broader base of subcontractors and bringing down energy costs, says Mr Donahue.

China, he adds, did a "fabulous job" of creating supply chains much earlier than Mexico. Although a central area of Mexico has taken off for manufacturers, its supply chains remain less developed and there are gaps to fill.

For example, makers of electrical wiring harnesses - used in the manufacture of tractors, cars, fridges and other appliances - need to source connectors and parts that are not made in Mexico because they are not labour-intensive to produce.

Energy costs in Mexico are also higher than in the US, although pipelines to bring more cheap US shale gas south of the border and Mexico's energy reform which is designed to boost domestic production, will gradually lower costs.

The country also needs to generate the type of labour that incoming industries will want, such as welders. But Mexico's demographic dividend - the average age of the population is 26 - and the fact that manufacturing is a respected industry suggest that it will be possible to find people willing and capable of acquiring the right skills.

The potential for Mexico is vast: Cidac has identified white goods, electronics and computing, plastics, metalworking, transport equipment, furniture, electronic equipment and medical equipment as attractive sectors.

"The window [for reshoring] is still open," says BCG's Mr Sirkin.

SERVICE SECTOR OUTSOURCING

According to the 2014 A. T. Kearney Global Services Location Index, the service sector outsourcing industry has grown significantly and now is in a third wave driven by automation.

> *Continual advances in technologies and communications infrastructure are allowing companies to gain access to pools of talent at locations across the globe that were previously inaccessible.*[84]

Clearly, an increasing number of firms are outsourcing white-collar jobs overseas in an attempt to reduce their overall costs. Indeed, the practice is not limited to large firms. Research by Gregorio et al. found that "Offshore outsourcing enhances international competitiveness by enabling SMEs to reduce costs, expand relational ties, serve customers more effectively, free up scarce resources, and leverage capabilities of foreign partners."[85]

Firms that outsource services usually enter overseas markets by setting up local offices, research laboratories, call centers, and so on to use the highly skilled but lower-wage **human capital**, which is available in countries such as India, the Philippines, and China, as well as the ability to offer global, round-the-clock service from different time zones.

Overall, it seems that India has benefited in information technology (IT), business-process outsourcing (BPO), and voice service jobs; as Bill Gates of Microsoft notes, "India is the absolute leader in IT services offered on the world market."[86] However, as Indians become more sophisticated at taking over high-skilled jobs outsourced from European and U.S. multinationals, they are starting to turn away call-center work, saying that it doesn't pay well any longer. In addition, companies are finding that salaries in India are increasing with the demand for jobs from MNCs and with the Indian technology companies themselves growing in global clout. Outsourcing of low-end office jobs may then migrate to other countries such as the Philippines or South Africa. In turn, both Indian and American IT service providers are opening offices in Hungary, Poland, and the Czech Republic to take advantage of the German and English-speaking workforce for European clients. Indeed, as the A. T. Kearney survey found, "[T]he geography of offshore delivery has expanded to include a large number of countries specializing in different parts of the service-production ecosystem."[87]

In a survey of the global outsourcing landscape in 50 countries and those countries' potential across three major categories—financial attractiveness, people skills and availability, and business environment—A. T. Kearney consultants identified the top countries for delivering IT, BPO, and voice services, shown in Exhibit 6-8.

The findings confirm that Asia continues to dominate, in particular in India, due to its highly educated and English-language staff availablility. Latin America as a region also does well, and Central Europe offers mature industry and highly skilled workers.[88]

Whether firms outsource (or offshore) white-collar or blue-collar jobs, they must consider the strategic aspects of that decision beyond immediate cost savings. In addition to the lack of

EXHIBIT 6-8 A.T. Kearney 2014 Global Services Location Index Ranks

Rank 2014	Change in Rank since 2011	Country
1	0	India
2	0	China
3	0	Malaysia
4	+2	Mexico
5	5	Indonesia
6	+1	Thailand
7	2	Philippines
8	+4	Brazil
9	+8	Bulgaria
10	−6	Egypt
11	+13	Poland
12	−4	Vietnam
13	−3	Chile
14	+4	United States
15	−1	Lithuania

Source: Selections from the A. T. Kearney 2014 Global Services Location Index.

consideration for factors other than production costs, sending jobs to a particular country is typically a short-term cost-reduction strategy, because at some point, competitive pressures will increase costs there, necessitating moving those jobs again to still lower-cost countries (a transition known as the race to the bottom.) In addition, as discussed previously, changing competitive, economic, and other conditions often necessitates reshoring or nearshoring.

Managers are in fact broadening their strategic view of sending skilled work abroad, now using the term *transformational outsourcing* to refer to the growth opportunities provided by making better use of skilled staff in the home office that are brought about by the gains in efficiency and productivity through leveraging global talent.[89] The risk of backlash from customers, community, and current employees necessitates careful consideration of the reasons for a company to go offshore. Managers also must consider the risk of losing control of proprietary technology and processes and must decide whether to set up the company's own subsidiary offshore (a *captive* operation) instead of contracting with outside specialists. Bank of America, for example, split its strategy by opening its own subsidiary in India but also allied with Infosys Technologies and Tata Consultancy Services for 30 percent of its IT resources to be outsourced.[90]

TURNKEY OPERATIONS

In a so-called **turnkey operation**, a company designs and constructs a facility abroad (such as a dam or chemical plant), trains local personnel, and then turns the key over to local management—for a fee, of course. Critical factors for success are the availability of local supplies and labor, reliable infrastructure, and an acceptable means of repatriating profits. There may also be a critical risk exposure if the turnkey contract is with the host government, which is often the case. This situation exposes the company to risks such as contract revocation and the rescission of bank guarantees.

MANAGEMENT CONTRACTS

A management contract gives a foreign company the rights to manage the daily operations of a business but not to make decisions regarding ownership, financing, or strategic and policy changes. Usually, management contracts are enacted in combination with other agreements, such as joint ventures. By itself, a management contract is a relatively low-risk entry strategy, but it is likely to be short term and provide limited income unless it leads to a more permanent position in the market.

INTERNATIONAL JOINT VENTURES

At a much higher level of investment and risk (though usually less risky than a wholly owned business), joint ventures present considerable opportunities unattainable through other strategies. A joint venture involves an agreement by two or more companies to produce a product or service together. In an **international joint venture (IJV)**, ownership is shared, typically by an MNC and a local partner, through agreed-upon proportions of equity. This strategy facilitates an MNC's rapid entry into new markets by means of an already established partner who has local contacts and familiarity with local operations. IJVs are a common strategy for corporate growth around the world. They also are a means to overcome trade barriers, to achieve significant economies of scale for development of a strong competitive position, to secure access to additional raw materials, to acquire managerial and technological skills, and to spread the risk associated with operating in a foreign environment.[91] Not surprisingly, larger companies are more inclined to take a high-equity stake in an IJV to engage in global industries and be less vulnerable to the risk conditions in the host country.[92] The joint venture reduces the risks of expropriation and harassment by the host country. Indeed, it may be the only means of entry into certain countries, such as Mexico and Japan, that stipulate proportions of local ownership and local participation.

In recent years, IJVs have made up about 20 percent of direct investments by MNCs in other countries, including such deals as the one between Mittal Steel of India and Arcelor of France in 2006—creating the world's biggest steel company.[93] Many companies have set up joint ventures with European companies to gain the status of an insider in the European Common Market. IJVs are quite common in India because the government encourages foreign collaborations to facilitate capital investments, import of capital goods, and transfer of technology.[94] Most of these alliances are not just tools of convenience but are important—perhaps critical—means to compete in the global arena, in particular to share in the immense costs involved and to share the risk burden. In a joint venture, the partners must work out the level of relative ownership and specific contributions. They must share management and decision making for a successful alliance. The company seeking such a venture must maintain sufficient control, however, because without adequate control, the company's managers may be unable to implement their desired strategies. Initial partner selection and the development of a mutually beneficial working agreement are, therefore, critical to the success of a joint venture. In addition, managers must ascertain that there will be enough of a fit between the partners' objectives, strategies, and resources—financial, human, and technological—to make the venture work. Unfortunately, too often the need for preparation and cooperation is given insufficient attention, resulting in many such marriages ending in divorce. About 60 percent of IJVs fail, usually because of ineffective managerial decisions regarding the type of IJV, its scope, duration, and administration as well as careless partner selection.[95] In 1998, the chief executive of Daimler-Benz, Jürgen Schrempp, said that its joint venture with Chrysler would be a "marriage made in heaven," but it ended in a messy divorce in 2007 because of cross-cultural conflicts and because the German company's luxury-car lineup had little in common with Chrysler's portfolio of vehicles.[96] IJVs, as well as the many forms of strategic global alliances, are further discussed in Chapter 7.

For companies in emerging markets or developing economies, joint ventures, mergers, and acquisition strategies provide opportunities to internationalize by gaining access to customers, supply networks, technology, local brand image and knowledge, and natural resources. The local alliances also typically provide to the new management a learning curve for manufacturing and management skills and technologies. Further discussion of joint ventures appears in Chapter 7.

FULLY OWNED SUBSIDIARIES

In countries where a **fully owned subsidiary** is permitted, an MNC wishing total control of its operations can start its own product or service business from scratch, or it may acquire an existing firm in the host country.

> *We acquire a company only if it gives us a new technology, new markets, new products,*
> *new customer bases or a new product development capability.*

PRAVEEN KADLE, TATA,
WWW.TATA.COM[97]

In September 2011, the South African company SABMiller announced it would buy Australia's Foster's—which commands 50 percent of the Australian beer market—for $10.15 billion, rounding out its global beer portfolio. South African Breweries bought Miller in 2002; since then, it has expanded into Latin America, Asia, and Africa.[98] Another deal that closed in 2011 was the purchase of Sara Lee by Grupo Bimbo, the Mexican-based bakery company, for $959 million; the deal allows Grupo Bimbo the right to sell Sara Lee baked goods everywhere except Western Europe, Australia, and New Zealand.[99]

Often the decision to acquire foreign companies will turn on opportunities presented by financial and economic situations at the time, as with companies that, for tax reasons, keep cash overseas. In 2011, for example, money sheltered from U.S. taxes resulted in cheaper acquisitions for a number of companies, including Apple, Cisco, and Pfizer, amounting to $174 billion in foreign asset purchases. Microsoft said it used $8.5 billion of offshore cash to acquire Luxembourg-based Internet–phone service Skype Technologies in May 2011. And in summer 2015 the strong dollar was presenting favorable exchange rates for overseas acquisitions as well as the opportunities to purchase cheaper supplies.

> *U.S. companies such as General Electric and Microsoft are using cash parked overseas to snap up foreign companies at more than double last year's pace. Through the first seven months of 2011, there have been about $174 billion in deals in which U.S. companies bought foreign assets.*[100]
>
> BLOOMBERG-BUSINESSWEEK
> *AUGUST 15–28, 2011*

The Tata Group, an Indian conglomerate for cars, steel, software, and tea, continues to make acquisitions around the world, including Corus, a European steel company, and Ford's Jaguar and Land Rover.[101] Such acquisitions by MNCs allow rapid entry into a market with established products and distribution networks and provide a level of acceptability not likely to be given to a foreign firm. These advantages somewhat offset the greater level of risk stemming from larger capital investments, compared with other entry strategies. At the highest level of risk is the strategy of starting a business from scratch in the host country—that is, establishing a new wholly owned foreign manufacturing or service company or subsidiary with products aimed at the local market or targeted for export. This strategy exposes the company to the full range of risk to the extent of its investment in the host country. As evidenced by events in the Middle East, political instability can be devastating to a wholly owned foreign subsidiary. Add to this risk a number of other critical environmental factors—local attitudes toward foreign ownership, currency stability and repatriation, the threat of expropriation and nationalism—and you have a high-risk entry strategy that must be carefully evaluated and monitored. There are advantages to this strategy, however, such as full control over decision making and efficiency as well as the ability to integrate operations with overall company-wide strategy.

E-BUSINESS

Discussed earlier as a global strategy, e-business is an entry strategy at the local level. As such, the failure risk of entry depends greatly on the country or region, even though it is relatively low globally. Yahoo!, for example, bought the largest Arabic-language web portal in August 2009. Although fewer than 50 million of the world's 320 million Arabic-language speakers are online, then-CEO Carol Bartz said that, "[E]merging markets and new languages are a key part of the strategy. Acquisition costs are modest, and while advertising spending is too low for immediate payback, the medium-term prospects for significant growth are surer than in more mature markets."[102]

Exhibit 6-9 summarizes the advantages and critical success factors of these entry strategies that must be taken into account when selecting one or a combination of strategies, depending on the location, the environmental factors and competitive analysis, and the overall strategy with which the company approaches world markets.

EXHIBIT 6-9 International Entry Strategies: Advantages and Critical Success Factors

Strategy	Advantages	Critical Success Factors
Exporting	Low risk No long-term assets Easy market access and exit	Choice of distributor Transportation costs Tariffs and quotas
Licensing	No asset ownership risk Fast market access Avoids regulations and tariffs	Quality and trustworthiness of licensee Appropriability of intellectual property Host-country royalty limits
Franchising	Little investment or risk Fast market access Small business expansion	Quality control of franchisee and franchise operations
Contract manufacturing/Offshoring	Limited cost and risk Short-term commitment	Reliability and quality of local contractor Operational control and human rights issues
Service-sector outsourcing	Lower employment costs	Quality control
Turnkey operations	Access to high skills and markets Revenue from skills and technology where FDI restricted	Domestic client acceptance Reliable infrastructure Sufficient local supplies and labor Repatriability of profits Reliability of any government partner
Management contracts	Low-risk access to further strategies	Opportunity to gain longer-term position
Joint ventures	Insider access to markets Share costs and risk Leverage partner's skill base, technology, local contacts	Strategic fit and complementarity of partner, markets, products Ability to protect technology Competitive advantage Ability to share control Cultural adaptability of partners
Wholly owned subsidiaries	Realize all revenues and control Global economies of scale Strategic coordination Protect technology and skill base	Ability to assess and control economic, political, and currency risk Ability to get local acceptance Repatriability of profits
E-Business	Rapid entry into (or exit from) new markets (often through alliance or purchase of local websites); relatively low-risk	Differences in business models, culture, language, and laws regarding intellectual property, consumer protection, and taxes.

STRATEGIC PLANNING FOR EMERGING MARKETS

Complex situational factors face the international manager as she or he considers strategic approaches to world markets along with which entry strategies might be appropriate. Emerging markets present particular complexity and unfamiliarity for managers to evaluate. The World Economic Forum report cautions that emerging markets are not a single homogenous group: "They develop differently, have different infrastructural, socio-economic and regulatory challenges, face different environmental and geographical constraints, and, to a certain extent, afford different opportunities for business. We argue that the lack of adequate development in the areas of trade facilitation and trade logistics can curtail the growth for these markets and the world."[103] The following *Management in Action: Strategic Planning for Emerging Markets* feature discusses these challenges and how managers can address them.

MANAGEMENT IN ACTION
Strategic Planning for Emerging Markets

There continue to be many indicators of the increasing business opportunities available for companies wanting to set up operations in or export to the emerging markets, in particular in light of the slowdown in growth in many developed economies brought about by economic problems.

In planning for global opportunities for retail businesses, for example, one can consider the A. T. Kearney Global Retail Development Index, which ranks 30 emerging countries on the urgency for retailers to enter the country and shows that countries such as Brazil, Uruguay, and Chile are prime candidates for expansion, based on economic and political risk, market attractiveness, market saturation, and time pressure. Although the study highlights the countries heading the list, Hana Ben-Shabat, A. T. Kearney partner and co-leader of the study, cautions that, because it started the annual study ten years ago, it has become clear that "there is no 'one size fits all' formula for global expansion. Different countries are at different levels of development and have different risk/return profiles, which require retailers to tailor their approaches accordingly and assemble a portfolio of markets to balance short-term risk with long-term growth aspirations."[104]

In jumping on the bandwagon, firms of all sizes, in particular small businesses, must realize that investing in developing economies usually entails considerably higher levels of risk than they are familiar with—in particular the risks of political turmoil, corruption, and contract enforcement. However, avoiding emerging markets will, over time, make firms less competitive than those who invest there in some form. The question is then how to minimize the risks without losing out to the competition and losing growth opportunities. After going through the steps of the strategic decision-making process as outlined in this chapter, including those operational factors in the institutional context such as infrastructure, availability of suppliers, labor markets, and capital markets (such as the effectiveness of banking and financial institutions), CEOs must then decide whether to enter that market and, if so, decide what needs to be changed. As Harvard Business Review authors Khanna, Palepu, and Sinha recommend, "[D]ecide whether to work around the country's institutional weaknesses, create new market infrastructures, or stay away because adapting your business model would be impractical and uneconomical."[105] Dell chose to adapt its business model in China when the company realized that consumers there did not order computers over the Internet, so it had to use Chinese ordering and supply chains rather than the company's usual model of just-in-time inventory. Financial MNCs have helped to improve the financial systems in Brazil and therefore their own firm's prospects. For its part, Home Depot has declined to enter markets with poor transportation and banking infrastructures because its model and its success depend on competitive inventory systems and employee stock ownership.[106]

However, as Washburn and Hunsaker note:

Too many companies in mature markets assume that the only reason to enter emerging countries is to pursue new customers. They fail to perceive the potential for innovation in those countries or to notice that a few visionary multinationals are successfully tapping that potential for much needed products and services.

HARVARD BUSINESS REVIEW,
SEPTEMBER 2011[107]

In their research, Washburn and Hunsaker have found that forward-thinking global managers (they call them bridgers) have identified and developed innovations in emerging markets (often with the insight of the local managers) and been able to integrate those ideas and improvements into their companies' product lines. Innovations percolating from emerging market companies already indicate the potential, such as Tata's $2,500 Nano car in India.[108]

In addition, when considering opportunities for firms within emerging markets, we can see that, for example, firms such as Tata and Infosys of India, BYD and Tencent Holdings of China, and Samsung Electronics of Korea have become prominent players in a number of technology-intensive industries that have traditionally been the domain of firms from the United States, Europe, and Japan.[109]

Entry Strategies

The following section discusses the findings of a study by Deloitte of 247 executives regarding the choices companies make among entry strategies for emerging markets, conceptualized in Fig. 6-1, along with a comparison of strategic objectives and operating strategies.

FIGURE 6-1 Emerging markets

Source: Deloitte Services LP

Strategic Expansion in Emerging Markets

[A study by Deloitte] involving interviews with several executives and a survey of 247 executives from consumer and industrial product companies with presence in emerging markets revealed that companies are increasingly making emerging geographic markets a centerpiece of their global business model. Over the next three years, upwards of 88 percent of companies plan to expand their presence in emerging markets. In fact, nearly half of these organizations expect 20 percent or more of their global revenues to have their origins in emerging markets. Furthermore, a third of these companies plan to place more than 20 percent of their investments in these regions. None of these figures suggest an imminent end to offshoring as we know it, but rather a renewed interest in its pursuit.

That's not to say manufacturers would call their endeavors business-as-usual in emerging markets. Forward-thinking companies have not been content to simply increase their presence in low-cost centers. They have become more strategic in their operations by establishing core functions of their value chains in these regions. While cost savings is still a key motivator for nearly three-quarters of manufacturing companies, it's no longer the sole reason to set up shop abroad. Almost seventy percent of the manufacturers in our study consider market expansion an important factor (see Exhibit 6-10).

EXHIBIT 6-10 Top Three Strategic Objectives for Establishing Functions in Emerging Markets

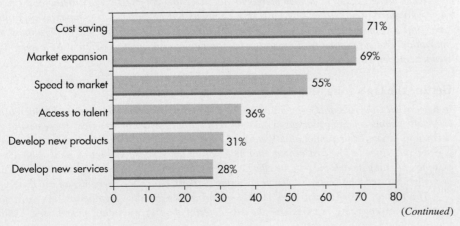

(Continued)

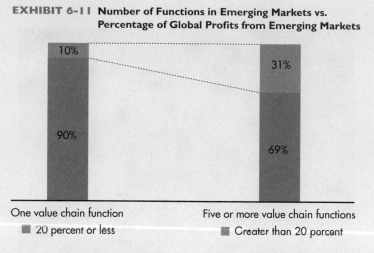

EXHIBIT 6-11 Number of Functions in Emerging Markets vs. Percentage of Global Profits from Emerging Markets

In fact, more than two-thirds of companies think it's equally important to cost savings. Similarly, 55 percent of manufacturing companies reported that they establish operations in emerging markets to improve their speed to market. Nokia has been in India since 1995, an early investment that earned it 50 percent of a mobile phone market—one that adds 8–10 million new users every month. D. Shivakumar, managing director of Nokia India, attributes this success to the company's completely localized value chain. Indian operations for everything from R&D to manufacturing, marketing, and sales give Nokia the power to launch new phones in a matter of weeks, rather than months, with designs that cater directly to the needs of its local customers.

Increasingly, organizations are broadening the scope of their pursuits in emerging economies. Nearly 40 percent of the companies in our study have established commercial operations in addition to their manufacturing endeavors that cater to global as well as local markets. After-sales service, material sourcing, and sales and marketing—relative newcomers to low-cost centers—are becoming increasingly prevalent. Forward-thinking companies are beginning to realize that future returns will depend on emulating global business models in emerging markets. Intuitively, a strong correlation exists between the number of functions a company establishes in emerging markets and the percentage of global profits that come from these regions. A third of the organizations in our study with five or more functions in emerging markets earn 20 percent or more of their global profits from these operations (see Exhibit 6-11). By comparison, the majority of manufacturers with only a single operation in these low-cost centers reported that they derive 10 percent or less of their global profits from their endeavors.

But these numbers don't paint a complete picture, either. Many manufacturers reported that they are increasing their expectations along with their investments in emerging markets. As a result, operational and financial performance goals can become as elusive as they are lofty. In fact, raw materials and manufacturing have become more expensive over the last three years for over 40 percent of the companies who cited cost savings as a key objective in their emerging market strategies. Likewise, only 13 percent of the companies that cited market expansion as their key objective have realized a significant increase in their global market share. The problem is a fundamental one: companies' endeavors in developing countries haven't kept pace with the evolving capacity and capabilities of these regions, and they're not part of a global business model. As a result, performance in these countries pales by comparison to other parts of their global business.

When companies were content merely to outsource low-complexity work to low-cost centers, strategies were narrow and straightforward. This simplicity has evaporated as companies begin to strategically shift specific functions of their value chains to account for new objectives pertaining to growth, innovation, and sustainability. From a strategy standpoint, three factors determine the emerging market business model: capacity, capability, and risk (see Exhibit 6-12).

Getting the Operating Model Right

In recent years, the rate of IJV (international joint venture) formation has continued to increase steadily, especially among emerging markets in Asia, Eastern Europe, and Latin America. These emerging markets account for about 70 percent of all IJV entries by multinational corporations. As companies deepen their business activities in low-cost centers and incorporate these endeavors into global value chains, their existing operating models may not be effective in emerging markets. According to our survey, 35 percent of companies used joint ventures to enter emerging markets, but only 21 percent still use them.

The type of business activities, market opportunities, country regulations, tax advantages, and experience in emerging markets are the key determinants of operating model (see Exhibit 6-13).

EXHIBIT 6-12 New Strategies for Emerging Markets

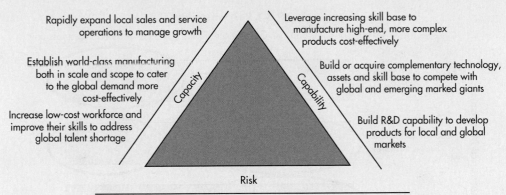

Rapidly expand local sales and service operations to manage growth

Establish world-class manufacturing both in scale and scope to cater to the global demand more cost-effectively

Increase low-cost workforce and improve their skills to address global talent shortage

Leverage increasing skill base to manufacture high-end, more complex products cost-effectively

Build or acquire complementary technology, assets and skill base to compete with global and emerging marked giants

Build R&D capability to develop products for local and global markets

Capacity

Capability

Risk

Diversify capabilities and capacity across multiple locations aligned with the strategic goals to manage cross-border business risks—exchange rate volatility, geopolitical uncertainty, demand and supply chain risk

Thirty-eight percent of manufacturing companies in our study reported that they currently use wholly owned subsidiaries in emerging markets. As they build complete product lines and develop new products, companies require a significant level of control over strategic business activities. For example, Sweden's Volvo group, the world's second largest truck manufacturer, owns a subsidiary in India that builds trucks to sell in India, Myanmar, Indonesia, Vietnam, and China. Volvo India has also established a product development center in Bangalore, India, that employs over 200 people. The wholly owned subsidiary model allows companies to take advantage of global brands and existing business processes and protects intellectual property by keeping development effectively in-house.

Similarly, companies expanding sales activities in emerging markets need access to deeper knowledge of local customers, support networks, distribution, and advertising. In many cases, companies choose joint ventures with experienced players in a local market, as noted earlier with Volvo's recently formed joint venture with Eicher Motors in India to sell heavy vehicles and leverage its network of over 200 service centers across the country.

In many cases, market opportunities also drive the choice of operating models in emerging markets. Multinational companies that struggle to stay competitive and innovative sometimes find emerging market companies with a new line of products that has potential to add significant cash flow. In such cases, the choice of operating model depends on size of investment, risk appetite, competition, and

EXHIBIT 6-13 Operating Model for Emerging Markets

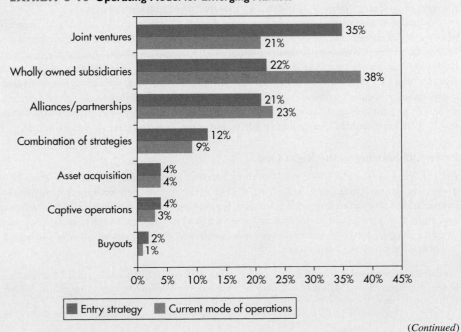

	Entry strategy	Current mode of operations
Joint ventures	35%	21%
Wholly owned subsidiaries	22%	38%
Alliances/partnerships	21%	23%
Combination of strategies	12%	9%
Asset acquisition	4%	4%
Captive operations	4%	3%
Buyouts	2%	1%

(Continued)

EXHIBIT 6-14 Disconnected Governance Model

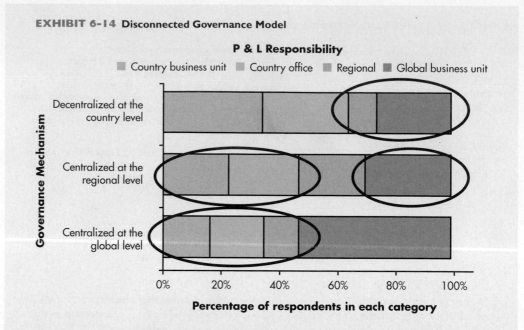

P & L Responsibility

■ Country business unit　■ Country office　■ Regional　■ Global business unit

Percentage of respondents in each category

expected return on the investment. Companies should choose between joint ventures and acquisitions only after thorough due diligence, depending on how these factors play out.

Country regulations and experience in specific countries also drive decisions about operating models. The types of operating model vary significantly by country. For example, in new and comparatively smaller emerging markets like Brazil, Czech Republic, and Mexico, more companies prefer wholly owned subsidiaries compared to China and India. Many countries have strict regulations on operating models for foreign direct investment to support protectionism and growth of domestic industries. However, as many countries are committed to becoming open market economies, these regulations are loosening. For instance, just a few years ago, China required all automotive companies to enter Chinese markets via joint venture. Over the years, as countries become economically stronger, they tend to ease such regulations on the operating model. However, to stay competitive over the long run, wholly owned subsidiaries might not be the best model for building an understanding of local markets.

Based on our study, companies with more experience in emerging markets tend to choose wholly owned subsidiaries to expand their presence. With the spotlight on emerging markets, thousands of studies have been commissioned by governments, private companies, and academia that now provide deep know-how of these markets. Based on our survey, more than half the companies that have been in the emerging markets for more than ten years choose "wholly owned subsidiary."

In addition to choosing the right operating model, alignment to the global governance model is also a critical success factor. Global governance models and P&L responsibilities are misaligned in over a third of manufacturing companies in our study (see Exhibit 6-14). For instance, almost 50 percent of the companies that have a governance model centrally managed by their global headquarters reported that they hold their local or regional businesses responsible for managing profit and loss. As a consequence, local or regional businesses do not have much flexibility to change policies that will be favorable to their region. Organizations that have misaligned governance models lose out on operational efficiencies and the chance to take advantage of emerging markets on a global scale.

From Off-Shoring to the Right One

For manufacturers, maybe the term "emerging market" is misleading. Emergence, after all, suggests a singular, upward path, but many companies are quick to call their operations a two-way street. If companies are to evolve along with host countries that are already becoming highly developed in their own right, they must take a closer look at how to adapt their operating models and global value chains and how to offset the risks and challenges associated with these locations, mindful of the fact that the competition is doing the same thing.

Source: Excerpted section from Deloitte Review, Issue 4 (January 2009) article titled "Rethinking Emerging Market Strategies: From Offshoring to Strategic Expansion," by Vikram Mahidhar, Craig Giffi, and Ajit Kambil, with Ryan Alvanos. Used with permission of the *Deloitte Review.*

Step 6. Decide on Strategy

The strategic choice of one or more of the entry strategies will depend on (1) a careful evaluation of the advantages (and disadvantages) of each in relation to the firm's capabilities and resources, (2) the critical environmental factors, and (3) the contribution that each choice would make to the overall mission and objectives of the company. Exhibit 6-9 summarized the advantages and the critical success factors for each entry strategy discussed. However, when it comes down to a choice of entry strategy or strategies for a particular company, more specific factors relating to that firm's situation must be taken into account. These include factors relating to the firm itself, the industry in which it operates, location factors, and venture-specific factors, as summarized in Exhibit 6-15.

After consideration of those factors for the firm as well as considering what is available and legal in the desired location, some entry strategies will no doubt fall out of the feasibility zone. With the options remaining, then, strategic planners need to decide which factors are more important to the firm than others. One method is to develop a weighted assessment to compare the overall impact of factors such as those in Exhibit 6-15 relative to the industry, the location, and the specific venture—on each entry strategy. Specific evaluation ratings, of course, would depend on the country conditions at a given point in time, the nature of the industry, and the local company.

Based on a study of more than 10,000 foreign entry activities into China, Pan and Tse concluded that managers tend to follow a hierarchy-of-decision sequence in choosing an entry mode. They found that the location choice—specifically the level of country risk—was the primary influence factor at the level of deciding between equity and non-equity modes. Host-country government incentives also encouraged the choice of equity mode. Managers first decide between non–equity based for high-risk locations and equity based where it is perceived there is lower risk. Then, non-equity modes are divided into contractual agreements such as franchising, licensing, outsourcing, e-business, and exporting; equity modes are split into wholly owned operations, acquisitions, offshoring, and equity joint ventures (EJVs) with varying levels of equity investment.[111]

EXHIBIT 6-15 Factors Affecting Choice of International Entry Mode[110]

Factor Category	Examples
Internal factors	Global experience of firm and managers
	Distinctive competencies, patents, technology
	Corporate culture and structure
	Global objectives
	Long-term strategy
	Financial assets
External factors	Industry globalization
	Industry growth rate
	Barriers to entry
	Level of global competition
	Opportunities and incentives
	Extent of scale and location economies
	Country risk—political, economic, legal
	Cultural distance
	Knowledge of local market
	Potential of local market
	Competition in local market
Venture-specific factors	Value of firm—assets risked in foreign location
	Ability to protect proprietary technology
	Costs of making or enforcing contracts with local partners
	Size of planned foreign venture
	Intent to conduct research and development with local partners

Source: Based on A. V. Phatak, *International Management Concepts and Cases*, 1997, Cincinnati, OH, Southwestern Publishing Company.

Gupta and Govindarajan also propose a hierarchy-of-decision factors sequence but consider two initial choice levels. The first is the extent to which the firm will export or produce locally; the second is the extent of ownership control over activities that will be performed locally in the target market.[112] There is an array of choice combinations within those two dimensions. Gupta and Govindarajan point out that, among the many factors to take into account, alliance-based entry modes are more suitable under the following conditions.

- Physical, linguistic, and cultural distance between the home and host countries is high.
- The subsidiary would have low operational integration with the rest of the multinational operations.
- The risk of asymmetric learning by the partner is low.
- The company is short of capital.
- Government regulations require local equity participation.[113]

The choice of entry strategy for McDonald's, for example, varies around the world according to the prevailing conditions in each country. As of August 2015, McDonald's had 36,000 restaurants in more than 100 countries, employing 1.9 million people worldwide.[114] In Europe, the company prefers wholly owned subsidiaries because European markets are similar to those in the United States and can be run similarly. Subsidiaries in the United States both operate company-owned stores and license out franchises. Approximately 80 percent of McDonald's stores around the world are franchised. In Asia, joint ventures are preferred to take advantage of partners' contacts and local expertise and their ability to negotiate with bureaucracies such as the Chinese government. McDonald's has more than 1,000 stores in Japan, and it continues its expansion in China in spite of conflicts with the Chinese government. In other markets, such as in Saudi Arabia, McDonald's prefers to limit its equity risk by licensing the name—adding strict quality standards—and keeping an option to buy later.

Timing Entry and Scheduling Expansions

As with McDonald's, international strategic formulation requires a long-term perspective. Entry strategies, therefore, need to be conceived as part of a well-designed, overall plan. In the past, many companies have decided on a particular means of entry that seemed appropriate at the time, only to find later that it was shortsighted. For instance, if a company initially chooses to license a host-country company to produce a product, then later decides that the market is large enough to warrant its own production facility, this new strategy will no longer be feasible because the local host-country company already owns the rights.

The Influence of Culture on Strategic Choices

Certain cultures are considered attractive to other cultures. A foreign culture's perceived attributes may be a major reason for the preferences expressed by potential partners and host countries.[115]

JOURNAL OF INTERNATIONAL BUSINESS
JANUARY 2012

It is clear that cultural distance (CD), or at least the perception of it, affects strategic choice. Potential partners and their host counterparts tend to feel more confident about their international allies when they seem culturally attractive, in particular when new to international business. The more similar the culture, the more likely managers are to select that region for investment—for example, between the United States and England. However, often that assumption of similarity leads to problems because preparation and allowance is not made for existing subtle differences. Shenkar gives the examples that the friction between dissimilar cultures is more likely in a merger or acquisition than in an IJV—because there is more interaction among parties in the former—whereas an IJV is set up as a separate entity with less interaction from the parent firms.[116] Managers armed with such insight might then choose an IJV over other strategic options that necessitate more cross-cultural interaction.

In addition, strategic choices at various levels often are influenced by specific cultural factors, such as a long-term versus a short-term perspective. Hofstede found that most people in such countries as China and Japan generally had a longer-term horizon than those in Canada and the United States.[117] Whereas Americans, then, might make strategic choices with a heavy emphasis on short-term profits, the Japanese are known to be more patient in sacrificing short-term results to build for the future with investment, research and development, and market share.

Risk orientation was also found to explain the choice between equity and nonequity modes.[118] Risk orientation relates to Hofstede's uncertainty avoidance dimension.[119] Firms from countries where, generally speaking, people tend to avoid uncertainty (for example, Latin American and African countries) tend to prefer nonequity entry modes to minimize exposure to risk. Managers from firms from low–uncertainty avoidance countries are more willing to take risks and are, therefore, more likely to adopt equity entry modes.[120]

The choice of the equity versus nonequity mode has also been found to be related to level of power distance. According to Hofstede, a high power-distance country (such as Arab countries and Japan) is one where people observe interpersonal inequality and hierarchy.[121] Pan and Tse found that firms from countries tending toward high power distance are more likely to use equity modes of entry abroad.[122]

These are but a few of the examples of the relationships between culture and the choices that are made in the strategic planning and implementation phase. They serve to remind us that it is people who make those decisions and that the ways people think, feel, and act are based on their ingrained societal culture. People bring that context to work, and it influences their propensity toward or against certain types of decisions.

CONCLUSION

The process of strategic formulation for global competitiveness is a daunting task in the volatile global arena and is further complicated by the difficulties involved in acquiring timely and credible information. However, early insight into global developments provides a critical advantage in positioning a firm for future success.

When an entry strategy is selected, the international manager focuses on translating strategic plans into actual operations. Often this involves strategic alliances; always it involves functional-level activities for strategic implementation. These subjects are covered in Chapter 7.

Summary of Key Points

- Companies go international for many reasons, both proactive and reactive. Companies that are proactive from their outset in establishing a presence in many countries are referred to as born globals. The Internet is facilitating companies of all sizes to expand around the world within a short time frame—thus leveling the field for small businesses relative to companies with greater resources.

- International expansion and the resulting realization of a firm's strategy are the products of both rational planning and responding to emergent opportunities. For example, those opportunities may develop because of economic, competitive, demographic, or political changes in other countries. Firms are increasingly taking advantage of opportunities for expansion into emerging markets such as the BRICs.

- The steps in the rational planning process for developing an international corporate strategy comprise defining the mission and objectives of the firm, scanning the environment for threats and opportunities, assessing

the internal strengths and weaknesses of the firm, considering alternative international entry strategies, and deciding on strategy. The strategic management process is completed by putting into place the operational plans necessary to implement the strategy and then setting up control and evaluation procedures.

- Competitive analysis is an assessment of how a firm's strengths and weaknesses vis-à-vis those of its competitors affect the opportunities and threats in the international environment. Such assessment allows the firm to determine where the company has distinctive competencies that will give it strategic advantage or where problem areas exist.

- Corporate-level strategic approaches to international competitiveness include globalization and regionalization. Many MNCs have developed to the point of using an integrative global strategy. Entry and ownership strategies are exporting, licensing, franchising, contract manufacturing, offshoring and reshoring, outsourcing services, turnkey operations, management contracts, joint ventures, and fully owned subsidiaries as well as the local level of e-business. Critical environmental and operational factors for implementation must be taken into account.

■ Companies of all sizes are increasingly looking to the Internet as a means of expanding their global operations, but localizing Internet operations is complex, involving various logistical and cultural challenges.

Discussion Questions

6-1. Discuss why companies go international, giving specific reactive and proactive reasons.

6-2. What effects on company strategy have you observed because of the global economic downturn?

6-3. Give examples of the impact of the Internet on small businesses.

6-4. Discuss the ways in which managers arrive at new strategic directions—formal and informal. Which is the best?

6-5. Explain the process of environmental assessment. What are the major international variables to consider in the scanning process? Discuss the levels of environmental monitoring that should be conducted. How well do you think managers conduct environmental assessment?

6-6. Discuss the impact of the rise of emerging-market countries on the strategic planning of firms around the world.

6-7. How can managers assess the potential relative competitive position of their firm to decide on new strategic directions?

6-8. Discuss the relative advantages of globalization versus regionalization/localization.

6-9. Compare the merits of the entry strategies discussed in this chapter. What is their role in an integrative global strategy?

6-10. Discuss the considerations in strategic choice, including the typical stages of the company and the need for a long-term global perspective.

Application Exercises

6-11. Choose a company in the social media industry or a chain in the fast-food industry. In small groups, conduct a multilevel environmental analysis, describing the major variables involved, the relative impact of specific threats and opportunities, and the critical environmental factors to be considered. The group findings can then be presented to the class, allowing a specific time period for each group so that comparison and debate of different group perspectives can follow. Be prepared to state what regions or specific countries you are interested in and give your rationale.

6-12. In small groups, discuss among yourselves and then debate with the other groups the relative merits of the alternative

entry strategies for the company and countries you chose in Exercise 6-11. You should be able to make a specific choice and defend that decision.

6-13. For this exercise, research (individually or in small groups) a company with international operations and find out the kinds of entry strategies the firm has used. Present the information you find, in writing or verbally to the class, describing the nature of the company's international operations, its motivations, its entry strategies, the kinds of implementation problems the firm has run into, and how those problems have been dealt with.

Experiential Exercise

6-14. In groups of four, develop a strategic analysis for a type of company that is considering entry into an

emerging market country. Which entry strategies seem most appropriate? Share your results with the class.

CASE STUDY

"Foreign Businesses Tread Carefully as Cuba Opens Up," by Marc Frank in Havana, FT.com, February 1, 2015.

Overseas business will have to tread carefully as the economy starts to open up.

With a view of the sea sparkling in the distance, Ceiba Investment enjoys some of the best corporate office space in Cuba's rundown capital city.

Complete with high-speed internet, boutiques, travel agencies and banks, the Miramar Trade Center, a sprawling complex of six modern edifices in an upmarket district of Havana, is home to international construction firms, Russian oil companies, Canadian and European banks and traders.

But even in this rarefied environment, success does not come easy for foreign companies on a Caribbean island that has a long history of communist rule and is only slowly opening up its economy. Businesses say they are hampered by regulations and US sanctions related to international finance.

As American companies begin to explore new opportunities here in the wake of the historic decision by Cuba and the US to renew diplomatic relations, they can learn much from those already with a foot in the door. International behemoths such as Bougyues, Nestlé and Anheuser-Busch InBev have interests in Cuba. There are 200 operating investment projects in Cuba, ranging from joint ventures to management agreements and oil exploration, according to government statistics.

But while many have been successful, some 60 per cent of the businesses set up by foreigners since the fall of communism in eastern Europe have closed, according to government statistics. Some of them, analysts and diplomats say, were forced out by the government.

"Cuba is one of the only places where every direct investment requires the authorisation of the highest government body. It's also different since nearly everything

Cuba

Deatonphotos/Shutterstock

is owned by the state," said Sabastiaan Berger, a Dutch corporate lawyer with more than 15 years' experience in Cuba and chief executive of Ceiba, whose investments include the Miramar Trade Center and hotels.

"Can you do business here?" asks Cameron Young, a Canadian lawyer and Mr Berger's partner. "Of course. The trade centre is full. But," he added: "Your state partner is also the supplier, the employer of your staff, the buyer, the regulating authority and the entity that taxes you. So it's a complex place to enter into a normal business transaction."

Just ask Michel Villand, a Frenchman who in the 1990s invested his fortune in a joint venture pastry business, Pain de Paris, with two factories and a number of retail outlets. He says he was forced out of business in 2007 because his venture was a success and his Cuban partners decided they wanted it all.

"Founding a joint venture in Cuba if you are a small or medium-sized foreign business is the same as putting a noose around your own neck," he wrote in his memoir *My Business Partner Fidel Castro*, which details the trials and tribulations he says he suffered.

The fate of Coral Capital, Ceiba's only real competitor in the country and a partner in Havana's upmarket Saratoga Hotel, also illustrates the pitfalls that await the unwary. The company was raided and closed in 2011 as part of a drive against corrupt trading practices.

Foreign executives, dozens of Cuban staff, officials and businessmen, found themselves behind bars. Some pleaded guilty, plea bargained and co-operated, others fought the charges. After being held without charges for more than a year, Coral capital's foreign managers were convicted of minor infractions in 2013 and deported.

Stephen Purvis, a British architect and former head of development projects at Coral Capital, said a defendant caught up in the corruption dragnet had falsely denounced him as part of a plea-bargain arrangement.

Initially accused of "revealing state secrets" and "illegal activities", he was held at the infamous Villa Marista state security interrogation centre for months. He eventually wound up at the Condesa prison for foreigners, charged with "economic crimes". He never saw the specific charges against him and a lawyer was not present during his interviews.

Mr Purvis described Cuba's legal system as Kafkaesque. "The process is contrary to any western concept of fairness and they blatantly ignore all the relevant international laws."

Patience, persistence and perseverance is the advice an Asian diplomat offers those eager to invest—advice veteran hotel manager Eric Peyre agrees with. He supervises three hotels in Cuba for the French firm Accor.

"In my more than 20 years working as foreign manager in the Cuban tourism industry, I have never seen anyone lose money at the end of the year," he said.

Success is certainly possible, says trade finance banker William White, the former head of the Republic Bank's office in Cuba. But, he adds: "Be ready to put up with a lack of economic information, delays in obtaining decisions from the state, and regulation which can hamper and delay business operations."

Source: FT.com, February 1, 2015.

Case Questions

6-15. Research updates on the business environment. Pick a company you are familiar with and do a SWOT analysis for considering entering the Cuban market.

6-16. What entry strategy do you think would work best for this company?

Endnotes

1. Jitender Miglani, "Amazon and Flipkart Are Betting Big on India eCommerce Growth," *Forbes*, August 7, 2014; Mahesh Sharma, "Amazon and eBay Inch into India," *Bloomberg Businessweek*, accessed September 17, 2014; Jitender Miglani, "Forester Research Online Retail Forecast 2014–2018," October 7, 2013, www.forrester.com/Forrester+Research+Online+Retail+Foreca st+2013+To+2018+Asia+Pacific, accessed September17, 2014; Laura Lorenzeti, "Amazon May Be Flying to India to Test Drone Deliveries," *Fortune*, August 20, 2014; Dhanya Ann Thoppil, "Regulator Looking into Amazon's Indian Subsidiary," *Wall Street Journal*, September 5, 2014; "Amazon India Entry Has Raised the Consolidation Pace in eCom," *Economic Times of India*, http://economictimes.indiatimes.com/, accessed September 20, 2014; Prasanto K. Roy, "Why Amazon and Flipkart Will Spend Billions in India," *BBC News*, http://www.bbc.com/news/world-asia-india-28772070, accessed September 20, 2014; "Amazon's Retail Practices in India Come Under Scrutiny" *Wall Street Journal*, September 5, 2014; PWC, "Evolution of e-Commerce in India," PWC, http://www.pwc.in/assets/pdfs/publications/2014/evolution-of-e-commerce-in-india.pdf, accessed September 20, 2014.
2. Pete Engardio, "Emerging Giants," *BusinessWeek*, July 31, 2006, pp. 41–49.
3. Ibid.
4. Eric Beinhocker, Ian Davis, and Lenny Mendonca, *Harvard Business Review* 87, No. 7/8 (2009), pp. 55–60.
5. A. MacDonald, A. Lucchetti, and E. Taylor, "Long City-Centric, Financial Exchanges Are Going Global," *Wall Street Journal*, May 27, 2006.
6. Kathrin Hille, "ZTE: Telecoms Manufacturer Makes Move to Latin America," www.FT.com/Reports, May 20, 2011.
7. Engardio.
8. A. K. Gupta and V. Govindarajan, "Managing Global Expansion: A Conceptual Framework," *Business Horizons* (March/April 2000).
9. Rob Ciccone, Vice President, American Express, "What Businesses Need to Know about Expanding Internationally," *Industrial Maintenance and Plant Operation*, June 1, 2011.
10. Angus Loten, "Firms Face Hurdles Overseas: Small Companies Seek Growth Abroad, but Lack Resources of Bigger Rivals," www.wsj.com, August 25, 2011.
11. Mark Scott, "Companies Born in Europe, but Based on the Planet," www.nytimes.com, June 12, 2012.
12. www.southafrica.info, accessed September 20, 2011.
13. Grant Thornton SA, www.gt.co.za, accessed March 15, 2015.
14. www.southafrica.info, accessed March 15, 2015.
15. Ibid.
16. Ibid.
17. www.expatexplorer.hsbc.com, accessed March 15, 2015.
18. 2013–2014 Global Competitiveness Index, www.worldeconomicforum.com, accessed March 15, 2014.
19. Bettina Wassener, "Nestlé to Buy Control of China's Biggest Confectioner," www.nytimes.com, DealBook, July 11, 2011.
20. Michael J. De La Merced and Mark Scott, "UPS to Buy TNT Express for $6.8 Billion," www.nytimes.com, March 18, 2012.
21. Adam Thomson, "Indebted Cemex Turns Corner," www.FT.com, April 26, 2010.
22. Priscilla Murphy, "Companies Rush to Complete M&A Deals in Brazil ahead of Uncertainty about Tax Break after 2009," www.mergermarket.com, February 19, 2009.
23. M. Maynard, "Foreign Makers, Settled in South, Pace Car Industry," *New York Times*, June 17, 2006.
24. Daniel Trotta, "Cuba Approves Law Aimed at Attracting Foreign Investment," *Reuters*, March 29, 2014.
25. Vivienne Walt, "Touch Times for a Favorite Tax Haven," *Fortune*, February 1, 2015, p.14.
26. Henry Mintzberg, "Strategy Making in Three Modes," *California Management Review* (Winter 1973), pp. 44–53.
27. http://www.panasonic.net/sanyo/corporate/profile/philosophy.html#managementSANYOName, accessed August 15, 2015.
28. http://www.siemens.com/annual/14/en/company-report/our-path/, accessed August15, 2015.
29. Helen Deresky and Elizabeth Christopher, *International Management* (Pearson Education Australia, 2008).
30. Michael Bird, "Moscow McDonald's Shuttered as Russian Government Intervenes," *Washington Post*, August 21, 2014, p. 17; "Russia Shuts Down McDonald's Branches in Moscow amid Ukraine Row," *Telegraph Online*, August 20, 2014; James Marson and Julie Jargon, "Russia Closes Four McDonald's Branches in Moscow," http://online.wsj.com/articles/russia-closes-four-mcdonalds-in-moscow-mcd-1408568948, August 20, 2014; Noah Rayman, "Russia Is Closing McDonald's Restaurants over Health Regulations," http://time.com/3153548/russia-mcdonalds-inspection-closed; Marsha Gessen, "The Other Big Mac Index," *International New York Times*, August 29,

2014; Maria Kiselyova, "McDonald's Says 12 Russian Branches Temporarily Closed," Reuters, August 29, 2014; Juergen Baetz, "EU Ministers Call for New Sanctions against Russia," Associated Press, Friday, August 29, 2014; Lily Kuo, "Moscow's Crackdown on McDonald's May Actually Bite Businesses in Russia," Reuters, August 21, 2014; http://news.mcdonalds.com/Corporate/Media-Statements/McDonald-s-Restaurants-in-Moscow.

31. This section contributed by Charles M. Byles, Professor, Virginia Commonwealth University, March 11, 2009.

32. Mike W. Peng, *Global Strategy*, 2nd ed., Southwestern, (Cengage Learning, 2009).

33. Douglass C. North, *Institutions, Institutional Change, and Economics Performance* (New York: Cambridge University Press, 1990); W. Richard Scott, *Institutions and Organizations* (Thousand Oaks, CA: Sage Publications, 1995).

34. Peng, 2009; Mike W. Peng, Denis YL Yang, and Yi Jiang, "An Institution-Based View of International Business Strategy: A Focus on Emerging Economies," *Journal of International Business Studies* 39, No. 5 (July–August 2008); *Economist*, "Order in the Jungle," March 13, 2008.

35. *Economist*, 2008.

36. Peng, 2009.

37. Ibid.

38. Ibid.

39. www.Mitsubishi.com, January 20, 2009.

40. Diane J. Garsombke, "International Competitor Analysis," *Planning Review* 17, No. 3 (1989), pp. 42–47.

41. C. K. Prahalad and Gary Hamel, "The Core Competence of the Corporation," *Harvard Business Review* (May–June 1990), pp. 79–91.

42. Ibid.

43. P. Ghemawat, "Distance Still Matters," *Harvard Business Review* 79, No. 8 (2001), pp. 137–147.

44. M. E. Porter, "Changing Patterns of International Competition," in *The Competitive Challenge*, D. J. Teece, ed. (Boston: Ballinger, 1987), pp. 29–30.

45. T. Chen, "Network Resources for Internationalization," *Journal of Management Studies* 40, pp. 1107–1130.

46. Porter, 1987.

47. P. W. Beamish et al., *International Management* (Homewood, IL: Irwin, 1991).

48. A. Palazzo, "B2B Markets—Industry Basics," www.FT.com, January 28, 2001.

49. "A Bigger World," *Economist*, September 20, 2008.

50. Ibid.

51. A. J. Morrison, D. A. Ricks, and K. Roth, "Globalization versus Regionalization: Which Way for the Multinational?" *Organizational Dynamics* 19 (Winter 1991).

52. "Wal-Mart Selling Stores and Leaving South Korea," www.nytimes.com, March 23, 2006.

53. Beamish et al.

54. www.nytimes.com, March 23, 2006.

55. Pankaj Ghemawat, *Redefining Global Strategy* (Boston: Harvard Business School Publishing, 2007).

56. www.panasonic.net, accessed October 6, 2012.

57. Ghemawat, 2007.

58. Thomas Friedman, *The World Is Flat* (New York: Farrar, Straus, and Giroux, 2005).

59. Yoram Wind and Susan Douglas, "International Portfolio Analysis and Strategy: The Challenge of the 1980s," *Journal of International Business Studies* (Fall 1991), pp. 69–82.

60. Daniel J. Isenberg, "The Global Entrepreneur," *Harvard Business Review*, December 2008.

61. Ibid.

62. "Technology Levels the Business Playing Field," www.nytimes.com, accessed September 10, 2011.

63. "China's E-commerce Market: The Logistics Challenges," research report, www.atkearney.com, accessed August 12, 2011.

64. Ibid.

65. Bob Tedeschi, "E-Commerce Report: Sensing Economic Opportunities, Many Developing Nations Are Laying the Groundwork for Online Commerce," www.nytimes, November 20, 2008.

66. Sorid, 2008.

67. P. Greenberg, "It's Not a Small eCommerce World, After All," www.ecommercetimes.com, February 23, 2001.

68. Ibid.

69. M. Porter, *The Competitive Advantage of Nations* (New York: Free Press, 1990).

70. Bruce Einhorn, "How China's Alibaba Is Surviving and Thriving," *BusinessWeek*, April 9, 2009.

71. M. Sawhney and S. Mandal, "Go Global," *Business 2.0*, May 2000.

72. Ibid.

73. B. Bright, "E-Commerce: How Do You Say 'Web?' Planning to Take Your Online Business International? Beware: E-Commerce Can Get Lost in Translation," *Wall Street Journal*, May 23, 2005.

74. Ibid.

75. Ibid.

76. U.S. Department of Commerce, "2011 Country Commercial Guide for U.S. Companies: Doing Business in China," www.export.gov, accessed September 20, 2011.

77. J. Mangier and P. Mercier, "What Happens When Offshoring Isn't So Cheap?" www.bcgperspectives.com, January 12, 2011.

78. Bill Vlasic, Hiroko Tabuchi, and Charles Duhigg, "In Pursuit of Nissan, a Jobs Lesson for the U.S. Tech Industry," www.nytimes.com, August 5, 2012.

79. U.S. Department of Commerce, 2005.

80. Peter Marsh, "Play the Home Advantage," *Financial Times*, November 26, 2008.

81. Ibid.

82. Harold L. Sirkin, James W. Hemerling, and Arindam K. Bhattacharya, *Globality: Competing with Everyone from Everywhere for Everything* (New York: Hachette Publishing Company, 2008).

83. Wendy L. Tate, Lisa M. Ellram, Tobias Schoenherr, and Kenneth J. Petersen, "Global Competitive Conditions Driving the Manufacturing Location Decision," *Business Horizons* 57 (2014), pp. 381–390.

84. The A. T. Kearney Global Services Location Index 2014, www.ATKearney.org, accessed March 17, 2014.

85. Dante Di Gregorio, Martina Musteen, and Douglas E. Thomas, "Offshore Outsourcing as a Source of International Competitiveness for SMEs," *Journal of International Business Studies* 40, No. 6 (August 2009), p. 969.

86. J. Johnson, "India at Center of Microsoft's World," *Financial Times*, December 8, 2005.

87. A. T. Kearney, 2014.

88. Ibid.

89. Manjeet Kripalani, "Call Center? That's So 2004," *BusinessWeek*, August 7, 2006, pp. 40–42.

90. Manjeet Kripalani, "Five Offshore Practices That Pay Off," *BusinessWeek*, January 30, 2006, p. 60.

91. S. Zahra and G. Elhagrasey, "Strategic Management of IJVs," *European Management Journal* 12, No. 1 (1994), pp. 83–93.

92. Yigang Pan and Xiaolia Li, "Joint Venture Formation of Very Large Multinational Firms," *Journal of International Business Studies* 31, No. 1 (2000), pp. 179–181.

93. R. Bream and Arkady Ostrovsky, "Merger Leaves Rivals Lagging Behind," *Financial Times*, June 27, 2006.

94. U.S. Department of Commerce: "Doing Business in India," www.export.gov, accessed September 21, 2011.

95. Zahra and Elhagrasey.

96. Bill Vlasic and Nick Bunkley, "Alliance with Fiat Gives Chrysler Another Partner and Lifeline," www.nytimes.com, January 21, 2009.

97. C. Rodrigues, "On the Fast Track," www.tata.com, April 2006.

98. Julia Werdigier, "SABMiller to Buy Foster's for $10.15 Billion," www.nytimes.com, September 21, 2011.

99. Adam Thomson, "Bimbo Advances in US," www.ft.com, October 25, 2011.

100. "Overseas Cash Fuels a Shopping Spree," *Bloomberg Businessweek*, August 15–28, 2011.

101. "A Bigger World," *Economist*, September 20, 2008.

102. Simeon Kerr, Joseph Menn, "Yahoo Buys Arabic Internet Portal," *Financial Times*. London (UK), August 26, 2009, p. 18.

103. World Economic Forum, http://www3.weforum.org/docs/WEF_GAC_LogisticsSupplyChain_Report_2010-11.

104. www.atkearney.com, accessed August 28, 2011.

105. Tarun Khanna, K. Palepu, J. Sinha, "Strategies That Fit Emerging Markets," *Harvard Business Review*, June 2005.

106. Ibid.

107. N. T. Washburn and B. T. Hunsaker, "Finding Great Ideas in Emerging Markets," *Harvard Business Review*, September 2011.

108. Ibid.

109. J. Li and R. K. Kozhikode, "Organizational Learning of Emerging Economy Firms," *Organizational Dynamics* (2011), doi:10.1016/ j.orgdyn.2011.04.009.

110. Based on A. V. Phatak, *International Management—Concepts and Cases* (Cincinnati, OH: South-Western College Publishing, 1997), pp. 270–275.

111. Yigang Pan and David K. Tse, "The Hierarchical Model of Market Entry Modes," *Journal of International Business Studies* 31, No. 4 (2000), pp. 535–554.

112. Gupta and Govindarajan.

113. Ibid.

114. www.McDonalds.com, accessed March 20, 2015.

115. Oded Shenkar, "Cultural Distance Revisited. Towards a More Rigorous Conceptualization and Measurement of Cultural Differences," *Journal of International Business* 43, January 2012, pp. 1–11.

116. Ibid.

117. G. Hofstede, *Cultures and Organizations: Software of the Mind* (London: McGraw-Hill, 1991).

118. Pan and Tse.

119. Hofstede.

120. Pan and Tse.

121. Hofstede.

122. Pan and Tse.

CHAPTER

7 Implementing Strategy
Strategic Alliances, Small Businesses, Emerging Economy Firms

OUTLINE

OBJECTIVES

7-1. To become familiar with the types of strategic alliances for international business, the challenges in implementing them, and guidelines for success in alliances.

7-2. To understand what is involved in implementing strategies, including those for small businesses and those involved in emerging economies.

7-3. To consider how to manage the firm's performance in international joint ventures, with attention to knowledge management, government and cultural influence, role of e-commerce.

Opening Profile: TAG Heuer in Smartwatch Alliance with Google and Intel

ADAM THOMSON - PARIS, FT.com, March 20, 2015

Oleksiy Mark/Fotolia

TAG Heuer has announced a partnership with Google and Intel to develop a smartwatch, signalling that they want to take the fight to Apple as the Californian company prepares to roll out its Apple Watch.

The Swiss watchmaker, owned by Paris luxury goods conglomerate LVMH, said that the alliance would create "a product that is both luxurious and seamlessly connected to its wearer's daily life".

The move marks the first time a top-end brand from the Swiss watch industry has joined the competition for smartwatches and leaves no doubt as to Google's determination to follow Apple into the high-end segment of wearable technology.

For chipmaker Intel, the alliance is an opportunity to make up for its failure in the smartphone market by leapfrogging into wearables.

Jean-Claude Biver, who heads LVMH's watches division, said yesterday that the transatlantic partnership between 155-year-old TAG Heuer and 17-year-old Google was "a marriage of technical innovation and watchmaking credibility".

Some industry analysts will see the irony of Mr Biver moving into the smartwatch business. He is largely credited with having saved the Swiss watch industry from the proliferation of quartz movements in the 1970s and 1980s by emphasising the virtues of handmade mechanical timepieces.

A 1980s campaign he launched as head of the Blancpain watchmaker he revived stated defiantly: "Since 1735 there has never been a quartz Blancpain watch. And there never will be."

But Mr Biver told the Financial Times yesterday: "We believe that TAG Heuer is an avant-garde brand and our customers belong to the younger generation. There is a demand for luxury connected watches and we want to satisfy that demand."

He said that the new watch, which will run on Google's operating platform, would probably go on sale in November. Mr Biver declined to give prices or any technical details. The average price of a conventional TAG Heuer watch is about €3,500.

Smartwatches have so far been relatively slow to catch on with activity-tracking wristbands from the likes of Jawbone and Fitbit proving more popular. But that could change next month as Apple prepares to launch its Watch, which it first unveiled last year.

Analysts have estimated that only watchmakers competing at lower price points - up to about €900 - could be affected by the product launch.

STRATEGIC ALLIANCES

As illustrated in the opening profile, sometimes it takes global strategic alliances to compete with behemoths such as Apple. **Strategic alliances** are partnerships between two or more firms that decide they can pursue their mutual goals better by combining their resources—financial, managerial, and technological—as well as their existing distinctive competitive advantages. Alliances—often called *cooperative strategies*—are transition mechanisms that propel the partners' strategies forward in a turbulent environment faster than would be possible for each company alone.[1] The explosion of international strategic alliances (ISAs) in the past has been caused by the need for organizations to respond to the globalization of markets and the opportunities presented by technological advances. However, the rush to take advantage of those opportunities has resulted in an estimated half of ISAs experiencing poor results or failing.[2] (These problems will be discussed later in this chapter.)

Alliances typically fall under one of three categories: joint ventures, equity strategic alliances, and non-equity strategic alliances, and they can be for various purposes such as sharing technology, marketing, or production joint ventures. Cross-border alliances frequently necessitate acquiring a local partner to counteract political risk factors and to take advantage of local knowledge and contacts. Indeed, Eli Lilly, realizing the need for a local partner in China, made an unprecedented deal between a Western drug manufacturer and a Chinese biotech company to co-develop and commercialize three cancer drugs and market to the growing consumer base there:

> *Indianapolis-based Lilly said it would pay $56 million upfront to Innovent Biologics Inc., a four-year-old startup near Shanghai, to co-develop at least three experimental cancer drugs—including one from Lilly's research labs and two from Innovent.*
>
> WALL STREET JOURNAL,
> *MARCH 20, 2015*[3]

It should be noted, however, that although the past decades brought a surge in companies seeking growth through mergers and acquisitions (M&As), joint ventures, and other alliances, the global economic downturn in 2008–2009 caused many companies to postpone or cancel such plans, often instead retrenching or de-merging. Examples were General Motors and Citigroup having to spin off partners as well as retrench operations to maintain sufficient cash flow. The rate of deals collapsing increased amid the credit crisis and global equity market volatility. Still other deals, made under duress, involved government alliances in an attempt to save companies and industries from default, as with a number of banks that become subject to partial nationalization.

Joint Ventures

> *MUMBAI, India—After years of studying the Indian market, Starbucks Coffee said Monday that it would open its first store here by September (2012) through a 50-50 joint venture with Tata Global Beverages, a unit of the largest business group in India.*
>
> NEW YORK TIMES
> *JANUARY 20, 2012*[4]

As discussed in Chapter 6, a **joint venture (JV)** is a new independent entity jointly created and owned by two or more parent companies. The JV agreement for a firm may comprise a majority JV (in which the firm has more than 50 percent equity), a minority JV (less than 50 percent equity), or a 50-50 JV (when two firms have equal equity). An international joint venture (IJV) is a joint venture among companies in different countries. In that case, the firm shares the profits, costs, and risks with a local partner (or a global partner) and benefits from the local partner's local contacts and markets. (Advantages and disadvantages of IJVs were discussed in Chapter 6). The Starbucks agreement with Tata Global Beverages is an example of a 50-50 equity IJV. "The announcement came a year after the company said it was going to enter the market and nearly two months after the Indian government fumbled an effort to attract more foreign investment in its retailing industry."[5]

Another example of a 50–50 equity IJV is that between France's PSA Peugeot-Citroen Group and Japan's Toyota at Kolin in the Czech Republic. As noted by Fujio Cho, president of Toyota Motors, the world's richest carmaker:

> *Each company has brought its own style, culture and way of thinking to this partnership—but our different approaches have benefited our joint venture enormously.*[6]

Among the benefits noted by the two companies are that Toyota "gains an insight into the mindset of one of Europe's biggest indigenous carmakers and knowledge of its suppliers and their capabilities."[7] And Peugeot-Citroen can gain experience from Toyota's lean manufacturing system. The companies acknowledge that the IJV has resulted in faster development and increased production capacity and that costs are shared without either company renouncing its independence.[8]

Equity Strategic Alliances

Brazilian firm 3G Capital and Buffett mastermind latest takeover in 7 year campaign. Heinz is to take over Kraft Foods to create one of North America's largest food companies.... The deal—the world's largest M&A transaction this year— marks another step in the conquest of the U.S. food industry by a Brazilian private equity group.

WWW.FT.COM
MARCH 26, 2015[9]

Two or more partners have different relative ownership shares (equity percentages) in the new venture in an equity strategic alliance. In the merger with Heinz and Kraft, which will create the fifth largest food and beverage company globally, Heinz will control 51 percent and Kraft 49 percent. Most global manufacturers have equity alliances with suppliers, sub-assemblers, and distributors, forming a network of internal family and financial links. Risk-sharing is often the motive behind equity alliances. Sometimes an international, or global, joint venture is part of a desperate strategy. This was the case in January 2009 when Chrysler reached for another lifeline in its equity deal to join forces with Italy's Fiat. The plan was for Fiat to get a 35 percent ownership stake in Chrysler with the goal of bringing its Fiat and Alfa Romeo brands back to the United States through Chrysler's dealership network. In return, Chrysler would try to stay alive by presenting a strategic partnership as part of its plan to the U.S. government in its quest for an additional $3 billion loan to allow it to stay in business.[10] However, further developments led to a change in plans when some creditors did not make concessions, and—as reported in the New York Times, President Obama announced on April 30, 2009:

> *Chrysler, the third-largest American auto company, will seek bankruptcy protection and enter an alliance with the Italian automaker Fiat, the White House announced Thursday.*[11]

However, the deal with Fiat would be intact after bankruptcy, with Fiat to take part in running Chrysler, provide technical operations, and build at least one vehicle in a Chrysler plant. Fiat did not put up any financing as part of the agreement. Considerable additional financing from the U.S. government was planned after Chrysler's restructuring, with the Canadian government also offering some financing.[12]

Non-equity Strategic Alliances

Uber Technologies Inc.'s biggest rivals around the world are banding together to launch a counterattack by linking their apps and effectively creating an international ride-hailing service.

WALL STREET JOURNAL,
17 SEPTEMBER, 2015[13]

As illustrated by the global ride-hailing alliance to defend their turf against Uber, agreements are carried out through contract rather than ownership sharing in a non-equity strategic alliance. Such contracts are often with a firm's suppliers, distributors, or manufacturers, or they may be for purposes of marketing and information sharing, such as with many airline partnerships. UPS, for example, is a global supply-chain manager for many companies around the world, such as Nike, that essentially do not touch their own products but contract with UPS to arrange the entire delivery process from factory to warehouse to customer to repair, even collecting the money.[14]

Global Strategic Alliances

Working partnerships between companies (often more than two) across national boundaries and increasingly across industries are referred to as global strategic alliances. A glance at the global airline industry, for example, tells us that global alliances have become a mainstay of competitive strategy. Not one airline is competing alone; each major U.S. carrier has established strategic links with non-U.S. companies. The Star Alliance, for example, has code sharing among 26 member airlines around the world.

Alliances are also sometimes formed between a company and a foreign government or among companies and governments. In addition, changing regulations and policies by governments and institutions lead to new opportunities for alliances with national industries abroad. Alliances may comprise full global partnerships, which are often joint ventures in which two or more companies, while retaining their national identities, develop a common, long-term strategy aimed at world leadership. The European Airbus Industrie consortium, for example, comprises France's Aerospatiale and Germany's Daimler-Benz Aerospace, each with 37.9 percent of the business; British Aerospace with 20 percent; and Spain's Construcciones Aeronauticas with 4.2 percent.

Whereas such alliances have a broad agenda, others are formed for a narrow and specific function such as production, marketing, research and development, or financing. More recently, these have included electronic alliances, such as Covisint, which is redefining the entire system of car production and distribution through a common electronic marketplace, as well as linking partners in other major industries involved in Business-to-Partner (B2P), Business-to-Customer (B2C) and Business-to-Enterprise (B2E) relationships.

Our customers have deployed our B2B Cloud Platform to connect to over 212,000 of their business partners and customers – transacting in excess of $1 trillion per year.

WWW.COVISINT.COM
MARCH 24, 2015[15]

Global and Cross-Border Alliances: Motivations and Benefits

Some of the typical reasons behind cross-border alliances are as follows.

- ***To avoid import barriers, licensing requirements, and other protectionist legislation:*** Japanese automotive manufacturers, for example, use alliances such as the GM–Toyota venture, or subsidiaries, to produce cars in the United States to avoid import quotas.

- ***To share the costs and risks of the research and development of new products and processes:*** In the semiconductor industry, for example, in which each new generation of memory chips is estimated to cost more than $1 billion to develop, those costs and the rapid technological evolution typically require the resources of more than one (or even two) firms. Intel, for example, has alliances with Samsung and NMB Semiconductor for technology (DRAM) development. Toshiba, Japan's third-largest electronics company, has more than two dozen major joint ventures and strategic alliances around the world, including partners such as Olivetti, Rhone-Poulenc, GEC Alstholm in Europe, LSI Logic in Canada, and Samsung in Korea. Fumio Sato, Toshiba's CEO, recognized long ago that a global strategy for a high-tech electronics company such as his necessitated joint ventures and strategic alliances.

- ***To gain access to specific markets, such as China and Russia, where regulations favor domestic companies:*** Firms often find that the only way—or, at least, the best way—to enter markets such as China and Russia is through alliances, as discussed elsewhere. In addition, in spite of the economic problems in the EU, firms around the world are still investing there and forming strategic alliances with European companies to bolster their chances of competing in the European Union (EU) and to gain access to markets in Eastern European countries as they further develop their businesses. Chun Joo Bum, chief executive of the Daewoo Electronics unit, acknowledged his desire for local partners in Europe for two reasons: (1) to provide sorely needed capital and (2) to help Daewoo navigate Europe's still disparate markets, saying, "I need to localize our management. It is not one market."[16]

- ***To reduce political risk while making inroads in a new market:***

  Carefully orchestrated partnerships with governments and other business groups are crucial to the [Disney] entertainment group's thrust into China and the rest of south-east Asia.

  BOB IGER
  PRESIDENT AND COO, WALT DISNEY[17]

Hong Kong Disneyland is jointly owned by the Chinese government with a 57 percent stake. Beijing is especially interested in promoting tourism through the venture and in facilitating employment for the 5,000 workers Disney employs directly as well as the estimated 18,000 workers in related services.[18] Coca-Cola—a global player with large-scale alliances—is not beyond using some very small-scale alliances to be political in China. The company uses senior citizens in the Chinese Communist Party's neighborhood committees to sell Coke locally.

- ***To gain rapid entry into a new or consolidating industry and to take advantage of synergies:*** Technology is rapidly providing the means and products—such as the iPad—for the overlapping and merging of traditional industries such as entertainment, computers, and telecommunications in new digital-based systems. Disney's business model of cellular partnerships and content sales, for example, created Disney mobile operations in Hong Kong, Taiwan, South Korea, Singapore, and the Philippines.[19] The company uses joint venture partners such as the Hong Kong government or licensees and distributors such as Oriental Land and NTT DoCoMo.[20]

In many cases, technological developments are necessitating strategic alliances across industries for companies to gain rapid entry into areas in which they have no expertise or manufacturing capabilities. Such was the case when Apple announced in September 2015 that it had acquired a "big data" analytics company, Mapsense, that will allow it to analyze the huge mass of location and mapping services required in cars.[21] Competition is so fierce that they cannot wait to develop those resources alone. Many of these objectives, such as access to new technology and new markets, are evident in AT&T's network of alliances around the world. Agreements with Japan's NEC, for example, gave AT&T access to new semiconductor and chip-making technologies, helping it learn how to integrate computers with communications better.

Challenges in Implementing Global Alliances

Effective global alliances are usually tediously slow in the making but can be among the best mechanisms to implement strategies in global markets. In a highly competitive environment, alliances present a faster and less risky route to global expansion and efficiency. It is extremely complex to fashion such linkages, however, especially when many interconnecting systems are involved, forming intricate networks. Many alliances fail for complex reasons. Many also end up in a takeover in which one partner swallows the other. McKinsey & Company, a consulting firm, surveyed 150 companies that had been in alliances and found that 75 percent of them had been taken over by Japanese partners. Problems with shared ownership, differences in national cultures, the integration of vastly different structures and systems, the distribution of power between the companies involved, and conflicts in their relative locus of decision making and control are but a few of the organizational issues that must be worked out. The *Financial Times* observed that "joint ventures start with smiles, but often end in tears."[22]

Often, the form of governance chosen for multinational firm alliances greatly influences their success, particularly in technologically intense fields such as pharmaceuticals, computers, and semiconductors. Thus, joint ventures are often the chosen form for such alliances because they provide greater control of proprietary technology as well as increased coordination in high-technology industries.

Cross-border partnerships, in particular, often become a race to learn—with the faster learner later dominating the alliance and rewriting its terms. In a real sense, an alliance becomes a new form of competition. In fact, according to researcher David Lei,

> Perhaps the single greatest impediment managers face when seeking to learn or renew sources of competitive advantage is to realize that co-operation can represent another form of unintended competition, particularly to shape and apply new skills to future products and businesses.[23]

All too often, cross-border allies have difficulty collaborating effectively, especially in competitively sensitive areas; this creates mistrust and secrecy, which then undermine the purpose of the alliance. The difficulty that they are dealing with is the dual nature of strategic alliances—the benefits of cooperation versus the dangers of introducing new competition through sharing their knowledge and technological skills about their mutual product or the manufacturing process. Managers may fear that they will lose the competitive advantage of the firm's proprietary technology or the specific skills that their personnel possess.

The cumulative learning that a partner attains through the alliance could be applied to other products or even other industries that are beyond the scope of the alliance and, therefore, would hold no benefit to the partner holding the original knowledge.[24] Some of the trade-offs of the duality of cross-border ventures are shown in Exhibit 7-1 and are illustrated by the 2011 joint venture between General Electric (GE) and Avic, a state-owned Chinese company. The alliance shows the tricky risk-and-reward calculations American corporations must increasingly make in their pursuit of the lucrative markets in China. This is a 50–50 venture with Avic planned for a 50-year duration. Additional risks are that such technology-sharing could advance the Chinese military-aviation status.

EXHIBIT 7-1 The Dual Role of Strategic Alliances

Cooperative	Competitive
Economies of scale in tangible assets (e.g., plant and equipment).	Opportunity to learn new intangible skills from partner, often tacit or organization-embedded.
Upstream–downstream division of labor among partners.	Accelerate diffusion of industry standards and new technologies to erect barriers to entry.
Fill out product line with components or end products provided by supplier.	Deny technological and learning initiative to partner via outsourcing and long-term supply arrangements.
Limit investment risk when entering new markets or uncertain technological fields via shared resources.	Encircle existing competitors and preempt the rise of new competitors with alliance partners in "proxy wars" to control market access, distribution, and access to new technologies.
Create a "critical mass" to learn and develop new technologies to protect domestic, strategic industries.	Form clusters of learning among suppliers and related firms to avoid or reduce foreign dependence for critical inputs and skills.
Assist short-term corporate restructurings by lowering exit barriers in mature or declining industries.	Alliances serve as experiential platforms to "demature" and transform existing mature industries via new components, technologies, or skills to enhance the value of future growth options.

Source: David Lei, "Offensive and Defensive Uses of Alliances," in Heidi Vernon-Wortzel and L. H. Wortzel, *Strategic Management in Global Economy*, 3rd ed. (New York: John Wiley & Sons, 1997), used with permission.

> *But doing business in China often requires Western multinationals like G.E. to share technology and trade secrets that might eventually enable Chinese companies to beat them at their own game—by making the same products cheaper, if not better.*[25]

The enticing benefits of cross-border alliances often mask the many pitfalls involved. In addition to potential loss of a company's technology and knowledge or skills base, other areas of incompatibility often arise such as conflicting strategic goals and objectives, cultural clashes, and disputes over management and control systems. Sometimes it takes a while for such problems to present themselves, particularly if insufficient homework has been done in meetings between the two sides to work out the implementation details.

Implementing Alliances between SMEs and MNCs

All countries have a large proportion of business enterprises, as well as NGOs, that are small or medium-sized enterprises (SMEs). But, increasingly, MNCs are dominating the markets in which SMEs operate, often crowding them out of business altogether. However, astute managers of SMEs can often find opportunities for alliances with those multinationals, providing "complementary resources and capabilities that can lead to, for instance, an innovative product offering being rolled out on a global scale, or a worldwide licensing agreement."[26] For example, MNCs often partner with local small enterprises to capture new ideas and innovations. Sun Microsystems, for instance, engaged with a number of small enterprises in Scotland on radio frequency identification (RFID) projects to bolster its competitiveness in this emerging area.[27] SMEs should seek out those opportunities to offer MNCs complementary technologies as well as local market networks. SABMiller, for example, helps the many small shop owners in Latin America with training and financing, which boosts beer sales for both the company and the *tiendas*.

Guidelines for Successful Alliances

As discussed earlier, many global companies, such as IBM, the Tata Group, and Toyota, build extensive alliance portfolios that involve multiple concurrent alliances. Oracle's Partner Network, for example, includes 19,500 partners. Alliance partners can provide synergies and value to corporate performance by providing access to new resources and markets, generating economies of scale and scope, reducing costs, sharing risks, and enhancing flexibility.[28] Unfortunately, the complexities involved in managing many alliances often means that many—around half by most estimates—are unsuccessful, often because of poor partner selections initially and then also because of poor management to ensure that the expected competencies and synergies are realized. Research by Dovev Lavie of 20,000 alliances involving about 8,800 unique partners provides some insight into how managers can manage their alliances in ways that will increase the likelihood of success. The results enabled the identification of "value-creation and value-capture strategies that can guide partner selection decisions, and developed alliance portfolio management practices to help managers extract more value from their alliance portfolios."[29] Value creation strategies include, for example, the importance of assimilating network resources to acquire new skills and capabilities. Value capture strategies caution that it is important to "avoid partners that compete in your industry if they enjoy superior bargaining power."[30] One key factor in managing alliance portfolios is to consider not only what each alliance partner will bring to the company but also how that partner will affect other partners in the portfolio.

It is clear that many difficulties arise in cross-border alliances in melding the national and corporate cultures of the parties, in overcoming language and communication barriers, and in building trust between the parties over how to share proprietary assets and management processes. Some basic guidelines, as follows, will help to minimize potential problems. However, nothing is as important as having a long courtship with a potential partner to establish compatibility strategically and interpersonally and set up a plan with the prospective partner. Even setting up some pilot programs on a short-term basis for some of the planned combined activities can highlight areas that may become problematic.

- Choose a partner with compatible strategic goals and objectives and with whom the alliance will result in synergies through the combined markets, technologies, and management cadre.

- Seek alliances where complementary skills, products, and markets will result. If each partner brings distinctive skills and assets to the venture, there will be reduced potential for direct competition in end products and markets. In addition, each partner will begin the alliance in a balanced relationship.[31]

- Work out with the partner how you will each deal with proprietary technology or competitively sensitive information—what will be shared, and what will not, and how shared technology will be handled. Trust is an essential ingredient of an alliance, particularly in these areas; but this must be backed up by contractual agreements.

- Recognize that most alliances last only a few years and will probably break up once a partner feels it has incorporated the skills and information it needs to go it alone. With this in mind, managers need to "learn thoroughly and rapidly about a partner technology and management: transfer valuable ideas and practices promptly into one's own operations."[32]

Some of the opportunities and complexities in cross-border alliances are illustrated in the following Comparative Management in Focus on joint ventures in the Russian Federation. Such alliances are further complicated by the different history of the two parties' economic systems and the resulting business practices, as well as political issues.

IMPLEMENTING STRATEGY

Implementing Strategy McDonald's Style

- *Form paradigm-busting arrangements with suppliers.*
- *Know a country's culture before you hit the beach.*
- *Hire locals whenever possible.*
- *Maximize autonomy.*
- *Tweak the standard menu only slightly from place to place.*
- *Keep pricing low to build market share. Profits will follow when economies of scale kick in.*[33]

Comparative Management in Focus
Joint Ventures in the Russian Federation

Russia ranks 53rd out of 139 countries covered by the 2014–2015 Global Competitiveness Index.
WORLD ECONOMIC FORUM[34]

GM says it will shut Russian plant; wind down Opel brand.

WWW.NYTIMES.COM
MARCH 18, 2015

"We are doing everything we can to continue development despite the slowdown of the Russian economy. We are still confident in Russia's long-term prospects."
MAURIZIO PATARNELLO, NESTLÉ RUSSIA CEO
WWW.NYTIMES.COM
MARCH 24, 2015[35]

Judging by the preceding quotes, it seems that Russia poses a number of contradictions to would-be investors. In 2011, as Disney pushed into Russia with a new Disney television channel, its CEO Bob Iger said "we really believe in Russia as a growth market."[36] However, as of 2015, both potential investors and those firms already in Russia were very concerned about Russia's continuing involvement in Ukraine (described in the Chapter 1 opening profile) and the negative impact on the economy of the stringent western sanctions. It has been clear for some time that foreign companies have started to think twice about investing in international joint ventures (IJVs) in Russia since President Putin's moves to take control of key industries, including banks, newspapers, and oil assets. In May 2008, President Putin signed the Strategic Industries Bill, which regulates foreign investment. The new law identifies 42 strategic sectors (compared to 16 in 2005) in which foreign investors have to seek special permission before investing.

In September 2014, the U.S. private equity investment group Blackstone gave up on Russia, citing a lack of investors' interest and limited investment opportunities after the widespread impact of the sanctions.[37] In spite of the recent negative climate, Russia—the world's largest country (see Map 7.1), spanning 11 time zones, clearly offers substantial opportunity for companies willing to go for the risk–return

MAP 7.1 Russia

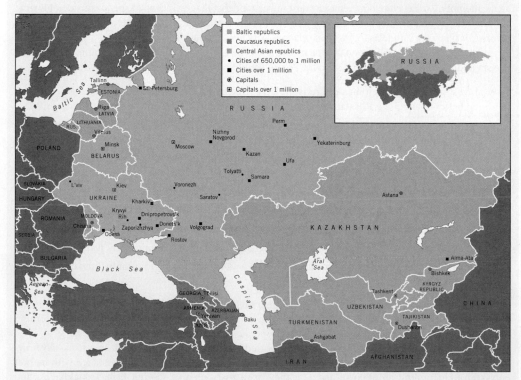

(Continued)

trade-off. However, its significant growth over the past decade has slowed considerably since the global economic downturn, making it less competitive than the other BRIC countries. According to the 2011 World Economic Forum Russia report, the most important single element explaining a country's medium-term growth performance is productivity; labor productivity in Russia is less than half the value achieved by workers in the OECD member states. The decline in manufacturing competitiveness in Russia "is due to the combination of an increase in real wages and shortcomings of the business climate, which puts Russia at a disadvantage in international comparison."[38] In addition, there is concern that the long-term business climate will remain for some time as an unbalanced, corruption-ridden, natural resource–based economy because of the persistent lack of formal institutions.

> *Russian managers have relied excessively on informal institutions, including personal networks, to conduct business due to the void created by the weak legitimacy of the country's formal institutions.*[39]

All in all, investors are confused, though many are determined to take advantage of the vast, underexploited natural-resource potential; a skilled, educated population; and a huge market. Indeed the abundance of technically skilled Russians has attracted a number of companies in the past, such as Intel, Cisco, Sun Microsystems, and Microsoft. Many MNCs claim that they must have a presence in Russia to be globally competitive.

In addition to the potential for corruption and the constant uncertainty in the business environment, firms doing business in Russia find that implementing a joint venture is very frustrating and time-consuming due to the all-consuming regulations and bureaucracy there. For these reasons, many foreign firms pick a local partner to help them navigate the myriad of negotiations to obtain permissions, get visas, acquire property, and so on. Other firms hire a security firm (Krisha), which smooths the way through the bureaucracy, often with payments.[40]

Until recently Moscow and other major cities have been experiencing a consumer boom, spurred on by rising incomes in the middle class, making Russia one of the fastest growing regions for global consumer giants such as Coca-Cola, Procter & Gamble, and Nestlé.[41] Indeed, the Swiss food giant, Nestlé confirmed its faith in the long-term prospects in Russia and that it would try to use more local content and ingredients to try to offset the currency problems, reinforcing the importance of local suppliers.[42] Nestlé has nine manufacturing facilities in Russia and opened a new factory for baby food in 2014. Many, like Bell Labs, have been involved in research and development, taking advantage of the Russians' high-level education and technical capabilities. Nevertheless,, Western managers need to recognize that cultural factors affect cross-border business, in particular, that Russians are distrustful of outsiders; managers attempting to develop joint ventures must understand that they will need to spend considerable time communicating and developing a trusting relationship. Reliance on their own networks and the use of favors (*blat*) present obstacles to business relations between Russians and outsiders.[43]

Overall, managers of foreign companies who are looking past the current economic problems in Russia and hoping to set up business in the future should carefully consider the following.

- Investigate whether a joint venture is the best strategy. If a lot of real estate is needed, it may be better to acquire a Russian business because of the difficulties involved in acquiring land.
- Set up meetings with the appropriate ministry and regional authorities well in advance. Have good communication about your business needs and build local relationships.
- Be sure to be totally above board in paying all relevant taxes to avoid crossing the Russian authorities.
- Set up stricter controls and accountability systems than usual for the company.
- Communicate clearly up front that your firm does not pay bribes.
- Assign the firm's best available managers and delegate to them enough authority to act locally.
- Take advantage of local knowledge by hiring appropriate Russian managers for the venture.
- Designate considerable funds for local promotion and advertising to establish the corporate image with authorities and consumers.[44]

Foreign managers' alliance strategy must also take into account the goals of potential Russian partners. An awareness and acceptance of the motivations of Russian firms for alliances with foreign companies will aid in finding and achieving a cooperative joint venture.

Researchers for the *Wall Street Journal* reported their findings about what local Russian firms want from an alliance with a foreign firm; they made it clear that they expect assistance with market entry through forming an alliance and that they need assistance in solving bribes, kickbacks, and other under-the-table transactions.[45]

Decisions regarding global alliances and entry strategies must now be put into motion with the next stage of planning: strategic implementation—also known as functional level strategies. Implementation plans are detailed and pervade the entire organization because they entail setting up overall policies, administrative responsibilities, and schedules throughout the organization to enact the selected strategy and to make sure it works. In the case of a merger or IJV, this process requires compromising and blending procedures among two or more companies and is extremely complex. The importance of the implementation phase of the strategic management process cannot be overemphasized. Until they are put into operation, strategic plans remain abstract ideas: verbal or printed proposals that have no effect on the organization.

Successful implementation requires the orchestration of many variables into a cohesive system that complements the desired strategy—that is, a *system of fits* that will facilitate the actual working of the strategic plan. In this way, the structure, systems, and processes of the firm are coordinated and set into motion by a system of management by objectives (MBO) whose primary objective is the fulfillment of strategy. Managers must review the organizational structure and, if necessary, change it to facilitate the administration of the strategy and coordinate activities in a particular location with headquarters (as discussed further in Chapter 8). In addition to ensuring the strategy-structure fit, managers must allocate resources to make the strategy work, budgeting money, facilities, equipment, people, and other support. Increasingly, that support necessitates a unified technology infrastructure to coordinate diverse businesses around the world and satisfy the need for current and reliable information. An efficient technology infrastructure can provide a strategic advantage in a globally competitive environment. Jack Welch, while CEO of General Electric (he retired in late 2001), was prescient when he referred to his e-commerce initiative, saying, "It will change relationships with suppliers. Within 18 months, all our suppliers will supply us on the Internet, or they won't do business with us."[46]

An overarching factor affecting all the other variables necessary for successful implementation is that of leadership; it is people, after all, who make things happen. The firm's leaders must skillfully guide employees and processes in the desired direction. Managers with different combinations of experience, education, abilities, and personality tend to be more suited to implementing certain strategies. In an equity-sharing alliance, sorting out which top managers in each company will be in which position is a sensitive matter. Who in which company will be CEO is usually worked out as part of the initial deal in alliance agreements. This problem seems to be frequently settled these days by setting up joint CEOs, one from each company. Setting monitoring systems into place to control activities and ensure success completes, but does not end, the strategic management process. Rather, it is a continuous process, using feedback to reevaluate strategy for needed modifications and updating and recycling plans.

Of particular note here, we should consider what is involved in implementing strategies for SMEs and the issues involved in the effective management of the global sourcing strategy. Then we will review what is involved in managing performance in international joint ventures because they are such a common form of global alliance, and yet they are fraught with implementation challenges.

Implementing Strategies for SMEs

For small businesses venturing abroad, however, the first step is often that of exporting. This can be a daunting task; however, many sources are available to help small-business managers embark on exporting, as discussed in the nearby feature, Under the Lens: Breaking Down Barriers for Small-Business Exports. Of particular note, China offers substantial opportunities for exports for SMEs (businesses with fewer than 500 employees), which have accounted for an estimated third of exports to China in recent years. Most exports to China include agricultural products leading the way, followed by computers and electronics, chemicals, non-electrical machinery, and waste and scrap.[47] China is the third largest export market for U.S. companies, after Canada and Mexico and followed by Japan and the United Kingdom. Further opportunities for SMEs will emerge once the new Trans Pacific Partnership Trade Deal between the U.S. and eleven Pacific Rim nations (announced October 2015) is ratified and in force.

For SME firms wishing to expand beyond their domestic markets and exporting, they typically need to find a market niche in the chosen countries between the MNCs and the local firms where they know they can compete. While they do not have the economies of scale and financial

UNDER THE LENS
Breaking Down Barriers for Small-Business Exports

Approximately 300,000 small or medium-sized businesses in the United States export goods or services abroad. Small businesses make up 97 percent of American companies that export, according to the U.S. Census Bureau, and their numbers are growing. The U.S. government is looking to boost small-business exports with the National Export Initiative (NEI)—an initiative started in January 2010 by U.S. President Barack Obama—which aimed to double U.S. exports and create millions of jobs in the United States by the end of 2015.

"To double exports we need to increase the number of small business exporters," said Richard Ginsburg, an international trade specialist with the U.S. Small Business Administration (SBA). Fifty-eight percent of roughly 250,000 U.S. small and medium-sized enterprise (SME) exporters ship to just one market. Ginsburg says one of the key goals of NEI is to help those firms ship to multiple markets.

China has been a growing market for American SMEs—companies with fewer than 500 employees. According to the U.S. International Trade Administration, the number of American SMEs exporting to China increased by 776 percent from 1992 to 2009. But there is still room for growth. Successful exporters to China emphasize the complexity, and that it is essential to meet your clients face-to-face at the beginning.

U.S. EXPORT ASSISTANCE CENTERS

Of the 20 U.S. government agencies involved in export assistance, SBA specifically aims to increase the number of small business exporters through programs delivered through U.S. Export Assistance Centers. Senior SBA trade and finance specialists—along with employees from the U.S. Commercial Service and the U.S. Export-Import (Ex-Im) Bank—staff 20 of more than 100 U.S. Export Assistance Centers in metropolitan areas around the country. The centers help "export-ready" companies begin to export or expand to new markets abroad by providing counseling, training, export insurance, and loans to these businesses; conducting market research; and facilitating contracts between U.S. exporters and foreign buyers.

Ginsburg says small business owners usually approach an Export Assistance Center when they want to make a deal with a foreign buyer or when they receive an order from a foreign buyer and have never exported before. The centers can help companies understand payment terms and conditions, help them handle logistics such as shipping, and refer them to translators. These transactions are often simple when doing business in the United States, but they can be complicated when crossing international borders.

Counseling, outreach, and loan programs help break down what Ginsburg calls the "psychological trade barriers" that prevent small businesses from exporting. "There are people who feel they can lose their business if they export," Ginsburg says. "The risks are so much more than shipping across town or across the state or across the country." For example, small-business owners sometimes fear that they will not be able to collect payments from overseas buyers.

Companies that want to export face barriers such as language and lack of knowledge of the foreign regulatory environment, and—specifically for businesses exporting to China—fear of intellectual property rights infringement, Ginsburg says.

EXPORT LOANS FOR SMALL BUSINESSES

In addition to counseling and training, SBA guarantees loans of up to $5 million, and the Ex-Im Bank provides export financing for amounts over $5 million. "It's a success story for SBA when we're working with a small-business exporter and they outgrow the small loan amount and need more than the $5 million SBA threshold," Ginsburg says.

SBA runs four loan programs for small-business exporters: the Export Express Program, the Export Working Capital Program, International Trade Loan Program, and SBA and Ex-Im Bank Co-Guarantee Program. The Export Express Program, formerly a pilot program, was made permanent in 2010 with the passage of the Small Business Jobs Act of 2010 to support the NEI goal of increasing small business exports. The program aims to streamline the export loan process for small businesses. SMEs that have been operating for at least 12 months can receive up to $500,000 to finance export activities, such as participating in foreign trade shows, purchasing equipment, and translating product literature. The law also permanently increased loan limits on export working capital and international trade loans.

and marketing resources of the MNCs; they also do not have the local connections, suppliers, and consumer knowledge of the small local companies. If those SMEs can find an opportunity, or niche, that the MNCs find too minor to bother with, and also that are not being targeted by local firms, they may be able to gain a foothold and establish their own reputation as leaders. Then, too, a later opportunity may arise with an MNC wanting to use that firm to gain inroads or to use the acquired knowledge or technology, as discussed earlier. Alternatively, seeking an alliance with a local partner would provide early access to hiring local talent, to local connections and suppliers, etc. In their research of successful Israeli small firms going global, Jonathan Friedrich, et al concluded first, that SMEs can take care not to awaken the gorillas by targeting a sufficiently minor opportunity that the MNCs decide is not worth their while, but which can be leveraged profitably across several international regions; and secondly, by bringing in superior technology and processing capabilities to keep out local players.[48]

Implementing a Global Sourcing Strategy: From Offshoring to Next-Shoring?

The entry strategy of global sourcing was discussed in Chapter 6. Outsourcing abroad—alliances with firms in other countries to perform specific functions for the firm (offshoring)—is often in the news because of the politically charged issue of domestic jobs apparently being lost to others overseas. Beyond finding lower-paid workers, however, the strategic view of global sourcing is to develop into transformational outsourcing—the view that, properly implemented, global sourcing can produce gains in efficiency, productivity, quality, and profitability by fully leveraging talent around the world.[49] Procter & Gamble, for example, having outsourced everything from IT infrastructure and Human Resource Department functions, such as staffing, training, compensation, and so on, around the world, announced that CEO Alan G. Lafley wanted 50 percent of all new P&G products to come from other countries.[50] However, implementing such a strategy is more difficult than it is made to seem in the press, because many companies have encountered unexpected problems when outsourcing. Advice on implementation from experiences by companies such as Dell, IBM, and Reuters Group PLC lead us to the following guidelines:

- *Examine your reasons for outsourcing:* Make sure that the advantages of efficiency and competitiveness will outweigh the disadvantages from your employees, customers, and community; don't outsource just because your competitors are doing it.

- *Evaluate the best outsourcing model:* Opening your own subsidiary in the host country (a captive operation) may be better than contracting with an outside firm if it is crucial for you to keep control of proprietary technology and processes.

- *Gain the cooperation of your management and staff:* Open communication and training is essential to get your domestic managers on board; uncertainty, fear, and disagreement from them can jeopardize your plans.

- *Consult your alliance partners:* Consult with your partners and treat them with the respect that made you decide to do business with them.

- *Invest in the alliance:* Plan to invest time and money in training in the firm's business practices, in particular those to deal with quality control and customer relations.[51]

Further advice comes from Josh Green, CEO of Panjiva, which is an information resource for companies doing business across borders. Green asks, "How healthy is your global partner?" because he noted that an increasing number of firms in developed economies were finding that their suppliers in Asia had gone out of business following the protracted global economic downturn that caused firms to reduce their demand from their suppliers. He notes that both buyers and suppliers have learned the hard way that in the future they need to investigate and evaluate their potential partners carefully. He suggests, for example, that both sides should do a background check on the financial health and future viability of the company; get references from other partners of the firm; be prepared to give those assurances and data about their own companies; and be prepared for problems by having alternate partners ready to fill in.[52] The need to be prepared for the unexpected was suddenly brought home on March 11, 2011, when the Japanese earthquake and tsunami struck—a disaster for the Japanese people and a problem for supply chains of companies around the world (see *Under the Lens: Global Supply Chain Risks—The Japanese Disaster*). The quake and tsunami left nearly 28,000 people dead or missing, thousands homeless, and Japan's northeast coast devastated. Clearly, the first responsibility for Japan was to its people, but this disaster also threatened the country economically—not the least because 15 percent of its GDP was in its supply chain business to global firms ranging from semiconductor makers to shipbuilding.[53]

UNDER THE LENS
Global Supply Chain Risks—The Japanese Disaster[54]

With different component parts for everything from cell phones to cars being sourced from various countries, supply chains have become longer and far more complex to manage than in the past. It is not surprising, then, that companies around the world, from Lenovo to General Motors, had to scramble to find alternate supply sources after the Japanese earthquake and tsunami on March 11, 2011, disrupted supplies. As well as being a disaster for the Japanese people, major problems arose due to the nuclear alert, power shortages, damaged infrastructure, and loss of port access. At Hewlett Packard, for example, Tony Prophet, senior VP for Operations, gathered his team in the wee hours of the morning to brainstorm back-up plans for its $65 billion a year global supply chain, saying,

"It's like being in an emergency room, doing triage."[55]

The auto industry in particular was hard hit. Japan exports 2.5 million engines and 8.5 million transmissions annually to assembly plants around the world, and 2,200 parts are used in the typical vehicle. Ironically, it was the Japanese automakers with plants in the U.S. and Europe who were the most disrupted, not expecting to be able to get up to full production again for several months. Toyota, for example, which sources about 15 per cent of its parts from Japan for its U.S. plants, was reduced to about 30 percent of its normal production capacity.

General Motors set up its disaster response teams in three crisis rooms at its Vehicle Engineering Center in Warren, Michigan. Problems included being able to identify tiers of sub-suppliers and what parts were affected. Shortages led to temporary plant shutdowns. Lack of information due to communication outages was a problem, so GM sent 40 employees to Japan to visit suppliers; determine what parts were being held up and why, such as the supplier's inability to get the steel it needed to make the parts or to acquire enough electricity to run its factories; and to offer help.

These days, sourcing risk is somewhat reduced because sourcing is done globally, and technological developments have enabled the ability to management of these complex networks through Internet communications, RFID tags, and sensors attached to valued parts. In addition, sophisticated software can now be used for tracking and orchestrating the flow of goods worldwide. However, as supply chains become longer—that is suppliers of suppliers of suppliers—control is more difficult and, therefore, the risk is greater. A further difficulty is the lack of alternative sources for the thousands of tiny specialized parts for those ubiquitous electronics such as connectors, speakers, microphones, batteries, and sensors. If any of these parts cannot be sourced, the entire plant might be put on hold. Five parts in the Apple iPad, for example, come from Japanese suppliers.

Clearly, executives around the world have learned that there are unforeseen risks in implementing a global sourcing strategy—in particular combined with the just-in-time inventory practice. As a result, they realize that they need to have backup sourcing plans to manage the risk of supply chain disruption.

THE NEXT WAVE

Elsewhere we pointed out that many companies are moving from a single strategy of outsourcing—or offshoring—manufacturing or service operations, towards nearshoring to closer geographic regions and markets, or to reshoring to the 'home' country. Increasing labor costs overseas, as well as the distance and risks of supply chains and transportation, have made offshoring less competitive overall. Two trends are converging towards this next strategy of global sourcing—which McKinsey Consultants call 'next-shoring'—the trend away from labor cost arbitrage, and the trend towards robotics as technological advances provide the opportunity to digitize operations through the Internet of Things.[56] In this way, companies can use the advantages of production facilities which are geographically closer to their markets so as to adapt products locally, while at the same time using innovation and technology to offset the previous advantages of economies of scale through distant outsourcing.

Nextshoring strategies encompass elements such as a diverse and agile set of production locations, a rich network of innovation-oriented partnerships, and a strong focus on technical skills.

McKinsey Quarterly,
January 2014[57]

Implementing Strategies for Emerging Economy Firms

Firms from emerging economies have, out of necessity, expanded globally through different paths and strategies than the traditional paths firms in the developed world followed. Their motives for expansion into developed countries often include the need to acquire specific resources, such as technological know-how, R&D capability, managerial skills, and global brands to make them competitive with established firms. It is interesting to observe how those firms are coping with strategic implementation. Rather than the gradual, staged internationalization process typical of traditional firms from the developed world, the emerging firms—of all sizes—are finding that they have to move quickly or skip various stages to expand into both developed as well as developing markets.[58] As a result, firms such as Brazil's Natura Cosmeticos, China's Lenovo, and Argentina's Tenaris—now significant global players—have tended to expand globally through acquisitions and alliances and have had to be more flexible organizationally. Mauro F. Guillén and Estaban García-Canal point out from their research that firms from emerging and developing countries "face a significant dilemma when it comes to international expansion because they need to balance the desire for global reach with the need to upgrade their capabilities. They can readily use their home-grown competitive advantages in other emerging or developing countries, but they must also enter more advanced countries in order to expose themselves to sophisticated, cutting-edge demand and develop their capabilities."[59] As Guillén and García-Canal demonstrate in Exhibit 7-2, those firms must decide how to balance their geographic expansion with their ability to upgrade their capabilities in the market because they lack the resources and capabilities of established MNEs; they must realize that "prioritizing global reach without improving firm competencies jeopardizes the capability upgrading process."[60] (This puts them in the Unsustainable region in the exhibit.) Huei-Ting Tsai and Eisingerich also note "the dual challenge faced by emerging market firms, namely, market creation and/or R&D knowledge creation."[61] They note that firms with less technological and selling capabilities tend to enter new markets one at a time. In addition, firms with strong technological capabilities often expand to overseas markets shortly after the firm is established, as with Infosys (featured in the Management in Action feature nearby) They found from the firms in their sample that those that were stronger technologically and had more financial resources would compete in the developed markets, whereas those with a smaller stable of competitive resources pursued less-competitive markets during the early stages of their internationalization.

EXHIBIT 7-2 Expansion Paths for Emerging Economy Firms

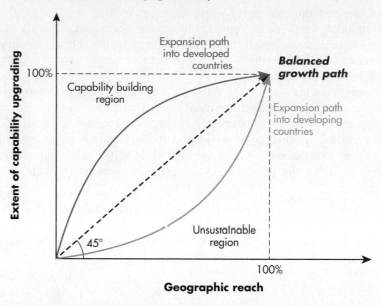

Source: Based on Mauro F. Guillén and Estaban García-Canal, "The American Model of the Multinational Firm and the 'New' Multinationals from Emerging Economies," *Academy of Management Perspectives*, May, 2009, pp. 23–35.

MANAGEMENT IN ACTION

Infosys's Path From Emerging Start-up to EMNE [62]

Infosys is one of the most fascinating success stories to come out of India—one of a start-up valued at $250 in 1981 to the over $36.1 billion (market cap as of Q3 2015) emerging market national enterprise (EMNE). It's path from a "born global" IT-services company to strategic alliances around the world is widely admired and reported.

Infosys was established by N. R. Narayana Murthy and six engineers in Pune, India, with an initial capital of $250. A central goal of Narayana Murthy's global strategy was the "global delivery model (GDM)," which focused on producing where it is most cost effective to produce and selling where it is most profitable to sell. As such, most of the software development work was done in India and the sales focused on the United States and other foreign markets. However, this model was competing with both foreign and Indian software companies such as Accenture, IBM Global Services, EDS, and TCS. From the beginning, Infosys focused the company on positioning it as a truly global company—global clients, global operations, global staff, and a global brand image. In 1987 the company opened its first international office in Boston, and in 1995 moved into the United Kingdom and Toronto, Canada. From there, global expansion happened rapidly as the company opened offices in Germany, Sweden, Belgium, Australia, and two development centers in the United States. As of 2015, Dr. Vishal Sikka is Infosys's CEO and Managing Director. The company has been a leader in establishing the Indian Business Process Outsourcing industry (BPO), now a global business. It is now the global leader in consulting, technology, and outsourcing solutions with 165,000 employees and clients in over 50 countries. The company's website emphasizes that its mission is based on "nurturing relationships that reflect our culture of unwavering ethics and mutual respect." In addition, Infosys is well recognized as a leader in sustainability efforts. Much of the company's success is attributed to its hybrid business models to include the best of the Indian culture and expectations, along with adapting to local business practices, and to the alliances and trust in developing new models with partners around the world.

In February 2015, Infosys bought U.S.-based Panaya in a $200 million deal in an effort to diversify away from its traditional outsourcing business into more lucrative opportunities in big data, cloud computing, and artificial intelligence.

Challenges in Implementing Strategies in Emerging Markets

Firms expanding into emerging, or developing, market countries are often unaware of the considerable differences from their home markets and the challenges they face in getting started. Because of their lack of familiarity and preparation for those challenges, foreign firms are often surprised that they cannot compete successfully with local firms. They may be operating under assumptions that firms from more developed countries have better experience, management knowledge, technology, and other resources than those in the target regions. Unfortunately, that mindset might lead foreign firms to enter those new markets without sufficient research and preparation for the differences and difficulties they may face. However, that is not the case with IKEA, the Swedish home furnishings giant. The company is absolutely committed to not expanding too rapidly; instead, it does extensive research on new locations. For example, it took six years before it opened its first store in South Korea.[63] The care the company takes to get familiar with the local area and the needs of the people there has certainly paid off; the company has 318 stores and around 50 franchised locations around the world and is one of the most profitable in the retail industry.

The initial challenge is likely to be how to navigate poor infrastructures, supply chains, and distribution networks—problems that local firms know how to navigate through experience and contacts. The same edge is enjoyed by local firms when dealing with the myriad regulations and bureaucracies prevalent in some developing economies.

Expansion into emerging markets also brings personnel challenges, especially at management levels. Here too, often the domestic companies have the advantage of knowing how to source, attract, and train local talent; those employees also tend to prefer to work for local companies that are perceived to be more invested in their future.[64] On the other hand, those employees often do not have the experience or familiarity with cross-border business compared with the foreign firms that may bring in their own talent.

Clearly, firms going into developing markets need to explore thoroughly how to navigate the infrastructure and institutions, evaluate the area for their personnel needs, and make local contacts to assess the feasibility of operating there and competing with local firms.

One firm, the global English-language social network LinkedIn, has found that it can make inroads in China through compromising on China's free-expression rules and developing local alliances with two Chinese venture-capital firms. Having local partners placates Chinese authorities and provides an incentive for the partners to make the venture a success. LinkedIn added a Chinese-language version, thereby adding about a million new members to the over four million it already had there.[65] Other technology firms, such as Facebook and Twitter, have been blocked from China, and Google is now in the authorities' bad books because of its about-face on its freedom of speech policies in 2010, as in no longer "cooperating" with the Chinese on what is allowed on the website. LinkedIn faced considerable backlash in the West for bowing to Chinese demands to take down content connected with the anniversary of the Tiananmen Square uprising.[66]

Managing Performance in International Joint Ventures

Much of the world's international business activity involves international joint ventures (IJVs) in which at least one parent is headquartered outside the venture's country of operation. IJVs require unique controls. Ignoring these specific control requisites can limit the parent company's ability to use its resources efficiently, coordinate its activities, and implement its strategy.

The term **IJV control** refers to the processes that management puts in place to direct the success of the firm's goals. Most of a firm's objectives can be achieved by careful attention to control features at the outset of the joint venture, such as the choice of a partner, the establishment of a strategic fit, and the design of the IJV organization. Howard Schultz, CEO of Starbucks, attributes its success in India to its joint venture with Tata Group, the largest coffee producer in Asia. This process followed a complicated six-year journey. Schultz acknowledged that Tata helped with finding highly desired locations, and the complex logistics and supply infrastructure, as well as the menus. Schultz admits there was much to learn, and that the key was finding a partner he could trust and with whom the firm could collaborate.[67]

Clearly the most important single factor determining IJV success or failure is the choice of a partner. Most problems with IJVs involve the local partner, especially in less-developed countries. In spite of this fact, many firms rush the process of partner selection because they are anxious to get on the bandwagon in an attractive market. In this process, it is vital to establish whether the partners' strategic goals are compatible (see Chapter 6). The strategic context and the competitive environment of the proposed IJV and the parent firm will determine the relative importance of the criteria used to select a partner.[68] IJV performance is also a function of the general fit between the international strategies of the parents, the IJV strategy, and the specific performance goals that the parents adopt.[69] Research has shown that, to facilitate this fit, the partner selection process must determine the specific task-related skills and resources needed from a partner as well as the relative priority of those needs.[70] To do this, managers must analyze their own firms and pinpoint any areas of weakness in task-related skills and resources that can be overcome with the help of the IJV partner.

Partnerships with companies in India present both positive and negative examples of IJV performance, although, overall, IJVs there run into considerable problems. McDonald's has had both experiences so far there. The company reported in February 2015 an ongoing legal battle with its 50 50 joint venture partner, Mr. Bakshi, in the north and east of the country due to a clash of business cultures and expectations which could take years to play out. However, its relationship with its 50–50 joint venture partner in the south and west, Amit Jatia, has been positive. In fact, Mr Jatia's Hardcastle Restaurants have now become a full franchisee, through a friendly buy-out of McDonald's share in the venture. Today, Hardcastle has 185 outlets, 85 of which opened in the past three years, and it plans to open between 175 and 250 more by 2020.[71] Of course both ventures were plagued in the early years by difficulty in adapting the menu to local tastes. Although India still insists on joint ventures in sectors such as telecommunications, agriculture, and insurance, it has lifted restrictions for other industries, allowing wholly owned operations in them. However, a number of recent IJVs have done poorly, especially for the Indian partner. On the other hand, an IJV between Indian engineering group Kirloskar and Japan's Toyota, for vehicle production, has had more positive results, with Mr. Kirloskar acknowledging that Toyota has been open in sharing ideas and improving the productivity of his firm.

Organizational design is another major mechanism for factoring in a means of control when an IJV is started. Beamish et al. discuss the important issue of the strategic freedom of an IJV. This refers to the relative amount of decision-making power that a joint venture will have, compared with the parents, in choosing suppliers, product lines, customers, and so on.[72] It is also crucial to consider beforehand the relative management roles each parent will play in the IJV because such decisions result in varying levels of control for different parties. An IJV is usually easier to manage if one parent plays a dominant role and has more decision-making responsibility than the other in daily operations. Alternatively, it is easier to manage an IJV if the local general manager has considerable management control, keeping both parents out of most of the daily operations.

International joint ventures are like a marriage: the more issues that can be settled before the merger, the less likely it will be to break up. Control over the stability and success of the IJV can be largely built into the initial agreement between the partners. The contract can specify who has what responsibilities and rights in a variety of circumstances, such as the contractual links of the IJV with the parents, the capitalization, and the rights and obligations regarding intellectual property. Of course, we cannot assume equal ownership of the IJV partners; where ownership is unequal, the partners will claim control and staffing choices proportionate to the ownership share. The choice of the IJV general manager, in particular, will influence the relative allocation of control because that person is responsible for running the IJV and for coordinating relationships with each of the parents.[73]

Where ownership is divided among several partners, the parents are more likely to delegate the daily operations of the IJV to the local IJV management—a move that resolves many potential disputes. In addition, the increased autonomy of the IJV tends to reduce many common human resource problems: staffing friction, blocked communication, and blurred organizational culture, to name a few, which all result from the conflicting goals and working practices of the parent companies.[74] Regardless of the number of parents, one way to avoid such potential problem situations is to provide special training to managers about the unique nature and problems of IJVs. The extent of control exercised over an IJV by its parent companies seems to be primarily determined by the decision-making autonomy that the parents delegate to the IJV management—which largely depends on staffing choices for the top IJV positions and thus on how much confidence the partners have in these managers. In addition, if top managers of the IJV are from the headquarters of each party, the compatibility of the managers will depend on how similar their national cultures are. This is because there are many areas of control decisions where agreement will be more likely between those of similar cultural backgrounds.[75]

Knowledge Management in IJVs

The most effective strategic leadership practices in the 21st century will be ones through which strategic leaders find ways for knowledge to breed still more knowledge.[76]

Managing the performance of an IJV for the long term, as well as adding value to the parent companies, necessitates managing the knowledge flows within the IJV network. When managed correctly, "alliances serve as a source of new knowledge for the firm."[77] Sirmon et al. contend that if firms can access and absorb this new knowledge, it can be used to alter existing capabilities or create new ones.[78] Yet, as found by Hitt et al., "cultural differences and institutional deficits can serve as barriers to the transfer of knowledge in alliance partnerships"[79] Clearly, then, managers need to recognize that it is critical to overcome cultural and system differences in managing knowledge flows to the advantage of the alliance.

Knowledge management, then, is "the conscious and active management of creating, disseminating, evolving, and applying knowledge to strategic ends."[80] Research on eight IJVs by Berdrow and Lane led them to define these processes as follows.

- *Transfer:* Managing the flow of existing knowledge between parents and from the parents to the IJV
- *Transformation:* Managing the transformation and creation of knowledge within the IJV through its independent activities
- *Harvest:* Managing the flow of transformed and newly created knowledge from the IJV back to the parents[81]

In particular, the sharing and development of technology among IJV partners provides the opportunity for knowledge transfer among individuals who have internalized that information, beyond any tangible assets; the challenge is to develop and harvest that information to benefit the parents through complementary synergies. IJVs that were successful in meeting that challenge were found to have personal involvement by the principals of the parent company in shared goals, in the activities and decisions being made, and in encouraging joint learning and coaching.[82]

The many operational activities and issues involved in strategic implementation—such as negotiating, organizing, staffing, leading, communicating, and controlling—are the subjects of other chapters in this book. Elsewhere, we include discussion of the many variables involved in strategic implementation that are specific to a particular country or region, such as goals, infrastructure, laws, technology, ways of doing business, people, and culture. In the following sections, the focus is on three pervasive influences on strategy implementation: government policy, societal culture, and the Internet.

Government Influences on Strategic Implementation

Host governments influence, in many areas, the strategic choices and implementations of foreign firms. The family-run Vermeer Company, for example, with its equipment-manufacturing factory in Pella, Iowa, earns about a third of its revenues from exports. However, the company realized its share of the market was falling rapidly due to competition from China, so it decided to open a plant in Beijing, taking a Chinese partner and drawing help for the venture from the Chinese. The chief executive, Ms. Mary Vermeer Andringa, noted that:

If we wanted to stay in the Chinese market, we needed to be there. That was the reality.[83]

The profitability of firms that set up operations abroad is greatly influenced, for example, by the level of taxation in the host country and by any restrictions on profit repatriation. Other important influences are government policies on ownership by foreign firms, on labor union rules, on hiring and remuneration practices, on patent and copyright protection, and so on. For the most part, however, if the corporation's managers have done the groundwork, all these factors are known beforehand and are part of the location and entry strategy decisions. However, what hurts managers is to set up shop in a host country and then have major economic or governmental policy changes after they have made a considerable investment. Vodafone, for example, the British mobile phone giant, bought an Indian wireless company in 2007 for $11 billion. However, it soon found the market was full of hazards—including a surprise tax bill of $2.5 billion and a corruption scandal over awarding contracts for additional wireless capacity.

> *In emerging markets "there are new hurdles every day, and they can change the rules of the market as you are playing it," Marten Pieters, the chief executive of Vodafone's India business, said.*
>
> *The lesson from India? "If you don't have the stomach for that," Mr. Pieters said, "please don't come."*

WWW.NYTIMES.COM
MARCH 27, 2011

Unpredictable changes in governmental regulations can be a death knell to businesses operating abroad. Recent changes in Russia causing uncertainty for foreign investors were already discussed. Another country that is often the subject of concern for foreign firms is China. Already one of the toughest countries for mergers and acquisitions, China recently added new restrictions on foreign investors, thus prolonging the time that a number of firms have to continue to wait to find out whether their deals will go through. "Acquisitions that will require the ministry's approval include companies with a well-known brand or those that could have an impact on 'China's economic security.'"[84] Although China contends it is more committed to a market economy since it joined the World Trade Organization (WTO) in November 2001, history shows that foreign firms need to be cautious about entering China, as illustrated in the chapter end case.

Running afoul of both governmental and cultural traditions is getting common among new-age companies, as exemplified by Uber, the $50 billion car-ride service operating in 60 countries:

> *Uber Collides With France—Company's growth snarled by entrenched business culture; 'a mockery of the French Republic'*

SAM SCHECHNER, WALL STREET JOURNAL,
SEPTEMBER 19, 2015[85]

Uber has created conflicts by rapidly entering markets and asking questions later, and, in the case of France, trying to overturn laws. After taxi drivers in Paris burned tires and stopped traffic, Uber managers realized the strength of the French business culture that favors government and local companies, when two of their executives were arrested for providing illegal taxi services. Beijing has another approach by launching a state-backed car-hailing app to compete with Uber.[86]

Cultural Influences on Strategic Implementation

When managers are responsible for implementing alliances among partners from diverse institutional environments, such as transition- and established-market economies, they are faced with the critical challenge of reconciling conflicting values, practices, and systems. Research by Danis shows how those important differences among Hungarian managers and Western expatriates can affect implementation. When considering key differences in practices, for example, Danis found that the Western expatriates evinced a team orientation, a consensual management style, and a future-planning mentality. This compared with the findings for the Hungarian managers, who showed an individual orientation, an autocratic management style, and a survival mentality.[87] Such advance knowledge can provide expatriate managers with valuable information to help them in successful local operations.

In other situations, the culture variable is often overlooked when deciding on and implementing entry strategies and alliances, particularly when we perceive the target country to be familiar to us and similar to our own. However, cultural differences can have a subtle and often negative effect. In fact, in a study of 129 U.K. cross-border acquisitions in continental

Europe, Schoenberg found that 54 percent of the acquiring firms cited poor performance resulting from the implementation of their acquisitions compared to their domestic mergers.[88] The researchers' study of those firms revealed six dimensions of national and corporate cultural differences between the management styles of the U.K. firms and the continental European firms.

CULTURAL DIFFERENCES IN U.K.–EUROPEAN ALLIANCES

- Organizational formality
- The extent of participation in decision making
- Attitude toward risk
- Systemization of decision making
- Managerial self-reliance
- Attitudes toward funding and gearing (financial leveraging)[89]

Among these dimensions, risk orientation was the key factor that affected the performance of the combined firm because risk-taking propensity affects managers' approach toward strategic options. Overall, risk-taking firms are likely to pursue aggressive strategies and deal well with change, whereas risk-averse companies are likely to tread more carefully and employ incremental strategies. Clearly, for companies entering into an IJV, successful implementation will depend largely on careful planning to take account of such differences, in particular that of risk orientation, to improve organizational compatibility. The greater the cultural distance between the allied firms, the more likely problems will emerge such as conflict regarding the level of innovation and the kinds of investments each firm is willing to pursue.

Because many of Europe's largest MNCs—including Nestlé, Electrolux, Grand Metropolitan, and Rhone-Poulenc—experience increasing proportions of their revenues from their positions in the United States and employ more than 2.9 million Americans, they have decided to shift the headquarters of some product lines to the United States. As they have done so, however, there is growing evidence that managing in the United States is not as easy as they anticipated it would be because of their perceived familiarity with the culture. Rosenzweig documents some reflections of European managers on their experiences of managing U.S. affiliates. Generally, he has found that European managers appreciate that Americans are pragmatic, open, forthright, and innovative. However, they also say that the tendency of Americans to be informal and individualistic means that their need for independence and autonomy on the job causes problems in their relationship with the head office Europeans. Americans simply do not take well to directives from a foreign-based headquarters.[90] Rosenzweig presents some comments from French managers on their activities in the United States.

FRENCH MANAGERS COMMENT ON THEIR ACTIVITIES IN THE UNITED STATES

- Americans see themselves as the world's leading country, and it's not easy for them to accept having a European in charge.
- It is difficult for Americans to develop a world perspective. It's hard for them to see that what may optimize the worldwide position may not optimize the U.S. activities.
- The horizon of Americans often goes only as far as the U.S. border. As a result, Americans often don't give equal importance to a foreign customer. If a foreign customer has a special need, the response is sometimes: It works here, why do they need it to be different?
- It might be said that Americans are the least international of all people, because their home market is so big.[91]

Other European firms have had more successful strategic implementation in their U.S. plants by adapting to U.S. culture and management styles. When Mercedes-Benz of Germany launched its plant in Tuscaloosa, Alabama, U.S. workers and German trainers had doubts. Lynn Snow, who works on the car-door line of the Alabama plant, was skeptical of whether the Germans and the

Americans would mesh well. Now, she proudly asserts that they work together, determined to build a quality vehicle. As Jürgen Schrempp, then CEO of Mercedes's parent, Daimler-Benz, observed, "'Made in Germany'—we have to change that to 'Made by Mercedes,' and never mind where they are assembled."[92]

The German trainers recognized that the whole concept of building a Mercedes quality car had to be taught to the U.S. workers in a way that would appeal to them. They abandoned the typically German strict hierarchy and instead designed a plant in which any worker could stop the assembly line to correct manufacturing problems. In addition, taking their cue from Japanese rivals, they formed the workers into teams that met every day with the trainers to problem solve. Out the window went formal offices and uniforms, replaced by casual shirts with personal names on the pocket. To add to the collegiality, get-togethers for a beer after work became common. "The most important thing is to bring together the two cultures," says Andreas Renschler, who has guided the M-Class since it began in 1993. "You have to generate a kind of ownership of the plant."[93] The local community has also embraced the mutual goals, often having beer fests and including German-language stations on local cable TV.

The impact of cultural differences in management style and expectations is perhaps most noticeable and important when implementing international joint ventures, mergers, or acquisitions. The complexity of such alliances requires managers from each party to learn to compromise to create a compatible and productive working environment, particularly when operations are integrated.

In China, too, strategic implementation necessitates an understanding of the pervasive cultural practice of *guanxi* in business dealings. Discussed in previous chapters, *guanxi* refers to the relationship networks that "bind millions of Chinese firms into social and business webs, largely dictating their success."[94] Tapping into this system of reciprocal social obligation is essential to get permits, information, assistance to access material and financial resources, and tax considerations. Nothing gets done without these direct or indirect connections. In fact, a new term has arisen—*guanxihu*—which refers to a bond between specially connected firms that generates preferential treatment for members of the network. Without *guanxi*, even implementing a strategy of withdrawal is difficult. Joint ventures can become hard to dissolve and as bitter as an acrimonious divorce. Problems include the forfeiture of assets and the inability to gain market access through future joint venture partners—all experienced by Audi, Chrysler, and Daimler-Benz. For example:

> Audi's decision to terminate its joint venture prompted its Chinese partner, First Automobile Works, to expropriate its car design and manufacturing processes. The result was an enormously successful, unauthorized Audi clone, with a Chrysler engine and a First Automobile Works nameplate.[95]

E-Commerce Impact on Strategy Implementation

> With subsidiaries, suppliers, distributors, manufacturing facilities, carriers, brokers, and customers all over the globe, global trade is complicated and fragmented. Shipments cross borders multiple times a day. Are they compliant with all the latest trade regulations? Are they consistently classified for each country? Can you give your buyers, customers, and service providers the latest information, on demand?[96]

As indicated in this quote, global trade is extremely complicated. Deciding on a global strategy is one thing; implementing it through all the necessary parties and intermediaries around the world presents a whole new level of complexity. Because of that complexity, many firms decide to implement their global e-commerce strategy by outsourcing the necessary tasks to **e-commerce enablers**, companies that specialize in providing the technology to organize transactions and follow through with the regulatory requirements. These specialists can help companies sort through the maze of different taxes, duties, language translations, and so on specific to each country. Such services allow small and medium-sized companies to go global without the internal capabilities to carry out global e-commerce functions These kinds of web-based services allow a company to manage an entire global trade operation, including automation of imports and exports by screening orders and generating the appropriate documentation, paying customs charges, complying with trade agreements, and so on.[97]

CONCLUSION

Cross-border strategic alliances are becoming increasingly common as innovative companies seek rapid entry into foreign markets and as they try to reduce the risks of going it alone in complex environments. Companies that do well are those that do their groundwork and pick complementary strategic partners. Too many, however, divorce because the devil is in the details—which is what happens when a marriage made in heaven runs into unanticipated problems, such as cultural clashes and government restrictions, during actual strategic implementation. Alliances in various forms are particularly important for emerging market firms to expand to developed economies. For SMEs, they too can work to ally with MNCs in the target locations to internationalize quickly.

Summary of Key Points

- Strategic alliances are partnerships with other companies for specific reasons. Cross-border, or global, strategic alliances are working partnerships between companies (often more than two) across national boundaries and, increasingly, across industries.
- Cross-border alliances are formed for many reasons, including market expansion, cost- and technology-sharing, avoiding protectionist legislation, and taking advantage of synergies.
- SMEs can overcome their resource constraints and accelerate their internationalization process by leveraging their network relationships with other companies—such as key clients or strategic partners. Strategies include forming MNC relationships, consolidating those relationships with MNCs, and then extending the relationships to other endeavors.
- Alliances may be short or long term; they may be full global partnerships, or they may be for more narrow and specific functions such as research and development sharing.
- Alliances often run into trouble in the strategic implementation phase. Problems include loss of technology and knowledge skill-base to the other partner, conflicting strategic goals and objectives, cultural clashes, and disputes over management and control systems.
- Emerging economy firms are finding that they have to move quickly or skip various stages to expand into both developed as well as developing markets. They tend to expand globally through acquisitions and alliances and have had to be more flexible organizationally. Their motives in developing alliances often include the need to access specific resources such as technology or management skills to compete globally.
- Successful alliances require compatible partners with complementary skills, products, and markets. Extensive preparation is necessary to work out how to share management control and technology and to understand each other's culture.
- Strategic implementation—also called *functional level strategies*—is the process of setting up overall policies, administrative responsibilities, and schedules throughout the organization. Successful implementation results from setting up the structure, systems, and processes of the firm as well as the functional activities that create a *system of fits* with the desired strategy.
- Differences in national culture and changes in the political arena or in government regulations often have unanticipated effects on strategic implementation.
- Strategic implementation of global trade is increasingly being facilitated by *e-commerce enablers*—companies that specialize in providing the software and Internet technology for complying with the specific regulations, taxes, shipping logistics, translations, and so on for each country with which their clients do business.

Discussion Questions

7-1. Discuss the reasons that companies embark on cross-border strategic alliances. What other motivations may prompt such alliances? What are the driving forces for firms in emerging economies to embark on strategic alliances? How can SMEs expand abroad through relationships with MNCs?

7-2. Why are there an increasing number of mergers with companies in different industries? Give some examples. What industry do you think will be the next for global consolidation?

7-3. Discuss the problems inherent in developing a cooperative alliance to enhance competitive advantage, which also incurs the risk of developing a new competitor.

7-4. What are the common sources of incompatibility in cross-border alliances? What can be done to minimize them?

7-5. Explain what is necessary for companies to implement a global sourcing strategy successfully.

7-6. Discuss the political and economic situation in the Russian Federation with your class. What has changed since this writing? What are the implications for foreign companies to start a joint venture there now?

7-7. What is involved in strategic implementation? What is meant by creating a *system of fits* with the strategic plan?

7-8. Explain how the host government may affect strategic implementation—in an alliance or another form of entry strategy.

7-9. How might the variable of national culture affect strategic implementation? Consider the earlier comments by French and British managers regarding Americans as examples to highlight some of these factors.

7-10. Discuss the importance of knowledge management in IJVs and what can be done to enhance the effectiveness of that process.

Application Exercise

7-11. Research some recent joint ventures with foreign companies situated in India or Russia. How are they doing? Bring your information to class for discussion. What is the climate for foreign investors in developing economies at the time of your reading this chapter?

CASE STUDY

Foreign Companies in China Under Attack[1]

Century Square, Nanjing Road, China

While China is still a very attractive and growing market for foreign businesses, a number of prominent companies are experiencing a sharp increase in problems while operating there. This was confirmed by the AmCham China Business Survey in 2014, which indicated that 60 percent of members feel less welcome than before, up from 41 percent a year ago. Their member firms report continuing challenges, including rising labor costs, inconsistent application of laws, confusing information, pressure from government-owned departments, political tensions, and slowing growth. In addition, a number of targeted attacks on foreign firms have deterred many European and U.S. firms from either new or increased investment in China.

In targeting technology companies through an antitrust investigation, China's National Development and Reform Commission concluded that the U.S. chip manufacturer Qualcomm had used monopoly tactics to set preferable licensing fees. The move was seen as giving preference to local companies, and the U.S. Chamber of Commerce has accused the Chinese government of protectionism and violating its commitments according to the World Trade Organization, which China joined in 2001. Microsoft was also the subject of yet another investigation in early September as Chinese officials made unannounced inspections of Microsoft's offices in Beijing, Shanghai, Guangzhou, and Chengdu. This move followed a purchasing ban on Microsoft's Windows 8 PC software in May by the Chinese government, supposedly over security concerns following the revelations of spying by the United States made by Edward Snowden.

Targeting other industries, the U.S. food processor OSI Group, supplier to a number of fast-food chains in China for over 20 years, was accused of using expired meat. Chinese regulators and persistent reporting of alleged problems on state media put a sudden halt to OSI's operations. The authorities closed down the plant, and restaurants such as McDonald's and Burger King cancelled further orders with OSI. While there may have been a problem, the company was treated very harshly given that no test results were given and there were no reports of illness from the OSI products.

Chinese regulators have been targeting various industries, as well as technology and food processing, including pharmaceuticals, car companies, and in particular, high-profile companies. The U.S. Chamber of Commerce has accused China of using the antimonopoly law to force foreign companies to cut prices. Mercedes-Benz staff, for example, were shocked when ten men from the antitrust investigators from China's National Development and Reform Commission (NDRC) roughly entered the company's east China sales office near Shanghai's Hongqiao international airport and subjected employees to intense questions for ten hours, rifling through the offices and demanding data and other information. More and more foreign companies have been subjected to early morning raids and had their desks, computers, safes, files, and so on inspected and "evidence" taken away, often downloading data from the companies' computers. Legal rights typical in Europe and North America are not acknowledged in China, and information is difficult to acquire about the processes there. It seems that China's antitrust enforcement agencies, the NDRC, and the State Administration for Industry and Commerce (SAIC), has become increasingly aggressive in seizing all evidence that could give them leads to other companies for antitrust violations or corruption.

For their part, the Chinese authorities claim that the investigations are to keep competition fair and to protect consumer rights. However, often the investigators advise foreign companies not to seek legal advice; in addition, European companies reporting to the European Chamber of Commerce claim that they have been intimidated into accepting punitive measures without requesting a court hearing. In fact, 61 percent of European companies that have a long tenure operating in China now say that doing business there is getting more difficult.

A number of Western firms blame poor regulation in the supply chains and stricter imposition of regulations than on Chinese firms. As a result, firms such as Walmart and others involved in food have set up their own supply sources and implemented their own inspection and oversight of their supply chains. These moves, however, raise the overall costs of their products.

While there are many challenges for foreign companies operating in China, the activities described here are blatant and have resulted in a considerable decline in firms wanting to operate there, according to the AmCham survey. The survey concluded that further deterioration of the investment climate would harm ventures and linkages among countries for some time.

Notes

1. **Andrew Browne, Laurie Burkitt**, "U.S. Firms Feel Unwelcome in China, According to Survey; U.S. Companies Say They Have Become Targets of China's Antimonopoly and Anticorruption Campaigns," *Wall Street Journal*, September 2, 2014; AmCham China 16th Annual Business Climate Survey, *http://www.amchamchina.org/businessclimate2014*, accessed September 2, 2014; Richard Waters, "China Probe Targets Microsoft," *Financial Times*, July 29, 2014; Laurie Burkitt, Andrew Browne, "After China Meat Scandal, Troubles for OSI Reflect Broader Perils for Business; Beijing's Scrutiny Increases as Bad Publicity's Effects Move Swiftly," *Wall Street Journal*, September 2, 2014; Michelle Price and Norihiko Shirouzu, "Food and flirting; how firms learn to live with China antitrust raids," *Reuters*, August 10, 2014; Laurie Burkitt, "China's Use of Antimonopoly Law May Violate Its WTO Commitments; U.S. Chamber of Commerce Report Says China's Use of Its Antimonopoly Law Has Been Subjective," *Wall Street Journal (Online) [New York, N.Y] 08 Sep 2014.*

Case Questions

7-12. What factors do you think are behind these events? Do some research to find out whether there have been more such problems since this writing. Is it just American companies that are being targeted?

7-13. What can firms currently operating in China, or considering investment there, do to lessen the likelihood of these problems for their managers?

Endnotes

1. D. Lei and J. W. Slocum, Jr., "Global Strategic Alliances: Payoffs and Pitfalls," *Organizational Dynamics* (Winter 1991).

2. Jung-Ho Lai, Shao-Chi Chang, and Sheng-Syan Chen, "Is Experience Valuable in International Strategic Alliances?" *Journal of International Management* 16 (2010), pp. 247–261; J. Walter, C. Lechner, F. W. Kellermanns, "Disentangling Alliance Management Processes: Decision Making, Politicality, and Alliance Performance," *Journal of Management Studies* 45, No. 3 (2008), p. 530.

3. Peter Loftus, "Lilly Joins with Chinese Biotech to Develop, Market Cancer Drugs," *Wall Street Journal*, March 20, 2015.

4. Vikas Bajaj, "After a Year of Delays, the First Starbucks Is to Open in Tea-Loving India This Fall," *New York Times*, January 20, 2012.

5. Ibid.

6. J. Griffiths, "A Marriage of Two Mindsets," *Financial Times*, March 16, 2005.

7. Ibid.

8. Ibid.

9. James Fontanella, "Buffett backs Brazil Private Equity Conquest of U.S. Food Industry," www.ft.com, March 26, 2015.

10. Bill Vlasic and Nick Bunkley, "Alliance with Fiat Gives Chrysler Another Partner and Lifeline," www.nytimes.com, January 21, 2009.

11. Micheline Maynard, "Chrysler Bankruptcy Plan Is Announced," www.nytimes.com, April 30, 2009.

12. Ibid.

13. Douglas Macmillan, Rick Carew, "Uber rivals form Global Alliance in Counterattack," Wall Street Journal, September 17, 2015.

14. Thomas Friedman, *The World Is Flat* (New York: Farrar, Straus and Giroux, 2005), p. 144.

15. www.covisint.com, accessed March 24, 2015.

16. www.e4engineering.com, January 4, 2001.

17. Tim Burt, "Disney's Asian Adventure," *Financial Times*, October 30, 2003.

18. Ibid.

19. Ibid.

20. Ibid.

21. Tim Bradshaw, "Apple Buys Big Data Analyser, Mapsense," FT.com, September 17, 2015.

22. Andres Parker and Gerrit Wiesmann, "Cross-border Sensitivities Give Grounds for Pessimism," *Financial Times*, September 9, 2009.

23. David Lei, "Offensive and Defensive Uses of Alliances," in Heidi Vernon-Wortzel and L. H. Wortzel, *Strategic Management in Global Economy*, 3rd ed. (New York: John Wiley & Sons, 1997).

24. Lei, 1997.

25. *New York Times*, January 17, 2011.

26. Shameen Prashantham and Julian Birkinshaw, "Dancing with Gorillas: How Small Companies Can Partner Effectively with MNCs," *California Management Review* 51, No. 1 (2008), pp. 6–23.

27. Ibid.

28. Dovev Lavie, "Capturing Value from Alliance Portfolios," *Organizational Dynamics* 38, No. 1 (2009), pp. 26–36.

29. Ibid.

30. Ibid.

31. Lei, 1997.

32. Wheelen and Hunger.

33. A. E. Serwer, "McDonald's Conquers the World," *Fortune*, October 17, 1994.

34. http://www3.weforum.org/docs/WEF_GCR_Russia_Report_2014.

35. Maria Kiselyova, "Nestle Keeps Faith with Russia Despite Turmoil," www.nytimes.com, March 24, 2015.

36. Ibid.

37. Henry Sender, Anne Sylvaine Chassaney, "Blackstone Calls it a Day in Russia After Sanctions Freeze Investor Appetite," *Financial Times*, September 22, 2015.

38. http://www3.weforum.org/docs/WEF_GCR_Russia_Report_2011.

39. Sheila M. Puffer and Daniel J. McCarthy, "Two Decades of Russian Business and Management Research: An Institutional Theory Perspective," *Academy of Management Perspectives*, May 2011, pp. 21–36.

40. "Russia's Retail Revolution," www.managementtoday.co.uk, June 1, 2008.

41. N. Buckley, "An Unmissable Opportunity," *Financial Times*, April 5, 2005.

42. Maria Kiselyova, "Nestle Keeps Faith with Russia Despite Turmoil," www.nytimes.com, March 24, 2015.

43. Puffer and McCarthy, May 2011.

44. N. Buckley, "Huge Gains but Also a Lot of Pain," *Financial Times*, October 11, 2005.

45. Garry Bruton, David Ahlstrom, Michael Young, and Yuri Rubanik, "In Emerging Markets, Know What Your Partners Expect," December 15, 2008.

46. Jack Welch (then CEO of GE) interviewed in *Fortune*, March 8, 1999.

47. "U.S. Exports to China Rebound in 2010," *China Business Review*, July–September, 2011.

48. Jonathan Friedrich, Amit Noam, Elie Nofek, "Right Up the Middle: How Israeli Firms Go Global," *Harvard Business Review*, May 2014.

49. P. Engardio, "The Future of Outsourcing," *BusinessWeek*, January 30, 2006, p. 50.

50. Ibid.

51. Based on M. Kripalani, D. Foust, S. Holmes, and P. Enga, "Five Offshore Practices That Pay Off," *BusinessWeek*, January 30, 2006, p. 60.

52. Josh Green, *Harvard Business Review* 87, No. 7/8 (2009), p. 19.

53. "Japan Seeks Russian Help to End Nuclear Crisis," *Financial Post* (Karachi), April 6, 2011.

54. Steve Lohr, "Stress Test for the Global Supply Chain," www.nytimes.com, March 19, 2011; Nick Bunkley, "G.M. Pieces Together a Japanese Supply Chain," www.nytimes.com, May 12, 2011; Anonymous, "Japan Earthquake: Global Supply Chains to Suffer Extensive Disruption," *Business Wire* (New York), March 17, 2011; Nigel Davis, "Japan's Crisis Affects Global Supply Chains," *ICIS Chemical Business*, March 28–April 3, 2011.

55. Steve Lohr.

56. Katy George, Sree Ramaswamy, and Lou Rassey, "Next-Shoring: A CEO's Guide," *McKinsey Quarterly*, January 2014.

57. Ibid.

58. Huei-Ting Tsai and Andreas B. Eisingerich, "Internationalization Strategies of Emerging Market Firms," *California Management Review*, 53, No. 1 (Fall 2010.).

59. Mauro F. Guillén and Estaban García-Canal, "The American Model of the Multinational Firm and the 'New' Multinationals from Emerging Economies," *Academy of Management Perspectives*, May 2009, pp. 23–35.

60. Ibid.

61. Huei-Ting Tsai, 2010.

62. www.infosys.com, accessed March 24, 2015; Sudheer Gupta and Daniel Shapiro, "Building and Transforming An Emerging Market Global Enterprise: Lessons from the Infosys Journey," *Business Horizons*, (2014) 57, 169–179.; James Crabtree, "Infosys Buys U.S. Technology Group Panaya," *FT.com*, February 17, 2015; http://www.icmrindia.org/free%20resources/casestudies/Narayana, accessed March 24, 2015.

63. Beth Kowitt, "It's Ikea's World," *Fortune*, March 15, 2015, 166–175.

64. "Mahindra and Mahindra (B): An Emerging Global Giant?" Case study from IBSCDC India.

65. Paul Mozur and Vindu Goel, "To Reach China LinkedIn Plays by Local Rules," www.nytimes.com, October 5, 2014.

66. "LinkedIn Faces Flak for Censoring onBehalf of China," Asia News Monitor [Bangkok] 06 June 2014.

67. Howard Schultz, "The Power of Partnership," in R*eimagining India: Unlocking the Potential of Asia's Next Superpower.* Copyright © 2013 by McKinsey & Company. Published by Simon & Schuster, Inc.

68. J. M. Geringer, "Strategic Determinants of Partner Selection Criteria in International Joint Ventures," *Journal of International Business Studies* (First Quarter 1991), pp. 41–62.

69. J. M. Geringer and L. Hebert, "Control and Performance of International Joint Ventures," *Journal of International Business Studies* 20, No. 2 (1989).

70. Geringer, 1991.

71. Amy Kazmin, "Indian Partnership Leaves Sour Taste for McDonald's: Culture Clash," *Financial Times*, February 13, 2015.

72. P. W. Beamish et al., *International Management* (Homewood, IL: Irwin, 1991).

73. J. L. Schaan and P. W. Beamish, "Joint Venture General Managers in Less Developed Countries," in *Cooperative Strategies in International Business*, F. Contractor and P. Lorange, eds. (Toronto: Lexington Books, 1988), pp. 279–299.

74. Oded Shenkar and Yoram Zeira, "International Joint Ventures: A Tough Test for HR," *Personnel* (January 1990), pp. 26–31.

75. R. Mead, *International Management* (Cambridge, MA: Blackwell Publishers, 1994).

76. R. Duane Ireland and M. A. Hitt, "Achieving and Maintaining Strategic Competitiveness in the 21st Century: The Role of Strategic Leadership," *Academy of Management Executive* 19, Nno. 4 (2005), p.: 63.

77. R. S. Bhagat, B. L. Kedia, P. D. Harveston, and H. C. Triandis, "Cultural Variations in the Cross-Border Transfer of Organizational Knowledge: An Integrative Framework," *Academy of Management Review* 27, No. 2 (2002), pp. 204–221.

78. D. G. Sirmon, M. A. Hitt, R. D. Ireland, in press. "Managing Firm Resources in Dynamic Environments to Create Value: Looking Inside the Black Box," *Academy of Management Review* 32., No. 1 (January 2007), pp. 273–292.

79. M. H. Hitt, V. Franklin, and Hong Zhu, "Culture, Institutions and International Strategy," *Journal of International Management* 12, No. 2 (2002), pp. 222–234.

80. I. Berdrow and H. W. Lane, "International Joint Ventures: Creating Value through Successful Knowledge Management," *Journal of World Business* 38, No. 1 (2003), pp. 15–30.

81. Ibid.

82. Ibid.

83. Louis Uchitelle, "Is Manufacturing Falling off the Radar?" *New York Times*, September 10, 2011.

84. "China's New Restrictions on Deals," *Financial Times*, August 10, 2006.

85. Sam Schechner, "Uber Collides With France—Company's Growth Snarled by Entrenched Business Culture; 'A Mockery of the French Republic,'" *Wall Street Journal* 19 Sep 2015: A.1.

86. Patti Waldmeir, "Beijing Joins Ranks of Car-Hailing Apps," FT.com, September 19, 2015.

87. W. M. Danis, "Differences in Values, Practices, and Systems among Hungarian Managers and Western Expatriates: An Organizing Framework and Typology," *Journal of World Business* (August 2003), pp. 224–244.

88. R. Schoenberg, "Dealing with a Culture Clash," *Financial Times*, September 23, 2006.

89. Ibid.

90. P. Rosenzweig, "Why Is Managing in the United States so Difficult for European Firms?" *European Management Journal* 12, No. 1 (1994), pp. 31–38.

91. Ibid.

92. "In Alabama, the Soul of a New Mercedes?" *BusinessWeek*, March 31, 1997.

93. Ibid.

94. J. A. Pearce II and R. B. Robinson Jr., "Cultivating *Guanxi* as a Foreign Investor Strategy," *Business Horizons* 43, No. 1 (2000), pp. 31.

95. Ibid.

96. www.NextLinx.com, September 10, 2001.

97. Ibid.

8 Organization Structure and Control Systems

OUTLINE

OBJECTIVES

8-1. To understand the importance of appropriate organizational structures to effective strategy implementation.

8-2. To become familiar with the types of organizational designs suitable for the level and scope of internationalization of the firm.

8-3. To understand the role of technology in the evolution of the networked structure and to appreciate the role of teams in achieving business goals.

8-4. To realize how organizational design affects the manager's job, for example, on the level and location of decision making.

8-5. To emphasize the role of control and monitoring systems suitable for specific situations and locations in the firm's international operations.

Opening Profile: BMG Signs Distribution Deal with Alibaba

CHARLES CLOVER IN BEIJING AND JEEVAN VASAGAR ROBERT COOKSON
FT.com, March 30, 2015

China's leading ecommerce group Alibaba has signed a distribution deal with music company BMG in the latest content deal featuring Chinese internet companies.

The value of the deal was not disclosed but includes digital rights to more than 2.5m recordings from artists that range from the Rolling Stones and Black Sabbath to Kylie Minogue and will.i.am.

The tie-up is an indication of Alibaba's intention to grow its share of the music market and comes in the wake of a similar deal by rival Tencent in November with Warner Music Group.

But the Alibaba deal also reflects optimism in the music industry that it is possible to make money in China, which has long been a centre for piracy.

BMG, which says it is the world's fourth-largest music rights company, said the deal is the latest step in a plan unveiled 12 months ago to make China a priority territory. BMG said the deal will put China "in the top 10 (countries) for revenue." Hitherto, he said, China was outside the top 25.

Over the past three years, the major record companies have signed licensing agreements with China's eight biggest online music services. A crackdown against sharing sites and "subtitle" sites that show copyrighted material has also been under way since the spring of last year.

The progress on intellectual property issues in China reflects the desire of Chinese internet groups to expand internationally into countries with tougher copyright regimes, making them more amenable to finding accommodation with intellectual property owners.

BMG chief executive Hartwig Masuch said in a statement released by the company that the internet and particular mobile media are giving an "answer to the music industry's long-time challenge of how to monetise the vast untapped potential of the Chinese market. We are delighted to link with such a powerful and dynamic partner as Alibaba."

Alibaba said its key asset in the deal would be troves of Chinese customer data that it has successfully begun mining to attract new customers.

Patrick Liu, president of Alibaba's Digital Entertainment business unit, said the model he envisaged "combines music with e-commerce in China's entertainment sector. Our rich experience in big data analysis will help us lead innovation in the music industry that ultimately enhances customer experience."

The alliance with Alibaba follows the announcement in November 2014 that BMG had struck a worldwide deal with Chinese independent music company Giant Jump to manage its music publishing and recording rights both domestically and internationally.

Strategic plans are abstract sets of decisions that cannot affect a company's competitive position or bottom line until they are implemented. Having decided on the strategic direction for the company, international managers must then consider two of the key variables for implementing strategy: the organizational structure and the control and monitoring mechanisms. The necessity of adapting organizational structures to facilitate changes in strategy, competitive moves, and changes in the environment is illustrated in this opening profile describing Alibaba's reorganization to accommodate new strategic directions in the music industry. Alibaba, founded by Jack Ma in his one-bedroom apartment, and which recently went public on the New York Stock Exchange (NYSE), is the largest e-commerce company in China and now a global online marketplace. Its organization connects manufacturers in China with small businesses globally. Alibaba's organization involves multiple marketplaces and business models organized in different sites and styles targeted at global audiences.[1] Clearly, any e-company such as Alibaba has technology as its organizational model, unlike traditional models. As we proceed through this chapter, we need to keep in mind the effects of the Internet and, in particular, the "Internet of Things." on how firms are structured and how that affects responsibilities.

With its emphasis on brokering transactions into and out of China, it {Alibaba} also promises to enable a new age of border hopping commerce that bypasses middlemen and erodes the ability of governments to regulate trade.

BLOOMBERG BUSINESS WEEK
AUGUST 15, 2014[2]

ORGANIZATIONAL STRUCTURE

There is no permanent organization chart for the world.... It is of supreme importance to be ready at all times to take advantage of new opportunities.

ROBERT C. GOIZUETA
(FORMER) CHAIRMAN AND CEO, COCA-COLA COMPANY[3]

Organizational structures must change to accommodate a firm's evolving internationalization in response to worldwide competition. Considerable research has shown that a firm's structure must be conducive to the implementation of its strategy.[4] In other words, the structure must fit the strategy, or it will not work. Managers are faced with how best to attain that fit in organizing the company's systems and tasks. The failure to adapt to changing market conditions both strategically and structurally is demonstrated by the short life span of even large companies. This is particularly apparent in times of radical change such as when new technologies appear and during the economic relapse that started in 2008 and resulted in many firms, such as Eastman Kodak Inc. and Borders Bookstores, going out of business or filing for Chapter 11 bankruptcy. Even General Motors, one of the largest global companies, was tipped over the edge into bankruptcy after decades of poor management, surviving only with radical downsizing and government aid. Comparatively, IBM has adapted in various ways. After realizing that the company had missed opportunities for growth initiatives, it developed its EBO (emerging business opportunities) model into three horizons—current core businesses, growth businesses, and future growth businesses.[5]

The design of an organization, as with any other management function, should be contingency based, taking into account the variables of that particular system at that specific point in time. Major variables include the firm's strategy, size, and appropriate technology as well as the environment where the firm operates. Given the increased complexity of the variables involved in the international context, it is no easy task to design the most suitable organizational structure and subsystems. In fact, research shows that most international managers find it easier to determine what to do to compete globally (strategy) than to decide how to develop the organizational capability (structure) to do it.[6] Additional variables affecting structural choices—geographic dispersion as well as differences in time, language, cultural attitudes, technology, and business practices—introduce further layers of complication. We will show how organizational structures need to, and typically do, change to accommodate strategies of increasing internationalization.

EVOLUTION AND CHANGE IN MNC ORGANIZATIONAL STRUCTURES

Historically, a firm reorganizes as it internationalizes to accommodate new strategies. The structure typically continues to change over time with growth and with increasing levels of investment or diversity and as a result of the types of entry strategy chosen. Internationalization is the process by which a firm gradually changes in response to international competition, domestic market saturation, and the desire for expansion, new markets, cost effectiveness, and diversification. As discussed in Chapter 6, a firm's managers weigh alternatives and decide on appropriate entry strategies. Perhaps the firm starts by exporting or by acting as a licensor or licensee and then, over time, continues to internationalize by engaging in joint ventures or by establishing service, production, or assembly facilities or alliances abroad, moving into a global strategy. At each stage, the firm's managers redesign the organizational structure to optimize the strategy's chances to work, making changes in the firm's tasks and relationships and designating authority, responsibility, lines of communication, geographic dispersal of units, and so forth. This model of **structural evolution** has become known as the **stages model**, resulting from Stopford's research on 187 U.S. multinational corporations (MNCs).[7] Of course, many firms do not follow the stages model because they may start their internationalization at a higher level of involvement—perhaps a full-blown global joint venture without ever having exported, for example, or a born global e company.

Even a mature MNC must make structural changes from time to time to facilitate changes in strategy—perhaps a change in strategy from globalization to regionalization (see Chapter 6) or an effort to improve efficiency or effectiveness. The reorganization of Aluminum Company of America (Alcoa), for example, split the company into smaller, more autonomous units, thereby giving more focus to growing businesses, such as automotive products, where the market for aluminum is strong. It also enabled Alcoa to link businesses with similar functions that are geographically divided—that is, to improve previously insufficient communication between Alcoa's aluminum operations in Brazil and its Australian counterparts. Alcoa, as with most MNCs, has found the need to adapt its structure continuously to accommodate global expansion and new ventures. Alcoa had a presence in 30 countries, employing 59,000 people worldwide. Indeed, in September 2015, Alcoa announced that it would split in two so as to separate its more profitable parts—making units from its raw aluminum operations. The move was a strategic response to greatly reduced demand for commodities from China.[8] Samsung Electronics also reorganized to become more efficient to deal with the economic downturn in 2009. Its network of 83 companies accounted for 13 percent of South Korea's exports.[9] The company integrated four business units—semiconductors, LCDs, mobile phones, and consumer electronics—into two divisions, regarded as parts and sets. This necessitated reassigning two-thirds of its executives and relocating 1,200 staff members.[10] As of March 2015, Samsung has a new generation of smartphones, the Galaxy 5 and 6, so time will tell of the success of its reorganization.[11]

The typical ways in which firms organize their international activities are shown in the following list. (Larger companies often use several of these structures in different regions or parts of their organization.) After the presentation of some of these structural forms, the focus will turn to transitional organizational arrangements.

- Domestic structure plus export department
- Domestic structure plus foreign subsidiary
- International division
- Global functional structure
- Global product structure
- Matrix structure

As previously stated, many firms—especially smaller ones—start their international involvement by exporting. They may simply use the services of an export management company for this, or they may reorganize into a simple *domestic structure plus export department*.

To facilitate access to and development of specific foreign markets, the firm can take a further step toward worldwide operations by reorganizing into a *domestic structure plus foreign subsidiary* in one or more countries (see Exhibit 8-1). To be effective, subsidiary managers should have a great deal of autonomy and be able to adapt and respond quickly to serve local markets. This structure works well for companies with one or a few subsidiaries located relatively close to headquarters.

With further market expansion, the firm may then decide to specialize by creating an *international division* organized along functional, product, or geographic lines. With this structure, the various foreign subsidiaries are organized under the international division, and the subsidiary managers report to its head, who is typically given the title of Vice President, International Division. This vice president, in turn, reports directly to the CEO of the corporation. The creation of an international division facilitates the beginning of a global strategy. It permits managers to allocate and coordinate resources for foreign activities under one roof and, thus, enhances the firm's ability to respond, both reactively and proactively, to market opportunities. Some conflicts may arise among the divisions of the firm because more resources and management attention tend to be channeled toward the international division than toward the domestic divisions and because of the different orientations of various division managers.

EXHIBIT 8-1 Domestic Structure Plus Foreign Subsidiary

Integrated Global Structures

To respond to increased product diversification and maximize benefits from both domestic and foreign operations, a firm may choose to replace its international division with an integrated global structure. This structure can be organized along functional, product, geographic, or matrix lines.

The **global functional structure** is designed on the basis of the company's functions—production, marketing, finance, and so forth. Foreign operations are integrated into the activities and responsibilities of each department to gain functional specialization and economies of scale. This form of organization is used primarily by small firms with highly centralized systems. It is particularly appropriate for product lines using similar technology and for businesses with a narrow spectrum of customers. This structure results in plants that are highly integrated across products and serve single or similar markets.

Much of the advantage resulting from economies of scale and functional specialization may be lost if the managers and the work systems become too narrowly defined to have the necessary flexibility to respond to local environments. An alternative structure can be based on product lines.

For firms with diversified product lines (or services) that have different technological bases and are aimed at dissimilar or dispersed markets, a **global product (divisional) structure** may be more strategically advantageous than a functional structure. In this structure, a single product (or product line) is represented by a separate division. Each division is headed by its own general manager, and each is responsible for its own production and sales functions. Usually, each division is a **strategic business unit** (**SBU**)—a self-contained business with its own functional departments and accounting systems. The advantages of this organizational form are market concentration, innovation, and responsiveness to new opportunities in a particular environment. It also facilitates diversification and rapid growth, sometimes at the expense of scale economies and functional specialization. H. J. Heinz Company CEO William R. Johnson came on board in April 1998 and decided that the company should restructure to implement a global strategy. He changed the focus of the company from a multidomestic international strategy using the global geographic area structure to a global strategy using the global product divisional structure. His goal was further growth overseas by building international operations; this structure also readily incorporated Heinz's Specialty Pet Food Division for marketing those products around the world.[12] Heinz is a global company with 35,000 employees in 30 countries, but in 2015, Heinz merged with Kraft Foods to form the Kraft Heinz Company, so, as of this writing, it remains to be seen what restructuring will take place.[13]

Particularly appropriate in a dynamic and diverse environment, the global product structure is illustrated in Exhibit 8-2.

With the global product (divisional) grouping, however, ongoing difficulties in the coordination of widely dispersed operations may result. One answer to this problem, particularly for large MNCs, is to reorganize into a global geographic structure.

EXHIBIT 8-2 Global Product (Divisional) Structure

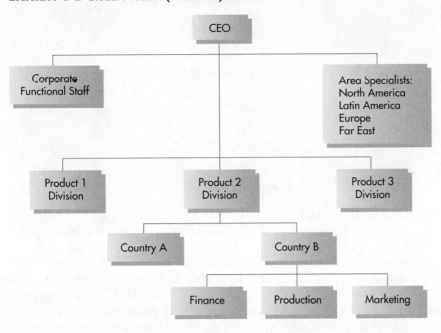

In the **global geographic (area) structure**—the most common form of organizing foreign operations—divisions are created to cover geographic regions (see Exhibit 8-3). Each regional manager is responsible for the operations and performance of the countries within a given region. In this way, country and regional needs and relative market knowledge take precedence over product expertise. Local managers are familiar with the cultural environment, government regulations, and business transactions. In addition, their language skills and local contacts facilitate daily transactions and responsiveness to the market and the customer. Although this is a good structure for consolidating regional expertise, problems of coordination across regions may arise.

With the geographic structure, the focus is on marketing because products can be adapted to local requirements. Therefore, marketing-oriented companies, such as Nestlé and Unilever, which produce a range of products that can be marketed through similar (or common) channels

EXHIBIT 8-3 Global Geographic Structure

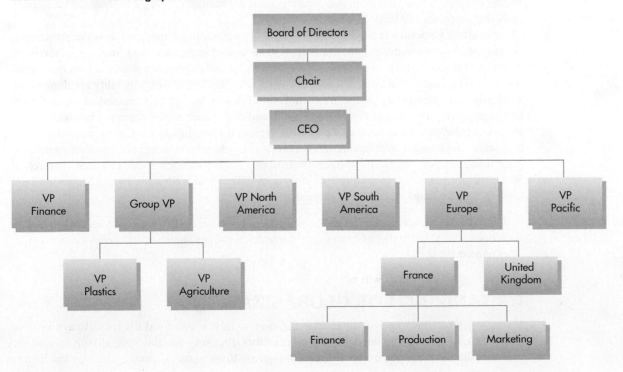

EXHIBIT 8-4 Matrix Geographic Structure

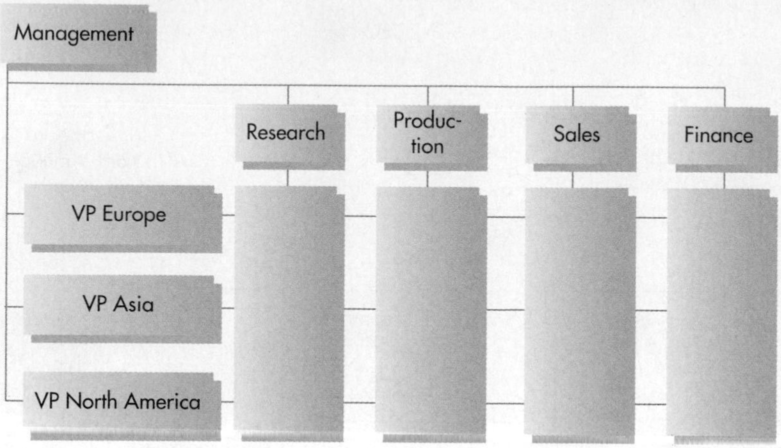

of distribution to similar customers, will usually opt for this structure. Nestlé SA, for example, uses this decentralized structure, which is more typical of European companies, because it is Nestlé's policy to generate most of its sales outside of Switzerland. The company strives to be an insider in every country in which it operates.[14] In 2005, Nestlé reinforced its global business strategy of emphasizing its brands by making its head of marketing responsible for Nestlé's seven strategic business units (SBUs)—dairy, confectionery, beverages, ice cream, food, pet care, and food services. Those SBUs help determine the company's regional business strategy, which then shapes the local market business strategies.[15] Still, Peter Brabeck-Letmathe, who was Nestlé's marketing manager, and later chairman, insisted that:

> *There is no such thing as a global consumer, especially in a sector as psychologically and cul-turally loaded as food.... This means having a local character.*[16]

Nestlé has a presence in almost every country in the world, including emerging markets, and it has various partnerships around the world—most recently with the Chinese confectionery company Hsu Fu Chi. The Nestlé company website describes the organization of the food and beverage business, with some product exceptions, as being managed by geographies in three zones—Europe, the Americas, and Asia/Oceania/Africa. The other products, such as Nestlé Purina Petcare, Nestlé Nutrition, and Nestlé Waters, are managed on a global basis; the company calls this group the Globally Managed Businesses.[17]

A **matrix structure** is a hybrid organization of overlapping responsibilities. The structure is developed to combine geographic support for both global integration and local responsiveness, and it can be used to take advantage of personnel skills and experience shared across both functional and divisional structures. In the matrix structure, the lines of responsibility are drawn both vertically and horizontally as illustrated in Exhibit 8-4. Although this method of management and organization maximizes the focus of skills and experience in the company brought to bear on a particular product as well as a particular region, it often brings confusion, communication problems, and conflict over having more than one boss to whom to report as well as stress over prioritizing time among overlapping and conflicting responsibilities. Indeed, in their research of 36 Dutch organizations, including subsidiaries of global firms, Strikwerda and Stoelhorst concluded from the majority of interviewees that:

> *[E]xecutives associate the matrix organization with unclear responsibilities, a lack of accountability, and political battles over resources, resulting in risk-averse behavior and loss of market share.*[18]

ORGANIZING FOR GLOBALIZATION

No matter what the stage of internationalization, a firm's structural choices always involve two opposing forces: the need for **differentiation** (focusing on and specializing in specific markets) and the need for **integration** (coordinating those same markets). The way the firm is organized along the differentiation–integration continuum determines how well strategies—along a localization–globalization continuum—are implemented. This is why the structural imperatives of various strategies such as globalization must be understood to organize appropriate worldwide systems and connections.

As previously presented, global trends and competitive forces have put increasing pressure on multinational corporations to adopt a strategy of **globalization**, a specific strategy that treats the world as one market by using a standardized approach to products and markets. The following are two examples of companies reorganizing to achieve globalization. IBM, for example, reorganized to achieve globalization by moving away from its traditional geographic structure to a global structure based on its 14 worldwide industry groups, such as banking, retail, and insurance, shifting power from country managers to centralized industry expert teams. Further restructuring to reduce overlapping functional responsibilities within Asia led IBM to develop its globally integrated enterprise model. In this way, previously country-based functions are now globalized. As examples, now "IBM's growth market operations are served by HR specialists in Manila, accounts receivable are processed in Shanghai, accounting is done in Kuala Lumpur, procurement in Shenzhen."[19]

And, in 2013, Microsoft, in a reversal of its divisional structure, disbanded its eight product divisions and created four new ones arranged around broader functional themes to streamline its technologies and compete better with Apple and Google in the global mobile and Internet markets. The goal was to reduce duplication and create more cooperative teamwork among the new managers.[20] "The earlier approach, intended to copy the success of companies such as General Electric, had left Microsoft ill-prepared for the fast-moving technology world," said Rob Helm, an analyst at Directions on Microsoft.[21]

Organizing to facilitate a globalization strategy typically involves rationalization and the development of strategic alliances. To achieve rationalization, managers choose the manufacturing location for each product based on where the best combination of overall cost - for example, labor, transportation, utillities, taxes - quality of products or services, technology, proximity to markets, and so on, can be attained. It often involves producing different products or component parts in different countries. Typically, it also means that the product design and marketing programs are essentially the same for all end markets around the world to achieve optimal economies of scale. The downside of this strategy is a lack of differentiation and specialization for local markets.

Organizing for global product standardization necessitates close coordination among the various countries involved. It also requires centralized global product responsibility (one manager at headquarters responsible for a specific product around the world), an especially difficult task for multiproduct companies. Henzler and Rall suggest that structural solutions to this problem can be found if companies rethink the roles of their headquarters and their national subsidiaries. Managers should center the overall control of the business at headquarters while treating national subsidiaries as partners in managing the business—perhaps as holding companies responsible for the administration and coordination of cross-divisional activities.[22]

Governments as well as firms may structure their holdings to attract and integrate strategic allies. Such was the case for Brazil's federal energy company Petrobas (NYSE: PBR) when it announced in February 2009 that it had created six wholly owned companies, along product lines, for the Rio de Janeiro Comperj petrochemical complex, commenting that:

> Petrobras will hold a 100% stake in the companies and voting capital at the initial stage while it integrates and defines the relationship between Comperj's component parts. By establishing these companies Petrobras is laying the foundations for the potential involvement of partners. Planned investments in Comperj are expected to total US$8.4bn and operations are scheduled to begin in 2012.[23]

A problem many companies face in the future is that their structurally sophisticated global networks, built to secure cost advantages, leave them exposed to the risk of environmental volatility from all corners of the world. Such companies must restructure their global operations to reduce the environmental risk that results from multicountry sourcing and supply networks.[24] In other words, the more links in the chain, the more chances for things to go wrong.

Organizing to Be Global, Act Local

In their rush to get on the globalization bandwagon, too many firms have sacrificed the ability to respond to local market structures and consumer preferences. Managers are now realizing that—depending on the type of products, markets, and so forth—a compromise must be made along the globalization–regionalization continuum, and they are experimenting with various structural configurations to be global and act local. One such company is Flipkart, an e-commerce company registered in Singapore and operating in India; it is often called the Amazon of India but uses a locally designed and operated complex pyramid structure to go local for its deliveries in India in a time-tested and accepted organization, as described in the accompanying Under the Lens feature.

UNDER THE LENS

Amazon of India Uses Curry-Carrying Dabawallas to Spice Up Parcel Delivery

JAMES CRABTREE - MUMBAI AVANTIKA CHILKOTI - LONDON, FT.COM, APRIL 10, 2015

While Amazon ponders whisking parcels to customers by drones, India's leading online retailer is launching a low-tech approach to deliveries - by joining forces with 5,000 dabbawallas, more famous for carting hot curry lunches around Mumbai.

In an unusual experiment in just-in-time logistics, Flipkart, often described as the "Amazon of India," is launching a tie-up with the city's network of bicycle-riding delivery-men, who ferry roughly 130,000 lunch boxes up and down India's financial capital each day.

The deliverymen are a near-ubiquitous sight on the city's teeming streets, picking up home-cooked meals in shiny silver tiffin boxes from residences each morning, before cramming on to trains to rush meals to workers in local offices.

From next week the often-elderly male riders will begin a new stage in their 120-year history by dropping into Flipkart's distribution centers to pick up everything from books to toys, for delivery where they also collect lunches.

The tie-up is the latest chapter of Flipkart's battle with Amazon, which last year began pouring $2bn into India's growing ecommerce market, in part to overhaul the lead enjoyed by its Bangalore-based rival in logistics and delivery.

It also comes amid rising interest in India's internet economy from global technology investors, who have begun pumping big sums into start-ups such as Flipkart, which won a valuation of about $11bn at its last fundraising.

Dmitry Kalinovsky/123RF GB Ltd

Dabbawallas' traditional approach to last-mile delivery has won glowing write-ups from management theorists at Harvard Business School and elsewhere, who laud the system's unerring timeliness and reliability.

Using a complex pyramid structure, the dabbawallas are organized into teams of 20, collecting lunch boxes, sorting them by destination and then loading them on to Mumbai's trains. Each tiffin box changes hands several times before arriving at its destination.

The system, which uses codes of numbers, letters, symbols and colors, has been likened to a "six sigma" process, a management term for a method with less than 3.4 errors per million.

"It is so hard to find reliable people who understand the local geographies," says Neeraj Aggarwal, an executive at Flipkart, who runs the dabbawalla partnership. "But for people in Mumbai, these guys are trusted, they are almost like family."

© 2015 The Financial Times Limited

Levi Strauss is another example of a company attempting to maximize the advantages of different structural configurations. The company employs a staff of approximately 16,700 people in 110 countries, including approximately 1,010 people at its San Francisco, California, headquarters. Approximately half of the company's revenues comes from outside the United States. The company is organized into three geographic divisions:

- Levi Strauss Americas (LSA), based in the San Francisco headquarters
- Levi Strauss Europe, Middle East, and North Africa (LSEMA), based in Brussels
- Asia Pacific Division (APD), based in Singapore

In the LSEMA division, there is a network of nine sales offices, six distribution centers, and three production facilities. The headquarters are located in Brussels, Belgium. The company's European franchise partners bring the products to consumers throughout the region.[25]

Levi Strauss & Co.'s Asia Pacific Division comprises subsidiary businesses, licensees, and distributors throughout the Asia Pacific region, the Middle East, and Africa.

Thus, through these various structural global–local formats, the company has ensured its ability to respond to local needs by allowing its managers to act independently; Levi's success turns on its ability to fashion a global strategy that doesn't snuff out local initiative. It's a delicate balancing act, one that often means giving foreign managers the freedom needed to adjust their tactics to meet the changing tastes of their home markets. The company's website in 2015 states that "our goal is to expand the Levi Strauss & Co. brands in India, China, Russia, Brazil and other emerging markets."[26] Independent contractors manufacture Levi's products in 30 countries and are required to adhere to the company's code of conduct.[27]

One well-known global consumer products company, Procter & Gamble, is succeeding with its global–local Four Pillars structure, as described in the accompanying Management in Action feature.

MANAGEMENT IN ACTION

Procter & Gamble's Think Globally–Act Locally Structure

In 2015, Procter & Gamble (P&G) attributes much of its success to its global/local Four Pillars organization structure. The well-known company melds its global scale efficiencies with a local focus in the 180 countries in which it operates. The company lauds its growth and competitive advantage in adopting new business models and in more than doubling of its capacity to innovate.

P&G touches the lives of people around the world three billion times a day with its broad portfolio of leading brands, including Pampers®, Tide®, Charmin®, Downy®, Crest®, Gillette®, and Braun®.[28]

P&G's organizational structure is broadly divided into three heads: GBU (Global Business Unit), SMOs (Selling and Market Operations), and GBS (Global Business Services). Upon the acquisition of Gillette, it was decided that the structure would change from business units based on geographic regions to GBUs based on product lines. "MDOs will develop market strategies to build business based on local knowledge and GBS will bring together business activities such as accounting, human resource systems, order management, and information technology, thus making it cost-effective."[29]

Since 2001, P&G has acquired three leading companies with leading brands in Clairol, Wella, and Gillette. The acquisition of Gillette in 2006 added five brands with annual sales in excess of $1 billion. CEO A. G. Lafley had expressed confidence that the company could deliver on a full decade of growth because of P&G's strategies and strengths and the company's unique organizational structure. P&G's structure makes it the only consumer-products company with global business unit profit centers, global market development organizations, and global shared services, all supported by innovative corporate functions. A description of P&G's organization structure as of 2015 follows, as provided in the company's corporate information description on its website.[30]

(Continued)

P&G's Global/Local Structure: 2015

Four pillars—Global Business Units (GBUs), Selling and Market Operations (SMOs), Global Business Services (GBS), and Corporate Functions (CF)—form the heart of P&G's organizational structure.

- Global Business Units (GBUs) build major global brands with robust business strategies.
- Selling and Market Operations (SMOs) build local understanding as a foundation for marketing campaigns.
- Global Business Services (GBS) provide business technology and services that drive business success.
- Corporate Functions (CFs) work to maintain our place as a leader of our industries.

P&G approaches business knowing that we need to Think Globally (GBUs) and Act Locally (MDOs). This approach is supported by our commitment to operate efficiently (GBS) and our constant striving to be the best at what we do (CFs). This streamlined structure allows us to get to market faster.

Global Business Units

Philosophy: Think Globally.
General Role: Create strong brand equities, robust strategies, and ongoing innovation in products and marketing to build major global brands.

GBUs:

- Baby Care, Family, and Feminine Care
- Beauty Care, Hair, Personal Care
- Fabric & Home Care
- Health and Grooming

Selling and Market Operations (SMOs)

Philosophy: Act Locally.
General Role: Interface with customers to ensure marketing plans fully capitalize on local understanding, to seek synergy across programs to leverage corporate scale, and to develop strong programs that change the game in our favor at point of purchase.

SMO Regions:

- Asia
- Europe
- India, Middle East, Africa (IMEA)
- Latin America
- North America

Global Business Services (GBS)

Philosophy: Enable P&G to win with customers and consumers.
General Role: Provide services and solutions that enable the Company to operate efficiently around the world, collaborate effectively with business partners, and help employees become more productive.

GBS Centers:

- GBS Americas located in Costa Rica
- GBS Asia located in Manila
- GBS Europe, Middle East, & Africa located in Newcastle

Corporate Functions (CF)

Philosophy: Be the Smartest/Best.
General Role: Ensure that the functional capability integrated into the rest of the company remains on the cutting edge of the industry. We want to be the thought leader within each CF.

Corporate Functions: (for example, IT, HR, R&D, Legal, Marketing).

Although strategy may be the primary means to a company's competitive advantage, the burden of realizing that advantage rests on the organizational structure and design; that structure, in turn, establishes the responsibilities and guides the decisions, actions, and communications of its employees. Because of the difficulties companies experience trying to be glocal companies (global and local), researchers are suggesting new, more flexible organizational designs involving interorganizational networks and transnational design.

EMERGENT STRUCTURAL FORMS

Companies are increasingly abandoning rigid structures in an attempt to be more flexible and responsive to the dynamic global environment. Some of the ways they are adapting are by transitioning to formats known as interorganizational networks, global e-corporation network structures, and transnational corporation network structures, described below. In addition, many firms are finding that specific team configurations can provide the flexibility and responsiveness they need to be competitive.

Teams as a Global–Local Structure

Similar to a matrix structure, but more fluid, flexible, independent, and often short-term, are the now common global teams that crisscross functional and geographic lines on any of the formalized structures described in this chapter. Discussed further in later chapters, global teams allow for flat, self-leading structural forms within otherwise hierarchical structures and provide for integrating local knowledge, contacts, and creativity with the firm's overall strategy. Often the teams are responsible for specific projects or trouble-shooting, but also they may be in place long-term for ongoing operations in multiple countries; as such, teams then create a depository of shared knowledge and experience of benefit to them and the firm. Most of their communication is virtual because of the time and costs involved in travel. Team leadership may move around to different countries, depending on the project or task involved.

An increasing number of companies, such as Cisco Systems and IBM, create customized structures according to the client needs. By selectively moving their skilled employees into cross-company teams, they can move rapidly and flexibly to take advantage of their portfolios of opportunities. To do this,

> They assemble and disassemble teams of hundreds of people from across the company who move from opportunity to opportunity. Their reconfigurable organizations consist of a stable part and a variable part. The stable structure is usually the functional and/or geographical home for nurturing talent.
>
> J. R. GALBRAITH
> 2010[31]

Other new structural formats are evolving as emerging market companies make their rapid entrée onto the global scene, as discussed in the following Comparative Management in Focus section.

Brazil is typical of developing markets for which both local and global firms must plan their strategy and organizational structures while considering the vast differences in macro- and micro-regions and infrastructures within the country. Sao Jose Dos Campos is home to Embraer, the world's third largest commercial aircraft manufacturing company, and Thales Alinear Space, the European telecommunications and space company; the city is one of the ten competitive micro-regions for doing business in Brazil, five of which are in the greater Sao Paolo metropolitan area. However, the farther one travels outside of that region, the less one sees of the infrastructure and pockets of competitive regions to attract businesses. Logistics and infrastructure are better in the south, but road quality is very substandard outside of the south and southeast. Firms therefore must realize that, although there are huge untapped markets in Brazil, they must recognize the nature of the emerging market needs for logistical and control systems.[34]

Comparative Management in Focus
Changing Organizational Structures of Emerging Market Companies

Rapidly changing competition and global business activities demand companies to run their worldwide operations efficiently and effectively, based on the right business models and organizational structures. Stable organizational structures and control systems are necessary to seek timely internationalization. The major variables involved in choosing the right organizational structure depend on a company's global involvement and degree of localization. Fast-growing companies from emerging markets (EMs), BRIC countries (Brazil, Russia, India, and China), and rapidly developing economies (RDEs) continue to internationalize their operations. Examples are CNOOC (China), Dr. Reddy's Laboratories (India), Embraer (Brazil), Gazprom (Russia), Haier Company (China), Infosys Technologies (India), Koc Holdings (Turkey), Lenovo Group (China), Tata Motors (India), and Wipro (India).[32] These developing market companies are the first wave of highly successful firms benefiting from the globalization phenomenon.[33]

Interestingly, the expansion models these emerging or developing market companies seek from Asia, Latin America, and Eastern Europe are unique and may not fit with today's mainstream multinational corporation (MNC) model because of the following three reasons. First, many emerging market companies are avoiding the traditional roadmap to internationalization and are instead capitalizing on the born-global phenomenon, which means running their operations and opening subsidiaries worldwide from the beginning. Second, they are finding niche businesses where competition is limited. Third, they are thriving in old-economy industries that have been abandoned by established MNCs from developed countries.

A new breed of companies in those geographic areas have excelled in global business because of their unique organizational structures and design. Like Korean chaebols (industrial conglomerates), most emerging market companies were started as family businesses and entrepreneurial entities in which ownership and control of the firms resided with the families. Therefore, the control mechanism is somewhat bureaucratic and headquarters-centered. Currently, a multitude of changes are in the pipeline that will force emerging market companies to redefine their family-based governance structures and rigid control systems.

Major structural changes include simplifying hierarchies, reducing family ownerships, providing more powers to subsidiaries, and seeking organizational structures based on either the traditional MNC model or company-specific hybrid structures. Interestingly, many emerging market companies have been following the model of "be global, act local" in becoming responsible citizens and adapting their products and services. Embraer, Haier Group, Lenovo, Mittal Steel, Orsacom, and others fit in this category. In addition, overseas Chinese business networks (OCBNs) are also changing to become part of the globalization phenomenon. Increasingly, emerging market companies from Asia, Latin America, Africa, and Eastern Europe will seek internationalization in their own unique ways, leading to hybrid structures and fast-growth entities. Of course, these newly emerging MNCs will become globally integrated, using multidomestic synergies and international/global/transnational strategies. Their future goals and scope of operations will determine organizational structures and global initiatives.

Source: Syed Tariq Anwar, Professor, West Texas A&M University, used with permission.

Interorganizational Networks

Whether the ever-expanding transnational linkages of an MNC consist of different companies, subsidiaries, suppliers, or individuals, they result in relational networks. These networks may adopt very different structures of their own because they operate in different local contexts within their own national environments. Similarly, Miles et al. describe the I-form as a collaborative, multi-firm network along with community-based structures, used by innovative firms such as Taiwan's Acer.[35] By regarding the MNC's overall structure as a network of interconnected relations, we can more realistically consider its organizational design imperatives at both global and local levels. Royal Philips Electronics of the Netherlands, one of the world's biggest electronics companies, has operating units in 100 countries, using a network structure. These units range from large subsidiaries, which might be among the largest companies in a country, to very small single-function operations, such as research and development or marketing divisions for one of Philips's businesses. Some have centralized control at Philips's headquarters; others are quite autonomous. As part of its Vision 2010, Philips simplified its overall business structure by creating three core sectors fully aligned with its markets: Philips Healthcare, Philips Lighting, and Philips Consumer Lifestyle.[36]

In yet another structural variation, Intel, in adapting to changes in the semiconductor industry, embarked on a wholesale reorganization of its businesses. Intel's executives decided that they wanted the company to focus more on what was going on outside the business and developed a structural focus they call Platformisation—that is, customizing a range of chips in a combination suitable for a particular target market, as a response to the increasing need for speedy adaptation to the market.[37] As the world's biggest semiconductor maker, with more than 82,500 employees worldwide, the company's general description of its approach to organizing, in response to an inquiry by this author, is as follows.

> *Intel is not a very hierarchical company so a formalized organizational structure is not a particularly good representation of how the company works. At the highest level, Intel is organized into largely autonomous divisions. Intel uses matrix management and cross-functional teams including IT, knowledge management, human resources, finance, legal, change control, data warehousing, common directory information management, and cost reduction teams (to name a few) to rapidly adapt to changing conditions.*

WWW.INTEL.COM[38]

The network framework makes clear that the company's operating units link vastly different environmental and operational contexts based on varied economic, social, and cultural milieus. This complex linkage highlights the intricate task of a giant MNC to rationalize and coordinate its activities globally to achieve an advantageous cost position while tailoring itself to local market conditions (to achieve benefits from differentiation).[39]

The Global E-Corporation Network Structure

The organizational structure for global e-businesses, in particular for physical products, typically involves a network of virtual e-exchanges and bricks-and-mortar services, whether those services are in-house or outsourced. This structure of functions and alliances makes up a combination of electronic and physical stages of the supply chain network, as illustrated in Exhibit 8-5.

EXHIBIT 8-5 A Global E-Corporation Network Structure

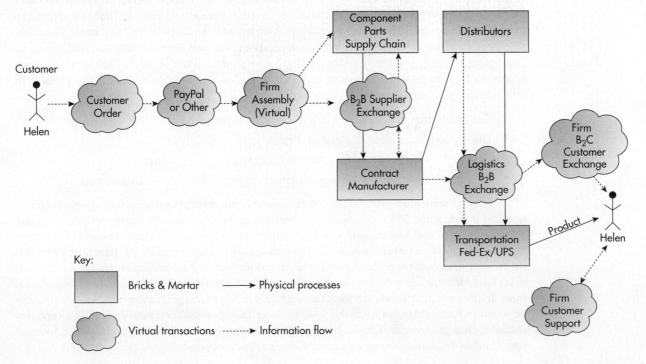

As such, the network comprises some global and some local functions. The centralized e-exchanges for logistics, supplies, and customers could be housed anywhere; suppliers, manufacturers, and distributors may be in various countries, separately or together, wherever efficiencies of scale and cost may be realized. The final distribution system and the customer interaction must be tailored to the customer-location physical infrastructure and payment infrastructure as well as to local regulations and languages.[40]

The result is a global e-network of suppliers, subcontractors, manufacturers, distributors, buyers, and sellers, communicating in real time through cyberspace. This spreads efficiency throughout the chain, providing cost-effectiveness for all parties.[41] Dell Computer is an example of a company that uses the Internet to streamline its global supply systems. It has a number of factories around the world that supply custom-built PCs to customers in that region. Customers' orders are received through call centers or Dell's own website. The order for components then goes to its suppliers, which have to be within a 15-minute drive of its factory. The component parts are delivered to the factory, and the completed customers' orders are collected within a few hours. Dell maintains Internet connections with its suppliers and connects them with its customer database so that they have direct and real-time information about orders. Customers also can use Dell's Internet system to track their orders as they go through the chain.[42]

Dell's organizational structure to implement its business model has evolved to what is known as a virtual company, or value web. Dell's strategy is to conduct critical activities in-house and outsource non-strategic activities.

The Transnational Corporation (TNC) Network Structure

To address the globalization–localization dilemma, firms that have evolved through the multinational form and the global company seek the advantages of horizontal organization in the pursuit of transnational capability—that is, the ability to manage across national boundaries, retaining local flexibility while achieving global integration.[43] This capability involves linking foreign operations to each other and to headquarters in a flexible way, thereby leveraging local and central capabilities. ABB (a global leader in power and information technologies, based in Zurich, Switzerland)is an example of such a decentralized horizontal organization. ABB operates in 100 countries with 150,000 employees and eight geographic region managers with only one management level separating the business units from top management. ABB prides itself on being a truly global company, with 11 board members representing seven nationalities. Thus, this structure is less a matter of boxes on an organizational chart and more a matter of a network of the company's units and their system of horizontal communication. This involves lateral communication across networks of units and alliances rather than in a hierarchy. The system requires the dispersal of responsibility and decision making to local subsidiaries and alliances. The effectiveness of that localized decision-making depends a great deal on the ability and willingness to share current and new learning and technology across the network of units. The matrix structure typical of the transnational company creates a complex coordination and control system as it attempts to combine:

- The capabilities and resources of a multinational corporation.
- The economies of scale of a global corporation.
- The local responsiveness of a domestic company.
- The ability to transfer technology efficiently, typical of the international structure.[44]

Whatever the names given to the organizational forms emerging to deal with global competition and logistics, the MNC organizational structure as we know it, with its hierarchical pyramid, subsidiaries, and world headquarters, is gradually evolving into a more fluid form to adapt to strategic and competitive imperatives. As is now well known, these more flexible forms are facilitated by the ever-developing technologies that enable various forms of electronic instant communication to connect elaborate networks of people and information around the world, regardless of their locations. In this new global web, the location of a firm's headquarters is unimportant. Various alliances tie together units and subunits in the web. Corning Incorporated (previously Corning Glass), for instance, changed from its national pyramid-like organization to a global web, enabling it to make optical cable through its European partner, Siemens AG, and medical equipment with Ciba-Geigy.

CHOICE OF ORGANIZATIONAL FORM

Two major variables in choosing the structure and design of an organization are the opportunities and need for (1) globalization and (2) localization. Exhibit 8-6 depicts alternative structural forms appropriate to each of these variables and the strategic choices regarding the level and type of international involvement the firm desires.

This figure thereby updates the evolutionary stages model to reflect alternative organizational responses to more recent environments and to the anticipated competitive environments ahead. The updated model shows that, as the firm progresses from a domestic to an international company—and perhaps later to a multinational and then a global company—its managers adapt the organizational structure to accommodate their relative strategic focus on globalization versus localization, choosing a global product structure, a geographic area structure, or perhaps a matrix form. The model proposes that, as the company becomes larger, more complex, and more sophisticated in its approach to world markets (no matter which structural route it has taken), it may evolve into a transnational corporation (TNC). The TNC strategy is to maximize opportunities for both efficiency and local responsiveness by adopting a transnational structure that uses alliances, networks, and horizontal design formats. The relationships between choice of global strategy and the appropriate structural variations necessary to implement each strategic choice are further illustrated in Exhibit 8-7.

EXHIBIT 8-6 Organizational Alternatives and Development for Global Companies

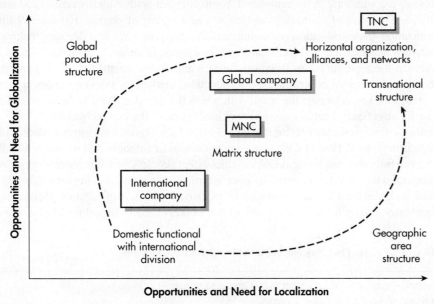

Sources: Based on models by R. E. White and T. A. Poynter, "Organizing for Worldwide Advantage," *Business Quarterly* 54 (Summer 1989); John M. Stopford and Louis T. Wells Jr., *Managing the Multinational Enterprise* (New York: Basic Books, 1972); C. A. Bartlett, "Organizing and Controlling MNCs," *Harvard Business School Case Study*, No.9 (March 1987), pp. 365, 375.

EXHIBIT 8-7 Structural Variables to Implement Global Strategies

Strategy	Organizational Structure	Delegation	Need to Coordinate	Organizational Culture
Multidomestic	Global area	To national unit	Low	Low impact
International	Intl. Division	Centralize core; rest to units	Medium	Medium
Global	Product Group	Locate where globally optimum	High	Important
Transnational	Global Matrix	Centralized and decentralized	Very High	Crucial

Source: Based on C. W. L. Hill and E. R. Jones, *Strategic Management: An Integrated Approach,* 3rd ed., (Boston, MA: Houghton Mifflin Company 1995), p. 390.

Organizational Change and Design Variables

When a company makes drastic changes in its goals, strategy, or scope of operations, it will usually also need a change in organizational structure. However, other, less obvious indications of organizational inefficiency also signal a need for structural changes; conflicts among divisions and subsidiaries over territories or customers, conflicts between overseas units and headquarters staff, complaints regarding overseas customer service, and overlapping responsibilities are some of these warning signals. Exhibit 8-8 lists some indications of the need for change in organizational design.

At persistent signs of ineffective work, a company should analyze its organizational design, systems, and work flow for the possible causes of those problems. The nature and extent of any design changes must reflect the magnitude of the problem. In choosing a new organizational design or modifying an existing structure, managers must establish a system of communication and control that will provide for effective decision making. At such times, managers need to localize decision making and integrate widely dispersed and disparate global operations.

Besides determining the behavior of the organization on a macro level (in terms of what the different divisions, subsidiaries, departments, and units are responsible for), the organizational design must determine behavior on a micro level. For example, the organizational design affects the level at which certain types of decisions will be made. Determining how many and what types of decisions can be made and by whom can have drastic consequences; both the locus and the scope of authority must be carefully considered. This centralization–decentralization variable actually represents a continuum. In the real world, companies are neither totally centralized nor totally decentralized. The level of centralization imposed is a matter of degree. Exhibit 8-9 illustrates this centralization–decentralization continuum and the different ways that decision making can be shared between headquarters and local units or subsidiaries. In general, centralized decision making is common for some functions (finance, research and development) that are organized for the entire corporation, whereas other functions (production, marketing, sales) are more appropriately decentralized. Two key issues are the speed with which the decisions have to be made and whether they primarily affect only a certain subsidiary or other parts of the company as well.

As noted, culture is another factor that complicates decisions on how much to decentralize and how to organize the work flow and the various relationships of authority and responsibility. Part 4 of this book more fully presents how cultural variables affect people's attitudes about working relationships and about who should have authority over whom. At this point, it is important merely to note that cultural variables must be taken into account when designing an organization. Delegating a high level of authority to employees in a country where workers usually regard the boss as the rightful

EXHIBIT 8-8   Changes That May Necessitate New Structural Designs

- New management with different goals and strategies
- Downturn in profitability or finances
- Lack of competitiveness; failure to meet goals or capitalize on opportunities
- Poor management, leadership, communication, delegation, or morale
- New strategic directions: growth, alliances, retrenchment; expanding globally from directing export activities to controlling overseas manufacturing and marketing units; a change in the size of operations on a country, regional, or worldwide basis; or failure of foreign operations to grow in accordance with plans and expectations
- Clashes among divisions, subsidiaries, or individuals over territories or customers in the field
- Divisive conflicts between overseas units and domestic division staff or corporate staff
- Underutilization of overseas manufacturing or distribution facilities
- Duplication of sales offices or geographic operational units within an area
- An increase in overseas customer service complaints
- Breakdowns in communications within and among organizations
- Bottlenecks, too many reporting layers, and ill-defined executive responsibilities
- Lack of innovation

Source: Based on Business International Corporation, *New Directions in Multinational Corporate Organization* (New York: Business International Corporation, 1981).

EXHIBIT 8-9 **Locus of Decision Making in an International Organization**

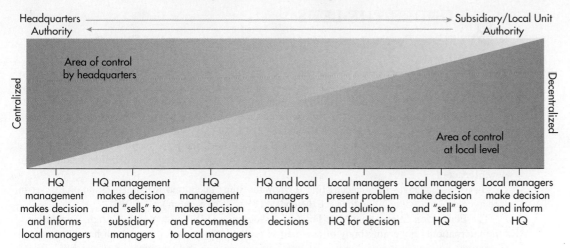

person to make all the decisions is not likely to work well. Clearly, managers must think through the interactions of organizational, staffing, and cultural issues before making final decisions.

In summary, no one way to organize is best. Contingency theory applies to organizational design as much as to any other aspect of management. The best organizational structure is the one that facilitates the firm's goals and is appropriate to its industry, size, technology, and competitive environment. Structure should be fluid and dynamic and highly adaptable to the changing needs of the company. The structure should not be allowed to be bogged down in the administrative heritage of the organization (that is, "the way we do things around here" or "what we've always done") to the point that it undermines the very processes that will enable the firm to take advantage of new opportunities.

Most likely, however, the future for the MNC structure, as well as for small businesses and born globals, lies in a global web of networked companies. Ideally, a company tries to organize in a way that will allow it to carry out its strategic goals; the staffing is then done to mesh with those strategic goals and the way the organizational structure has been set up. In reality, however, the existing structural factors often affect strategic decisions, so the result may be a trade-off of desired strategy with existing constraints. So, too, with staffing. Ideal staffing plans have to be adjusted to reflect the realities of assigning managers from various sources and the local regulations or cultural variables that make some organizing and staffing decisions more workable than others.

What may at first seem a linear management process of deciding on strategy, then on structure, and finally on staffing is actually an interdependent set of factors that must be taken into consideration and worked out as a set of decisions. Chapter 9 explores how staffing decisions are—or should be—intricately intertwined with other decisions regarding strategy, structure, and so forth. A unique set of management cadre and skills in a particular location can be a competitive advantage in itself, so it may be a smart move to build strategic and organizational decisions around that resource rather than risk losing that advantage. The following sections present some other processes that are involved in implementing strategy and are interconnected with coordinating functions through organizational structure.

CONTROL SYSTEMS FOR GLOBAL OPERATIONS

To complement the organizational structure, the international manager must design efficient coordinating and reporting systems to ensure that actual performance conforms to expected organizational standards and goals. The challenge is to coordinate far-flung operations in vastly different environments with various work processes; rules; and economic, political, legal, and cultural norms. The feedback from the control process and the information systems should signal any necessary change in strategy, structure, or operations in a timely manner. Often the strategy, the coordinating processes, or both, need to be changed to reflect conditions in other countries. Organizations may also restructure and set up reporting systems to avoid problems preemptively that would negatively affect its processes and image. Such was the case when FIFA decided to set up a structure to provide decision oversight and transparency to its worldwide activities, as explained in the following Under the Lens feature.

UNDER THE LENS
FIFA—Restructuring for Governance Oversight of Ethics [45]

Most sports organizations developed on a small scale but have now grown in size and complexity to organizations similar to multinational corporations. As such, those sports organizations should have a structure and a set of policies in place to oversee anticorruption and conflict-of-interest compliance; this awareness has grown in particular in the wake of the scandal surrounding the International Olympic Committee (IOC) and the Salt Lake City Olympics. However, the governance structure of FIFA, for example, had not previously encompassed the responsibility for ethical behavior in the organization. In October 2011, FIFA restructured and took the steps as described below and on www.FIFA.com.

Have these changes been successful? Review the steps taken and the organization charts set in place to control these issues and then see the update below as of September 1, 2015.

The Fédération Internationale de Football Association (FIFA), located in Zurich, Switzerland, is the international governing body of association football. The association, which has 208 national associations within six regional areas, oversees the governance and organization of the FIFA World Cup; the last one was held in Brazil in 2014. The administrative organization chart is shown in Exhibit 8-10.

Following the proposals made by the FIFA President, Joseph S. Blatter, at the FIFA Congress on June 1, 2011, in terms of good governance, transparency, and zero tolerance toward wrongdoing on and off the pitch (during games or at any time), the FIFA Executive Committee, meeting on October 20–21, 2011, at the home offices of FIFA in Zurich, agreed on the following measures:

• The creation of four task forces, mandated to propose reforms: *Task Force Revision of Statutes*, chaired by Dr. Theo Zwanziger (Germany); *Task Force FIFA Ethics Committee*, chaired by the

EXHIBIT 8-10 **FIFA Administrative Organization Chart**

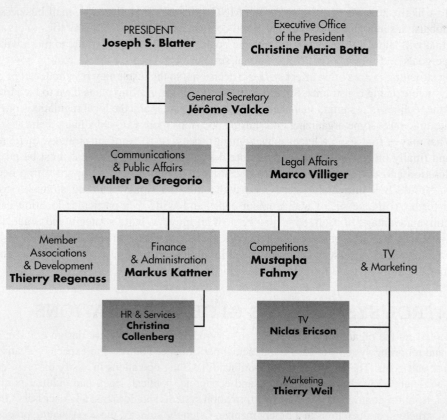

Source: Administrative Organization Chart, www.FIFA.com, accessed February 1, 2012.

EXHIBIT 8-11 **Independent Governance Committee**

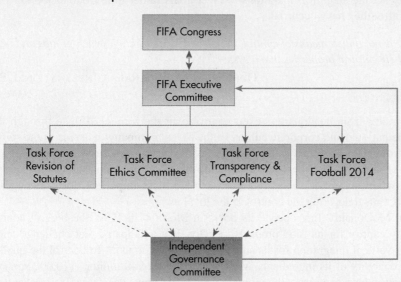

Source: www.FIFA.com, accessed February 1, 2012, used with permission.

Chairman of the Ethics Committee, Claudio Sulser (Switzerland); *Task Force Transparency and Compliance*, chaired by Juan Ángel Napout (President of the Paraguayan FA) and Frank Van Hattum (President of the New Zealand FA); and *Task Force Football 2014* (operating since May 2011), chaired by Franz Beckenbauer (Germany).

- The creation of an Independent Governance Committee (see Exhibit 8-11) which, among other tasks, will oversee reforms FIFA undertakes. It comprises representatives not only from the international football family but also from other spheres.

- The establishment of a "FIFA Good Governance" road map between October 2011 and the 2013 FIFA Congress.

UPDATE: On May 28, 2015, the United States indicted nine FIFA officials and five sports executives on charges of taking millions in bribes in a culture of "rampant, systemic, deep-rooted corruption,"[46] following arrests of the executives in a dawn raid on a Swiss Hotel. The indictment followed investigations into the awarding of the 2010 World Cup to South Africa, the 2011 FIFA presidential election (and since then a probe into the 2014 Cup in Brazil.) Questions are also being raised regarding the decisions to grant Russia the 2018 World Cup, and Qatar (with exceedingly hot summer temperatures) in 2022. Regardless of these events, Sepp Blatter was relected the FIFA President two days later. Shortly after, Blatter resigned. And on September 18, 2015, the Wall Street Journal reported that Jerome Valcke, FIFA's secretary-general and its second-highest ranking official was suspended amid accusations that he sought to profit personally through the sale of a cache of World Cup tickets he controlled in 2014.[47] Subsequently, the FIFA Ethics Committee launched an investigation!

Evaluate the restructuring. Was it too little, too late? Were there other factors at play which could not be resolved by reorganizing? What else has happened since September 2015? Has this changed your interest in the sport?

The design and application of coordinating and reporting systems for foreign subsidiaries and activities can take any form that management wishes. MNCs usually employ a variety of direct and indirect coordinating and control mechanisms suitable for their organization structure. For example, in the transnational network structure, decision-making control is centralized to key network nodes, greatly reducing emphasis on bureaucratic control. Other specific mechanisms are summarized in the next sections.[48]

Direct Coordinating Mechanisms

Direct mechanisms that provide the basis for the overall guidance and management of foreign operations include the design of appropriate structures (discussed previously in this chapter) and the use of effective staffing practices (discussed in Chapters 9 and 10). Such decisions proactively set the stage for operations to meet goals rather than troubleshooting deviations or problems after they have occurred.

> *Staffing is not only a means of control, but also a venue through which groups and individuals bring their cultural properties into a system.*[49]
>
> ODEDSHENKAR, JOURNAL OF INTERNATIONAL BUSINESS
> *JANUARY 2012*

Expatriates from headquarters exert control over the foreign affiliate through the expectations of the national and corporate culture of the parent company; whereas, if the staffing assignment is through third-country nationals, it is likely that somewhat less of the corporate culture might be brought to bear locally and certainly less of the national culture of the parent.[50] In situations where parent control might be considered less important, local managers would be considered, thus delegating the control to the local level.

When McDonald's first opened its doors in Moscow in 1990, the biggest control problem was quality control for its food products. McDonald's anticipated that challenge and adopted a strategy of vertical integration for its sourcing of raw materials.[51] To control the quality, distribution, and reliability of its ingredients, McDonald's built a $40 million, 110,000-square-foot plant in a Moscow suburb to process the required beef, milk, buns, vegetables, sauces, and potatoes. In addition, the company brought the managers to Toronto, Canada, for five months of training.[52] Top management at McDonald's anticipated difficulties with the setup and daily operations of this IJV and, indeed, had been working toward the opening day for 13 years. Through careful planning for the control of crucial operational factors, they solved the sourcing, distribution, and employment problems inherent in the former Soviet Union.[53]

Other direct mechanisms are visits by head-office personnel and regular meetings to allow employees around the world to consult and troubleshoot. Increasingly, those meetings comprise videoconferences to allow face-to-face, if not physical, interaction among managers around the world to enable faster and less-expensive frequent meetings. Top executives from headquarters may use periodic visits to subsidiaries to check performance and help anticipate future problems. The meetings allow each general manager to keep in touch with her or his associates, with the overall mission and strategy of the organization, and with comparative performance data and new problem-solving techniques. Increasingly, the tools of technology are being applied as direct mechanisms to ensure up front that operations will be carried out as planned, in particular in countries where processes such as efficient infrastructure and goods forwarding cannot be taken for granted. An example of this is the logistics monitoring system Air Express International set up in Latin America to minimize its many problems there.

Indirect Coordinating Mechanisms

Indirect coordinating mechanisms typically include sales quotas, budgets, and other financial tools as well as feedback reports, which give information about the sales and financial performance of the subsidiary for the last quarter or year.

Domestic companies invariably rely on budgets and financial statement analyses, but for foreign subsidiaries, financial statements and performance evaluations are complicated by *financial variables in MNC reports*, such as exchange rates, inflation levels, transfer prices, and accounting standards.

To reconcile accounting statements, MNCs usually require three sets of financial statements from subsidiaries. One set must meet the national accounting standards and procedures prescribed by law in the host country. This set also aids management in comparing subsidiaries in the same country. A second set must be prepared according to the accounting principles and standards the home country requires. This set allows some comparison with other MNC subsidiaries. The third set of statements translates the second set of statements (with certain adjustments) into the currency of the home country for consolidation purposes, in accordance with FASB Ruling Number 52 of 1982. A foreign subsidiary's financial statements must be consolidated line by line with those of the parent company, according to International Accounting Standard Number 3, adopted in the United States.

Researchers have noted comparative differences between the use of direct versus **indirect controls** among companies headquartered in different countries. One study by Egelhoff examined the practices of 50 U.S., U.K., and European MNCs over their foreign subsidiaries. It compared the use of two mechanisms—the assignment of parent-company managers to foreign subsidiaries and the use of performance reporting systems (that is, comparing behavior mechanisms with output reporting systems).[54] The results of this study show that considerable differences exist in practices across MNC nationalities. For example, U.S. MNCs monitor subsidiary outputs and rely more on frequently reported performance data than do European MNCs. The latter tend to assign more parent-company nationals to key positions in foreign subsidiaries and can count on a higher level of behavior control than their U.S. counterparts.[55]

These findings imply that the U.S. system, which measures more quantifiable aspects of a foreign subsidiary, provides the means to compare performance among subsidiaries. The European system, on the other hand, measures more qualitative aspects of a subsidiary and its environment, which vary among subsidiaries—allowing a focus on the unique situation of the subsidiary but making it difficult to compare its performance to other subsidiaries.[56]

MANAGING EFFECTIVE MONITORING SYSTEMS

Management practices, local constraints, and expectations regarding authority, time, and communication are but a few of the variables likely to affect the **appropriateness of monitoring (or control) systems**. The degree to which headquarters' practices and goals are transferable probably depends on whether top managers are from the head office, the host country, or a third country. In addition, information systems and evaluation variables must all be considered when deciding on appropriate systems.

The Appropriateness of Monitoring and Reporting Systems

One example of differences in the expectations regarding monitoring practices, and therefore in the need for coordination systems, is indicated by a study of Japanese and U.S. firms. Ueno and Sekaran state that their research shows that "the U.S. companies, compared to the Japanese companies, tend to use communication and coordination more extensively, build budget slack to a greater extent, and use long-term performance evaluations to a lesser extent."[57] Furthermore, Ueno and Sekaran conclude that those differences in reporting systems are attributable to the cultural variable of individualism in U.S. society, compared to collectivism in Japanese society. For example, U.S. managers are more likely to use formal communication and coordination processes, whereas Japanese managers use informal and implicit processes. In addition, U.S. managers, who are evaluated on individual performance, are more likely to build slack into budget calculations for a safety net than their Japanese counterparts, who are evaluated on group performance. The implications of this study are that managers around the world who understand the cultural bases for differences in control practices will be more flexible in working with those systems in other countries.

The Role of Information Systems

Reporting systems, such as those described in this chapter, require sophisticated information systems to enable them to work properly—not only for competitive purposes but also for purposes of performance evaluation. Top management must receive accurate and timely information regarding sales, production, and financial results to be able to compare actual performance with goals and to take corrective action where necessary. Most international reporting systems require information feedback at one level or another for financial, personnel, production, and marketing variables.

The specific types of functional reports, their frequency, and the amount of detail required from subsidiaries by headquarters will vary. Neghandi and Welge surveyed the types of functional reports 117 MNCs in Germany, Japan, and the United States submitted.[58] They found that U.S. MNCs typically submit about double the number of reports as do German and Japanese MNCs, with the exception of performance reviews. The Japanese MNCs put far less emphasis on personnel performance reviews than do the U.S. and German MNCs—a finding consistent with the Japanese culture of group decision making, consensus, and responsibility.

Unfortunately, the accuracy and timeliness of information systems are often less than perfect, especially in less-developed countries, where managers typically operate under conditions of extreme uncertainty. Government information, for example, is often filtered or fabricated; other sources of data for decision making are usually limited. Employees are not used to the kinds of sophisticated information generation, analysis, and reporting systems common in developed countries. Their work norms and sense of necessity and urgency may also confound the problem. In addition, their available technology, and the ability to manipulate and transmit data, are usually limited. The **MIS adequacy** in foreign affiliates is a sticky problem for headquarters managers in their attempt to maintain efficient coordination of activities and consolidation of results. Another problem is the **noncomparability of performance data across countries**—the control problem caused by the difficulty of comparing performance data across various countries because of the variables that make that information appear different—which hinders the evaluation process.

The Internet has, of course, made the availability and use of information attainable instantaneously. Many companies are starting to supply Internet MIS systems for supply-chain management. European partners Nestlé S.A. and the Danone Group, world leaders in the food industry, set up Europe's first Internet marketplace for e-procurement in the consumer goods sector, called CPGmarket.com:

> *CPGmarket.com will enhance the efficiency of logistics while at the same time reducing procurement costs for businesses producing, distributing and selling consumer goods. CPG (based on mySAP.com e-business platform) allows companies not only to buy and sell, but also to access industry information.*[59]

Evaluation Variables across Countries

A major problem that arises when evaluating the performance of foreign affiliates is the tendency by headquarters managers to judge subsidiary managers as if all of the evaluation data were comparable across countries. Unfortunately, many variables can make the evaluation information from one country look very different from that of another country, owing to circumstances beyond the control of a subsidiary manager. For example, one country may experience considerable inflation, significant fluctuations in the price of raw materials, political uprisings, or governmental actions. These factors are beyond the manager's control and are likely to have a downward effect on profitability—and yet, that manager may, in fact, have maximized the opportunity for long-term stability and profitability compared with a manager of another subsidiary who was not faced with such adverse conditions. Other variables influencing profitability patterns include transfer pricing, currency devaluation, exchange-rate fluctuations, taxes, and expectations of contributions to local economies.

One way to ensure more meaningful performance measures is to adjust the financial statements to reflect the uncontrollable variables peculiar to each country where a subsidiary is located. This provides a basis for the true evaluation of the comparative return on investment (ROI), which is an overall control measure. Another way to provide meaningful, long-term performance standards is to take into account other nonfinancial measures. These measures include market share, productivity, sales, relations with the host-country government, public image, employee morale, union relations, and community involvement.[60]

CONCLUSION

The structure, control, and coordination *processes* are the same whether they take place in a domestic company, a multinational company with a network of foreign affiliates, or a specific IJV. It is the extent, the focus, and the mechanisms used to organize those activities that differ. More coordination is needed in global companies and MNEs because of uncertain working environments and information systems and because of the variable loci of decision making. Headquarters managers must design appropriate systems to take into account those variables and evaluate performance.

Summary of Key Points

- An organization must be designed to facilitate the implementation of strategic goals. Other variables to consider when designing an organization's structure include environmental conditions, the size of the organization, and the appropriate technology. The geographic dispersion of operations as well as differences in time, language, and culture affect structure in the international context.

- The design of a firm's structure reflects its international entry strategy and tends to change over time with growth and increasing levels of investment, diversity, or both.

- Global trends are exerting increasing pressure on MNCs to achieve economies of scale through globalization. This involves rationalization and the coordination of strategic alliances.

- MNCs can be regarded as interorganizational networks of their own dispersed operations and other strategic alliances. Such relational networks may adopt unique structures for their particular environment while also requiring centralized coordination.

- The transnational structure allows a company to be global and act local by using networks of decentralized units with horizontal communication. This permits local flexibility while achieving global integration.

- Indications of the need for structural changes include inefficiency, conflicts among units, poor communication, and overlapping responsibilities.

- Coordinating and monitoring systems are necessary to regulate organizational activities so that actual performance conforms to expected organizational standards and goals. MNCs use a variety of direct and indirect controls.

- Financial monitoring and evaluation of foreign affiliates are complicated by variables such as exchange rates, levels of inflation, transfer prices, and accounting standards.

- The design of appropriate monitoring systems must take into account local constraints, management practices and expectations, uncertain information systems, and variables in the evaluation process.

- Two major problems in reporting for subsidiaries must be considered: (1) inadequate management information systems and (2) the noncomparability across countries of the performance data needed for evaluation purposes.

Discussion Questions

8-1. What variables have to be considered in designing the organizational structure for international operations? How do these variables interact, and which do you think are most important?

8-2. Explain the need for a firm to be global and act local. How can a firm design its organization to enable this?

8-3. What is a transnational organization? Because many large MNCs are moving toward this format, it is likely that you could at some point be working within this structure. How do you feel about that?

8-4. Discuss the implications of the relative centralization of authority and decision making at headquarters versus local units or subsidiaries. How would you feel about this variable if you were a subsidiary manager?

8-5. As an international manager, what would make you suggest restructuring your firm? What other means of direct and indirect monitoring systems do you suggest?

8-6. What is the role of information systems in the reporting process? Discuss the statement, "Inadequate MIS systems in some foreign affiliates are a control problem for MNCs."

Application Exercises

8-7. If you have personal access to a company with international operations, try to conduct some interviews and find out about the personal interactions involved in working with the organization's counterparts abroad. In particular, ask questions about the nature and level of authority and decision making in overseas units compared with headquarters. What kinds of conflicts are experienced? What changes would your interviewees recommend?

8-8. Do some research on monitoring and reporting issues facing an MNC with subsidiaries in (1) a country in Asia, and (2) a country in South America. Discuss problem areas and

your recommendations to the MNC management as to how to control potential problems.

8-9. Find out about a foreign company with an IJV in the United States. Google some articles, email the company for information, and if possible visit the company and ask questions. Present your findings on the company's major control issues to the class—both at the beginning of the venture and now. What is the company doing differently in its control process compared to a typical domestic operation? Are the control procedures having the desired results? What recommendations do you have?

Experiential Exercise

In groups of four, consider a fast-food chain going into Brazil. Decide on your initial level of desired involvement in Brazil and your entry strategy. Draw up an appropriate organizational design, taking into account strategic goals, relevant variables in Brazil, technology used, size of the firm, and so on. At the next class, present power points of your organization chart and describe the operations and rationale. What are some of the major control issues to be considered?

CASE STUDY

HSBC in 2015: Complex Global Operations and Downsizing

Originally known as Hong Kong Shanghai Banking Corp., HSBC was founded in Hong Kong and Shanghai in 1865. During the past 150 years, HSBC grew by leaps and bounds and became one of the largest banks in the world. In 2014, HSBC had 6,300 offices in 75 countries and was headquartered in London, U.K. During the same year, HSBC was rated the second largest bank in the world with total assets of $2.68 trillion after Industrial and Commercial Bank of China ($2.95 trillion). Other top banks on the list included Deutsche Bank (Germany), Credit Agricole (France), BNP Paribas (Spain), Mitsubishi UFJ Financial (Japan), Barclays (U.K.), and Chase (U.S.).[1] The pace of change and competition in the global banking industry is always dynamic and fierce. In emerging markets and developed countries, HSBC continued to be a visible brand name and dealt with the industry's traditional retail sector, commercial banking, global banking, and global private banking. In 2014, HSBC's market capitalization stood at $176.44 billion with revenues of $74.59 billion, and it employed 266,000 workers worldwide. No wonder HSBC's operations remained in major parts of the world and its main revenues came from commercial banking, retail banking, wealth management, and private banking.

During the 2008 global financial crisis, HSBC did lose money but was not bailed out in Europe and Asia and remained a visible business entity in the banking industry.[2] The financial crisis created havoc in the banking industry, which witnessed *systematic distress* as well as *spillover effects*.[3] The crisis also affected HSBC, which ended up losing money and customers. Unlike American banks, HSBC's operations were somewhat spared, but growth remained stagnant during this period. The bank closed its money-losing operations and sold a few assets. This was a major disruption in HSBC's history and weakened the bank's well-established business model. To deal with the 2008 financial crisis, HSBC embarked on a major reorganization that changed its strategy, corporate structure, and growth patterns. In 2011, HSBC trimmed its North American operations because of losses in the area of subprime lending.[4] At the same time, HSBC started expanding in emerging markets of Asia. China was selected to be the bank's major market for future growth. Other reorganization took place that aimed at mostly downsizing and trimming operations.

In February 2012, HSBC announced its financial results and said the bank had increased its net by 27 percent. This was clearly the result of HSBC's 2010 restructuring plan, which was designed in the post-financial crisis period. Whereas HSBC trimmed its operations in North America, the bank's Asian markets witnessed a good increase in revenues because of growth in emerging markets.[5] *Financial Times* called HSBC "the world's Asian bank."[6] No wonder HSBC planned a major expansion in China and announced increasing its share in China's Bank of Communications. HSBC also expanded its branches in China from 110 locations to 800.[7] This was a major part of the bank's reorganization that was initiated by HSBC's CEO Stuart Gulliver and his team from 2009 to 2010.[8] Although competition was heightened because of the arrival of local and multinational banks,[9] markets were available to financial institutions that carried efficient business models and networks. Because of its long history and operations, the bank's restructuring initiatives resulted in tangible growth and expansion. In a special research report ("The World in 2050: Quantifying the Shift in the Global Economy"), Karen Ward, HSBC's chief economist observed:

> *[Nineteen] of the 30 largest economies will be emerging economies; the emerging economies will collectively be bigger than the developed economies; Global growth will accelerate*

thanks to the contribution from the emerging economies.... Asia will continue demonstrating extremely strong growth rates and those with large population will overtake Western powerhouses."[10]

This clearly showed HSBC's long-term ambitions in emerging markets of Asia where markets were available to banks that carried prudent policies and networks. Like other banks, HSBC expanded in financial services and became more efficient by providing online banking, accessibility of large-scale and real-time data, useful analytics, and other technologies on hand. This was helpful to HSBC when dealing with competitive markets. In 2012, *Hoovers.com* made the following statement that perfectly reflected HSBC's diverse and archetypical operations in global business:

> *HSBC would be a real alphabet soup if the company's name reflected its geographic diversity. One of the world's largest banking groups by assets, HSBC Holdings owns subsidiaries throughout Europe, Hong Kong and the rest of the Asia/Pacific region, the Middle East and Africa, and the Americas.*[11]

Although HSBC had been known for its effective internationalization and growth, by March 2015, HSBC's global operations had become more complex and puzzling. These issues had to be dealt with because of HSBC's fast growth, diverse and complex organizational structure, and control systems in the post-financial crisis period. Robert Jenkins in *Financial Times* observed:

> *Is Europe's biggest bank too big to manage? Or have its management and board simply not been up to the job? Politicians and pundits are pressing the issue. HSBC's senior executives are ducking the question. Yes, they acknowledge, mistakes were made, controls were lax, practices were inappropriate and the organization's structure was flawed. But it was not their fault and they are working hard to put things right.*[12]

Andrew Hill further added in *Financial Times*:

> *HSBC chief executive Stuart Gulliver declared this week that he could not possibly be accountable for the actions of all the staff employed by the bank. Does he have a point? ... But HSBC's difficulties still raise a worrying question: Have some companies become too big to manage?*[13]

The preceding problems that HSBC and other multinational banks encountered after 2012 made widespread headlines in the global media and brought negative publicity and criticism. In 2012, HSBC paid a fine of $1.92 billion to U.S. regulators. This was the result of corporate lapses, money laundering problems in Mexico, and lax operations and control. Moreover, in March 2015, it was disclosed that HSBC's unit in Switzerland had been involved in tax evasion.[14] In 2015, these and other developments forced HSBC to trim down its operations in emerging markets. Interestingly, HSBC's model of "world's local bank" did not work after 2008. In fact, in the coming years, HSBC may become "simpler and smaller" when seeking growth expansion in global markets.[15] Martin Arnold and Patrick Jenkins in *Financial Times* predicted that HSBC will "shrink and simplify" ... it is abandoning once-prized markets, has sold dozens of companies and shed thousands of jobs."[16]

Although the global banking industry is a major strategic industry in world business, it is unevenly regulated. Historically, the industry's growth has been based on regions and country-specific strategies because of national developmental agendas, ideologies, and business growth. Banks may be global in their operations, but they thrive mostly because of national identities, networks, and financial resources. In conclusion, firms' organizational structures, networks, and control and monitoring systems are always on the move because of the complexity of global markets and expansion. In the global banking industry, large-scale multinational banks thrive on strategic locations, networks, and customer service. The same areas can become complex and cumbersome when growth is sought in the presence of lax controls, weakened monitoring system, and haphazard corporate expansion.

Notes

1. D. Fuscaldo, "The 10 Largest Banks in the World," Bankrate
   .com (2015), http://www.bankrate.com/finance/banking/largest-
   banks-in-the-world-1.aspx, accessed April 23, 2015.
2. For detail, see YahooFinance, HSBC Holdings, plc. (2015),
   http://finance.yahoo.com/q/pr?s=HSBC+Profile, accessed April
   23, 2015; Wikipedia, "HSBC," (2015), http://en.wikipedia.org/
   wiki/HSBC, accessed April 23, 2015.
3. For more discussion on these topics, see K. Giesecke & B. Kim,
   "Systemic Risk: What Defaults Are Telling Us," *Management
   Science* 57, No. 8 (2011), pp. 1387–1405.
4. See J. Menon, "HSBC Rues Household Deal, Halts U.S.
   Subprime Lending (Update1)," *Bloomberg* (March 2, 2009),
   http://www.bloomberg.com/apps/news?pid=newsarchive&sid=a
   jBfkUKrgsZY), accessed March 5, 2012.
5. For detail, see P. Jenkins and S. Goff, "HSBC Progress Fails to
   Rally Investors," *Financial Times* (February 28, 2012), p. 17;
   S. S. Munoz and M. Colchester, "HSBC Profit Climbs, So Do
   Costs," *Wall Street Journal* (February 28, 2012), p. C3.
6. "The World's Asian Bank," *Financial Times* (February 28,
   2012), p. 14.
7. H. Sender, "HSBC to Build China Presence by Seeking to Raise
   Stake in BoCom," *Financial Times* (February 15, 2012), p. 13.
8. "Gulliver's travels," *Economist* (April 16, 2011), p. 75.
9. T. Alloway and R. Wigglesworth, "New Lenders Move to Fill
   the Gap Left by Ailing Banks," *Financial Times* (October 6,
   2011), p. 22.
10. K. Ward, *The World in 2050: Quantifying the Shift in the Global
    Economy* (London, U.K.: HSBC Plc, 2011), pp. 1, 21.
11. Hoovers.com, "HSBC Holding, Plc.," http://www.hoovers.com/
    company/HSBC_Holdings_plc/crksif-1-1njht4-1njfaq.html,
    (2012), accessed March 3, 2012.
12. R. Jenkins, "How the HSBC Chairman Can Restore Accountability
    at His Bank," *Financial Times* (March 11, 2015), p. 9.
13. A. Hill, "Too Big to Manage," *Financial Times* (March 1, 2015),
    p. 7.
14. M. Arnold, P. Jenkins, and H. Sender, "Pressure Mounts on
    HSBC Leadership," *Financial Times* (February 25, 2015),
    p. 16.
15. P. Jenkins and M. Arnold, "HSBC Speeds Up Exit from
    Emerging Markets," *Financial Times* (April 17, 2015), http://
    www.ft.com/cms/s/0/85642fcc-e50d-11e4-bb4b-00144feab7de
    .html#axzz3YGfzQGkn, accessed April 22, 2015.
16. M. Arnold and P. Jenkins, "Shrink and Simplify," *Financial
    Times* (April 23, 2015), p. 5.

Case Questions

8-10. How do you evaluate HSBC's global reorganization after the 2008 global financial crisis, its position in 2015, and its current position?

8-11. Compare and contrast HSBC and other multinational banks in global business.

8-12. What did you learn from HSBC's case when applying concepts and theories from this chapter?

Source: Copyright © 2015 by Syed Tariq Anwar, West Texas A&M University, used with permission.

Endnotes

1. Brad Stone, "The Alibaba Invasion," *Bloomberg Businessweek*,
   August 15, 2014.
2. Ibid.
3. Roberto C. Goizueta, (Former) Chairman and CEO, Coca-Cola
   Company.
4. A. D. Chandler, *Strategy and Structure: Chapters in the History of
   the American Industrial Enterprise* (Cambridge, MA: MIT Press,
   1962); R. E. Miles et al., "Organizational Strategy, Structure, and
   Process," *Academy of Management Review* 3, No. 3 (1978), pp.
   546–562; and J. Woodward, *Industrial Organization: Theory and
   Practice* (Oxford University Press, 1965).
5. Charles A. O'Reilly III, J. Bruce Harreld, and Michael L.
   Tushman, "Organizational Ambidexterity: IBM and Emerging
   Business Opportunities," *California Management Review* 51,
   No. 4 (2009), pp. 75–99.
6. C. A. Bartlett and S. Ghoshal, *Managing across Borders*
   (Boston: Harvard Business School Press, 1989).
7. J. M. Stopford and L. T. Wells Jr., *Managing the Multinational
   Enterprise* (New York: Basic Books, 1972).
8. John W. Miller, "Alcoa Will Divide in Two," Wall Street Journal,
   September 29, 2015, B1.
9. Leaders, "Asia's New Model Company"; "Samsung and Its
   Attractions," *Economist*, October 1, 2011, p. 14.
10. Kelly Olsen, "Samsung Electronics Reorganizes to Fight
    Slump," www.nytimes, January 16, 2009.
11. "Samsung Firestorm," *Financial Times*, March 3, 2015.
12. "Heinz's Johnson to Divest Operations, Scrap Management of
    Firm by Regions," *Wall Street Journal*, December 8, 1997.
13. "H. J. Heinz Company and Kraft Foods Group Sign Definitive
    Merger Agreement to Form the Kraft Heinz Company," www.heinz
    .com, release date Wednesday, March 25, 2015, 06:02 A.M. EDT.
14. www.Nestle.com, December 7, 2000.
15. *Financial Times*, February 22, 2005.
16. Ibid.
17. www.Nestle.com, April 15, 2012.
18. J. Strikwerda and J. W. Stoelhorst, "The Emergence and
    Evolution of the Multidimensional Organization," *California
    Management Review* 51, No. 4 (2009), pp. 11–31.

19. Toby Gibbs, Suzanne Heywood, and Leigh Weiss, "Organizing for an Emerging World," *McKinsey Quarterly*, June 2012.

20. Nick Wingfield, "Microsoft Reorganizes the Apple Way," www.nytimes.com, July 11, 2013.

21. Richard Waters, "Microsoft Rejigs Management," *Financial Times* [London (UK)], July 12, 2013, p. 11.

22. H. Henzler and W. Rall, "Facing Up to the Globalization Challenge," *McKinsey Quarterly* (Fall 1986), pp. 52–68.

23. "Petrobras Creates 6 Companies for Comperj Project—Brazil," *Business News Americas*, February 5, 2009.

24. T. Levitt, "The Globalization of Markets," *Harvard Business Review* (May–June 1983), pp. 92–102; and S. P. Douglas and Yoram Wind, "The Myth of Globalization," *Columbia Journal of World Business* (Winter 1987), pp. 19–29.

25. www.levistrauss.com, accessed April 18, 2015.

26. http://www.levistrauss.com/about/global-workplaces, accessed April 18, 2015.

27. Ibid.

28. www.pg.com, news releases, November 22, 2006.

29. "P&G Corporate Information: How the Structure Works," www.pg.com, accessed April 18, 2015.

30. "P&G Corporate Information: How the Structure Works," www.pg.com, accessed April 18, 2015.

31. J. R. Galbraith, "The Multidimensional and Reconfigurable Organization," *Organizational Dynamics* 39, No. 2 (2010), pp. 115–125.

32. For more detail, see *The New Global Challengers: How 100 Top Companies from Rapidly Developing Economies Are Changing the World* (Boston, MA: The Boston Consulting Group, 2006); *Organizing for Global Advantage in China, India, and Other Rapidly Developing Economies* (Boston, MA: The Boston Consulting Group, 2006); Khanna, Tarun, and Krishna Palepu, "Emerging Giants: Building World-Class Companies in Developing Countries," *Harvard Business Review* (October 2006), pp. 60–69.

33. See Syed T. Anwar, "Global Business and Globalization," *Journal of International Management* 71 (2007); "Emerging Giants," *BusinessWeek*, July 31, 2006, pp. 40–49.

34. Joe Leahy, "Brazil Competitive Profile: Investors Urged to Spread Net," FT.com, March 26, 2015.

35. Raymond E. Miles, Miles Grant, Charles C. Snow, Kirsimarja Blomqvist, and Hector Rocha, "The I-form Organization," *California Management Review* 51, No. 4 (2009), pp. 61–76.

36. http://www.philips.com/global/, accessed April 19, 2015.

37. *Financial Times*, February 9, 2005.

38. www.Intel.com, August 18, 2005.

39. S. Ghoshal and C. A. Bartlett, "The Multinational Corporation as an Interorganizational Network," *Academy of Management Review* 15, No. 4 (1990), pp. 603–625.

40. Mohanbir Sawhney and Sumant Mandal, "Go Global," *Business 2.0* (May 5, 2001), pp. 178–213.

41. J. D. Daniels, L. H. Radebaugh, and D. P. Sullivan, *Globalization and Business* (Upper Saddle River, NJ: Prentice Hall, 2002).

42. Deloitte & Touche, "Energizing the Supply Chain," *The Review*, January 17, 2000, p. 1.

43. C. A. Bartlett and S. Ghoshal, "Organizing for Worldwide Effectiveness: The Transnational Solution," *California Management Review* (Fall 1988), pp. 54–74.

44. Ibid.

45. Sources include Mark Pieth, "FIFA Must Finally Show a Red Card to Corruption in Football," *Financial Times*, January 20, 2012, p. 13; Grant Wahl, "Rotten All Around: FIFA's Year of Corruption Shows That Real Change Will Only Come When the Man at the Top Leaves," http://sportsillustrated.cnn.com/vault/article/magazine/MAG1193195/index.htm, December 26, 2011; http://en.wikipedia.org/wiki/FIFA, accessed February 1, 2012; www.FIFA.com, accessed February 1, 2012.

46. Kara Scannell, "FIFA Officials Accused of 'rampant, systemic, deep-rooted corruption," *FT.com*, May 28, 2015.

47. Matthew Futterman, "FIFA suspends its No.2. Official," Wall Street Journal, September 18, 2015, A.7.

48. John B. Cullen and K. Praveen Parboteeah, *Multinational Management: A Strategic Approach*, 3rd ed. (Cincinnati: South-Western, 2005), p. 281.

49. Oded Shenkar, "Cultural Distance Revisited: Towards a More Rigorous Conceptualization and Measurement of Cultural Differences," *Journal of International Business*, 43, No. 1 (January 2012).

50. Ibid.

51. www.McDonalds.com, February 20, 2001.

52. Andrew Jack, "Russians Wake up to Consumer Capitalism," www.FT.com, January 30, 2001.

53. Ibid.

54. W. G. Egelhoff, "Patterns of Control in U.S., U.K., and European Multinational Corporations," *Journal of International Business Studies* (Fall 1984), pp. 73–83.

55. Ibid.

56. Ibid.

57. S. Ueno and U. Sekaran, "The Influence of Culture on Budget Control Practices in the U.S.A. and Japan: An Empirical Study," *Journal of International Business Studies* 23 (Winter 1992), pp. 659–674.

58. A. R. Neghandi and M. Welge, *Beyond Theory Z* (Greenwich, CT: J.A.I. Publishers, 1984), p. 18.

59. www.Nestle.com, press release, March 21, 2000.

60. A. V. Phatak, *International Dimensions of Management*, 2nd ed. (Boston: PWS-Kent, 1989).

PART 3: Comprehensive Cases

AMITY
RESEARCH CENTERS
HEADQUARTER
BANGALORE

Case 5 Alibaba versus Tencent: The Battle for China's M-Commerce Space

Abstract: Mobile e-commerce or m-commerce was growing fast in China. By 2018, China was anticipated to rank as the second largest m-commerce market in the world. The rising m-commerce market had lured many Internet players, including Chinese web giants Tencent and Alibaba. Tencent, which started off as an instant messaging platform in 1998, had gradually grown into a leading Internet service portal in the country. Alibaba, which began its business in 1999 as an online B2B model, gradually adopted B2C and C2C business models and was ranked as the leading player in the Chinese e-commerce market. Since October 2013, both Alibaba and Tencent had been involved in various frenzied acquisitions to outpace each other in the online markets particularly in the m-commerce segment. The rivalry was more visible in 2014 particularly with the taxi-calling apps *Didi Dache* backed by Tencent and *Kuadi Dache* of Alibaba. The quick shift in consumers' behavior from desktop to mobile devices, coupled with the development of mobile Internet further intensified the competition between the Internet giants in the country. In 2014, Tencent launched a mobile payment platform, and more than 200 million users signed up for the service within 15 days. In an effort to stave off competition, Alibaba also adopted several strategies. Against this background, it remained to be seen who, ultimately, would win the battle in China's m-commerce space.

Pedagogical Objectives

The case study helps to understand and analyze:

- The m-commerce market in China.
- The rivalry between Alibaba and Tencent in China's m-commerce market.
- The impact of rivalry in reviving the country's m-commerce market.

Case Study

"In China shopping is a social activity. You want to tell friends about it, recommend it—it's a smartphone activity, and whoever owns that organizational ability also has a hold over how a person shops."[1]

–FRANK LAVIN
CEO, Export Now[2]

This case was written by Dr. Suchitra Mohanty, Amity Research Centers Headquarters, Bangalore. It is intended to be used as the basis for class discussion rather than to illustrate either effective or ineffective handling of a management situation. The case was compiled from published sources.
© 2014, Amity Research Centers Headquarters, Bangalore.

"The penguin [Tencent's corporate mascot] has walked out of the Antarctic. They are trying to adapt to hot weather, and to force the world to adapt to their preferred conditions too. It is time for Ali to hit out, either on the offensive or the defensive."[3]

–JACK MA
Founder, Alibaba

"The wind is blowing against Alibaba and the biggest risk is coming from the mobile sector....Firms are all lining up—the school of Tencent or the school of Alibaba—and the camps are forming."[4]

–ZHANG CHENHAO
Executive Director, Gold Sand Capital[5]

Tencent, one of the most successful Internet players in the country, was introduced by Huateng Ma in 1998, and Alibaba, the key player in the Chinese e-commerce market, was founded by Jack Ma (Ma) in 1999.[6] Alibaba, which started its business as an online B2B model, had gradually adopted B2C and C2C business models and was known as the leading e-commerce portal in China. Alibaba had launched online business platforms such as Taobao, Tmall, group buying platform Juhuasuan and Aliexpress, and so on.[7] Tencent had also introduced a variety of social platforms, including QQ, WeChat, QQ games, Qzone, and so on.[8]

The Chinese m-commerce market was growing at a faster rate.[9] In 2014, out of 618 million[10] Internet users, around 80 percent were accessing the web on mobile phones; 85 percent were interested in buying various products through Internet-enabled mobile handsets.[11] Besides, China was anticipated to rank as the second largest mobile commerce (m-commerce) market in the world after the United States by 2018.[12] The rising m-commerce market coupled with the quick shift in consumers' preferences toward mobile shopping and the

[3]Jiying Chen and Zhihui Xu, "Digital Warfare," http://www.newschinamag.com/magazine/digital-warfare, April 2014.

[4]"As Giant U.S. IPO Nears, Alibaba's China E-commerce Crown Slips," op. cit.

[5]Gold Sand Capital was one of the popular e-commerce investment advisory firms.

[6]Kim Gittleson, "Tencent and Alibaba Battle for Internet Dominance in China," http://www.bbc.com/news/business-26540666, March 18, 2014.

[7]"Company Overview," http://news.alibaba.com/specials/aboutalibaba/aligroup/index.html.

[8]"About Tencent," http://www.tencent.com/en-us/at/abouttencent.shtml.

[9]"IDC: Mobile E-Commerce to Become the Focus of Competition in Chinese E-Commerce Market," http://www.idc.com/getdoc.jsp?containerId=prCN24764014, March 25, 2014.

[10]"Tencent and Alibaba Battle for Internet Dominance in China," op. cit.

[11]"IDC: Mobile E-Commerce to Become the Focus of Competition in Chinese E-Commerce Market," op. cit.

[12]Michelle Evans, "China's M-Commerce Market to Triple by 2018," http://blog.euromonitor.com/2014/01/chinas-m-commerce-market-to-triple-by-2018.html, January 3, 2014.

[1]Adam Jourdan, "As Giant U.S. IPO Nears, Alibaba's China E-commerce Crown Slips," http://www.reuters.com/article/2014/03/17/us-china-ecommerce-idUSBREA2G04Z20140317, March 17, 2014.

[2]Export Now offered a group of interrelated online services to the customers that facilitated export and sales of various items on the web. © 2014, Amity Research Centers HQ, Bangalore. All rights reserved.

EXHIBIT I China: Growth of M-Commerce

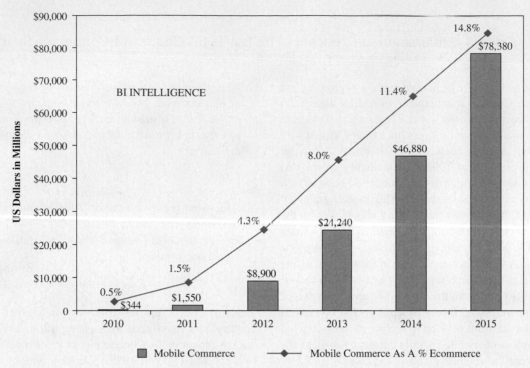

Source: John Heggestuen, "China's Smartphone Explosion: The Top Opportunities in the World's Largest Mobile Market," http://www.businessinsider.in/Chinas-Smartphone-Explosion-The-Top-Opportunities-In-The-Worlds-Largest-Mobile-Market/articleshow/24949669.cms, October 30, 2013.

development of mobile Internet further attracted many Internet players toward the Chinese m-commerce market.[13]

In 2014,[14] Tencent launched a mobile payment platform, and more than 200 million users signed up for the service within 15 days. Analysts highlighted that for both Tencent and Alibaba, a big challenge was how to design a strong mobile business strategy to stay competitive in the mobile Internet business segment in the country. Against this background, the case study tried to unravel the strategic battle between Alibaba and Tencent to gain the top slot in the Chinese m-commerce market.

M-Commerce in China: An Overview

M-commerce, or mobile e-commerce, referred to the payment transactions for the purchase of various goods and services by a mobile handset.[15] The size of the m-commerce market in China was projected to reach $78,380 million in 2014 from $344 million in 2010[16] (Exhibit I). By 2018,[17] China was anticipated to be the second biggest m-commerce market in the world next to the United States. Within five years (2014–2018), the size of the m-commerce market was forecasted to increase by more than three times in the country. According to the projections of Euromonitor International, the size of the m-commerce market would touch $134.3 billion[18] in the United States and $123.8 billion in China by 2018. Besides, China had the largest number of mobile subscribers as well as smartphone users in the world, which further provided remarkable opportunity for m-commerce in the Asian country[19] (Exhibit II).

In 2013,[20] IDC[21] estimated that more than 360 million smartphones were purchased by Chinese consumers. According to the China Internet Network Center[22] (CNNIC), as of June 2013, around 78.5 percent of the Chinese netizens had surfed the Internet through their handsets, which was comparatively higher than the people who visited the web on desktops (69.5%) and laptops (46.9%).[23] Moreover, the rapid developments in 3G network with 300 million 3G subscribers, the widely accessible Wi-Fi spots in the country, along with the reasonably priced handsets acted as a fuel for the growth of m-commerce in China.[24] "Mobile purchasing aligns with the

[13]Charles Clover, "Chinese Internet: Mobile Wars," http://www.ft.com/intl/cms/s/2/56a160aa-a86f-11e3-a946-00144feab7de.html#axzz2wTprNHt8, March 19, 2014.

[14]"Tencent and Alibaba Battle for Internet Dominance in China," op. cit.

[15]"China's M-Commerce Market to Triple by 2018," op. cit.

[16]John Heggestuen, "China's Smartphone Explosion: The Top Opportunities in the World's Largest Mobile Market," http://www.businessinsider.in/Chinas-Smartphone-Explosion-The-Top-Opportunities-In-The-Worlds-Largest-Mobile-Market/articleshow/24949669.cms, October 30, 2013.

[17]"China's M-Commerce Market to Triple by 2018," op. cit.

[18]Ibid.

[19]Ibid.

[20]Julia Q. Zhu, "China's E-Commerce Goes Mobile in 2014," http://www.techinasia.com/china-ecommerce-goes-mobile-2014/, December 30, 2013.

[21]International Data Corporation, founded in 1964, was one of the popular market research firms that specialized in information technology.

[22]Founded in 1997, CNNIC was an administrative agency for Internet affairs in China.

[23]"China's E-Commerce Goes Mobile in 2014," op. cit.

[24]Ibid.

EXHIBIT II   M-Commerce in the Asia Pacific

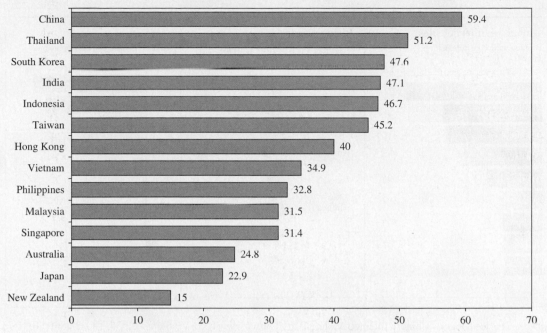

Source: Jim Erickson, "What's Driving China's M-Commerce Boom [Charts]," http://www.alizila.com/whats-driving-chinas-m-commerce-boom-charts, February 26, 2014.

Chinese consumer's desire for speed and the convenience for 'any time' shopping....The trend toward smarter and more functional phones and tablets, coupled with the rising use of social media platforms to inform and connect consumers, is likely to fuel the continued rise in the number and proportion of so-called m-commerce transactions in the Chinese e-commerce market,"[25] explained KPMG (Exhibit III). However, critics also pointed out that despite the favorable growth projections, the m-commerce market in China was at a nascent stage. The mobile payment market in the country was highly fragmented.[26]

Alibaba, Baidu, and Tencent, the big three online rivals in China, popularly known as BAT, were aiming to play actively in the emerging m-commerce market of the country.[27] The Internet giants were ranked among the top ten web companies in the world (Exhibit IV) and were enjoying a natural monopoly in their respective domains. However, for the six months after October 2013, the online rivals, particularly Alibaba and Tencent, were engaged in aggressive acquisitions to expand their businesses in different segments of the market (such as online taxi reservation, online payment through handsets, etc.) to compete with each other. Arthur Kroeber of Gavekal Dragonomics stated that, "Before, each of these companies had a distinct sphere, but with the arrival of mobile Internet there is more and more convergence on a single model, and more areas of overlap. That's where the battle lines are now."[28]

[25]Jim Erickson, "What's Driving China's M-Commerce Boom [Charts]," http://www.alizila.com/whats-driving-chinas-m-commerce-boom-charts, February 26, 2014.
[26]"China's M-Commerce Market to Triple by 2018," op. cit.
[27]"Chinese Internet: Mobile Wars," op. cit.
[28]Ibid.

EXHIBIT III   M-Commerce Growth Opportunities in China

- **Mobile commerce**   By the end of 2013, China's mobile commerce market—e-commerce transacted on smartphones or tablets—will reach $24.2 billion in value and account for 11 percent of all e-commerce, a proportion that is on par with the U.S. market.
- **Mobile transactions and payments**   Sixty-nine percent of Chinese consumers said that they had purchased a product or service with their smartphone, compared with 46 percent in the United States.
- **Mobile advertising**   Mobile e-commerce will account for $2.1 billion in spending or 13 percent of all online ad spending in China this year. That's also on par with U.S. levels. (In the first half of 2013, U.S. online ad spending was 15 percent mobile.)
- **Smartphones**   China is currently responsible for 38 percent of global smartphone shipments. The country is near the smartphone tipping point. In just over a year, smartphone subscriptions will outpace feature phone shipments.
- **Mobile platforms**   Android is dominant. It accounted for 72 percent of smartphone sales compared to Apple's 21 percent in the 12 weeks through August 2013.
- **App stores**   China is already responsible for 15 percent of global Apple app store downloads.

Source: John Heggestuen, "China's Smartphone Explosion: The Top Opportunities in the World's Largest Mobile Market," http://www.businessinsider.in/Chinas-Smartphone-Explosion-The-Top-Opportunities-In-The-Worlds-Largest-Mobile-Market/articleshow/24949669.cms, October 30, 2013.

EXHIBIT IV   Top Ten Internet Players in the World

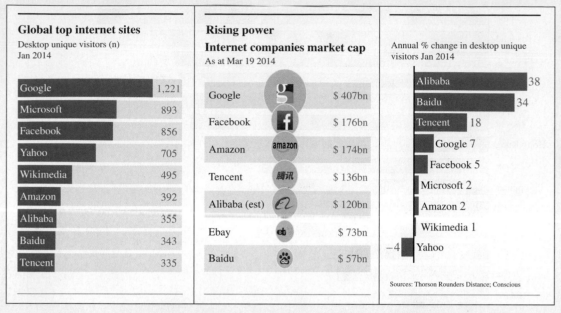

Global top internet sites		Rising power		Annual % change in desktop unique	

Global top internet sites
Desktop unique visitors (n)
Jan 2014

Google	1,221
Microsoft	893
Facebook	856
Yahoo	705
Wikimedia	495
Amazon	392
Alibaba	355
Baidu	343
Tencent	335

Rising power
Internet companies market cap
As at Mar 19 2014

Google	$ 407bn
Facebook	$ 176bn
Amazon	$ 174bn
Tencent	$ 136bn
Alibaba (est)	$ 120bn
Ebay	$ 73bn
Baidu	$ 57bn

Annual % change in desktop unique visitors Jan 2014

Alibaba	38
Baidu	34
Tencent	18
Google	7
Facebook	5
Microsoft	2
Amazon	2
Wikimedia	1
Yahoo	−4

Sources: Thorson Rounders Distance; Conscious

Source: Charles Clover, "Chinese Internet: Mobile Wars," http://www.ft.com/intl/cms/s/2/56a160aa-a86f-11e3-a946-00144feab7de.html#axzz2wTprNHt8, March 19, 2014.

Alibaba versus Tencent: The Digital War

The Alibaba group, which started its journey in 1999,[29] was the largest e-commerce group in China. The company was founded by Jack Ma, a teacher from Hangzhou, China. In 2003, Alibaba introduced Taobao, an online marketplace. In 2008, the group started Tmall.com as part of Taobao.com and, in 2010, it introduced AliExpress, an online retail marketplace targeted at global customers. Later in 2011, Tmall started working as an independent online marketplace of Alibaba and was ranked largest B2C online platform in China by iResearch. Besides, in February 2014, Taobao was recognized as the leading m-commerce app in the country by Alexa.com.[30]

In 2013,[31] Alibaba had forayed into the online education marketplace and introduced Tongxue, a vertical site through Taobao. Tongxue offered various online education materials and online videos for different courses in the country. It also offered materials prepared by tutors for various exams, materials for vocational training such as bakery lessons, makeup tips, and so on. Analysts pointed out that the online education market, valued at 72.3 yuan in 2012, was anticipated to reach 174.5 billion yuan by 2015.[32] Alibaba also launched smart TVs in the Chinese market in 2013 with an aim to extend the e-commerce business to the living rooms of the people.[33]

However, Tencent, one of the biggest rivals of Alibaba, was an early entrant in the e-commerce space.[34] It was founded in 1998[35] by Huateng Ma with the objective of connecting young users on the Net and introduced the popular instant messenger platform QQ. In 2004,[36] Tencent was listed in the Hong Kong Stock Exchange as Tencent Holdings Limited. Gradually, Tencent introduced other innovative messenger platforms such as WeChat, QQ.com, QQ Games, Qzone, 3g.QQ.com, SoSo, PaiPai, and Tenpay.[37] In 2005,[38] the web firm collaborated with the global search engine leader, Google. The collaboration enabled Tencent to include Google Web Search in its Internet-based services. "Cooperation with Google is part of our efforts to further strengthen our Internet-based offerings. We believe Google Web Search will provide our users with a high-quality search experience and increase the stickiness of our user community. In addition, Google's targeted advertising programme, Google AdSense, will contribute to our revenue growth,"[39] emphasized David Wallerstein, senior executive VP of Tencent. In the same year, the company also signed an agreement with China Mobile to provide mobile value-added service 161 Mobile Chat.[40] In 2006, QQ reached a new milestone with 20

[29]"Company Overview," op. cit.
[30]Ibid.
[31]Jing Meng, "Taobao Launches Online Education Marketplace," http://www.chinadaily.com.cn/china/2013-12/04/content_17152461.htm, April 12, 2013.
[32]Ibid.
[33]Kaylene Hong, "Alibaba Launches 55-Inch and 42-Inch Smart TVs in China to Extend E-Commerce into the Living Room," http://thenextweb.com/asia/2013/09/10/alibaba-launches-55-inch-and-42-inch-smart-tvs-in-china-to-extend-e-commerce-into-the-living-room/, September 10, 2013.

[34]"Tencent and Alibaba Battle for Internet Dominance in China," op. cit.
[35]Ibid.
[36]"About Tencent, http://www.tencent.com/en-us/at/abouttencent.shtml.
[37]Ibid.
[38]"Tencent Announces Alliance with Google in Web Search and Targeted Advertising," http://www.tencent.com/en-us/content/ir/news/2005/attachments/20050204.pdf, February 4, 2005.
[39]Ibid.
[40]"Tencent Signs New '161 Mobile Chat' Agreement with China Mobile," http://www.tencent.com/en-us/content/ir/news/2005/attachments/20050118.pdf, January 18, 2005.

million online users account. By 2014, QQ became the largest messenger platform in the world with more than a billion user accounts.[41]

Earlier in 2012,[42] Tencent reorganized its business entity into six subgroups: Corporate Development Group (CDG), Interactive Entertainment Group (IEG), Mobile Internet Group (MIG), Online Media Group (OMG), Social Network Group (SNG) and Technology and Engineering Group (TEG). "Through the reorganization, we hope to unleash the Company's potential capabilities to capture the opportunities of the evolving Internet industry. Our goals are: to strengthen our social networking services, to embrace the expanding global online games market, to extend our presence in mobile Internet, to integrate our online media platforms, to nurture our search business, to build out our e-commerce platforms, and to enhance our capabilities to incubate new businesses. At the same time, we will pool certain of our technology and engineering teams to further develop core technologies and operational platforms so as to better support future business growth,"[43] said Huateng Ma.

In 2013,[44] Tencent invested around $448 million and entered into a strategic collaboration with Sogou Inc in China. Analysts said that the collaboration further strengthened the position of Tencent on the mobile front. "We believe Sogou is the ideal partner for Tencent to develop search opportunities further within China. This reinforces our 'open, win–win' philosophy of working with leading teams to create innovative products for users, and build a healthy, diversified ecosystem for the industry," stated Huateng Ma. He further added that, "We have high regard for Sogou's strong innovation capabilities and successful execution track record. We are confident that Sogou, after combination with Soso, will deliver superior search experiences to users on our social, browser and content platforms, especially on the mobile front."[45]

To compete with Alibaba, Tencent also launched its own online education site with the help of QQ IM in 2013.[46] Through the education site, Tencent offered services such as group video chatting, PowerPoint presentations, and so on[47] (Exhibit V).

Will the Rivalry Revive the Industry?

"The world's major tech companies are realizing that having a really popular mobile messenger has simply become table stake for competing in this era of computing....If you want to play in mobile, you need to have a popular mobile messenger. You don't have one? You don't get to play,"[48] stressed Ted Livingston, CEO, Kik Messenger.[49] Alibaba, the leading player in the $1.6 trillion Chinese e-commerce market, might have lost its battle with opponent Tencent in China's mobile Internet market.[50] Tencent had gradually ruled the smartphone screens of the users in the country with the help of its popular social messaging platforms, WeChat and Weixin. Analysts noted that the m-commerce battle between Tencent and Alibaba gained prominence soon after the acquisition of the mobile messaging firms WhatsApp[51] by Facebook and Viber[52] by Rakuten.[53] The acquisitions signaled that the mobile messaging platform would play an important role, particularly in users' experience in their smartphone screens.[54]

In China, Alibaba was struggling with its mobile business. The Laiwang mobile messaging app of the company had not shown any remarkable progress so far (both as a chat app and as a mobile gaming portal). By November 2013, Laiwang had registered only 10 million users compared to the 272 million users of WeChat as of September 2013. The WeChat users employed its services for booking taxis, topping up phone credit, investing in wealth management products, and so on through the messaging platform. "WeChat has won China....It's going to be the dominant application there. Tencent controls the channel, the customer relationship (and) that means they can promote their services and e-commerce offerings to the exclusion and detriment of Alibaba," said Ben Thompson, technology writer, stratechery.com. Besides Wandoujia, the Chinese app store reported that the games introduced by WeChat were the most-downloaded ones through its app store.[55]

Alibaba also introduced few interesting promotional measures for Laiwang. For example, it sent a memo to its employees to sign up at least 100 new users to obtain the New Year bonus at Alibaba.[56] Alibaba was also planning to build a mobile gaming platform to compete with rival Tencent in the country. Wang Shuai (Shuai), spokesman for Alibaba, emphasized that the games introduced through the Laiwang platform were mainly to compete with the rival WeChat. "We're unhappy with Tencent's monopoly in this industry....We have to help to fight for a healthy environment for game development,"[57] explained Shuai.

[41]Ibid.

[42]"Tencent Forms Six Business Groups to Embrace Future Internet Opportunities," http://www.tencent.com/en-us/content/ir/news/2012/attachments/20120518.pdf, May 18, 2012.

[43]Ibid.

[44]"Sohu, Sogou and Tencent Jointly Announce Strategic Cooperation," http://www.tencent.com/en-us/content/ir/news/2013/attachments/20130916.pdf.

[45]Ibid.

[46]Xiang Tracey, "Tencent Finally Taps into Online Education Market, with a Live Video Course Feature Added to QQ IM," http://technode.com/2013/11/15/tencent-finally-taps-into-online-education-marketwith-a-live-video-course-feature-added-to-qq-im/, November 2013.

[47]Ibid.

[48]Denny Thomas and Paul Carsten, "What's Up for Alibaba's Mobile App Strategy?" http://in.reuters.com/article/2014/02/24/tech-mobile-alibaba-idINL3N0LQ2NJ20140224, February 25, 2014.

[49]An instant messaging application for mobile devices started in 2009.

[50]"What's Up for Alibaba's Mobile App Strategy?" op. cit.

[51]Facebook acquired WhatsApp in 2014 for $19 billion; it was known as the biggest acquisition in the tech industry.

[52]Viber was an instant messaging voice-over-Internet application Talmon Marco founded in 2010.

[53]Rakuten was the largest e-commerce company in Japan on the basis of sales volume.

[54]"What's Up for Alibaba's Mobile App Strategy?" op. cit.

[55]Ibid.

[56]"Bloggers Weigh In as the War for China's Chatters Gets Dirty," https://www.youtube.com/watch?v=c1sRdDffMgk, October 28, 2013.

[57]"What's Up for Alibaba's Mobile App Strategy?" op. cit.

EXHIBIT V Alibaba versus Tencent

Alibaba	Specification	Tencent
Laiwang	Messaging	WeChat (355 million active users as of March 2014)
Sina Weibo (Alibaba won 18% of Sina Weibo having 129 million active users)	Weibo	Tencent Weibo
Tabao (119 million active shopping accounts)	C2C Commerce	Paipai
Tmall (50.6% market share 2013 2nd Quarter)	B2C Commerce	Jingdong
Alipay (300 million registered users more than the TenPay)	3rd Party Payment	Tenpay
Juhuasuan (1/3rd of the daily deal markets)	Daily Deals	Dianping
Alipay Credit Card	Virtual Credit Cards	Tenpay Credit Card
Taobao, Qyer	Travel Booking	E Long, 17u
Kuaide Dache	Taxi Hailing	Didi Dache (almost twice the market share of Kuaide)
Haier	E-Commerce Logistics	China South City
Aliyun, Yahoo	Search	Sogou, Soso
Aliyun, Kanbox	Cloud Storage	Weiyun (having 300 million registered users)
Autonavi	Navigation	Tencent Map
Aliyun OS	Android Rom	CyanogenMod
Aliyun App Store	App Stores	Tencent MyApp
Laiwang, Taobao (as operators)	Gaming	Tencent Games, Riot Games, Epic Games
Xiami	Music	QQ Music (250 million registered users)
Skyworth, Wasu Rainbow, Aliyun OS (2013)	Smart TV	Le TV, Future TV, Weixin TV (in 2013)
Tutorgroup, Taobao Tongxue (in April, 2013)	Education	QQ group (in November, 2013)

Source: Compiled by the author from Paul Bischoff, "Tencent versus Alibaba: A Complete Guide to an Increasingly Fierce Rivalry (INFOGRAPHIC)," http://www.techinasia.com/tencent-alibaba-complete-guide-increasingly-fierce-rivalry-infographic/, March 19, 2014.

In 2014,[58] Tencent invested around HK$1.5 billion dollars ($193.5 million[59]) in the logistic firm, China South City Holdings. The investment allowed Tencent to obtain around 9.9 percent stake in the logistics firm. The company also had an option to increase its stake up to 13 percent by 2016. Soon after the deal, the shares of Tencent rose more than 5 percent on the Hong Kong stock exchange. Analysts said the China South City deal would support Tencent's plans to expand its e-commerce business. "Chinese small-to-medium-sized enterprises have huge demand to expand their businesses online.... Cooperation with China South City enables us to jointly facilitate such enterprises migrating online, utilising China South City's physical locations and logistics capabilities,"[60] revealed Martin Lau Chi Ping, president of Tencent. Besides, both Tencent and China South City were planning to work on online payment services, warehousing, and delivery services.[61] Critics added that until early 2014,[62] Alibaba and Tencent were working closely to develop their own area of expertise such as Alibaba on the e-commerce sites and Tencent on the instant messaging services sites. However, during 2014, both Tencent and

[58]"Tencent Shares Rise to Record on China South City Deal," http://www.bbc.com/news/business-25754894, January 16, 2014.

[59]"Update 1: Tencent Grows E-Commerce Ops Via China South City Investment," http://www.reuters.com/article/2014/01/15/tencent-chinasouthcity-idUSL3N0KP39920140115, January 15, 2014.

[60]"Tencent Shares Rise to Record on China South City Deal," op. cit.

[61]Ibid.

[62]Eric Pfanner, "E-Commerce War Intensifies in China between Rivals Tencent and Alibaba," http://retail.economictimes.indiatimes.com/news/e-commerce/e-tailing/e-commerce-war-intensifies-in-china-between-rivals-tencent-and-alibaba/28945144, January 17, 2014.

Alibaba were trying to encroach on each other's traditional boundaries.[63] Bryan Wang, an analyst with Forrester Research, while commenting on Tencent's alliance with China South City Holdings, stated that, "Tencent is absolutely trying to get more aggressive in the e-business space, challenging Alibaba, as most of their services are now overlapping."[64]

The battle between the Internet giants Tencent and Alibaba to capture the emerging mobile payment market of China became more intense with the cab-calling services.[65] Wang Ran, founder of China eCapital, quoted the rivalry between the two web giants as the "the first battle in the first world war of the Internet."[66] The two popular cab-calling smartphone apps, Didi Dache (Didi) supported by Tencent and Kuaidi Dache (Kuaidi) of Alibaba, were competing with each other to provide cab services through their online booking facilities. Didi proclaimed 12 yuan (US$1.96) price subsidy to the passengers if the taxi fare was paid by WeChat. Within a few hours, Kuaidi publicly announced that it would reduce the price one yuan more than its rival if the payment were received by Alipay. Alipay was a dominant player in the mobile payment market with almost 300 million registered users. In 2013, Alibaba had earned around 900 billion yuan (US$147.7 billion) through mobile payments from 2.78 billion transactions.[67]

Further, analysts felt that the warfare in the mobile Internet market might be unavoidable due to the increasing demand of the consumers to be connected all the time. Around 81 percent of the country's Internet population had browsed the net through mobile phones in 2013. Hu Yanping (Hu), Director of Data Center of China Internet[68] (DCCI), further justified that, "Most Chinese netizens are not satisfied in using the Internet sitting down at a table. They want to use it anytime anywhere....This is the reason why the two firms are promoting mobile Internet products. Mobile Internet services will make people's lives more comfortable and convenient." Both Alibaba and Tencent were adopting different approaches to lure the customers to use mobile payments. Money transfer and credit card payment were the main attraction of Alipay, whereas Tencent drew the customers for mobile payment with its mobile social-networking and game apps.[69]

The m-commerce market in China was still at a nascent stage and upon maturity the m-commerce market would be almost four times the size of the e-commerce market. Besides the cab-calling services, there would be huge competition in associated services such as personal finance products, maps, meal-ordering, social-networking apps, mobile gaming platforms, e-commerce, and so on. In 2014, Tencent also acquired a 20 percent stake in Dianping, a lifestyle and group buying platform to provide services from online to offline. Alibaba also acquired AutoNavi, a digital mapping entity that would offer various navigation and location-based solutions to the users through the Net. It would also help the smartphone users in locating their favorite services and products.[70]

In a sudden turn of events in March 2014, the People's Bank of China banned the use of QR codes and virtual credit cards due to security concerns.[71] The suspension of mobile payments through the QR codes and virtual credit cards created a further new hurdle for both Tencent and Alibaba. "This seems to be a knee-jerk reaction by China's central bank in response to rising payment security concerns worldwide....Certainly this announcement is a big deal for mobile payments and represents the first time the QR code has been thrown into the security spotlight on such a large scale," remarked concerned Jordan McKee (McKee), an analyst for Yankee Group. However, McKee added that, "I don't anticipate the QR code ban will be long-term....Rather, I suspect the government will investigate the procedures of companies like Alibaba and Tencent and lift the ban, permitted there are no blatant security flaws."[72]

Industry analysts predicted that the battle between Alibaba and Tencent would have a significant impact on China's m-commerce market and would facilitate a rapid expansion of the mobile Internet market in the country. "Companies will seek ways to integrate all mobile services to make profits and even change people's lifestyle,"[73] added Hu. Besides, Deloitte released a report[74] and mentioned that, "The adoption of mobile payment is low and application scenarios are limited. The players are very active, but the majority of mobile payment services and products are still in the pre-commercial phase."[75] However, Hu added that the various acquisitions by Alibaba and Tencent were only the first steps toward the development of the mobile Internet market.[76] "It's too early to say which will top the mobile payment market as two thirds of the market has not been developed yet,"[77] emphasized Hu.

Case Questions

1. Give a brief overview of China's m-commerce market and its major players.
2. Discuss the competition between Alibaba and Tencent.
3. Discuss the opportunities and challenges for Alibaba and Tencent in China's m-commerce market.

[63]"Tencent Shares Rise to Record on China South City Deal," op. cit.
[64]"E-Commerce War Intensifies in China between Rivals Tencent and Alibaba," op. cit.
[65]"China Internet Giants on a Collision Course over E-Payments," http://www.youtube.com/watch?v=B3Z0cTfhXjQ, March 17, 2014.
[66]"Chinese Internet: Mobile Wars," op. cit.
[67]"Tencent and Alibaba's Mobile Payment War Escalates," http://www.wantchinatimes.com/news-subclass-cnt.aspx?id=20140223000057&cid=1102, February 23, 2014.
[68]Data Center of China Internet was an independent third party institute based in China focused on Internet research and Internet measurement.
[69]"Tencent and Alibaba's Mobile Payment War Escalates," op. cit.

[70]"Tencent and Alibaba's mobile payment war escalates," op.cit.
[71]Borison Rebecca, "China bank's mpayments ban throws a curveball at Alibaba, Tencent", http://www.mobilecommercedaily.com/china-banks-mpayments-ban-highlights-growing-security-concerns, March 18th 2014
[72]Ibid.
[73]"Tencent and Alibaba's mobile payment war escalates," op.cit.
[74]Trends and Prospects of Mobile Payment Industry in China 2012-2015 was a report by Deloitte China that covered the various opportunities and challenges of the Chineses mobile payment market.
[75]"Tencent and Alibaba's mobile payment war escalates," op.cit.
[76]ibid.
[77]ibid.

By Debapratim Purkayastha and Syed Abdul Samad

We are very determined but very patient at the same time. We started this journey six years ago. Things are finally moving and we are satisfied with the progress so far ...
I truly believe that the IKEA format is going to work. What is an IKEA store? An IKEA store has more than 9000 different articles for the entire family. We offer an experience for the whole family. Also remember, at IKEA we don't sell products, we sell inspiration.[1]

JUVENCIO MAEZTU
IKEA's Country Manager for India, 2013

After a year of lobbying, negotiating with, and convincing the Indian politicos and bureaucrats, IKEA's €1.5 billion investment proposal to set up its stores in India was finally accepted by the local government on May 2, 2013. However, as of July 2013, Juvencio Maeztu (Maeztu), IKEA's country manager for India, found he still had a colossal task ahead of him.

IKEA, the Netherlands-based Swedish company, was the largest furniture retailer in the world, with a presence in 44 countries around the globe in countries such as the United States, the U.K., Russia, the European Union region, Japan, China, Australia, and so on. However, it did not enter the Indian market until 2013, though the company had had a presence in the country since the 1980s as a sourcing destination for its global stores. It had even opened its regional procurement office in Gurgaon, India, in 2007. In 2009, IKEA tried to enter the country to establish its stores, but its attempts were thwarted by India's stringent Foreign Direct Investment (FDI) regulations. It again applied for permission for entry in June 2012 after India made some changes in its FDI rules. However, IKEA had to wait another year, hitting many roadblocks on the way, before it was able to obtain the Indian government's approval to establish its stores. The company also had to tweak its global store model to fit the Indian FDI, sourcing outlines, and Indian consumer preferences.

While Maeztu was tasked with tapping the Rs.[1] 925 billion Indian furniture and furnishings market, analysts were keenly waiting to see what strategies the furniture giant would come up with to win the highly fragmented, price-sensitive Indian market; many Indian middle-class families preferred to have their furniture custom-made from small retailers or local carpenters. No two Indian homes had the same kind of furniture; Indians in general showed more of an affinity for unique woodwork and designs than for flat geometric furniture. "Living room in India is different from any other country—a place for socializing and every activity is around the food. In some countries it is the kitchen and in some countries living room is used for sleeping,"[2] said Maeztu. More important was the fact that the Indian customer did not like the concept of do-it-yourself (when buyers had to assemble different pieces of the product themselves), a key part of IKEA's globally successful business model. Analysts opined that although the company managed to impress the Indian government, getting into the homes of Indian consumers would be an entirely different ballgame.

About IKEA

IKEA was a privately held company. It designed and sold ready-to-assemble furniture, home appliances, and accessories. From humble beginnings in 1943, the company went on to become the world's largest furniture retailer by the 2000s.[3] In the financial year 2001, the company earned revenue of €10.4 billion. **(Refer to Exhibit I for IKEA's growth in revenue.)** By 2012, the company's revenues increased to €27.6 billion with a net income of €3.202 billion. **(Refer to Exhibit II for IKEA's income statement.)** By August 31, 2012, the IKEA Group had operations in 44 countries, including 30 service trading offices in 25 countries, 33 distribution centers, and 11 customer distribution centers. By the same date, the IKEA Group had a total of 298 stores in 26 countries and employed 139,000 people.[4] Globally, the company had doubled its sales to €27.6 billion in the past decade and further planned to double them again by 2020 and to open 20 to 25 stores a year from 2015.

IKEA was founded in Sweden in 1943 by 17-year-old Ingvar Kamprad (Kamprad). IKEA was an acronym of Ingvar Kamprad, Elmtaryd (the farm where he grew up) and Agunnaryd (his hometown in Småland, South Sweden). The company's products were well known for their modern architecture and eco-friendly designs. In addition, the firm paid attention to cost control, operational details, and continuous product development, which allowed it to lower its prices. Instead of selling pre-assembled products, the company designed furniture that could be assembled by the customer. This helped it cut down on costs

*This case was written by **Syed Abdul Samad**, under the direction of **Debapratim Purkayastha**, IBS Hyderabad. It was compiled from published sources, and is intended to be used as a basis for class discussion rather than to illustrate either effective or ineffective handling of a management situation.*
2014, IBS Center for Management Research. All rights reserved.

To order copies, call +91 9640901313 or write to IBS Center for Management Research (ICMR), IFHE Campus, Donthanapally, Sankarapally Road, Hyderabad 501 504, Andhra Pradesh, India or email: info@icmrindia.org
www.icmrindia.org

[1]"After Long Wait, IKEA in No Rush for Quick Launch of Stores," www.moneycontrol.com, June 2, 2013.

[2]Rasul Bailay and Chaitali Chakravarty, "IKEA Ready to Wait for Years for Perfect Locations: CEO," http://articles.economictimes.indiatimes.com, May 16, 2013.
[3]"IKEA Mulls Joint Venture with Bosnia Furniture Maker," www.reuters.com, January 8, 2008.
[4]"Welcome Inside: IKEA Group Yearly Summary FY12," www.ikea.com/ms/en_CA/pdf/yearly_summary/ys_welcome_inside_2012_final.pdf.

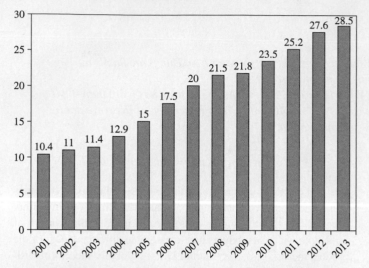

Source: Adapted from IKEA Group Yearly Summary FY12, FY13 and other sources.

and packaging. The company's website featured around 12,000 products, which represented its entire range.

Corporate Structure

IKEA was structured in such a way as to prevent any kind of takeover of the company and to protect the Kamprad family from taxes. Although Kamprad was the founder, he did not technically own IKEA. He wanted an ownership structure that stood for independence, long-term approach, and continuity. Therefore in 1982, Kamprad created Stichting INGKA Foundation, a nonprofit organization registered in Leiden in the Netherlands. In 1984, Kamprad transferred 100% of IKEA equity as an irrevocable gift to the Foundation. IKEA was privately held by this Foundation. Its purpose was to hold shares, reinvest in the IKEA Group, and to fund charity through it. It also protected IKEA from family squabbling and its inheritance in whole or part by the Kamprad family. Kamprad said, "My family will never have the chance to sell or destroy the company."[5] The foundation

was controlled by a five-member executive committee that was chaired by Kamprad and included his wife and attorney; however, it was only controlled (not owned) by the Kamprad family. It did own INGKA Holding BV, a private, for-profit, Dutch company that controlled IKEA's operations.

IKEA's structure was a complicated array of not-for-profit and for-profit organizations. It had two main components: operations and franchising. Operations included the management of its stores, the design and manufacture of its furniture, and purchasing and supply functions, which INGKA Holding oversaw. As of August 31, 2012, only 30 of the 298 IKEA stores were run by franchisees; the remaining stores were run by INGKA Holding.[6]

The franchising part (trademark and concept) was owned by a separate Dutch company called Inter IKEA Systems. All IKEA stores (franchised and those run by INGKA Holding) shared 3 percent of their revenue with Inter IKEA Systems as a franchise fee. Inter IKEA Systems was owned by Inter IKEA Holding of Luxembourg, which in turn belonged to Interogo Foundation in Liechtenstein. This foundation was also controlled by the Kamprad family. Apart from these holdings, the food joints that operated in IKEA stores were directly owned by the Kamprad family and represented a major part of the family income. This corporate structure allowed Kamprad to maintain tight control over the operations of INGKA Holding and IKEA stores. **(Refer to Exhibit III for IKEA's Corporate Structure.)**

Going Global

In 1943, after founding IKEA, Kamprad increased his product range to include pens, wallets, picture frames, table runners, watches, jewelry, and nylon stockings at reduced prices. He initially made individual sales calls to sell the merchandise. When his business grew, he advertised in local newspapers and operated via the mail-order service using the local milk van to deliver the products to his customers. In 1948, he introduced furniture into the IKEA range. The furniture was made by local manufacturers closer to his home. The furniture met with good response, and Kamprad decided to expand his range. However, the company's sales were threatened by the price wars among

EXHIBIT II   IKEA's Consolidated Income Statement (2008–2013)
In million € (for September 1–August 31 of)

	2013	2012	2011	2010	2009	2008
Revenue	28,506	27,628	25,173	23,539	21,846	21,534
Cost of sales	15,786	15,723	13,773	12,454	11,878	11,802
Gross profit	12,720	11,905	11,400	11,085	9,968	9,732
Operating cost	8,709	8,423	7,808	7,888	7,198	7,078
Operating income	4,011	3,482	3,592	3,197	2,770	2,654
Net income	3,302	3,202	2,966	2,688	2,538	2,280

Source: Adapted from www.ikea.com, IKEA annual reports and other sources.

[5]"IKEA Corporate Structure," www.ikeafans.com/articles/1000-ikea-corporate/330-ikea-corporate-structure-.html.

[6]"Welcome Inside: IKEA Group Yearly Summary FY12," www.ikea.com/ms/en_CA/pdf/yearly_summary/ys_welcome_inside_2012_final.pdf.

EXHIBIT III **IKEA's Corporate Structure**

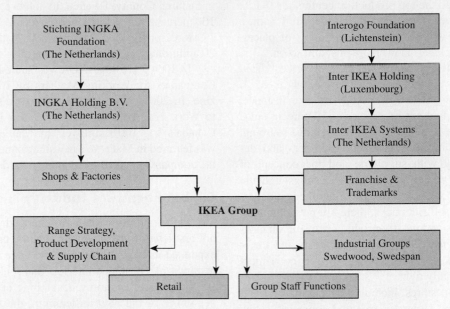

Source: Adapted from "Welcome Inside: Yearly Summary FY09," and other sources.

the competitors. Therefore, in 1953, he opened a showroom in Älmhult, Sweden so that his customers could look at the furniture before placing an order. This helped the company because customers chose the products with the best value for their money. However, the pressure that competitors exerted on suppliers to boycott IKEA led the company to design its own furniture. When IKEA began exploring the packaging of its furniture, one of the workers disassembled a table to fit it into a car for transportation. This led to the invention of flat packs and the do-it-yourself assembly concept, which became a huge success.

In 1958, the company opened its first IKEA store, Möbel-IKÉA, in Älmhult, Småland, Sweden, with 6,700 square meters of home furnishings, the largest furniture display in the Scandinavian region during those times. In 1960, it added a restaurant to the store, which over time became an integral part of the store concept and layout. However, after this, the company began looking at markets other than in its home country. In 1963, the first store outside Sweden was opened in Oslo, Norway. Later in 1969, it entered Denmark with its store at Copenhagen. The company then spread out to other parts of Europe in the 1970s. In 1973, it went outside the Scandinavian region and opened a store in Switzerland, followed by a store in Germany in 1974. The global expansion of IKEA stores took place at a rapid pace during the 1970s and 1980s. Stores were soon opened in other parts of the world, including Japan (1974), Australia and Hong Kong (1975), Canada (1976), and Singapore (1978). In the 1980s, IKEA further expanded its store network to France and Spain (1981), Belgium (1984), the United States (1985), the UK (1987), and Italy (1989), among other areas. It further expanded into more countries in the 1990s and 2000s. In 1998, it entered China by setting up a store in Beijing. In 2010, the company also entered the Latin American region with a store in Santo Domingo, Dominican Republic. However, the company did not have much of a presence in the developing countries.

Germany, with 44 stores, was IKEA's biggest market, followed by the United States with 37 stores. The IKEA store at Stockholm Kungens Kurva, Sweden, with an area of 55,200 square meters was the largest in the world, followed by the stores in Shanghai, China (49,400 m^2), Shenyang, China (47,000 m^2), Tianjin, China (45,736 m^2), and Berlin Lichtenberg, Germany (45,000 m^2).[7] The IKEA store located in Tempe, Sydney, was the biggest store in the southern hemisphere with an area of 39,000 square meters.[8] By the end of 2013, IKEA planned to open its first warehouse in Croatia and its first shopping center in Vilnius, Lithuania, which would be the biggest furniture-selling mall in the Baltic states.

Manufacturing and Other Initiatives

Unlike the traditional retail stores, where the customer could directly go to the needed section, IKEA encouraged its customers to go through its store in its entirety. Therefore, its stores were designed in a one-way layout in the counterclockwise direction. Most of the IKEA stores were very large buildings decorated in blue and yellow patterns. However, the newer stores used more glass for functional and aesthetic purposes to give a better impression of the product and a better look to the store and to use more natural light to reduce energy costs. The stores required customers first to go through the display, making note of the required items, proceed to the open shelves to make smaller purchases, and then to the self-serve warehouse to collect the previously noted products. They were then directed to the in-house warehouse or external warehouse to collect the products and make a payment.

All the IKEA products were designed in Sweden but were largely manufactured in developing countries. The company

[7]"About IKEA: Facts & Figures," www.ikea.com.
[8]"IKEA Tempe Opens for Business," www.dynamicbusiness.com.au, November 3, 2011.

had 50 suppliers, mostly in Europe and Asia. China, Poland, Italy, and Sweden formed the top production centers for IKEA. Most of its products were identified by single word names, which were Scandinavian in origin such as names of places, men and women, rivers, lakes, flowers, plants, and so on.

"People flock to IKEA stores because of price,"[9] said Debashish Mukherjee, partner and vice president at A. T. Kearney, a global management consulting firm. For instance, in China, the company had cut its prices by 60 percent since it entered in 1998. The secret lay in its designing, sourcing, and packaging. The company's product developers and designers worked directly with suppliers, and the concept of do-it-yourself drastically reduced its cost. Devangshu Dutta (Dutta), chief executive of Third Eyesight, a retail consultancy, explained, "When they sell flat packs, there are no assembling costs, no shipment costs and mostly products are sold on catalogues, which helps them reduce operational costs and lower prices. Those flat packs work well with young consumers whose budgets are normally tight."[10]

Most of the IKEA stores included restaurants serving traditional Swedish food. However, in some countries, a few varieties of the local cuisine and beverages were served besides the Swedish staples. For instance, the IKEA restaurant in Austria offered a free refill policy for soft drinks, a practice that was otherwise unknown in the country. Another important feature of the IKEA stores was Småland (Swedish for "small lands"), where parents dropped off their children at a gate to the playground and picked them up at another gate after shopping. IKEA also launched a loyalty card called IKEA Family, which was free of charge and could be used to take advantage of discounts on a special range of IKEA products.

IKEA was involved in various charity and social initiatives. The INGKA Foundation was involved in several international charitable causes such as helping the tsunami victims in Indonesia, Sri Lanka, and India; the cyclone-affected in Burma; Somali refugees; earthquake victims in Pakistan and China; donating to schools in Liberia; saving and restoring forests; and reducing pollution. In September 2005, the IKEA Social Initiative was formed to manage the company's social involvements on a global level. The main partners to IKEA's Social Initiative were UNICEF and Save the Children. IKEA also took a proactive stance on environmental issues and developed an environmental action plan in 1990, which was adopted in 1992. The company's environmental measures included elimination of polyvinylchloride (PVC) from its products and packaging and minimizing the usage of formaldehyde, chromium, cadmium, lead, PCB, PCP, and Azo pigments. The company used wood from responsibly managed forests and stopped providing plastic bags to customers but offered reusable bags. In August 2008, it created IKEA GreenTech, a €50 million venture capital fund, to invest in 8 to 10 companies with a focus on solar panels, alternative light sources, product materials, energy efficiency, and water saving and purification.

In February 2011, IKEA announced its plans for a wind farm in Dalarna County, Sweden, to achieve the goal of running on 100 percent renewable energy. As of June 2012, IKEA had 17 stores powered by solar panels in the United States, with 20 additional installations in progress.

In 2004 and 2005, IKEA was named as one of the 100 Best Companies for Working Mothers by *Working Mothers* magazine. In 2006, it ranked 96 in Fortune's 100 Best Companies to Work For. In 2008, IKEA Canada LP was named one of Canada's Top 100 Employers by Mediacorp Canada Inc., and was featured in Maclean's newsmagazine.[11] In addition to these, the company received many more awards and recognitions.

Global Furniture Industry

The global furniture industry changed over the years. It was not restricted to the making of chairs, tables, and beds but had expanded into the production of a wide range of furniture, furnishings, and designed interiors that spelled style and elegance. With the world economy developing at a faster rate since the beginning of the new millennium, the furniture industry witnessed a boom with new markets opening up. Although every country had a unique style in its furniture design and usage, globalization, increasing migration, changing lifestyles, and disposable incomes all contributed to the increased demand for stylish and quality furniture and, in turn, to the growth of the furniture industry.

Because of the long established production capacity, advances in science and technology, greater availability of funds, and management experiences, the traditional furniture-making countries in the West took up over 70 percent of the global market. However, developing countries, such as China, the Philippines, Indonesia, Malaysia, Singapore, Thailand, Korea, Taiwan, India, Poland, and Mexico, were growing and showing great potential in furniture production. With their newly identified competitive advantages, these countries took up the remaining 30 percent of the world market. The European region, on the other hand, accounted for about half of the world's furniture production valued at around €82 billion, with Germany taking the lead with 27 percent of the total European Union production, followed by Italy (21.6%), France (13.5%), and the UK (10.4%).[12] Whereas the United States and Canada were the largest importers at 15 percent purchase of the global production, China was the world's largest exporter, recording exports of US$38,882 billion in 2011, up by 15.31 percent year-on-year and accounting for 35.3 percent of global furniture trade.[13]

By 2015, the global furniture market was expected to reach US$436.5 billion.[14] With a steady improvement in the economy and living standards, Asia was expected to become

---

[9]Raghavendra Kamath, "What IKEA Brings to the Table," www.business-standard.com, July 13, 2012.
[10]Ibid.

[11]"Corporate Awards and Recognition," http://info.ikea-usa.com/centennial/pdfs/9-IKEA%20Awards%20and%20Achievements.pdf.
[12]"World Furniture Industry," www.furnituremanufacturers.net/world-furniture-industry.html.
[13]"Global Furniture Industry Overview 2013," www.businessvibes.com/blog/global-furniture-industry-overview-2013.
[14]"A Review of the World Furniture Summit 2012," www.furniturenews.net, January 11, 2013.

the center for long-term growth of the global furniture market. According to a study by the World Bank, the organized furniture industry was expected to grow by 20 percent[15] a year, and the demand for luxury furniture was expected to rise in countries such as China, Russia, Brazil, and India.

Furniture Industry in India

India was home to rich traditional handicrafts and artistic works in wood. Indian art and design had earned a worldwide reputation for themselves. The supreme quality, exceptional designs, and luxurious trends lent elegance to the Indian furniture segment. However, with the passage of time, the preferences of the Indian consumer changed, and the furniture industry too had changed to suit the consumer needs. The industry produced a wide range of products related to office, living room, bedroom, kitchen, garden, and school furniture as well as mattresses, furnishings, upholstery, parts of furniture, and so on, using a wide variety of raw materials such as wood, rattan, steel, plastic, and metal and, more recently, silver.

Based on the raw material used, the furniture market in India was regionally concentrated. According to research by IKON Marketing Consultants, the furniture market in India was estimated at around Rs. 700 billion in 2010.[16] However, it was considered an unorganized sector because handicraft production accounted for about 85 percent to 90 percent of the total furniture production in the country.[17] The market was highly fragmented, and production came from small regional firms or individual artisans; only 10 percent to 15 percent came from the organized sector comprising leading manufacturers, importers, dealers, and distributors. Within the Indian furniture market, home furniture was the largest segment, accounting for 65 percent of the industry sales, followed by the office segment with 20 percent and the contract segment taking the remaining 15 percent.[18]

However, Indian imports of furniture were growing at a considerable rate, catering to the need of the urban middle class for stylish homes in compact apartments. Countries such as Germany, Italy, Korea, Japan, and, recently, China and Thailand had been major suppliers of furniture to India. With a promising market potential in place, several international brands such as Arredo Classic, Art Design Group, B.T.C. International, Bizzarri, Cantori, Desirée, Girasole, Gold Line, Presotto, and Reflex were trying to enter the Indian market. Top domestic companies such as Godrej, BP Ergo, Featherlite, Hanworth, Style Spa, Zuari, Durian, and Millenium Lifestyles also had a presence in the industry (**refer to Exhibit IV for the top 10 furniture companies in India**). The entry of international brands and changing consumer preference led to the emergence of furniture retailing in India. IKON Marketing

Consultants estimated that with India's robust economy, spurt in real estate and housing activity, burgeoning information technology and services, and the Indian middle class aspiring to better lifestyles, there would be a further boom in the Indian furniture industry in the near future, the demand mainly coming from the metropolitan cities of the country.

IKEA'S Entry Into India

Retailing accounted for 14 percent of India's GDP. The industry consisted mostly of small shops with organized retail stores accounting for only 4 percent of the industry. After liberalization in the 1990s, many foreign companies set their sights on the Indian market. However, until 2011, FDI in multi-brand retail was forbidden by the Indian government and FDI in single-brand retail was permitted only up to 51 percent. In November 2011, the FDI reforms were announced but, due to opposition from different political parties and activists, they were kept on hold. In January 2012, India allowed 100 percent FDI in single-brand retail on the condition that the retailer should mandatorily source 30 percent of their goods from India's micro, small, and medium enterprises (MSMEs); 51 percent FDI was allowed in multi-brand retailing in December 2012. After the reforms, IKEA, which had been trying for a long time to expand into the Indian market, applied for permission in June 2012 to invest US$1.9 billion (€1.5 billion or Rs. 105 billion) and set up 25 retail stores in India in two stages.[19]

However, this was not IKEA's first tryst with India. India had served IKEA as a low-cost sourcing destination since the 1980s. Every year, the company sourced around US$600 million worth of goods (textiles, rugs, lighting, ceramics, and carpets) from 70 suppliers and 1,450 sub-suppliers in India.[20] In August 2003, when the company was on an expansion drive, it set up a raw material trading division in India to ensure better cost management. Because the yield of cotton (per hectare) was very low in India (and therefore higher priced), IKEA sourced cotton from Australia and China where yields were much higher. This reduced price pressures on its exports from India. The setup in India was its first trading division to offer the service of raw material sourcing.

Later, in May 2007, IKEA set up an office in Gurgaon in northern India to carry out market research and initiate talks with Indian players for an alliance. IKEA was then planning for an Indian debut in 2009. IKEA group president and CEO Anders Dahlvig said, "We will be there eventually, I'm sure. It is a question of how and when. I think it will mostly depend on things like legislation and infrastructure development."[21] However, FDI restrictions and local sourcing conditions prevailing during those times. IKEA tried to persuade the Indian government to ease the FDI rules and seemed hopeful of a breakthrough in 2008, but the company failed. The company anticipated that the opening

[15]"World Furniture Industry," www.furnituremanufacturers.net/world-furniture-industry.html.

[16]Taruna Sondarva, "Furniture Market in India: Boom Time Ahead," www.ikonmarket.com, February 2010.

[17]"Indian Furniture Industry," www.indianmirror.com/indian-industries/furniture.html.

[18]Taruna Sondarva, "Furniture Market in India: Boom Time Ahead," www.ikonmarket.com, February 2010.

[19]S. Arun, "IKEA to Invest € 1.5 B in 2 Stages," www.thehindubusinessline.com, June 22, 2012.

[20]Manu Kaushik, "Home Run," http://businesstoday.intoday.in, July 22, 2012.

[21]"Ikea in JV Talks with Local Cos," http://articles.economictimes.indiatimes.com, May 1, 2007.

EXHIBIT IV   Top 10 Furniture Companies in India

	Brand	Company	Head Office	Product Categories	Store Locations
1	Godrej Interio	Godrej & Boyce Mfg. Co. Ltd.	Mumbai	Bedroom, Living Room, Study Room, Dining, Kids, Kitchen, Home Accessories, Mattresses, Seating, Desks, Storage, Carpet, Health Care, Lab, Marine	Across India
2	Usha Lexus	Usha Shriram Enterprises Pvt. ltd.	New Delhi	Bedroom, Living Room, Dining Room, Study Room, Office	Srinagar, Delhi, Jammu, Dehradun, Noida, Lucknow, Muradabad, Jaunpur, Varanasi, Allahabad, Patna, Guwahati
3	Zuari	KK Birla Group	Chennai	Home Furniture, Soft Furnishing, Home accessories, Lighting, Kitchens	Across India
3	Home Town	Future Group/ Pantaloon Retail	Mumbai	Home Furniture, Soft Furnishing, Home Accessories, Lighting, Kitchens	Across India
4	Durian	Durian Industries Ltd.	Mumbai	Home Furniture, Office Furniture, Laminates, Veneers, Turnkey Solutions, Plywood, Doors	Across India
5	Damro	Damro Furniture Pvt. Ltd.	Chennai	Bedroom, Living Room, Study Room, Dining, Kids, Seating, Storage	Across India
6	Wipro Furniture	Wipro Group	Bengaluru	Home and Office Furniture and Interior Products	Across India
7	Evok	Somany Group/ Hindware (HSIL)	Gurgaon	Home Furniture, Soft Furnishing, Home Decor, Flooring, Modular Kitchens, Bath, Decorative Lighting	Across India
8	@home	Nilkamal Ltd.	Mumbai	Home Furniture, Soft Furnishing, Home Accessories, Lighting, Kitchens	Pune, Surat, Vadodara, Mumbai, Kochi, Hyderabad, Ghaziabad, Ahmedabad, Chennai, Coimbatore, Bengaluru
9	Style Spa	Adventz Group of Companies	Chennai	Home Furniture, Soft Furnishing, Home Accessories, Lighting, Kitchens	Across India
10	Housefull	Housefull Furniture Pvt. Ltd.	Mumbai	Bedroom, Living Room, Dining, and Kitchen, Office and Study, Storage, Décor	Ahmedabad, Vadodara, Bengaluru, Chennai, Hyderabad, Mumbai, Nashik, Pune, Surat

Source: Compiled from various sources.

of the Indian sector would take more time and abandoned its efforts to set up stores in India with an investment of €300 million. However, IKEA could not ignore the Indian furniture and furnishings market. According to some estimates, the market was Rs. 925 billion[22] of which only 7 percent belonged to organized retail. IKEA made it clear that it would only enter India when 100 percent FDI was allowed.

In the meantime, IKEA continued with its production and sourcing in India. In September 2010, the company's CEO, Mikael Ohlsson (Ohlsson), visited India to ensure that its suppliers were not employing young children or forcing people to work in difficult conditions. IKEA had spent millions of dollars to create sustainable audit and transparency networks in India. It also worked in partnership with the United

[22]Amit Bagaria, "Why IKEA Will Opt for Standalone Suburban Stores in India," www.dnaindia.com, February 8, 2012.

Nations Development Program and UNICEF on grassroots development programs such as female empowerment, health awareness, education, water and sanitation, and industry-based programs that benefited 100 million women and children. Ohlsson also proposed doubling production in India. Speaking about the possibility of IKEA setting up its stores in partnership with Indian firms, Ohlsson said, "A joint venture is simply not an option. IKEA has spent years streamlining costs, making investment money go further, and cutting out middlemen. As a result, introducing a foreign partner into the mix now is not something that is under consideration."[23]

In January 2012, India approved reforms to allow 100 percent FDI in single-brand retail. In welcoming the change, an IKEA spokesperson said, "The IKEA Group welcomes the Indian government's decision to allow 100 percent foreign direct investment for single-brand retailers. We will now over the next few days look into the details of the decision and we expect to present more information shortly about our intention to establish retail operations. India is long since a strong and growing purchase market for IKEA."[24] Industry experts were expecting that IKEA might announce its Indian entry sometime soon. Ohlsson too welcomed the change but stated that India's requirement for foreign single-brand retailers to source 30 percent of goods from local small and medium-sized establishments came in the way of its proceeding with its investment. IKEA spokeswoman Josefin Thorell (Thorell) said, "India is still a very interesting potential retail market for the IKEA Group, but we need to understand what the guidelines will mean for us. We have found that the conditions applied to local sourcing from [small and midsize enterprises] might be difficult for us to live up to."[25] Some other companies and analysts too voiced the same concern. Abhay Gupta, CEO and founder of Luxury Connect, a retail consultancy, said, "Companies like IKEA and Nike have raised concern on the sourcing clause. Every brand would like to go alone but this is a major bottleneck as it is difficult to find expertise among small vendors. Also, companies will have to go to more suppliers so that they are less than $1 million. This will create supply chain inconsistencies."[26] Arvind Singhal, chairman of Technopak, also supported the concern and said, "This condition (on sourcing) is highly impractical and illogical. Big brands entering India would not like to source from SME players as they cannot match up to the standards of global retailers. We believe that the government cannot force this condition on brands wishing to scale up in India."[27] But the Indian government ruled out any changes in the local sourcing clause.

On June 22, 2012, Ohlsson met the Indian commerce, industry, and textiles minister, Anand Sharma (Sharma), at St. Petersburg in Russia and confirmed its investment and sourcing plans. IKEA filed its application seeking the Indian government's permission to establish 25 stores. The application also sought permission to engage in import, export, distribution, marketing, and warehousing and to have standard IKEA store features such as cafés, restaurants, food marts, nursing homes, children's play area, and publications under its brand name. In the first tranche, the company planned to invest €600 million (Rs. 42 billion) in opening 10 stores, followed by the remaining €900 million (Rs. 63 billion)[28] for setting up 15 more stores later. However, stating its concerns over sourcing norms, the company in its statement said, "We will source at least 30 percent of the purchase value of products sold in India from our direct and indirect supply chain comprising Indian small industries. In the longer term, however, the mandatory sourcing of 30 percent of the value of goods sold in India from domestic small industries remains a challenge."[29]

IKEA's decision to enter India was met with mixed reactions. Although the backers of the reforms opined that this investment would help modernize the country's infrastructure and manufacturing and supply chain, the critics said that the entry of such companies would put millions of small-time shops out of business. In addition, the country's GDP growth was only 5.3 percent during the first quarter of 2012, and there was a widening trade gap with a current account deficit of 4 percent of GDP, requiring international capital to overcome the gap. Hence, the pressure on the Indian government to implement the economic reforms announced earlier that year continued, but this move faced opposition from critics. Seema Desai, India analyst for the risk-advisory firm Eurasia Group, said, "It doesn't take the pressure off the government; India's balance-of-payments situation requires some more reforms for foreign-direct-investment flows to strengthen."[30] However, it was still not clear when India would respond to the proposal.

Overcoming Regulatory and Political Roadblocks

In July 2012, IKEA sought a 10-year window (instead of one year) to comply with the sourcing rules. IKEA also expressed concerns that if it procured from MSMEs (firms with a total investment less than US$1 million), they would soon grow and become large setups. Then the company would have to find other MSMEs, which would affect its product quality and supply-chain setup. There were speculations in the media that the sourcing clause might be relaxed. On the other hand, industry experts opined that India had laid out a welcome mat for single-brand retailing, but only theoretically, and opined that a compromise solution had to be found. Saloni Nangia (Nangia), president of retail consultancy Technopak, said, "Keeping in mind IKEA's stature, I'm sure the government will work out

[23]Nidhi Dutt, "Ikea Makes Steps in India's Growth Market," www.bbc.co.uk, September 21, 2010.

[24]Tuhina Anand, "IKEA, Carrefour Welcome FDI," www.mxmindia.com/2011/11/ikea-carrefour-welcome-fdi/.

[25]Amol Sharma, "IKEA Remains Wary of Entering India," http://online.wsj.com, January 24, 2012.

[26]Bindu D. Menon, "Govt Retains Sourcing Clause for Single Brand Retailers," www.thehindubusinessline.com, April 10, 2012.

[27]Ibid.

[28]"IKEA Set to Enter India with Euro 1.5 Billion Investment," http://articles.timesofindia.indiatimes.com, June 22, 2012.

[29]S. Arun, "IKEA to Invest € 1.5 b in 2 Stages," www.thehindubusinessline.com, June 22, 2012.

[30]Amol Sharma and Jens Hansegard, "IKEA Says It Is Ready to Give India a Try," http://online.wsj.com, June 24, 2012.

something. Meeting the 30% sourcing target will take time—Ikea just wants some latitude."[31]

In September 2012, the Indian government tweaked its sourcing clause. It changed "mandatory sourcing from MSMEs" to "preferably from MSMEs" and said that foreign firms expecting a relaxation in the 30 percent procurement norms would have to set up a manufacturing facility in India. After these reforms, the government asked IKEA to revise and resubmit its application. On October 8, 2012, IKEA submitted its final paperwork to start its retail operations in India. The company, in its application, also gave the assurance that the old furniture collected from Indian customers in exchange for new ones would not be resold in the market but donated to needy families or third-party small businesses through charitable organizations. Ohlsson said, "Once our application is approved we will develop a solid plan for the establishment of IKEA stores for many years to come, generating investments and new employment. At the same time, we will continue to increase our sourcing in India from both existing and new suppliers building on long-term relations and shared values."[32]

A day after it filed the application, IKEA appointed Juvencio Maeztu (Maeztu) as its country manager for India, with a responsibility to find the right real estate and hire talent for its India foray. The outskirts of Indian metropolitan cities such as Delhi, Mumbai, Bangalore, Hyderabad, and Chennai were expected to be its store locations. Maeztu opined that the Indian market was different in terms of the varied tastes and said, "So we have to slightly tweak our model with designs and pricing, keeping in mind the Indian consumers and the dynamics of the retail industry here."[33]

On November 20, 2012, India's Foreign Investment Promotion Board (FIPB) approved IKEA's proposal to start its operations in India. However, it imposed the following conditions: IKEA should not operate food and beverage outlets within the store; it should not sell 18 categories of items (of the 30 initially applied categories) such as gift items, home and office products, apparel, leather products, fabrics, textile goods, books, toys, travel and lifestyle items, and consumer electronics; it should not sell any products that it did not brand, including secondhand furniture. Citing the reason for the conditions, a government spokesperson said that according to the norms, a single-brand retailer could not be a marketplace with such a wide range of products and could not sell food items.

Citing the restrictions, some analysts opined that the company might have to change its business model. Ankur Bisen, vice president of retail and consumer products at retail consultancy Technopak Advisors, said, "IKEA is known to open 'big-box' stores (above 200,000 sq. ft.) with a standardized design. So far, they have not tweaked the model anywhere in the world.

But India is such a strong pull, they will not mind opening stores without food courts."[34] Other industry experts opined that a restriction on so many categories was not a good idea. Harminder Sahni, managing director of Wazir Advisors, said, "Home improvement is still the bread and butter for IKEA. The home furnishing category is all about experience. People do not mind travelling extra to buy IKEA products."[35] The company also opined that all its product categories were sold across stores in 44 countries, and it was not demanding anything extra from India. Replying to the government's concerns about in-house cafés, the company opined that because the stores would be located on the outskirts of the city, there would not be any displacement of small food retailers. The company wrote to the Department of Industrial Policy and Promotion (DIPP) stating that to keep the "IKEA experience" intact, the company must be allowed to operate its global model.

On January 22, 2013, FIPB cleared IKEA's business proposal and permitted it to sell non-furniture items and run cafés in India. Although FIPB permitted food and beverages to be sold at IKEA's in-store restaurants/cafés, it restricted the retailing of any food item off the shelf in any other part of the store. It also said that IKEA could not use its global procurement of products to satisfy the Indian demand of mandatory sourcing (30%) from the country. However, India had given a five-year window (from the time of the company's initial launch in the country) to fully comply with the sourcing requirements. Other conditions included the restriction of e-commerce sales and used-furniture sales. After FIPB's clearance, the proposal was put before the Cabinet Committee on Economic Affairs (CCEA) for final approval because the FIPB had the authority to make a decision only on investments less than Rs. 12 billion. On May 2, 2013, CCEA approved IKEA's investment proposal. Maeztu added, "We feel very welcome in India. This is a big step in our journey to open IKEA stores in India."[36]

Working with Suppliers

After the company got the approval to set up its stores in India, an IKEA spokeswoman, Ylva Magnusson, said, "It will be another four to five years before Indians can purchase the company's iconic flat-pack furniture."[37] IKEA's planned investment was until then the largest by a foreign retailer in India. IKEA's spokesperson, Josefin Thorell, said, "The Swedish retailer's presence in India will, in a major way, help improve availability of high quality, low-price products, increase sourcing of goods from India and increase the competitiveness of Indian enterprise through access to global designs, technologies, skill development, and global best practices."[38] However, the promoter of

[31]"Ikea's India Plans Hit Snag over Sourcing Issue," www.thelocal.se, July 8, 2012.

[32]"IKEA Files Fresh Application to Start Retail Operations," www.thehindubusinessline.com, October 8, 2012.

[33]"IKEA to Tweak Product Design for India," www.thehindubusinessline.com, October 11, 2012.

[34]Manu Kaushik, "Ikea to Comply with Riders on its India Investment Proposal," http://m.businesstoday.in, December 23, 2012.

[35]Ibid.

[36]"CCEA Paves Way for IKEA's Rs. 10,500-Crore Investment Plan in India," http://articles.economictimes.indiatimes.com, May 3, 2013.

[37]Roy Rajesh, "Indian Clears IKEA's $1.95 Billion Investment Plan," http://online.wsj.com, May 2, 2013.

[38]Raghavendra Kamath, "What IKEA Brings to the Table," http://www .business-standard.com, July 13, 2012.

a Ludhiana-headquartered home-furnishing unit (an ex-IKEA supplier) was not too enthusiastic about IKEA's entry and said, "IKEA engages in predatory trade practices. In the first year, they offer excellent margins. In subsequent years, the margins reduce to a level that turns a unit into an unprofitable venture."[39]

After the approval of its application by the CCEA, Ohlsson, said while commenting on the development, "This is a very positive development. IKEA already sources products from the country and will continue to increase our sourcing in India from both existing and new suppliers, building on long-term relations and shared values."[40] India had been IKEA's sourcing destination for textiles and carpets for a long time. However, the company was interested in further tying up with Indian suppliers in the plastics, steel, lighting, and natural fiber categories as well. Analysts opined that this investment by IKEA had come at a time when the Indian furniture market lacked big brands and was sure to shake things up for the benefit of the Indian consumer.[41]

IKEA already had 70 suppliers and 1450 sub-suppliers in India. After the company got clearance from the cabinet, it invited all its suppliers to its Gurgaon office and discussed its plans for the future. It focused its discussion on growth and doubling its sourcing from Indian suppliers. In response to these developments, IKEA's Indian suppliers began gearing up to face the sudden surge in order volumes. For instance, V Ashok Ram Kumar, managing director of Asian Fabricx, said, "We certainly need more people when there's a sudden increase in order volumes. To beat labor shortage, automation is being focused on."[42] Some change in the processes was also taken up by the suppliers. For instance, earlier 80 percent of the yarn was dyed before weaving into fabric; but now, to reduce costs, most of the weaving was done without the yarn being dyed.

Apart from these benefits, analysts expected IKEA's entry to have a great impact on the industry as a whole. They expected large box retail formats, which would be located on the outskirts of big cities, to be introduced and gain popularity with other retailers in India. An increase in the competition between large box furniture retailers that had little or no differentiation and a partial or total wipe-out of the low-cost imported furniture market was also expected. However, retailers or brands that maintained sharp differentiation in their products and services were expected to survive the competition. IKEA, since its founding, had played on the price sensitivity of the customer and low-cost furniture. The company's website stated, "We design the price tag first and then develop the product to suit that price."[43] According to Thorell, "Product developers and designers work directly with suppliers to ensure that creating the low prices starts on the factory floor."[44]

Challenges

IKEA lobbied hard with the Indian politicos and bureaucrats to overcome the initial hurdles and obtain permission to open its stores in the country with its global model intact. However, this was only one part of the problem; the company expected to face more challenges after its entry.

A major challenge for the company in establishing its stores was the availability of retail space and its cost. IKEA stores in India were unlikely to be smaller than 350,000 square feet. Some of its biggest stores around the world had an area of 606,000 square feet. The accommodation of such a huge area in any mall in India was highly unlikely. Moreover, any IKEA store had 6–8 unloading bays and 300–400-foot-long customer vehicle loading bays, with 20-foot high ceilings.[45] IKEA's 2006 initiative of 100 percent renewable energy usage required its stores to be supplied with either wind power or energy from solar panels. Its stores in Germany, France, Sweden, and at forty more places used either power from their own wind turbines or from solar panels. The possibility of Indian real estate developers meeting such stringent energy requirements was also doubtful. IKEA planned to open nine stores in seven years: two stores each in the National Capital Region (NCR), Mumbai, and Bangalore, and one store each at Chennai, Hyderabad, and Pune. Therefore, with the existing space constraints, analysts opined that it was more likely for IKEA to opt for standalone suburban stores. "In India, the cost of real estate is high, retail space availability is an issue and overall store efficiency is a big challenge. They can't cut and paste their global model here. They have to develop India-specific strategy,"[46] said Dutta of Third Eyesight. Other industry players opined that though IKEA might opt for suburban locations, it would be difficult to obtain such large chunks of land, and the price would be high. D. K. Jairath (Jairath), deputy managing director of Style Spa, pointed out, "This kind of land tract will only be available on the city outskirts and IKEA will have to join hands with land parcel owners if it is keen to acquire such large land parcels for its use."[47] Experts opined that land acquisition through public auction through government or through individual owners would turn out to be a greater challenge for the company in acquiring such huge chunks of land.

IKEA had started its hiring activities and vendor negotiations to start its operations in India. However, the organized Indian players—including Landmark's Home Centre, Hindware's Evok, Future Group's Home Town, Godrej's Interio, K. K. Birla's Style Spa, and others—claimed that they did not feel threatened by the entry of the ultra big-box retailer IKEA. Anil S. Mathur, COO of Godrej Interio, said, "There will be initial euphoria on IKEA's entry into India. However, they will have to work hard on getting market share in India."

[39]Manu Kaushik, "Home Run," http://businesstoday.intoday.in, July 22, 2012.

[40]Roy Rajesh, "Indian Clears IKEA's $1.95 Billion Investment Plan," http://online.wsj.com, May 2, 2013.

[41]Bindu D. Menon, "IKEA's India Foray, a Boost for Single-Brand Retail," www.thehindubusinessline.com, June 22, 2012.

[42]Nivedita Mookerji, "Asian Fabricx Gears Up for IKEA's India Operations," www.business-standard.com, June 11, 2013.

[43]"Our Business Idea," www.ikea.com/ms/en_CA/about_ikea/the_ikea_way/our_business_idea/index.html.

[44]Raghavendra Kamath, "What IKEA Brings to the Table," www.business-standard.com, July 13, 2012.

[45]Amit Bagaria, "Why IKEA Will Opt for Standalone Suburban Stores in India," www.dnaindia.com, February 8, 2012.

[46]Raghavendra Kamath, "What IKEA Brings to the Table," www.business-standard.com, July 13, 2012.

[47]Bindu D. Menon, "IKEA May Have to Overcome Infrastructure Bottlenecks," www.thehindubusinessline.com, November 20, 2012.

Jairath added, "There is no collision course with IKEA. It will definitely add competition to the market as IKEA is an ultra big-box retailer. If it has to survive in India, it will have to play on the volume metrics. Real estate costs are highly prohibitive and they will have to create products suited for the Indian climate and style."[48]

Apart from these two main challenges, IKEA was likely to face many others. Because the stores were likely to be located in the suburban areas of big cities and customers had to travel long distances to make purchases from IKEA, A. T. Kearney's Mukherjee opined that the company might have to face last-mile supply chain issues (from IKEA store to home transportation). People in Western countries had large cars, houses, and parking lots where folded and packed furniture could be accommodated, but Indians had compact cars and homes that would make it difficult for consumers to stock and transport their products. Moreover, low levels of car ownership and a patchy road network would make it harder for consumers to shop at IKEA, and the company might feel the need to locate its stores nearer urban centers, which in turn would increase its set-up costs and render real estate acquisition more difficult. Apart from that, IKEA's do-it-yourself (DIY) concept might be a hit globally, but people in India preferred readymade furniture or getting it made by their carpenters. Moreover, Indians expected shop assistants to guide them around the store, and the lack of such staff would come as a shock to them. Vivek Iyer, a 38-year-old lawyer from south Delhi, said, "I'd go with my driver and he could be doing the loading and carrying I suppose. Then I could get someone in to build it all. But [the] point of a shop is that someone will be doing that for you, isn't it?"[49] Analysts opined that IKEA's DIY model might suffer if faced with such consumer behavior.

It was felt that IKEA's anti-corruption policy might prove to be another hindrance in its growth in India. For instance in Russia, the company could open only 14 stores in 12 years because of this policy. According to the Transparency International Corruption Perceptions Index, and the World Bank's Ease of Doing Business reports, India ranked 95th and 132nd respectively,[50] which indicated that the company might face difficulties with the Indian bureaucratic setup. However, analysts opined that the success or failure of the company lay in the hands of the next generation of customers, whose reception of the company's products was unpredictable.

Looking Ahead

According to retail consultancy Technopak Advisors, the highly fragmented Indian furniture market was expected to grow from US$10 billion in 2009 to US$15 billion by 2014.[51] Nevertheless, the working of IKEA's core concept, the DIY

model, in India remained a question. However, IKEA still felt that its prospects were bright in the country and that it was ready to tweak its model to win over the Indian consumers. It was tweaking its product range and showrooms and adding services to accommodate a new culture. In places where people lived in smaller rooms, it modeled its showrooms smaller. Ohlsson said, "Most people don't really know and can hardly imagine that we visit thousands of homes round every store in the world every year. We sit down in the kitchen and talk to them…. That's the way we try to learn and understand. 'What are you annoyed with? What are your frustrations? What would you like to have? How much can you afford? What are your alternatives?'"[52] In developed markets, IKEA was positioned as a low-priced product, but in emerging markets like India, it planned to target its products at the growing middle class that aspired to an international lifestyle.

In India, the company planned to open 10 stores by 2023 and 15 more in the next phase. The company might also take into consideration the consumers' concerns. As Ridhika Mandavia, a playschool teacher in Mumbai, said, "I'm not sure if I will want to travel to the end of the city to buy their furniture. Plus I have heard about how you are encouraged to pack your furniture up and then take it home and set it up yourself, and that is not something we Indians are used to. So if they can change that model and help pack and deliver furniture at no extra cost, it may work."[53] In India, should IKEA consider building larger stores closer to customers' homes as it did in China? Should it do away with the do-it-yourself (DIY) concept altogether in India?

Country Manager Maeztu also acknowledged the challenge that store locations posed in India. Because the whole investment was made from internal accruals, Maeztu said, "An ideal location for us would be 10 acres space (it could be between 5 and 15 acres), close to a highway with good visibility so it is not three kilometers inside and with public transport infrastructure. When I talk of public transport, in India it has to be metro connectivity because you can have a bus stop and if you are struck in the traffic for two hours then you are not properly accessible. We are looking to cater to the real middle class in India. We will never compromise on a good location. So even if it takes five years to locate a place it is no problem. The future is much more important for us than 1 to 2 years. My job or my salary does not depend on how quickly I open stores. We try to do it right on a long-term basis. We don't depend on banks or on investors and we don't need to show (quick results) to our investors or banks."[54]

As of July 2013, with the approval of the Indian government on opening its stores in India, the company was busy understanding the Indian culture to introduce the best possible

[48]Ibid.

[49]Jason Burke, "Food Fight Complicates Ikea's Entry into India," www.guardian.co.uk, December 28, 2012.

[50]Matthew Stych, "IKEA Sets Sights on India," www.stores.org, August 2012.

[51]Manu Kaushik, "Home Run," http://businesstoday.intoday.in, July 22, 2012.

[52]"One Size Doesn't Fit All: IKEA Goes Local for India, China," http://in.reuters.com/article/2013/03/07/ikea-expansion-india-china-idINDEE92603L20130307, March 7, 2013.

[53]Ibid.

[54]Rasul and Chaitali Chakravarty, "IKEA Ready to Wait for Years for Perfect Locations: CEO," http://articles.economictimes.indiatimes.com, May 16, 2013.

and workable IKEA model in the country and hired a consulting and a market research company to map the demographics and economic parameters of consumers in the top ten cities. Maeztu personally visited about 20 families in the Delhi region, Mumbai, and Bangalore. The question was whether IKEA could tweak its globally successful business model to suit the requirements of India without breaking the model?

Case Questions

1. Analyze the reasons for IKEA's delayed entry into the Indian market.
2. Discuss the market entry strategy of IKEA for the Indian market. What are the advantages and disadvantages of adopting the wholly-owned subsidiary route in entering the market?
3. Describe the key elements of IKEA's globally successful business model. What are the sources of IKEA's competitive advantage?
4. Describe the bureaucratic and cultural challenges faced by IKEA in gaining approval to enter India. How did the company overcome these?
5. Discuss the challenges that IKEA could face down the line in establishing its stores in the Indian market. What steps should IKEA take to succeed in the Indian furniture market?

Endnote

i. Rs. = Indian rupees or INR. As of 2013, US$1 was approximately equal to Rs. 62; €1 was approximately equal to Rs. 85.

Africa is awakening. It's a huge market of almost a billion people with huge resources and a young population. People spend when they're young.[1]

–CHRISTO WIESE
Chairman, Pepkor Ltd.[a] *(Pepkor), August, 2012*

Whenever Walmart enters a new market, it introduces its global operating belief that being a responsible global citizen begins with being a responsible local citizen.[2]

–DOUG MCMILLON
Wal-Mart International CEO, June, 2011

Walmart, with sales of more than $405bn [£258bn—more than South Africa's GDP] in 2010, has massive power to dominate the world's global supply chains, and national retail sectors, and to dictate the conditions of trade to thousands of supply firms in other sectors.[3]

–A UNION SPOKESMAN, COSATU
A South African Trades Union, 2011

On March 9, 2012, the Competition Appeal Court of South Africa ruled that U.S.-based Wal-Mart Stores, Inc. (Wal-Mart), the world's biggest retailer, could go ahead with its US$2.4 billion purchase of stake in the South African retailer Massmart Holdings Limited (Massmart).[4] By ruling in favor of the deal, the Competition Appeal Court upheld the 2011 ruling of South Africa's Competition Tribunal.[b] Wal-Mart had started expanding into international markets in 1991. It experienced successes in international markets such as Mexico and bitter failure in markets such as Germany and South Korea. The financial crisis of 2008 resulted in Wal-Mart putting even more emphasis on the international markets to fuel its growth as there were limited growth opportunities in the domestic sector. Wal-Mart started to focus on Africa as other markets with good potential like India were still closed to foreign players.[c] Africa remained the last major market yet to be explored by big MNCs like Wal-Mart. Despite political instability and poor economic conditions plaguing the continent, some countries in Africa offered good potential for growth due to their stable political environment and rising disposable incomes.

Wal-Mart decided to expand its presence in Africa in an inorganic way and made a preliminary offer to buy South African retailer, Massmart. Massmart was the second biggest retailer in

South Africa and its operations were spread across many African countries. Wal-Mart's offer was accepted by Massmart's shareholders and South Africa's Competition Tribunal in June 2011. The deal was cleared with some conditions. But Wal-Mart quickly ran into trouble as the deal was opposed by some trade unions and government departments of South Africa. The coalition that was opposing the deal alleged that WM's entry would lead to huge job losses and adversely affect the domestic manufacturing sector of South Africa. Wal-Mart refuted the allegations and said that it was willing to create 15,000 new jobs within three years of the takeover. Wal-Mart's past record of being a low-wage, low-benefit employer, which discouraged its employees from forming labor unions, compounded the fears of the opposition coalition. While some analysts expressed optimism that Wal-Mart's low-price model could prove successful in Africa due to its poverty and low income levels, others were skeptical. They said that much of the population in Africa lived below the poverty line and might not have good buying potential. Analysts also warned Wal-Mart of repeating the mistakes it had committed in Germany and South Korea like trying to use the same business model as it followed in the U.S. market without understanding the needs of the local market.

Background Note

Wal-Mart was founded in 1962 by Samuel Moore Walton (Walton) in Rogers, Arkansas, USA. Walton worked at JC Penney Corporation, Inc.[d] before starting Wal-Mart. He also ran a franchise of Ben Franklin stores.[e] When working with other retailers and later running a franchise, the conviction grew on Walton that the changing buyer behavior in the United States made discount stores the future of retailing, especially in the smaller towns. He traveled across the United States before starting his own discount store and was convinced that Americans wanted a new type of discount store, which would offer more discounts than the traditional discount stores. Wal-Mart was founded on the principle of passing on the discounts that retailers could manage from the wholesalers to the consumers and making money through the higher volumes

This case was written by Adapa Srinivasa Rao, under the direction of Debapratim Purkayastha, IBS Hyderabad. It was compiled from published sources, and is intended to be used as a basis for class discussion rather than to illustrate either effective or ineffective handling of a management situation. 2014, IBS Center for Management Research. All rights reserved.

To order copies, call +91 9640901313 or write to IBS Center for Management Research (ICMR), IFHE Campus, Donthanapally, Sankarapally Road, Hyderabad 501 504, Andhra Pradesh, India or email: info@icmrindia.org www.icmrindia.org

[1]Sikonathi Mantshantsha, "Billionaire Wiese Targets Nigeria as Wal-Mart Enters Africa," http://www.businessweek.com, August 12, 2011.

[2]Max Clarke, "Walmart Enters Africa Despite Union Opposition," http://www.freshbusinessthinking.com, June 1, 2011.

[3]Richard Wachman, "South Africa Resists March of Walmart," http://guardian.co.uk, October 10, 2011.

[4]Donna Bryson, "Wal-Mart Gets Go-Ahead in South Africa," http://news.yahoo.com, March 9, 2012.

EXHIBIT I   Criticisms against Wal-Mart

Issues	Description of Issues
Anti-unionist	Since the 1970s, Wal-Mart had been anti-unionist, taking the stand that it was adhering to an open-door employee policy.
Employee discrimination	The company was charged with discrimination against women employees in 2003.
Employee surveillance	A former employee of Wal-Mart contended that the retailer carried out a large surveillance operation involving employees, shareholders, critics, etc.
Poor working conditions	Wal-Mart was accused of forcing its workers to work off the clock, denying overtime payments, child-labor laws infringements, and employing illegal immigrant workers.
Low wages	The retail giant was charged with discouraging labor costs and of paying lower wages to its workforce.
Health insurance	Critics alleged that employees were paid so little that they could not afford health insurance, and if they could afford it, they preferred the state's health insurance program to Wal-Mart's.
Overseas labor concerns	Critics accused Wal-Mart of poor supervision of overseas operations, where issues like poor working conditions, employing prison labor, low wages, etc., were allegedly prevalent.
Predatory pricing and supplier issues	The company was also accused of intentionally selling the merchandise at low costs, driving competitors away from the market. It was also alleged that it used its scale to squeeze the margins of its suppliers.

Source: Adapted from various sources.

achieved.[5] Walton's business clicked, and Wal-Mart made better profits than many of its competing stores. By 1967, Wal-Mart had 24 stores with sales of US$12.6 million. By 1968, it had expanded to Oklahoma and Missouri. Wal-Mart was incorporated as a company under the name Wal-Mart Stores, Inc. in 1969.

Wal-Mart achieved significant growth during the 1970s. It opened its first distribution center and Wal-Mart Home Office in Bentonville in the first year of the decade. In 1977, Wal-Mart acquired 16 Mohr-Value stores based in Michigan and Illinois—its first acquisition. Wal-Mart expanded its business into other retail formats in 1978 and set up pharmacy, auto service center, and jewelry divisions. In 1979, Wal-Mart's annual sales reached US$1 billion, and it became the first company to reach that goal within the quickest time. It had expanded its stores to 276 by 1980. In the years 1981 and 1982, Wal-Mart entered new states in the United States such as Georgia, South Carolina, Florida, and Nebraska and expanded its reach. It opened its first Sam's Club in Midwest City, Oklahoma, in the year 1983. Sam's Club, a chain of membership-only warehouse clubs, proved highly successful. It was later expanded across 47 states in the United States. Strong customer demand in small towns drove the rapid growth of Wal-Mart in the 1980s. In the 1980s, the number of Wal-Mart stores expanded to 640 with annual sales of US$4.5 billion.

Walton appointed David Glass (Glass) as the new CEO of Wal-Mart in 1988. Soon after taking over, Glass started a joint venture with Cullum Companies (a Dallas-based supermarket chain) called Hypermart USA. Wal-Mart bought out Cullum Companies' stake in the joint venture in 1989. Hypermart USA was a discount store/supermarket chain with an average space of over 200,000 sq. ft. It featured branch banks, fast food outlets, photo developers, and playrooms for shoppers'

children. Hypermart USA stores were later renamed Wal-Mart Supercenters. In 1990, Wal-Mart became the largest retailer in the United States after it entered California, Nevada, North Dakota, Pennsylvania, South Dakota, and Utah.[6] In the same year, it acquired McLane Company (a grocer and retail distributor) and launched a new retail format, Bud's Discount City. Walton died in 1992 after a prolonged illness, but Wal-Mart continued its impressive growth under the leadership of Glass. After Walton's death, Sam Robson Walton (Robson), Walton's eldest son, was named the chairman of the company. In 1997, Wal-Mart's annual sales crossed the US$100 billion mark. Even as Wal-Mart was enjoying successes, controversies regarding its business practices and labor issues began to surface. Wal-Mart faced several criticisms relating to its business practices (refer to Exhibit I for criticisms faced by Wal-Mart).

Apart from following the strategy of selling products at a lower cost, Wal-Mart followed several unique practices in the United States to emerge as the leader. It developed a strategy by which it did not allow retailers any control over its merchandise. It limited the percentage of merchandise that it sourced from a single supplier to have good bargaining power over it. Wal-Mart was one of the first retailers to use information technology to its advantage. In the early 1980s, it adopted the barcode technology to track sales of items in its stores on specific days and to manage its inventory better than any other business in the world. The adoption of barcode technology helped the company in the communication process with its suppliers. It saved a lot of money through inventory management practices. Wal-Mart also started using a new technology called RFID[f] to track its merchandise better. Over the years, it used technology to gain good control over its supply chain. It hired some of the best people in the area of logistics and supply chain management. Wal-Mart

[5]T. A. Frank, "A Brief History of Wal-Mart," http://www.reclaimdemocracy.org.

[6]"History Timeline," http://www.walmartstores.com.

developed the largest commercial satellite system in the world to collect and give information to its vendors. The vast amounts of data that Wal-Mart was able to gather gave it good control over its vendors. Through these practices, Wal-Mart could stock the latest merchandise in its stores and replenish it faster. The use of the latest technology also facilitated recruitment of employees who did not need to be trained heavily to handle store operations. This kept its employee recruitment and training costs under control. The savings that resulted from the use of technology, good logistics, supply chain management practices, and lower employee costs were passed on to the consumers in the form of lower prices. This helped Wal-Mart and cemented its leadership position in the U.S. market.

The 1990s also saw Wal-Mart expanding into international markets. In 1991, the company opened its first overseas store in Mexico City, Mexico. It entered Mexico through a joint venture with Mexican company Cifra and opened its first Sam's Club in the country. Wal-Mart's global expansion got a boost when an international division was created in 1993. Wal-Mart entered Canada in 1993 after acquiring 122 former Woolco stores from Woolworth in Canada. During the first five years of its global expansion (1991–1995), Wal-Mart concentrated on markets like Mexico, Canada, Argentina, and Brazil, which were close to its home market. For the fiscal year 2002, Wal-Mart's revenue stood at US$218 billion, and it overtook ExxonMobil[g] as the biggest company in the world on the *Fortune* 500[h] list of 2002. By 2005, Wal-Mart had expanded to 10 countries across the world. It had 1,991 stores, which included 1,175 discount stores, 285 Super Centers, 91 Sam's Clubs, and 36 Neighbourhood Markets. But global expansion showed mixed results. Athough it had good results in some countries, it faced many problems in some countries and even had to exit some. Wal-Mart exited South Korea and Germany in 2006. Cultural discrepancies and intense competition from local retailers were cited as the reasons for its failure in these markets. At the same time, Wal-Mart experienced tremendous success in some global markets. It emerged as the largest retailer in Mexico, Argentina, Canada, and Puerto Rico. By 2005, it had emerged as one of the top three retailers in the UK. By 2012, Wal-Mart had a presence in 27 countries across the world with 10,130 retail stores (Refer to Exhibit II for the list of countries in which Wal-Mart operated in 2012). Its revenues for the fiscal year 2012 were US$ 443.85 billion (Refer to Exhibit III for Consolidated Income Statement of Wal-Mart from Fiscal Years 2010–2012).[7]

Wal-Mart's Past Experience in International Markets

Wal-Mart had mixed results in its operations in foreign countries. It operated very successfully in rich markets like Mexico, Canada, and the U.K. (refer to Exhibit IV for the socioeconomic data of key countries where Wal-Mart operated). It operated in Mexico through its subsidiary called Wal-Mart de Mexico. Right from the time it first started its overseas operations in Mexico in 1991 through a joint venture with a local retailer called Cifra, it had grown in size to become the biggest

[7]"About Us," http://www.walmartstores.com/AboutUs/.

EXHIBIT II Countries in Which Wal-Mart Operated in 2012

Country	Year of Entry
Argentina	1995
Botswana	2011
Brazil	1995
Canada	1994
Chile	2009
China	1996
Costa Rica	2005
El Salvador	2005
Ghana	2011
Guatemala	2005
Honduras	2005
India	2007
Japan	2002
Lesotho	2011
Malawi	2011
Mexico	1991
Mozambique	2011
Namibia	2011
Nicaragua	2005
Nigeria	2011
South Africa	2011
Swaziland	2011
Tanzania	2011
Uganda	2011
United Kingdom	2000
Zambia	2011

Source: "Saving People Money So They Can Live Better—Worldwide," http://www.walmartstores.com.

retailing company in the whole of Latin America. In 1997, Wal-Mart increased its stake in the joint venture with Cifra and acquired 51 percent in Cifra. After the acquisition of majority stake in Cifra, Wal-Mart expanded its operations across Mexico under different brands like Walmart, Superama, Suburbia, VIPS, Sam's Club, and Bodega Aurrerá. By the end of 2011, it had a total of 2,037 outlets and restaurants in Mexico. It was also the biggest employer in Mexico by the end of 2011. Though highly successful in Mexico, Wal-Mart faced fierce competition from local competitors. Some of Mexico's local retailers formed a purchasing association in 2004 called Sinergia to face up to the tremendous purchasing ability of Wal-Mart.[8]

Wal-Mart had also been operating successfully in Canada since it entered the Canadian market in 1993. By the end of January 2012, it operated 333 discount stores and supercenters across Canada through its subsidiary, Walmart Canada Corp.[9] Wal-Mart employed 82,000 people in Canada and was one of its largest employers. It was expected to face severe

[8]"Mexican Retailers Unite against Wal-Mart," http://www.expresstextile.com, July 29, 2004.
[9]Allison Martell and Jessica Wohl, "Target to Test Wal-Mart's Mettle in Canada," http://www.reuters.com, April 11, 2011.

EXHIBIT III   Consolidated Income Statement of Wal-Mart for Fiscal Years 2010–2012 (in US$ millions)

	2012	2011	2010
Net sales	443,854	418,952	405,132
Membership and other income	3,096	2,897	2,953
Cost of sales	335,127	314,946	304,106
Operating, selling, general and administrative expenses	85,265	81,361	79,977
Operating Income	26,558	25,542	24,002
Interest	2,160	2,004	1,884
Income from continuing operations before income taxes	24,398	23,538	22,118
Provision for income taxes	7,944	7,579	7,156
Consolidated net income	16,387	16,993	14,883

Source: Wal-Mart 2012 Annual Report.

EXHIBIT IV   Socio-Economic Data of Key Countries Where Wal-Mart Operated

Country	GDP (US$ trillion)	GDP- Per Capita (US$)	GDP- Real Growth Rate	GNI- Per Capita (US$)	Population	Literacy Rate	Unemployment Rate
U.S.	15.04	48,100	1.5%	47,310	313,847,465	99%	9%
Mexico	1.657	15,100	3.8%	14,400	114,975,406	86.1%	5.2%
Canada	1.389	40,300	2.2%	38,370	34,300,083	99%	7.5%
U.K.	2.25	35,900	1.1%	35,840	63,047,162	99%	8.1%
Japan	4.389	34,300	–0.5%	34,610	127,368,088	99%	4.6%

Sources: https://www.cia.gov/library/publications/the-world-factbook, http://data.worldbank.org/indicator/NY.GNP.PCAP.PP.CD/countries.

competition in Canada with Target[i] announcing its intentions to enter the Canadian market by the spring of 2013.[10]

Wal-Mart experienced similar success in the U.K. market after it entered there through the acquisition of the third largest supermarket chain in the U.K., Asda Stores Ltd., in 1999. Even after the takeover, Wal-Mart continued its operations in the U.K. under the Asda brand. Very soon, it opened the American-style supercenters in the U.K., which got a good response from customers. Wal-Mart expanded its operations in the U.K. quickly and very soon emerged as the second largest supermarket chain in the country. However, it experienced some problems in the U.K., related to labor issues, because it was accused of following illegal practices. It was fined in 2006 for offering its staff a pay rise in return for their giving up a collective union agreement. But it quickly sorted out these issues before they escalated out of its control. Wal-Mart had 544 retail units including 32 supercenters in the U.K. as of May 31, 2012.[11]

On the other hand, Wal-Mart experienced its biggest fiasco in Germany. It entered Germany by acquiring the 21 hypermarket stores of Wertkauf in 1997.[12] It later acquired

74 hypermarket stores of another local retailer to increase its presence in Germany. But analysts pointed out that Wal-Mart had failed to understand the German market right from the beginning and had tried to implement the business model it followed in the United States unchanged. Though it offered lower prices to German customers like it did in the United States, its local competitors could easily match its prices. Germany was the most price sensitive market in Europe, and Germans were accustomed to lower prices from domestic retailers. Wal-Mart also failed to build a good image for its stores in the German market. The stores Wal-Mart acquired when entering Germany had a poor reputation, which compounded its problems. While not being able to differentiate itself on the price front, Wal-Mart also failed in offering any compelling value proposition to the German customers to visit its stores. Wal-Mart's vendors in Germany opposed the centralized distribution system followed by Wal-Mart globally. Another operational problem Wal-Mart faced in Germany was labor unrest. Wal-Mart paid lower wages and didn't encourage its employees to form unions. Wal-Mart's employees organized a two-day strike in protest against employee lay-offs and store closures in 2002, which further tarnished its reputation in Germany. Wal-Mart also faced problems on the legal front and was accused of violating various German competition laws. In May 2000, Wal-Mart reportedly sold some goods in its stores at a price that was

[10]Ibid.
[11]www.walmartstores.com/AboutUs/275.aspx.
[12]Christine Lepisto, "Walmart Leaves Germany: Blame Smiles, Love or Plastic Bags," http://www.treehugger.com, June 30, 2006.

lower than the cost price at which it bought them. Apart from regulatory issues, Wal-Mart also faced problems in integrating its culture with the culture of the retail businesses it acquired in Germany. Wal-Mart strongly discouraged office romance between employees in its stores, which many employees found to be intrusive. Commenting on Wal-Mart's attitude when it entered the German retail market, Bryan Roberts, an analyst at Planet Retail,[j] said, "Wal-Mart was not very humble when they went in. They wanted to impose their own culture."[13] Analysts said that even by 2003, five years after it entered the German market, Wal-Mart was losing nearly US$200–300 million per annum. It remained a secondary player in the German retail market and was never able to recover.[14] Unable to understand the German market, Wal-Mart exited the country in 2006.

Wal-Mart similarly exited from the South Korean market retail in 2006 and struggled to establish itself in the Japanese retail market. It entered the South Korean market in 1998 and implemented its U.S. business model of low prices just as it did in Germany, but the South Korean customers did not like Wal-Mart's offerings. The South Korean retail market was highly sophisticated with lavish stores and the South Korean customers did not like the "warehouse style" environment of Wal-Mart's stores. Housewives were not satisfied with the food and beverage offerings in Wal-Mart's stores.[15] As a result, sales did not pick up in Wal-Mart's South Korean stores, and the retailer could not open new stores in the country. Limited operations prevented Wal-Mart from extracting better discounts from its suppliers.[16] Analysts said that Wal-Mart failed to localize its operations to suit the needs of the South Korean market, unlike the other global retailing giant Tesco.[k] Homeplus, the South Korean subsidiary of Tesco, emerged as the second biggest retailer in South Korea by 2006 by localizing its operations to suit the needs of South Korean customers. Wal-Mart Korea reported sales of just US$800 million and a loss of US$10 million in 2005.[17] Unable to sustain its operations in South Korea, Wal-Mart sold its 16 stores in the country for US$882 million and exited the market in 2006.[18] Wal-Mart struggled to establish itself in Japan since it entered the Japanese retail market in 2002, but it later started adjusting its business model to suit the needs of the Japanese retail market. Japanese customers initially equated Wal-Mart's lower prices and unsophisticated stores to inferior products.[19] Wal-Mart rectified its problems in Japan through some measures like renovating its stores to look better

and creating better consumer awareness about the quality of its products. Later, Wal-Mart expanded its operations in Japan and acquired a 100 percent stake in its Japanese subsidiary in 2008.

Wal-Mart Embarks On An African Safari

Wal-Mart started putting more emphasis on the international markets to drive its expansion since the financial crisis of 2008.[1] The main reason for its enhanced international focus was the limited growth opportunities in its domestic (U.S.) market since the financial crisis. Strong sales growth and a record number of new stores opened made its international segment grow faster. Wal-Mart's international segment grew by 15.2 percent year on year for the fiscal year 2012.[20] Its operating income from international operations for the fiscal year ending January 31, 2012, was US$6,241 million (refer to Exhibit V for Wal-Mart's operating income from international operations for the fiscal years 2010–2012). According to an estimate by *Forbes* magazine,[m] Wal-Mart's international segment was contributing approximately 40 percent to its stock price in March 2012. This estimate highlighted the importance of international operations for Wal-Mart. It had been trying for a long time to enter the Indian retail market due to the tremendous growth opportunities for the retail sector there. The Indian retail sector was projected to grow from US$396 billion in 2012 to US$785 billion by 2015.[21] However, the Indian retail market was still closed to foreign multi-brand retailers, and Wal-Mart's operations were limited to some wholesale outlets there. That had left Wal-Mart to focus on Africa as another most important growth opportunity.

With most of the developed Western markets reaching saturation levels and the Asian markets becoming highly competitive, many big multinational companies (MNCs) were turning their attention toward Africa. Africa was being considered the last major emerging market left to be captured by the MNCs. The unstable political environment in most of African countries made it unviable for businesses to set up shop there, but some African countries like South Africa and Nigeria with elected governments and rule of law were seen as viable options for big MNCs to enter the African continent. Wal-Mart decided

EXHIBIT V Operating Income from International Operations for Fiscal Years 2010–2012 (in US$ millions)

Fiscal Year	Operating Income from International Operations	Percentage of Total Operating Income
2012	6,214	23.4
2011	5,606	21.99
2010	4,901	20.4

Source: Wal-Mart 2012 Annual Report.

[13]Kate Norton, "Wal-Mart's German Retreat," http://www.businessweek.com, July 28, 2006.
[14]"Wal-Mart: Struggling in Germany," http://www.businessweek.com, April 11, 2005.
[15]Daniel Workman, "Wal-Mart Finally Gets It: Lessons from South Korea & Germany," http://daniel-workman.suite101.com, July 31, 2006.
[16]Choe Sang-Hun, "Wal-Mart Selling Stores and Leaving South Korea," http://www.nytimes.com, May 23, 2006.
[17]Daniel Workman, "Wal-Mart Finally Gets It: Lessons from South Korea & Germany," http://daniel-workman.suite101.com, July 31, 2006.
[18]Kelly Olsen, "Wal-Mart Pulls Out of South Korea, Sells 16 Stores," http://www.usatoday.com, May 22, 2006.
[19]Matthew Boyle, "Wal-Mart's Painful Lessons," http://www.businessweek.com, October 13, 2009.

[20]"Wal-Mart's Africa and India Plans Boost its International Outlook," http://www.forbes.com, March 25, 2012.
[21]Ibid.

to gain a foothold in the African market in an inorganic way by acquiring an established retailing company. Since 2008, Wal-Mart had been on the lookout for an acquisition target in Africa. South Africa had some sophisticated retailers, such as Shoprite Holdings[n] (Shoprite), Massmart, Pick 'n Pay Stores Ltd.[o] (Pick 'n Pay), Spar,[p] and Woolworths.[q] In September 2010, Wal-Mart announced that it had made a preliminary offer to buy the South African retailer, Massmart.[22] Analysts felt that Wal-Mart had gone in for Massmart rather than Africa's biggest grocer, Shoprite, because Massmart had rapidly increased its presence in the food-retailing business and, by then, operated 40 grocery stores in South Africa.[23]

South Africa had a relatively mature organized retail market, and some of South Africa's leading retailers like Pepkor were planning to expand their operations to other African markets like Nigeria.[24] Commenting on the preference given by Wal-Mart to South Africa, Andy Bond (Bond), executive vice president of Wal-Mart, said, "South Africa presents a compelling growth opportunity for Wal-Mart and offers a platform for growth and expansion in other African countries."[25] The preliminary offer was nonbinding to Wal-Mart, and it could withdraw the offer anytime after conducting due diligence.

Massmart was the second biggest retailer in Africa and owned several established local retail brands like Game, Makro, Builders' Warehouse, and CBW.[26] Massmart was founded in 1990 and the group comprised nine wholesale and retail chains (refer to Exhibit VI for the list of major retailers in South Africa). The group functioned through four operating divisions: Massdiscounters, Masswarehouse, Massbuild, and Masscash. Even though most of Massmart's operations were concentrated in South Africa, Massmart had operations across many sub-Saharan countries (refer to Exhibit VII for the list of countries in which Massmart operated in 2012). Wal-Mart hoped to gain an instant footprint across Africa through the acquisition of Massmart. Saying that "Walmart likes emerging markets and South Africa in particular,"[27] Bond said that Massmart hoped to open 40 new outlets a year in countries, including South Africa, Nigeria, Malawi, and Zambia. It was also looking at opportunities in countries like Senegal, Cameroon, and Angola. The retailer said that its aim was not to change Massmart's strategy, but simply "to put the foot on the accelerator."[28]

However, the news of Wal-Mart's entry in South Africa led to huge protests from powerful trade unions and some government departments in South Africa who contended that

---

EXHIBIT VI Major Retailers in South Africa

No.	Company
1	Shoprite
2	Massmart
3	Pick n Pay
4	SPAR
5	Steinhoff International
6	Woolworths

Source: http://www.prnewswire.com/news-releases/south-africa-retail-direct-selling-b2c-e-commerce-report-2012-150747085.html.

Wal-Mart's entry would drive down wages and lead to unemployment. They threatened to respond with strike action, demonstrations, and boycotts. Faced with such opposition, Wal-Mart defended itself and warned that it would walk away from the deal.[29]

After the negotiations were completed in June 2010, Wal-Mart's offer was accepted by the shareholders of Massmart and South Africa's Competition Tribunal in May 2011.[30] According to the tribunal, "The merging parties contend that the merger will indeed be good for competition by bringing lower prices and additional choice to South African consumers. We accept that this is a likely outcome of the merger based on Walmart's history in bringing about lower prices. However, the extent of this consumer benefit is by no means clear—Walmart itself has not been able to put a number to this claim, only that it is likely."[31]

According to the figures of the United Nations Conference on Trade and Development, Wal-Mart's entry helped boost South Africa's foreign direct investment in 2011 to US$4.5 billion.[32]

Initial Hiccups

Wal-Mart's offer was to buy a controlling stake of 51 percent in the South African retailer. Its offer was accepted with some conditions. First of all, Wal-Mart would be restrained from cutting any jobs in Massmart for two years after the merger. Wal-Mart was also to give preference to the 503 Massmart employees who had been retrenched in June 2010 in its future recruitments.[r] Wal-Mart agreed to honor labor bargaining rights for at least three years after the merger. In a move to develop the local manufacturing sector, Wal-Mart agreed to implement a program to improve the competitiveness of local suppliers within three years of the merger approval date. It earmarked 100 million rand (US$13.37 million) for a supply-chain training program.[33]

---

[22]Stephanie Clifford, "Wal-Mart Bids for Massmart to Expand into Africa," http://www.nytimes.com, September 27, 2010.

[23]"Walmart in South Africa: The Beast in the Bush," www.economist.com, February 17, 2011.

[24]Sikonathi Mantshantsha, "Billionaire Wiese Targets Nigeria as Wal-Mart Enters Africa," www.businessweek.com, August 12, 2011.

[25]Stephanie Clifford, "Wal-Mart Bids for Massmart to Expand into Africa," www.nytimes.com, September 27, 2010.

[26]Tiisetso Motsoeneng, "Massmart Could Open Up to 20 Stores in Nigeria," http://af.reuters.com, February 22, 2012.

[27]Richard Wachman, "South Africa Resists March of Walmart," http://guardian.co.uk, October 10, 2011.

[28]"Walmart in South Africa: The Beast in the Bush," www.economist.com, February 17, 2011.

[29]David Smith, "Walmart Gets First Foothold in Africa," http://guardian.co.uk, May 31, 2011.

[30]Jennifer Booton, "Wal-Mart Enters South Africa with Massmart Deal," http://www.foxbusiness.com, June 20, 2011.

[31]David Smith, "Walmart Gets First Foothold in Africa," http://guardian.co.uk, May 31, 2011.

[32]Devon Maylie, "Wal-Mart, Massmart Merger Approved in South Africa," http://online.wsj.com, March 9, 2012.

[33]Ibid.

EXHIBIT VII List of Countries in Which Massmart Operated in 2012

Country	No. of Stores
Botswana	9
Lesotho	2
Ghana	1
Malawi	2
Mauritius	1
Mozambique	1
Namibia	3
Nigeria	1
South Africa	188
Tanzania	1
Uganda	1
Zambia	1

Source: http://www.massmart.co.za/pdf/massmarts_operations_in_Africa_2011.pdf.

Wal-Mart hoped to create at least 15,000 new jobs within three years of the merger,[34] but it started to run into trouble from various quarters in Africa that were opposed to the deal. The opposition to the deal was similar to the ones faced in markets like India against foreign participation in the retail sector. The main opposition was from some trade unions and government departments that feared job losses in the retail sector. People who were opposed to the deal included the organized labor unions of South Africa like the Congress of South African Trade Unions, the South African Commercial, and the Catering and Allied Workers Union. Opposition to the deal also came from three government departments: Economic Development; Trade and Industry; and Agriculture, Forestry, and Fisheries. In addition to the fear of job losses, the opposition was also opposed to some of the terms of the merger.

The opposition coalition to the deal claimed that there would be huge job losses due to the entry of Wal-Mart because it might import a large part of its merchandise from cheaper markets like China. It claimed that 4,000 jobs would be lost immediately even if Wal-Mart imported just one percent of its merchandise. It also claimed that importing the merchandise from cheaper markets like China would hit the manufacturing sector in South Africa. The main reason for opposition to Wal-Mart's entry into South Africa stemmed from the high levels of unemployment prevailing in that country. The South African government was wary of Wal-Mart's entry leading to huge job losses. The manufacturing and agriculture sectors in South Africa had been declining just before Wal-Mart decided upon entering South Africa. According to a report on the South African labor market published by the Development Policy Research Unit[s] (DPRU), the employment rate in the South African agriculture, forestry, and fishing sector contracted by 13 percent, and the employment rate in the manufacturing

sector contracted by 11 percent between the second quarter of 2009 and the second quarter of 2010.[35] However, Wal-Mart refuted the allegations made by the opposition coalition. Many analysts too supported the deal, arguing that the fears expressed by the opposition coalition were ill founded. Some said that the fears raised by the opposition were misguided because the retrenchment ban forming part of the terms of the deal made it difficult for Wal-Mart to cut any jobs for at least two years after the merger. Some industry observers said that the supplier development program agreed upon by Wal-Mart at the time of the merger would help in improving the efficiency of South Africa's manufacturing sector.

Wal-Mart was also known for being a low-wage and low-benefit employer in the United States. Its founder, Walton, feared and hated worker unions, and Wal-Mart's workers were often discouraged from forming themselves into any labor unions. The opposition coalition feared that Wal-Mart might bring the same work culture to South Africa and other African countries. African countries like South Africa, Kenya, and Nigeria traditionally had a culture of very strong labor unions.

The three government departments opposed to the deal criticized South Africa's Competition Tribunal approval of the deal, saying that the commission had failed to consider some vital issues relating to public interest. Many labor unions in South Africa too voiced their opposition to the deal. Patrick Craven, spokesperson for the South African workers' union, Cosatu, said, "Walmart however is more likely to destroy jobs, by using its competitive advantage to force its competitors out of business, and destroying South African manufacturing businesses, which will not be able to compete with a flood of cheap imports...."[36] The group opposed to the deal approached the Competition Appeal Court of South Africa for a review of the ruling by South Africa's Competition Tribunal. However, the Competition Appeal Court of South Africa ruled in favor of the deal on March 9, 2012, saying that the fears expressed over the deal were unfounded. The ruling by the appeals court finally paved the way for Wal-Mart to enter the South African retail market. Ruling in favor of the deal, the appeals court said, "There was insufficient evidence to conclude that the detrimental effects of the merger would outweigh the clear benefits."[37] As part of the ruling, the appeal court also ordered Wal-Mart to conduct a study to determine the best possible way to safeguard the interests of small producers who would not be able to compete against low-cost foreign producers from which Wal-Mart would be importing goods at cheaper rates.[38] Based on this study, the court would decide how Wal-Mart should use the 100 million rand fund that it had earmarked for improving the competitiveness of local industry. The court also ordered the retailer to reinstate the 503 workers who had been fired just before the merger.[39]

[34]Olumide Taiwo and Jessica Smith, "Big Box vs. Spring Boks: Wal-Mart's Troubles Entering the South African Retail Market," www.brookings.edu, November 1, 2011.

[35]Ibid.
[36]Max Clarke, "Walmart Enters Africa Despite Union Opposition," http://www.freshbusinessthinking.com, June 1, 2011.
[37]Donna Bryson, "Wal-Mart Gets Go-Ahead in South Africa," http://news.yahoo.com, March 9, 2012.
[38]Ibid.
[39]Devon Maylie, "Wal-Mart, Massmart Merger Approved in South Africa," http://online.wsj.com, March 9, 2012.

EXHIBIT VIII   Socio-Economic Data of Countries Where Massmart Operated

Country	GDP (US$ billion)	GDP- Per Capita (US$)	GDP- Real Growth Rate	GNI- Per Capita (US$)	Population	Literacy Rate	Unemploy-ment Rate
Botswana	30.09	16,300	6.2%	13,700	2,098,018	81.2%	7.5%
Lesotho	3.672	1,400	5.2%	1,970	1,930,493	84.8%	45%
Ghana	74.77	3,100	13.5%	1,620	25,241,998	57.9%	11%
Malawi	13.77	900	4.6%	860	16,323,044	62.7%	NA
Mauritius	19.28	15,000	4.2%	13,980	1,313,095	84.4%	7.8%
Mozambique	23.87	1,100	7.2%	930	23,515,934	47.8%	21%
Namibia	15.5	7,300	3.6%	6,420	2,165,828	85%	51.2%
Nigeria	414.5	2,600	6.9%	2,240	170,123,710	68%	21%
South Africa	554.6	11,000	3.4%	10,360	48,810,427	86.4%	24.9%
Tanzania	63.44	1,500	6.1%	1,440	43,601,796	69.4%	NA
Uganda	45.9	1,300	6.4%	1,250	35,873,253	66.8%	NA
Zambia	21.93	1,600	6.7%	1,380	14,309,466	80.6%	14%

Source: https://www.cia.gov/library/publications/the-world-factbook, http://data.worldbank.org/indicator/NY.GNP.PCAP.PP.CD/countries.

Smooth Ride?

As the court was deliberating on the appeal against the merger, Wal-Mart and Massmart were busy moving ahead with their integration, which included aligning product sourcing.[40] McMillon said, "Massmart is currently located in 12 markets so that's our focus. Building our business in the markets that we are currently in is our primary focus.... We are excited about the region. We have a long-term view."[41]

Analysts were divided in their opinion about Wal-Mart's prospects in Africa. Just before the Competition Appeal Court of South Africa ruled in favor of Wal-Mart's deal with Massmart, Massmart announced that it was going to expand and open 20 more stores in Nigeria. Nigeria was another major market for retailing business in Africa, with a population of 160 million. Announcing the expansion plans in Nigeria, Grant Pattison, CEO of Massmart, said that Nigeria had the potential to be a bigger market than South Africa. He said, "By all simple metrics, Nigeria has the potential to be larger than South Africa, but it has some way to go in terms of infrastructure and political stability."[42] This showed Massmart's desire to expand in all the major markets across Africa, which could ultimately benefit Wal-Mart in its quest to gain a foothold across the African continent. Some analysts said that Wal-Mart's financial muscle could help Massmart expand across the continent faster.

Nevertheless, some analysts expressed the view that Wal-Mart could face more problems in Africa than it had faced in countries like Germany. Because the market potential of many individual African countries was limited, Wal-Mart would have to expand its operations to many countries across Africa to achieve good economies of scale and make its operations viable. Rampant poverty and low income levels would make operations in some African countries simply unviable to Wal-Mart, they said (refer to Exhibit VIII for the socio-economic data of countries where Massmart operated). Nearly 61 percent of Nigeria's population lived on less than US$1 per day, which could limit the country's potential.[43] Some other problems cited by critics to the deal were the unstable political environment and poor infrastructure in many parts of Africa that might hit Wal-Mart's ambitions there. David Strasser, an analyst at Janney Montgomery Scott,[44] said, "For this deal to drive returns, we believe it is essential to succeed by using this acquisition as a springboard. For every relatively stable country like Botswana, there is a Zimbabwe."[45]

Some analysts were optimistic about the viability of Wal-Mart's U.S. business model in Africa. They said that its business model of offering everyday low pricing for its customers would be very successful in a market like Africa where high poverty and very low income levels prevailed. Wal-Mart might not face the problem of being seen as a low-quality retailer as it was seen in countries like Germany and South Korea. However, others warned Wal-Mart against repeating the mistakes it had made in countries like Germany and South Korea like failing to understand the needs of the local markets and trying to follow the same business model it followed in the United States.

Case Questions

1. What were the reasons for Wal-Mart shifting its focus to Africa? Do you think Africa offers good growth prospects for Wal-Mart in the future?

---

[40]Ibid.

[41]"Wal-Mart Focused on Existing Africa Markets," www.reuters.com, May 10, 2012.

[42]"Massmart Could Open Up to 20 Stores in Nigeria," http://af.reuters.com, February 22, 2012.

[43]Ibid.

[44]Janney Montgomery Scott, headquartered in Philadelphia, Pennsylvania, U.S., was a full-service financial services firm.

[45]Stephanie Clifford, "Wal-Mart Bids for Massmart to Expand into Africa," http://www.nytimes.com, September 27, 2010.

2. Why did Wal-Mart face opposition from trade unions and other government departments over its acquisition of Massmart? Do you think the opposition coalition had a valid point in opposing the deal? Justify your answer.

3. What strategies should Wal-Mart follow to succeed in a market like Africa with its low income levels and high poverty incidence? Do you think its low-cost model will be successful in Africa? Give reasons to support your answer.

Endnotes

a. Pepkor Ltd., headquartered in Cape Town, South Africa, is the biggest clothing company in South Africa.

b. The Competition Tribunal is the government agency of South Africa charged with promoting competition and protection of consumers.

c. Wal-Mart entered into a joint venture with Indian major Bharti Enterprises to operate in India. As of early 2012, the JV operated 17 stores across the country. Multi-brand retailers like Wal-Mart were not allowed to sell directly to consumers in India. They were also required to invest at least US$100 million, half of which had to be spent on developing back-end infrastructure (Source: "Wal-Mart's Africa and India Plans Boost Its International Outlook," www.forbes.com, March 25, 2012).

d. JC Penney Company, Inc., headquartered in Plano, Texas, U.S., was a chain of American mid-range department stores.

e. Ben Franklin Stores was a chain of discount stores mostly spread across small towns in the United States.

f. Radio-frequency identification (RFID) is a wireless technology that facilitates automatic identification and tracking.

g. Exxon Mobil, headquartered in Irving, Texas, USA, is an American multinational oil and gas corporation. It was formed after the merger of two major corporate entities, Exxon and Mobil, in 1999.

h. *Fortune* 500 is the annual list of top 500 companies based on their gross revenue published by *Fortune* magazine.

i. Target Corporation, headquartered in Minneapolis, Minnesota, U.S., is one of the leading retail companies in the world.

j. Planet Research, based in the U.K., is a leading retail analyst firm in the world.

k. Tesco, headquartered in Cheshunt, England, U.K., is a multinational grocery and general merchandise retailer.

l. The 2008 financial crisis was a major financial crisis that resulted in the meltdown of the global financial markets.

m. *Forbes* magazine is a biweekly business magazine published by the American publishing and media company Forbes.

n. Shoprite Holdings, headquartered in Cape Town, South Africa, is a leading retail and fast food company. It has operations across 16 countries in Africa and the Indian Ocean Islands.

o. Pick 'n Pay, headquartered in Cape Town, is the second largest supermarket chain in South Africa.

p. Spar, headquartered in Amsterdam, Netherlands, is a leading retailer with operations across the globe. In Africa, its operations are spread across Nigeria, South Africa, Botswana, Namibia, Zimbabwe, Zambia, Swaziland, and Mauritius.

q. Woolworths Group plc, headquartered in London, England, is a leading retail and distribution company.

r. Massmart CEO Grant Pattison claimed that the retailer's decision to lay off workers had long preceded the merger talks with Wal-Mart.

s. The Development Policy Research Institute is a research unit at the University of Cape Town, Cape Town, South Africa.

Case 8 Fiat Chrysler Automobiles N.V. (2015)[1]: From an Alliance to a Cross-Border Merger

From an Alliance to a Cross-Border Merger

In 2015, Fiat Chrysler Automobiles N.V. (hereafter FCA) was the seventh-largest manufacturer of automobiles in the world. The company sold passenger and commercial vehicles in global markets. The Group's automotive brands included Abarth, Alfa Romeo, Chrysler, Dodge, Fiat, Fiat Professional, Jeep, Lancia, Ram, SRT, Ferrari and Maserati. The Group also managed operations of production systems (Comu), components (Magneti Marelli), and iron and castings (Teksid). The company was formed in 2014 when Fiat from Italy and Chrysler from the United States sought a cross-border merger and created a new automotive entity.[2] Table 1 briefly provides FCA's history and brand portfolio.

In 2012, Chrysler and Fiat created a successful strategic alliance to share technology, manufacturing platforms, and other corporate resources. Unlike other corporate tie-ups and cooperative links, the Chrysler–Fiat alliance survived because of the companies' sharing of knowledge and resources. In addition, the two firms enjoyed a solid growth in their post-alliance integration. Chrysler manufactured the Chrysler brand, Jeep, Dodge, Ram, SRT, and other products and was headquartered in Auburn Hills, Michigan. Chrysler was founded as Chrysler Corporation in 1925. Fiat, on the other hand, sold a variety of brands that included Fiat, Alfa Romeo, Lancia, Fiat Professional, and Maserati and Ferrari sports cars. Fiat first started manufacturing cars in Turin, Italy, in 1899. After 2012, the two auto companies survived their financial exigencies and operational problems. The whole process forced the companies to go through restructuring and corporate changes that took place on both sides of the Atlantic. Chrysler's alliance with Fiat initially provided the company with a tangible lifeline by which Fiat initially took 20 percent ownership in Chrysler.[3]

Chrysler in North America

Business history reveals that Chrysler was always a marginal player among the three automakers in North America because of its quality problems, weakened market share, and old technology. The company remained behind GM and Ford in its quality rankings and sales. In the area of consumer satisfaction, Chrysler had problems making satisfactory scores. Right from its inception, Chrysler concentrated on those segments

This case was written by Syed Tariq Anwar. The material in this case is intended to be used as a basis for classroom/academic discussion rather than to illustrate either effective or ineffective handling of a managerial situation or business practices.
© 2015: Syed Tariq Anwar

[1] Naamloze vennootschap (abbreviation: N.V.) is used for a public company having operations in the Netherlands, Belgium, Indonesia, and Suriname. See Wikipedia, *NV* (2015), http://en.wikipedia.org/wiki/Naamloze_vennootschap.
[2] Wikipedia (2015), *Fiat Chrysler Automobiles*, http://en.wikipedia.org/wiki/Fiat_Chrysler_Automobiles, accessed May 9, 2015.
[3] Ibid.

TABLE 1 Group Information, History, and Brand Portfolio of Fiat Chrysler Automobiles (2015)

- Heritage/Years in Operation
  - Fiat: 1899–2011
  - Chrysler: 1925–2012
  - Fiat Chrysler Automobiles N.V.: 2012–present
- Global ranking in the automobile industry: 7
- Manufacturing in 40 countries; sales operations in 150 countries
- Automotive sectors: Passenger cars, light commercial vehicles, and parts and services
- Brand Portfolio:
  - Alfa Romeo
  - Chrysler
  - Dodge
  - Fiat
  - Fiat Professional
  - Jeep
  - Lancia
  - Ram Truck
  - Abarth
  - Mopar
  - Street and Racing Technology
  - Ferrari
  - Maserati
  - Comau
  - Magneti Marelli
  - Teksid

Source: Fiat Chrysler Automobiles N.V. (2015), company website, http://www.fcagroup.com/en-US/Pages/home.aspx, accessed on May 9, 2015.

that required inexpensive autos by middle-income consumers. The company was further left behind in the auto industry with the arrival of Japanese competitors such as Toyota, Honda, and Nissan. No wonder Chrysler remained synonymous with its low quality image and distant competitor. At the same time, in minivans and the Jeep brand, the company was a competitive player and witnessed solid growth in North America.

Fiat's Long-Term Plans and Corporate Strategies (2014–2018)

In May 2014, FCA announced a five-year plan (2014–2018) that aimed at reinvigorating the company in the global auto industry. FCA projected that its sales would surpass seven million vehicles, eventually reaching revenues of 132 billion euro. The company planned to use its Jeep brand as the main growth vehicle because of its visibility and market share. FCA plans to use its Alfa Romeo brand to compete with Mercedes-Benz, BMW, and other luxury automotive manufacturers.

Fiat is a visible automotive brand from Italy and carries a rich history in global business regarding its brand portfolio, business model, and growth. The company had survived corporate disruptions, labor crises, and new competitors. Most of Fiat's problems arose from Italian labor laws, weakened business environment, and cost issues. From business history perspectives, Fiat had come a long way in the European market regarding dealing with quality areas and reputation.[4] The company reinvented itself by fixing its brand portfolio and quality areas.

Like Chrysler, Fiat's evolutionary growth and survival encountered problems in the areas of technology and quality standards. The company history has been unique and reflects Italy's industry-specific problems and rigid labor laws. Fiat was founded in 1899 and employed 35 workers in 1900. Between 1980 and 1985, the company reduced its labor force by cutting 100,000 jobs. In 1986, Fiat acquired Alfa Romeo from the Italian government and became the largest automaker in Europe.

In 2004, Fiat recruited a well-known turnaround executive Sergio Marchionne to become its CEO. In 2005, Fiat and GM dissolved their five-year partnership when GM paid Fiat $2 billion in cash to get out of the partnership.[5] In 2007, Fiat introduced its iconic Cinquecento 500 model after 32 years. In early 2009, Fiat announced a deal to acquire 20 percent of Chrysler in exchange for a technology-sharing pact and distribution networks in Europe and North America. During the same period, Marchionne also showed interest in acquiring GM's Opel and Vauxhall brands in Germany and the U.K.

Global Auto Industry in 2015

The global auto industry has been one of the largest industries in the world that affects countries, regions, cities, and businesses in every major nation and emerging market. In the United States, Japan, and Europe, auto companies often became part of their country-specific policies and national prides.[6] The global auto market is somewhat *uneven* regarding its technologies, quality standards, and growth patterns.[7] The market is also witnessing *mobility customers, innovative concepts*, and efficient value chains that bring efficiencies and growth. Other factors that affect the global auto industry are cost issues, diverse markets, new technologies, and supplier-related issues.[8] The auto industry is also an amalgam of complex and modular technologies and assembly-line operations that includes suppliers/parts manufacturers, raw material providers, and outsourcing firms. At the global level, these entities are highly diverse, intertwined, and dynamic. Small disruptions in the industry can cause major delays in the industry's value chains and technology platforms.[9]

The auto industry has witnessed cross-border alliances, joint ventures, and other corporate tie-ups that mostly aimed at economies of scale and market expansion.[10] In 2015, only three American auto manufacturers prevailed in North America (General Motors, Ford, and Chrysler), and Japan had three major firms: Toyota, Honda, and Nissan. Europe has been left with four large auto companies (Daimler, Volkswagen, Fiat, and Renault–Nissan). The auto industry has witnessed major structural changes in the forms of strategic alliances and collaborative activities, R&D networks, distribution agreements, joint ventures, and equity stakes. The reasons behind these changes are the industry's evolutionary processes, revenues, net profit, and economies of scale in manufacturing. As of 2015, the auto industry is in the process of reaching out to Silicon Valley regarding sharing mobile technologies from the smartphone industry and its related areas.[11] Table 2 and Table 3 compare and contrast this data from 2014 to 2016 and provide industry-level rankings on seven auto manufacturers in the industry.

[4] For more discussion on Fiat's history and its evolutionary growth and company-related issues, see F. Fauri, "The Role of Fiat in the Development of the Italian Car Industry in the 1950s," *Business History Review*, 70, No. 1 (1996), pp. 167–206; F. Garibaldo, "A Company in Transition: Fiat Mirafiori of Turin," *International Journal of Technology and Management*, 8, No. 2 (2008), pp. 185–193; G. Maielli, "The Machine That Never Changed: Intangible Specialization and Output-Mix Optimization at Fiat, 1960s–1990s," *Competition & Change* 9, No. 3 (2005), pp. 249–276; J. Whitford, and A. Enrietti, "Surviving the Fall of King: The Regional Institutional Implications of Crisis at Fiat Auto," *International Journal of Urban and Regional Research* 29, No. 4 (2005), pp. 771–795.

[5] A.Galloni, and G. L. White, "Fiat Head Sees GM Write-Off as Tuneup to Bid," *Wall Street Journal*, October 11, 2002, p. A2.

[6] See P. Collins, "Special Report—Cars: Gloom and Boom," *Economist* (April 20, 2013), pp. 1–16; E. Levy, *Industry Surveys: Autos and Auto Parts* (New York: S&P Capital IQ, 2014), pp. 1–45.

[7] See S. Nishitateno, "Global Production Sharing and the FDI-Trade Nexus: New Evidence from the Japanese Automobile Industry," *Journal of Japanese and International Economies* 27 (2013), pp. 64–80; Strategy&, *2015 Auto Industry Trends*, PWC (2015), http://www.strategyand.pwc.com/perspectives/2015-auto-trends, accessed May 20, 2015.

[8] For detail, see G. Klink et al., "The Contribution of the Automobile Industry to Technology and Value Creation," A. T. Kearney, (2013), https://www.atkearney.com/documents/10192/2426917/The+Contribution+of+the+Automobile+Industry+to+Technology+and+Value+Creation.pdf/8a5f53b4-4bd2-42cc-8e2e-82a0872aa429, accessed May 20, 2015; KPMG, KPMG's Global Automotive Executive Survey 2015, https://www.kpmg.com/Global/en/IssuesAndInsights/ArticlesPublications/global-automotive-executive-survey/Documents/2015-report-v1.pdf, accessed May 20, 2015; D. Mohr et al., *The Road to 2020 and Beyond: What's Driving the Global Automotive Industry?* (New York: McKinsey & Co, 2013).

[9] For detail, see *New York Times*, "Japan Makes More Cars Elsewhere," (August 1, 2005), pp. C1&C9; *Financial Times*, "Fitting Together a Modular Approach," (August 15, 2002), p. 6; *Financial Times*, "FT: Motor Industry," (September 28, 2006), pp. 1–4; M. Symonds, "A Global Love Affair: A Special Report on Cars in Emerging Markets," *Economist*, (November 15, 2008), pp. 1–20.

[10] For more discussion on cross-border alliances, joint ventures, and mergers and acquisition, see the following recent studies: M. Y. Brannen and M. F. Paterson, "Merging without Alienating: Interventions Promoting Cross-Cultural Organizational Integration and Their Limitations," *Journal of International Business Studies*, 40 (2009), pp. 468–489; C. Haeussler, H. Patzelt, and S. A. Zahra, "Strategic Alliances and Product Development in High Technology New Firms: The Moderating Effect of Technological Capabilities," *Journal of Business Venturing* 27, No. 2 (2012), pp. 217–233; X. Jiang, Y. Li, and S. Gao, "The Stability of Strategic Alliances: Characteristics, Factors and Stages," *Journal of International Management*, 14 (2008), pp. 173–189; T. Keil, and T. Laamanen, "When Rivals Merge, Think before You Follow Suit," *Harvard Business Review* (December 2011), pp. 25–27; S. Kumar, and J. Park, "Partner Characteristics, Information Asymmetry, and the Signaling Effects of Joint Ventures," *Managerial & Decision Economics* 33, No. 2 (2012), 127–145; B. Tjemkes et al., "Response Strategies in an International Strategic Alliance Experimental Context: Cross-Country Differences," *Journal of International Management* 18, No. 1 (2012), pp. 66–84.

[11] A.Sharman, and S. Mishkin, S. "Detroit Dinosaurs Hit the Road to Silicon Valley," *Financial Times* (February 7–8, 2015), p. 10; A. Sharman, "Tyred and wired," *Financial Times* (April 4–5, 2015), p. 5.

TABLE 2 Financial Data and Ranking of Global Auto Manufacturers Based on Revenues (2014–2016)*

	2014	2015	2016**
Toyota Motor			
Revenues ($ million)	241002	250000	250000
Net profit ($ million)	19548	20025	20700
Net profit margin (%)	8.1	8.2	8.3
Earnings per share/ADR***	12.31	12.60	13
Daimler AG			
Revenues ($ million)	168848	162000	174000
Net profit ($ million)	8742.4	9560	10480
Net profit margin (%)	5.2	5.5	5.7
Earnings per share/ADR***	8.14	8.90	8.75
General Motors			
Revenues ($ million)	155929	159250	159250
Net profit ($ million)	5054.2	7500	8365
Net profit margin (%)	3.2	4.8	5.3
Earnings per share/ADR***	3.05	4.45	4.90
Ford Motor			
Revenues ($ million)	144077	146000	154000
Net profit ($ million)	4698.5	7250	7300
Net profit margin (%)	3.3	4.2	4.6
Earnings per share/ADR***	1.16	1.55	1.80
Fiat Chrysler			
Revenues ($ million)	116898	131385	139900
Net profit ($ million)	692.0	1035	1215
Net profit margin (%)	.6	.8	.9
Earnings per share/ADR***	.57	.85	1.00
Honda Motor			
Revenues ($ million)	105390	115415	122915
Net profit ($ million)	4357.7	4410	4775
Net profit margin (%)	4.1	3.8	3.9
Earnings per share/ADR***	2.42	2.45	2.65
Nissan Motor			
Revenues ($ million)	94793	100000	105500
Net profit ($ million)	3806.5	4095	4400
Net profit margin (%)	4.0	4.1	4.2
Earnings per share/ADR***	1.82	1.95	2.10

Sources: I. Dalavagas, *Toyota Motor* (New York: Value Line Publishing LLC, 2015); I. Dalavagas, *Daimler AG* (New York: Value Line Publishing LLC, 2015); M. Ferro, *Fiat Chrysler* (New York: Value Line Publishing LLC, 2015); M. Ferro, *General Motors* (New York: Value Line Publishing LLC2015); M. Ferro, *Ford Motor* (New York: Value Line Publishing LLC, 2015); M. Ferro, *Honda Motor* (New York: Value Line Publishing LLC, 2015); M. Ferro, *Nissan Motor* (New York: Value Line Publishing LLC, 2015).

Note: *Companies were ranked by their 2015 revenues. **2016 forecast. ***American Depository Receipts.

TABLE 3 Company-Specific Market Share in the U.S. Automotive Market (2012–2014)

	2012	2013	2014*
Passengers Cars			
U.S. Manufacturers:			
General Motors	14.2%	14.1%	14.3%
Ford	10.5	11.0	10.7
Fiat Chrysler	6.9	7.3	6.4
Japanese Manufacturers:			
Honda	10.8	11.0	11.0
Mazda	2.5	2.2	2.3
Mitsubishi	0.4	0.3	0.4
Nissan	9.3	9.5	10.7
Subaru	1.8	1.7	1.8
Suzuki	0.3	0.1	0.0
Toyota	16.6	16.6	16.8
Other Foreign Manufacturers:			
BMW	3.2	3.3	3.2
Hyundai	7.9	7.8	7.4
Kia	5.3	5.1	5.6
Mercedes/Daimler	2.6	2.8	2.8
Volkswagen	5.3	4.8	4.2
Others	2.3	2.4	2.5
Light Trucks			
U.S. Manufacturers:			
General Motors	21.7%	21.6%	21.0%
Ford	20.1	20.1	18.5
Fiat Chrysler	15.9	15.6	18.1
Foreign Manufacturers:			
Honda	8.9	8.7	8.0
Hyundai	1.8	1.8	1.8
Isuzu	0.0	0.0	0.1
Kia	2.4	1.8	1.8
Mazda	1.3	1.5	1.5
Mitsubishi	0.4	0.5	0.5
Nissan	6.5	6.6	6.7
Subaru	2.8	3.7	4.2
Suzuki	0.1	0.0	0.0
Toyota	12.3	12.3	12.4
Others	4.2	4.1	3.8

Source: E. Levy, *Industry Surveys: Autos and Auto Parts* (New York: S&P Capital IQ, 2014), p. 4.
Note: *Ten months (October)

Changing demographics and rising costs have compelled large-scale auto manufacturers to move assembly plants to low cost economies. In addition, consumer demand in emerging markets has forced large auto manufacturers to move facilities abroad to take advantage of cheaper labor and market opportunities. Auto analysts believe that in the coming years, only a small number of auto manufacturers will be left at the global level because of consolidations and mergers. Companies maintaining strong quality standards and competitive technologies will be able to compete and survive. At the same time, the global auto industry will continue to see consolidation in its major markets.

Synergies and Challenges Faced by Fiat Chrysler Automobiles

Since 2013, Fiat and Chrysler have made major structural changes to meet their integration goals. Academic and practitioner studies authenticate that strategic alliances link two or more companies' operations by combining manufacturing resources and knowledge.[12] These tie-ups combine R&D, produce development, distribution networks, and other areas in knowledge sharing. Strategic alliances mostly aim at seeking economies of scale and improving productivity.[13] Interorganizational cooperation is a unique competitive weapon that helps companies to expand their managerial and financial resources.[14] This was the same situation with the Chrysler–Fiat strategic alliance in 2012 that brought changes to the companies. The alliance allowed Chrysler and Fiat not only to survive in the auto industry but also to expand in global markets. In its initial phase in 2009, Fiat owned 20 percent of Chrysler and later raised its stake to 58.6 percent in 2011. Table 4 provides information on the Chrysler–Fiat alliance, which saw a diverse array of changes and developments between 2010 and 2013.

The Chrysler–Fiat strategic alliance was heavily influenced by competition in the auto industry, which had witnessed downsizing, massive losses, and weak consumer demand. The auto manufacturers from North America have been heavily burdened with debt and expensive labor union contracts. Chrysler was in a dire situation and saw Fiat as the only available partner for survival. Other factors that helped form the alliance were R&D opportunities, access to markets, and long-term rationalization in manufacturing. Within the global auto industry, we now discuss the status of FCA and its alliance and future developments as follows.

---

[12] For more information on alliances and collaboration, see S. T. Anwar, (2015) "Strategic Alliances, JVs/IJVs, M&As, Interorganizational Cooperation & Related Links," http://wtfaculty.wtamu.edu/~sanwar.bus/otherlinks .htm#StrAlliances_JV_MAs, accessed May 9, 2015.

[13] For more discussion on the concepts, theories and problems of strategic alliances, see: Y. L. Doz and G. Hamel, *Alliance Advantage: The Art of Creating Value through Partnering* (Boston, Massachusetts: Harvard Business School Press, 1998); J. H. Dyer, N. W. Hatch, "Relation-Specific Capabilities and Barriers to Knowledge Transfers: Creating Advantage through Network Relationships," *Strategic Management Journal* 27 (2006), pp. 701–719; F. A. Kuglin, *Building, Leading and Managing Strategic Alliances* (New York: AMACOM, 2002).

[14] R. P. Lynch, *Business Alliances Guide: The Hidden Competitive Weapon* (New York: John Wiley & Sons, 1993).

TABLE 4 **Major Developments and Timeline of the Chrysler–Fiat Alliance (2010–2013) and Fiat Chrysler Automobiles N.V. (2014–2015)**

Chrysler–Fiat Alliance (2010–2013)

- Fiat used its alliance with Chrysler to seek a high-profile entry into the U.S. market.
- Fiat made major changes in its quality control and manufacturing.
- Chrysler established Fiat dealerships in the United States to sell the Fiat 500 brand.
- Fiat bought 20 percent of Chrysler.
- Fiat shareholders approved the Group to spin off and demerge automotive operations and Fiat Industrial.
- Fiat raised its Chrysler share to 25 percent.
- Chrysler–Fiat repaid $7.6 billion of its bail-out loans to the U.S. and Canadian governments.
- The Chrysler–Fiat alliance was praised by analysts for its cost-cutting synergies and useful integration.
- Fiat started to redo its brand portfolio.
- Fiat S.p.A. (automotive unit) and Fiat Industrial S.p.A. were separated.
- Fiat brought in a team of 22 international managers, and the alliance started to take off.
- Fiat successfully managed its labor relations in Italy, and the labor contract was negotiated.
- The Fiat 500 model was launched in the United States; a major publicity campaign was run to unveil the brand.
- Fiat raised its ownership in Chrysler to 58.5 percent. This was a major breakthrough.
- The top leadership in the alliance brought good synergies.
- The alliance was based on equal partnership.
- In 2013, Fiat made major changes and restructuring plans in the two companies.

Fiat Chrysler Automobiles (2014–2015)

- In 2014, the Chrysler–Fiat alliance sold over six million vehicles worldwide.
- In January 2014, Fiat bought the remaining 41.5 percent of Chrysler to complete its 100 percent ownership. The new company was incorporated in the Netherlands and domiciled in the U.K.
- FCA listed its shares on the New York Stock Exchange; it will also be listed in Milan.
- After completing the merger, the two companies chose a new name: Fiat Chrysler Automobiles (FCA).
- In October 2014, FCA announced the launch of 30 new car and truck models in global markets.
- FCA plans to concentrate on Jeep, Maserati, and Alfa Romeo.
- FCA will target emerging markets with newer models.
- FCA will have to deal with competition in the United States, Europe, and emerging markets.
- In 2015, Sergio Marchionne raised the issue of restructuring and additional consolidation in the global auto industry.

Sources: Automotive News; Economist; Financial Times; Fortune; New York Times; Wall Street Journal (various issues).

1. **What went well in the alliance?** After the alliance, the top managers of Chrysler and Fiat planned and came up with major synergies that aimed at a common R&D platform, restructuring, streamlining global operations,

and image building in both companies (see Table 2). Both Chrysler and Fiat raised their quality ratings and established dealer networks in Europe and the United States. Although downsizing was pursued to cut cost and operations, this did not cause the companies to lose sales. Both firms developed common assembly platforms in those sectors where technologies were similar. By 2014, the alliance had brought major cost savings and simplified R&D-related activities that helped suppliers and dealers (see Table 4).

2. **Problems that surfaced in the post-alliance integration**
   In the post-alliance integration, Fiat's sales declined in the European markets in 2011 because of the economic downturn. Dealing with labor unions in Italy and their work ethic–related issues also hampered corporate efficiencies in the alliance. Chrysler's U.S. operations mostly went well because of stable financial resources and sales (see Table 4).

3. **Globalization and the changing global auto industry**
   Globalization is a major force affecting countries and their industries.[15] The same applies to the global auto industry that continues to be dynamic yet highly competitive in sales and market shares. Regardless of the auto industry's consolidations and mergers and acquisitions, opportunities are available to those companies that bring new technologies and auto models. After the merger, both companies have the potential to target new markets in North America, Europe, and emerging markets (see Table 4).

4. **Leadership of Sergio Marchionne**   As of 2015, Marchionne enjoys a great reputation in Italy and North America because of his turnaround and managerial qualities. Under his leadership, the alliance worked well and helped the two companies merge. Originally trained as a chartered accountant and solicitor, Marchionne joined Fiat in 2004 and was able to convince the board to seek major changes in difficult times.[16] Marchionne sought a planned and systematic restructuring of Fiat by concentrating on new technologies and models. Fiat successfully realigned its management structure and was able to show profit (see Table 4).

5. **Brand portfolio and new models**   In 2015, FCA's brand portfolio seems compatible within the global auto industry. Both companies manufacture small cars that are in demand because of high gasoline prices and cost issues. In their alliance, the companies have successfully pooled their resources to consolidate brand portfolios that aim at significant cost savings in R&D and technology platforms. The companies' joint dealer networks have brought required savings and efficiencies as well (see Table 4).

6. **Issues related to the new company**   History books tell us that Fiat left the North American market in the eighties because of its weakened market share, quality problems, and mismanagement. To reenter the North American market, Fiat needed a well-established auto manufacturer that knew the market and had the technology to compete. Chrysler was the only choice available for this growth plan. As we evaluate the alliance and the companies' merger, it is evident that the tie-up was a logical choice on the part of Fiat, which desperately wanted to come back to North America for future expansion and growth (see Table 4).

7. **Status of Fiat Chrysler automobiles in 2015**   Table 4 provides information on the status of FCA since 2013. In 2014, the new company listed its shares on the New York Stock Exchange and plans to list on the Milan Stock Exchange (Borsa Italiana) as well. Although complex in its form and structure because of Italian and American corporate cultures, the cross-border merger has stood well in the industry and will continue to grow in coming years. FCA was incorporated in the Netherlands, domiciled in the U.K., and listed its shares on the New York Stock Exchange. The company is slowly reducing its Italian heritage and would like to grow as a global player that operates like a multinational corporation. At the same time in the United States and emerging markets, FCA has had to deal with its aging brand portfolio and weakened quality standards.[17] This may lead to additional alliances and possibly another merger with an auto manufacturer.[18] In March 2015, Marchionne proposed a *mega merger* to General Motors executives but was declined.[19] The company plans to sell five million vehicles by 2018 and would have new automotive models.[20] This is an ambitious plan that could see competitive headwind because of the overcrowded markets and cost efficiencies (see Table 4).

[15] See S. T. Anwar, "Global Business and Globalization," *Journal of International Management* 13, No. 1 (2007), pp. 78–89; S. T. Anwar, "Internationalization, Investment Opportunities, Expansion Strategies, and the Changing Telecom Industry in the MENA Region," *Journal of World Investment & Trade* 12, No. 6 (2011), 891–917; S. T. Anwar, "Super-Connectors: A New Model of Internationalization from the MENA Region," *Thunderbird International Business Review*, 57, No. 2 (2015), pp. 163–180.

[16] S. Marchionne, "Fiat's Extreme Makeover," *Harvard Business Review*, (December 2008), pp. 45–48.

[17] G. Blacet, G. Commisso, and G. Calabrese, "Structuring and Restricting Fiat-Chrysler: Can Two Weak Carmakers Jointly Survive in the New Automotive Arena?" *International Journal of Automotive Technology and Management* 13, No. 2 (2013), pp. 183–197.

[18] See H. W. Jenkins, Jr., "Chrysler Shops for Its New Bailout," *Wall Street Journal* (May 6, 2015), p. A13.

[19] Reuters, "Fiat Chrysler CEO Approaches GM about a Merger, Was Rebuffed: NTY," (May 23, 2015), http://www.reuters.com/article/2015/05/24/us-gm-fiat-chrysler-idUSKBN0O900D20150524, accessed May 24, 2015.

[20] A. Sharman and R. Wright, "Fiat and Chrysler Line Up 30 New Models," *Financial Times* (October 13, 2014), p. 17.

Case Questions

1. What are your views of the Chrysler–Fiat strategic alliance in 2009?
2. Analyze and evaluate the new company, Fiat Chrysler Automobiles (FCA), and its strengths and weaknesses in global markets.
3. Compare and contrast Fiat Chrysler automobiles with three other auto manufacturers (Toyota, General Motors, and Ford) in the global auto industry.
4. What do you anticipate beyond 2016 regarding the growth of FCA in the automotive industry?
5. What did you learn from the Fiat–Chrysler automobiles case?

9 Staffing, Training, and Compensation for Global Operations

OUTLINE

OBJECTIVES

9-1. To understand the strategic importance to the firm of the IHRM function and its various responsibilities.

9-2. To learn about the major staffing options for global operations and the factors involved in those choices.

9-3. To emphasize the need for managing the performance of expatriates through careful selection, training, and compensation.

9-4. To discuss the role of host country managers and the need for their training and appropriate compensation packages.

Opening Profile: Staffing Company Operations in Emerging Markets[1]

Ⅰn the 2015 Brookfield Global Relocation Trends Survey (GRTS), firms' human resources (HR) staffs from 143 MNCs were asked to identify the top three countries that represented new assignment locations for them. They were China, Brazil, and the UAE. Those that were considered the most challenging for assigning people, as well as for the assignees, were Brazil, India and China, followed by Russia.[2]

Frontpage/Shutterstock

However, distinction was made between relatively developed cities, such as Mexico City, pictured here, and less-developed locations in other areas of those countries.

In addition to the challenge of assigning and maintaining expatriates in emerging market economies, the ability to staff subsidiaries in emerging market economies with local managers has become a major challenge in the race for recruiting and retaining local talent. Emerging economies such as Brazil, Russia, India, and China have been developing so rapidly and have so attracted increasing overseas investment that they have outpaced the supply of suitable mid- and upper-level managers in their own markets. Foreign firms wishing to expand their investments in such economies are competing for what talent is available with both local companies and other global companies; however, they are falling behind the curve in not recognizing that they need different approaches than those they use domestically.

The problem is so acute that many companies have had to reconsider how fast they can expand in developing economies. According to *The Economist*:

> *In a recent survey, 600 chief executives of multinational companies with businesses across Asia said a shortage of qualified staff ranked as their biggest concern in China and South-East Asia. It was their second-biggest headache in Japan (after cultural differences) and the fourth-biggest in India (after problems with infrastructure, bureaucracy and wage inflation).*[3]

Reasons for the shortage of upper-level managers vary by country. Research by Ready et al. shows that although Brazil has an influx of new graduates available to staff at the low- to mid-management level, there is a deficit at the upper levels. In India, there is also a surplus at the lower level but a deficit starting at the middle levels; one additional explanation is the brain drain, in particular in the technology industry. In Russia, there is a deficit at all management levels because of decades of operating under a planned economy, together with the great increase in demand by foreign companies. In China, there is a sizable surplus at the entry level—though of varying quality—but a considerable deficit at all levels up from there.[4]

> *Competition for talent in emerging markets is heating up. Global companies should groom local highfliers—and actively encourage more managers to leave home.*[5]

Clearly, the competition for talent has become global, as has the competition for jobs. The brain drain from emerging economies has contributed to the dearth of local talent available. Over a million Chinese went to the United States to study between 1978 and 2006, and 70 percent of them did not go back. Exacerbating the problem is the high turnover of those highly sought managers and, because of that, the escalating salary requirements.[6] In addition, local firms in developing economies such as China are growing rapidly and becoming global themselves, thereby attracting local talent for their own companies. Added to these variables, as of 2015, there has been a decline in the willingness of managers from developed economies to take assignments abroad, perhaps because of global turmoil and uncertainty and concerns for their families' safety in some areas, as well as a growing concern

(Continued)

about the spouse/partner's career. For these reasons, the challenge to companies operating around the world is not only to recruit capable local managers but also to retain them. Problems regarding immigration and cultural adaptation persist.[7] Advice from professionals includes growing your own—that is, to provide sufficient training and career mentoring to elicit loyalty with managers; and, in particular, to balance local human resource needs with global standards. This may require tailoring employment packages to local markets to attract and keep top talent rather than applying global policies for the sake of global consistency.[8]

Ready et al. suggest a framework for attracting and retaining talent that recognizes that managers in developing markets are motivated by factors that are a function of their culture, business practices, and personal goals and usually dissimilar to what is expected in the home office. They conclude that successful companies offer more than a good salary and comprise four distinguishing characteristics that provide meaning for potential recruits in emerging markets:[9]

- *Brand:* That is, a global name brand known for its excellence and with a distinctive competence in a particular area, for example, technology, in which new recruits would have confidence in their future.
- *Purpose:* That is, a company that is breaking into new markets with new models and strategy, giving new employees a chance to be part of something meaningful.
- *Opportunity:* That is, a company that provides a fast-track training and career path for new recruits.
- *Culture:* That is, a company that has an organizational culture of openness and transparency for employees, with support for their work and career development.[10]

THE ROLE OF IHRM IN GLOBAL STRATEGY IMPLEMENTATION

We believe the war for talent will continue to be the major human resource issue to 2020, when the people pipeline looks to be the most crucial variable separating winners and losers in the marketplace…. Global mobility will play a key role in solving the labor availability conundrum.

PRICEWATERHOUSECOOPERS' 14TH
ANNUAL *CEO SURVEY*[11]

Hello? Anyone in HQ Listening? Why Asian Executives of Western Multinationals So Often Quit.

HARVARD BUSINESS REVIEW
APRIL 1, 2015[12]

This chapter's opening profile describes the challenges involved in assigning, recruiting, and retaining suitable managers to staff operations in emerging markets, where the burgeoning demand by both foreign and local companies is outstripping the supply. In addition, retention of local managers requires continuing effort; the high turnover rate in Asia, for example, is largely attributable to local managers feeling that those in the firm's headquarters don't understand them and their roles.[13] Other challenges for companies around the world include growing workforce mobility and the increasing trend of outsourcing service and professional jobs, which have now joined manufacturing jobs in the category of boundaryless human capital (discussed in previous chapters).

The need to outsource employees is just one of the complex issues for international human resource (IHR) managers as they seek to support strategic mandates (see Chapter 6). Global firms are finding that their practices of outsourcing skilled and professional jobs have implications for their human resource practices at home and around the world. Consequently, a firm such as Infosys, one of India's top outsourcing companies, also experiences complex human resource challenges involved in recruiting, training, and compensating increasingly sophisticated employees in its attempt to meet the escalating demand for its services; in addition, Infosys has the same challenges with its operations abroad.

It is clear, then, that a vital component of implementing global strategy is *international human resource management* (IHRM). Executives questioned about the major challenges the HR function faces in the global arena cited "(1) enhancing global business strategy, (2) aligning HR issues with business strategy, (3) designing and leading change, (4) building global corporate cultures, and (5) staffing organizations with global leaders."[14] IHRM is therefore increasingly being recognized as a major determinant of success or failure in international business. In a highly competitive global economy, where the other factors of production—capital, technology, raw materials, and information—can increasingly be duplicated, "the caliber of the people in an organization will be the only source of sustainable competitive advantage available to U.S. companies."[15] Corporations operating overseas need to pay careful attention to this most critical resource—one that also provides control over other resources. In fact, increasing recognition is being given to the role of *strategic human resource management (SHRM)*—that is, the two-way role of HRM in both helping to determine strategy and implementing it. That role in helping the organization develop the necessary capabilities to enact the desired strategy includes the reality that strategic plans are developed in large part based on the resources the firm possesses, including the human resources capabilities.[16] IBM is one company that clearly uses its global workforce to convey and implement its strategy of a globally integrated company—doing business with clients in whatever location is appropriate rather than in its previous structure of 160 subsidiaries.[17] The majority of IBM's employees are in countries such as India, Japan, Britain, and Brazil. The company uses various staffing modes and considers international assignments important to its goal of global integration.

The IHRM function comprises varied responsibilities involved in managing human resources in global corporations, including recruiting and selecting employees, providing preparation and training, and setting up appropriate compensation and performance management programs. Although firms would like to harmonize their IHRM practices around the world, considerable and powerful variables confound that goal, making it either impractical or undesirable for many localities. Among these are the complexities of local government laws and regulations, varying cultural norms and practices, and the long-entrenched and accepted business practices in the local area. Some examples are shown in Exhibit 9-1. These

EXHIBIT 9-1 Influences on Local HRM Practices

```
        ┌──────────────┐
        │  STRATEGY    │
        └──────┬───────┘
               ↓
        ┌──────────────┐
        │  STRUCTURE   │
        └──────┬───────┘
               ↓
```

Local Laws and Practices ⟶	IHRM ⟵	Cultural Norms and Practices
Qualifications vs Nepotism	**Recruitment & Selection**	Individualism
Collectivism		
Equal Employment vs Women's Roles		Masculinity
Laws re hiring local employees		Obligation
Skill levels, certification requirements	**Training & Development**	
Gov't pressure for training (e.g., China)		Long/short-term orientation
HQ vs local training		
Education (U.S.) vs Apprentice/OJT (Germany)		Power Distance
Achievement vs Seniority (e.g., Japan)	**Performance Appraisal**	Source of Power/Status
Locally accepted measures		Face-saving; privacy issues
Local standards; minimum wages; benefits	**Compensation**	Uncertainty Avoidance
Group-based vs Individual Performance vs seniority		Loyalty/harmony/seniority/face
Unemployment compensation		
Local labor laws, restrictions	**Labor Relations**	Attitudes toward work
Union power (e.g., high in India)		Attitudes toward unions
Union structure (Germany's "codetermination")		Loyalty/group harmony (e.g., Japan)
Collective bargaining process		Paternalism (e.g., Mexico)
Federation of trade unions (e.g., Sweden)		Nature of employee relations
Joint Venture union regulations (e.g., China)		

factors, in turn, are influenced by national variables in the political, economic, legal, and institutional arena as well as by competitive factors. Of particular importance to the IHRM function is the management of expatriates—employees assigned to a country other than their own, discussed in this chapter and the next and working within host-country practices and laws are discussed in the following chapter.

At the first level of planning, decisions are required on the staffing policy suitable for a particular kind of business, its global strategy, and its geographic locations. Key issues involve the difficulty of control in geographically dispersed operations, the need for local decision making independent of the home office, and the suitability of managers from alternate sources.

The interdependence of strategy, structure, and staffing is particularly worth noting. Ideally, the desired strategy of the firm should dictate the organizational structure and staffing modes considered most effective for implementing that strategy. In reality, however, there is usually considerable interdependence among those functions. Existing structural constraints often affect strategic decisions; similarly, staffing constraints or unique sets of competencies in management come into play in organizational and, sometimes, strategic decisions. It is thus important to achieve a system of fits among those variables that facilitates strategic implementation.

STAFFING FOR GLOBAL OPERATIONS

Globalization in the 21st century has resulted in an even higher demand for businesses to send the right talent to the right place at the right time.

KPMG 2012 GLOBAL ASSIGNMENT SURVEY[18]

WWW.KPMG.COM

Despite concerns about the weaker global economy and the costs of international assignment programs, the results of the PricewaterhouseCoopers' CEO Survey found that CEOs forecast a 50 percent growth of assignments over the next decade.[19] Those executives made it clear that when competing in global markets, global experience and expertise are critical to the success of the organization and employee. Colgate, for example, requires all new hires in its marketing field to have international experience.

In addition to the global war for talent, there are now considerable strategic competitive challenges for some firms regarding the need to "(a) reduce and remove talent in order to lower the costs of operations, (b) locate and relocate operations around the world, and (c) obtain equally competent talent anywhere in the world at lower wages."[20] Firms use short-term assignments and commuter assignments to nearby countries to reduce costs.[21]

Depending on the firm's primary strategic orientation and stage of internationalization, as well as situational factors, managerial staffing abroad falls into one or more of the following staffing modes—ethnocentric, polycentric, regiocentric, and global. When the company is at the internationalization stage of strategic expansion, and has a centralized structure, it will likely use an **ethnocentric staffing approach** to fill key managerial positions with people from headquarters—that is, **parent-country nationals (PCNs)**. Among the advantages of this approach, PCNs are familiar with company goals, products, technology, policies, and procedures—and they know how to accomplish things through headquarters. This policy is also likely to be used when a company notes the inadequacy of local managerial skills and determines a high need to maintain close communication and coordination with headquarters. For German companies, the most important reason for assigning expatriates was "to develop international management skills." For companies in Japan and the United Kingdom, it was "to set up a new operation," and in the United States, it was "to fill a skill gap."[22]

Frequently, companies use PCNs for the top management positions in the foreign subsidiary—in particular, the chief executive officer (CEO) and the chief financial officer (CFO)—to maintain close control. PCNs are usually preferable when a high level of technical capability is required. They are also chosen for new international ventures requiring managerial experience in the parent company and when there is a concern for loyalty to the company rather than to the host country—such as when proprietary technology is used.

In addition, the strategic goal of understanding the needs and opportunities in emerging markets has led an increasing number of top-level executives, including board members and CEOs, to assign themselves to Asia. As an example, in 2011, John Rice, vice chairman of GE and president and chief executive of global growth and operations, relocated to Hong Kong with his wife. Saying his motives were part substance and part symbolism, Mr. Rice conceded that, "Being outside the United States makes you smarter about global issues. It lets you see the world through a different lens."[23] He noted that he had learned more about China since moving there 18 months ago than he had in the 100 or so times he had visited before. According to a survey by the Economist Corporate Network, 45.3 percent of respondents expected to have board members in Asia by 2016.[24] Others in the survey noted that their continuing presence gave them more access to key leaders who regarded them as more committed to the region.

Generally speaking, however, there can be important disadvantages to the ethnocentric approach, including (1) the lack of opportunities or development for local managers, thereby decreasing their morale and their loyalty to the subsidiary; and (2) the poor adaptation and lack of effectiveness of expatriates in foreign countries. Procter & Gamble, for example, routinely appointed managers from its headquarters for foreign assignments for many years. After several unfortunate experiences in Japan, the firm realized that such a practice was insensitive to local cultures and underused its pool of high-potential, non-American managers.[25] Furthermore, an ethnocentric recruiting approach does not enable the company to take advantage of its worldwide pool of management skill. This approach also perpetuates particular personnel selections and other decision-making processes because the same types of people are making the same types of decisions.

With a **polycentric staffing approach**, local managers—**host-country nationals (HCNs)**—are hired to fill key positions in their own country. This approach is more likely to be effective when implementing a multinational strategy. If a company wants to act local, staffing with HCNs has obvious advantages. These managers are naturally familiar with the local culture, language, and ways of doing business, and they already have many contacts in place. In addition, HCNs are more likely to be accepted by people both inside and outside the subsidiary, and they provide role models for other upwardly mobile personnel. For these and other reasons, Tata Consultancy Services (TCS) follows this staffing policy for some of its subsidiaries, as detailed in the accompanying Under the Lens section.

With regard to cost, it is usually less expensive for a company to hire a local manager than to transfer one from headquarters, frequently with a family and often at a higher rate of pay. Transferring from headquarters is a particularly expensive policy when the manager and her or his family do not adjust and have to be transferred home prematurely. Rather than opening their own facilities, some companies acquire foreign firms as a means of obtaining qualified local personnel. Local managers also tend to be instrumental in staving off or more effectively dealing with problems in sensitive political situations. Some countries, in fact, legally require a specific proportion of the firm's top managers to be citizens of that country.

One disadvantage of a polycentric staffing policy is the difficulty of coordinating activities and goals between the subsidiary and the parent company, including the potentially conflicting loyalties of the local manager. Poor coordination among subsidiaries of a multinational firm could constrain strategic options. An additional drawback of this policy is that the headquarters managers of multinational firms will not gain the overseas experience necessary for any higher positions in the firm that require the understanding and coordination of subsidiary operations.

In the **global staffing approach**, the best managers are recruited from within or outside of the company, regardless of nationality. This practice—recruiting **third country nationals (TCNs)**—has been used for some time by many European multinationals. Now, HRM professionals everywhere are realizing that "the emergence of a global talent pool following China and India's decade of growth will increasingly influence talent development and acquisition."[26]

UNDER THE LENS
Tata's Staffing Challenges in the United States[27]

Tata Consultancy Services (TCS) provides IT services, business solutions, and outsourcing around the world. The Indian company, which sends thousands of employees abroad to work in client locations, is part of the Tata Group—one of India's largest industrial conglomerates—and operates in 43 countries. In 2008, TCS decided to buy a facility in Milford, Ohio, to be closer to a number of *Fortune* 500 clients in the area and to hire American graduates from the several nearby universities. TCS's strategy is to compete with consultancy giants such as IBM and Accenture on their home turf. More than half of TCS's revenue is from North America, with about 16,000 employees. TCS was anxious to compete for the estimated $52 billion in U.S. federal contracts. In 2011, TCS had 450 employees in Ohio, nearly all American, partly because of the difficulty of getting visas for Indians, and the company had plans to hire a further 500-plus, adding to its 215,000-strong global workforce.[28]

Factors affecting TCS's staffing practices in the United States include the Ohio government's ban in September 2010 of outsourcing government contracts to overseas operations, and the difficulty in finding sufficient numbers of qualified engineers in the United States. Even so, TCS faces a cost increase of around seven times for a U.S. worker compared with one hired to do similar work in India.

Clearly, the staffing challenges TCS faces in its U.S. subsidiary are just the tip of the iceberg for an IT company needing highly qualified employees around the world. In its attempt to attract and retain skilled local talent continually, Tata's HR vice president stresses the importance of recognizing the varying factors that will motivate people in its different locations. The company "has a tailored employee value proposition for each of its major markets."[29] The company understands, for example, that quality is of paramount importance to its managers in India; that in China, its managers are primarily interested in opportunities for personal development; and that the United States managers look for interesting jobs.

A global staffing approach has several important advantages. First, this policy provides a greater pool of qualified and willing applicants from which to choose, which, in time, results in further development of a global executive cadre. As discussed further in Chapter 10, the skills and experiences those managers use and transfer throughout the company result in a pool of shared learning that is necessary for the company to compete globally.

Second, where third country nationals are used to manage subsidiaries, they usually bring more cultural flexibility and adaptability to a situation, as well as bilingual or multilingual skills, than parent-country nationals, especially if they are from a similar cultural background as the host-country coworkers, and are accustomed to moving around. In addition, when TCNs are placed in key positions, employees perceive them as acceptable compromises between headquarters and local managers; thus, appointing them works to reduce resentment.

Third, it can be more cost-effective to transfer and pay managers from some countries than from others because their pay scale and benefits packages are lower. Indeed, those firms with a truly global staffing orientation are phasing out the entire ethnocentric concept of a home or host country. In fact, as globalization increases, terms such as *TCNs, HCNs*, and *expatriates* are becoming less common because of the kind of situation in which a manager may leave her native Ireland to take a job in England, then be assigned to Switzerland, then to China, and so on, without returning to Ireland. As part of that focus, the term **transpatriate** is increasingly replacing the term *expatriate*. Firms such as Philips, Heinz, Unilever, IBM, and ABB have a global staffing approach, which makes them highly visible and seems to indicate a trend.

Overall, firms still tend to use expatriates in key positions in host countries that have a less familiar culture and in less-developed economies. Clearly, this situation arises out of concern about uncertainty and the ability to control implementation of the corporation's goals. However, given the generally accepted consensus that staffing, along with structure and systems, must fit the desired strategy, firms desiring a truly global posture should adopt a global staffing approach. That is easier said than done. As shown in Exhibit 9-2, such an approach requires the firm to overcome barriers such as the availability and willingness of high-quality managers to transfer frequently around the world, dual-career constraints, time and cost constraints, conflicting requirements of host governments, and ineffective human resource management policies.

In a **regiocentric staffing approach**, recruiting is done on a regional basis—say, within Latin America for a position in Chile. This staffing approach can produce a specific mix of PCNs, HCNs, and TCNs, according to the needs of the company or the product strategy.

More recently, a staffing option known as **inpatriates** has been used to provide a linking pin between the company's headquarters and local host subsidiaries. Inpatriates are managers with global experience who are transferred to the organization's headquarters country so that their overseas business and cultural experience and contacts can facilitate interactions among the country's far-flung operations.[30]

> *Because power will always reside at world headquarters, you have to "inpatriate" foreign executives if you want to ensure that those in leadership positions know and trust them.*
>
> HARVARD BUSINESS REVIEW
> SEPTEMBER 2010[31]

Inpatriate managers can provide communication of strategic goals, change processes, and provide continuity among revolving expatriates and host nationals; in addition, they can facilitate multicultural management teams in global organizations.[32] Nestlé, for example, brings in managers at all levels from around the world to its Swiss headquarters to ensure that its executives become acquainted with the firm's best talent. The inpatriates are also happy to do this because they gain relationships all around and can network with one another in addition to gaining the knowledge and familiarity with the firm's headquarters people and processes.[33] Other companies that have brought inpatriate managers into their headquarters operations are Quaker Chemical Company (Guus Lobsen, Holland); Coca-Cola Co. (John Hunter, Australia); and Sara Lee Corporation (Cornelis Boonstra, Holland).

A critical success factor in the use of an inpatriate is the ability of that person to develop acceptance and trust among the people in the various locations, making it imperative for the

EXHIBIT 9-2 Maintaining a Globalization Momentum

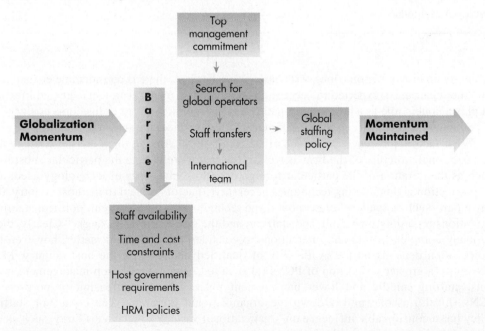

Source: Based on and adapted from D. Welch, "HRM Implications of Globalization," *Journal of General Management* 19, No. 4 (Summer 1994), pp. 52–69, used with permission of Braybrooke Press, 2011.

EXHIBIT 9-3 Key Advantages and Drawbacks of Global Staffing Practices

	Advantages	Drawbacks
PCNs	• Transfer and control firm strategy	• Costly to relocate family
	• Assignments abroad develop managers	• Little development of HCNs
	• Integrate knowledge firm-wide	• Lack local familiarity/contacts
	• Suitable managers not available locally	• PCN/family adaptation problems
	• Protect proprietary technology	• Limits use of global skills/ideas
HCNs	• Firm "acts local"; develops HCNs	• May have short-term loyalty
	• Familiarity with culture, procedures, politics, language, contacts, laws	
	• Fulfill government hiring requirements	
	• Can hit the ground running vs PCNs	
	• Likely to be less costly	• Less firm-wide coordination
	• Local role model; employee morale	• Possible conflict of interests
	• Business may be more accepted	
TCNs	• Broad global experience	• Little development of HCNs
	• Pool of shared learning	• May lack local contacts
	• Cultural flexibility and adaptability	• Complex to manage and harmonize
	• Language skills	
	• Often more acceptable than PCNs	• Less acceptable than HCNs
	• Often less-costly transferees	• Costly compared to HCNs
	• Liaison between HQ and local firm	
Inpatriates	• Linking pin between firm HQ and local host subsidiaries	• Does not replace need for PCNs or HCNs
	• Utilizes overseas experience and contacts to coordinate global operations	• Probably still perceived as an HQ manager
	• Provide continuity among revolving PCNs and HCNs	• Difficulty in gaining trust
	• Facilitate global multicultural teams	

firm to retain him or her on a long-term basis.[34] For her part, there is considerable challenge in that "the inpatriate is expected to become a parent country manager in language and lifestyle, yet play a double role as a host country national when returning to her or his home country."[35]

Some of the pros and cons of the different staffing practices are shown in Exhibit 9-3.

What factors influence the choice of staffing policy? Among them are the strategy and organizational structure of the firm as well as the factors related to the particular subsidiary (such as the duration of the particular foreign operation, the types of technology used, and the production and marketing techniques necessary). Factors related to the host country also play a part (such as the level of economic and technological development, political stability, regulations regarding ownership and staffing, and the sociocultural setting).[36] Clearly, there are many complex factors and interactions to consider. As a practical matter, however, the choice often depends on the availability of qualified managers in the host country. Most MNCs use a greater proportion of PCNs (also called expatriates) in top management positions, staffing middle and lower management positions with increasing proportions of HCNs (locals) as one moves down the organizational hierarchy. The choice of staffing policy has a considerable influence on organizational variables in the subsidiary, such as the locus of decision-making authority, the methods of communication, and the perpetuation of human resource management practices. These variables are illustrated in Exhibit 9-4. The ethnocentric staffing approach, for example, usually results in a higher level of authority and decision making in headquarters compared to the polycentric approach.[37]

EXHIBIT 9-4 Relationships among Strategic Mode, Organizational Variables, and Staffing Orientation[38]

Aspects of the Enterprise	Orientation			
	Ethnocentric	Polycentric	Regiocentric	Global
Primary strategic orientation/stage	International	Multidomestic	Regional	Transnational
Perpetuation (recruiting, staffing, development)	People of home country developed for key positions everywhere in the world	People of local nationality developed for key positions in their own country	Regional people developed for key positions anywhere in the region	Best people everywhere in the world developed for key positions everywhere in the world
Complexity of organization	Complex in home country; simple in subsidiaries	Varied and independent	Highly interdependent on a regional basis	"Global Web": complex, worldwide alliances/network
Authority; decision	High in headquarters	Relatively low in headquarters	High in regional headquarters and/or high collaboration among subsidiaries	Collaboration of headquarters and subsidiaries around the world
Evaluation and control	Home standards applied to people and performance	Determined locally	Determined regionally	Globally integrated
Rewards	High in headquarters; low in subsidiaries	Wide variation; can be high or low rewards for subsidiary performance	Rewards for contribution to regional objectives	Rewards to international and local executives for reaching local and worldwide objectives based on global company goals
Communication; information flow	High volume of orders, commands, advice to subsidiaries	Little to and from headquarters; little among subsidiaries	Little to and from corporate headquarters, but may be high to and from regional headquarters and among countries	Horizontal; network relations; "virtual" teams
Geographic identification	Nationality of owner	Nationality of host country	Regional company	Truly global company, but identifying with national interests ("glocal")

Without exception, all phases of IHRM should support the desired strategy of the firm. In the staffing phase, having the right people in the right places at the right times is a key ingredient of success in international operations. An effective managerial cadre can be a distinct competitive advantage for a firm.

The initial phase of setting up criteria for global selection, then, is to consider which overall staffing approach or approaches would most likely support the company's strategy, as previously discussed—such as HCNs for localization, the (multilocal) strategic approach, and transpatriates and inpatriates for a global strategy. These are typically just starting points using idealized criteria, however. In reality, other factors creep into the process, such as host-country regulations, stage of internationalization, and—most often—who is both suitable and available for the position. It is also vital to integrate long-term strategic goals into the selection and development process, especially when rapid global expansion is intended. Insufficient projection of staffing needs for global assignments will likely result in constrained strategic opportunities because of a shortage of experienced managers suitable to place in those positions.

The selection process is set up as a decision tree in which the progression to the next stage of selection or the type of orientation training depends on the assessment of critical factors regarding the job or the candidate at each decision point. The simplest selection process involves choosing a local national because minimal training is necessary regarding the culture or ways of doing business locally.[39] However, to be successful, local managers often require additional training in the MNC company-wide processes, technology, and corporate culture. If a local national cannot fill the position, yet the job requires a high level of interaction with the local community, careful screening of candidates from other countries and a vigorous training program are necessary.

Most MNCs tend to start their operations in a particular region by selecting primarily from their own pool of managers. Over time, and with increasing internationalization, they tend to move to a predominantly polycentric or regiocentric policy because of (1) increasing pressure (explicit or implicit) from local governments to hire locals (or sometimes legal restraints on the use of expatriates) and (2) the greater costs of expatriate staffing, particularly when the company has to pay taxes for the parent-company employee in both countries.[40] In addition, in recent years, MNCs have noted an improvement in the level of managerial and technical competence in many countries, negating the chief reason for using a primarily ethnocentric policy in the past. One researcher's comment represents a growing attitude: "All things being equal, a local national who speaks the language, understands the culture and the political system, and is often a member of the local elite should be more effective than an expatriate alien."[41] However, concerns about the need to maintain strategic control over subsidiaries and to develop managers with a global perspective remain a source of debate about staffing policies among human resource management professionals. A globally oriented company such as ABB (Asea Brown Boveri), for example, has 500 roving transpatriates who are moved every two to three years, thus developing a considerable management cadre with global experience.[42]

For MNCs based in Europe and Asia, human resource policies at all levels of the organization are greatly influenced by the home-country culture and policies. For Japanese subsidiaries in Singapore, Malaysia, and India, for example, promotion from within and expectations of long-term loyalty to and by the firm are culture-based practices transferable to subsidiaries.

MANAGING EXPATRIATES

The survey identified three significant challenges facing corporations: finding suitable candidates for assignments, helping employees—and their families—complete their assignments, and retaining these employees once their assignments end.[43]

If some of your expatriates are about to jump ship because they are not getting paid on time, their families are miserable or their taxes are fouled up, it may be time to move beyond low-tech tools.

HR MAGAZINE,
APRIL 2015[44]

An important responsibility of IHR managers is that of managing expatriates—employees they assign to positions in other countries—whether from the headquarters country or third countries. Most multinationals underestimate the importance of the human resource function in the selection, training, acculturation, and evaluation of expatriates. However, although the number of employers sending staff abroad is on the rise, only half actually have policies in place to govern these assignments, research shows. In fact, the Brookfield Global Relocation Trends Survey in 2014 concluded that, although career management was stated as a challenging international assignment management issue by company respondents, only 22 percent indicated that they had a formal career management process in place, and only 19 percent had an international assignment candidate pool in place.[45]

In addition, too often, HR managers are not aware that expatriates are unhappy until they find out they are losing valuable, experienced managers to another company. So, in addition to ensuring that there is personal contact with expatriates, a number of firms are turning to technological applications to keep track of visas and immigration status, payroll and compensation packages, taxes, housing, and so on, which can make or break the family's situational satisfaction.[46]

Expatriate Selection

The selection of personnel for overseas assignments is a complex process. While matching the firm's criteria for selection with the motivation and suitability of potential candidates, it is also useful to bear in mind the reasons candidates might have for taking the assignment. In their survey of reasons people would consider a foreign assignment, the Boston Consulting Group (BCG), with a sample size of 203,756 from respondents around the world, found a high level of willingness to work abroad (64 percent) among those looking for new job opportunities; the top ten reasons were: broaden personal experience, acquire work experience, better career opportunities, an overall attractive job offer, improved salary prospects, better standard of living, ability to live in a different culture, for the challenge, learn a new language, and meet new people to build new networks.[47]

From the firm's perspective, criteria for selection are based on the same success factors as in the domestic setting, but additional criteria must be considered, relative to the specific circumstances of each international position. Unfortunately, many HRM directors have a long-standing, ingrained practice of selecting potential expatriates simply on the basis of their domestic track records and their technical expertise.[48] The need to ascertain whether potential expatriates have the necessary cross-cultural awareness and interpersonal skills for the position is too often overlooked.

Research by Mansour Javidan points to three major global mind-set attributes that successful expatriates possess.

- Intellectual capital, or knowledge, skills, understanding, and cognitive complexity
- Psychological capital, or the ability to function successfully in the host country through internal acceptance of different cultures and a strong desire to learn from new experiences
- Social capital, or the ability to build trusting relationships with local stakeholders, whether they are employees, supply chain partners, or customers[49]

It is also important to assess whether the candidate's personal and family situation is such that everyone is likely to adapt to the local culture. Studies have shown that there are five categories of success for expatriate managers: job factors, relational dimensions such as cultural empathy and flexibility, motivational state, family situation, and language skills. However, deciding before the expatriate goes on assignment whether he or she will be successful in those dimensions poses considerable problems for recruitment and selection purposes. Whereas language skills, for example, may be easy to ascertain, characteristics such as flexibility and cultural adjustment—widely acknowledged as most vital for expatriates—are difficult to judge beforehand. To address the problem of predicting how well an expatriate will perform on an overseas assignment, Tye and Chen studied factors that HR managers used as predictors of expatriate success. They found that the greatest predictive value was in the expatriate characteristics of stress tolerance and extraversion and less in domestic work experience, gender, or even international experience. The results indicate that a manager who is extraverted (sociable, talkative) and who has a high tolerance for stress (typically experienced in new, different contexts such as in a foreign country) is more likely to be able to adjust to the new environment, the new job, and interaction with diverse people than those without those characteristics. HR selection procedures, then, often include seeking out managers with those characteristics because they know there will be a greater chance for successful job performance and less turnover likelihood.[50]

These expatriate success factors are based on studies of American expatriates. One could argue that the requisite skills are the same for managers from any country—and particularly so for third-country nationals. A study of expatriates in China, for example, found that expatriate success factors included performance management, training, organizational support, willingness to relocate, and strength of the relationship between the expatriate and the firm.[51]

Expatriate Performance Management

Deciding on a staffing policy and selecting suitable managers are logical first steps, but they do not alone ensure success. When staffing overseas assignments with expatriates, for example, many other reasons, besides poor selection, contribute to *expatriate failure* among U.S. multinationals. A large percentage of these failures can be attributed to poor preparation and planning for the entry and reentry transitions of the manager and his or her family. One important variable, for example, often given insufficient attention in the selection, preparation, and support phases, is the suitability and adjustment of the spouse (discussed further in chapter 10). The inability of the spouse to adjust to the new environment has been found to be a major—in fact, the most frequently cited—reason for expatriate failure in U.S. and European companies.[52] Despite these obvious concerns, few companies include the spouse in the interviewing process. The following is a synthesis of the factors researchers and firms frequently mention as the major causes of expatriate failure.

- Selection based on headquarters criteria rather than assignment needs
- Inadequate preparation, training, and orientation prior to assignment
- Alienation or lack of support from headquarters
- Inability to adapt to local culture and working environment
- Problems with spouse and children—poor adaptation, family unhappiness
- Insufficient compensation and financial support
- Poor programs for career support and repatriation

In considering the overall family adjustment and happiness, it is important to pay attention to the trailing spouse—that is, the spouse or partner of the person taking the assignment overseas. Whether the situation is that the spouse wants to work in the new location but has not found a position or that the couple has made a decision for the spouse to devote the time to the children and household, HR should attempt to help the couple, or family, have a positive experience and thus retain the employee and facilitate a successful assignment. Although most assignees are still men, especially expats from the more masculine cultures, women are increasingly taking the position, and the husband becomes the trailing spouse, creating a unique situation for him to settle into, as illustrated in the following Under the Lens section describing how some men created their own solutions.

UNDER THE LENS
Tales from Trailing Husbands

Stay-at-home men who accompany their wives on overseas postings are looking for support, writes Alicia Clegg.

It is Friday lunchtime. Inside Le Baron, a bar on the outskirts of Brussels, George from Canada and Henri from South Africa are setting the world to rights over cappuccino and Jupiler beer. Among their companions the talk is of iPhones, golf and Prince Harry. Welcome to Spouses Trailing Under Duress Successfully, an expatriate network-cum-social club for men who follow their wives on overseas postings, otherwise known as STUDS.

Once a rarity, women now comprise 23 per cent of workers on overseas assignments according to the latest report from U.S.-based Brookfield Global Relocation Services. But while many international cities have long-established clubs for expat wives, the social needs of accompanying husbands have traditionally been overlooked. STUDS aims to change that, creating a space in which businessmen-turned-stay-at-home-spouses can swap war stories and indulge in some man talk.

The group began in the mid-1990s, when Brussels's expatriate population was expanding. Groups of trailing males can also be found, from Switzerland to China. Eric Johnson, co-organiser of Shanghai-based Guy Tai—a play on taitai, Chinese for "lady who lunches"—says he knows of trailing male groups in the early stages in Beijing, Hong Kong and Zurich. "As [expat spouses] move on to other cities, they start to form local groups. Someone knows someone else and they say, 'let's do things together.'"

Michael Shevlin, a British national, put his career as an animator on hold to look after his two toddlers when his wife had a chance to work in Geneva. As the only man in weekday playgrounds, he hankered for weekends when he could push his kids on the swings without feeling "judged"; he says: "There's a certain look that [says] 'why aren't you at work?'"

He hoped the expat mothers whom he overheard arranging coffee dates around their offspring's play dates would invite him into their circle. But the invitations never came. Instead, with the help of Catherine Nelson-Pollard, an expat blogger and broadcaster, who knew of other expat husbands scattered across the region, he set up a trailing spouse group for men. Two years on, the group still meets in a microbrewery in Nyon, pulling in trailing males from nearby Geneva, Lausanne and across the French border.

In an alien environment, says Yvonne McNulty, author of *Managing Expatriates: A Return on Investment Approach*, people seek out others with whom "they might have something in common." This puts trailing husbands, who will typically be far outnumbered by trailing wives, at an immediate disadvantage. "When it turns out that you're the stay-at-home and your wife has the big career … people can feel awkward because they don't quite know where you fit in."

Differences between gender roles today and the norms with which people grew up create other problems, says David Schiesher, a Geneva-based psychotherapist, recalling a couple who consulted him. The wife's job involved repeated overseas postings, hindering the husband's career. He became resentful and depressed; she thought he needed to make a bigger effort. "Even though she was comfortable being the provider, there was still this old programming that told her that he should be doing more."

Mr. Shevlin says meeting other men who had also come to Switzerland "on the back of their wives' contracts" made his life less lonely. However, having sat in on a few gatherings of expat wives in which—on more than one occasion—a mother "going through hell" began crying, he thinks the emotional lows that both sexes go through are more on display when women get together.

Although some men will share their insecurities with peers, he says, others do not want to. Some become "ultra-blokey" when the conversation takes a personal turn, possibly to signal to the group that emotional matters are off-limits: "In a guys' group you just wouldn't see [tears]."

Likewise, Mr. Johnson—a part-time international development consultant and stay-at-home father from the U.S., who is married to a corporate lawyer—says the emphasis at Guy Tai is on sharing local know-how rather than giving each other overt emotional support: "Because we are in a novel situation we spend a lot of time [helping each other] figure things out." Subjects include bureaucracy or what air purifier to choose. Like the group in Nyon, Guy Tai meets in a microbrewery. It also organises sports activities, factory tours and lunches.

Such groups can also help uprooted spouses restart careers. Mr. Johnson says some Guy Tais have sidelines, but few look for regular employment. Settling in a family in China is a job in itself and opportunities for highly qualified westerners are scarce. By contrast, Mr. Shevlin, who now teaches animation, says that among his group trailing spouses who find jobs act as a grapevine, providing tip-offs when employers are recruiting, for instance.

One risk with any expat spouse group is that members do not learn the local language or make friends and contacts outside the coterie. When you are newly arrived and know nobody, joining a ready-made buddy group may seem like "a cure for social isolation," says Mr. Schiesher, especially if you are the only male at the school-gate and rarely get the chance to talk to other men. He advises trailing males to look upon spouse groups as stepping stones to exploring local life.

This is the approach that Kevin Anderson, a retired high-school band director who followed his accountant wife from Texas to Brussels, has taken. When their radiators sprang a leak, Mr. Anderson found an English-speaking plumber through STUDS, but he is learning French and asks members to suggest cultural events, such as jazz festivals, to help him connect to the local scene.

As more women are posted abroad, some male spouse groups see opportunities to recruit members through HR departments, and thereby solve a problem for employers. When assignments go badly, one frequent explanation is that the family failed to adjust. Yet, according to research done for Lloyds TSB International, only 10 per cent of expat employers provide networking opportunities for spouses. "My impression is that employers like [us] because if spouses feel comfortable, employees are more likely to be happy," says Mr. Johnson, adding that Guy Tai has a flyer that relocation agencies and employers are starting to give to newly arrived female staff.

Alan Welch, a former British naval officer who joined STUDS when his wife's career took them to Brussels, thinks employers would do better to publicise groups such as Guy Tai and STUDS than host socials of their own. "[At your spouse's workplace], you need to keep in mind to whom you're talking…. With a group like STUDS it's more like meeting [friends] in the pub—and you're not relying on your wife for a social life," he says.

Starting a men's group

- Look for clever locations. Meeting in centrally situated Nyon, rather than Geneva or Lausanne, allows Michael Shevlin's group to pull in trailing males from both cities.

- Keep to the same day, time and place, so people don't get confused. Fit around school runs and office hours so that working wives can relieve stay-at-home dads.

- Publicise meetings through expat forums, establish an email list and do not assume everyone is on Facebook or Twitter. Many older spouses aren't (yet).

- Offer something extra. Guy Tai and the Nyon group both meet in microbreweries with unusual ales. Le Baron overlooks a popular farmer's market selling cheese, fish and patisserie. It also sells fresh flowers—"handy if you're in the doghouse" at home, says Kevin Anderson.

Source: Alicia Clegg, *Financial Times* [London (UK)], June 11, 2013, p. 14.

After careful selection based on the specific assignment and the long-term plans of both the organization and the candidates, plans must be made for the preparation, training, and development of expatriate managers. In the following sections, we discuss training and development and then compensation. However, it is useful to note that these should be components of an integrated performance management program, specific to expatriates, which includes goal setting, training, performance appraisal, and performance-related compensation. Some insight into the variability of performance management functions can be gleaned from the accompanying Comparative Management in Focus feature.

Global Team Performance Management

Global teams are discussed more fully in Chapter 10. But here, we must recognize that expatriate performance often includes performance as a team, typically based on discussions and decisions made with team members in various countries, cultures, and time zones, thus most often conducted virtually through teleconferencing, Skyping, and various social media, but also sometimes personally. As with any HR decision, care must go into the selection and training of the people who will comprise the team so that the advantages of insight, local knowledge, and group creativity will support the firm's strategic plans. Clearly, as described throughout this book, a first is to include cross-cultural training specific to team members with whom the interactions will take place. This can be followed up by an initial face-to-face group meeting to develop trust, feel out communication styles, and iron out practical matters such as the language to use and the time of day for virtual meetings that would work for everyone. From the team leader's perspective, it is also important to find a way to mesh leadership styles and be creative about how the team as a whole can adapt to one another.[53] Often, differences in the relative emphasis and leadership styles depend on the stage of the project at hand. For example, as concluded from a study by Zhang et al. on the scope of the project management process, team members from the Netherlands wanted a very pre-determined and formal process, compared with team members from China, who preferred flexibility in the project goals and scope.[54]

EXPATRIATE TRAINING AND DEVELOPMENT

It is clear that preparation and training for cross-cultural interactions are critical. A Global Relocation Trends Survey revealed that attrition rates for expatriates were more than double the rate of non-expatriates. It found that 21 percent of expatriates left their companies during the assignments, and another 23 percent left within a year of returning from the assignment.[55] Moreover, about half of those who remain longer in their overseas assignment function at a low

Comparative Management in Focus
Expatriate Performance Management Practices:
Samples from Five Countries

Hsi-An Shih et al. conducted a study in which they interviewed expatriates and human resource professionals in global information technology companies headquartered in five countries. These were Applied Materials (American) with 16,000 employees in 13 countries, Hitachi High Technologies (Japanese) with 470,000 employees in 23 countries, Philips Electronics (Dutch) with 192,000 employees in 60 countries, Samsung (Korean) with 173,000 employees in 20 countries, and Winbond Electronics (Taiwanese) with 47,000 employees in six countries. Shih et al. found that those companies used standardized forms from headquarters rather than tailoring them to the host environment; as such, they reflected the company culture but not the local culture in which those expatriates were operating. There also was lack of on-the-job training from those companies.[56] The differences in procedures for goal setting, performance appraisal, training, and performance-related pay among those five companies are detailed in Exhibit 9-5.

EXHIBIT 9-5 Expatriate Performance Management from MNEs of Five National Origins

Company	Goal Setting	Performance Appraisal	Training and Development	Performance-related Pay
AMT (American)	Short-term: sending unit's general manager Long term: host country's general manager	Annual performance appraisal Open feedback Interview	Applied global university Seldom take training programs while on assignment No clear connection between performance result and career development	Clear link between performance and compensation Cash bonuses and stock options
Hitachi (Japanese)	Self-setting, then finalized by host-country manager	Annually for managerial purposes, biannually for development purposes; One-way feedback discussion Seldom take training programs while on assignment	Orientation Language training Can apply to host location supervisor No clear connection between performance result and career development	Link between performance and compensation not clear Seniority-based pay system Cash bonuses
Philips (Dutch)	Self-setting, then finalized by host-country manager	Biannual performance appraisal; Open feedback in interview	Orientation Seldom take training programs while on assignment No clear connection between performance result and career development	Clear link between performance and compensation Cash bonuses and stock options
Samsung (Korean)	Self-setting, then finalized by host-country manager	Biannually for managerial purposes, annually for development purposes; Open feedback in interview	Orientation Language training Can apply to host location supervisor No clear connection between performance result and career development	Clear link between performance and compensation Senior managers: cash bonuses and stock options Ordinary expatriates: cash bonuses
Windbond (Taiwanese)	Self-setting, then finalized by host-country manager	Biannual performance appraisal; Feedback depends on manager	Orientation Seldom take training programs while on assignment Can apply to host location supervisor No clear connection between performance result and career development	Clear link between performance and compensation Cash bonuses and stock options

Source: Adapted from His-An Shih, Yun-Hwa Chiang, and In-Sook Kim, "Expatriate Performance Management from MNEs of Different National Origins," *International Journal of Manpower* 26, No. 2 (2005), pp. 161–162. Reprinted with permission of Emerald Group Publishing Ltd, 2011.

level of effectiveness. The direct cost alone of a failed expatriate assignment is estimated to be from $200,000 to $1.2 million. The indirect costs may be far greater, depending on the expatriate's position. Relations with the host-country government and customers may be damaged, resulting in a loss of market share and a poor reception for future PCNs.

Both cross-cultural adjustment problems and practical differences in everyday living present challenges for expatriates and their families. Examples are evident from a survey of expatriates in which they ranked the countries that presented the most challenging assignments to them, along with some pet peeves from their experiences.

China: A continuing problem for expatriates; one complained that at his welcome banquet, he was served duck tongue and pigeon head.

Brazil: Expatriates stress that cell phones are essential because home phones don't work.

India: Returning executives complain that the pervasiveness of poverty and street children is overwhelming.

Indonesia: Here you need to plan ahead financially because landlords typically demand rent two to three years in advance.

Japan: Expatriates and their families remain concerned that, although there is excellent medical care, the Japanese doctors reveal little to their patients.[57]

Even though cross-cultural training has proved to be of high value in making the assignment a success, only 20 percent of companies surveyed had formal cross-cultural training for expatriates.[58] Much of the rationale for this lack of training is an assumption that managerial skills and processes are universal. In a simplistic way, a manager's domestic track record is used as the major selection criterion for an overseas assignment.

In most countries, however, the success of the expatriate is not left so much to chance. Foreign companies provide considerably more training and preparation for expatriates than U.S. companies do. Therefore, it is not hard to understand why Japanese expatriates experience significantly fewer incidences of failure than their U.S. counterparts, although this may be partially because fewer families accompany Japanese assignees. Japanese multinationals typically have recall rates of below 5 percent, signifying that they send abroad managers who are far better prepared and more adept at working and flourishing in a foreign environment.[59] The demands on expatriate managers have always been as much a result of the multiple relationships that they have to maintain as they are of the differences in the host-country environment. Those relations include family relations; internal relations with people in the corporation, both locally and globally, especially with headquarters; external relations (suppliers, distributors, allies, customers, local community, etc.); and relations with the host government. It is important to pinpoint any potential problems that an expatriate may experience with those relationships so that these problems may be addressed during predeparture training. Problem recognition is the first stage in a comprehensive plan for developing expatriates. The three areas critical to preparation are cultural training, language instruction, and familiarity with everyday matters.[60] In the model shown in Exhibit 9-6, various development methods are used to address these areas during predeparture training, postarrival training, and reentry training. These methods continue to be valid and used by many organizations. Two-way feedback between the executive and the trainers at each stage helps to tailor the level and kinds of training to the individual manager. The desired goal is the increased effectiveness of the expatriate because of familiarity with local conditions, cultural awareness, and his or her family's needs in the host country.

Cross-Cultural Training

Training in language and practical affairs is quite straightforward, but cross-cultural training is not; it is complex and deals with deep-rooted behaviors. The actual process of cross-cultural training should result in the expatriate learning both content and skills that will improve interactions with host-country individuals by reducing misunderstandings and inappropriate behaviors.

CULTURE SHOCK

The goal of training is to ease the adjustment to the new environment by reducing **culture shock**, a state of disorientation and anxiety about not knowing how to behave in an unfamiliar culture. The cause of culture shock is the trauma people experience in new and different cultures, where they lose the familiar signs and cues that they had used to interact in daily life and where they must learn to cope with a vast array of new cultural cues and expectations.[61]

EXHIBIT 9-6 IHRM Process to Maximize Effectiveness of Expatriate Assignments

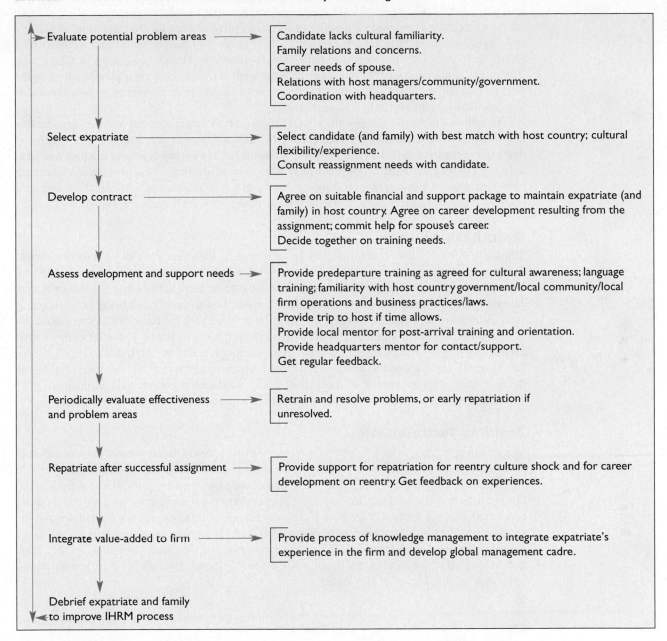

The symptoms of culture shock range from mild irritation to deep-seated psychological panic or crisis. The inability to work effectively, stress within the family, and hostility toward host nationals are the common dysfunctional results of culture shock—often leading to the manager giving up and going home.

It is helpful to recognize the stages of culture shock to understand what is happening. Culture shock usually progresses through four stages, as described by Oberg: (1) *honeymoon*, when positive attitudes and expectations, excitement, and a tourist feeling prevail (which may last up to several weeks); (2) *irritation and hostility*, the crisis stage when cultural differences result in problems at work, at home, and in daily living—expatriates and family members feel homesick and disoriented, lashing out at everyone (many never get past this stage); (3) *gradual adjustment*, a period of recovery in which the expatriate gradually becomes able to understand and predict patterns of behavior, use the language, and deal with daily activities, and the family starts to accept its new life; and (4) *biculturalism*, the stage in which the manager and family members grow to accept and appreciate local people and practices and become able to function effectively in two cultures.[62] Many never get to the fourth stage—operating acceptably at the third stage—but those who do report that their assignment is positive and growth oriented. In recognition of the importance of helping expatriates adapt to the local environment, companies such as PepsiCo provide a number of localized programs to aid the transition. PepsiCo's 600 expats and their families are encouraged to join the company's health and wellness programs and various local sports programs such as soccer in Dubai, ping-pong in China, and Zumba in Latin countries. The company believes such activities help their people adjust to the new culture and get involved in the local community. In addition, the company provides families language lessons and help with child tuition.[63]

In addition to family and organizational support, HCN coworkers can provide considerable help for expatriate adjustment. A recent study by Ashish Mahajan and Soo Min Toh concluded that expatriates who sought advice from HCN coworkers whom they felt were credible and likeable reported greater satisfaction with their work and adjustment.[64] Clearly, most expatriates have a number of avenues at their disposal to help in the adjustment process for them and their families if they seek them out and take advantage of the local coworkers and friends.

SUBCULTURE SHOCK

Similar to culture shock, though usually less extreme, is the experience of **subculture shock**. This occurs when a manager is transferred to another part of the country where there are cultural differences—essentially from what she or he perceives to be a majority culture to a minority one. The shock comes from feeling like an immigrant in one's own country and being unprepared for such differences. For instance, someone going from New York to Texas will experience considerable differences in attitudes and lifestyle between those two states. These differences exist even within Texas, with cultures that range from roaming ranches and high technology to Bible-belt attitudes and laws and to areas with a mostly Mexican heritage.[65] As with other regions in the world, expatriates coming to the United States might need considerable adjustment after working in, say, San Francisco, California, and then being posted to somewhere in Alabama.

Training Techniques

Many training techniques are available to assist overseas assignees in the adjustment process, although too often programs include only some language coaching and introduction to the host country.

Most training programs take place in the expatriate's own country prior to leaving. Although this is certainly a convenience, the impact of host-country programs can be far greater than those conducted at home because there is no better way for someone to experience the culture and the local people than actually being there. Some MNCs are beginning to recognize that there is no substitute for on-the-job training (OJT) in the early stages of the careers of managers they hope to develop into senior-level global managers. Exhibit 9-7 shows some global management development programs for junior employees.

EXHIBIT 9-7 Corporate Programs to Develop Global Managers

- ABB (Asea Brown Boveri) rotates about 500 managers around the world to different countries every two to three years in order to develop a management cadre of transpatriates to support their global strategy.
- PepsiCo has an orientation program for its foreign managers, which brings them to the United States for one-year assignments in bottling division plants.
- British Telecom uses informal mentoring techniques to induct employees into the ways of their assigned country; existing expatriate workers talk to prospective assignees about the cultural factors to expect (www.FT.com).
- Honda of America Manufacturing gives its U.S. supervisors and managers extensive preparation in Japanese language, culture, and lifestyle and then sends them to the parent company in Tokyo for up to three years.
- General Electric likes its engineers and managers to have a global perspective whether or not they are slated to go abroad. The company gives regular language and cross-cultural training for them so that they are equipped to conduct business with people around the world (www.GE.com).

In addition, according to Eduardo Caride, Telefonica's regional manager in Latin America, there is no better training than the experience managers get by working in one country and then being able to use that knowledge and experience in another country; in addition, the relationships that are made around the world greatly facilitate business transactions.[66] After assignments in Miami, Telefonica's head office in Spain, and then Argentina, he says:

> *I can tell you, it helps to have been on both sides of the world.*
>
> EDUARDO CARIDE TELEFONICA, HARVARD BUSINESS REVIEW
> *SEPTEMBER 2014*[67]

INTEGRATING TRAINING WITH GLOBAL ORIENTATION

In continuing our discussion of strategic fit, it is important to remember that training programs, like staffing approaches, should be designed with the company's strategy in mind. Although it is probably impractical to break down those programs into many variations, it is feasible at least to consider the relative level or stage of globalization that the firm has reached, because obvious major differences would be appropriate—for example, from the initial export stage to the full global stage. Exhibit 9-8 suggests levels of rigor and types of training content appropriate for the firm's managers, as well as those for host-country nationals, for four globalization stages—export, multidomestic, multinational, and global. It is noteworthy, for example, that the training of host-country nationals for a global firm has a considerably higher level of scope and rigor than that for the other stages and borders on the standards for the firm's expatriates.

As a further area for managerial preparation for global orientation—in addition to training plans for expatriates and for HCNs separately—there is a particular need to anticipate potential problems with the interaction of expatriates and local staff. In a study of expatriates and local staff (inpatriates) in Central and Eastern European joint ventures and subsidiaries, Peterson found that managers reported a number of expatriate behaviors that helped them integrate with

EXHIBIT 9-8 Stage of Globalization and Training Design Issues[68]

Export Stage	**MNC Stage**
Training Need: Low to moderate	*Training Need:* High moderate to high
Content: Emphasis should be on interpersonal skills, local culture, customer values, and business behavior.	*Content:* Emphasis should be on interpersonal skills, two-way technology transfer, corporate value transfer, international strategy, stress management, local culture, and business practices.
Host-Country Nationals: Train to understand parent-country products and policies.	*Host-Country Nationals:* Train in technical areas, product and service systems, and corporate culture.
MDC Stage	**Global Stage**
Training Need: Moderate to high	*Training Need:* High
Content: Emphasis should be on interpersonal skills, local culture, technology transfer, stress management, and business practices and laws.	*Content:* Emphasis should be on global corporate operations and systems, corporate culture transfer, customers, global competitors, and international strategy.
Host-Country Nationals: Train to familiarize with production and service procedures.	*Host-Country Nationals:* Train for proficiency in global organization production and efficiency systems, corporate culture, business systems, and global conduct policies.

EXHIBIT 9-9 Factors That Facilitate or Hinder the Integration of Expatriate Staff with Local Staff

Facilitates Integration	Hinders Integration
Relationship-building	Not using team concept
Speaking the local language	Not learning local language
Knowledge sharing	Withholding useful information
Cultural adaptability/flexibility	Spouse and family problems in adjusting
Respect	Superior and autocratic behavior
Overseas experience	Limited time in assignment
Develop local value-added from venture	Headquarters mentality
Encourage local innovation	Dominate from head office

Source: Based on R. B. Peterson, "The Use of Expatriates and Inpatriates in Central and Eastern Europe Since the Wall Came Down," *Journal of World Business* 38 (2003), pp. 55–69.

local staff but also some that were hindrances (see Exhibit 9-9).[69] Clearly, this kind of feedback from MNC managers in the field can provide the basis for expatriate training and help HCNs anticipate and work with the expatriates to meet joint strategic objectives.

Compensating Expatriates

If you're an expatriate working alongside another expatriate and you're being treated differently, it creates a lot of dissension.

CHRISTOPHER TICE
MANAGER, *GLOBAL EXPATRIATE OPERATIONS, DUPONT INC*[70]

The significance of an appropriate compensation and benefits package to attract, retain, and motivate international employees cannot be overemphasized. Compensation is a crucial link between strategy and its successful implementation. There must be a fit between compensation and the goals for which the firm wants managers to aim. So that they will not feel exploited, employees need to perceive equity and goodwill in their compensation and benefits, whether they are PCNs, HCNs, or TCNs. The premature return of expatriates or the unwillingness of managers to take overseas assignments can often be traced to their knowledge that the assignment is detrimental to them financially and usually to their career progression. One company that recognizes the need for a reasonable degree of standardization in its treatment of expatriates is DuPont. The company has centralized programs in its Global Transfer Center of Expertise for its approximately 400 annual international relocations so its expatriates know that everyone is getting the same package.

From the firm's perspective, the high cost of maintaining appropriate compensation packages for expatriates has led many companies—Colgate-Palmolive, Chase Manhattan Bank, Digital Equipment, General Motors, and General Electric among them—to find ways to cut the cost of PCN assignments as much as possible. "Transfer a $100,000-a-year American executive to London—and suddenly he [or she] costs the employer $300,000," explains the *Wall Street Journal.* "Move him to Stockholm or Tokyo, and he [or she] easily becomes a million-dollar [manager]."[71]

Firms try to cut overall costs of assignments by either extending the expatriate's tour, since turnover is expensive—especially when there is an accompanying family to move—or assigning expatriates to a much shorter tour as an unaccompanied assignment.

Designing and maintaining an appropriate compensation package is more complex than it would seem because of the need to consider and reconcile parent- and host-country financial, legal, and customary practices. The problem is that although little variation in typical executive salaries at the level of base compensation exists around the world, a wide variation in net spendable income is often present. U.S. executives abroad may receive more in cash and stock, but they have to spend more for what foreign companies provide, such as cars, vacations, and entertainment allowances. In addition, the manager's purchasing power with that net income is affected by the relative cost of living. The cost of living is considerably higher in most of Europe than in the United States. In designing compensation and benefit packages for PCNs, then, the challenge to IHRM professionals is to maintain a standard of living for expatriates equivalent to their colleagues at home, plus compensating them for any additional incurred costs. This policy is referred to as "keeping the expatriate whole."[72]

To ensure that expatriates do not lose out through their overseas assignment, the **balance sheet approach**, or **home-based method** (see Exhibit 9-10 for an example), is often used to equalize the standard of living between the host country and the home country and add some compensation for inconvenience or qualitative loss. In fact, 78 percent of the firms in the 2015 Brookfield survey stated that they used the home-based approach for long-term assignments.[73] However, recently, some companies have begun to base their compensation package on a goal of achieving a standard of living comparable to that of host-country managers, which does help resolve some of the problems of pay differentials.

In fairness, the MNC is obliged to make up additional costs that the expatriate would incur for taxes, housing, and goods and services. The tax differential is complex and expensive for the company, and MNCs generally use a policy of tax equalization. This means that the company pays any taxes due on any type of additional compensation that the expatriate receives for the assignment; the expatriate pays in taxes only what she or he would pay at home. The burden of foreign taxes can be lessened, however, by efficient tax planning—a fact small firms often overlook. The timing and methods of paying people determine what foreign taxes are incurred. For example, a company can save on taxes by renting an apartment for the employee instead of providing a cash housing allowance. All in all, MNCs have to weigh the many aspects of a complete compensation package, especially at high management levels, to effect a tax equalization policy. The total cost to the company can vary greatly by location; for example:

> *Expatriates in Germany may incur twice the income tax they would in the U.S., and they are taxed on their housing and cost-of-living allowances as well. This financial snowball effect is a great incentive to make sure we really need to fill the position with an expatriate.*[74]

Managing expatriate compensation is a complex challenge for companies with overseas operations. All components of the compensation package must be considered in light of both home- and host-country legalities and practices. Those components include:

Salary: Local salary buying power and currency translation, as compared with home salary; bonuses or incentives for dislocation

Taxes: Equalizing any differential effects of taxes as a result of expatriate's assignment

EXHIBIT 9-10 The Balance Sheet Approach to Expatriate Compensation Package—Hypothetical Examples (Estimates in U.S. Dollars)

Sample Components for Expat	Chicago	Tokyo	Mexico City
Base Salary + COLA	$100,000	$150,000	$75,000
Relocation Allowance (20%)		30,000	15,000
Housing Allowance (20%)		30,000	15,000
Private Education for two children		30,000	20,000
Two trips per year home for four		12,000	10,000
	$100,000	252,000	135,000

Additional costs not estimated here include any local tax differential, health insurance, placement services for spouse, moving expenses and home sale, predeparture training and preparation, etc., as well as other negotiated items. In some "dangerous" locales, there will be additional costs pertaining to the safety of personnel, such as insurance, security guards, etc.

Allowances: Relocation expenses; cost-of-living adjustments (COLA); housing allowance for assignment and allowance to maintain house at home; trips home for expatriate and family; private education for children

Benefits: Health insurance; stock options

The **localization**, or **going-rate, approach** pays the expatriate the going rate for similar positions in the host country, plus whatever allowances and benefits for the assignment that the manager negotiates. With the basic pay similar to other managers in the host country, no matter where they come from, there is less resentment and more opportunity for open cooperation. However, when the going rate in a location is less than that in the home country—which is likely the case of a U.S.-based expatriate—she or he is likely to be reluctant to accept that assignment unless there are considerable perks in addition to the salary.

With the increasing number of companies that operate around the world and assign and move personnel (whether one calls them expatriates, transpatriates, or inpatriates) from one country to another, the design of equitable pay scales has become exceedingly complex. In an International Assignments Policies and Practices Survey by KPMG, companies noted the need to "review mobility policies to focus on harmonization of the treatment of globally mobile employees."[75] Should those managers in similar positions who come from different countries to a host country be paid according to the MNE headquarters location, or the host location, or that manager's home location? Or should they all be paid the same according to a globally determined rate for that job? Further complications arise from any legal or cultural restrictions on compensation in a particular location.

Most important, to be strategically competitive, the compensation package must be comparatively attractive to the kinds of managers the company wishes to hire or relocate. Some of those managers will, of course, be local managers in the host country. This, too, is a complex situation requiring competitive compensation policies that can attract, motivate, and retain the best local managerial talent. In many countries, however, it is a considerable challenge to develop compensation packages appropriate to the local situation and culture while also recognizing the differences between local salaries and those expatriates or transpatriates expect (that difference itself often being a source of competitive advantage).

TRAINING AND COMPENSATING HOST-COUNTRY NATIONALS

Training HCNs

The continuous training and development of HCNs and TCNs for management positions is also important to the long-term success of multinational corporations. As part of a long-term staffing policy for a subsidiary, the ongoing development of HCNs will facilitate the transition to an indigenization policy. Furthermore, multinational companies like to have well-trained managers with broad international experience available to take charge in many intercultural settings, whether at home or abroad, and, increasingly, in developing countries. Kimberly-Clark, for example, with more than 60,000 employees around the world, has steadily increased its talent development and training programs in all countries but, more recently, has focused on developing markets. "In Latin America, the average employee has gone from receiving practically no training time to about 38 hours each year. By contrast, workers in Europe now receive 40 hours per year—eight hours more than in 1996."[76]

Training for HCNs by foreign companies operating in the United States can be quite surprising for managers operating in their own country when they have to learn new ways. Toyota is an example of how employees at all levels must be trained in the Toyota Way. As recounted by Ms. Newton, a 38-year-old Indiana native who joined Toyota after college 15 years ago and now works at the North American headquarters in Erlanger, Kentucky:

For Americans and anyone, it can be a shock to the system to be actually expected to make problems visible. Other corporate environments tend to hide problems from bosses.[77]

What Ms. Newton is referring to are the colored bar charts against a white bulletin board, which represent the work targets of individual workers, visibly charting their successes or failures to meet those targets. This is part of the Toyota Way. The idea is not to humiliate but to alert coworkers and enlist their help in finding solutions. Ms. Newton, now a general manager in charge of employee training and development at Toyota's North American manufacturing subsidiary, said it took a while to accept that fully, but now she is a firm believer.[78]

Certainly, there is no arguing with success—in 2009, Toyota became the largest global automaker in sales. The training institute in Mikkabi has trained more than 700 foreign executives, including cultural orientation with the same intensity as its training in the production processes. Core concepts such as ownership of problems and visibility are impressed upon new employees. A sense of shared purpose is conveyed with open offices—often without even cubicle partitions between desks.[79]

Many multinationals, in particular chains, wish to train their local managers and workers to bridge the divide between, on the one hand, the firm's successful corporate culture and practices and, on the other, the local culture and work practices. One example of how to do this in China is the Starbucks firm described in the *Management in Action feature, "Success! Starbucks' Java Style Helps to Recruit, Train, and Retain Local Managers in Beijing."*

MANAGEMENT IN ACTION

Success! Starbucks' Java Style Helps to Recruit, Train, and Retain Local Managers in Beijing

When we first started, people didn't know who we were and it was rough finding sites. Now landlords are coming to us.

DAVID SUN,
PRESIDENT OF BEIJING MEI DA COFFEE COMPANY (FORMER STARBUCKS' PARTNER FOR NORTHERN CHINA) ECONOMIST *OCTOBER 6, 2001*

As we see from the preceding quote, Starbucks has achieved a remarkable penetration rate in China, given that it is a country of devoted tea drinkers who do not take readily to the taste of coffee.

Starbucks is no stranger to training leaders from around the world into the Starbucks style. As of June 2015, Starbucks has 22,519 both store-owned and licensed locations in 66 countries, as detailed here:

Starbucks' Global Presence

United States Stores

50 states, plus the District of Columbia
7,087 company-operated stores
4,081 licensed stores

International Stores

65 countries outside the United States

Company Operated

Australia, Canada, Chile, China (Northern China, Southern China), Germany, Ireland, Puerto Rico, Singapore, Thailand, and the United Kingdom

Joint Venture and Licensed Stores

Austria, the Bahamas, Bahrain, Brazil, Canada, China (Shanghai/Eastern China), Cyprus, Czech Republic, Denmark, Egypt, France, Greece, Hong Kong, Indonesia, Ireland, Japan, Jordan, Kuwait, Lebanon, Macau S.A.R., Malaysia, Mexico, the Netherlands, New Zealand, Oman, Peru, the Philippines, Qatar, Romania, Russia, Saudi Arabia, South Korea, Spain, Switzerland, Taiwan, Turkey, the United Arab Emirates, and the United Kingdom.[80]

(Continued)

FIGURE 9-1 A Starbucks Coffee Shop in Old Beijing-Style Building in Beijing, China

Source: © Jack Young-Places/Alamy

Company managers nevertheless have had quite a challenge in recruiting, motivating, and retaining managers for its Beijing outlets (and, more recently, in its Qunguang Square outlet in Central China). Starbucks' primary challenge has been to recruit good managers in a country where the demand for local managers by foreign companies expanding there is far greater than the supply of managers with any experience in capitalist-style companies. Chinese recruits have stressed that they are looking for opportunity to train and advance in global companies rather than for money. They know that managers with experience in Western organizations can always get a job. The brand's pop-culture reputation is also an attraction to young Beijingers.

To expose the recruits to java-style culture as well as to train them for management, Starbucks brings them to Seattle, Washington, for three months to give them a taste of the West Coast lifestyle and the company's informal culture, such as Western-style backyard barbecues.

Then they are exposed to the art of cappuccino making at a real store before dawn and concocting dozens of fancy coffees. They get the same intensive training as anyone else anywhere in the world. One recruit, Mr. Wang, who worked in a large Beijing hotel before finding out how to make a triple grande latte, said that he enjoys the casual atmosphere and respect. The training and culture are very different from what one would expect at a traditional state-owned company in China, where the work is strictly defined and has no challenge for employees.

Starbucks has found that motivating their managers in Beijing is multifaceted. They know that people won't switch jobs for money alone. They want to work for a company that gives them an opportunity to learn. They also want to have a good working environment and a company with a strong reputation. The recruits have expressed their need for trust and participation in an environment where local nationals traditionally are not expected to exercise initiative or authority. In all, what seems to motivate them more than anything else is their dignity.

Source: www.Starbucks.com, Corporate Information: June 28, 2015; Associated Press, "Starbucks Reorganizes for Growth," www.nytimes.com; J. Adamy, "Starbucks Raises New-Stores Goal, Enters iTunes Deal," *Wall Street Journal*, October 6, 2006; "China: Starbucks Opens New Outlet in Beijing," Info-Prod (Middle East) Ltd., July 20, 2003; "Coffee with Your Tea? Starbucks in China," *Economist*, October 6, 2001.

Many HCNs are, of course, receiving excellent training in global business and Internet technology within their home corporations. For example, the German media company Bertelsmann has specialized training programs to develop and retain local managers. In India, for example, its high-potential employees can apply for an INSEAD Global Executive MBA.[81]

Whether in home corporations, MNC subsidiaries, or joint ventures in any country, managerial training to facilitate e-business adoption is taking on increasing competitive importance to take advantage of new strategic opportunities. Although large companies are well ahead of the curve for information and communication technologies (ICT), there is considerable need for small and medium-sized enterprises (SMEs) to adopt such knowledge-creating capabilities.

Managerial training in ICT is particularly critical for firms in new economy and emerging markets and, taken together, can provide advantage for rapid economic growth in regions such as Eastern Europe. Research by Damaskopoulos and Evgeniou addressed these needs by surveying more than 900 SME managers in Slovenia, Poland, Romania, Bulgaria, and Cyprus. Although most managers recognized the opportunities in implementing e-business strategies, they also noted the urgent need for training to take advantage of those opportunities. Some of the training needs and issues those SME managers perceived are shown below. Some of these factors are at the firm level, whereas other issues relate to the market and regulatory levels, such as the need to increase security for commercial activity on the Internet.[82] Such findings highlight the need to recognize the strategy-staffing-training link and its importance to the overall growth of emerging economies.

Training Priorities for E-Business Development[83]

- How to develop a business plan and an e-business strategy
- How to develop the partnerships and in-house expertise for e-business
- How to finance e-business initiatives
- Addressing security and privacy concerns
- How to set up electronic payments
- How to develop good customer relations on the Internet
- Training in technology management
- How to collect marketing intelligence online

In another common scenario also requiring the management of a mixture of executives and employees, American and European MNCs presently employ Asians as well as Arab locals in their plants and offices in Saudi Arabia, bringing together three cultures: well-educated Asian managers living in a Middle Eastern, highly traditional society who are employed by a firm reflecting Western technology and culture. This kind of situation requires training to help all parties effectively integrate multiple sets of culturally based values, expectations, and work habits.

Compensating HCNs

How do firms deal with the question of what is appropriate compensation for host-country nationals, given local norms and the competitive needs of the firm? For the most part, firms adjust pay according to market conditions and design methods for job grading and incentive plans.[84]

Of course, no one set of solutions can be applicable in any country. Many variables apply—including local market factors and pay scales, government involvement in benefits, the role of unions, the cost of living, and so on. In Eastern Europe, for example, Hungarians, Poles, and Czechs spend a considerable portion of their disposable income on food and utilities. Therefore, East European managers must have cash for about 65 to 80 percent of their base pay, compared to about 40 percent for U.S. managers (the rest being long-term incentives, benefits, and perks). In addition, they still expect the many social benefits the old government provided. To be competitive, MNCs can focus on providing goods and services that are either not available at all or are extremely expensive in Eastern Europe. Such upscale perks can be used to attract high-skilled workers.

In Japan, in response to a decade-long economic slump, companies are revamping their HRM policies to compete in a global economy. The traditional lifetime employment and guaranteed tidy pension are giving way to the more Western practices of competing for jobs, of basing pay on performance rather than seniority, and of making people responsible for their own retirement fund decisions.[85]

A key concern of Western managers in China and India, as well as of the firms that outsource there, are the rapidly rising pay rates in those countries and a shortage of top talent. This shortage of talent is especially problematic in India. With the considerable growth in emerging markets, foreign firms trying to get on the bandwagon there are finding themselves in a war for talent. With that kind of supply–demand ratio for local skilled managers, salaries are being pushed up; that situation then lowers the rationale for hiring local managers instead of sending expatriates.

According to Citigroup, it is also imperative to make clear what benefits, as well as salary, come with a position because of the way compensation is perceived and regulated around the world.[86] In Latin America, for example, an employee's pay and title are associated with what type of car he or she can receive.

CONCLUSION

The IHRM function is a vital component of implementing the global strategy of a firm. In particular, managing the IHRM functions for and in emerging and developing markets presents complex challenges at all employee levels; these include the war for talent for managerial and professional people and the issues of outsourcing employees in those markets. Careful decisions regarding the appropriate staffing policy for foreign locations are crucial to the success of the firm's operations, particularly because of the lack of proximity to and control by headquarters executives. In particular, the ability of expatriates to initiate and maintain cooperative relationships with local people and agencies will determine the long-term success, even the viability, of the operation. In a real sense, a company's global cadre represents its most valuable resource. Proactive management of that resource by headquarters will result in having the right people in the right place at the right time, appropriately trained, prepared, and supported. MNCs using these IHRM practices can anticipate the effective management of the foreign operation, the fostering of expatriates' careers, and, ultimately, the enhanced success of the corporation.

Summary of Key Points

- Global human resource management is a vital component of implementing global strategy and is increasingly recognized as a major determinant of success or failure in international business.
- The main staffing alternatives for global operations are the ethnocentric, polycentric, regiocentric, and global approaches; the use of inpatriates supplements those choices. Each approach has its appropriate uses, according to its advantages and disadvantages and, in particular, the firm's strategy.
- The causes of expatriate failure include the following: poor selection based on inappropriate criteria, inadequate preparation before assignment, alienation from headquarters, inability of manager or family to adapt to local environment, inadequate compensation package, and poor programs for career support and repatriation.
- The three major areas critical to expatriate preparation are cultural training, language instruction, and familiarity with everyday matters.
- Appropriate and attractive compensation packages must be designed by IHRM staffs to sustain a competitive global expatriate staff. Compensation packages for host-country managers must be designed to fit the local culture and situation as well as the firm's objectives.

Discussion Questions

9-1. What are the major alternative staffing approaches for international operations? Explain the relative advantages of each and the conditions under which you would choose one approach over another.

9-2. Why is the HRM role so much more complex, and important, in the international context?

9-3. Discuss the challenges involved in staffing operations in emerging markets.

9-4. Explain the common causes of expatriate failure. What are the major success factors for expatriates? Explain the role and importance of each.

9-5. What are the common training techniques for managers going overseas? How should these vary as appropriate to the level of globalization of the firm?

9-6. Explain the balance sheet approach to international compensation packages. Why is this approach so important? Discuss the pros and cons of aligning the expatriate compensation package with the host-country colleagues compared to the home-country colleagues.

9-7. Discuss the importance of a complete program for expatriate performance management. What are the typical components for such a program?

Application Exercises

9-8. Make a list of the reasons you would want to accept a foreign assignment and a list of reasons you would want to reject it. Do they depend on the location? Compare your list with a classmate and discuss your reasons.

9-9. Research a company with operations in several countries and ascertain the staffing policy used for those countries. Find out what kinds of training and preparation are provided for expatriates and what kinds of results the company is experiencing with expatriate training.

Experiential Exercise

This can be done in groups or individually. After the exercise, discuss your proposals with the rest of the class.

You are the expatriate general manager of a British company's subsidiary in Brazil, an automobile component parts manufacturer. You and your family have been in Brazil for seven years, and now you are being reassigned and replaced with another expatriate—Ian Fleming. Ian is bringing his family: Helen, an instructor in computer science, who hopes to find a position; a son, age twelve; and a daughter, age fourteen. None of them has lived abroad before. Ian has asked you what he and his family should expect in the new assignment. Remembering all the problems you and your family experienced in the first couple of years of your assignment in Brazil, you want to facilitate their adjustment and have decided to do two things.

9-10. Write a letter to Ian, telling him what to expect both on the job and in the community. Tell him about some of the cross-cultural conflicts he may run into with his coworkers and employees and how he should handle them.

9-11. Set up some arrangements and support systems for the family and design a support package for them, with a letter to each family member telling him or her what to expect.

CASE STUDY

Kelly's Assignment in Japan

Well, it's my job that brought us here in the first place … I am going to have to make a decision to stick with this assignment and hope I can work things out or to return to the United States and probably lose my promised promotion after this assignment—maybe even my job.

As she surveyed the teeming traffic of downtown Tokyo from her office window, Kelly tried to assess the situation her family was in, how her job was going, and what could have been done to lead to a better situation four months ago when she was offered the job.

As a program manager for a startup Internet services company, she had been given the opportunity to head up the sales and marketing department in Tokyo. Her boss said that "the sky's the limit" as far as her being able to climb the corporate ladder if she was successful in Tokyo. She explained that she did not speak Japanese and that she knew nothing about Japan, but he said he had confidence in her because she had done such a great job in Boston and in recent short assignments to London and Munich. Moreover, the company offered her a very attractive compensation package that included a higher salary, bonuses, a relocation allowance, a rent-free apartment in Tokyo, and an education allowance for their two children, Lisa and Sam, to attend private schools. She was told she had two days to decide, and that they wanted her in Tokyo in three weeks because they wanted her to prepare and present a proposal for a new account opportunity there as soon as possible. Her boss said they would hire a relocation company to handle the move for her.

That night Kelly excitedly discussed the opportunity with her husband, Joe. He was glad for her and thought it would be an exciting experience for the whole family. However, he was concerned about his own job and what the move would do to his career. She told him that her boss had said that Joe would probably find something or be transferred there, but that her boss did seem unconcerned about that. In the end, Joe felt that Kelly should have this opportunity, and he agreed to the move. He talked to his boss about a transfer and was told that the manager would look into that and get back to him. However, he knew that his company was having layoffs because of the economic decline that was taking its toll on profits. The problem was that Kelly had to make a decision before he could fully explore his options, so Kelly and Joe decided to go ahead with the plans. To sweeten the deal, Kelly's company had offered to buy her house in Boston since the housing market decline had her concerned about whether she could sell without taking a loss.

After the long trip, they arrived at their apartment in Tokyo; they were tired but excited, but did not anticipate that the apartment would be so tiny, given the very high rent that the company was paying for it. Kelly realized at once that they had included way too much in their move of personal belongings to be able to fit into this apartment. Undaunted, they planned to spend the weekend sightseeing and looked forward to some travel. Japan was beautiful in the spring, and they were anxious to see the area.

On Monday, Kelly took a cab to the office. She had emailed requesting a staff meeting at 9 A.M. She knew that her immediate staff would include seven Japanese, two Americans, and two Germans—all men. Her assistant, Peter, to whom she had not yet spoken, was an American who had also just arrived, coming from an assignment in London. He greeted her at the elevator, looking surprised, and they proceeded to the conference room, where everyone was awaiting the new boss. Kelly exchanged the usual handshake greetings with the Westerners and then bowed to the Japanese; an awkward silence and exchange took place, with the Japanese looking embarrassed. While she attempted a greeting in her limited Japanese that she had studied on the plane, she was relieved to find that the Japanese spoke English, but they seemed very quiet and hesitant. Peter then told her that they all thought that "Kelly" was a man, and they all attempted a laugh.

After that, Kelly decided that she would just meet with Peter and postpone the general meeting until the next day. She asked them each to prepare a short presentation for her on their ideas for the new account. Whereas the Americans and Germans said they would have it ready, the Japanese seemed reluctant to commit themselves.

Meanwhile, at home Joe was looking into the schools for the children and trying to make some contacts to look for a job. Travelling, getting information, and shopping for groceries proved bewildering, but they decided that they would soon get acquainted with local customs.

At the office the next day, Kelly received a short presentation from the Westerners on the staff, but when it came to the Japanese, they indicated that they had not yet had a chance to meet with their groups and other contacts to come to their decisions. Kelly asked them why they had not told her the day before that they needed more time, and when could they be ready. They seemed unwilling to give a direct answer and kept their eyes lowered. In an attempt to lighten the atmosphere and get to know her staff, Kelly then began chatting casually and asked several of them about their families. The Americans chatted on about their children's achievements, the Germans talked about their family positions, and the Japanese went silent, seemingly very confused and offended.

Still attempting to get everyone's ideas for an initial proposal to the potential new client, Kelly later asked one of the Americans who had been there for some time what he thought was the problem and delay in getting presentations from the Japanese. He told her that they did not like to do individual presentations, but rather wanted to gain consensus among themselves and their contacts and present a group presentation. Having learned her lesson, but feeling irritated, she asked him to intervene and have the presentations ready for the next week. When that time came, the Japanese made the rest of the presentations but, oddly, they seemed to be addressed primarily to Peter. Later, Kelly decided to finalize her own presentation to put forth a proposal for the client, which she set up for the following week.

At home, Joe said that he had not heard anything from his company in Boston and asked Kelly to contact her company again to request some networking in Tokyo that might lead to job opportunities for him. Kelly said she would do that, but that there didn't seem to be any one person back home who was keeping up with her situation or giving any support about that or about her job.

The children, meanwhile, complained that, although their schools were meant to be bilingual English–Japanese, a majority of the children were Japanese and did not speak English; Lisa and Sam felt confused and left out. They were disoriented by the different customs, classes, and foods for lunch. At home, they complained that there was no backyard to go out to play, and they could not get their programs on the television or understand the Japanese programs.

Back at the office, Kelly worked with her staff to finalize the proposal but noticed a strained atmosphere. Peter told her that some of them would drop by a local bar for a drink after work, which helped the whole group to relax together. However, she felt that she could not do that, nor that she would be accepted as a female.

The next week, as arranged, Kelly and Peter went to the offices of the client; she knew that a lot was riding on getting this big new contract. She had asked Peter to let them know ahead of time that she is a woman, yet the introductions still seemed strained. She planned to get straight down to business, so when the client company's CEO handed her his business card, she put it in her pocket without a glance and did not give him her card. Again, she noticed some shock and embarrassment all around. (She found out much later that a business card is very important to a Japanese businessman because it conveys all his accomplishments and position without having to say it himself.) Flustered, she tried to make light of the situation, patted him on the back, and asked him what his first name was, saying, rather loudly, that hers was Kelly. He went quiet again, backed away from her, and, with his head bowed, whispered, "Michio." He glanced around at his Japanese colleagues rather nervously.

After a period of silence, Michio pointed to the table of refreshments, and indicated that they sit and eat; however, Kelly was anxious to present her power-point slides and went to the end of the table where the equipment was and asked Peter to set up the slides. As she proceeded to go through the proposal, telling them what her company could do for them, she paused and asked for questions. However, when Michio and his two colleagues asked questions, they directed them to Peter, not to her. In fact, they made little eye contact with her at all. She tried to remain cool, but insisted on answering the questions herself. In the end, she sat down and asked Michio what he thought of the proposal. He bowed politely and said, "Very good," and that he would discuss it with his colleagues and get back to her. However, Kelly did not hear from them, and after a couple of weeks, she asked Peter to follow up with them. He did that but reported that they were not going to pursue the contract. Frustrated, she said, "Well, why did Michio say that it looked very good, then?" She knew that it was a very competitive proposal and felt that something other than the proposed contract was to blame for the loss of the contract.

Disillusioned, but determined not to give up without success in the assignment, Kelly took a cab to go home and think about it, but the driver misunderstood her and went the wrong way and got stuck in traffic. She felt discouraged and wished that she had some female American friends to whom she could confide her problems.

When Kelly got home, Peter was angrily trying to fix dinner, complaining about the small appliances and inability to understand the food packages or how to prepare the food. He said he needed something else to do, but that a job did not seem to be on the horizon for him. He was also concerned about continuing to live in such a high-cost city on only one salary.

Kelly went to the other room to see the children; they were fighting and complaining that they had nothing to do and wanted to go home. Kelly felt that the three months they had been there was not a fair trial and was wondering what to do. She wished she had had more time to prepare for this assignment, and whenever she contacted the home office, no one seemed able to advise her.

Case Questions

9-12. Explain the clashes in culture, customs, and expectations that occurred in this situation.

9-13. What stage of culture shock is Kelly's family experiencing?

9-14. Turn back the clock to when Kelly was offered the position in Tokyo. What, if anything, should have been done differently and by whom?

9-15. You are Kelly. What should you do now?

Endnotes

1. 2015 Brookfield Global Relocation Trends Survey, www.brookfieldgrs.com, accessed August 24, 2015; www.McKinsey.com/mgi/; "Capturing Talent," *Economist*, August 18, 2007, pp. 59–61; Douglas A. Ready, Linda A. Hill, and Jay A. Conger, "Winning the Race for Talent in Emerging Markets," *Harvard Business Review* (November 2008); Harold L. Sirkin, "Need Global Talent? Grow Your Own," *BusinessWeek* Online, September 17, 2008; "Talent Retention: Ongoing Problem for Asia-Pacific Region," T+D 61, No. 3 (2007), p. 12.

2. 2015 Brookfield Global Relocation Trends Survey, www.brookfieldgrs.com, accessed August 24, 2015.

3. www.McKinsey.com/mgi/; "Capturing Talent," *Economist*, August 18, 2007, pp. 59–61.

4. Douglas A. Ready, Linda A. Hill, and Jay A. Conger, "Winning the Race for Talent in Emerging Markets," *Harvard Business Review* (November 2008).

5. Martin Dewhurst, Matthew Pettigrew, and Ramesh Srinivasan, "How Multinationals Can Attract the Talent They Need," *McKinsey Quarterly*, June 2012.

6. Sirkin, 2008.

7. 2015 Brookfield Global Relocation Trends Survey, www.brookfieldgrs.com, accessed August 24, 2015.

8. Sirkin, 2008.

9. Ready et al., 2008.

10. Ibid.

11. www.pricewaterhousecoopers.com, accessed November 19, 2011.

12. "Retention: Hello? Is Anyone at HQ Listening?" *Harvard Business Review*, April 1, 2015.

13. Ibid.

14. J. E. Mendenhall, R. J. Jensen, J. S. Black, and H. B. Gregerson, "Seeing the Elephant: Human Resource Management Challenges in the Age of Globalization," *Organizational Dynamics* 32, No. 3 (2003), pp. 261–274.

15. J. L. Laabs, "HR Pioneers Explore the Road Less Traveled," *Personnel Journal* (February 1996), pp. 70–72, 74, 77–78.

16. Friso Den Hertog, Ad Van Iterson, and Christian Mari, "Does HRM Really Matter in Bringing about Strategic Change? Comparative Action Research in Ten European Steel Firms," *European Management Journal* 28, No. 1 (2010), pp. 14–24.

17. www.ibm.com, accessed December 1, 2011; S. Hamm, "International Isn't Just IBM's First Name," www.businessweek.com, January 28, 2008, pp. 36–40.

18. KPMG 2012 Global Assignment Survey, www.kpmg.com, accessed August 9, 2012.

19. *The 2011 PricewaterhouseCoopers' 14th Annual CEO Survey.*

20. J. Stewart Black and Allen J. Morrison, "A Cautionary Tale for Emerging Market Giants," *Harvard Business Review*, September 2010.

21. Ibid.; "International Assignments Remain on the Upswing Despite Economic Concerns, Says KPMG," Anonymous, *PR Newswire*, December 3, 2008.

22. Ibid.

23. Bettina Wassener, "Living in Asia Appeals to More Company Leaders," *New York Times* [New York, NY] June 21, 2012, p. B.3.

24. Ibid.

25. C. A. Bartlett and S. Ghoshal, "Matrix Management: Not a Structure, a Frame of Mind," *Harvard Business Review* (July–August 1990).

26. Lynda Gratton, "Workplace 2025—What Will It Look Like?" *Organizational Dynamics* 40 (2011), pp. 246–254.

27. www.tcs.com, accessed November 21, 2011; Stefan Wagstyl, "Indian Outsourcers in U.S. Hiring Push," FT.com, September 21, 2010; R. Jai Krishna and R. Guha, "U.S. Visa Rejections Hit TCS," July 18, 2011, *Wall Street Journal*, July 18, 2011; Bruce Einhorn, "Demand Grows Despite H-1B Fight, TCS Exec Says," www.bloombergbusinessweek.com, August 18, 2010; Charlie Adith, "TCS, IBM back in US' Fast-Track Visa Facility," *Hindu Business Line*, June 13, 2010; "Business: From Mumbai to the Midwest; TCS in America," *Economist* 401. 8758 (November 5, 2011), p. 74.

28. Ibid.

29. Martin Dewhurst, Matthew Pettigrew, and Ramesh Srinivasan, "How Multinationals Can Attract the Talent They Need," *McKinsey Quarterly*, June 2012.

30. M. Harvey et al., "Developing Effective Global Relationships through Staffing with Inpatriate Managers: The Role of Interpersonal Trust," *Journal of International Management*, 2011, doi:10.1016/j.intman 2011.01.02.

31. J. Stewart Black and Allen J. Morrison, "A Cautionary Tale for Emerging Market Giants," *Harvard Business Review*, September 2010.

32. M. Harvey, M. M. Novivenic, C. Speier, "Strategic Global Human Resource Management: The Role of Inpatriate Managers," *Human Resource Management Review*, 10, No. 2 (2000), pp. 153–175.

33. Ibid.

34. M. Harvey, 2011.

35. Michael Harvey, Helene Mayerhofer, Linley Hartmann, and Miriam Moeller, "Corralling the 'Horses' to Staff the Global Organization of the 21st Century," *Organizational Dynamics*, 39, No. 3 (2010), pp. 258–268.

36. S. B. Prasad and Y. K. Krishna Shetty, *An Introduction to Multinational Management* (Upper Saddle River, NJ: Prentice Hall, 1979).

37. Rochelle Kopp, "International Human Resource Policies and Practices in Japanese, European, and United States Multinationals," *Human Resource Management* 33, No. 4 (1994), pp. 581–599.

38. Based on, updated, and adapted by H. Deresky, from original work by D. A. Heenan and H. V. Perlmutter, *Multinational Organization Development* (Reading, MA: Addison-Wesley, 1979), pp. 18–19.

39. R. L. Tung, "Selection and Training of Personnel for Overseas Assignments," *Columbia Journal of World Business* (Spring 1981), pp. 68–78.

40. P. Dowling and R. S. Schuler, *International Dimensions of Human Resource Management* (Boston: PWS-Kent, 1990).

41. S. J. Kobrin, "Expatriate Reduction and Strategic Control in American Multinational Corporations," *Human Resource Management* 27, No. 1 (1988), pp. 63–75.

42. Company information, www.ABB.com, accessed July 26, 2004.

43. www.GMACGlobalrelocation.com, accessed March 1, 2009.

44. Ed Hannibal, Yvonne Traber, Paul Jelinek, "Tracking Your Expatriate Workforce," *HRMagazine* 60, No. 3 (April 2015), pp. 63–65.

45. 2014 Global Mobility Talent Trends Survey, Brookfield Global Relocation Services, www.brookfieldgrs.com, accessed April 21, 2015.

46. *HRMagazine* 60, No. 3 (April 2015), pp. 63–65.

47. "Decoding Global Talent," *Boston Consulting Group*, The Network, 2014.

48. M. Mendenhall and G. Oddou, "The Dimensions of Expatriate Acculturation: A Review," *Academy of Management Review* 10, No. 1 (1985), pp. 39–47.

49. Theresa Minton-Eversole, "Best Expatriate Assignments Require Much Thought, Even More Planning," SHRM's 2009 Global Trend Book, *HRMagazine* (2009), pp. 74–75.

50. M. G. Tye and P. Y. Chen (2005), "Selection of Expatriates: Decision-Making Models Used by HR Professionals," *Human Resource Planning* 28, No. 4, pp. 15–20.

51. D. Erbacher, B. D'Netto, and J. Espana, "Expatriate Success in China: Impact of Personal and Situational Factors," *Journal of American Academy of Business* 9, No. 2 (2006), p. 183.

52. Rosalie Tung, "American Expatriates Abroad: From Neophytes to Cosmopolitans," *Journal of World Business* 33 (1998), pp. 125–144.

53. His-An Shih, Yun-Hwa Chiang, and In-Sook Kim, "Expatriate Performance Management from MNEs of Different National Origins," *International Journal of Manpower* 26, No. 2 (2005), pp. 161–162.

54. "Managing Global Virtual Teams," http://executive-education. insead.edu/managing_global_virtual_teams, accessed April 26, 2015.

55. Ying Zhang, Christopher Marquis, Sergey Filippov, Henk-Jan Haasnoot, Martijn van der Steen, "The Challenges and Enhancing Opportunities of Global Project Management: Evidence from Chinese and Dutch Cross-Cultural Project Management," Harvard Business School Working Paper 15-063- February 11, 2015.

56. *Business Wire*, 2006.

57. Ibid.

58. Ibid.

59. Tung, 1998.

60. Mendenhall and Oddou.

61. K. Oberg, "Culture Shock: Adjustments to New Cultural Environments," *Practical Anthropology* (July–August 1960), pp. 177–182.

62. Ibid.

63. Lynette Clemetson, "The Pepsi Challenge: Helping Expats Feel At Home," *Workforce Management* 89, No. 12 (December 2010), p. 36.

64. Ashish Mahajan and Soo Min Toh, "Facilitating Expatriate Adjustment: The Role of Advice-Seeking from Host Country Nationals," *Journal of World Business* 49 (2014), pp. 476–487.

65. Ibid.

66. Eduardo Caride, "Diversifying Talent to Suit the Market," *Harvard Business Review*, September 2014.

67. Ibid.

68. R. B. Peterson, "The Use of Expatriates and Inpatriates in Central and Eastern Europe since the Wall Came Down," *Journal of World Business* 38 (2003), pp. 55–69.

69. Based on J. S. Black, Mark. E. Mendenhall, Hal B. Gregersen, and Linda K. Stroh, *Globalizing People through International Assignments* (Reading, MA: Addison Wesley Longman, 1999).

70. Christopher Tice, Manager, Global Expatriate Operations, DuPont Inc., quoted in Mark Schoeff, "International Assignments Best Served by Unified Policy," *Workforce Management* 85, No. 3 (2006), p. 36.

71. "Living Expenses," www.economist.com, July 22, 2000; "Runzheimer International Compensation Worksheet," www.runzheimer.com, 2000.

72. B. W. Teague, *Compensating Key Personnel Overseas* (New York: Conference Board, 1992).

73. 2015 Brookfield Global Relocation Trends Survey, www.brookfieldgrs.com, accessed August 24, 2015.

74. S. F. Galc, "Taxing Situations for Expatriates," *Workforce* 82, No. 6 (2003), p. 100.

75. International Assignment Policies and Practices Survey, 2011, www.kpmg.com, accessed November 11, 2011.

76. Gina Ruiz, "Kimberly-Clark: Developing Talent in Developing World Markets," *Workforce Management* 85, No. 7 (2006), p. 34.

77. Martin Fackler, "The 'Toyota Way' Is Translated for a New Generation of Foreign Managers," www.nytimes.com, February 17, 2007.

78. Ibid.

79. Ibid.

80. Company website, www.starbucks.com, accessed March 5, 2012.

81. Martin Dewhurst, Matthew Pettigrew, and Ramesh Srinivasan, "How Multinationals Can Attract the Talent They Need," *McKinsey Quarterly*, June 2012.

82. P. Damaskopoulos and T. Evgeniou, "Adoption of New Economy Practices by SMEs in Eastern Europe," *European Management Journal* 21, No. 2 (2003), pp. 133–145.

83. Based on Damaskopoulos and Evgeniou, 2003.

84. Fay Hansen, "The Great Global Talent Race: One World, One Workforce: Part 1 of 2," *Workforce Management* 85, No. 7 (2006), p. 1.

85. Y. Ono and W. Spindle, "Japan's Long Decline Makes One Thing Rise: Individualism," *Wall Street Journal*, January 3, 2001.

86. "Personnel Demands Attention Overseas," *Mutual Fund Market News* (March 19, 2001), p. 1.

10 Developing a Global Management Cadre

OUTLINE

OBJECTIVES

10-1. To appreciate the importance of international assignments in developing top managers with global experience and perspectives

10-2. To recognize the need to design programs for the careful preparation, adaptation, and repatriation of the expatriate and any accompanying family, as well as programs for career management and retention, thereby also transferring knowledge to and from host operations

10-3. To become familiar with the use of global management teams to coordinate host country and cross-border business

10-4. To recognize the varying roles of women around the world in international management

10-5. To understand the variations in host-country labor relations systems and the impact on the manager's job and effectiveness

Opening Profile: The Expat Life[1]

Expats Flee Moscow as Tensions Flare

WALL STREET JOURNAL, JUNE 10, 2015.

What is it like to take an assignment abroad? Well, if you were one of the expats from the west who were living the good life in Moscow, for example, life took an abrupt turn when they were recalled in 2014–2015 because so many western companies were pulling out as a result of the sanctions on Russia. This situation makes it clear that expat lives are vulnerable to sudden changes in the political and business climate around the world. But, if you were an expat from China you were one of the sudden surge of people moving to Moscow to take up the slack in business opportunities left open by western companies.

Would you like to be an expat (expatriate)? Is it an adventure or a hardship? (The young man from Asia pictured in Fig. 10-1 seems to be excited about his assignment in London.) Experiences of those who have done a stint abroad are mixed, but it is clear that it is very likely an opportunity that will present itself at some point during your career. Most companies with global business transactions want their top employees to have overseas experience. At Procter & Gamble, for example, 39 of the company's top 44 global officers have had an international assignment, and 22 were born outside the United States. According to the 2015 Brookfield Relocation Trends Survey of 143 firms, 43 percent of assignees were relocated to or from a non-headquarters country.

Experiences vary by job type, especially by location. Adjustment is easier for those who go to places where the culture and business practices are similar to their own. Those transitioning between Western Europe and the United States or Canada, for example, typically adapt easier than those going to China or Yemen, as related below. Some expatriates enjoy perks that they do not get at home, and others find they fare worse financially, either while overseas or when they return home. In addition, with more firms expanding operations in emerging economies, expats often face considerable challenges such as inefficient infrastructure; limited housing, medical, or educational facilities; security risks; and political instability. Such conditions often mean that the assignment is turned down or that the manager will decide to go without his or her family. In most places, assignees expect the assignment to be career-broadening and hope it will leverage them to a promotion. Some expat experiences are described below.

As an example of how quickly the changing global environment can affect expats, we can look at the typical expat life for Wall Street executives as described in the *New York Times* in 2008: "When Wall Streeters pack their bags for Dubai or Shanghai, for example, they get much more than a plane ticket and coverage of per-diem expenses. These days, moving abroad can mean scoring a nanny, a driver, or even a bodyguard."[2] In Shanghai, there are 70,000 expatriates from around the world, in various capacities. For those in the finance industry, the expat package typically includes round trips home a year; fees for a real estate agency; moving expenses; at least one month of temporary

FIGURE 10-1 Enjoying London

Rawpixel/Fotolia

accommodation; and language classes if required. For an accompanying family, fees for private schools, for example, are usually included as well as help for the spouse to find a job. A cost of living adjustment is typically included as well as an adjustment for tax equalization. A very nice assignment—however, in spring 2009, the *New York Times* was then reporting about the number of expats in the banking and finance industry who were being laid off.

> *Losing your job anywhere is disorienting, but imagine being laid off when you work in a foreign country. Not only is your source of income, and perhaps a good part of your identity, suddenly yanked away, but often you lose your right to remain in the country.*[3]

That, however, was an unusual development; for most expats, the overseas assignment has been very rewarding in terms of both personal and job experience.

In many circumstances, the adventure that started out with many concerns turns out to be one that the expats and their families do not want to end. According to the Global Relocation Trends Survey, 26 percent of expats opt to continue their overseas assignment when the original term ends. Those people have settled in to their position and life in the host country and enjoy their situations.

One reporter assigned to Beijing commented, "That's why we recently decided to extend our stay for a fourth year. For me, it was an easy decision. The three years that seemed so ominous turned out to be not nearly enough time to settle into a new life." The family wanted to do more travelling as well as really understand and enjoy the culture of Beijing.[4]

Assignments in some locations can turn out to be more challenging. One example is that of Mr. Deffontaines, who moved to Yemen in 2008 as the local manager for Total, the French oil giant, along with his family. Since then, Mr. Deffontaines has seen his main export pipeline damaged by terrorists, endured devastating flash floods, and sent expatriate families back home because of security concerns.

Recounting some of the interesting challenges he had faced there, Mr. Deffontaines, a 43-year-old Parisian, described "negotiating with tribal leaders and sending actors to remote villages to stage a play about the hazards of gas pipelines. In meetings with government officials to thrash out problems, participants typically chew khat, a mildly narcotic plant that is widely consumed in Yemen but banned in many places around the world."[5]

A particularly difficult decision, in response to growing security concerns, was to send the families of his workers back to France. His own wife, son, and twin daughters were among those forced to depart.

Robert Kneupfer, a lawyer, reflects that, in spite of inconveniences such as the 17-year wait for a telephone line and the absence of any McDonald's restaurants, the five years he spent in Budapest with his family on behalf of the international law firm Baker & McKenzie were a "defining moment both personally and professionally." The 56-year-old partner, now based in Chicago, didn't speak the language, and his children had been reluctant to leave family and friends. His advice: "Don't sweat the small stuff. You need to appreciate the bigger-picture experience."[6] To do that, he makes it clear that preparation is important for a positive experience. His advice follows that of many others as discussed throughout this chapter and the preceding chapter. First and foremost, you and any accompanying family members must familiarize yourselves ahead of time with the local people and their culture, their language and communication style, and their ways of living and doing business. Most important, prepare your family for the stages of adjustment they will go through so that they know what to expect; plans must be made to integrate them as quickly as possible into the local schools, church, social life, and so on. It also helps if you can meet with other expat families in the area who will provide both practical and emotional support. In addition, research shows that part of the pre-departure training should include setting up a mentor in the headquarters office or in the local area so that regular support will be available as well as some visibility for your career continuity.

Further advice from a well-travelled expat comes from Philip Shearer, Group President, Clinique, Estee Lauder. His mother was French, his father British, and he was born in Morocco. After going to college in France and then business school in the United States, he worked at a pharmaceutical company in Minneapolis. Then he worked in France, Mexico, Britain, Japan, and again in the United States for companies such as L'Oréal and the Elizabeth Arden division of Eli Lilly.

Shearer's advice melds with that of other successful expats who seem to be able to distill their experiences and travels to arrive at common themes. They recommend that, above all, you should be yourself and gain a reputation for being trustworthy. In that way, people will trust you and relate to you no matter where you are from. Shearer warns, however, that Americans generally show off too much. "But in the end, you have to deliver. And that's the same all over the world."[7]

> *After investing over a million dollars in my overseas experience, I thought someone, somewhere in the organization would want to know what I have learned. I was wrong.*
>
> INTERNATIONAL MANAGER[8]

A crucial factor in global competitiveness is the ability of the firm to maximize its global human resources in the long term. In the globalized economy, the knowledge and management resources, as well as the skilled and non-skilled employee resources, required for the firm to succeed are no longer concentrated in a single region but are distributed around the world. There are various categories of those resources—both people and processes—that IHR managers and others must develop and maintain; in particular it is essential for them to:

- Maximize long-term retention and benefits of an international cadre through career management so that the company can develop a top management team with global experience.
- Develop effective global management teams.
- Understand, value, and promote the role of women in international management to maximize those underused resources.
- Work with the host-country labor relations system to effect strategic implementation and employee productivity.

EXPATRIATE CAREER MANAGEMENT

Martin Walker, senior director of the Global Business Policy Council at A. T. Kearney, a consultancy, maintains that the dearth of talent is mainly evident at the very top: "Shortages do exist most notably, of people with the internationalized business skills to thrive at senior management level in global companies.

THE GLOBAL TALENT INDEX REPORT: THE OUTLOOK TO 2015
HEIDRICK & STRUGGLES[9]

It is clear from the preceding quote that the road to the top necessitates managers to have overseas experience. For the firm, the ability to develop a top management team, globally experienced, depends largely on the success of expatriates' assignments—and that depends on the ability to manage the transitions for the expatriate and any accompanying family members well. The importance of this was determined by the 2015 Global Relocation Trends Survey, which found that "only 18% of respondents had formal career-management processes for international assignees and 19% of respondents had a formal candidate pool for international assignments."[10]

Preparation, Adaptation, and Repatriation

The top family challenges identified as very critical to companies were partner resistance (40%), family adjustment (40%), children's education (40%).[11]

THE 2015 BROOKFIELD GLOBAL RELOCATIONS TRENDS SURVEY

Effective human resource management of a company's global cadre does not end with the overseas assignment. It ends with the successful repatriation of the executive into company headquarters. A study by Heidrick & Struggles, the international headhunting firm, revealed that international experience has become much more important to get to the top of the FTSE (London Stock Exchange) 100 companies than a decade ago. "Chief executives such as Mark Tucker at Prudential, who has experience in the United States and Asia, and Unilever's Patrick Cescau, who has worked in Europe, Asia and the United States, are becoming the norm in top companies."[12] Clearly, those executives and their companies have paid careful attention to what is necessary for successful assignments, career management, and repatriation of their experiences and skills. Such firms realize that long-term, proactive management of such critical resources should begin with the end of the current assignment in mind—that is, it should begin with plans for the repatriation of the executive as part of his or her career path. The management of the reentry phase of the career cycle is as vital as the management of the cross-cultural entry and training. Otherwise, the long-term benefits of that executive's international experience may be negated. Shortsightedly, many companies do little to minimize the potential effects of **reverse culture shock** (return shock). In fact, a KPMG survey concluded that "25 percent of organizations surveyed do not know if assignees have left the organization within 12 months of returning from international assignment. For repatriated assignees that are tracked as leaving the organization soon after returning from assignment, the overriding reason cited is the lack of an appropriate job after repatriation."[13] For smaller companies, little, if any pre- or post-assignment counseling was provided.

A study by Lazarova and Caligiuri with 58 expatriates from four North American companies found that repatriates who received supportive practices from their firms felt that their companies had an interest in their careers and well-being and so were more likely to stay with the firm upon reentry. The expatriates cited the following HRM practices as important to them.

- Visible signs that the company values international experience
- Career planning sessions
- Communications with home office of details of the repatriation process
- Continuous communications with the home office
- Agreement about position upon repatriation[14]

Reverse culture shock occurs primarily because of the difficulty of reintegrating into the organization but also because, generally speaking, the longer a person is away, the more difficult it is to get back into the swing of things. Not only might the manager have been overlooked and lost in the shuffle of reorganization, but her or his whole family might have lost social contacts or jobs and feel out of step with their contemporaries. These feelings of alienation from what has always been perceived as home—because of the loss of contact with family, friends, and daily life—delay the resocialization process. Such a reaction is particularly serious if the family's overall financial situation has been hurt by the assignment and if the spouse's career has also been kept on hold while he or she was abroad.

For companies to maximize the long-term use of their global cadre, they need to make sure that the foreign assignment and the reintegration process are positive experiences. This means careful career planning, support while overseas, and use of the increased experience and skills of returned managers to benefit the home office

The Role of the Expatriate Spouse

We began to realize that the entire effectiveness of the assignment could be compromised by ignoring the spouse.

STEVE FORD
CORPORATION RELOCATIONS, HEWLETT-PACKARD[15]

Many companies are beginning to recognize the importance of providing support for spouses and children—in particular because both spouses are often corporate fast-trackers and demand both sets of needs to be included on the bargaining table. Research shows that 83 percent of married expatriates were accompanied by their spouses. However, although about half of the spouses were employed before the assignment, only 11 percent were employed during the assignment.[16] "That's underscored by the fact that 61 percent of respondents noted that the impact of family issues on early returns from assignment was very critical or of high importance."[17] The 2015 Brookfield Survey found that candidates' "knowledge of career concerns is the second most noted reason for assignment refusal, and 35% of respondents indicated that spouse/partner career concerns were having an impact on their ability to attract employees for international assignments."[18]

Firms often use informal means, such as intercompany networking, to help find the trailing spouse a position in the same location. They know that with the increasing number of dual-career couples, if the spouse does not find a position, the manager will very likely turn down the assignment. They decline because they cannot afford to lose the income or because the spouse's career may be delayed entirely if he or she is out of the workforce for a few years. As women continue to move up the corporate ladder, the accompanying (trailing) spouse is often male. Companies such as Hewlett-Packard, Shell, Medtronic, and Monsanto offer a variety of options to address the dual-career dilemma.

Clearly, then, the selection process must include spouses, partners, and entire families. Global assignments must take account of the expatriate's personal concerns and future career; otherwise, the company will face the possibility of early return and a possible doubling of the chances for employee attrition. The GMAC survey revealed that the annual turnover rate is 13 percent for all employees but 25 percent for expatriate employees during assignments and 27 percent within one year of completing assignments. Those assignees indicated that they felt their firms did not appreciate the difficulties of their overseas stints; nor did they fully use the expatriates' skills on return to the home country.[19]

At Procter & Gamble, employees and spouses destined for China are sent to Beijing for two months of language training and cultural familiarization. Nissho Iwai, a Japanese trading company, gets together managers and spouses who are leaving Japan with foreign managers and spouses who are on their way there. In addition, the firm provides a year of language training and information and services for Japanese children to attend schools abroad.

Expatriate Retention

Managers returning from expatriate assignments are two to three times more likely to leave the company within a year because attention has not been paid to their careers and the way they fit back into the corporate structure back home.[20]

Firms must design support services to provide timely help for the manager and, therefore, are part of the effective management of an overseas assignment. The overall transition process experienced by the company's international management cadre over time comprises three phases of transition and adjustment that must be managed for successful socialization to a new culture and resocialization back to the old culture. These phases are (1) the exit transition from the home country, the success of which will be determined largely by the quality of preparation the expatriate has received; (2) the entry transition to the host country, in which successful acculturation (or early exit) will depend largely on monitoring and support; and (3) the entry transition back to the home country or to a new host country, in which the level of reverse culture shock and the ease of re-acculturation will depend on previous stages of preparation and support.[21]

A company may derive many potential benefits from carefully managing the careers of its expatriates. By helping managers make the right moves for their careers, the company will be able to retain people with increasing global experience and skills.

However, from the individual manager's perspective, most people understand that no one can look out better for one's interests than oneself. With that in mind, managers must ask themselves, and their superiors, what role each overseas stint will play in career advancement and what proactive role each will play in one's own career. Retaining the returning expatriate within the company (assuming he or she has been effective) is vitally important to gain the knowledge and benefit from the assignment. Yet, as discussed earlier, the attrition rate for expatriates is about double that of non-expatriates for the following reasons.

- Expatriates are more marketable and receive more attractive offers from other employers.
- Expatriates find that their compensation packages on overseas assignments are more generous than at home and go from one company to another to take advantage of that.
- Expatriates feel unappreciated and dissatisfied both during and after the assignment and leave the company.[22]

It is essential, therefore, for the company to pay careful attention to maintaining and retaining the expatriate by managing both the assignment and the repatriation of the expatriate and the family.

THE ROLE OF REPATRIATION IN DEVELOPING A GLOBAL MANAGEMENT CADRE

In the international assignment, both the manager and the company can benefit from the enhanced skills and experience the expatriate gains. Many returning executives report an improvement in their managerial skills and self-confidence. Some of these acquired skills, as reported by Adler, include the following.

- **Managerial skills, not technical skills:** Learning how to deal with a wide range of people, to adapt to their cultures through compromise, and not to be a dictator
- **Tolerance for ambiguity:** Making decisions with less information and more uncertainty about the process and the outcome
- **Multiple perspectives:** Learning to understand situations from the perspective of local employees and businesspeople
- **Ability to work with and manage others:** Learning patience and tolerance—realizing that managers abroad are in the minority among local people; learning to communicate more with others and empathize with them[23]

Knowledge Transfer

In addition to the managerial and cross-cultural skills expatriates acquire, the company benefits from the knowledge and experience those managers gain about how to do business overseas and about new technology, local marketing, and competitive information. Expatriates have long served as facilitators of intra-firm knowledge transfer and application. Traditionally, it has been assumed that the role of expatriates is partly to bring knowledge from the corporate headquarters to subsidiaries; however, it is clear that there is a potential strategic advantage when expatriates acquiring knowledge while on international assignment bring it back to the center of the organization or disseminate it across other subsidiaries.[24] Consider, for example, Claire Molyneux, Associate Marketing Director for P&G West Africa. Claire, who was born and raised in England, started her P&G career there in 1998 as an assistant brand manager. Over the years, she worked for P&G in Geneva and Israel. In 2008, Claire was assigned to Nigeria as marketing director for Ariel detergent, Duracell batteries, and Gillette razors and to lead research into West Africa's consumers. Claire has taken up the challenge, saying, "Africa has this huge diversity. Our job is to find the similarities."[25] Consider the wealth of knowledge and information she has gathered in those ten years—cultural, consumer- and product-related, and technical as well as her contacts around the world—that she is transferring across subsidiaries and benefiting the organization. Claire's situation is an example of the five types of knowledge gained abroad that Berthoin discusses.

- Knowledge about **what** (such as differences in customer preferences)
- Knowledge about **why** (e.g., understanding how cultural differences affect cross-cultural understanding)
- Knowledge about **how** (e.g., management skills such as delegating responsibilities)
- Knowledge about **when** (e.g., knowledge about the effect of timing)
- Knowledge about **who** (e.g., relationships created over the life of an assignment)[26]

Berthoin also points out that expatriate experience not only brings knowledge about culture differences but also creates insights about HQ–subsidiary relations, from which ideas about improving business could be derived.[27] However, as Lazarova and Tarique found, "repatriates' motivation to contribute to collective organizational learning is primarily driven by the fit between their individual career objectives and the career development opportunities offered by the organization upon return."[28] They found that several conditions have to be met to transfer knowledge successfully. First, the repatriates have to (a) have valuable knowledge to transfer and (b) be motivated to transfer that knowledge; secondly, organizations need to (a) have the right tools to capture knowledge, and (b) create the right incentives for repatriates to share their knowledge. Knowledge transfer is optimized when the type of knowledge repatriates gain is matched by the right knowledge transfer mechanisms—for example, by assigning repatriates to strategic teams—and when career opportunities the organization provides are congruent with

EXHIBIT 10-1 **Variables Influencing Success of Knowledge Transfer from Repatriated Manager**

Knowledge Acquired:
cultural, local business
acumen, political, negotiating

↓

Retention of manager in firm

↓

GO/NO GO

↓

Manager's willingness to share;
ability to transfer/communicate

↓

GO/NO GO

↓

Firm value placed on
knowledge transfer

↓

GO/NO GO

↓

Organizational knowledge
transfer processes

↓

HOW EFFECTIVE?

↓

Level of integration of
knowledge/repatriated manager

↓

Knowledge Management

↓

Organizational Value Added

Source: Based on M. Lazarova and Ibraiz Tarique, "Knowledge Transfer Upon Repatriation," *Journal of World Business*, 40, 4 (2005): 361–373.

repatriate career goals and aspirations.[29] Exhibit 10-1 illustrates the conditions and process by which knowledge may be successfully integrated into the organization.

The company should therefore position itself to benefit from that enhanced management knowledge if it wants to develop a globally experienced management cadre—an essential ingredient for global competitiveness—in particular when there is a high degree of shared learning among the organization's global managers. If the company cannot retain good returning managers, their potential shared knowledge is not only lost but also conveyed to another organization that hires that person. This can be very detrimental to the company's competitive stance. Some companies are becoming quite savvy about how to use technology to employ shared knowledge to develop their global management cadre, to service their customers better, and—as a side benefit—to store the knowledge and expertise of their managers around the world in case they leave the company. That knowledge, it can be argued, is an asset in which the company has invested large amounts of resources. A successful repatriation program, then, starts before the assignment. The company's top management must set up a culture that conveys the message that the organization regards international assignments as an integral part of continuing career development and advancement and that it values the skills of the returnees. The company's objectives should be reflected in its long-range plans, commitment, and compensation on behalf of the expatriate. Unfortunately, as indicated by the respondents in the 2015 Brookfield survey, most companies do very little to minimize attrition by returning international assignees, with only 14 percent guaranteeing a position upon the assignee's return.[30] However, GE is one company that sets a model for effective expatriate career management. With its 500 expatriates worldwide, it takes care to select only the best managers for overseas jobs and then commits to placing them in specific positions upon reentry. The following Under the Lens section illustrates some expatriates' experiences that contribute to their firms' store of knowledge.

UNDER THE LENS
Expatriates' Careers Add to Knowledge Transfer[31]

Brazil's distinctive culture, the lack of English spoken at street level and the country's labyrinthine politics and bureaucracy make it hard to import foreign talent. Meanwhile, the global financial crisis is also prompting more Brazilian expatriates to consider going back.[32]

Developments around the world and in an expatriate's original country can redirect an expatriate's career choices in unexpected ways and, at the same time, affect the firms involved. Such was the case for Casio Calil. As reported in the *Financial Times*, he left Brazil in 1987, in very poor economic times, to seek his fortune elsewhere. After stints in Japan, Australia, and Ireland, he went to New York and, in 2005, took a job with J. P. Morgan's investment bank. Since then, through his business contacts in Brazil, he realized that the expanding economy and opportunities in Brazil made a move back home very attractive. Therefore, in 2011, he found himself head of J. P. Morgan Asset Management in Sao Paulo. He is now one of many Brazilians bringing their international experience and knowledge back to help a rapidly growing country with a shortage of management talent.[33]

Sometimes those world developments are less positive, causing unwanted upheaval to the lives of expats and their families. Such has been the case in Libya. After booming with international businesses taking advantage of the oil-rich country, the war to overthrow Col. Gaddafi drove out foreign businesses and their expatriates and families, some of whom had come to regard it as home. In 2012, after a year of disrupted lives, those expatriates were gradually going back and hoping that the business climate would improve after elections in June 2012. If not:

The challenges for conducting business in Libya under its old rules are daunting. Regulators required companies to hire large proportions of Libyan workers and managers even if they were unqualified. Land ownership was impossible. Even majority ownership in joint ventures did not translate into authority over strategic decisions.[34]

Similar upheavals were experienced by expatriates in Japan and, of course, the Japanese themselves during their triple disaster in 2011 composed of the earthquake, tsunami, and nuclear meltdown. Foreign companies naturally wanted to bring their staff out of danger, and the expatriates wanted to get their families out of harm's way, when the U.S. embassy sent in planes to ferry them out. However, the Japanese felt betrayed by the expatriates leaving while they worked through the crisis. In their anger, they were calling those who left *flyjin* as a take-off on their term *gaijin*, meaning foreigner. The anger the Japanese felt toward those who left is largely based on the difference between the cultural attitude of the Japanese that the company and the family are almost one entity, compared with that in the West, where family comes before the company. One expat clearly recognized this.

If I had left as the president, my role as a leader would have been diminished," said Gerry Dorizas, the president of Volkswagen AG's operations in Japan, who has been in that role four years. "We've been very transparent."[35]

There is no doubt that the events in Japan and Libya, rare as they are, have proven to add valuable experience and knowledge transfer for those expatriates and their companies about how to prepare for and deal with such events and their repercussions.

GLOBAL MANAGEMENT TEAMS

MNCs realize it is essential to maximize their human assets in the form of global management teams so they can share resources and manage the transnational transfer of knowledge. The term **global management team** describes a collection of managers in or from several countries who must rely on group collaboration if each member is to experience optimum success and goal achievement. Whirlpool International, for example, is a U.S.–Dutch joint venture with administrative headquarters in Comerio, Italy, where it is managed by a Swede and a six-person management team from Sweden, Italy, Holland, the United States, Belgium, and Germany. To achieve the individual and collective goals of the team members, international teams must have a global perspective but at the same time share the expectations of the corporate culture; they also must be glocal—able to respond to the local market while still be adept at coordinating the parts of the firm. The role and importance of international teams increase as the firm progresses in its scope of international activity. Similarly, the manner in which multicultural interaction affects the firm's operations depends on its level of international involvement, its environment, and its strategy.

The team's ability to work effectively together is crucial to the company's success. In addition, technology facilitates effective and efficient teamwork around the world. This was found by the Timberland U.K. sales conference planning team. In the past, the company's large sales conferences were cumbersome to organize because their offices were in France, Germany, Spain, Italy, and the United Kingdom. Then the team started using the British Telecom (BT) Conference Call system for the arrangements, which saved them much travel and expense. The company subsequently adopted the BT Conference Call system for the executive team's country meetings. Teleconferencing and videoconferencing are now much of the way of life for global businesses. However, research indicates that face-to-face meetings are the best way to kick off a virtual team project so that the members can agree on goals and schedules and who is responsible for what. IBM project teams start with all members in a personal meeting to help to build an understanding of the other members' cultures and set up a trusting relationship.[36]

For global organizations and alliances, the same cross-cultural interactions hold as in MNCs and, in addition, considerably more interaction takes place with the external environment at all levels of the organization. Therefore, global teamwork is vital, as are the pockets of cross-cultural teamwork and interactions that occur at many boundaries.[37] For the global company, worldwide competition and markets necessitate global teams for strategy development, both for the organization as a whole and for the local units to respond to their markets.

When a firm responds to its global environment with a global strategy and then organizes with a networked glocal structure (see Chapter 8), various types of cross-border teams are necessary for global integration and local differentiation. These include teams between and among headquarters and subsidiaries; transnational project teams, often operating on a virtual basis; and teams coordinating alliances outside the organization.[38] In joint ventures, in particular, multicultural teams work at all levels of strategic planning and implementation as well as on the production and assembly floor. Clearly, the team's success is highly dependent on the members' ability to understand the culture and communication style of members in other countries. The United Kingdom is one example where considerable differences in behavior, expectations of business protocol, and communication are often dismissed by other Westerners because of the assumption of similarity between English-speaking countries. This brings to mind a quote often attributed to Winston Churchill, "Britain and America are two nations divided by a common language."

Virtual Transnational Teams

Virtual groups, whose members interact through computer-mediated communication systems (such as desktop video conferencing systems, email, group support systems, the Internet, and intranets), are linked across time, space, and organizational boundaries.[39]

As illustrated in the diagram, advances in communication now facilitate virtual global teams formed of people working from home or work, while travelling, or anywhere in the world, using their laptops or tablets, Wi-Fi, and smartphones. **Virtual global teams**, a horizontal networked structure with people around the world conducting meetings and exchanging information through the Internet, enable the organization to capitalize on 24-hour productivity. In this way, too, knowledge is shared across business units and across cultures.[40] The advantages and cost savings of virtual global teams are frequently offset by their challenges—including cultural misunderstandings and the logistics of differences in time and space, as shown in Exhibit 10-2. Group members must build their teams while bearing in mind the group diversity and the need for careful communication.[41]

Virtual Transnational Teams

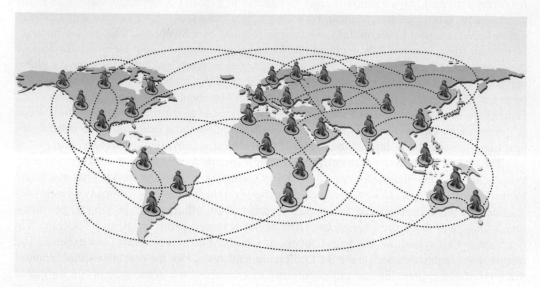

Source: Janos Levente/Shutterstock

EXHIBIT 10-2 Operational Challenges for Global Virtual Teams

Geographic Dispersal:	The complexity of scheduling communications such as teleconferences and video conferences across multiple time zones, holidays, and so on. Lack of face-to-face meetings to establish trust or for cross-interaction processes such as brainstorming.
Cultural Differences:	Variations in attitudes and expectations toward time, planning, scheduling, risk taking, money, relationship building, and so on. Differences in goal sets and work styles arising out of such variables as individualism/collectivism; the relative value of work compared with other life factors; and variable sets of assumptions, norms, patterns of behavior.
Language and Communications:	Translation difficulties, or at least variations in accents, semantics, terminology, or local jargon. Lack of personal and physical contact, which greatly inhibits trust and relationship building in many countries; the social dynamics change. Lack of visibility of nonverbal cues makes interpretation difficult and creates two-way noise in the communication process.
Technology:	Variations in availability, speed, acceptability, and cost of equipment necessary for meetings and communications through computer-aided systems. Variable skill levels and willingness to interact through virtual media.

Source: Some of this content is based on Kenneth W. Kerber and Anthony F. Buono, "Leadership Challenges in Global Virtual Teams: Lessons from the Field," *SAM Advanced Management Journal* 69, no. 4 (2004): 4–10.

Virtual team leaders from Alcoa Company's operations in 20 diverse countries have noted many of these challenges. (Alcoa is the world leader in the production of aluminum and has 63,000 employees in 31 countries.) The teams are called parallel Global Virtual Teams (pGVTs)—teams that operate outside the formal structure, focusing on innovation and improvement. All their meetings are conducted electronically through videoconferencing, teleconferencing, discussion boards, email, instant messaging, knowledge repositories, and planning and scheduling tools.

There is clearly a cross-cultural issue here—one that is particularly important to the success of pGVTs as, more than other forms of team, their success vitally depends on all members contributing and debating ideas.

"LESSONS FROM ALCOA,"
ORGANIZATIONAL DYNAMICS[42]

Cordery et al.'s studies of Alcoa's teams highlighted leadership problems. One GVT leader described the problems in not always being able to interpret or understand the subtleties of language being expressed and respond accordingly when sharing ideas because of the inability to observe the body language of members. She observed, "People from some cultures will say, 'yes' even if they have not understood. They do not feel comfortable asking you to repeat what they have not understood, being in such a large group. Others will commit to do almost anything (quite willingly) in the meeting, but it doesn't get done."

A survey of 200 of Alcoa's virtual team members by Cordery et al. revealed that they view successful team leaders as having the following skills: *interpersonal facilitation*—the ability to build teams and resolve conflicts; *task facilitation*—the ability to convey goals and train team members to use the collaborative technology effectively; *resource acquisition;* and *external alignment/vision*—that is, the ability to mesh the team's activities with the organization's goals.[43]

In a separate survey of 440 training and development professionals across a variety of industries conducted by Rosen, Furst, and Blackburn, the respondents indicated which training techniques for virtual teams were more effective than others and reported which of those programs were most needed in the future. The relative priority of the training modules is shown in Exhibit 10-3.[44]

EXHIBIT 10-3 Virtual Team Training

Importance of Virtual Team Training Modules (in order of value and effectiveness)
Training on how to lead a virtual team meeting
Leader training on how to coach and mentor team members virtually
Training on how to monitor team progress, diagnose team problems, and take corrective actions
Training to use communications technologies
Leader training on how to manage team boundaries, negotiate member time commitments with local managers, and stay in touch with team sponsors
Training on how to establish trust and resolve conflicts in virtual teams
Communications skills training—cultural sensitivity, etc.
Team-building training for new virtual teams
Training to select the appropriate technologies to fit team tasks
Leader training on how to evaluate and reward individual contributions on the virtual team
Training on how to select virtual team members, establish a virtual team charter, and assign virtual team roles
Realistic preview of virtual team challenges
Training on what qualities to look for in prospective virtual team members and leaders

Source: Based on B. Rosen, S. Furst, and R. Blackburn, "Training for Virtual Teams: An Investigation of Current Practices and Future Needs," *Human Resources Management* 45, No. 2 (2006), pp. 229–247.

Managing Transnational Teams

The ability to develop and lead effective transnational teams (whether they interact virtually, physically, or, as is most often the case, a mixture of both) is essential in light of the increasing proliferation of foreign subsidiaries, joint ventures, and other transnational alliances. The primary corporate question is how to integrate a diverse pool of cultural values, traditions, and norms in order to be competitive. These challenges were experienced when Nomura, Japan's largest investment bank, acquired most of Lehman Brothers' operations in Asia, Europe, and the Middle East in October 2008, after Lehman's collapse. Nomura had to absorb hundreds of Lehman employees immediately. Although Nomura is the acquirer, it is trying to transform its own culture to be more globally competitive. As observed by one manager:

> Nomura has "a completely domestic culture"... one based on Japanese customs of employment, and where company loyalty is strong, decision-making is slow and tolerance for risk is low.[45]

Both the Japanese and the Americans trying to work together felt the cultural divide. In particular, the Japanese were shocked when Nomura's management introduced American-style pay and career structures.[46]

Teams comprising people located in far-flung operations are faced with often-conflicting goals of achieving greater efficiency across those operations, responding to local differences, and facilitating organizational learning across boundaries; conflicts arise based on cultural differences, local work norms and environments, and varied time zones. A study by Joshi et al. of a 30-member team of human resource (HR) managers in six countries in the Asia-Pacific region showed that network analysis of the various interactions among team members can reveal when and where negative cross-cultural conflicts occur and, thus, provide top management with information for conflict resolution so that a higher level of synergy may be attained among the group members. The advantages of synergy include a greater opportunity for global competition (by being able to share experiences, technology, and a pool of international managers) and a greater opportunity for cross-cultural understanding and exposure to different viewpoints. The disadvantages include problems resulting from differences in language, communication, and varying managerial styles; complex decision-making processes; fewer promotional opportunities; personality conflicts, often resulting from stereotyping and prejudice; and greater complexity in the workplace.[47] In the Joshi study, the greatest conflict and, therefore, lack of synergy, was not, as one would expect, resulting from the headquarters subsidiary power divide. Rather, the critical conflicts were between the Country A subsidiary and Country B subsidiary, given the required communication and workflow patterns between them. What are other ways that management can ascertain how well its international teams are performing and what areas need to be improved? In recognizing the areas needing better team management, executives in a study by Govindarajan and Gupta ranked five key tasks based on their level of importance, as follows.

Tasks for Global Business Teams[48]

- Cultivating trust among members
- Overcoming communication barriers
- Aligning goals of individual team members
- Obtaining clarity regarding team objectives
- Ensuring that the team possesses necessary knowledge and skills

The managers also rated the level of difficulty to accomplish that task. The researchers concluded from their study that the ability to cultivate trust among team members is critical to the success of global business teams if they want to minimize conflict and encourage cooperation.[49]

Following are some general recommendations the researchers make for improving global teamwork.

- Cultivate a culture of trust; one way to do this is by scheduling face-to-face meetings early on, even if later meetings will be virtual.
- Rotate meeting locations; this develops global exposure for all team members and legitimizes each person's position.
- Rotate and diffuse team leadership.
- Link rewards to team performance.
- Build social networks among managers from different countries.[50]

What other techniques do managers actually use to deal with the challenge of achieving cross-cultural collaboration in multinational horizontal projects? A comparative study of European project groups in several countries by Sylvie Chevrie revealed three main strategies.[51]

- **Drawing upon individual tolerance and self-control:** In this R&D consortium, the Swiss manager treated all team members the same, ignoring cultural differences, and the team members coexisted with patience and compromise. Many of the members said they were used to multinational projects and just tried to focus on technical issues.
- **Trial-and-error processes coupled with personal relationships:** This is a specific strategy in which the project manager sets up social events to facilitate acquaintance of the team members with one another. Then, they discover, through trial and error, what procedures will be acceptable to the group.
- **Setting up transnational cultures:** Here the managers used the common professional, or occupational, culture, such as the engineering profession, to bring the disparate members together within a common understanding and process.

The managers in the study admitted their solutions were not perfect but met their needs as best they could in the situation. Chevrie suggests that, where possible, a "cultural mediator" should be used who helps team members interpret and understand one another and come to an agreement about processes to achieve organizational goals.[52]

THE ROLE OF WOMEN IN INTERNATIONAL MANAGEMENT

Whether in global management teams, as expatriates, or as host-country nationals, the importance of women as a valuable, and often-underused resource should not be overlooked in IHRM efforts to maximize the company's global management cadre. On February 26, 2015, Christine Lagarde, Managing Director of the International Monetary Fund (IMF), explained on various news programs its committee's action plan to discuss with heads of state what can be done to improve their country's economic progress by removing or lessening the roadblocks to females working there—cultural and practical. For example, in Japan, she proposed that more women could take jobs if the government instituted a child-care plan. And, in fact, in August 2015, Prime Minister Shinzo Abe announced a new law requiring companies with over 300 employees to set targets for hiring more women managers - although child-care was not addressed and remains an obstacle; at that time women comprised only 11 percent of supervisory or management positions. This move was heralded as:

A Step Forward for 'Womenomics' in Japan.

THE WALL STREET JOURNAL
AUGUST 28, 2015[53]

The changing roles of women in management is explored in the following Management in Action feature.

MANAGEMENT IN ACTION
Women in Management Around the World

More CEOs, More Industries, More Power, More Challenges

FORTUNE.COM[54]

Although it is clear that women are increasingly making their way into the international management cadre, their numbers and clout vary greatly around the world.

The 2015 ranking by *Fortune* magazine of the most powerful women in business in the United States includes a record 27 CEOs of large companies. At the top of the list are Mary Barra, CEO of General Motors; and Indra Nooyi, PepsiCo Chairman and CEO, the Indian-born strategist and former CFO and president, followed by Ginni Rommetty, Chairman, CEO, and President of IBM—and at number 51—Taylor Swift, singer, Music and Technology Industry Disrupter! The article also includes a separate list of "Most Powerful Women: International." For the EMEA region, with 10 of the top 25 based in England, the list includes Ana Botin, Chairman Banco Santander, Spain; and Maria Ramos, Group CEO, Barclays Africa. For the Asia-Pacific region, first was Chanda Kochhar, Managing Director and CEO, ICICI Bank, India; and includes Chua Sock Koon, Group CEO of Singapore Telecommunications, along with eleven from Mainland China.' Eighteen of the top 25 most powerful women of the Asia-Pacific region were in India or China. *Fortune* also pointed out that Alibaba is a great company for fostering talented women and featured Maggie Wu, CFO of Alibaba, and Lucy Peng, Alibaba's head of HR and the affiliated Small and Micro Financial Services Co, which owns Alipay.[55]

However, although women's advancement in some global companies is impressive, it is still true that there are limitations on managerial opportunities for many women in their own country—some more than others—and there are even more limitations on their opportunities for expatriate assignments

A report by the World Economic Forum stated that companies in the United States, Spain, Canada, and Finland lead the world in employing the largest numbers of women from entry level to senior management. Yet the report also found that, "despite increasing awareness of gender disparities in the workplace, women at many of the world's top companies continued to lag behind their male peers in many areas, including pay and opportunities for professional advancement."[56] In addition, the study found that overall only 5 percent of the chief executives of the 600 companies surveyed were women. Finnish companies were at the top with 13 percent, Norway and Turkey with 12 percent, and Italy and Brazil with 11 percent.[57]

Gender diversity is gaining ground in Latin America, yet women in the region are still greatly under-represented in top management—even though they are more likely than men to say they want to advance their careers.

MCKINSEY GLOBAL SURVEY RESULTS
AUGUST 2013[58]

The reasons for the different opportunities for women among various countries can often be traced to the cultural expectations of the host countries—the same cultural values that keep women in these countries from the managerial ranks. For example, in a McKinsey 2013 survey of what gender-diversity measures CEOs are taking, the results for Latin America showed a considerable discrepancy by country. In Brazil, 59 percent say they have programs to recruit and retain women; in Chile, only 10 percent acknowledge they have taken such steps.[59]

Cultural expectations may also contribute to different opportunities for women at the top levels between northern and southern Europe. For example, Maitland reported in an article entitled "the North–South Divide in Europe, Inc.", that "[w]omen are far more likely to serve on the boards of Scandinavia's biggest companies than Italy's or Spain's, and attitudes to their promotion remain deeply split."[60]

In their research in 32 countries on the cultural indicators of the reasons for the variation in the participation of women in management around the world, Toh and Leonardelli found a relationship between loose and tight cultures and the presence of women in the firms of those countries. They conclude that in tight cultures, such as Germany and South Korea, the norms of expected behavior are more clear and rigid, with norms of traditional male attitudes, and thus have far fewer women in leadership positions than those in loose cultures such as New Zealand and Hungary.[61] In loose cultures, people are more open to change and variations in expectations, so the general attitude in the leadership of firms in those cultures is one of a more open and positive perspective of women leaders.

Men from Australia, a looser culture, were more likely to rate the leadership styles of women leaders as effective, compared to men from Malaysia, a tighter culture.

SOO MIN TOH AND GEOFFREY J. LEONARDELLI
2013[62]

The problem is even more acute at the boardroom level. Whereas in top boardrooms only 5 percent were female in Italy, and 10 percent in Spain, women occupied 32 percent of board seats in the largest companies in Norway and 27 percent in Sweden. Overall, over half of major European companies have no female representation on their executive committees.[63] The female composition on executive committees in 2010 was similarly divided although overall lower than the female board composition. Whereas Sweden had 17 percent representation, followed by the United States and Britain with 14 percent, at low end was Brazil with 6 percent and Germany with 2 percent.[64]

Given the powerful figure at the top in Germany—Chancellor Angela Merkel—it seems surprising to see the low female participation at the top levels, "but a decade of earnest vows from the corporate sector has not dented male-dominated Deutschland AG…all 30 DAX companies are run by men."[65] Clearly, traditional cultural values about gender roles in Germany, as well as lifestyle and laws, can account for much of the disparity in Germany. For example, most children attend school only in the mornings, which restricts the ability for both parents to work. Nevertheless, in spite of considerable recent government encouragement in its attempts to capitalize on females as an economic resource, only about 14 percent of German mothers with one child resume full-time work and only 6 percent of those with two children. Even though the German birthrate—at 1.39—is the lowest in Europe, and even though there is a generous 14-month shared parental leave after childbirth, conservative family values that expect mothers to stay home with their children still predominate.

Opportunities for indigenous female employees to move up the managerial ladder in a given culture depend on the values and expectations regarding the role of women in that society. In Japan, for example, the workplace has traditionally been a male domain as far as managerial careers are concerned (although rapid changes are now taking place, as previously pointed out). To the older generation, a working married woman represented a loss of face to the husband because it implied that he was not able to support her. The younger generation and increased global competitiveness have brought some changes to traditional values regarding women's roles in Japan. More than 60 percent of Japanese women are now employed, including half of Japanese mothers, but largely in part-time and temporary positions. How and when the new law, and cultural changes will affect the number of Japanese women in managerial positions remains to be seen. Currently, only about 11 percent are in managerial positions, compared with about 45 percent in the United States and 30 percent in Sweden, for example. One can understand the problems Japanese women face when trying to enter and progress in managerial careers when we review the experiences of Yuko Suzuki, who went into business for herself after the advertising company she worked for went bankrupt. However, she could not gain respect or even attention from customers, who often asked her who her boss was after she finished a presentation. She eventually hired a man to accompany her, which increased her sales, but, to her dismay, customers would only establish eye contact with him, even though she was doing the talking and he had nothing to do with the company.[66] Japanese labor economists observe that, "Japan has gone as far as it can go with a social model that consists of men filling all of the economic, management and political roles."[67]

Although the variation in women's roles around the world can be attributed to complex social and cultural issues, firms ought to be aware of the effects on their bottom line. Research by Catalyst showed that—of the 353 Fortune 500 companies they surveyed—the quartile with the largest proportion of women in top management had a return on equity of 35.1 percent higher than the quartile with the lowest female representation.[68]

The lack of expatriates who are female or represent other minority groups does not reflect their lack of desire to take overseas assignments. Indeed, studies indicate women's strong willingness to work abroad and their considerable success on their assignments. For example, Adler's major study of North American women working as expatriate managers in countries around the world showed that they are, for the most part, successful.[69]

Women and minorities represent a significant resource for overseas assignments—whether as expatriates or as host-country nationals—a resource that U.S. companies underuse. Adler studied this phenomenon regarding women and recommends that businesses (1) avoid assuming that a female executive will fail because of the way she will be received or because of problems female spouses experience; (2) avoid assuming that a woman will not want to go overseas; and (3) give female managers every chance to succeed by giving them the titles, status, and recognition appropriate to the position— as well as sufficient time to be effective.[70]

WORKING WITHIN LOCAL LABOR RELATIONS SYSTEMS

If you have to close a plant in Italy, in France, in Spain or in Germany, you have to discuss the possibility with the state, the local communities, the trade unions; everybody feels entitled to intervene…even the Church.

JACOB VITTORELLI
FORMER DEPUTY CHAIRMAN OF PIRELLI[71]

An important variable in implementing strategy and maximizing host-country human resources for productivity is that of the labor relations environment and system within which the managers of a multinational enterprise (MNE) will operate in a foreign country. Differences in economic, political, and legal systems result in considerable variation in labor relations systems across countries. It is the responsibility of the IHRM function to monitor the labor relations systems in host countries and advise local managers accordingly. In fact, that information should be considered one input to the strategic decision of whether to operate in a particular country or region.

The Impact of Unions on Businesses

European businesses, for example, continue to be undermined by their poor labor relations and by inflexible regulations. As a result, businesses have to move jobs overseas to cut labor costs, resulting from a refusal of unions to grant any reduction in employment protection or benefits to keep the jobs at home. In addition, non-European firms wishing to operate in Europe have to weigh carefully the labor relations systems and their potential effect on strategic and operational decisions, as illustrated by Ford's experiences, described in the accompanying Under the Lens feature.

UNDER THE LENS

Ford's Bitter Struggle to Close a Plant in Belgium[72]

When Ford announced that it would close its factory in Genk, Belgium, at the end of 2014, and move its production to Spain, its 4,300 employees, the approximately 5,000 associated suppliers and works, the community, and Ford, paid a high price.

The economic downturn in Europe severely restricted consumer demand for cars, resulting in the need to close three European plants, including Genk, to cut about 18 percent of its productive capacity. (Ford also has plants in Germany, Spain, and the United Kingdom, totaling 15,000 employees.) The news triggered violent protests in Cologne, Germany, at the site of Ford's European headquarters. At the Genk factory, union representatives announced the decision over loudspeakers as soon as it was announced, resulting in workers barricading factory gates, thus restricting any movement of about 6,000 newly built Mondeo cars, S-Max minivans, and Galaxy vans that had already been ordered. This caused a backlog, which halted production for months. About 20,000 people staged a protest in Genk; the factory workers there were joined by workers from other factories who traveled to join the protest. The proposal was met with shock throughout Belgium because of the likely negative impact on the Belgian economy and because Ford had committed to operating there until 2020. The proposal also sparked criticism because a statute in Belgium requires firms planning large cutbacks to consult with employees to seek other options.

The three trade unions decided right away to accept the closure in favor of securing a favorable deal, but the workers disagreed and staged walkouts, angry that they had been left out of the negotiations between management and unions, resulting in the assignment of a government arbitrator. The workers did not accept the proposals. Protests and picketing by the workers and suppliers followed. As of January 2013, the Genk plant had been shut for three months due to no resolution with the workers, and Ford tried to meet orders from existing inventory. Even after management and unions had an agreement that the workers approved, production could not resume because protestors blocked access to supply deliveries. Other staged protests blocked the union leaders from leaving the building after a meeting at Ford's headquarters in Cologne.

In the end, Ford settled with a labor agreement that allowed the company to close the plant, but at a high price. In all, five unions were involved in the protracted negotiations, and Ford ended up paying $750 million in severance pay to its workers at the Genk plant—about 11,000 workers, including suppliers. The Genk workers received about $190,000. In all, Ford's bill for closing the Genk plant and two in England was estimated at about $1 billion, but it compared that to the losses of about $1 billion in 2013, which would have continued.

Ford is one of few companies to go up against the fierce resistance of Europe's powerful unions and its politicians, illustrating the difficulty and expense of closing auto plants in Europe compared with those in the United States. Few companies dared close plants in Europe after the 2008–2009 financial crisis, compared with more than a dozen plants in the United States. The European labor laws support unions, even in their protests, far more than in the United States.

These situations raise a number of issues for managers regarding strategic decisions for overseas plant locations, relationships with host unions and communities, and sustainability and social responsibility.

With the economic downturn in Europe, however, recent changes bring relief to businesses in Europe as some unions grant concessions to firms to keep their jobs. Unions in Germany, France, and Italy have been losing their battle to derail labor-market reforms by the governments in those countries, which are increasingly concerned that excess regulation and benefits to workers are smothering growth opportunities. Firms such as the Swedish furniture company IKEA, for example, have set up plants abroad. IKEA opened its non-unionized plant in Danville, southern Virginia, where the unemployment rate is very high, and received incentive grants of $12 million. However, in July 2011, employees at the plant voted 221 to 69 to allow the International Association of Machinists and Aerospace Workers union to negotiate salary and benefits with the retailer's manufacturing subsidiary, Swedwood. The union organizers claimed that IKEA's high corporate standards for employees stopped at the U.S. border and that employees were "grossly underpaid compared to their Swedish counterparts, suffer high injury rates, are forced to work overtime, and demoted or fired for expressing union sympathies."[73]

The term **labor relations** refers to the process through which managers and workers determine their workplace relationships. This process may be through verbal agreement and job descriptions or through a union's written labor contract, which has been reached through negotiation in **collective bargaining** between workers and managers. The labor contract determines rights regarding workers' pay, benefits, job duties, firing procedures, retirement, layoffs, and so on.

The prevailing labor relations system in a country is important to the international manager because it can constrain the strategic choices and operational activities of a firm operating there. The three main dimensions of the labor-management relationship that the manager will consider are (1) the participation of labor in the affairs of the firm, especially as this affects performance and well-being; (2) the role and impact of unions in the relationship; and (3) specific human resource policies in terms of recruitment, training, and compensation.[74] Constraints take the form of (1) wage levels that are set by union contracts and leave the foreign firm little flexibility to be globally competitive, (2) limits on the ability of the foreign firm to vary employment levels when necessary, and (3) limitations on the global integration of operations of the foreign firm because of incompatibility and the potential for industrial conflict.[75]

Organized Labor around the World

The percentage of the workforce in trade unions in industrialized countries has declined in the past decade, most notably in Europe. In the United States, union membership fell from a 20.1 percent in 1983 to 11.1 percent in 2014.[76] This global trend is attributable to various factors, including an increase in the proportion of white-collar and service workers to manufacturing workers, a rising proportion of temporary and part-time workers, offshoring of jobs to gain lower wage costs, and a reduced belief in unions by the younger generations. In addition, the global economic decline and loss of jobs has put downward pressure on union demands and power when the focus changed to job retention rather than increased benefits.

The numbers do not show the nature of the system in each country. In most countries, a single dominant industrial relations system applies to almost all workers. Both Canada and the United States have two systems—one for the organized and one for the unorganized. Each, according to Adams, has "different rights and duties of the parties, terms and conditions of employment, and structures and processes of decision making." In North America, an agent represents unionized employees, whereas unorganized employees can only bargain individually, usually with little capability to affect major strategic decisions or policies or conditions of employment.[77]

The traditional trade union structures in Western industrialized societies have been in *industrial unions*, representing all grades of employees in a specific industry, and *craft unions*, based on certain occupational skills. More recently, the structure has been conglomerate unions, representing members in several industries—for example, the metalworkers unions in Europe, which cut across industries, and general unions, which are open to most employees within a country.[78] The system of union representation varies among countries. In the United States, most unions are national and represent specific groups of workers—for example, truck drivers or airline pilots—so a company may have to deal with several national unions. A single U.S. firm—rather than an association of firms representing a worker classification—engages in its own negotiations. In Japan, on the other hand, it is common for a union to represent all workers in a company. In recent years, company unions in Japan have increasingly coordinated their activities, leading to some lengthy strikes.

Industrial labor relations systems across countries can be understood only in the context of the variables in their environment and the sources of origins of unions. These include government regulation of unions, economic and unemployment factors, technological issues, and the influence of religious organizations. Any of the basic processes or concepts of labor unions, therefore, may vary across countries, depending on where and how the parties have their power and achieve their objectives, such as through parliamentary action in Sweden. For example, collective bargaining in the United States and Canada refers to negotiations between a labor union local and management. However, in Europe, collective bargaining takes place between the employer's organization and a trade union at the industry level.[79] This difference means that North America's decentralized, plant-level, collective agreements are more detailed than Europe's industry-wide agreements because of the complexity of negotiating myriad details in multi-employer bargaining. In Germany and Austria, for example, such details are delegated to works councils by legal mandate.[80]

The resulting agreements from bargaining also vary around the world. A written, legally binding agreement for a specific period, common in Northern Europe and North America, is less prevalent in southern Europe and Britain. In Britain, France, and Italy, bargaining is frequently informal and results in a verbal agreement valid only until one party wishes to renegotiate.[81]

Other variables of the collective bargaining process are the objectives of the bargaining and the enforceability of collective agreements. Because of these differences, managers in MNEs overseas realize that they must adapt their labor relations policies to local conditions and regulations. They also need to bear in mind that, although U.S. union membership has declined by about 50 percent in the past 30 years, in Europe, overall, membership is still quite high, particularly in Italy and the United Kingdom—though it, too, has been falling, but from much higher levels.

Most Europeans are covered by collective agreements, whereas most Americans are not. Unions in Europe are part of a national cooperative culture among government, unions, and management, and they hold more power than in the United States. Increasing privatization will make governments less vulnerable to this kind of pressure. It is also interesting to note that some labor courts in Europe deal separately with employment matters from unions and works councils.

In Japan, labor militancy has long been dead since labor and management agreed 40 years ago on a deal for industrial peace in exchange for job security. Unions in Japan have little official clout, especially in the midst of the Japanese recession. In addition, not much can be negotiated because wage rates, working hours, job security, health benefits, overtime work, insurance, and the like have traditionally been legislated. However, global competition is putting pressure on companies to move away from guaranteed job security and pay. Often, however, the managers and labor union representatives are the same people, a fact that limits confrontation, as does the cultural norm of maintaining harmonious relationships.

In the industrialized world, tumbling trade barriers are also reducing the power of trade unions because competitive multinational companies have more freedom to choose alternative production and sourcing locations. Most new union workers—about 75 percent—will be in emerging nations such as China and Mexico, where wages are low and unions are scarce. However, in some countries, such as India, outmoded labor laws are very restrictive for MNEs, making it difficult to lay off employees under any circumstances and forcing foreign companies to be very careful in their selection of new employees.

In China, for example, in a surprising move, the government passed a new law that will grant power to labor unions, in spite of protests by foreign companies with factories there. The order was in response to a sharp rise in labor tension and protests about poor working conditions and industrial accidents.[82] The All-China Federation of Trade Unions claimed that foreign employers often force workers to work overtime, pay no heed to labor-safety regulations, and deliberately find fault with the workers as an excuse to cut their wages or fine them. The move, which underscores the government's growing concern about the widening income gap and threats of social unrest, is setting off a battle with American and other foreign corporations that have lobbied against it by hinting that they may build fewer factories in China.[83]

Protests arose after Walmart, the world's biggest retailer, was forced to accept unions in its Chinese outlets; other MNCs then joined the effort to get the Chinese government to reverse its decision. State-controlled unions in China have traditionally not wielded much power; however, after years of reports of worker abuse, the government seems determined to give its union new powers to negotiate worker contracts, safety protection, and workplace ground rules.[84] However, in spite of such well-publicized incidences, the union situation in China is generally regarded as *The Economist* states in the following:

> *In name, the All-China Federation of Trade Unions (ACFTU) is a vast union bureaucracy run-ning from the national level to small enterprises. In practice it is controlled by the Communist Party at the national level and, in companies, is mostly a tool of the management.*
>
> THE ECONOMIST[85]

Chinese managers often ignore workers' basic rights for reasonable working conditions, safety, and even the right to be paid.

> *Less than two years after the worker suicides at electronics giant Foxconn and a strike at Honda suppliers in Guangdong province, labor troubles are again roiling China.*[86]
>
> BUSINESS WEEK
> DECEMBER 19, 2011

At Foxconn Technology, for example, which is a major supplier to several electronics giants such as Hewlett Packard, Apple, and Microsoft, there were large protests in January 2012 by workers at its Wuhan plant that involved threats from some workers to commit suicide. The employees were protesting that they had been forced to work long hours under poor conditions with little pay. Foxconn resolved the dispute and, under pressure from Apple and other compa-nies, pledged to improve working conditions in China.[87] Increasing protests and strikes across China are partly attributed to more awareness of labor laws as well as to inflationary pressures. The next day, Apple, following the lead of companies such as Intel and Nike, released a list of its major suppliers, including a list of troubling practices at some of those.[88]

> *Apple said in the report that it recently became the first technology company to join the Fair Labor Association, a nonprofit group that aims to improve conditions in factories around the world.*
>
> INTERNATIONAL HERALD TRIBUNE
> JANUARY 14, 2012

However, because problems occur in factories from which Apple's suppliers outsource, or that supply parts to the suppliers, retaining control and oversight is very difficult. Perhaps, as discussed in Chapter 2, the improved social responsibility of foreign firms operating in China might exert pressure for better working conditions for Chinese employees. Policymakers want 80% of all companies to have collective bargaining agreements by 2013."[89]

Historically, the existence of unions in the West has been linked closely to improved social responsibility toward workers, and countries around the world are beginning to catch up as far as improved conditions for workers. This happens when unions are permitted and have some power or when governments exert pressure to improve life for workers so that unions will not take hold. However, strict adherence to union regulations is often traded off by all parties for the local factory to remain competitive and viable and thus provide jobs and a reasonable level of living conditions compared to those experienced previously. This connection is illustrated in the following Under the Lens feature, "Vietnam: The Union Role in Achieving Manufacturing Sustainability and Global Competitiveness."

Convergence versus Divergence in Labor Systems

> *The world trade union movement is poised to follow the lead of transnational companies, by extending its reach and throwing off the shackles of national boundaries. Unions are about to go global.*[90]

In October 2006, the International Trade Union Confederation (ITUC) was formed in Vienna, comprising the affiliated organizations of the former ICFTU (International Confederation of Free Trade Unions) and WCL (World Confederation of Labor) and eight other national trade union organizations, to form a global body.[91] The ITUC is the world's largest trade union and, as of 2012, represents 168 million workers through its 308 affiliated organizations in 155 countries and territories.[92] Its objective is to provide "a countervailing force in a society that has changed

UNDER THE LENS

Vietnam: The Union Role in Achieving Manufacturing Sustainability and Global Competitiveness

In most aspects, Vietnam has been gone from the attention of Americans for an entire generation. The country is, however, open for business—and business is booming. Capital is flowing in large amounts from Asia Pacific interests based in Singapore, Japan, Australia, Taiwan, and South Korea. The U.S. is Vietnam's seventh-largest foreign direct investment country, primarily through apparel and footwear manufacturing.

FAST DEVELOPMENT SINCE 2000

Vietnam's appearance as a global competitor is comparatively recent. After the North and South were united in 1975, the country languished for ten years. Finally, in 1986, the Vietnamese government woke up and initiated an overall economic renewal policy, known as *doi moi*. Business privatization was encouraged, commerce restrictions came down, and relations with other countries were normalized. It has only been since 2000 that their stock market has been established. Moving rapidly from there, they have been admitted to the Association of Southeast Asian Nations (ASEAN) Free Trade Area (AFTA) and to the World Trade Organization (WTO). Trade relations with the U.S. were normalized in 2006. The results are that Vietnam has gone from triple-digit annual inflation and the inability to grow enough food even for its own use, to single-digit inflation and becoming a mass exporter of both agricultural and manufactured goods.

Major components of their manufacturing for export are footwear and apparel. Unfortunately, most of what the West sees of these types of manufacturing operations comes through non-governmental organizations (NGOs), whose agendas are often far from being unbiased. The purpose of this author's visit in June, 2011 was to see if low labor costs are synonymous with exploitation of workers.

It is important to note that footwear and apparel manufacturing sites in Vietnam are frequently offshored operations owned by outsourced contractors from Taiwan and South Korea. This puts the actual production and labor management considerably removed from the oversight and control of the companies whose brands are being manufactured. Images of sweatshops and exploitation are generally associated with offshored apparel manufacturing.

MODERN INDUSTRIAL PARKS

In visiting Ho Chi Minh City in 2011, the industrial developments look quite modern. Closest to the city is the Saigon High Tech Park, which is in the early stages of developing a world-class industrial park. Intel is in the process of a $1 billion investment on those grounds. A few kilometers further out are the Linh Trung Processing Zone, Vietnam Singapore Industrial Park, and Song Than Park. Along with Western firms, such as Siemens and Kimberly Clark, are various apparel and footwear manufacturers owned by Asian outsourcers. The industrial parks are very similar to Western-style developments in terms of the grounds, infrastructure, cleanliness, and the spaciousness of the layouts. The main difference is the size of the buildings, some of which are enormous four-level structures containing as many as 10,000 workers at any given time. At 6:00 a.m. a sea of humanity floods the roadways, mostly on foot but many on motorbikes carrying up to three passengers. Workers clock in for 12-hour shifts, and factories operate on a 24-hour basis when orders and deadlines are high. Employment turnover is very high, but jobs are plentiful. Interestingly, the high turnover and high need for workers has not led to fast wage growth. Employers are finding an adequate supply of workers to keep their lines running.

WAGES AND HOUSING

The typical factory worker comes from farming provinces in order to earn higher wages. Workers start at $80–85 per month, with more for experience and productivity. This is often double the potential in their home towns. Many workers will take the option to work 7-day weeks and beyond their 12-hour shifts when factory orders are high. They send as much of their wages home as possible. Workers like to take a yearly 20-day holiday to return home, often on a very long bus ride to the north of the country. Research by Dr. Rhys Jenkins found the migrant textile workers to be appreciative of their job situation, as it had raised their standard of living.[93]

In a tour and interview with a Vietnamese housing owner, as well as several current tenants, the workers were observed to have satisfactory living accommodations, although understandably modest. Workers' rooms rent for $30 per month, and are usually shared by four workers, making their housing

FIGURE 10-2 Not the Comfort Inn, But Even the Bosses Don't Live This Well Back on the Rice Farm

Source: Photo by Dr. Robert Buchanan, used with permission.

cost about 25 cents per day or $8 per month. This is just 10% of base wages. The rooms are clean, austere, and approximately the size of a budget hotel room, with an upper deck for sleeping. Residents cook and have running water downstairs, with a communal bathroom down the hall. The rooms are in single-story buildings, situated along covered, secure corridors. Out on the street, a multitude of vendors serve the food and service needs of this demographic. We observed nothing about these living arrangements that would be characterized as inhumane or even depressing. The housing owners are typically hard-working locals who bought the properties from their own savings, live on-site, and have a congenial, patriarchal relationship with their tenants.

GOVERNMENT OVERSIGHT AND CSR

The general consensus is that the Vietnam government is providing effective levels of oversight and threats to keep factories from being exploitative. Better Work Vietnam is an NGO sponsored by the World Bank and the International Labor Organization (ILO). It has been vocal and credible in its reporting. Their most recent report indicates widespread noncompliance with government overtime standards, as well as health and safety standards. They did not find child labor in any of the large factories. While labor unions are commonplace and protected by law, the reality is that the union officers in many factories are managerial staff. This fails the non-interference test.

Corporate Social Responsibility (CSR) is a luxury that only the largest manufacturers can afford. Nonetheless, the emergence of CSR to benefit Vietnamese workers can be quite similar to those of developed nations. An April, 2011 "Fun Run" in Ho Chi Minh City to raise safety awareness was sponsored by the ILO along with such companies as Abercrombie & Fitch, Levi's, Nike, and The Walt Disney Company. Entertainment, education, and an appearance by a Vietnam Idol winner were sponsored.

CONCLUSIONS

The upshot of these observations is that Vietnam appears to be a successful model for sustainable low-cost labor manufacturing. While it is debatable whether large apparel manufacturers really contribute much to the country overall, there is no question that the jobs they provide are beneficial to that category of worker. Hopefully unions can improve the conditions further for the workers while those plants can remain competitive and retain the jobs locally.

Source: Dr. F. Robert Buchanan, University of Central Oklahoma, used with permission.

enormously, with workers' rights being flouted under the pressure created by the current trajectory of 'race to the bottom' globalization."[94]

Political changes, external competitive forces, increased open trade, and frequent moves of MNCs around the world are forces working toward convergence in labor systems. **Convergence** occurs as the migration of management and workplace practices around the world reduce workplace disparities from one country to another. This occurs primarily as MNCs seek consistency and coordination among their foreign subsidiaries and as they act as catalysts for change by exporting new forms of work organization and industrial relations practices.[95] It also occurs as harmonization is sought, such as for the EU countries, and as competitive pressures in free-trade zones, such as the NAFTA countries, eventually bring about demands for some equalization of benefits for workers.[96] It would appear that economic globalization is leading to labor transnationalism and will bring about changes in labor rights and democracy around the world.

Other pressures toward convergence of labor relations practices around the world come from the activities and monitoring of labor conditions worldwide by various organizations. One of these organizations is the International Labor Organization (ILO)—comprising union, employer, and government representation—whose mission is to ensure that humane conditions of labor are maintained. Other associations of unions in different countries include various international trade secretariats representing workers in specific industries. The activities and communication channels of these associations provide unions and firms with information about differences in labor conditions around the world.[97]

However, there are considerable forces for continued divergence of unions. These include government attitudes toward unions; union competition to attract foreign investment and provide jobs locally; different approaches to structuring unions and how to organize collective bargaining and deal with workers' rights. Exhibit 10-4 shows the major forces for and against convergence in labor relations systems.

Adapting to Local Industrial Relations Systems

Although forces for convergence are found in labor relations systems around the world (as discussed previously), for the most part, MNCs still adapt their practices largely to the traditions of national industrial relations systems, with considerable pressure to do so. Those companies, in fact, act more like local employers, subject to local and country regulations and practices. Although the reasons for continued divergence in systems seem fewer, they are very strong. Not the least of these reasons are political ideology and the overall social structure and history of industrial practices. In the European Union (EU), where states are required to maintain parity in wage rates and benefits under the Social Charter of the Maastricht Treaty, a powerful defense of cultural identity and social systems still exists, with considerable resistance by unions to comply with those requirements. Managers in those MNCs also recognize that a considerable gap often exists between the labor laws and the enforcement of those laws—in particular in less-developed countries.

EXHIBIT 10-4 Trends in Global Labor Relations Systems

Forces for Global Convergence →	Dynamic Forces Acting on Current System ←	Forces to Maintain or Establish Divergent Systems
Global competitiveness		National labor relations systems and traditions
MNC presence or consolidation initiatives		Social systems
Political change		Local regulations and practices
New market economies		Political ideology
Free-trade zones: harmonization		Cultural norms
(EU), competitive forces (NAFTA)		Competition for jobs
Technological standardization, IT		Collective bargaining methods
Declining role of unions		
Agencies monitoring world labor practices		

NAFTA and Labor Relations in Mexico

About 40 percent of the total workforce in Mexico is unionized, with about 80 percent of the workers unionized in industrial organizations that employ more than 25 workers. However, government control over union activities is very strong, and although some strikes occur, union control over members remains rather weak. Most labor unions are affiliated with the Institutional Revolutionary Party (PRI) through the Confederation of Mexican Workers (Confederación de Trabajadores Mexicanos—CTM). In April 2011, the Teamsters Union charged that Mexico's oligarchs, led by President Felipe Calderon, were trying to take away workers' collective bargaining rights through various labor law reforms. The union charged that:

> *In reality, the growing power of corporations (enabled by NAFTA) has undermined those rights, especially in the maquiladora district in northern Mexico. Half of all Mexicans live in poverty, and even those with a formal job don't make much money.*[98]

> TEAMSTER NATION
> APRIL 21, 2012

MNCs are required by government regulation to hire Mexican nationals for at least 90 percent of their workforce; preference must be given to Mexicans and to union personnel. In reality, however, the government permits hiring exceptions. The HSBC Bank, for example, found the following.

The owner must employ a minimum of 90 percent Mexican workers in accordance with Mexican Federal Labor Law (MFLL). In the case of technicians and professional workers, they must be Mexican; in the event that Mexican technicians or professional workers are not available, the business may temporarily hire a foreign worker, but both will then have the obligation to train a Mexican technician or professional worker in order to comply with the MFLL. For management or director levels, the rule does not apply.[99]

Many foreign firms set up production in Mexico—using the advantages of NAFTA—at least in part for the lower wages and lower overall cost of operating there, as well as low transportation costs to the United States - and the Mexican government wants to continue to attract that investment as it has for many years before NAFTA. Mexican workers claim that some of the large U.S. companies in Mexico violate basic labor rights and cooperate with pro-government labor leaders in Mexico to break up independent unions. Workers there believe that MNCs routinely use blacklists, physical intimidation, and economic pressure against union organizations and independent labor groups that oppose Mexican government policies or the pro-government Confederation of Mexican Workers (CTM).

This example illustrates the complexities of labor relations when a firm operates in other countries—particularly when there are linkages and interdependence among those countries, such as through NAFTA or the EU. Of interest are the differences among NAFTA nations in labor law in the private sector. For example, although the minimum wage in Mexico is far less than that in Canada or the United States, a number of costly benefits for Mexican workers are required, such as 15 days of pay for a Christmas bonus and 90 days of severance pay. For comparison, the accompanying Comparative Management in Focus feature examines labor relations in Germany.

Comparative Management in Focus

Labor Relations in Germany

> *IG Metall yesterday settled on a 3.4 percent pay rise for a year from April for employees in Baden-Württemberg, one of Germany's richest states, where unemployment is just 4.2 per cent. The deal is seen as a bellwether for negotiations in the rest of the country.*

> FINANCIAL TIMES
> FEBRUARY 25, 2015[100]

Given the continuing economic problems in Europe at that time, there was considerable commitment to Germany's largest union, IG Metall, at its 2011 annual congress in Karlsruhe. "The union's executive used the occasion to confirm and celebrate its policy of class collaboration. Federal President Christian Wulff and Chancellor Angela Merkel (both from the Christian Democratic Union—CDU) came to the gathering to pay their respects."[101]

(Continued)

It is noteworthy that the German economy has done very well over the past few years—while the rest of Europe staggered—leading Angel Gurría, the OECD's secretary general, to say in a speech in Berlin in February 2012 that Germany's "growth model has been so successful in navigating through the stormy waters of the crisis."[102] The German unemployment level fell to the lowest level in decades, whereas it went up in the rest of Europe. Part of that result is because, in the labor system in Germany, companies tend to move employees to part-time status and give them continued training the rest of the time rather than laying them off. In addition, the company often banks the overtime pay of employees to use when times are difficult and they have to reduce employees' hours. Unfortunately, many of the younger generation workers do not have permanent jobs; rather they have contract (temporary) jobs, which makes it easier for companies to let them go when the term of the contract ends.[103]

In spite of the commitment to IG Metall, Germany's **codetermination** law *(mitbestimmung)* is coming under pressure from German companies dealing with global competition and the results of global trends of outsourcing, industrial restructuring, and the expansion of the service sector.[104] That pressure is increasingly taking the form of concession bargaining to keep jobs at home. Still, some companies—tired of restrictions on their strategic decisions and necessary job cuts—are sidestepping those restrictions by registering as public limited companies in the United Kingdom.[105]

Mitbestimmung refers to the participation of labor in the management of a firm. The law mandates representation for unions and salaried employees on the supervisory boards of all companies with more than 2,000 employees and works councils of employees at every work site. Companies with 2,000 or more staff have to give employees half the votes; those with 500 employees or more have to give a third of supervisory board seats to union representatives.[106] Unions are well integrated into managerial decision-making and can make a positive contribution to corporate competitiveness and restructuring; this seems different from the traditional adversarial relationship of unions and management in the United States. However, the fact is that German firms, in the form of affiliated organizations of companies, have to contend with negotiating with powerful industry-wide unions. Employment conditions that would be negotiated privately in the United States, for example, are subject to federal mandates in Germany—a model unique in Europe. Germans on average work fewer hours than those in any other country than the Netherlands.[107] Under pressure from global competition, German unions incurred huge membership losses. In 2010, there were 7.9 million members, 40 percent fewer than in 1990, but that includes about 20 percent of retired union members.[108] In fact, only 20 percent of employees in Germany are union members, compared to 28 percent in the United Kingdom and 67 percent in Denmark.[109] As a result, the unions are now more willing to make concessions and trade flexibility for increased job security.

Union membership in Germany is voluntary, usually with one union for each major industry, and union power traditionally has been quite strong. Negotiated contracts with firms by the employers' federation stand to be accepted by firms that are members of the federation, or used as a guide for other firms. These contracts, therefore, result in setting the pay scale for about 90 percent of the country's workers.[110]

The union works councils play an active role in hiring, firing, training, and reassignment during times of reorganization and change.[111] Because of the depth of works council penetration into personnel and work organization matters, as required by law, its role has been described by some as "co-manager of the internal labor market."[112] This situation has considerable implications for how managers of MNCs plan to operate in Germany.

IG Metall (*Industriegewerkschaft Metall*—Industrial Union of Metalworkers) had nearly 3.7 million members as of February 2015, representing workers at Germany's biggest companies. IG Metall has traditionally negotiated guidelines regarding pay, hours, and working conditions on a regional basis. IG Metall's proactive role on change illustrates the evolving role of unions by leading management thinking instead of reacting to it. In addition, management and workers tend to work together because of the unions' structure. Indeed, such institutional accord is a powerful factor in changing deeply ingrained cultural traits. Codetermination has clearly helped to modify German managerial style from authoritarian to something more akin to humanitarian without, it should be noted, altering its capacity for efficiency and effectiveness.[113] This system compares to the lack of integration and active roles for unions in the U.S. auto industry—for example, conditions that limit opportunities for change.

Pay for German production workers has been among the highest in the world, about 150 percent of that in the United States and about ten times that in Mexico. German workers also have the highest number of paid vacation days in the world and prefer short workdays.

Foreign companies operating in Germany also have to be aware that termination costs—including severance pay, retraining costs, time to find another job, and so on—are very high, and that is assuming the company is successful in terminating the employee in the first place, which is very difficult

MAP 10.1 **Germany and Western Europe**

Legend:
- ■ EU members using the euro
- ■ EU members using own national currency
- ■ Countries not members of the EU
- ■ Cities over 1 million
- ⊞ Capitals over 1 million

Source: Deloitte Services LP

to do in Europe. This was brought home to Colgate-Palmolive when it tried to close its factory in Hamburg. The company offered the 500 employees an average severance of $40,000 each, but the union would not accept, and eventually Colgate had to pay a much higher (undisclosed) amount.

To the extent that the West German unions have established the high-wage, high-skill, and high-value-added production pattern, they have also become dependent on the continued presence of that pattern.[114]

Conflicting opinions over the value of codetermination are increasingly evident as business practices become increasingly subject to EU policies. A major concern was that firms from other countries that were considering cross-border mergers would be discouraged by the EU statute that would oblige them to incorporate codetermination if the new company includes significant German interests.

CONCLUSION

The role of the IHRM department has expanded to meet the strategic needs of the company to develop a competitive global management cadre. Maximizing human resources around the world requires attention to the many categories and combinations of those people, including expatriates, inpatriates, host-country managers, third-country nationals, global teams, and local employees. Competitive global companies need top managers with global experience and understanding. To that end, attention must be paid to the needs of expatriates before, during, and after their assignments to maximize their long-term contributions to the company.

Summary of Key Points

- Expatriate career management necessitates plans for retention of expatriates during and after their assignments. Through retention, the firm can benefit from the knowledge and experiences attained on assignments; otherwise, the next firm that hires the returnee will benefit from that knowledge. Support programs for expatriates should include information from and contact with the home organization as well as career guidance and support after the overseas assignment.

- The expatriate's spouse plays a crucial role in the potential retention and effectiveness of the manager in host locations. Companies should ensure the spouse's interest in the assignment, include him or her in the predeparture training, and provide career and family support during the assignment and upon return.

- Global management teams offer greater opportunities for competition—by sharing experiences, technology, and international managers—and greater opportunities for cross-cultural understanding and exposure to different viewpoints. Disadvantages can result from communication and cross-cultural conflicts and greater complexity in the workplace.

- Virtual global teams enable cost-effective, rapid knowledge sharing and collaboration but are fraught with cross-cultural and logistical challenges.

- Women represent an underused resource in international management. One reason for this situation is the assumption that culturally based biases may limit the opportunities and success of female managers and employees.

- The labor relations environment, system, and processes vary around the world and affect how the international manager must plan strategy and maximize the productivity of local human resources.

- Labor unions around the world are becoming increasingly interdependent because of the operations of MNCs worldwide, the outsourcing of jobs around the world, and the leveling of the playing field for jobs.

Discussion Questions

10-1. What steps can the company's IHRM department take to maximize the effectiveness of the expatriate's assignment and the long-term benefit to the company?

10-2. Discuss the role of reverse culture shock in the repatriation process. What can companies do to avoid this problem? What kinds of skills do managers learn from a foreign assignment, and how can the company benefit from them? What is the role of repatriation in the company's global competitive situation?

10-3. What are the reasons for the small numbers of female expatriates? What more can companies do to use women as a resource for international management?

10-4. What is a virtual global management team? How do the members interact? Discuss the advantages and the challenges these teams face. Suggest some ways to maximize the effectiveness of virtual teams across borders.

10-5. Discuss the reasons behind the growing convergence and interdependence of labor unions around the world.

Application Exercise

10-6. Interview one or more managers who have held positions overseas. Try to find a man and a woman. Ask them about their experiences both in the working environment and in the foreign country generally. How did they and their families adapt? How did they find the stage of reentry to headquarters, and what were the effects of the assignment on their career progression? What differences do you notice, if any, between the experiences of the male and the female expatriates?

Experiential Exercise

Form groups of six students, divided into two teams, one representing union members from a German company and the other representing union members from a Mexican company. These companies have recently merged in a joint venture, with the subsidiary to be located in Mexico. These union workers, all line supervisors, will be working together in Mexico. You are to negotiate six major points of agreement regarding union representation, bargaining rights, and worker participation in management, as discussed in this chapter. Present your findings to the other groups in the class and discuss. (It may help to read the *Comparative Management in Focus: Motivation in Mexico* feature in Chapter 11.)

CASE STUDY

Expatriate Management at AstraZeneca Plc

Over the years, AstraZeneca Plc (AstraZeneca) has developed a strong reputation for its expatriate management practices. Expatriate management at AstraZeneca went beyond tackling issues such as compensation, housing, issues related to the spouse's career abroad, and so on. It also took care to ensure that employees on international assignment were able to adapt well to the new environment and achieve a work–life balance. With the global economic situation continuing to be grim, AstraZeneca also began placing emphasis on a "more thoughtful planning and selection process" of candidates for international assignments.[1]

Source: Deloitte Services LP

AstraZeneca is the world's fifth-largest pharmaceutical company by global sales.[2] It is headquartered in London, UK, and Södertälje, Sweden. For the year 2013, AstraZeneca's revenues were US$25.7 billion, and it employed around 51,500 employees. As of 2013, AstraZeneca had around 350 employees working on international assignments in 140 countries worldwide. These were employees who were on short-term, long-term, or commuter assignments.[3] According to Ashley Daly (Daly), senior manager of international assignments for AstraZeneca in the United States, the company's employees were mainly concentrated in Belgium, the United States, and the United Kingdom, but they "also have a significant presence in the Asia-Pacific and Latin America regions."[4] AstraZeneca's policy stipulates that for any international assignment, there had to be a business rationale. The company saw to it that the costs involved were acceptable and that the career management of the employee during the assignment was consistent with personal development goals as well as business needs. The contractual arrangements for the assignment were also centrally managed.[5] "From the outset, if there is not a clear sense of how the international assignment experience can be applied at the end of the assignment term—at least in broad terms—the business should strongly consider whether an international assignment should even move forward,"[6] said Daly.

Once an assignment offer was made to a potential expat, AstraZeneca paired the employee up with an international assignment manager (IA manager), who briefed him or her on company policy and opportunities for cultural and language training. Before leaving for the international assignment, the employee was trained in a workshop that focused on relevant issues (such as leaving the destination location and returning to the home country). The expat was given information about the culture of the destination country—particularly differences with the home country—as well as social considerations and do's and don'ts. If necessary, the employee and his or her spouse were given training in the local language. Tessi Romell (Romell), research and development projects and HR effectiveness leader at AstraZeneca, said that the company also helped connect new expats with those who had already served in that location.

Sometimes, follow-up workshops were held in the host country. Once on assignment, expats stayed in touch with their IA manager in addition to the manager they reported to in the home country. AstraZeneca saw to it that expats were given the necessary flexibility to achieve a work–life balance. "AstraZeneca is really good at allowing people to manage their own time and being aware that we are working across different time zones. It's always something that we try to take into consideration so we don't have people [taking care of work matters] in the middle of the night,"[7] said Romell.

With AstraZeneca taking various initiatives on this front, there were few complaints about work–life balance among the company's expat population. Romell attributed this to the mechanisms the company had put in place to prepare the employees for life in a different country. "It's a combination of things that the company is doing and having a culture that is supportive of work–life balance, as well as encouraging individuals themselves to think about their own work–life balance,"[8] she said. Experts, too, felt that the practices AstraZeneca followed, such as preparing the employees for international assignments, providing them with support, and assigning IA managers, were effective. They lauded AstraZeneca's practices, which were in contrast to those of many companies that rushed employees to foreign assignments without adequate support. Chris Buckley, manager of international operations for St. Louis–based Impact Group Inc., pointed out that the expats knew that the organization was spending a lot of money on them and they might be wary about coming up with any complaints regarding their new assignment with their boss. In such a scenario, contact with the IA manager was useful because it could encourage them to open up.

With the economic situation around the globe still gloomy, experts felt that organizations would be forced to take a second look at the costs associated with international staffing. Some felt that organizations would send fewer people on international assignments or allot them to shorter terms abroad. They even predicted that the high compensation and benefits generally associated with foreign assignments could also see cuts. While AstraZeneca had also taken measures to cut costs (specifically tax costs) by sending employees on short-term assignments, Daly noted that this was not always possible. When the expat had a family and was being posted for a longer term, Daly pointed out that some of the elements of AstraZeneca's expat packages, such as comprehensive destination support and educational counseling for expatriate children, played a critical role in ensuring the employee's productivity. These supports ensured that the expatriate family could settle down in the host country. Not providing them might prevent employees from focusing on their new job, putting the company's investment at risk, so the company was not looking at this issue in terms of expenditures alone. The company also did not have any plans to decrease the number of its staff deployed internationally. According to Daly, "Our recent focus has been less on reducing numbers of international assignees and more on making the right decisions about who goes on assignment; why they go; and perhaps most important, how the skills and experience gained abroad will be leveraged in their next role, post assignment."[9]

Notes

1. Tanya Mohn, "When U.S. Home Isn't Home Anymore," www.mydigitalfc.com, March 10, 2009.
2. "The Pharm Exec 50," www.pharmexec.com, May 2009.
3. www.ideas.astrazeneca.com.
4. Susan Ainsworth, "Expatriate Programs," http://pubs.acs.org, April 6, 2009.
5. "AstraZeneca Global Policy: People," www.astrazeneca.com.
6. Susan Ainsworth, "Expatriate Programs," http://pubs.acs.org, April 6, 2009.
7. Julie Cook Ramirez, "Finding Balance Abroad," www.hreonline.com, August 1, 2009.
8. Ibid.
9. Susan Ainsworth, "Expatriate Programs," http://pubs.acs.org, April 6, 2009.

Case Questions

10-7. Critically analyze AstraZeneca's expatriate management practices.

10-8. Surveys show that most expats report feeling the strain of managing the demands of work and home while adjusting to the foreign environment, leading to more anxieties at home and at the workplace. What steps can an organization take to mitigate this?

10-9. What decisions related to expatriates can organizations take to maximize the benefits to the company despite the economic downturn? Do you think a company that paid more careful attention to selection could further boost its chances of success?

This case was written by Debapratim Purkayastha, ICMR Center for Management Research (ICMR). It was compiled from published sources and is intended to be used as a basis for class discussion rather than to illustrate either effective or ineffective handling of a management situation. © 2010, ICMR. All rights reserved. Used with permission, 2012.

Endnotes

1. Thomas Grove, "Expats Flee Moscow as Tensions Flare," Wall Street Journal, June 10, 2015, B1. Julia Werdigier, "Paychecks and Passports," *New York Times*, April 2, 2008; Doreen Carvajal, "Paid in Dollars, Some Americans Are Struggling in Europe," *New York Times*, December 15, 2007; Alan Paul, "The Expat Life: Clock Counts Down as Decision Weighs: Should I Stay or Go?" www.wallstreetjournal, February 28, 2008; Monica Ginsburg, "Getting Ahead by Going Abroad," *Crain's Chicago Business* 31, No. 50 (2008), p. 20; Philip Shearer and Abby Ellin, "Foreign from the Start," www.nytimes.com, September 21, 2003; Jad Mouawad, "Total, the French Oil Company, Places Its Bets Globally," www.nytimes.com, February 22, 2009; www.Global Relocation Trends Survey, www.brookfieldgrs.com, accessed March 1, 2009; Keith Bradsher and Julia Werdigier, "Abruptly Expatriate Bankers Are Cut Loose," www.nytimes.com March 4, 2009.

2. Werdigier.

3. Bradsher and Werdigier.

4. *Wall Street Journal*, February 28, 2008.

5. www.nytimes.com, February 22, 2000.

6. Ginsburg.

7. Shearer and Ellin.

8. Garry Oddou et al., "Repatriates as a Source of Competitive Advantage, *Organizational Dynamics* (2013), pp. 42, 257–266.

9. The *Global Talent Index Report: The Outlook to 2015* was written by the Economist Intelligence Unit and published by Heidrick & Struggles.

10. 2015 Global Relocation Trends Survey, www.brookfieldgrs.com, accessed August 26, 2015.

11. Ibid.

12. A. Maitland, "Top Companies Value Overseas Experience," www.Financial Times, July 3, 2006.

13. "International Assignments Remain on the Upswing Despite Economic Concerns, Says KPMG," *PR Newswire*, December 3, 2008; www.kpmglink.com.

14. M. Lazarova and P. Caligiuri, "Retaining Repatriates: The Role of Organizational Support Practices," *Journal of World Business* 36, No. 4 (2001), pp. 389–401.

15. Charlene M. Solomon, "One Assignment, Two Lives," *Personnel Journal* (May 1996), pp. 36–44.

16. 2015 Global Relocation Trends Survey, www.brookfieldgrs.com, accessed August 26, 2015.

17. Ibid.

18. Ibid.

19. 2011 Global Relocation Trends Survey, accessed March 1, 2011.

20. www.FT.com, March 5, 2001.

21. P. Asheghian and B. Ebrahimi, *International Business* (New York: HarperCollins, 1990), p. 470.

22. Global Relocation Trends Survey, 2011.

23. N. J. Adler, *International Dimensions of Organizational Behavior*, 4th ed. (Boston: PWS-Kent, 2002).

24. J. Bonache and C. Brewster, "Knowledge Transfer and the Management of Expatriation," *Thunderbird International Business Review* 43, No. 1 (2001), pp. 145–168.

25. David Holthaus, "P&G at Work: Key Managers in Africa," *Cincinnati Enquirer*, April 16, 2011; www.pg.com, accessed December 9, 2011.

26. Berthoin-Antal, "Expatriates' Contributions to Organizational Learning," *Journal of General Management* 26, No. 4 (2001), pp. 62–84.

27. Ibid.

28. Mila Lazarova and Ibraiz Tarique, "Knowledge Transfer upon Repatriation," *Journal of World Business* 40, No. 4 (2005), pp. 361–373.

29. Ibid.

30. 2015 Global Relocation Trends Survey, www.brookfieldgrs.com, accessed August 26, 2015.

31. Joe Leahy, "Brazil Hosts a Homecoming," *Financial Times*, August 23, 2011, p. 8; Guy Chazan, "Middle East: Oil Firms Suspend Libyan Operations," *Wall Street Journal*, February 22, 2011, p. A.11; Borzou Daragahi, "Expats Trickle Back to Libya but Business Remains Slow," *Financial Times*, London (UK), February 11, 2012, pp. 2; Mariko Sanchanta, "Disaster in Japan: Expatriates Tiptoe Back to the Office," *Wall Street Journal*, March 23, 2011, p. A.7.

32. *Financial Times*, August 23, 2011.
33. Ibid.
34. *Financial Times*, February 11, 2012.
35. *Wall Street Journal*, March 23, 2011.
36. J. Conger and E. Lawler, "People Skills Still Rule in the Virtual Company," *Financial Times*, August 26, 2005.
37. Based largely on Adler, 2002.
38. T. Gross, E. Turner, and L. Cederholm, "Building Teams for Global Operations," *Management Review* (June 1987), p. 34.
39. T. R. Kayworth and D. E. Leidner, "Leadership Effectiveness in Global Virtual Teams," *Journal of Management Information Systems* 18, No. 3 (2001–2002), pp. 7–40.
40. C. Solomon, "Building Teams across Borders," *Global Workforce* (November 1998), pp. 12–17.
41. Ibid.
42. J. Cordery, C. Soo, B. Kirkman, B. Benson, and J. Mathieu, "Leading Parallel Virtual Teams: Lessons from Alcoa," *Organizational Dynamics* 38, No. 3 (2009), pp. 204–216.
43. Ibid.
44. B. Rosen, S. Furst, and R. Blackburn, "Training for Virtual Teams: An Investigation of Current Practices and Future Needs," *Human Resources Management* 45, No. 2 (2006), pp. 229–247.
45. Michiyo Nakamoto, "Cultural Revolution in Tokyo," www.ft.com, September 17, 2009.
46. Ibid.
47. A. Joshi, G. Labianca, and P. M. Caligiuri, "Getting along Long Distance: Understanding Conflict in a Multinational Team through Network Analysis," *Journal of World Business* 37 (2002), pp. 277–284.
48. V. Govindarajan and A. K. Gupta, "Building an Effective Global Business Team," *MIT Sloan Management Review* 42, No. 4 (2001), p. 63.
49. Ibid.
50. Ibid.
51. S. Chevrier, "Cross-Cultural Management in Multinational Project Groups," *Journal of World Business* 38, No. 2 (2003), pp. 141–149.
52. Ibid.
53. Eleanor Warnok, "A Step Forward for Economics in Japan," *The Wall Street Journal*, August 28, 2015.
54. "The Most Powerful Women in Business 2015," *Fortune.com*, accessed September 20, 2015.
55. Ibid.
56. Nicola Clark, "Awareness Rises, but Women Still Lag in Pay," www.nytimes.com, March 8, 2010.
57. Ibid.
58. "Why Top Management Eludes Women in Latin America," *McKinsey Global Survey Results*, August 2013.
59. Ibid.
60. Alison Maitland, "The North–South Divide in Europe, Inc.," *Financial Times*, June 14, 2004.
61. Soo Min Toh and Geoffrey J. Leonardelli, "Cultural Constraints on the Emergence of Women Leaders: How Global Leaders Can Promote Women in Different Cultures," *Organizational Dynamics* (2013), pp. 42, 191–197.
62. Ibid.
63. Katrin Bennhold, "Women Nudged Out of German Workforce," www.nytimes.com, June 28, 2011.
64. Based on selected data from Bennhold, June 28, 2011, and McKinsey's 2010 "Women Matter" Report.
65. Bennhold.
66. Japan's Neglected Resource—Female Workers," www.nytimes.com, July 24, 2003.
67. Ibid.
68. Maitland, 2004.
69. M. Jelinek and N. Adler, "Women: World Class Managers for Global Competition," *Academy of Management Executive* 11, No. 1 (February 1988), pp. 11–19.
70. Ibid.
71. Jacob Vittorelli, Former Deputy Chairman of Pirelli.
72. Deepa Seetharaman, "Ford to Pay $750 Million Severance to Workers at Belgium Plant," www.reuters.com, March 19, 2013; Jack Ewing, "Ford Pays a High Price for its Factory Closing in Belgium," www.nytimes.com, November 5, 2013; Dietmar Henning, "Unions Suppress Opposition to Closure of Belgian Ford Plant," http://www.wsws.org/en/articles/2013/02/14/genk-f14.html, "Ford Confirms Plans to Close Belgian Factory," http://www.bbc.com/news/business-20054924, October 24, 2012; John Reed in London and James Fontanella-Khan in Brussels, "Ford to Close Belgian Plant," www.ft.com, October 24, 2012; Chris Reiter and Keith Naughton, "Ford's Genk Plant Remains Shut on Strikes at Suppliers," www.bloomberg.com/news, January 18, 2013; Mike Ramsey and Marietta Cauchi, "Vote Nears at Troubled Ford Plant in Belgium," *Wall Street Journal*, March 13, 2013.
73. Stuart Pfeifer, "Workers at IKEA's First U.S. Factory O.K. Union," *Los Angeles Times*, July 29, 2011.
74. "A New Deal in Europe?" www.businessweek.com, July 14, 2003.
75. M. R. Czinkota, I. A. Ronkainen, and M. H. Moffett, *International Business*, 3rd ed. (New York: Dryden Press, 1994).
76. Bureau of Labor Statistics news release, January 23, 2014.
77. R. J. Adams, *Industrial Relations under Liberal Democracy* (University of South Carolina Press, 1995).
78. J. S. Daniels and L. H. Radebaugh, *International Business*, 10th ed. (Reading, MA: Addison-Wesley, 2004).
79. P. J. Dowling, R. S. Schuler, and D. E. Welch, *International Dimensions of Human Resource Management*, 2nd ed. (Belmont CA: Wadsworth, 1994).
80. Adams.
81. Ibid.
82. D. Barboza, "China Passed Law to Empower Unions and End Labor Abuse," *New York Times*, October 12, 2006.
83. David Barboza, www.nytimes.com, October 12, 2006.
84. Ibid.
85. Anonymous, "Asia: Arbitration Needed: China's Labour Laws," *Economist* 392, No. 8642 (2009), p. 37.
86. Dexter Roberts, "Using Propaganda to Stop China's Strikes," *BusinessWeek* (Dec 19, 2011), p. 1.
87. David Barboza, "Foxconn Resolves a Dispute with Some Workers in China," *International Herald Tribune*, January 12, 2012.
88. Nick Wingfield and Charles Duhigg, "Apple Lists Its Suppliers for the First Time," *International Herald Tribune*, January 14, 2012.
89. *BusinessWeek*, 2011.
90. R. Jenkins, "Globalisation of Production, Employment and Poverty: Three Macro-Meso-Micro Studies," *European Journal of Development Research* 17, No. 4, (2005), pp. 601–625.
91. B. Barber, "Workers of the World Are Uniting," *Financial Times*, December 7, 2004.
92. International Confederation of Free Trade Unions, www.icftu.org, accessed August 29, 2015.
93. Ibid.

94. www.ituc-csi.org, accessed August 29, 2015.

95. M. M. Lucio and S. Weston, "New Management Practices in a Multinational Corporation: The Restructuring of Worker Representation and Rights?" *Industrial Relations Journal* 25, No. 2 (2004), pp. 110–121.

96. D. B. Cornfield, "Labor Transnationalism?" *Work and Occupations* 24, No. 3 (August 1997), p. 278.

97. Daniels and Radebaugh.

98. "Mexico Prez Trying to Crush Labor Unions Legally," *Teamster Nation*, April 21, 2011.

99. "Maximum Number of Permitted Foreign Employees," HSBC Bank, www.hsbc.com, accessed October 3, 2011.

100. Claire Jones: Frankfurt, and Jeevan Vasagar: Berlin, "IG Metall-Bellwether Deal: Germany's Largest Union Agrees Above-Inflation Pay Rise," *Financial Times*, February 25, 2015.

101. Dietmar Henning, "IG Metall Union and German Government Reaffirm Their Collaboration," www.wsws.org, October 21, 2011.

102. Floyd Norris, "Germany vs. the Rest of Europe," *New York Times*, February 16, 2012.

103. Ibid.

104. R. Milne and H. Williamson, "Selective Bargaining: German Companies Are Driving a Hidden Revolution in Labour Flexibility," *Financial Times*, January 6, 2006.

105. Gerrit Wiesmann, "Germans Eye U.K. Listings as a Way Out of Worker Law," *Financial Times*, May 24, 2006.

106. Ibid.

107. "A New Deal in Europe?" www.businessweek.com; BW Online, July 14, 2003.

108. http://www.worker-participation.eu/National-Industrial-Relations/Countries/Germany/Trade-Unions, accessed August 22, 2012.

109. http://www.worker-participation.eu, accessed August 22, 2012.

110. J. Hoerr, "What Should Unions Do?" *Harvard Business Review* (May–June 1991), pp. 30–45.

111. H. C. Katz, "The Decentralization of Collective Bargaining: A Literature Review and Comparative Analysis," *Industrial and Labor Relations Review* 47, No. 1 (1993), pp. 3–22.

112. Williamson, *Financial Times*, July 22, 2004.

113. www.nytimes.com, July 24, 2004.

114. Wofgang Streeck, "More Uncertainties: German Unions Facing 1992," *Industrial Relations* (Fall 1991), pp. 30–33.

11 Motivating and Leading

OBJECTIVES

11-1 To understand the complexity and the variables involved in cross-cultural motivation and leadership

11-2 To learn how to use the research on cultural dimensions as tools to understand how to motivate people in different cultural contexts

11-3 To become familiar with the global leader's role and environment and what makes a successful global leader

11-4 To discuss the research on leadership and how leadership styles and practices vary around the world

11-5 To understand the variables that necessitate contingency leadership: culture, context, people, and situations

Opening Profile: The EU Business Leader—Myth Or Reality?

> *The eurozone crisis means "the already shaky European identity will weaken further...[causing] reemergence of hard-edged national identities."*
>
> INTERNATIONAL HERALD TRIBUNE[1]

Is the EU business leader a myth or reality? The European Union now comprises a 28-nation unified market of over 400 million people. Can a businessperson have an effective leadership style across such diverse contexts and people? Not according to a survey of 200 chief executives in France, Germany, and the United Kingdom. Steve Newhall, of DDI Europe, an international human resources consultancy, notes that "the danger for any leader is only being able to operate within one of these styles. If you take an autocratic style into a culture that expects a more democratic or meritocratic style, the chances are that you will trip up."[2] In 2012, in particular, conflicts brought about by the euro crisis heightened ethnic differences in attitudes; and in 2015, economic problems continue to cause strife and changing attitudes toward Greece, for example. In addition, attitudes clashed regarding rescuing and accommodating the mounting numbers of refugees from war-torn countries.

Perhaps some people can lead well in firms that stretch across countries in the EU, but consider the complexity in its many forms: different histories and languages, government systems, business practices, educational systems, religions, organizations, and, not least, national cultures. We have already examined, in this book, the many dimensions of culture along which societies differ and that determine how people behave on the job—their attitudes toward work and their superiors, their perspectives on time and scheduling, their level of motivation, and so on. In addition, countries in the EU are fiercely defensive of any incursions on national culture and identity. Given those factors, the prospect of convergence of leadership styles across the EU countries seems dim. On the other hand, argue Kets de Vries and Korotov:

> *Can European organizations afford not to have some form of European leadership? Can an organization remain Belgian, or Polish, or Italian and not include a "toolset" of European capabilities?*[3]

The strategic argument for convergence of leadership styles for EU business executives is that, whereas the Japanese or Americans, for example, can succeed domestically with their predominantly local leadership style, it is not a good option for executives in most EU companies. For them, retaining national styles and processes will not lead to those companies being competitive in the EU and global markets because of the blending of labor, goods, services, and processes across the EU countries. Rather, EU leaders need an EU style that will work across their markets.[4]

With that lofty goal in sight—whether one considers that goal desirable or undesirable—research shows that differences in leadership style still dominate. The DDI survey on leadership asked 200 executives what they liked or disliked about being a leader. It was found that, for example, the French are three times more likely than the British and eight times more likely than the Germans to regard being in a position of power as important.[5] In other words, there are differences in attitude toward being a leader and making decisions. Whereas French leaders liked to make decisions unilaterally, German executives indicated their concern about the responsibility of their decisions; leaders in the United Kingdom, however, seemed less troubled about their decisions.[6]

Research on the German culture, for example, tells us that German leaders most likely will evince high assertiveness and high individualism but low humane orientation.[7] Their primary focus is on structured tasks and performance and less on relationships. Although very organized, based on technical expertise, they have been criticized for lack of innovation as leaders.[8]

The status of leaders in France is known to be based on position and the educational institutions that they attended, known as the *grand écoles*. Title and position are attained through this elite status and thus are paramount over advancement through skills or training. French leadership style is very hierarchical and autocratic. French managers do not typically use a participative leadership style.[9] These conclusions about French leaders are supported by Javidan et al., who found that:

> *To French managers, people in positions of leadership should not be expected to be sensitive or empathetic, or to worry about another's status because such attributes would weaken a leader's resolve and impede decision making. Leaders should make decisions without being distracted by other considerations.*
>
> JAVIDAN, DORFMAN, DE LUQUE, AND HOUSE[10]

We also see a predominantly autocratic style in the United Kingdom. Top positions of leadership are usually attained through the old-boy network as a function of the tripartite class system that still permeates British society (upper-, middle-, and working class). In this respect, leadership is based on traits, not skills, and there tends to be a highly cynical attitude throughout this style.[11]

These brief glimpses of leadership style in three of the EU countries indicate the difficulty, at least for now, of being an EU leader. Clearly, however, any leaders in positions in which they deal with people and processes in several EU countries need to consider the context and cultures where they are operating and try to be flexible with their leadership style.

As the opening profile illustrates, leadership—at any level and in any location—is complicated by the norms and expectations of the people involved and by the local business practices. A successful leader must be an effective motivator, a process that is also culturally contingent. We review the processes of motivating and leading in this chapter, bearing in mind that they are intricately entwined.

Motivating

The Westerners can't understand that we need the fork on our neck, not all these nice words and baby techniques. The Technique is the fork.

RUSSIAN MIDDLE MANAGER[12]

After managers set up a firm's operations by planning strategy, organizing the work and responsibilities, and staffing those operations, they turn their attention to everyday activities. This ongoing behavior of individual people carrying out various daily tasks enables the firm to accomplish its objectives. Getting those people to perform their jobs efficiently and effectively is at the heart of the manager's challenge.

Motivation—and therefore appropriate leadership style—is affected by many powerful variables (societal, cultural, and political). When considering the Japanese culture, for example, as discussed throughout this book, it is not surprising to find that Fujitsu uses some motivational techniques very different from those used in the West, such as when it cut the salaries of around 14,000 managers to motivate them and their subordinates to work harder. Fujitsu management said that if the company met their profit goal for the year the managers might have their full salaries restored. The logic was to build a sense of urgency and team spirit. Japanese workers typically feel a strong kinship to their employers and will work harder if they see their managers making similar sacrifices for the group goals.[13] Clearly, Fujitsu's decision to cut pay is based on the Japanese tradition of sink or swim, coworkers and employer together, and its collectivist culture.

Our objective in this chapter is to consider motivation and leadership in the context of diverse cultural milieus. We need to know what, if any, differences exist in the societal factors that elicit and maintain behaviors leading to high employee productivity and job satisfaction. Are effective motivational and leadership techniques universal or culture based?

CROSS-CULTURAL RESEARCH ON MOTIVATION

Motivation is very much a function of the context of a person's work and personal life. That context is greatly influenced by cultural variables, which affect the attitudes and behaviors of individuals (and groups) on the job. The framework of this context was described in Chapter 3 and illustrated in Exhibit 3-1.

This perspective of the overall context of a person's life on motivation was confirmed by a recent research study by Irem Uz, published in 2015, of the concept of cultural tightness and looseness (CTL) among 68 countries, which found:

[T]raditional societies to be tighter, and industrialized societies to be looser.

JOURNAL OF CROSS-CULTURAL PSYCHOLOGY[14]

A tight culture is one with pervasive norms and practices of sanctioning deviance from norms; people's values, norms, and behavior are similar to one another. People in tight societies preferred to live near those who are similar to them; and they tend to feel better when there is order and predictability in their lives; they tend to be risk-averse. Uz found the five most "tight" countries to be Morocco, Indonesia, Egypt, Bangladesh, and Jordan. Loose cultures, then, are at the opposite end of the range of CTL; the most loose, according to the study were Belgium, Luxembourg, France, Great Britain, and Sweden.[15] Of course, there is a wide range of differences between tight and loose; and, as always, we caution that any such findings do not take account of individual or regional differences. That is, we cannot stereotype, only generalize to show some ideas of how to lead in various environments.

These findings have considerable implications for both motivation and leadership in that managers must recognize the impact of the commonly accepted norms of behavior in a society and how it affects work attitudes and relationships on the job.

Some overlap with Uz's findings can be observed by applying Hofstede's research on the cultural dimensions of individualism—uncertainty avoidance, masculinity, and power distance, for example—which allows us to make some generalized assumptions about motivation such as the following.

- High uncertainty avoidance suggests the need for job security, whereas people with low uncertainty avoidance would probably be motivated by more risky opportunities for variety and fast-track advancement.

- High power distance suggests motivators in the relationship between subordinates and a boss, whereas low power distance implies that people would be more motivated by teamwork and relations with peers.

- High individualism suggests people would be motivated by opportunities for individual advancement and autonomy; collectivism (low individualism) suggests that motivation will more likely work through appeals to group goals and support.

- High masculinity suggests that most people would be more comfortable with the traditional division of work and roles; in a more feminine culture, the boundaries could be looser, motivating people through more flexible roles and work networks.

More recent research, based on Hofstede's dimensions of individualism and masculinity, was conducted by Gelade, Dobson, and Auer. They compared what 50,000 workers in a global pharmaceutical company in 29 nations valued most in their jobs and how that positively affected their company. The results, based on Hofstede's individualism dimension, showed that the higher the level of national individualism (such as is typical in the United States), the more employees valued their autonomy, opportunities for personal achievements, and a work–life balance. This compared with employees in the more collectivistic countries (such as in China and Singapore), who apparently were more motivated when they felt that their jobs fully used their skills and when they felt that the company was providing them with good working conditions, fringe benefits, and training.[16] The findings based on the masculinity dimension were that the higher the level of masculinity (such as in Japan and Mexico), the more motivated employees were when given opportunities for high pay, personal accomplishment, and job advancement. This compared with those from more feminine cultures (such as in Denmark and Sweden), who claimed that factors related to their relationships with their managers and coworkers provided more commitment to the organization. The authors conclude that:

These findings show that the sources of organizational commitment are culturally conditioned and that their effects are predictable from Hofstede's value dimensions.

JOURNAL OF CROSS-CULTURAL PSYCHOLOGY 39[17]

Misjudging the importance of these cultural variables in the workplace may result not only in a failure to motivate but also in demotivation. Rieger and Wong-Rieger present the following example.

In Thailand, the introduction of an individual merit bonus plan, which runs counter to the societal norm of group cooperation, may result in a decline rather than an increase in productivity from employees who refuse to openly compete with each other.[18]

In considering what motivates people, we have to understand their needs, goals, value systems, and expectations. No matter what their nationality or cultural background, people are driven to fulfill needs and achieve goals, but what are those needs, what goals do they want to achieve, and what can motivate that drive to satisfy their goals?

The Meaning of Work

Because the focus in this text is on the needs that affect the working environment, it is important to understand first what work means to people from different backgrounds. For most people, the basic meaning of work is tied to economic necessity (money for food, housing, and so forth) for the individual and for society. However, the additional connotations of work are more subjective, especially about what work provides other than money—achievement, honor, social contacts, and so on.

Another way to view work, however, is through its relationship to the rest of a person's life. The Thais call work *ngan*, which is the same as the Thai word for "play," and they tend to introduce periods of play in their workdays. On the other hand, most people in China, Germany, and the United States have a more serious attitude toward work. Especially in work-oriented China, seven-day workweeks with long hours and few days off are common. A study of average work hours in various countries conducted by Steers found that Koreans worked longer hours and took fewer vacation days than workers in most countries.[19] The conclusion was that the Koreans' hard work was attributable to loyalty to the company, group-oriented achievement, and emphasis on group harmony and business relationships.

Studies on the meaning of work in eight countries were carried out by George England and a group of researchers who are called the Meaning of Work (MOW) International Research Team.[20] Their research sought to determine a person's idea of the relative importance of work compared to that of leisure, community, religion, and family. They called this concept of work **work centrality**, defined as "the degree of general importance that working has in the life of an individual at any given point in time." The results showed, for example, that the Japanese hold work to be very important in their lives; the Brits, on the other hand (in this author's birth country), seem to like their leisure time more than those in the other countries surveyed. However, given the complexity of cultural and economic variables involved in people's attitude toward work, the results are difficult to generalize, in particular as concerns the implications of on-the-job work motivation. More relevant to managers (as an aid to understanding culture-based differences in motivation) are the specific reasons for valuing work. What kinds of needs does the working environment satisfy, and how does that psychological contract differ among populations?

The MOW research team provided some excellent insights into this question when it asked people in the eight countries what they valued about work and what needs their jobs satisfied. Their research results showed the relative order of importance overall as follows.

- A needed income
- Interest and satisfaction
- Contacts with others
- A way to serve society
- A means of keeping occupied
- Status and prestige.[21]

Note the similarities of some of these functions with Maslow's need categories[22] and Herzberg's categories of motivators and maintenance factors. (Frederick Herzberg's research focused on how some people are motivated by internal aspirations and life goals, whereas others are primarily motivated by the job conditions.[23]) Clearly, these studies can help international managers anticipate what attitudes people have toward their work, what aspects of work in their life context are meaningful to them, and therefore what approach the manager should take in setting up motivation and incentive plans.

In addition to the differences among countries within each category—such as the higher level of interest and satisfaction derived from work by the Israelis as compared with the

Germans—it is interesting to note the within-country differences. Although income was the most important factor for all countries, it apparently has a far greater importance than any other factor in Japan. In other countries, such as the Netherlands, the relative importance of different factors was more evenly distributed.

The broader implications of such comparisons about what work means to people are derived from considering the total cultural context. The low rating the Japanese give to the status and prestige found in work, for instance, suggests that those needs are more fully satisfied elsewhere in their lives, such as within the family and community. In the Middle East, religion plays a major role in all aspects of life, including work. The Islamic work ethic is a commitment toward fulfillment, so business motives are held in the highest regard.[24] The origin of the Islamic work ethic is in the Muslim holy book, the Qur'an.

Muslims feel that work is a virtue and an obligation to establish equilibrium in one's individual and social life. The Arab worker is defined by his or her level of commitment to family, and work is perceived as the determining factor in the ability to enjoy social and family life.[25] A study of 117 managers in Saudi Arabia by Ali found that Arab managers are highly committed to the Islamic work ethic and that there is a moderate tendency toward individualism.[26]

Exhibit 11-1 shows the results of the study and gives more insight into the Islamic work ethic. A different study by Kuroda and Suzuki found that Arabs are serious about their work and that favoritism, give and take, and paternalism have no place in the Arab workplace. They contrasted this attitude to that of the Japanese and Americans, who consider friendship to be an integral part of the workplace.[27]

Other variables affect the perceived meaning of work and how it satisfies various needs, such as the relative wealth of a country. When people have a high standard of living, work

EXHIBIT 11-1 The Islamic Work Ethic: Responses by Saudi Arabian Managers

Item*	Mean*
Islamic Work Ethic	
1. Laziness is a vice.	4.66
2. Dedication to work is a virtue.	4.62
3. Good work benefits both one's self and others.	4.57
4. Justice and generosity in the workplace are necessary conditions for society's welfare.	4.59
5. Producing more than enough to meet one's personal needs contributes to the prosperity of society as a whole.	3.71
6. One should carry work out to the best of one's ability.	4.70
7. Work is not an end in itself but a means to foster personal growth and social relations.	3.97
8. Life has no meaning without work.	4.47
9. More leisure time is good for society.	3.08
10. Human relations in organizations should be emphasized and encouraged.	3.89
11. Work enables man to control nature.	4.06
12. Creative work is a source of happiness and accomplishment.	4.60
13. Any man who works is more likely to get ahead in life.	3.92
14. Work gives one the chance to be independent.	4.35
15. A successful man is the one who meets deadlines at work.	4.17
16. One should constantly work hard to meet responsibilities.	4.25
17. The value of work is derived from the accompanying intention rather than its results.	3.16

*On a scale of 1–5 (5 = highest)
Source: Based on Abbas J. Ali, *Journal of Psychology* 126, No. 5 (1992), pp. 507–519.

can take on a meaning different from simply providing the basic economic necessities of life. Economic differences among countries were found to explain variations in attitudes toward work in a study by Furnham et al. of more than 12,000 young people from 41 countries on five continents. Specifically, the researchers found that young people in Far East and Middle Eastern countries reported the highest competitiveness and acquisitiveness for money, whereas those from North America and South America scored highest on work ethics and mastery (that is, continuing to struggle to master something).[28] Such studies show the complexity of the underlying reasons for differences in attitudes toward work—cultural, economic, and so on— which must be taken into account when considering what needs and motivations people bring to the workplace. All in all, research shows a considerable cultural variability affecting how work meets employees' needs.

The Needs Hierarchy in the International Context

How can a manager know what motivates people in a specific country? Certainly, by drawing on the experiences of others who have worked there and by inferring the likely type of motivational structure present by studying what is known about the culture in that region.

People's opinions of how best to satisfy their needs vary across cultures also. One clear conclusion is that managers around the world have similar needs but show differing levels of satisfaction of those needs derived from their jobs. Variables other than culture may be at play, however. One of these variables may be the country's stage of economic development. Whatever the reason, many companies that have started operations in other countries have experienced differences in the apparent needs of the local employees and how they expect work to be recognized. Mazda, of Japan, experienced this problem in its Michigan plant. Japanese firms tend to confer recognition in the form of plaques, attention, and applause, and Japanese workers are likely to be insulted by material incentives because such rewards imply that they would work harder to achieve them than they otherwise would. Instead, Japanese firms focus on group-wide or company-wide goals, compared with the American emphasis on individual goals, achievement, and reward.

When considering the cross-cultural applicability of Maslow's hierarchy of needs theory, then, it is not the needs that are in question as much as the ordering of those needs in the hierarchy. The hierarchy reflects the Western culture, where Maslow conducted his study; he concluded that people progress from satisfying basic needs on to satisfying belongingness and esteem needs, and then to self-actualization needs.[29] However, different hierarchies might better reflect other cultures. For example, Eastern cultures focus more on the needs of society rather than on the needs of individuals. It is difficult to observe or measure the individual needs of a Chinese person because, from childhood, these are meshed with the needs of society. Clearly, however, along with culture, the political beliefs at work in China dominate many facets of motivation. Traditionally, workers have been given exact and detailed prescriptions of what is expected of them as members of a factory, workshop, or work unit. This results in conformity at the expense of creativity. Workers are accountable to their group, which is a powerful motivator. Because being unemployed has not been an option in China until recently, it has been important for employees to maintain themselves as cooperating members of the work group, and this cultural norm still largely prevails in much of China.[30] Money is also a motivator, stemming from the historical political insecurity and economic disasters that have perpetuated the need for a high level of savings.[31]

Although more cross-cultural research on motivation is needed, one can draw the tentative conclusion that managers around the world are motivated more by intrinsic than by extrinsic factors. Considerable doubt remains, however, about the universality of Western theories because it is not possible to take into account all the relevant cultural variables when researching motivation. Different factors have different meanings within the entire cultural context and must be considered on a situation-by-situation basis. The need to consider the entire national and cultural context is shown in the Comparative Management in Focus: Motivation in Mexico feature, which highlights motivational issues for Mexican workers and indicates the meaning of work to them.

Research shows that little conclusive information is available to answer a manager's direct question of exactly how to motivate in any particular culture. The reason is that we cannot

Comparative Management in Focus
Motivation in Mexico

In Mexico, everything is a personal matter, but a lot of managers don't get it. To get anything done here, the manager has to be more of an instructor, teacher, or father figure than a boss.

ROBERT HOSKINS
MANAGER, LEVITON MANUFACTURING, JUAREZ

Latin Americans tend to score high on personal authority and collective or group-related cultural dimensions and values relative to people in the United States or Europe.

DAVILA AND ELVIRA, *JOURNAL OF WORLD BUSINESS*, OCTOBER 2012[32]

To understand the cultural milieu in Mexico, we can draw on research concluding that the Mexican people as a whole rank high on both power distance (the acknowledgment of hierarchical authority) and on uncertainty avoidance (a preference for security and formality over risk). In addition, they rank low on individualism, preferring collectivism, which values the good of the group, family, or country over individual achievement.[33] Recent research by Davila and Elvira concluded that, "This cultural trend has given rise to a 'paternalistic' leadership style in which personal and social relationships are key to working and leading employees effectively."[34]

It is important for managers to recognize that Mexican society is very hierarchical, with a clear power structure for family, religion, business, politics, and other areas of life. People are accorded respect according to their age, sex, and rank or position.[35]

The Mexican culture, generally, is being-oriented, compared to the doing-oriented culture that prevails in the rest of North America; business takes a backseat to socializing.[36] Integral to the being-orientation is the high-context and implicit communication style of most Mexicans; much takes place on the level of nonverbal cues, and the assumption of unspoken communication is based on the personal relationships and trust developed with colleagues. Implicit communication is also based on the importance attached to respect, whereas any conflict would lose face for all concerned.[37] On the other hand, they maintain a small personal space with others and are a "touching" society. They are also frequently very expressive and passionate communicators. In addition, that being-orientation leads to a rather fluid attitude toward time, whereas relationships and commitment to individuals frequently take precedence over scheduled time commitments.[38]

It is said that Mexicans work to live compared to those in the United States, for example, who live to work. One reason for that is that in Mexico the family is of central importance; loyalty and commitment to family and friends frequently determine employment, promotion, or special treatment for contracts. Decisions and actions are usually based on what is good for the family and the group.[39] For many Mexican males, the value of work lies primarily in its ability to fulfill their culturally imposed responsibilities as head of household and breadwinner rather than to seek individual achievement. Machismo (sharp role differentiation based on gender) and prestige are important characteristics of the Mexican culture.

As a people, speaking very generally, Mexicans are very proud and patriotic; *respeto* (respect) is important to them, and a slight against personal dignity is regarded as a grave provocation.[40] Mexican workers expect to be treated in the same respectful manner that they use toward one another. As noted by one U.S. expatriate, foreign managers must adapt to Mexico's "softer culture"; Mexican workers "need more communication, more relationship-building, and more reassurance than employees in the U.S."[41] The Mexican people are very warm and have a leisurely attitude toward time; face-to-face interaction is best for any kind of business, with time allowed for socializing and appreciating the Mexicans' cultural artifacts, buildings, and so forth. Taking time to celebrate a worker's birthday, for instance, will show that you are a *simpático* boss and will increase workers' loyalty and effort. The workers' expectations of small considerations that seem inconsequential to U.S. managers should not be discounted. Personal relationships are of utmost importance to the Mexican people, usually taking priority over work goals. Trust in friends and family takes precedence over purely business relationships, so that networking through personal contacts is the best way to do business. Following are some general guidelines on the Mexican culture to guide foreign managers in Mexico.

- Family and friends are first priority; maintaining those relationships and trust takes precedence over outsiders, thus are important for business success.

- The Mexican employee works to live; scheduling and time management is secondary.

(Continued)

- Mexicans are fatalistic, based on strong religious influence.
- Mexicans are nationalistic; history and tradition are important.
- Work harmony is important; Mexicans are sensitive to conflict situations and need to maintain face.
- Mexicans are very proud; status is evidenced by title, position, and formality in dress and etiquette.

Most managers in Mexico find that the management style that works best there is authoritative and paternal. Paternalism is expected; the manager is regarded as *el patrón* (pronounced "pah-trone"), or the father figure, whose role it is to take care of the workers as an extended family.[42] Employees expect managers to be the authority; they are the elite—power rests with the owner or manager and other prominent community leaders. Frequently, if not told to do something, the workers will not do it, nor will they question the boss or make any decisions for the boss.[43] Nevertheless, employees perceive the manager as a person, not as a concept or a function, and success often depends on the ability of a foreign manager to adopt a personalized management style, such as by greeting all workers as they arrive for their shifts. To be effective, managers need to realize that a psychological contract between the manager and the worker encompasses the work group and the community as a whole. This should include:

- Investment in employees, including salary, benefits, education, training, and development.
- Cooperative efforts in labor relations.
- Community-centered CSR practices.[44]

Generally speaking, many Mexican factory workers doubt their ability to influence the outcome of their lives personally. They are apt to attribute events to the will of God or to luck, timing, or relationships with higher authority figures. For many, decisions are made on the basis of ideals, emotions, and intuition rather than on objective information. However, individualism and materialism are increasingly evident, particularly among the upwardly mobile high-tech and professional Mexican employees.

Corrective discipline and motivation must occur through training examples, cooperation, and, if necessary, subtle shaming. As a disciplinary measure, it is a mistake to insult a Mexican directly; an outright insult implies an insult to the whole family. As a motivation, one must appeal to the pride of the Mexican employees and avoid causing them to feel humiliated. Given that, getting ahead is often associated more with outside forces than with one's own actions; the motivation and reward system becomes difficult to structure in the usual ways.

Past experiences have indicated that, for the most part, motivation through participative decision-making is not as effective as motivation through the more traditional and expected autocratic methods. With careful implementation, however, the mutual respect and caring that the Mexican people have for one another can lead to the positive team spirit needed for the team structure to be used successfully by companies. One example is GM's highest-quality plant in the world in Ramos Arizpe, near Saltillo, Mexico.[45] In a study by Nicholls et al, the Mexican executives surveyed gave some suggestions for implementing work teams. They suggested the following.

- Foster a culture of individual responsibility among team members.
- Anticipate the impact of changes in power distribution.
- Provide leadership from the top throughout the implementation process.
- Provide adequate training to prepare workers for teamwork.
- Develop motivation and harmony through clear expectations.
- Encourage an environment of shared responsibility.[46]

For the most part, Mexican workers expect that authority will not be abused but rather will follow the family model in which everyone works together in a dignified manner according to their designated roles.[47] Any event that may break this harmony, or seems to confront authority, will likely be covered up. This may result in a supervisor hiding defective work, for example, or, as in the case of a steel conveyor plant in Puebla, a total worker walkout rather than using the grievance process.[48] Contributing to these kinds of problems is the need to save face for oneself and to respect others' place and honor. Public criticism is regarded as humiliating. Employees like an atmosphere of formality and respect. They typically use flattery and call people by their titles rather than their names to maintain an atmosphere of regard for status and respect.

The business culture in Mexico is also attributable to prevailing economic conditions in Mexico, which include low levels of education, training, and technical skills. A context of continuing economic problems and a relatively low standard of living for most workers help explain why Maslow's higher-order needs (self-actualization, achievement, status) are generally not very high on most Mexican workers' lists of needs. In discussing compensation, Mariah de Forest, who consults for American firms in Mexico, suggests the following.

Rather than an impersonal wage scale, Mexican workers tend to think in terms of payment now for services rendered now. A daily incentive system with automatic payouts for production exceeding quotas, as well as daily/monthly attendance bonuses, works well.[49]

Global economic problems and cutbacks in auto manufacturing have also affected Mexico, making money a pressing motivational factor for most employees. Benefits that most workers cannot afford are prized. For example, since workers highly value the enjoyment of life, many companies in Mexico provide recreation facilities—a picnic area, a soccer field, and so forth. Bonuses are expected regardless of productivity. In fact, it is the law to give Christmas bonuses of 15 days of pay to each worker. Fringe benefits are also important to Mexicans; because most Mexican workers are poor, the company provides the only source of such benefits for them. In particular, benefits that help to manage family-related issues are positive motivators for employees at least to show up for work. To this end, companies often provide on-site health care facilities for workers and their families, nurseries, free meals, and even small loans in crisis situations.[50] In addition, companies that understand the local infrastructure problems often provide a company bus to minimize the pervasive problems of absenteeism and tardiness.

The foregoing statements are broad generalizations about Mexican factory workers. Increasing numbers of American managers are in Mexico because NAFTA has encouraged more U.S. businesses to move operations there. For firms on U.S. soil, managers may employ many Mexican-Americans in an intercultural setting, and they have become known to be very hard-working people in both business and societal settings. As the second-largest and fastest-growing ethnic group in the United States, Mexican-Americans represent an important subculture requiring management attention as they take an increasing proportion of the jobs there and continue to move up the managerial ladders.

assume the universal applicability of the motivational theories, or even concepts, that have been used to research differences among cultures. Furthermore, the entire motivational context must be taken into account. For example, Western firms entering markets in both Russia and Eastern Europe invariably run into difficulties in motivating their local staffs. Except for the younger generation, most workers have been accustomed to working under entirely different circumstances and usually do not trust foreign managers. Typically, then, the work systems and responsibilities must be highly structured because workers in Eastern Europe and Russia are less likely to use their own judgment in making decisions and because managerial skills are less developed.[51] Russia, for example, while rapidly becoming Westernized in the big cities, still presents foreign managers challenges regarding motivation and leadership styles, as discussed in the accompanying Under the Lens feature.

In sum, motivation is situational, and savvy managers use all they know about the relevant culture or subculture—consulting frequently with local people—to infer the best means of motivating in that context. Furthermore, tactful managers consciously avoid an ethnocentric attitude in which they make assumptions about a person's goals, motivations, or work habits based on their own frames of reference, and they do not make negative value judgments about a person's level of motivation because it differs from their own.

Many cultural variables affect people's sense of what is attainable and thus affect motivation. One example is how much control people believe they have over their environment and their destiny—whether they believe that they can control certain events and not just be at the mercy of external forces. Although people in the United States typically feel a strong internal locus of control, others attribute results to, for example, the will of God (in the case of Muslims) or to the good fortune of being born in the right social class or family (in the case of many Latin Americans). For example, whereas most Westerners feel that hard work will get the job done, many Hong Kong Chinese believe that outcomes are determined by *joss*, or luck. Clearly, then, managers must use persuasive strategies to motivate employees when they do not readily connect their personal work behaviors with outcomes or productivity.

UNDER THE LENS

Managing in Russia—Motivation and Leadership Challenges

A principal rule in the [Russian] workplace is "Superiors know better."

SNEJINA MICHAILOVA[52]

As of this writing in 2015, the business and economic climate in Russia is under considerable pressure because of falling oil prices and Western sanctions following the conflict in the Ukraine, as discussed in Chapter 1 and elsewhere. Although many companies have been holding back on investment there, and a number of them are withdrawing until things settle down, long term, there are always opportunities for foreign investors in Russia because of its vast natural resources, its educated workforce, and a growing middle class of consumers. However, for foreign managers, there are considerable differences and challenges in how best to adapt their styles to motivate and lead employees as well as the company.

A study by Michailova concluded that many Russian employees are still used to the management style that prevailed in a centrally planned economic system. This context resulted in vertically managed hierarchies, one-man authority, and anti-individualism. The continued prevalence of the authoritative, paternalistic leadership style restricts innovation and teamwork. The employees in the study experienced conflict when faced with different managerial styles from their Russian and Western managers in joint venture situations. Those employees were in traditional industries, were on average 45 years old, and were more motivated by the authoritarianism of their Russian managers than the attempts at empowerment by their Western managers. More important, the conflicting motivational techniques left them in a double bind, as shown in Exhibit 11-2 Conflicting Motivational Techniques Western-Russian Joint Ventures.[53]

From his studies of Russian managers, Carl Fey found that, typically, they "simply want employees to carry out designated tasks set by top management rather than to think creatively about those tasks."[54] The employees themselves would say:

You don't understand. Workers work and managers make decisions.[55]

From his interviews and research, Fey makes a number of suggestions for leaders. For example, employees must be given training and information about the company's challenges and goals and the reasons for them. Employees then must be encouraged to share ideas and concerns by providing multiple channels for them to do so without fear of reprisals, and there must be involvement by the managers. Constructive feedback must be given in a timely manner, and a reward system should be set up.[56]

Additional insight can be gleaned from Fey and Stanislav Shekshnia, who have worked and consulted in Russia for 15 years and recently interviewed 36 executives from foreign firms operating in Russia. (Examples are IKEA, Microsoft, SAP, Huawei, Cisco, and Ericsson.) Their paper, based on those interviews, gave a number of recommendations, as discussed in the following paragraph.

EXHIBIT 11-2 Conflicting Motivational Techniques in Western–Russian Joint Ventures

Western Managers to Russian Employees	Russian Managers to Russian Employees
Be independent; have initiative	Stick to the rules and procedures
Learn from mistakes and move on	Mistakes are not allowed and should be punished
Take the long-term perspective	Focus on the present
Be a team member	Stick to your own job and business

Source: Based on S. Michailova, "When Common Sense Becomes Uncommon: Participation and Empowerment in Russian Companies with Western Participation," *Journal of World Business 37* (2002): 180–187.

Foreign managers can provide meaning for employees by practicing authoritative, not authoritarian, leadership. The researchers conclude that Russians are motivated by powerful, charismatic leaders who reflect leaders in their history, so they respect managers they perceive to have the authority of proven competence. The employees expect foreign managers to be more competent than local managers, and if that expectation is met, they are then more motivated.[57] In addition, because of Russia's tradition of limited empowerment of employees and severe punishment for mistakes, Fey and Shekshnia concluded that considerable motivation and success can be achieved by gradually creating an empowered organization. This means that managers should encourage employees to make decisions and allow them to make mistakes without criticism; in this way employees will gradually understand and accept the value of empowerment.[58] Recall that the GLOBE study found that Russian culture was among the least performance oriented and the least future oriented.[59] Since that time, Russia's transitioning society and the influence of more proactive management processes and leadership will, it is hoped, have more positive outcomes for business there. In the past, the owner and manager were usually the same, and little value was placed on management techniques such as motivating. Further, as noted in an interview with Russian entrepreneur Ruben Vardanian, Russian companies have traditionally not considered employees very important—to the extent that there have been no HR people on boards, and no real HR systems in place.[60] Because of the continuing level of uncertainty in Russian society, the main motivation for employees and managers is still often just to work for a large company—and thus to feel secure.

In another study, this one by Puffer and McCarthy in 2011, the authors determined that Russian leaders rely on informal personal networks to conduct business due to the weak legitimacy of the country's formal institutions. Therefore, it is important for Western leaders in Russia to realize that it is informal networks and institutions that drive business and decision making in Russia. Through those networks, people are hired as board members, and contacts with officials are made to speed up the bureaucratic permissions process for business. Foreign leaders are likely to experience a lack of trust by Russians toward them, creating a barrier to communication and therefore to motivation and leadership; they will need to take time to develop relationships and build trust with employees and others in their business and personal interactions while there.[61] In particular, it is essential to develop a network of contacts with people in government agencies at all levels. The Russian word *svyasi* means "connections" and refers to having friends in high places, which is often required to cut through red tape.[62]

The role of culture in the motivational process is shown in Exhibit 11-3. An employee's needs are determined largely by the cultural context of values and attitudes—along with the national variables—in which he or she lives and works. Those needs then determine the meaning of work for that employee. The manager's understanding of what work means in that employee's life can then lead to the design of a culturally appropriate job context and reward system to guide individual and group employee job behavior to meet mutual goals.

Reward Systems

"The rewards must be 100 percent street-level local," says Derek Irvine, Globoforce's vice president, client strategy and consulting. *"Our motto is: 'Think global, thank local.'"*

WORKFORCE MANAGEMENT
SEPTEMBER 2011[63]

EXHIBIT 11-3 The Role of Culture in Job Motivation

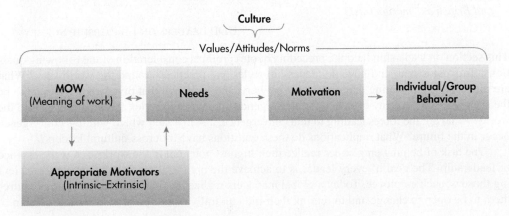

Incentives and rewards are an integral part of motivation in a corporation. Recognizing and understanding different motivational patterns across cultures leads to the design of appropriate reward systems. In the United States, there are common patterns of rewards, varying among levels of the company and types of occupations and based on experience and research with Americans. Rewards usually fall into five categories: financial, social status, job content, career, and professional. The relative emphasis on one or more of these five categories varies from country to country. In Japan, for example, reward systems are based primarily on seniority, and much emphasis is put on the bonus system. In addition, a distinction is made there between the regular workforce and the temporary workforce, which traditionally comprises women expected to leave when they start a family. As is usually the case, the regular workforce receives considerably more rewards than the temporary workforce in pay and benefits and the allocation of interesting jobs.[64] For the regular workforce, the emphasis is on the employee's long-term effectiveness in terms of behavior, personality, and group output. Rewarding the individual is frowned on in Japan because it encourages competition rather than the desired group cooperation. Therefore, specific cash incentives are usually limited. In Taiwan, recognition and affection are important; company departments compete for praise from top management at their annual celebration. O. C. Tanner, a consultant firm on such matters, found in its research, for example, that:

> [C]locks or watches, popular gifts in the U.S. for employees celebrating a workplace anniversary, are taboo in Asian countries because timepieces are reminders of mortality. In France, O. C. Tanner learned that workers tend to scoff at effusive gratitude and view thank you notes with skepticism.

WORKFORCE MANAGEMENT
SEPTEMBER 2011[65]

In contrast, the entire reward system in China is very different from that of most countries. The low wage rates are compensated for by free housing, schools, and medical care. Although egalitarianism still seems to prevail, the recent free-enterprise reform movements have encouraged *duo lao, duo de* (more work, more pay). One important incentive is training, which gives workers more power. One approach used in the past—and one that seems quite negative to Americans—is best illustrated by the example of a plaque award labeled "Ms. Wong—Employee of the Month." Although Westerners would assume that Ms. Wong had excelled as an employee, actually this award given in a Chinese retail store was for the worst employee; the plaque was designed to shame and embarrass her.[66] Younger Chinese in areas changing to a more market-based economy have seen a shift toward equity-based rewards, most likely resulting from a gradual shift in work values.[67]

No doubt culture plays a significant role in determining the appropriate incentive and reward systems around the world. Employees in collectivist cultures such as Japan, Korea, and Taiwan would not respond well to the typical U.S. merit-based reward system to motivate employees because that would go against the traditional value system and would disrupt the harmony and corporate culture.

Leading

Research results label French captains of industry as "autocrats," Germans as "democrats," and British as "meritocrats."

DDI, LEADERS ON LEADERSHIP SURVEY[68]

This section on leadership (and the preceding quote) prompts consideration of the following questions: To what extent, and how, do leadership styles and practices around the world vary? What are the forces perpetuating that divergence? Where, and why, will that divergence continue to be the strongest? Is there any evidence for convergence of leadership styles and practices around the world? What are the forces leading to that convergence, and how and where will this convergence occur in the future? What implications do these questions have for cross-cultural leaders?

The task of helping employees realize their highest potential in the workplace is the essence of leadership. The goal of every leader is to achieve the organization's objectives while achieving those of each employee. Today's global managers realize that increased competition requires them to be open to change and to rethink their old culturally conditioned modes of leadership.

THE GLOBAL LEADER'S ROLE AND ENVIRONMENT

"I don't want to change Sony's culture to the point that it's unrecognizable from the founder's vision," he observed. "That's the balancing act." He thought for a moment and then concluded, "You can't go through a Japanese company with a sledgehammer."

HOWARD STRINGER
CEO SONY CORPORATION, QUOTED IN ORGANIZATIONAL DYNAMICS, *2011*[69]

The greatest competitive advantage global companies in the twenty-first century can have is effective global leaders. Yet this competitive challenge is not easy to meet, as observed by the astute British-born leader Howard Stringer when asked to take over as CEO of Tokyo-based Sony Corporation and revitalize its competitive position. People tend to rise to leadership positions by proving themselves able to lead in their home-country corporate culture and meeting the generally accepted behaviors of that national culture. However, global leaders must broaden their horizons, both strategically and cross-culturally, and develop a more flexible model of leadership that can be applied anywhere—one that is adaptable to locational situations around the world.[70]

In a survey of 197 global HR executives, Thomas et al. found that those executives "believe that tomorrow's leaders will need to be more diverse than today's—especially in terms of thought styles and work experiences."[71] The study highlighted the need for global experience, industry experience, and thought styles.

The critical factors necessary for successful leadership abroad have come to be known as the global mind-set. Typically, that mind-set compares with the traditional mind-set in the areas of general perspective, organizational life, work style, view of change, and learning.[72] Harvard Business School authors Javidan et al. describe a leader with a global mind-set as having three major qualities.

- "Intellectual capital: the general knowledge and capacity to learn, including global business savvy

- Psychological capital: the openness to differences and capacity to change, such as a thirst for adventure

- Social capital: the ability to build trusting relationships with and among people who are different from you, including intercultural empathy and diplomacy"[73]

Other researchers describe the attributes in terms of the manager's personal work style and general perspective; they articulate some of the typical actions and attitudes of a leader with a global mind-set as shown in Exhibit 11-4.

EXHIBIT 11-4 **The Global Mind-set of Successful Leaders**

Personal work style	High "cultural quotient" (CQ)
	Open-minded and flexible
	Effective cross-cultural communicator and collaborator
	Team player in a global matrix
	Supports global objectives and balances global with local goals and practices
General perspective	Broad, systems perspective
	Personal autonomy and emotional resilience
	Change is welcomed and facilitated
	Enables boundaryless organizations
	Operates easily in cross-cultural and cross-functional environments
	Global learning is sought and used for career development

Source: Based on Walker et al., 2003; and Gary P. Ferraro, *The Cultural Dimension of International Business,* 5th ed. (Upper Saddle River, NJ: Prentice Hall, 2006).

One successful leader with a global mind-set is Carlos Ghosn, a French businessman and CEO of Nissan and Renault as well as the chairman and CEO of the Nissan–Renault alliance. He was born in Brazil of Lebanese parents and educated in France. While at Renault, he was sent to Japan to turn around the ailing auto company, Nissan, which he did very successfully, surprising everyone that he could work so well within the intricate culture of Japanese business. Ghosn was voted Man of the Year 2003 by *Fortune* magazine's Asian edition; he also sits on the boards of Alcoa, Sony, and IBM. This global leader and multicultural manager conveyed his high cultural quotient (CQ) when interviewed by *Newsweek*.

> *Companies are going global, but the teams are divided and scattered all over the planet....You have to know how to motivate people who think very differently than you, who have different kinds of sensitivities, so I think the most important message is to get prepared to deal with teams who are multicultural.*[74]

Morrison, Gregersen, and Black found further information regarding leadership effectiveness abroad; their research involved 125 global leaders in 50 companies. They concluded that effective leaders must have global business and organizational savvy. They explain global business savvy as the ability to recognize global market opportunities for a company and having a vision of doing business worldwide. Global organizational savvy requires an intimate knowledge of a company's resources and capabilities to capture global markets as well as an understanding of each subsidiary's product lines and how the people and business operate on the local level. Morrison et al outline four personal development strategies through which companies and managers can meet these requirements of effective global leadership: travel, teamwork, training, and transfers (the four Ts).[75]

Travel, of course, exposes managers to various cultures, economies, political systems, and markets. Working on global teams teaches managers to operate on an interpersonal level while dealing with business decision-making processes that are embraced by differences in cultural norms and business models. Although formal training seminars also play an important role, most of the global leaders interviewed said that the most influential developmental experience in their lives was the international assignment. Increasingly, global companies are requiring their managers who will progress to top management positions to have overseas assignment experience. The benefits accruing to the organization depend on how effectively the assignment and repatriation are handled, as discussed in Chapter 10. Many top leaders in the world, for example, have had their start with both a homegrown training and an international assignment, which provided them with considerable skills to operate in the global marketplace, as illustrated in the accompanying Under the Lens: Interview, Yoshiaki Fujimori: Lixil Builds a New Style of Japanese Multinational feature.

Effective global leadership involves the ability to inspire and influence the thinking, attitudes, and behavior of people anywhere in the world. The importance of the leadership role cannot be overemphasized, because the leader's interactions strongly influence the motivation and behavior of employees and, ultimately, the entire climate of the organization. The cumulative effects of one or more weak managers can have a significant negative impact on the ability of the organization to meet its objectives.

Managers on international assignments try to maximize leadership effectiveness by juggling several important, and sometimes conflicting, roles as (1) a representative of the parent firm, (2) the manager of the local firm, (3) a resident of the local community, (4) a citizen of either the host country or of another country, (5) a member of a profession, and (6) a member of a family.[76]

The leader's role comprises the interaction of two sets of variables—the content and the context of leadership. The content of leadership comprises the attributes of the leader and the decisions to be made; the context of leadership comprises all those variables related to the particular situation.[77] The increased number of variables (political, economic, and cultural) in the context of the managerial job abroad requires astute leadership. Some examples of the variables in the content and context of the leader's role in foreign settings are given below.[78] The multicultural leader's role thus blends leadership, communication, motivational, and other managerial skills within unique and ever-changing environments. We will examine the contingent nature of such leadership throughout this section.

UNDER THE LENS

Interview: Yoshiaki Fujimori: Lixil Builds a New Style of Japanese Multinational

Robin Harding and Kana Inagaki - Tokyo FT.com April 22, 2015

Merged construction products group defies predictions of a disastrous clash of cultures.

What do you get when you take five proud but domestic Japanese companies, merge them, and then add four large foreign acquisitions in the space of a few years?

You might expect an almighty mess. The actual result is Lixil, one of the world's largest makers of building products, and an unprecedented attempt to forge a Japanese multinational out of a declining domestic industry.

The outcome of the experiment is unclear - with operating margins of just 4 per cent last year, Lixil has a long way to go - but under chief executive Yoshiaki Fujimori the group has defied predictions of a disastrous clash of cultures.

"I think we are extremely far ahead from the original state," says Mr. Fujimori. Of the ten board directors, he says, four are non-Japanese and only one is a survivor from the pre-merger days.

But he says there is further to go, that Lixil is still an internationalized Japanese company and not yet truly global. "It's still the mind of the people. The Germans are still German, the Japanese are still Japanese, the Americans are still American—we're trying to create one global company," he says.

The original companies were Tostem, which made building materials; Inax, a plumbing specialist; Toyo Exterior, a seller of carports and conservatories; Shin Nikkei, a provider of interior fittings; and Sun Wave, which made kitchens. All traditional Japanese operations, they agreed to combine in 2011 in pursuit of survival as their market declines.

That merger was followed by an overseas acquisition spree including American Standard Brands bathroom products for $342m; Permasteelisa, the Italian group that made the façades for London's Shard, for €573m; and largest of all, Grohe, a German bathroom products group, for €3.06 billion. The deals have boosted sales by 34 percent to $13.5 billion.

Mr. Fujimori, an executive at General Electric in Asia and the United States for 25 years, is an unusual leader for any Japanese company: blunt, forceful and not afraid of a little trash-talking. He says that further acquisitions in plumbing or exteriors would be add-ons in emerging markets; but Lixil's kitchen segment still needs to move into global markets.

"We've acquired the top three big ones already - there's none left. If Toto wants to sell to us, we'll buy," says Mr. Fujimori. His minder winces: Toto is Lixil's main competitor in Japan, so while it is a joke, it is a joke with an edge.

Hiroki Kawashima, SMBC Nikko Securities analyst, likens Lixil to a "mini-SoftBank" for its acquisitive nature, but he says the real test is to come: "Mr. Fujimori can add the firms together, but creating synergy is another matter. Remember that the original Tostem-Inax merger [in 2001] took a decade to bear fruit."

Mr. Fujimori is not daunted by the challenge. He is outspoken about the need for corporate Japan to change and calls on his fellow chief executive officers to "be gutsy".

"The risk of doing nothing is the highest. It's the highest crime. So don't be afraid, don't be afraid of change," he says. Many Japanese leaders bemoan the conservatism of their staff, he says, but Mr. Fujimori urges them to look in the mirror before telling employees to change: "In my heart - you've got to be that before you tell your people."

One of the big problems for Lixil is growth and profits at home. With Japan's population falling the market for new housing is in decline. Its annual net profit for the year through March is tipped to have fallen as much as 45 percent due to weak domestic demand, and analysts are calling for more job cuts.

The answer, says Mr. Fujimori, is refurbishment - which he predicts will grow because of ageing, energy policy and the threat of earthquakes.

As people get older, they "don't want to build new homes, they want to live where they are", but many will require elderly-friendly adaptations. The shutdown of nuclear power after the Fukushima disaster, meanwhile, requires a renewed focus on energy efficiency.

"Japan is probably the only country where you're allowed to build with single glazing. We have not been so energy conscious in terms of how you build houses," says Mr. Fujimori.

He attacks the government's feed-in tariff for renewable energy as a "horrible" policy and says there should be mandates for homes to generate their own energy instead.

Most of all, though, Mr. Fujimori is calling for Japan to change its ways, moving past the "internationalization" of exports and foreign subsidiaries and creating truly global companies.

"We will fail most of the time if we stick to Japanese management and stick to the Japanese way," he says.

"If we don't accept diversity, don't value diversity and don't utilize global intellectual capital - then we'll fail."

The Leader and the Job[79]

- Leadership experience and technical knowledge
- Cultural adaptability
- Clarity of information available in host area
- Level of authority and autonomy
- Level of cooperation among partners, government, and employees

The Job Context

- Level of authority granted to leader
- Physical location and local resource availability
- Host professional contacts and community relations
- Organizational structure, scope of internationalization, technology, and so on
- Business environment. social-cultural, political-economic, level of risk
- Systems of staffing, coordination, reward system and decision making, locally and in home office

Women in Global Leadership Roles

As we consider the variables of the leader, the job, and the job context in the international arena, and the fact that women in leadership positions around the world encounter specific sets of these variables, it is useful to gain some insight into their particular sets of circumstances and challenges, as illustrated in the following Under the Lens section.

Global Team Leadership

As discussed in previous chapters, global teams have become common means of organizing management projects and ongoing operations around the world. Their complexity is evident because the teams comprise people from several countries, various cultures, and probably different languages; add to that multicultural cauldron the usual virtual communication mode, and the leadership challenge is considerable without the personal contact and individual contexts that typically give the leader clues and cement relationships. Studies have concluded that to be effective in such a multicultural mix, teams should be composed of managers willing both to lead and to follow, to have open discussion and decision making; that is to use a team model of shared leadership in which the leadership role can be fluid and flexible as it passes from one to another according to the team goals.[80] A study by Lisak and Erez concluded that "individuals who scored high on the three global characteristics—of cultural intelligence, global identity, and openness to cultural diversity—were significantly more likely to emerge as leaders than were other team members."[81] They recommend that the selection of team members and leaders take particular account of the specific global work culture in which the teams will need to operate to succeed; therefore selection of leaders should:

> [F]ocus on building the norms and values in their multicultural teams that will be shared by all culturally diverse team members to facilitate their adaptation in the global work context.[82]
>
> JOURNAL OF WORLD BUSINESS 50 (2015), pp. 3–14

The Role of Technology in Leadership

Globalization and technology have been and continue to be the two great drivers of change in the content and context of leaders' jobs at all levels. Although some say that the pace of globalization is slowing down, as discussed in Chapter 1 there is no doubt that all agree that the pace of technological change continues to accelerate, and thus affects leadership.

> The Internet of Things—the computers and other inanimate objects that communicate with each other and with people through mobile technologies, sensors, and software—challenges every business model in every industry everywhere.
>
> BCG.COM PERSPECTIVES, APRIL 8, 2015.[83]

UNDER THE LENS
Women in Business Leadership

CLARITY AND COURAGE ARE VITAL ON THE GLASS CLIFF

"Leadership: Women who make it to the top can find themselves very isolated," writes Charlotte Clarke.

Sushma Rajagopalan was working in the United States when she was offered the opportunity to become the first female chief executive of ITC Infotech in Bangalore, India. She did not hesitate. It meant a long-distance relationship with her husband, but she wanted a leadership role. "I'm also the first chief executive from outside the

Indra Nooyi (center), Chairman and Ceo Pepsico

group," she says, adding that her brief at the IT services company, since joining in August 2014, is to turn it into a multibillion-dollar enterprise.

In recent years, there has been a proliferation of headlines beginning, "The first woman to…" Last year alone, stories along these lines featured Tsakani Ratsela as South Africa's first deputy auditor-general, Paula Schneider as the first to take control of U.S. retailer American Apparel, and Patrice Merrin as the first woman director of Glencore, which was the last FTSE 100 company to have an all-male board.

Furthermore, Jean-Claude Juncker, president of the European Commission, promised high-profile roles to women once he was appointed, and he promptly made Sweden's Cecilia Malmstrom trade commissioner and appointed Margrethe Vestager, from Denmark, competition commissioner.

But the benefit of these leadership roles to women is open to debate. For many, each milestone is a step towards gender equality and something to celebrate. Some argue it provides evidence that women are better crisis managers. Others, however, see cause for concern.

Jean Stephens, chief of RSM International, a professional services firm, says, "Women have natural skills of collaboration and consensus building that could fit into the corporate environment in times of difficulty."As RSM's first female chief executive, Ms. Stephens mentors women worldwide. "The role of women in senior positions is evolving," she says. "In every country, the journey is the same. In China, for example, women are at the table, making decisions."

One high-profile woman is Ana Botin. She became head of Banco Santander within 24 hours of her father's death and inside two months had engineered a decisive change of leadership, promoting the finance director to chief executive.

Alex Haslam, by contrast, a professor who with a colleague coined the term "glass cliff" to describe the precariousness of women currently being given roles at the top, believes it could amount to a form of gender discrimination. "The first wave [of gender discrimination] was about quantity. The second wave is about quality," he says. Initially, women were not getting any leadership positions at all; now they are, but "it is not the cushy jobs that are plain sailing, they are [subject to] a lot of pressure, stress, and criticism." Their tenure, he adds, also tends to be briefer than for men, and he cites a 2005 study that suggests male chief executives in the United States hold their jobs for approximately twice as long as their female counterparts.

One leader currently under significant pressure is Elvira Nabiullina, Russia's central bank governor. While trying to facilitate growth in an economy badly hurt by geopolitical tension and a sliding oil price, she is faced with criticism from all directions. The fact that Ms. Nabiullina and others are able to ride out this pressure is beside the point, says Professor Haslam. They should not be put under such pressure to begin with.

Mireia Gine, professor of financial management at IESE Business School in Spain, agrees with this view. "When we talk about women who reach the top, this is a subsample that may not share the characteristics of the general population," she says.

(Continued)

It is true that women at the top are still very isolated. According to a report by the World Economic Forum, there are only 26 female chief executives in this year's *Fortune* 500 companies and only 54 in the top 1,000.

Allyson Zimmermann, executive director of Catalyst Europe, a nonprofit group, says the best way forward—now that opportunities for women leaders are increasing—is talent management. "If not managed well, diversity can be a disaster," says Ms. Zimmermann. "Tokenism doesn't work [and] you can't blame it for failure." She points to research produced by her organisation that reveals a positive return on equity occurs when boards consist of about 30 percent women. "This is when critical mass is achieved."

Ms. Rajagopalan is even more direct. She recommends four things to every leader: "clarity of thought, courage to act, charisma to influence, and character—always."

Source: Charlotte Clarke, *Financial Times* [London (UK)] March 5, 2015, p. 4.

© 2015 The Financial Times Limited

Clearly, the leader's role at all levels is rapidly changing along with each new technological development. Affecting leaders' plans and decisions, for example, is the Internet of Things, permitting computer-to-computer instructions and decisions, often controlling a complex global supply chain; the use of robotics in manufacturing, health care, engineering, and so on; and firms' intranets, which permit knowledge sharing and product information throughout global operations. It is clear that big data analytics (cloud-based intelligence for businesses to collect and analyze large amounts of data) is here to stay and bring considerable benefits to firms' managers. There is no turning back, and for all leaders, "new technologies will force you to reconfigure your strategy, your operations, and your whole approach to business."[84]

Individual managers are realizing that the Internet is changing their leadership styles and interactions with employees as well as their strategic leadership of their organizations. They have to adapt to the hyperspeed environment of e-business as well as to the need for visionary leadership in a whole new set of competitive industry dynamics. Some of these new-age leadership issues are discussed in the following feature, Management in Action: Leadership in a Digital World.

CROSS-CULTURAL RESEARCH ON LEADERSHIP

Numerous leadership theories focus in various ways on individual traits, leader behavior, interaction patterns, role relationships, follower perceptions, influence over followers, influence on task goals, and influence on organizational culture.[85] Here it is important to understand how the variable of societal culture fits into these theories and what implications can be drawn for international managers as they seek to provide leadership around the world. Although leadership is a universal phenomenon, what makes effective leadership varies across cultures.

In addition to research studies that indicate variations in leadership profiles, the generally accepted image that people in different countries have about what they expect and admire in their leaders tends to become a norm over time, forming an idealized role for these leaders. Industry leaders in France and Italy, for example, are highly regarded for their social prominence and political power. In Latin American countries, leaders are respected as total persons and leaders in society, and appreciation for the arts is important. In Germany, polish, decisiveness, and a wide general knowledge are respected, with their leaders granted a lot of formality by everyone. Foreigners are often surprised at the informal off-the-job lifestyles of executives in the United States and would be surprised to see them pushing a lawn mower, for example.

Most research on U.S. leadership styles describes managerial behaviors on, essentially, the same dimensions, variously termed *autocratic* versus *democratic, participative* versus *directive, relations-oriented* versus *task-oriented,* or *initiating structure* versus *consideration continuum.*[86] These studies were developed in the West, and conclusions regarding employee responses largely reflect the opinions of U.S. workers. The democratic, or participative, leadership style has been recommended as the one more likely to have positive results with most U.S. employees.

MANAGEMENT IN ACTION
Leadership in a Digital World

What does leadership mean in a digital world in which organizations are flexible and fluid and the pace of change is extremely rapid? What's it like to lead in an e-business organization? Jomei Chang of Vitria Technology describes it as follows: "There's no place to hide. [The Internet] forces you to be on your toes every minute, every second." Is leadership in e-businesses really all that different from traditional organizations? Managers who've worked in both think it is. How? Three differences seem to be most evident: the speed at which decisions must be made, the importance of being flexible, and the need to create a vision of the future.

Making Decisions Fast

Managers in all organizations never have all the data they want when making decisions, but the problem is multiplied in e-business. The situation is changing rapidly and the competition is intense. For example, Meg Whitman, then-president and CEO of eBay, said, "We're growing at 40 percent to 50 percent per quarter. That pace absolutely changes the leadership challenge. Every three months we become a different company. In one year, we went from 30 employees to 140, and from 100,000 registered users to 2.2 million. At Hasbro [where she was previously an executive], we would set a yearlong strategy, and then we would simply execute against it. At eBay, we constantly revisit the strategy—and revise the tactics."

Leaders in e-businesses see themselves as sprinters and their contemporaries in traditional businesses as long-distance runners. They frequently use the term "Internet time," which is a reference to a rapidly speeded-up working environment. "Every [e-business] leader today has to unlearn one lesson that was drilled into each one of them: You gather data so that you can make considered decisions. You can't do that on Internet time."

Maintaining Flexibility

In addition to speed, leaders in e-businesses need to be highly flexible. They have to be able to roll with the ups and downs. They need to be able to redirect their group or organization when they find that something doesn't work. They have to encourage experimentation. This is what Mark Cuban, president and co-founder of Broadcast.com, had to say about the importance of being flexible. "When we started, we thought advertising would be the core of our business. We were wrong. We thought that the way to define our network was to distribute servers all over the country. We were wrong. We've had to recalibrate again and again—and we'll have to keep doing it in the future."

Focusing on the Vision

Although visionary leadership is important in every organization, in a hyperspeed environment, people require more from their leaders. The rules, policies, and regulations that characterize more traditional organizations provide direction and reduce uncertainty for employees. Such formalized guidelines typically don't exist in e-businesses, and it becomes the responsibility of the leaders to provide direction through their vision. For instance, David Pottruck, co-CEO of Charles Schwab, gathered nearly 100 of the company's senior managers at the southern end of the Golden Gate Bridge. He handed each a jacket inscribed with the phrase "Crossing the Chasm" and led them across the bridge in a symbolic march to kick off his plan to turn Schwab into a full-fledged Internet brokerage. Getting people to buy into the vision may require even more radical actions. For instance, when Isao Okawa, chairman of Sega Enterprises, decided to remake his company into an e-business, his management team resisted—that is, until he defied Japan's consensus-charged, lifetime-employment culture by announcing that those who resisted the change would be fired, risking shame. Not so amazingly, resistance to the change vanished overnight.

Source: S. P. Robbins and M. Coulter, Management, 7th ed. (Upper Saddle River, NJ: Prentice Hall, 2001), used with permission.

CONTINGENCY LEADERSHIP: THE CULTURE VARIABLE

Modern leadership theory recognizes that no single leadership style works well in all situations.[87] A considerable amount of research, directly or indirectly, supports the notion of cultural contingency in leadership. This means that, as a result of culture-based norms and beliefs about how people in various roles should behave, what is expected of leaders, what influence they have, and what kind of status they are given vary from nation to nation. Clearly, this has implications for what kind of leadership style a manager should expect to adopt when going abroad.

The GLOBE Project

Research by the Global Leadership and Organizational Behavior Effectiveness (GLOBE) research program comprised a network of 170 social scientists and management scholars from 62 countries for the purpose of understanding the impact of cultural variables on leadership and organizational processes. Using both quantitative and qualitative methodologies to collect data from 18,000 managers in those countries, representing the majority of the world's population, the researchers wanted to find out which leadership behaviors are universally accepted and which are culturally contingent. Not unexpectedly, they found that the positive leadership behaviors generally accepted anywhere are behaviors such as being trustworthy, encouraging, an effective bargainer, a skilled administrator and communicator, and a team builder; the negatively regarded traits included being uncooperative, egocentric, ruthless, and dictatorial.[88] Leadership styles and behaviors found to be culturally contingent are charismatic, team-oriented, self-protective, participative, humane, and autonomous.

The results for some of the countries researched are shown in Exhibit 11-5. The first column *(N)* is the sample size within that country. The scores for each country on those leadership

EXHIBIT 11-5 Culturally Contingent Beliefs Regarding Effective Leadership Styles

Country	N	Charisma	Team	Self-Protective	Participative	Humane	Autonomous
Australia	345	6.09	5.81	3.05	5.71	5.09	3.95
Brazil	264	6.01	6.17	3.50	6.06	4.84	2.27
Canada (English-speaking)	257	6.16	5.84	2.96	6.09	5.20	3.65
China	160	5.57	5.57	3.80	5.05	5.18	4.07
Denmark	327	6.01	5.70	2.82	5.80	4.23	3.79
Egypt	201	5.57	5.55	4.21	4.69	5.14	4.49
England	168	6.01	5.71	3.04	5.57	4.90	3.92
Greece	234	6.02	6.12	3.49	5.81	5.16	3.98
India	231	5.85	5.72	3.78	4.99	5.26	3.85
Ireland	157	6.08	5.82	3.01	5.64	5.06	3.95
Israel	543	6.23	5.91	3.64	4.96	4.68	4.26
Japan	197	5.49	5.56	3.61	5.08	4.68	3.67
Mexico	327	5.66	5.75	3.86	4.64	4.71	3.86
Nigeria	419	5.77	5.65	3.90	5.19	5.48	3.62
Philippines	287	6.33	6.06	3.33	5.40	5.53	3.75
Poland	283	5.67	5.98	3.53	5.05	4.56	4.34
Russia	301	5.66	5.63	3.69	4.67	4.08	4.63
Singapore	224	5.95	5.77	3.32	5.30	5.24	3.87
South Korea	233	5.53	5.53	3.68	4.93	4.87	4.21
Spain	370	5.90	5.93	3.39	5.11	4.66	3.54
Sweden	1,790	5.84	5.75	2.82	5.54	4.73	3.97
Thailand	449	5.78	5.76	3.91	5.30	5.09	4.28
Turkey	301	5.96	6.01	3.58	5.09	4.90	3.83
USA	399	6.12	5.80	3.16	5.93	5.21	3.75

Note: Scale 1 to 7 in order of how important those behaviors are considered for effective leadership (7 = highest).
Source: Based on selected data from Den Hartog, R. House et al. (GLOBE Project) *Leadership Quarterly* 10, No. 2 (1999).

dimensions are based on a scale from 1 (the opinion that those leadership behaviors would not be regarded favorably) to 7 (that those behaviors would substantially facilitate effective leadership). Note that reading from top to bottom on a single dimension allows comparison among those countries on that dimension. For example, being a participative leader is regarded as more important in Canada, Brazil, and Austria than it is in Egypt, Hong Kong, Indonesia, and Mexico. In addition, reading from left to right for a particular country on all dimensions allows development of an effective leadership style profile for that country. In Brazil, for example, one can conclude that an effective leader is expected to be very charismatic, team-oriented and participative, and relatively humane but not autonomous.

The charismatic leader shown in this research is someone who is, for example, a visionary, an inspiration to subordinates, and performance-oriented. A team-oriented leader is someone who exhibits diplomatic, integrative, and collaborative behaviors toward the team. The self-protective dimension describes a leader who is self-centered, conflictual, and status conscious. The participative leader is one who delegates decision making and encourages subordinates to take responsibility. Humane leaders are those who are compassionate to their employees. An autonomous leader is, as expected, an individualist, so countries that ranked participation as important tended to rank autonomy in leadership as relatively unimportant. In Egypt, participation and autonomy were ranked about equally.[89]

This broad, path-breaking research by the GLOBE researchers can be very helpful to managers going abroad, enabling them to exercise culturally appropriate leadership styles. In another stage of this ongoing research project, interviews with managers from various countries led the researchers, headed by Robert House, to conclude that the status and influence of leaders vary a great deal across countries or regions according to the prevailing cultural forces. Whereas Americans, Arabs, Asians, the English, Eastern Europeans, the French, Germans, Latin Americans, and Russians tend to glorify leaders in both the political and organizational arenas, those in the Netherlands, Scandinavia, and Germanic Switzerland have very different views of leadership.[90] Following are some sample comments made by managers from various countries.

- Americans appreciate two kinds of leaders. They seek empowerment from leaders who grant autonomy and delegate authority to subordinates. They also respect the bold, forceful, confident, and risk-taking leader, as personified by John Wayne in his movies.

- The Dutch place emphasis on egalitarianism and are skeptical about the value of leadership. Terms like *leader* and *manager* carry a stigma. If a father is employed as a manager, Dutch children will not admit it to their schoolmates.

- Arabs worship their leaders—as long as they are in power!

- Iranians seek power and strength in their leaders.

- Malaysians expect their leaders to behave in a manner that is humble, modest, and dignified.

- The French expect leaders to be cultivated—highly educated in the arts and in mathematics.[91]

Subsequently, further conclusions were drawn from the GLOBE results by Javidan et al. about which leadership variables are found to be universally effective, about universal impediments to effectiveness, and culturally contingent attributes. Their findings are listed in Exhibit 11-6, with the corresponding GLOBE dimension in parentheses.

In phase three of their follow-up research, the GLOBE team surveyed and interviewed 1060 CEOs and surveyed their more than 5,000 direct reports in 24 countries. Among their many and groundbreaking results, we highlight the one that the team concluded, that:

Leaders who behave according to expectations are effective.
THE GLOBE TEAM, JOURNAL OF WORLD BUSINESS 47 (2012), PP. 504–518.[92]

In other words, if the leadership style meets the expectations of those reporting to him or her, there is acceptance and an effective balance for success in meeting goals. The most effective leaders are those who do not violate cultural norms.[93] We can interpret this finding as confirming other research described here that cross-cultural, cross-border leadership style needs to blend with the norms, values, and expectations of the host people and institution to be successful.

EXHIBIT 11-6 Cultural Views of Leadership Effectiveness

Behaviors and Traits Universally Considered Facilitators of Leadership Effectiveness

- Trustworthiness (integrity)
- Visionary (charismatic-visionary)
- Inspirational and motivating (charismatic-inspirational)
- Communicative (team builder)

Behaviors and Traits Universally Considered Impediments to Leadership Effectiveness

- Being a loner and asocial (self-protective)
- Non-cooperative (malevolent)
- Dictatorial (autocratic)

Culturally Contingent Endorsement of Leader Attributes

- Individualistic (autonomous)
- Status-conscious (status-conscious)
- Risk-taking (charismatic: self-sacrificial)

Source: Based on Mansour Javidan, Peter W. Dorfman, Mary Sully de Luque, and Robert J. House, "In the Eye of the Beholder: Cross Cultural Lessons in Leadership from Project GLOBE," *Academy of Management Perspectives* 20, No. 1 (2006), p. 75.

Earlier Leadership Research

Other research also provides insight on the relative level of preference for autocratic versus participative leadership styles. For example, Hofstede's four cultural dimensions (discussed in Chapter 3) provide a good starting point to study leader–subordinate expectations and relationships. We can assume, for example, that employees in countries that rank high on power distance (i.e., India, Mexico, the Philippines) are more likely to prefer an autocratic leadership style and some paternalism because they are more comfortable with a clear distinction between managers and subordinates than with a blurring of decision-making responsibility.

Employees in countries that rank low on power distance (Sweden and Israel) are more likely to prefer a consultative, participative leadership style, and they expect superiors to adhere to that style. Hofstede, in fact, concludes that participative management approaches recommended by many American researchers can be counterproductive in certain cultures.[94] The crucial fact to grasp about leadership in any culture, he points out, is that it is a complement to subordinateship (employee attitudes toward leaders). In other words, perhaps we concentrate too much on leaders and their unlikely ability to change styles at will. Much depends on subordinates and their cultural conditioning, and it is that subordinateship to which the leader must respond.[95] Hofstede points out that his research reflects the values of subordinates, not the values of superiors.

In another part of his research, Hofstede ranked the relative presence of autocratic norms in the following countries, from lowest to highest: Germany, France, Belgium, Japan, Italy, the United States, the Netherlands, Britain, and India. India ranked much higher than the others on autocracy.[96]

In the Middle East, in particular, little delegation occurs. A successful company there must have strong managers who make all the decisions and who go unquestioned. Much emphasis is placed on the use of power through social contacts and family influence, and the chain of command must be rigidly followed.[97]

Exhibit 11-7 depicts an integrative model of the leadership process that pulls together the variables described in this book and in the research on culture, leadership, and motivation—and shows the powerful contingency of culture as it affects the leadership role. Reading from left to right, Exhibit 11-7 presents contingencies from the broad environmental factors to the outcomes affected by the entire leadership situation. As shown, the broad context in which the manager operates necessitates adjustments in leadership style to all those variables relating to the work and task environment and the people involved. Cultural variables (values, work norms, the locus

EXHIBIT 11-7 The Culture Contingency in the Leadership Process: An Integrative Model

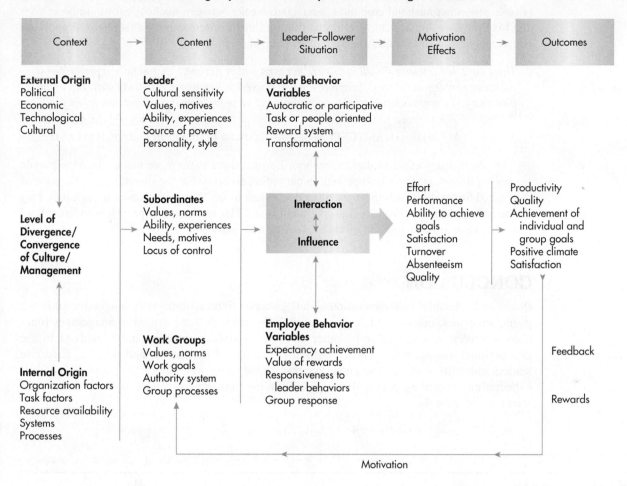

of control, and so forth), as they affect everyone involved—leader, subordinates, and work groups—then shape the content of the immediate leadership situation.

The leader–follower interaction is then further shaped by the leader's choice of behaviors (autocratic, participative, and so on) and by the employees' attitudes toward the leader and the incentives. Motivation effects—various levels of effort, performance, and satisfaction—result from these interactions, on an individual and a group level. These effects determine the outcomes for the company (productivity, quality) and for the employees (satisfaction, positive climate). The results and rewards from those outcomes then act as feedback (positive or negative) into the cycle of the motivation and leadership process.

Clearly, then, international managers should take seriously the culture contingency in their application of the contingency theory of leadership. They must adjust their leadership behaviors according to the context, norms, attitudes, and other variables in that society. As noted, leadership refers not just to the manager–subordinate relationship but also to the important task of running the whole company, division, or unit for which a manager is responsible. When that is a global responsibility, it is vital to be able to adapt one's leadership style to the local context on many levels. Nancy McKinstry, an American leader in Europe, is very sensitive to that imperative. Since she moved to Europe, charged with the task of turning around the troubled Wolters Kluwer, the Dutch publishing group, she "has had plenty of experience of the way national and cultural differences can both bedevil and enliven business."[98] One immediate difference she noticed is that she is one of few women in senior management in Holland. (Since then, as of 2015, the number of women in leadership positions has increased from 20 percent to 50 percent.) That fact, added to the focus of the Dutch media on the executive as a person and the views of the employees rather than the focus on the company, as in the

United States, was surprising to her. As she continues her restructuring plan, Ms. McKinstry (whose physician husband commutes every two weeks between his hospital job in New York and his family in Amsterdam) has found that there is a misconception that she will apply an American, bottom-line leadership style. However, she says:

> *There isn't that one-size-fits-all approach, not even within Europe....If you have a product or a customer problem in France, there might be an approach that works extremely well. But if you took that same approach and tried to solve the exact same problem in Holland, you might fail.*[99]

NANCY MCKINSTRY
CHAIRMAN AND CEO, WOLTERS KLUWER PUBLISHING GROUP, HOLLAND[100]

Ms. McKinstry explains that in southern Europe, there is far more nuance to what people are saying than in northern Europe and, in particular, compared to the direct, optimistic style of the United States. She finds that they often don't want to say "No" to her, even though they may not be able to achieve what she is asking them to do. Her leadership approach is to listen hard and ask, "How are you going to go about meeting this goal?"[101]

CONCLUSION

Because leadership and motivation entail constant interactions with others (employees, peers, superiors, outside contacts), cultural influences on these critical management functions are very strong. Certainly, other powerful variables are intricately involved in the international management context, particularly those of economics and politics. Effective leaders carefully examine the entire context and develop sensitivity to others' values and expectations regarding personal and group interactions, performance, and outcomes—and then act accordingly.

Summary of Key Points

- Motivation and leadership are factors in the successful implementation of desired strategy. However, although many of the basic principles are universal, much of the actual content and process are culture-contingent—a function of an individual's needs, value systems, and environmental context.

- One problem in using content theories for cross-cultural research, such as Maslow created, is the assumption of their universal application. Because they were developed in the United States, even the concepts, such as achievement or esteem, may have different meanings in other societies, resulting in a noncomparable basis of research.

- Implicit in motivating an employee is understanding which of the employee's needs are satisfied by work. Studies on the meaning of work indicate considerable cross-cultural differences.

- A reexamination of motivation relative to Hofstede's dimensions of power distance, uncertainty avoidance, individualism, and masculinity provides another perspective on the cultural contexts that can influence motivational structures.

- Incentives and reward systems must be designed to reflect the motivational structure and relative cultural emphasis on five categories of rewards: financial, social status, job content, career, and professional.

- Effective leadership is crucial to the ability of a company to achieve its goals. The challenge is to decide what is effective leadership in different international or mixed-culture situations.

- The perception of what makes a good leader—both traits and behaviors—varies a great deal from one society to another. The GLOBE leadership study across 62 countries provides considerable insight into culturally appropriate leadership behaviors.

- Contingency theory is applicable to cross-cultural leadership situations because of the vast number of cultural and national variables that can affect the dynamics of the leadership context. These include both leader–subordinate and group relations, which are affected by cultural expectations, values, needs, attitudes, perceptions of risk, and loci of control.

- Joint ventures with other countries present a common but complex situation in which leaders must work together to anticipate and address cross-cultural problems.

Discussion Questions

11-1. What have you learned from the research on work centrality and the relative importance of work dimensions to people around the world?

11-2. What are the implications for motivation of Hofstede's research findings on the dimensions of power distance, uncertainty avoidance, individualism, and masculinity?

11-3. Explain what is meant by the need to design culturally appropriate reward systems. Give some examples.

11-4. Develop a cultural profile which might be applicable to many workers in Mexico and discuss the management style you would use.

11-5. Describe the variables of content and context in the leadership situation. What additional variables are involved in cross-cultural leadership? What are the major elements of a "global mind-set?"

11-6. Explain the theory of contingency leadership and discuss the role of culture in that theory.

11-7. How can we use Hofstede's four dimensions—power distance, uncertainty avoidance, individualism, and masculinity—to gain insight into leader–subordinate relationships around the world? Give some specific examples.

11-8. Describe the autocratic versus democratic leadership dimension. Discuss the cultural contingency in this dimension and give some examples of research findings indicating differences among countries.

11-9. Discuss how you would develop a profile of an effective leader from the research results of the GLOBE project. Give an example.

11-10. Can there be an effective EU leader? Is this a realistic prospect? Discuss the factors involved with this concept. What role has the financial crisis in the Eurozone played in this concept?

Application Exercises

11-11. Using the material on motivation in this chapter, design a suitable organizational reward system for the workers in your company's plant in Mexico.

11-12. Choose a country and do some research (and conduct interviews if possible) to create a cultural profile. Focus on factors affecting behavior in the workplace. Integrate any findings regarding motivation or work attitudes and behaviors. Decide on the type of approach to motivation you would take and the kinds of incentive and reward systems you would set up as manager of a subsidiary in that country. Use the theories on motivation discussed in this chapter to infer motivational structures relative to that society. Then decide what type of leadership style and process you would use. What major contingencies did you take into account?

11-13. Try to interview several people from a specific ethnic subculture in a company or in your college regarding values, needs, expectations in the workplace, and so on. Sketch a motivational profile of this subculture and present it to your class for discussion.

Experiential Exercise

Meet with another student, preferably one whom you know well. Talk with that person and draw up a list of leadership skills you perceive him or her to possess. Then consider your research and readings regarding cross-cultural leadership. Name two countries where you think the student would be an effective leader and two where you think there would be conflict. Discuss those areas of conflict. Then reverse the procedure to find out more about yourself. Share with the class if you wish.

CASE STUDY

Interview: Carlo D'Asaro Biondo, Google's Europe Strategy Chief in Charm Offensive

RICHARD WATERS - LONDON FT.com *APRIL 28, 2015*

The group has woken up to the fact that the way it operates in the continent must change.

Google needs more friends in Europe. That message was brought home with a vengeance earlier this month when the European Commission lodged an antitrust complaint against the internet search company and started a second investigation into the Android mobile operating system.

But Google privately woke up to the fact that it needed to change the way it was operating in Europe last summer, according to Carlo D'Asaro Biondo, the French-Italian executive leading the group's new charm offensive.

"We realised in the last years we had a problem," he says.

In Mr. D'Asaro Biondo's analysis, Google should have offered a helping hand to all kinds of European industries as the digital world put increasing pressure on their business models. That did not happen.

"In Europe we were not organized to value [partnerships]," he says. "We were more organised to sell advertising."

That neglect has had a high price. A series of running battles with the media and entertainment industries over copyright issues has expanded into wider competition complaints, resulting in this month's action in Brussels.

Now, with the digital world encroaching far beyond media and communications, anxiety about Google's influence - whether it is friend or foe of industries from healthcare to cars - is rising.

"Maybe we didn't make enough effort to understand our partners...in developing relationships," says Mr. D'Asaro Biondo, speaking in his first extended interview since he was handed the job of managing European strategic relationships in February.

He has the task of convincing companies in other industries that Google is a reliable ally rather than the leader of a digital invasion from Silicon Valley bent on wiping them out.

Mr. D'Asaro Biondo says he plans to start by telling other industries why they have nothing to fear as Google expands into new markets.

For instance, carmakers should not be worried that the internet company is building its own prototype driverless vehicle, he maintains.

"We can't develop things alone to replace them. I don't believe in that. Developing a car requires skills and know-how that we don't have."

Google would not want to become a carmaker in its own right, for instance, he says.

"It would stop innovation, because instead of focusing on what we do, we would have to try to learn things we don't know."

His comments at times sound as though they run counter to the large ambition emanating from the company's headquarters in Mountain View, California, as it eyes new markets far beyond internet search.

But in the version of Google Mr. D'Asaro Biondo is bringing to would-be partners in Europe, the company's horizons sound far more limited. He says he will become a champion for ideas developed with partners in Europe, taking them back to Mountain View to help shape the group's global product development.

Mr. D'Asaro Biondo's unenviable first task will be to persuade Europe's news publishers, have long been counted among the company's strongest critics, that it has their interests at heart. The challenge extends beyond news publishers to other old media companies trying to make money online.

TV executives like Bertelsmann's Thomas Rabe, for instance, grumble that the economics of platforms like Google's YouTube simply don't generate enough money for broadcasters.

"I think the model is going to work for everybody over time because the internet grows and YouTube grows," counters Mr. D'Asaro Biondo.

One of his overtures involves Android, the smartphone operating system. Linking a system that is on 85 per cent of smartphones with new devices like watches, glasses, cars and TVs creates opportunities for various industries to develop stronger links with customers.

"Making those machines speak together is an incredible development of services," he says. "There's huge value for the ecosystem."

The focus on Android comes in the shadow of an antitrust probe into the operating system in Brussels. Mr. D'Asaro Biondo claims, though, that the regulatory challenge would not slow the company's Android ambitions.

His message to Google detractors is straightforward. "I can make the cake bigger for everybody. If we can look each other in the eye with respect, I think we can do incredible things in Europe."

Case Questions

11-14. What is the history of Google's clashes with European authorities and people? Give some examples. What cultural factors have been involved in these clashes?

11-15. What is Biondo's overall strategy when he says, "I can make the cake bigger for everybody"?

11-16. What has happened since the writing of this case? How is Biondo doing?

Endnotes

1. Nicholas Sambanis, "The Euro Crisis as Ethnic Conflict," *International Herald Tribune*, August 27, 2012.
2. A. Maitland, "Le patron, der Chef and the Boss," *Financial Times*, January 9, 2006.
3. M. Kets de Vries and K. Korotov, "The Future of an Illusion: In Search of the New European Business Leader," *Organizational Dynamics* 34, No. 3 (2005), pp. 218–230.
4. Ibid.
5. Maitland.
6. Ibid.
7. R. J. House, *Culture, Leadership and Organizations: The GLOBE Study of 62 Societies* (Thousand Oaks, CA: Sage, 2004).
8. F. C. Brodbeck, M. Frese, and M. Javidan, "Leadership Made in Germany: Low on Compassion, High on Performance," *Academy of Management Executive* 16, No. 1 (2002).
9. R. House and M. Javidan, "Cultural Acumen for the Global Manager: Lessons from Project GLOBE," *Organizational Dynamics* (2001).
10. Mansour Javidan, Peter W. Dorfman, Mary Sully de Luque, Robert J. House, "In the Eye of the Beholder: Cross Cultural Lessons in Leadership from Project GLOBE," *The Academy of Management Perspectives* 20, No. 1 (2006).
11. N. Payton, "Leaderships Skills Hold Britain Back," *The Guardian*, February 22, 2003.
12. S. Michailova, "When Common Sense Becomes Uncommon: Participation and Empowerment in Russian Companies with Western Participation," *Journal of World Business* 37 (2002), pp. 180–187.
13. "Fujitsu Uses Pay Cuts as a Motivational Tool," www.nytimes.com, January 27, 2004.
14. Irem Uz, "The Index of Cultural Tightness and Looseness Among 68 Countries," *Journal of Cross-Cultural Psychology* 46, No. 3 (2015), pp. 319–335.
15. Ibid.
16. Garry A. Gelade, Paul Dobson, and Katharina Auer, "Individualism, Masculinity, and the Sources of Organizational Commitment," *Journal of Cross-Cultural Psychology* 39 (2008), p. 599.
17. Ibid.
18. F. Rieger and D. Wong-Rieger, "A Configuration Model of National Influence Applied to Southeast Asian Organizations," *Proceedings of the Research Conference on Business in Southeast Asia*, May 12–13, 1990, University of Michigan.
19. R. M. Steers, *Made in Korea: Chung Ju Yung and the Rise of Hyundai* (New York: Routledge, 1999).
20. Meaning of Work International Research Team, *The Meaning of Working: An International Perspective* (New York: Academic Press, 1985).
21. Ibid.
22. A. H. Maslow, *Motivation and Personality* (New York: Harper and Row, 1954).
23. F. Herzberg, *Work and the Nature of Man* (Cleveland: Cleveland World Press, 1966).
24. D. Siddiqui and A. Alkhafaji, *The Gulf War: Implications for Global Businesses and Media* (Apollo, PA: Closson Press, 1992), pp. 133–135.
25. Ibid.
26. A. Ali, "The Islamic Work Ethic in Arabia," *Journal of Psychology* 126 (1992): 507–19.
27. Yasamusa Kuroda and Tatsuzo Suzuki, "A Comparative Analysis of the Arab Culture: Arabic, English and Japanese Language and Values," paper presented at the 5th Congress of the International Association of Middle Eastern Studies, Tunis (September 20–24, 1991), quoted in Siddiqui and Alkhafaji.
28. A. Furnham, B. D. Kirkcaldy, and R. Lynn, "National Attitudes to Competitiveness, Money, and Work among Young People: First, Second, and Third World Differences," *Human Relations* 47, No. 1 (1994), pp. 119–132.
29. Abraham Maslow, *Motivation and Personality* (New York: Harper & Row, 1954).
30. R. L. Tung, "Patterns of Motivation in Chinese Industrial Enterprises," *Academy of Management Review* 6, No. 3 (1981), pp. 481–489.
31. Swee Hoon Ang, "The Power of Money: A Cross-Cultural Analysis of Business-Related Beliefs," *Journal of World Business* 35, No. 1 (2000), p. 43.
32. Anabella Davila and Marta M. Elvira, "Humanistic Leadership: Lessons from Latin America," *Journal of World Business* 47, No. 4 (October 2012), pp. 548ser.
33. Geert Hofstede, "National Cultures in Four Dimensions," *International Studies of Management and Organization* (Spring–Summer 1983).
34. Davila and Elvira, 2012.
35. D. Walker, T. Walker, and J. Schmitz, *Doing Business Internationally*, 2nd ed. (New York: McGraw-Hill, 2003).
36. Ibid.
37. Ibid.
38. Ibid.
39. M. B. Teagarden, M. C. Butler, and M. Von Glinow, "Mexico's Maquiladora Industry: Where Strategic Human Resource Management Makes a Difference," *Organizational Dynamics* (Winter 1992), pp. 34–47.
40. John Condon, *Good Neighbors: Communication with the Mexicans* (Yarmouth, ME: Intercultural Press, 1985).
41. G. K. Stephens and C. R. Greer, "Doing Business in Mexico: Understanding Cultural Differences," *Organizational Dynamics* (Summer 1995), pp. 39–55.
42. Teagarden, Butler, and Von Glinow.
43. Stephens and Greer.
44. David and Elvira, 2012.
45. Ibid.
46. Ibid.
47. Mariah E. de Forest, "Thinking of a Plant in Mexico?" *Academy of Management Executive* 8, No. 1 (1994), pp. 33–40.
48. Ibid.
49. Ibid.
50. Teagarden, Butler, and Von Glinow.
51. Malgorzata Tarczynska, "Eastern Europe: How Valid Is Western Reward/Performance Management?" *Benefits and Compensation International* 29, No. 8 (2000), pp. 9–16.
52. Snejina Michailova, "When Common Sense Becomes Uncommon: Participation and Empowerment in Russian Companies with Western Participation," *Journal of World Business* 37 (2002), pp. 180–187.
53. S. Michailova, "When Common Sense Becomes Uncommon: Participation and Empowerment in Russian Companies with Western Participation," *Journal of World Business* 37 (2002), pp. 180–187.

54. Carl Fey, "Overcoming a Leader's Greatest Challenge: Involving Employees in Firms in Russia," *Organizational Dynamics* 37, No. 3 (2008), pp. 254–265.
55. Ibid.
56. Ibid.
57. Carl F. Fey, Stanislav Shekshnia, "The Key Commandments for Doing Business in Russia," *Organizational Dynamics* 40 (2011), pp. 57–66.
58. Ibid.
59. M. Javidan and R. J. House, "Cultural Acumen for the Global Manager: Lessons from Project GLOBE," *Organizational Dynamics* (Spring 2001), pp. 289–305.
60. Stanislav Shekshnia, Manfred Kets de Vries, "Interview with a Russian Entrepreneur: Ruben Vardanian," *Organizational Dynamics* 37, No. 3 (2008), pp. 288–299.
61. Sheila M. Puffer and Daniel J. McCarthy, "Two Decades of Russian Business and Management Research: An Institutional Theory Perspective," *Academy of Management Perspectives,* May, 2011.
62. "Doing Business in Russia," www.kwintessential.co.uk, accessed May 1, 2012.
63. Rita Pyrillis, "Just a Token of Your Appreciation? Avoid Cultural Faux Pas When Rewarding International Employees," *Workforce Management* 90, No. 9 (September 2011), pp. 3–6.
64. M. A. Von Glinow and Byung Jae Chung, "Comparative HRM Practices in the U.S., Japan, Korea and the PRC," in *Research in Personnel and HRM—A Research Annual: International HRM,* A. Nedd, G. R. Ferris, and K. M. Rowland, eds. (London: JAI Press, 1989).
65. Pyrillis, 2011.
66. A. Ignatius, "Now If Ms. Wong Insults a Customer, She Gets an Award," *Wall Street Journal,* January 24, 1989.
67. T. Saywell, "Motive Power: China's State Firms Bank on Incentives to Keep Bosses Operating at Their Peak," *Far Eastern Economic Review* (July 8, 2000), pp. 67–68.
68. A. Maitland, "Le patron, der Chef and the Boss," *Financial Times,* January 9, 2006.
69. Carlos Sanchez-Runde, Luciara Nardon, Richard M. Steers, "Looking beyond Western Leadership Models: Implications for Global Managers," *Organizational Dynamics* 40, No. 4 (2011), pp. 207–213.
70. A. Morrison, H. Gregersen, and S. Black, "What Makes Savvy Global Leaders?" *Ivey Business Journal* 64, No. 2 (1999), pp. 44–51; and *Monash Mt. Eliza Business Review* 1, No. 2 (1998).
71. Robert J. Thomas, Joshua Bellin, Claudy Jules, and Nandani Lynton, "Developing Tomorrow's Global Leaders," *Sloan Management Review,* Fall 2013.
72. D. Walker, T. Walker, and J. Schmitz, *Doing Business Internationally* (New York: McGraw-Hill, 2003).
73. Mansour Javidan and Mary Teagarden, "Making It Overseas," *Harvard Business Review,* April 2010.
74. "In the Driver's Seat," *Newsweek,* June 30, 2008.
75. A. Morrison, H. Gregersen, and S. Black, "What Makes Savvy Global Leaders?" *Ivey Business Journal* 64, No. 2 (1999), pp. 44–51; and *Monash Mt. Eliza Business Review* 1, No. 2 (1998).
76. R. H. Mason and R. S. Spich, *Management: An International Perspective* (Homewood: IL: Irwin, 1987).
77. Ibid., p. 184.
78. Ibid., p. 186.
79. Based on and excerpted from Mason and Spich.
80. Kendall Herbert, Audra I. Mockaitis, and Lena Zander, "An Opportunity for East and West to Share Leadership: A Multicultural Analysis of Shared Leadership Preferences in Global Teams," *Asian Business & Management* 13, No, 3, (2015) pp. 257–282,
81. Alon Lisak, Miriam Erez, "Leadership Emergence in Multicultural Teams: The Power of Global Characteristics," *Journal of World Business* 50 (2015), pp. 3–14.
82. Ibid.
83. Hans-Paul Bürkner, Vincent Chin, and Ranu Dayal, "There's No Such Thing as Corporate DNA," www.bcgperspectives.com, April 8, 2015.
84. Ibid.
85. B. M. Bass, *Bass & Stogdill's Handbook of Leadership* (New York: Free Press, 1990).
86. D. McGregor, *The Human Side of Enterprise* (New York: McGraw-Hill, 1960). See, for example, R. M. Stogdill, *Manual for the Leader Behavior Description Questionnaire—Form XII* (Columbus: Ohio State University, Bureau of Business Research, 1963); R. R. Blake and J. S. Mouton, *The New Managerial Grid* (Houston: Gulf Publishing, 1978).
87. F. E. Fiedler, "Engineering the Job to Fit the Manager," *Harvard Business Review* 43, No. 5 (1965), pp. 115–122.
88. Den Hartog, N. Deanne, R. J. House, Paul J. Hanges, P. W. Dorfman, S. Antonio Ruiz-Quintanna, et al., "Culture Specific and Cross-Culturally Generalizable Implicit Leadership Theories: Are Attributes of Charismatic/Transformational Leadership Universally Endorsed?" *Leadership Quarterly* 10, No. 2 (1999), pp. 219–256.
89. Ibid.
90. R. House et al., "Cultural Influences on Leadership and Organizations: Project GLOBE," *Advances in Global Leadership,* 1 (JAI Press, 1999).
91. Ibid.
92. Peter Dorfman, Mansour Javidan, Paul Hanges, Ali Dastmalchian, and Robert House, "GLOBE: A Twenty-Year Journey into the Intriguing Word of Culture and Leadership," *Journal of World Business* 47 (2012), pp. 504-518.
93. Ibid.
94. Geert Hofstede, "Motivation, Leadership and Organization: Do American Theories Apply Abroad?" *Organizational Dynamics* (Summer 1980): 42–63.
95. Ibid.
96. Geert Hofstede, "Value Systems in Forty Countries," *Proceedings of the 4th International Congress of the International Association for Cross-Cultural Psychology* (1978).
97. M. K. Badawy, "Styles of Mid-Eastern Managers," *California Management Review* (Spring 1980), p. 57 various newscasts, 2001.
98. Alison Maitland, "An American Leader in Europe," leadership interview with Nancy McKinstry, Wolters Kluwer, *Financial Times,* July 15, 2004.
99. Ibid.
100. Ibid.
101. Ibid.

INSEAD
The Business School
for the World®

Case 9 Leading Across Cultures at Michelin

*"I had managed teams in six countries for large companies and had worked in a multicultural environment my entire career.
I looked forward to moving to the US and working with Americans. With my fluent English and my six years' experience in
the UK, I assumed that it would be an easy transition and I would fit right in."*

OLIVIER CHALON,
President of a large business unit, Michelin North America

Greenville, South Carolina, 2004

How did it come to this?
Olivier Chalon leant back in his chair and let out a frustrated sigh. For the first time in years he was starting to question his leadership style. Jeff Armstrong, the head of human resources for Michelin's North American operations and whom Chalon knew personally, had just left his office. He had mentioned to Chalon that several of his colleagues and subordinates had bitterly complained about Chalon's management approach. Some individuals thought they were going to be fired or were seeking other positions within the company.

Chalon was shocked by the complaints people had made to Armstrong. Was it really true that people felt his leadership style was demoralising? That he lacked people skills? That he was an arrogant manager? Chalon was dumbfounded. Throughout his career he had been known for his ability to motivate teams to accomplish great things and attain outstanding results. In his previous position he had successfully motivated a workforce of over 1,500 European employees to restructure a €1.2 billion business, leading to a profit increase of over 50% on a quarterly basis. The outstanding career success he had enjoyed over the last decade was largely built on his strong interpersonal skills and his ability to mobilise large groups of employees. Where could this criticism be coming from? Chalon knew he had to better understand this situation and to make some changes. *"I need to address this before things get out of control and really damage the business,"* he thought. He was concerned that his new position might be in jeopardy just six months after moving to Michelin. The stakes were high at Michelin and he was in charge of an important division that was in the midst of a turnaround.

Chalon's Background
Up until now, Chalon had had a long and very successful track record in the corporate world as a talented leader who consistently delivered top results. Trained as an engineer at one of France's highly selective and prestigious *Grandes Ecoles*, he had started out in sales with the Paris office of a European integrated oil company with vast global operations. He transferred to the London office as a business analyst, then worked in strategy for three years, and one year in the Netherlands. Over an 18-year career at the company, he had held several top-level management positions in different business units in six countries, including heading the company's Spanish operations in the late 1990s.

Chalon was fluent in four languages, including English, and had lived for six years in the UK. He had enjoyed working with colleagues from different countries and considered himself to have had a very multicultural professional experience. But he had grown weary of moving every few years: *"I had relocated a number of times over the years and I wanted to move back, so I started to look for opportunities that would allow me to settle down in France."*

In 2002, he joined an international automotive spare parts company headquartered in Paris, where he headed a large globally-positioned business unit and helped set up a number of global subsidiaries. By 2004, he was ready for new opportunities. He was interested when Michelin approached him to lead a large division in North America. Although the position would be based out of their North American headquarters in Greenville, South Carolina, it was an exciting new challenge and Chalon jumped at the chance to work for the group. He expected the transition to be smooth: *"I felt I knew the US well and figured the move to be easy. My sister-in-law is American, and with my fluent English, I felt prepared to work in an American environment."*

The Michelin Group
Founded in the 1800s in Clermont-Ferrand, France, the Companie Générale des Etablissements Michelin was the leading tyre manufacturer in the world with 19.2% market share for tyres in 2004 and was a global powerhouse with sales in 170 countries. Famous the world over for its road atlases, restaurant and hotel guides, and its iconic mascot, the Michelin Man, the company's reputation was built on technical innovation and a focus on long-term growth. It employed over 120,000 people, including over 20,000 in North America.[1] Within the industry it had a long-held reputation for excellence and for nurturing the careers of its employees.

Winner of the 2010 European Case Clearing House Award in the category "Human Resource Management/Organisational Behaviour"
This case was prepared by Erin Meyer, Adjunct Professor of Organisational Behaviour at INSEAD and case writer Sapna Gupta. It is intended to be used as a basis for class discussion rather than to illustrate either effective or ineffective handling of personal or professional circumstances.

[1]In 2007, Michelin had over 121,000 employees, operated 69 production sites in 19 countries, and had sales operations in 170 countries. The company held 17.2% of the world's market share for tyres in 2008. (Source: Michelin 2007 Annual Report and Michelin Worldwide 2008 Factsheet.)

The company was organised along eight major product lines, including the car and light truck product line, the truck product line, and the specialities product line (comprising the aircraft, earthmover, agricultural, two-wheel, and component product lines). Michelin reached €15.69 billion in sales in 2004, with North American operations (comprising operations in the US, Canada, and Mexico) accounting for 33% of 2003 sales. The company's shares had traded on the Paris Bourse (Paris stock exchange) since 1946 and its market capitalisation as of 31 December 2002 was €5.22 billion.[2] Michelin stock was part of the CAC 40 and Euronext 100 indices.

In 2004, the North American business unit to which he was assigned faced several challenges: the company was trailing competitors in the aftermarket business and had experienced sliding sales and poor financial results several quarters in a row. The line of business was critical to Michelin and generated close to $2 billion in annual sales. The Boston Consulting Group (BCG) had been brought in to conduct a comprehensive assessment of the unit's operations, and it had strongly recommended that Michelin change course and alter its strategy in the tyre service business. This strategy had put the company in direct competition with its own long-time customers and required a significant realignment of the sales and marketing approach.

Michelin had hired Chalon to lead a division with several plants and 4,000 employees under his management. Even before accepting the position, he knew about the challenges facing the group. Furthermore, he was fully aware that he was expected to implement a turnaround by reinvigorating the sales and marketing teams by having them enthusiastically support the new sales strategy, placating existing clients (most of them very large dealers) who would now see Michelin as a competitive threat rather than a supplier, and regaining lost market share. Chalon felt fully prepared to meet this new challenge. He wanted to work for Michelin precisely because the position would require his unwavering focus and ability to motivate personnel. *"This could be the culmination of two decades of hard-won experience motivating people and achieving results,"* he thought.

Olivier Chalon's Management Style

Chalon considered himself a tough but fair manager – he was results-driven, disciplined, and he demanded complete accountability from his team. That was precisely why Michelin had hired him. He had to change the way business was done in his division and he expected some initial resistance from his team and subordinates. In his experience, being demanding and setting very high standards was the best way to mobilise a team to attain the desired results.

Nevertheless, Armstrong's comments suggested something deeper than resistance to changing how business was conducted in his division. These complaints were about him as a leader, about the way he interacted with employees. Perhaps he had been too blunt during meetings? However, important decisions had to be made and he had been careful to seek consensus and not make any decision on his own. He had been put in charge for a reason. Arrogant? Certainly not. In fact, he

²Michelin's market capitalisation was €11.29 billion as of 31 December 2007.

considered himself close and open to his staff's issues. Lacking the ability to motivate teams? Never! Of all the things Chalon could be accused of, this was certainly the most surprising. Given all that he had accomplished in his career, the accusation was ludicrous.

Armstrong had also relayed complaints about Chalon being cold and distant, and that he had not made an effort to get to know people at work. Chalon was taken aback. He had been making an effort to walk around the office and to get to know his colleagues. He had an open-door policy with regard to his staff dropping by, and considered himself to be very accessible. He believed he was very transparent in the way he worked and he certainly did not hoard information.

At least Jeff had highlighted and praised Chalon's client skills. Most of Michelin's clients in the tyre service business were people who had built their companies from the ground up, and Chalon had made a point of meeting them to personally allay their fears about Michelin entering the business. He was able to relate to them remarkably well and explain Michelin's new strategy while building their loyalty. It seemed to Chalon that the issues Armstrong had brought up were not about being unable to get along with Americans. Rather, the difficulties seemed to stem from his management style and how he interacted with his team and subordinates.

Chalon briefly wondered if there was something unique about Michelin's corporate culture, which was different from the more confrontational, almost rough-and-tumble culture at his previous company. Somehow, though, he felt that the problem was not due to just a difference in corporate style. In his former positions he had successfully instituted similar transformations without this level of complaint or resistance. Chalon reviewed carefully in his mind his interactions with staff since arriving in his new post. These statements that Armstrong had recounted – where could they be coming from? *"How did it come to this?"* he wondered. *"Why had my colleagues not confronted me and why hadn't they brought this up earlier?"*

Chalon recalled his first few months in Greenville:

"I was charged with turning around the division and that had the full support of the company CEO and president. The changes were necessary in order to turn the business around and we couldn't deviate from the strategy, even if it meant stepping on the toes of some long-time managers. I demanded that we do things differently, from the way we looked at our market to how we presented the market analysis. That is why Michelin had put me in charge: to make difficult decisions and change how we did business. Not everyone agreed with how I decided to implement the changes, but it is impossible to have 100% agreement, especially in the beginning.

I instituted a monthly performance review of our sales team, and in these reviews I made it absolutely clear that I meant business. Often, my subordinates would present information that was below their capabilities and this, I made 100% clear, was unacceptable. I frequently insisted my reports go back to the drawing board and present a more structured, detailed presentation, and prepare an in-depth analysis of the risks and opportunities down to the last dollar. I demanded a great level of detail about our market and I was upfront with my disapproval when I didn't get what I was expecting. If I was displeased, I let them know it.

I was straightforward with my criticism and apparently I surprised some people with my direct style. But I was always upfront, and I knew from experience that the leader who demands the most from his people is the leader who will achieve the greatest results. Even when I was pleased with their results, I tried not to show it. I needed my team to push themselves further than ever before, and I didn't want to encourage complacency by stroking people on the back. I was asking my team to give 110% percent of themselves to this new strategy, and I knew they were capable of it. My colleagues and subordinates were very smart and they worked very hard. I wouldn't have been so demanding if I felt they weren't up to the task.

Of course I was surprised that people complained that I was distant! I had made a point of frequently walking around the office and talking informally to my colleagues and subordinates. In truth, I was often a bit taken aback by the intrusiveness of the American culture. People asked one another such personal questions. Individuals I barely knew would ask me questions about my wife or our newborn son, which I found both surprising and inappropriate. I was not used to sharing this level of personal information at work, and now I began to wonder if this might have given people the impression that I was distant or cold.

Chalon wondered if he could have been misreading the cues his colleagues had been sending. Maybe he had been misled, fooled into thinking that his fluent English and two decades' experience in a global work environment had prepared him for managing an American operation, even if it was the division of a French company. Perhaps he had miscalculated how to motivate this team. Would his first assignment in the US end in disaster? What could he do to regain his disgruntled colleagues' loyalty and support?

Since moving into the general manager position in Greenville, Chalon had demanded greater accountability and realigned the division's sales efforts. He had not been aware of any deep dissatisfaction among some of the key executives who reported to him. He had used the same tactics and methods that had worked to fire up his staff while leading teams across Europe, and had not realised that they had fallen flat in this new environment. He felt blind-sided by the comments that Armstrong had passed along.

Chalon was, of course, aware that different skills were needed to motivate teams in different cultural environments. The US was not so different from Europe or the other environments he had worked in. Or was it? Could this be a French vs. American cultural issue?

Headquarters were expecting a turnaround within two years. Chalon was under pressure to show results – but without the goodwill and energy of every single member of his team it would be impossible to implement the turnaround.

He needed to find a way to motivate his colleagues while regaining their trust and goodwill. During their conversation, Armstrong had suggested that Chalon meet with a cross-cultural consultant who specialised in helping European managers adapt their leadership style to an American context. Other managers in France and America had struggled with cross-cultural issues, and Armstrong had attended a presentation given by this consultant. He found that it had helped him work better with his French colleagues in Clermont-Ferrand, even after spending almost two decades at Michelin working alongside French people.

Chalon was initially sceptical but his conversation with Armstrong had touched a nerve and he very much wanted to turn things around. He picked up the phone and called Armstrong. His initial one-on-one meeting with the consultant was scheduled for the following week.

1. Discussion question: What differences in American and French value systems might be at the root of the difficulties Chalon is facing as he implements a new strategy?

Maybe I'm stupid or old fashioned, but I really want to go to bed at night saying I haven't succumbed to this.[1]

RATAN TATA
Chairman, Tata Group, on paying bribes

"Ratan Tata has set an example with his transparency and integrity. In a milieu haunted by wheeler-dealers and a business climate where companies will stop at nothing to pouch contracts, [Ratan] Tata is an inspiration for young entrepreneurs."[2]

RAJEEV CHANDRASEKHAR
An independent member of the Indian Parliament and a former telecom entrepreneur

"[W]e have endeavoured to uphold a value system that has been part of our tradition, and we've been disadvantaged repeatedly in that we have lost projects, projects have been delayed …," said Ratan Naval Tata (Ratan), Chairman of Tata Sons Ltd., the holding company of the Tata Group, on the difficulties of doing business in his home country, India. "And in that sense, we would like to keep the Group ferociously protecting this one asset…."[3] As he prepared to hand over the reins of the group to his successor by the end of 2012, Ratan's job was to ensure that his successor carried forward the legacy of the Tatas and did not view its ethical standards and values as a burden while operating in this key emerging market.

Ratan was credited with transforming the Tata Group under his leadership and bringing it into the 21st century. Although the septuagenarian was applauded as an astute leader and for continuing the Tatas' tradition of ethical leadership, his name was also drawn into the infamous 2G scam that surfaced in India in 2010. Allegations that the Tata Group had not "walked the talk" and that it was involved in what was being described as India's biggest scam, had dented the image of the group. For generations of Indians and even outside the country, the word Tata had been synonymous with "trust" and "integrity." The group was well known for its corporate social responsibility and principles such as the "Tatas don't bribe" and the "Tatas don't indulge in politics."[4] Strict adherence to these principles had led to the group prospering under the predecessors of Ratan and under his reign becoming the best-known Indian group in the world.

On his commitment not to indulge in corruption, Ratan said this had resulted in his group getting a raw deal because he had had to forsake a significant amount of business. He lamented that he had not been able to expand more in his home country due to bureaucratic delays, arbitrary regulatory decisions, and widespread corruption in such sectors as steel, power, aviation, and telecommunications. Despite this, the group upheld the traditions of the Tata Group and did not indulge in corruption, he said.

About the Tata Group

The Tata Group, which was founded by Jamsetji Tata in 1868, had grown to comprise over 100 companies in seven business sectors: communications and information technology, engineering, materials, services, energy, consumer products, and chemicals. Initially inspired by the spirit of nationalism, the group had pioneered several industries of national importance in India: steel, power, hospitality, and airlines. As of early 2012, the major Tata companies were Tata Steel, Tata Motors, Tata Consultancy Services, Tata Power, Tata Chemicals, Tata Global Beverages, Tata Teleservices, Titan, Tata Communications, and Indian Hotels. The group had operations in 80 countries across the globe, and its companies exported products and services to 85 countries. It had revenues of US$83.3 billion in 2010–2011, with 58 percent of this coming from business outside India. Tata companies employed over 425,000 people worldwide. The Tata Group's contribution to the Indian exchequer for the year 2010–2011 was US$6.93 billion out of the total US$210.26 billion[5] (refer to Exhibits I and II).

Each enterprise in the Tata Group operated independently, with its own board of directors and shareholders. These enterprises had a combined market capitalization of about US$80.59 billion (as of January 19, 2012) and a shareholder base of 3.6 million. The Tata Group had had a series of illustrious leaders—Jamsetji Tata (1868–1904), Sir Dorab Tata (1904–1932), and JRD Tata (1932–1991)—who spurred the growth of the company, taking it into newer businesses. However, it was Ratan Tata, who took over the reins of the company in 1991, who was credited with making Tata a truly global group.

Ratan, great grandson of the founder, was a graduate from Cornell University in architecture and structural engineering. He turned down a position at leading IT company,

This case was written by Debapratim Purkayastha, IBS Hyderabad. It was compiled from published sources, and is intended to be used as a basis for class discussion rather than to illustrate either effective or ineffective handling of a management situation.

This case won the Third prize in the BLR Case Study Competition, organized by Business Leadership Review, the official journal of the Association of MBAs (AMBA), UK.

2013, IBS Center for Management Research. All rights reserved.

To order copies, call +91 9640901313 or write to IBS Center for Management Research (ICMR), IFHE Campus, Donthanapally, Sankarapally Road, Hyderabad 501 504, Andhra Pradesh, India or email: info@icmrindia.org. www.icmrindia.org

[1] Amol Sharma, "India's Tata Finds Home Hostile," http://online.wsj.com, April 13, 2011.

[2] "Tata Juggernaut Stirring," *Business India*, www.tata.com, April 30–May 13, 2001.

[3] Shekhar Gupta, "'The Most Noise Usually Comes from the People Who Have the Most to Hide'," www.indianexpress.com, November, 28 2010.

[4] Girish Nikam, "Is Ratan Tata as Clean as He Claims: Why Is Niira Radia Talking to Karunanidhi's Wife?" http://indiasreport.com, November 28, 2010.

[5] http://www.tata.com/htm/Group_Investor_GroupFinancials.htm.

EXHIBIT I Financial Snapshot of Tata Group

Year	2010–11 (US $ billion)	2009–10 (US $ billion)	% change
Total revenue	83.3	67.4	23.6
Sales	82.2	65.6	25.3
Total assets	68.9	52.8	30.5
International revenues	48.3	38.4	25.8
Profit after tax	5.8	1.74	233.3
Net forex earnings	1.0	–0.16	–

(In Rs. million)

Year	Total turnover	Sales turnover	Value of assets	Gross block	Exports
2010–11	3,796,753	3,746,872	3,139,601	3,343,376	378,521
2009–10	3,195,339	3,111,290	2,501,786	2,922,475	317,210
2008–09	3,253,340	3,218,490	2,372,470	2,612,760	339,870
2007–08	2,515,430	2,474,156	1,772,931	1,935,072	252,801
2006–07	1,299,940	1,283,770	1,135,730	866,127	236,350
2005–06	9,67,230	9,47,140	7,97,660	6,81,690	2,36,430
2004–05	7,99,130	7,82,750	6,80,180	6,00,290	2,05,870
2003–04	6,54,240	6,14,340	5,50,630	4,58,840	1,41,360
2002–03	5,42,270	5,21,337	5,09,270	4,34,809	1,30,764
2001–02	4,94,568	4,79,999	4,91,622	4,03,647	1,25,738

Market Capitalization

(Rs. million)	2009 (End March)	2010 (End March)	2011 (End March)	As on Jan 19, 2012
Tata group	124,97.7 ($24.5bn)	344,13.9 ($76.2bn)	469,96.4 ($105.4 bn)	404,89.2 ($80.59bn)
Bombay Stock Exchange	3,086,07.6 ($605.7bn)	6,261,78.7 ($1387.2bn)	6,907,78.8 ($1550.0 bn)	5,893,15.2 ($1,173bn)

Compiled from various sources including Tata Group's website.

IBM, to join the Tata Group in 1962 in Tata Iron and Steel Company (TISCO, later renamed Tata Steel). After initially working on the shop floor alongside blue-collar employees, he was made Director-in-charge of The National Radio and Electronics Company (NELCO) in 1971 and continued in that position until 1974. In 1975, he completed an advanced management program at Harvard Business School. In 1977, Ratan was elevated to the position of chairman of TISCO. He became the chairman of Tata Engineering and Locomotive Company (TELCO, later renamed Tata Motors) and Tata Industries[i] in 1981. A decade later, he became chairman of Tata Sons.

It was around this time that the Indian government began to initiate a series of reforms to open up the economy.[ii] The Tata Group companies, like most other Indian companies at that time, were not globally competitive and found themselves facing the threat of competition from multinational companies.[6] Moreover, the group seemed on its way to disintegration, with powerful CEOs running some of the group companies like their personal fiefdoms and challenging the core structure of the group. Over a period of four years, Ratan managed to oust most of these CEOs.[7] To bring in greater integration among the group companies, Ratan created the Group Executive Office, whose members were represented on the boards of the Tata companies. To protect individual companies from hostile takeovers, he also increased the stake of Tata Sons in each company.

Recognizing that the culture and the work ethic at the group were no longer relevant to the more competitive post-liberalization era, Ratan shook things up. In 1998, at a gathering of heads and

[6]"Complementing for Complexity: Leading through Managing," www.etmgr.com, January–March, 2005.

[7]Robyn Meredith, "Tempest in a Teapot," www.forbes.com, February 14, 2005.

EXHIBIT II Tata Group's Revenues by Segment

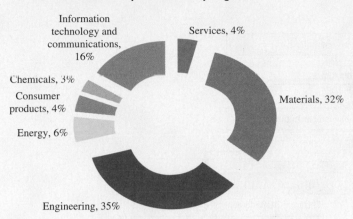

Information technology and communications, 16%

Services, 4%

Chemicals, 3%

Consumer products, 4%

Energy, 6%

Materials, 32%

Engineering, 35%

Adapted from Tata Group's Annual Reports.

senior officials of group companies, he made a speech on the changes in the external environment and cautioned the senior management that inaction would cost them dearly. He introduced the Tata Business Excellence Model (TBEM), a customized version of the globally renowned Malcolm Baldrige model, to support the group's largest change initiative. Once a company signed up, it was annually evaluated on seven criteria: leadership, strategic planning, customer and market focus, information and analysis, process management, human resource focus, and business results. Each of these criteria was allotted points, totaling 1,000. Each participating company aimed to earn 600 points, at the least, over five years. Ratan also established the Group Corporate Center, an apex body that was to review the Group operations on a monthly basis. Using the TBEM framework, Ratan was able to transform the Tata Group's companies into much leaner and agile companies.

When Ratan assumed leadership of the Tata Group, it was involved in many businesses: automobiles, steel, tea, oil mills, chemicals, cosmetics, power, and so on. In 1997, the group had 84 companies; however, only a few large companies contributed significantly to the group's revenues and profits.[8] In order to bring in greater focus, Ratan divested the group of businesses that he felt did not fit in with his vision for the group. In subsequent years, the group sold its stakes in Merind (including Tata Pharma), Goodlass Nerolac (a paint company), Lakmé (a cosmetics company), and ACC (a cement company). In addition to this and in order to create a single brand image, all the group companies that had earlier had individual logos began to use one common logo in 1999. Some of the group companies were also renamed.

Ratan's broad direction for growth of the group was two-pronged. One was targeting the emerging mass market in India through product development and innovation. The other was to globalize, wherein the group planned to expand the markets for its existing products. Ratan strongly believed that to achieve growth at the Tata Group, it was necessary to create technologically superior and exciting products. According to him, the Tata Group would have to distinguish itself from other companies through innovation and low costs. Under his leadership, the group companies came up with several new and

innovative products. For example, Tata Steel patented several new kinds of equipment such as a fuel and reducing gas generator and an emulsion atomizer and processes such as the inert gas shrouding process and the corrosion-resistant steel production process. More importantly, the company started selling its products, which until then had been sold as commodities under the Tata brand. Tata Motors, until then known for its bulky trucks, launched India's first indigenous car, the Indica, in December 1998. The Nano car project too required Tata Motors to come up with innovative solutions to bring down costs so that the car could be priced at an almost unimaginably low price of Rs.[iii] 100,000.[9] The Nano was finally launched in 2009.

Despite its strong position in India, the Tata Group's overseas ventures had never been large enough to be worth a mention. Ratan was keen on the group companies entering new markets to take advantage of global opportunities.[10] He felt that global operations would make them more competitive and efficient. Ratan said, "Perhaps the most graphic moment came in 1997–1998 or 2000 when we had that economic downturn and when Tata Motors, at that time, produced that [Rs. 5 billion] loss. That told me that we had to do something where we would not in the future be dependent on one economic cycle, but we had to have more irons in the fire in different economies and if one economic cycle was down, the chances are that the other might be up. That accelerated the move to go and search, not for acquisitions, but for markets in a serious way."[11] In 2001, Ratan acquired a controlling stake in VSNL, a government company. In 2004, VSNL (renamed as Tata Communications), purchased Switzerland-based Tyco International's undersea telecom cables to become the world's biggest carrier of international phone calls. In the same year, Tata Motors acquired South Korean conglomerate Daewoo's commercial vehicles operations, making it the first Indian company to acquire a major foreign automobile company. In 2005, the group acquired Incat International, a major vendor for American auto and aerospace companies. In this period, India Hotels Company, the group's hotel business, acquired renowned hotels like The Pierre (New York), the Ritz-Carlton Boston, and Camden Place (San Francisco). In January 2007, Tata Steel acquired the Anglo-Dutch steel company Corus. In March 2008, Tata Motors acquired the iconic car brands Jaguar and Land Rover from Ford Motor Company. Ratan's perspective on going global was not just to increase the turnover; it was also to engage creatively in the development of the countries in which the group entered. Keeping this perspective in view, the group ventured into developing and emerging countries such as Bangladesh and Sri Lanka.

As of early 2012, the Tata Group was a globally renowned name with its brand ranked 41st among the world's 100 most valuable brands in 2011. *BusinessWeek* ranked Tata 17th on the 50 Most Innovative Companies list, and the Reputation Institute, USA, in 2009, rated it 11th on its list of the world's most reputable companies.

[9]Kunal N. Talgeri and Sriram Srinivasan, "The Countdown Begins Now ..." www.outlookbusiness.com, February 9, 2008.

[10]"Driving Global Strategy," www.tata.com.

[11]"I Always Envisaged Tata Could be a Global Group: Ratan Tata," http://markets.moneycontrol.com, December 8, 2007.

[8]"The New Raj at Tata," *BusinessWeek*, www.tata.com, November 27, 1997.

EXHIBIT III   Tata Group – Leadership with Trust

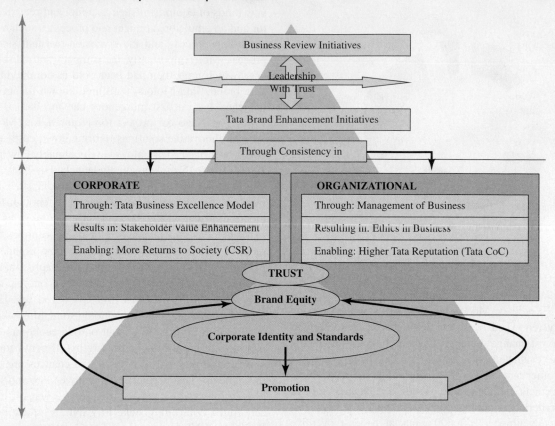

Adapted from "The Tata Group: Integrating Social Responsibility with Corporate Strategy," www.icmrindia .org, 2005.

Leadership with Trust

Since its inception, the Tata Group sought to function with ethics, integrity, social consciousness, and fairness. According to Ratan, these values were an integral part of the group, and the questions one needed to ask while making decisions were: "Does this stand the test of public scrutiny in terms of what I said earlier? As you think the decision through, you have to automatically feel that this is wrong, incorrect, or unfair. You have to think of the advantages or disadvantages to the segments involved, be it employees or stakeholders."[12] The group's strategy of "Leadership with Trust" sought to achieve higher value for its stakeholders, better returns for society, and an ethical model of business (refer to Exhibit III).

The guiding mission of the Tata Group was stated by JRD Tata in the following words: "No success or achievement in material terms is worthwhile unless it serves the needs or interests of the country and its people."[13] Even before him, Jamsetji Tata had said that, "Community is not just another stakeholder in business but is in fact the very purpose of its existence."[14] The group had always been recognized as a value-driven organization. The company's values were imbibed from the founder

of the group and his successors who took on the leadership of the group (refer to Exhibit IV).

Considered pioneers in the area of CSR in India, the Tata Group had played an active role in nation building and socio-economic development. A unique feature of the group was that 63 percent of the equity capital of Tata Sons was held by Tata trusts, which were philanthropic in nature. At a time when rival group Reliance Industries Ltd.'s Mukesh Ambani featured among the richest people in the world and was in the news for building a 27-story home with three helipads, a health club, and 50-seat movie theater, Ratan wasn't even counted among India's billionaires. He had a stake of less than 1 percent in Tata Sons.[15] According to JRD Tata, "The wealth gathered by Jamsetji Tata and his sons in half a century of industrial pioneering formed but a minute fraction of the amount by which they enriched the nation. The whole of that wealth is held in trust for the people and used exclusively for their benefit. The cycle is thus complete; what came from the people has gone back to the people many times over."[16] Over the decades, these trusts had promoted a number of public institutions of national interest, including hospitals, education and research centers, and scientific and cultural establishments. Besides the trust activities, individual

[12]"View from the Top," www.tata.com. June 2002.
[13]"'Visionaries,' CSR Initiatives of Tata Group," www.indianngos.com, December 2004.
[14]Ibid.

[15]Amol Sharma, "India's Tata Finds Home Hostile," http://online.wsj.com, April 13, 2011.
[16]"The Quotable Jamsetji Tata," www.tata.com, March 2008.

EXHIBIT IV Tata Group's Purpose and Core Values

Purpose

At the Tata Group we are committed to improving the quality of life of the communities we serve. We do this by striving for leadership and global competitiveness in the business sectors in which we operate.

Our practice of returning to society what we earn evokes trust among consumers, employees, shareholders, and the community. We are committed to protecting this heritage of leadership with trust through the manner in which we conduct our business.

Core Values

Tata has always been values-driven. These values continue to direct the growth and business of Tata companies. The five core Tata values underpinning the way we do business are:

- **Integrity:** We must conduct our business fairly, with honesty and transparency. Everything we do must stand the test of public scrutiny.

- **Understanding:** We must be caring, show respect, compassion, and humanity for our colleagues and customers around the world, and always work for the benefit of the communities we serve.

- **Excellence:** We must constantly strive to achieve the highest possible standards in our day-to-day work and in the quality of the goods and services we provide.

- **Unity:** We must work cohesively with our colleagues across the group and with our customers and partners around the world, building strong relationships based on tolerance, understanding, and mutual cooperation.

- **Responsibility:** We must continue to be responsible, sensitive to the countries, communities, and environments in which we work, always ensuring that what comes from the people goes back to the people many times over.

Adapted from www.tata.com and various sources.

group companies had taken up community development initiatives based on the needs of the local community. The combined development-related expenditure of the trusts and the companies amounted to around 3 percent of the group's net profits in 2011. The group was engaged in social welfare and environment-related projects worth US$59.7 million for the FY2011.[17]

Employee welfare measures were also one of the major focus areas of the group. The Tatas had initiated several labor welfare measures in their group companies even before these were made mandatory by law. Environment protection also figured high on the list of priorities of the Tata Group. "The kind of company one would want to emulate is one where products and technology are at the leading edge, dealings with customers are very fair, services are of a high order, and business ethics are transparent and straightforward. A less tangible issue involves the work environment, which should not be one where you are stressed and driven to the point of being drugged,"[18] said Ratan Tata.

Way back in 1895, Jamsetji Tata had stated, "We do not claim to be more unselfish, more generous, or more philanthropic than others, but we think we started on sound and straightforward business principles considering the interests of the shareholders, our own, and the health and welfare of our employees … the sure foundation of prosperity."[19] JRD Tata strongly believed that the CSR initiatives of the Tata Group should be institutionalized. Therefore, suitable amendments were made to the Articles of Association of the major Tata Group companies in the 1970s to include: "Company shall be mindful of its social and moral responsibilities to consumers, employees, shareholders, society and the local community."[20] In addition to this, a clause was put into the group's Code of Conduct (CoC), which stated that group companies had to assist actively in improving the quality of life in the communities in which they operated. All the group companies were signatories to this code. To ensure that the CSR measures started by the group were sustained, a social audit of companies was also carried out. The companies were required to conduct periodic surveys, institute community programs as part of the annual business plans, and earmark a budget for this purpose in advance, so that these expenses were built into the cost of business as for any other cost like material, labor, and so on. The CSR programs undertaken by member companies had to be aligned with their core competencies and capabilities, and the CEO and operational heads acted as facilitators in the process.

Taking these initiatives forward, Ratan formed Tata Council for Community Initiatives (TCCI) in 1996 that acted as a facilitator for the group's CSR initiatives as a whole. By 2000, TCCI had developed the Tata Model for Social Audit. The development of a business-compatible procedure to evaluate the impact of community programs in terms of their outcomes on human development was another area of focus for TCCI. This procedure was titled "Tata Social – Evaluation, Responsibility, and Accountability (Social – ERA)." In 2000, TCCI also developed a first-of-its-kind CSR index in India called the Tata Index for Sustainable Human Development, which was adopted by fifteen group companies.[21]

In the following year, TCCI appointed one Corporate Head – Social Responsibility for each of the group companies. TCCI's effort toward community development was based on the concept of volunteering. TCCI's approach was to shift the community from welfare-based dependence to self-reliance, and the company from social work to developmental work. TCCI also established the Tata Group Environment Network in 2000 for coordinating the group-level network on the environment, conservation of natural resources, and related initiatives.[22] As of 2012, 42 Tata companies were signatories to the UN Global Compact, the highest in the world from a single business group.

In order to align its CSR initiatives with business processes, the Tata Group made efforts to develop mechanisms for integrating

---

[17] www.tata.com.
[18] "Ratan Tata's Words of Inspiration," http://parsikhabar.net, August 27, 2008.

[19] "Beyond Business—Back to the People," www.tata.com, December 2004.
[20] R Gopalakrishnan, "Improving the Quality of Life," *The Economic Times*, September 1, 2001.
[21] "Tatas Index their Social Conscience," *Times of India*, March 27, 2004.
[22] Anant Nadkarni, "Convergence Process," *Tata Workout*, www.hdrc.undp.org.in, June 2002.

social responsibility with corporate excellence. The group focused on developing partnerships for benchmarking with the United Nations Development Program, Global Reporting Initiative, The Global Compact, World Business Council for Sustainable Development, Ford Foundation, and the Confederation of Indian Industry. In June 2002, a workshop titled "Towards Creating a Sustainable World" was conducted to assist Tata companies in developing a common system for social and environmental reporting. The participants discussed the linkage between CSR and the TBEM and how the business excellence processes could be institutionalized to create value for all stakeholders while focusing on achieving long-term sustained competitive success. One of the core values of TBEM was social responsibility and citizenship.[23]

Ratan felt that doing business in India could be an exercise fraught with frustration due to the role of the bureaucracy. "It takes more time in India to undertake projects or to set up or develop mergers and acquisitions. A deal [like] Corus in India may not have been possible [because of government bureaucracy],"[24] he said. Despite that, he tried to ensure that group companies did not indulge in corruption and bribery to quicken the pace of work or secure permissions. There are certain clauses in the group's Code of Conduct that explicitly stated this (Refer to Exhibit V). Ratan said, "You often have young employees who ask me, 'Why don't you just do it (give bribe),' but my reply to that is I would rather like to hold my head high."[25]

2G Scam and the Tatas

The Tatas were one of the first private players to foray into the Indian telecom sector. This sector had witnessed unparalleled growth since the dawn of the new millennium, attracting the attention of Indian as well as global telecom companies.[26] The growth of the Indian telecom sector was often attributed to the country's good telecom policies. However, there were murmurs in certain sections that the leading players in the sector had grown by taking advantage of the government's ignorance of the telecom sector in the earlier years of the rollout of services. For instance, they said that companies had manipulated the government's policy by acquiring the bulk of the scarce spectrum[iv] for a very cheap price. The Indian companies operating in this market had a good understanding of the market and many of them were led by powerful people who had immense clout in India. Analysts felt that these people had no qualms about manipulating the public policy to their advantage.[27] Some experts even suggested that many of these executives might owe their riches to "oligopolistic access to scarce resources" rather than to entrepreneurship.[28]

[23]BG Deshmukh, "Tata Workout," www.hdrc.undp.org.in, June 2002.
[24]Elliot Wilson, "Tata's Global Ambitions Show No Sign of Abating," www.asiamoney.com, July 2007.
[25]"Corruption in India Has Become Worse: Ratan Tata," www.thehindubusinessline.com, August 24, 2011.
[26]Ayush Kanwar, "Boom in the Indian Telecom Sector Here to Stay," http://theviewspaper.net, January 15, 2010.
[27]M. Rajendran, "The Great War," www.businessworld.com, February 15, 2008.
[28]Bala Murali Krishna, "Time to Tame India's 'Robber Barons'," http://asiancorrespondent.com, February 21, 2011.

EXHIBIT V   Excerpts from Tata Code of Conduct

Clause: 3
Competition
"A Tata company shall fully support the development and operation of competitive open markets and shall promote the liberalization of trade and investment in each country and market in which it operates. Specifically, no Tata company or employee shall engage in restrictive trade practices, abuse of market dominance, or similar unfair trade activities. [...]"

Clause: 5
Gifts and donations
"A Tata company and its employees shall neither receive nor offer or make, directly or indirectly, any illegal payments, remuneration, gifts, donations, or comparable benefits that are intended, or perceived, to obtain uncompetitive favors for the conduct of its business. The company shall cooperate with governmental authorities in efforts to eliminate all forms of bribery, fraud and corruption. [...]"

Clause: 6
Government agencies
"A Tata company and its employees shall not, unless mandated under applicable laws, offer or give any company funds or property as donation to any government agency or its representative, directly or through intermediaries, in order to obtain any favorable performance of official duties. A Tata company shall comply with government procurement regulations and shall be transparent in all its dealings with government agencies."

Clause: 7
Political non-alignment
"A Tata company shall be committed to and support the constitution and governance systems of the country in which it operates.

"A Tata company shall not support any specific political party or candidate for political office. The company's conduct shall preclude any activity that could be interpreted as mutual dependence/favor with any political body or person, and shall not offer or give any company funds or property as donations to any political party, candidate, or campaign."

Adapted from www.tata.com.

In 2010, the 2G scam broke out in India, and Tata Teleservices was also dragged into it.[v] It was alleged that the Minister of Communications and Information Technology, Andimuthu Raja (Raja), had granted telecom operating licenses[vi] and allotted spectrum arbitrarily on a first-come-first-served basis. Across the world, spectrum, which was treated as a scarce natural resource, was generally auctioned and given to the highest bidders, but in India, the Ministry of Communications and Information Technology (MCIT) allocated spectrum to various companies between November 2007 and December 2010 at price levels agreed to in 2001 without any bids being called for. A preliminary report by the Comptroller and Auditor General of India (CAG), a federal agency for auditing public accounts in India, computed the loss to the exchequer at around US$40 billion (Rs. 1760 billion)[vii] due to the MCIT favoring allocation rather than open auctioning.[29] Further, it was also alleged that the MCIT had flouted guidelines and eligibility conditions, altered cut-off dates (for receiving applications), and tweaked procedural conditions, resulting in certain companies getting an unfair advantage. Following the allegations, Raja was forced to step down from the MCIT and, since early 2011, faced corruption charges.[viii] Tata Teleservices was also named along with several Indian telecom companies that had come under the scanner for alleged irregularities in the grant of licenses and spectrum allocation: Videocon, Loop Telecom, Dishnet Wireless, S-Tel, Uninor, Allianz Infra, Sistema Shyam Teleservices, Idea Cellular, Etisalat (Swan), and Vodafone-Essar.[30] In January 2011, the apex court in India, the Supreme Court, issued notices to these 11 private telecom companies on charges that they had been granted licenses despite allegedly being ineligible to secure telecom licenses per regulations or having failed to roll out services within a stipulated time frame per regulatory obligations.[31]

According to Rajeev Chandrashekar, "The impressive economic growth numbers hide an extremely dysfunctional and skewed economic model. On the one hand, we have governments with wide administrative discretion, little oversight, and huge budget. On the other hand, entrepreneurs and companies act as proxies of politicians. This combination, if allowed to grow unfettered, represents a clear and present danger to the whole concept of Indian democracy and free markets."[32] It was widely reported that political leaders and bureaucrats were hand in glove with the corporate leaders and that corporate lobbyists were mediating between the two groups on the matter. Corporate lobbying, though not legal in India, was not considered an offense if no rule was broken in the process. Niira Radia (Radia), head of Vaishnavi Corporate Communications, was one such business lobbyist who had interacted with the MCIT on behalf of prominent wireless services providers such as Tata Teleservices and had allegedly influenced spectrum allocation decisions of the ministry in favor of her clients. According to the affidavit filed by the government in the Supreme Court against her, she had built up a Rs. 3 billion business empire within a short span of nine months.[33]

The Income Tax Department, with the approval of the Home Ministry, had tapped Radia's telephone conversations between 2008 and 2009 to ascertain the accuracy of her tax filings. These tapes were leaked to the media in late 2010. (Who leaked the tapes was kept a secret.) Two news magazines, *Outlook* and *Open*, published extracts from those tapes, triggering a

controversy as the content brought out the nexus between corporate-media-political houses to show undue regulatory support to certain businesses at the cost of public welfare. As the *New York Times* observed, "The incestuous world revealed in the telecom scandal—one in which ethical lines are blurred between journalists, lobbyists, and politicians, and corporate bosses curry favor with the ministers—has reinforced the perception of an Indian economy dominated by a small, tightly connected elite."[34] It was also believed that Radia had lobbied for the appointment of Raja as Minister of Communications and Information Technology. From the tapped conversations, it appeared that "companies owned by Radia not only manage media but try to influence policy changes and decision of the various government departments to suit the commercial requirements of their clients."[35] Some observers alleged that the lobbying carried out by Radia had helped Tata Teleservices bag spectrum at lower prices. Radia's taped conversations indicated that she had lobbied with Raja, his personal secretary RK Chandolia—one of the key suspects in 2G scam—and other officials belonging to the Department of Telecom (DoT) and ensured that the spectrum was allocated to Tata Teleservices at the same rate as to Reliance Communications, Swan Telecom, and Unitech Wireless.[36]

It was alleged that Radia had gathered inside information about policy changes and decisions from key bureaucrats in the DoT and other regulatory authorities, including the Telecom Regulatory Authority of India, and shared the information with Ratan and other senior Tata Teleservices employees. For instance, during a conversation on July 8, 2009, with Madhav Joshi, chief legal officer and company secretary of Tata Teleservices, Radia had passed on critical information about a key committee's recommendations that was likely to influence the DoT's future policy on spectrum pricing.[37] One of the tapes of a conversation between Radia and Tarun Das, former head of the Confederation of Indian Industry, revealed how Radia was trying to sort out the antagonism between Ratan Tata and Sunil Mittal (chairman of the Bharti Group that owned Bharti Airtel Ltd.), so that they would align forces for effective lobbying to win spectrum from the MCIT. In that conversation, Radia also stated that she was talking to Raja every day over spectrum allocation: "I am talking to Raja every day and I know, I can see his body language. Raja will be very cautious with what he has to do but we have to step in. Tatas and Mittals (are) telling him that we will take you all the way."[38]

In a taped conversation with Sunil Arora, former Indian Airlines chief, during June 2009 Radia claimed, "My client Tata Teleservices has also been a beneficiary in this (read 2G scam)."[39]

[29]"DoT Begins Survey of 2G Scam-Hit Cos," www.businesstoday.intoday.in, November 22, 2010.

[30]"2G Scam: SC Reserves Order on Cancellation of Licences," http://ibnlive.in.com, March 17, 2011.

[31]"2G Scam: Supreme Court Issues Notice to Centre, 11 Telecom Companies," www.merinews.com, January 10, 2011.

[32]Rama Lakshmi, "Corruption Scandals in India Fuel Fears of Crony Capitalism," www.washingtonpost.com, December 17, 2010.

[33]"How Radia Built Her R 300 cr Empire," http://daily.bhaskar.com, December 11, 2010.

[34]Jim Yardley and Heather Timmons, "Telecom Scandal Plunges India Into Political Crisis," www.nytimes.com, December 13, 2010.

[35]"Radia Admits to Liaising with Raja for Clients," http://indiatoday.intoday.in, November 25, 2010.

[36]Unitech Wireless sold 60% interests to Telenor of Norway for Rs. 61.2 billion and was subsequently renamed Uninor.

[37]Ashish Khetan, "My Client Tata Teleservices Has Also Been a Beneficiary in 2G: Radia," http://indiatoday.intoday.in, December 3, 2010.

[38]"Too Close For Disclosure," http://indiatoday.intoday.in, December 3, 2010.

[39]Ashish Khetan, "My Client Tata Teleservices Has Also Been a Beneficiary in 2G: Radia," http://indiatoday.intoday.in, December 3, 2010.

Industry observers alleged that Tata Teleservices had benefited in two ways. First, Radia effectively lobbied for GSM spectrum across 18 telecom circles for Tata Teleservices at lower prices. The DoT allotted 4.4 MHz GSM spectrum to Tata Teleservices at the 2001 price, for which the company paid around Rs. 16 billion. The CAG report stated that the same amount of spectrum could have cost Tata Teleservices anywhere between Rs. 90 billion and Rs. 200 billion, had the DoT auctioned it. Second, Tata Teleservices was allegedly given undue preference in license allocation. It was granted the license (ahead of 343 applicants) though it had submitted its application on October 20, 2007. The license was granted despite the MCIT advancing the cut-off date for submitting applications from October 1, 2007, to September 25, 2007, due to inadequate spectrum availability. After the license allocation, the net worth of Tata Teleservices had shot up. In November 2008, Tata Teleservices sold 26 percent stake to Japanese telecom major NTT Docomo for US$2.8 billion and launched its services under the brand Tata Docomo.[40]

Following this, the Central Bureau of Investigation (CBI), a government agency of India, also started investigations on a Tata Group company's transaction of Rs.16 billion with Unitech in 2007, months before the allocation of the licenses, and the Voltas land deal with the Karunanidhi[ix] family.[41] There were also allegations that in November 2007, Ratan had written a letter to M. Karunanidhi, the then chief minister of Tamil Nadu and leader of the DMK party, praising A. Raja.[42] It was alleged that, in a handwritten letter, Ratan had praised Raja for his "rational, fair, and action-oriented" leadership and "legally sound, rational, and well reasoned" policies on the issue of spectrum allocation.[43]

Ratan Tata's Response

Ratan vehemently denied the allegations that Tata Teleservices had been a beneficiary of the 2G scam. Rather, he claimed that it was a victim. According to him, as Tata Teleservices complied with all application requirements, rivals with better political connections had jumped ahead in the queue and taken most of the spectrum. For getting its share of the spectrum, the company had had to fight an 83-day legal battle with the government. "We haven't had a level playing field. We're still waiting for spectrum. We're still behind the eight ball on several of the things that we should get,"[44] claimed Ratan Tata.

In late 2010, Ratan approached the Supreme Court, claiming that the Radia tapes infringed upon his right to privacy. He alleged that some of the conversations between him and Radia were personal in nature and were not related to the 2G scam investigation.[45] His petition said that taping of conversations should be used for investigations only and could not be used for "unauthorized publication." According to him, "the government has been given a special right to be able to invade people's privacy for national security or for enforcement of law. So they can do so. That additional power is a very special power which has to be exercised with a sense of responsibility. The content needs to be held for prosecution purposes and not to be misused and certainly not to go out and have a field day with."[46] Some observers found it hypocritical that Ratan, on the one hand spoke of high moral and ethical standards while on the other, he wanted to deny the right of the Indian public for transparency in the Radia matters just because she was handling PR work for the group. They questioned why the group that could get the best talent in its payroll should hire someone like Radia to do its PR work.[47]

In April 2011, CBI gave a clean chit to the Tata Group.[48] In the same month, Ratan faced questions about the group's relationship with the DMK party and a number of related issues from the parliament's Public Accounts Committee, which was probing the 2G scam separately. Ratan confirmed that it was his voice in the Radia tapes and that in November 2007 he had written a letter to M. Karunanidhi praising A. Raja.[49] Ratan Tata also reiterated that his group did not believe in paying bribes.[50]

Taking the fight to its critics, the group argued that some of the transcripts of the Radia tapes had shown how the group had been disadvantaged in its mining-related projects in Jharkhand and Madhya Pradesh.[51] In 2010, Ratan said that the group had had an ambition to get back into the airline business, which it had pioneered in India in 1932, but that had been nationalized in 1953. However, this ambition had been repeatedly thwarted for seven years as the group refused to pay bribes, leading to the group withdrawing its application in 1998, he alleged. "We went through three governments, three prime ministers, and each time there was a particular individual that thwarted our efforts,"[52] Ratan said.

On February 2, 2012, the Supreme Court ordered the scrapping of 122 telecom licenses including those issued to Tata Teleservices. Some of the telecom operators were also fined. For instance, Tata Teleservices, Unitech Wireless, and Etisalat were fined Rs. 50 million each for selling equity in their respective companies to foreign companies after acquiring additional spectrum in 2008.[53]

[40]Ibid.

[41]Pradip R. Sagar, "2G Scam: Tata Group Gets Clean Chit," DNA, April 3, 2011.

[42]"Ratan Tata Confirms Praising Raja in Letter to Tamil Nadu CM," www.indiaeveryday.in, April 4, 2011.

[43]Ibid.

[44]Amol Sharma, "India's Tata Finds Home Hostile," http://online.wsj.com, April 13, 2011.

[45]Kian Ganz, "Ratan Tata Claims Radia Tapes Violated Privacy: Karanjawala, Perhaps Salve, to Rep," www.legallyindia.com, November 29, 2010.

[46]"Ratan Tata & Right to Privacy?" www.moneycontrol.com, November 30, 2010.

[47]Dave Makkar, "Ratan Tata's Double Standards on Corruption," www.indiatribune.com, January 31, 2011.

[48]Pradip R. Sagar, "2G Scam: Tata Group Gets Clean Chit," DNA, April 3, 2011.

[49]"Ratan Tata Confirms Praising Raja in Letter to Tamil Nadu CM," www.indiaeveryday.in, April 4, 2011.

[50]"PAC Questions Ratan Tata, Radia: Key Takeaways," www.moneycontrol.com, April 4, 2011.

[51]Amol Sharma, "On Radia Tapes, Tata's Frustrations Show," http://online.wsj.com, April 13, 2011.

[52]Amol Sharma, "India's Tata Finds Home Hostile," http://online.wsj.com, April 13, 2011.

[53]Nikhil Kanekal and Shauvik Ghosh, "Ruling Disconnects Telcos ...," Mint, February 3, 2012.

Time for a Leadership Transition

Going forward, the Tata Group focused on new technologies and innovation to drive its business in India and internationally. The aim of the group was to build multinational businesses that would achieve growth through excellence and innovation while balancing the interests of shareholders, employees, and civil society. Ratan believed that one of the biggest challenges for the group was retaining its value systems as it grew bigger and more diverse. He believed that the group had to expand the managerial perspective while retaining the same ethical and moral standards.

Ratan's age and the fact that he was a bachelor gave rise to concerns that his departure might result in the group's breakup.[54] There were also concerns that the value systems of the Tata Group might be lost because Ratan might be the last Tata to oversee the group. Some were of the view that after him, the future managers of the group might view the development projects and philanthropy as burdens during tougher times.

In August 2010, the Tata Group created a five-member committee to find a successor to Ratan. In late 2011, the committee zeroed in on Cyrus P. Mistry, a director of Tata Sons and the son of Pallonji Shapoorji Mistry, a construction tycoon who was the single largest shareholder of Tata Sons with an 18 percent stake. Mistry was also a relative of Ratan. On Mistry's selection, Morgen Witzel, the management writer who authored *Tata: The Evolution of a Corporate Brand*, said, "One of the key tasks of the leader of the Tata group is to act as guardian of the group's traditions and values and reputation, which are in turn a powerful part of its brand. An internal candidate will already have absorbed all of this, and be much more connected with the group."[55]

The Road Ahead

Under the two-decade reign of Ratan, the Tata Group had been transformed into a global company while still retaining its pre-eminent position in India. However, the belief that "Integrity" and "Tata" were synonymous had come into question following the 2G scam. At the end of his illustrious career, Ratan himself seemed to be frustrated with the level of corruption in his home country, which, he argued, had held his group back. In his words: "I think corruption has become worse and if you choose not to participate in this, you leave behind a fair amount of business…. You have a non-level playing field and those who do not participate in this (paying bribes) live at a disadvantage."[56]

In this scenario, one of Ratan's prime concerns was how to deal with the problem of bureaucratic delays, arbitrary regulatory decisions, and widespread corruption. His successor, Mistry, would soon have to decide which approach he wanted to take while managing the group. What if he considers corruption a normal part of doing business, especially while operating in emerging markets like India? How to ensure that his successors carried forward the legacy of ethical leadership of the Tata Group and do not view it as a burden?

Case Questions

1. Is corruption a normal part of business?
2. Corruption is often linked to the qualities of a particular country and society. Are some countries more corrupt and prone to crony capitalism than others?
3. What is your opinion about the Tata Group? What role did ethical leadership play in the success of the group?
4. What do you think of Ratan Tata's leadership? Do you think that Ratan was able to carry forward the legacy of the Tatas in letter and spirit?
5. What should Ratan Tata do to ensure that the group carries forward the legacy of ethical leadership of the Tata Group and does not view it as a burden while operating in emerging markets like India?

Endnotes

i. Tata Industries was set up by Tata Sons in 1945 as a managing agency for the businesses it promoted. Following the abolition of the managing agency system in the 1980s, Tata Industries' mandate was to promote the group's entry into new and high-tech areas.

ii. Until 1991, the Indian economy was mired in the so-called *license raj*, with government intervening quite a bit in normal businesses through quotas and sanctions on private business. All major industries were run by the government, including the telecommunications industry. This, coupled with the dire fiscal condition of the country, left India on the verge of bankruptcy and with foreign currency reserves sufficient for only two weeks of imports. In 1991, the economy was liberalized with most of the sectors and industries being privatized and government intervention being limited to only the issuing of mandatory permissions and allocating of resources wherever necessary.

iii. Rs. = Indian rupees. As of early 2012, US$1 was approximately equal to Rs. 50.

iv. Radio spectrum, a part of the atmosphere that transmits electromagnetic waves, enables transmission of all types of wireless signals. Spectrum is used to transmit all signals, including satellite, radar, mobile, and fixed telecommunications and broadcasting. Spectrum being a finite resource and vital for communications, government controls its usage by allocating each lode for specific transmission purposes. In this way, some part of it is allocated to commercial mobile communications, which in turn is allocated to mobile carriers based on certain criteria.

v. In May 2009, Telecom Watchdog, an NGO, submitted a complaint to the Central Vigilance Commission, an apex Indian governmental body to address governmental corruption, pointing out irregularities and requesting for an enquiry.

vi. The Indian telecom sector is divided into 23 service areas (commonly called circles) consisting of 19 state telecom circles and 4 metro service areas for providing Unified Access Services (UAS). Operators need to procure a separate license from the government to operate in each service area or circle.

[54]Pete Engardio and Nandini Lakshman, "The Last Rajah," www.business-week.com, August 13, 2007.

[55]PR Sanjai and John Satish Kumar, "Surprise Pick Mistry to Succeed Ratan Tata," www.livemint.com, November 24, 2011.

[56]"Corruption in India Has Become Worse: Ratan Tata," www.thehindubusinessline.com, August 24, 2011.

vii. Calculation of loss was based on the 3G auction in 2010.

viii. It was alleged that Raja had amassed bribes to the tune of Rs. 30 billion for favoring several telecom companies in the allocation of the 2G spectrum. (Source: "2G Scam: 'Raja Used Wife's a/c to Stash Bribe Money Abroad'," www.daijiworld.com, March 2, 2011.)

ix. M Karunanidhi was the then chief minister of Tamil Nadu. He was the leader of the DMK party to which A. Raja belonged. His daughter, Kanimozi, a member of the Indian parliament, was also arrested on charges of being associated with the 2G scam. The DMK party was a coalition partner of the United Progressive Alliance that was in power in India.

1 Integrative Term Project
2 IKEA in Russia: Emerging Market Strategies and Ethical Dilemmas

Integrative Term Project

This project requires research, imagination, and logic in applying the content of this course and book.

In groups of three to five students, create an imaginary company that you have been operating in the domestic arena for some time. Your group represents top management, and you have decided it is time to go international.

* Describe your company and its operations, relative size, and so forth. Give reasons for your decision to go international.

* Decide on an appropriate country in which to operate, and give your rationale for this choice.

* State your planned entry strategy, and give your reasons for this strategy.

* Describe the environment in which you will operate and the critical operational factors that you must consider and how they will affect your company.

* Give a cultural profile of the local area in which you will be operating. What are the workers going to be like? What kind of reception do you anticipate from local governments, suppliers, distributors, and so on?

* Draw up an organization chart showing the company and its overseas operations, and describe why you have chosen this structure.

* Decide on the staffing policy you will use for top-level managers, and give your rationale for this policy.

* Describe the kinds of leadership and motivational systems you think would be most effective in this environment. Give your rationale.

* Discuss the kinds of communication problems your managers might face in the host-country working environment. How should they prepare for and deal with these problems?

* Explain any special control issues for this overseas operation that concern you. How do you plan to deal with them?

* Identify the concerns of the host country and the local community regarding your operations there. What plans do you have to deal with their concerns and to ensure a long-term cooperative relationship?

"IKEA consistently combats corruption. All of our divisions operate completely transparently. The company has adopted a strict code of conduct and its provisions are binding not only for rank-and-file employees and executives, but also for business partners. These regulations are uniform throughout the world and Russia is no exclusion."[1]

– IKEA's Press Release following investigation of bribery cases
against former employees of IKEA Russia, July 2012

"People in the West know astonishingly little about Russia. Those who call themselves Russia experts usually don't understand the first thing about it. People who say they don't know much about Russia come much closer to understanding it."[2]

– Lennart Dahlgren,
Former Russia Country Manager for IKEA, February 2011

Introduction

In July 2012, a Turkish national, Okan Yunalan (Yunalan), who acted as an intermediary for Carl Ola Ingvaldsson (Ingvaldsson), former Head of the Leasing Department in IKEA's Russian subsidiary (IKEA MOS), to extract a bribe, was sentenced to five years in a high-security prison. Yunalan was found guilty of large-scale extortion after he demanded 6.5 million ruble (US\$ 225,000) from a company that sought to lease two premises at IKEA's Mega shopping complex in Tyoply Stan, a suburb in Moscow. Ingvaldsson and another accomplice managed to leave the country and Russia was seeking their extradition.

IKEA stated that it welcomed the investigation by Russian authorities into the incident and would co-operate fully with them. This was not the first instance of corruption seeping into its Russian operations negating its tough stance against the all-pervasive corrupt business environment in Russia.[3] IKEA was known for its uncompromising attitude toward corruption but it had not always been successful in ensuring that its employees adhered to its ethical standards.

The same year, the company came under the scanner of global environmental agencies when an investigative report revealed that it was utilizing ill-defined Russian logging rules to cut down old growth forests.[4] This raised questions about its claims of being an ecologically sensitive company that believed in sustainable logging practices.

[1]"IKEA Cooperates with Investigation in Cases against Executives," www .rapsinews.com, July 18, 2012.
[2]Svetlana Smetanina, "Addicted to Russia," http://rbth.ru, February 23, 2011.
[3]Augusto Come, "Corruption, Corruption, Corruption," www.opendemocracy .net, November 29, 2012.
[4]Old growth forests are those that have been left undisturbed for about 300 to 600 years, resulting in them exhibiting unique ecological features.

It was in the late 1990s that IKEA decided to enter the Russian market as part of its global expansion strategy. From its early days, the company had displayed a non-tolerance for corruption. This standpoint meant that it had to face several setbacks when setting up stores, inaugurating them, and even while advertising for them. However, there were also instances of support from authorities, whether local or federal, and of difficulties being smoothed out, which enabled the company to get things done faster than in any other country in the world.

Over the years, the company expanded and experienced success with its stores in Russia. Some of them, in fact, became the top grossers in the world for IKEA. It was also in Russia that the company introduced its successful new business model, wherein its furniture stores were operated not as standalone stores but as part of large shopping and entertainment complexes.

Though the company continuously faced and overcame the serious hurdles caused by the corrupt bureaucratic system, it finally decided to halt all expansion in Russia in 2009. The decision came in the wake of permission being denied to setup two if its stores, allegedly after it refused to pay bribes to safety inspectors. However, the top Russian ministry officials convinced the company to go ahead with its expansion in 2011.

As of 2012, with 14 existing stores (**See Exhibit I for more Information about Russia's IKEA Stores**), the company's expansion plan in Russia was on track, and it had plans to open several new stores and even a retail bank.

Background Note

IKEA, founded in Sweden was the most successful entrepreneurial venture of its founder Ingvar Kamprad (Kamprad). Kamprad was just a boy in the 1920s, when he began selling matches. He later graduated to selling flower seeds, greeting cards, Christmas tree decorations, pencils, and then ball-point pens.

In 1943, Kamprad set up a business with money given by his father. He called it IKEA (representing his own initials (I.K.), in addition to the first letter of his farm, Elmtaryd (E), and the village where he spent his childhood Agunnaryd (A)). IKEA started out selling products such as pens, wallets, picture frames, table runners, watches, jewelry, and nylon stockings, at discounted prices. In 1948, furniture made by local manufacturers was also sold through the business.

EXHIBIT I Russia's IKEA Stores

Store Location	Opened
Moscow Khimki	2000
Moscow Teply Stan	2001
St Petersburg Dybenko	2003
Kazan	2004
Moscow Belaya Dacha	2005
Nizhniy Novgorod	2006
St Petersburg Parnas	2006
Yekaterinburg	2006
Novosibirsk	2007
Rostov-on-Don	2007
AdygeaAdygea Kuban	2008
Omsk	2009
Samara	2009
Ufa	2010

Source: www.ikea.com

Over the years, the company took to advertising its products by various methods, including through catalogs. In 1953, the first IKEA furniture showroom was opened in Älmhult, Sweden. In 1956, the company took to designing its own furniture, adopting flat packaging and enabling self-assembly of the furniture. In the early 1960s, the 'IKEA Concepts'[5] of form, function, and price were created, with furniture designed accordingly.

Over the next three decades, the company launched some highly successful products such as the POÄNG armchair, the SKOPA chair, the ÖGLA chair, the BILLY Bookcases, the KLIPPAN sofa, the LACK table, the MOMENT, sofa and the STOCKHOLM furnishings. IKEA gradually expanded its footprint across Europe and North America, opening stores in Norway (1963), Denmark (1969), Switzerland (1973), Germany (1974), Australia (1975), Canada (1976), Austria (1977), the Netherlands (1979), France (1981), Belgium (1984), the US (1985), the UK (1987), and Italy (1989).

In 1982, the Stichting INGKA Foundation, based in the Netherlands, became the owner of the newly formed 'The IKEA Group'. In 1984, the customer club, 'IKEA Family', was launched. In 1991, the company started the industrial group, Swedwood, to produce wood-based furniture and wooden components. In addition, IKEA purchased several sawmills and production plants.

In 1997, IKEA launched its website, www.ikea.com. The same year, the company also launched Children's IKEA, with the focus on providing home furnishing solutions to cater to families having young children. In 2000, IKEA launched e-shopping in Sweden and Denmark. Over a period of time, it began providing this facility in several other countries.

The company continued its global expansion endeavor, opening stores in Hungary (1990), the Czech Republic, and Poland (1991), Spain (1996), China (1998), Russia (2000), Portugal (2004), and Japan (2006). The company also entered

into several partnerships to execute numerous social and environmental projects.

The company's business concept in all its markets was to offer furniture of simple designs at affordable prices. Though the company designed its own furniture and other items, it manufactured only a minimal portion; most of the supplies were made through a global network of contract manufacturers (a significant quota of these were located in emerging markets). The company's business strategy could be summed up as cheap labor, combined with expedient retail pricing.

With regard to human resources, IKEA claimed that it gave precedence to values and beliefs over skills, academics, or work experience in all of its standard jobs interviews. Prospective employees were expected to even take a culture quiz to determine if they fit in with the corporate culture.

IKEA strove hard to project itself as an environmentally conscious, ethical company. It took measures to ensure that the materials it used were sustainably sourced and the labor it employed met international labor regulations. By 2012, it hoped to fully implement the "IKEA Way", a roster of rules and regulations for its suppliers. It was also against child labor being used at its supplier's operations. The idea behind these rules was to provide the world with a clear picture on the origin, volume, and kind of wood used in IKEA's products.

Over the years, IKEA won several awards for its ethical practices. As of 2010, it had been recognized by the Ethisphere Institute[6] as one of the "World's Most Ethical Companies" in specialty retail for four consecutive years.

As of 2012, IKEA had 338 stores in 40 countries. Of IKEA's revenues, 80% came from Europe and the company had future plans to expand into Asian markets, especially India. By the end of the decade, IKEA expected to increase the number of its stores by 50% (to 500 stores) and to double its sales figures and customer numbers. IKEA was judged the "2012 World Retail Congress International Retailer of the Year" because of its superiority as compared to its peers in global profitability, branding, and strategizing.

Foray into Russia

Kamprad had been quite keen to do business in Russia since the 1960's, when it was still The Soviet Union.[7] However, he was unable to do so for quite a few decades for several reasons. IKEA's first attempt to begin Russian operations was stalled due to the collapse of the Soviet Union in 1991. A later attempt failed due to the 'Russian constitutional crisis of 1993[8] and the country's subsequent unfavorable economic scenario.

---

[5]IKEA believed in the practice of providing its products at prices which made them affordable to everyone. It was this belief that dictated the way it sourced its raw materials (maximizing their use), its production processes (cost effective and innovative) and its retail practices (reasonable pricing).

[6]The research-based Ethisphere Institute based in New York is concerned with the creation, advancement, and sharing of best practices in business ethics, corporate social responsibility, anti-corruption, and sustainability. It publishes a quarterly called the "Ethisphere Magazine".

[7]The Soviet Union or USSR (Union of Soviet Socialist Republics) was in existence between 1922 and 1991. It constituted 15 socialist states, which were ruled collectively by the Communist Party.

[8]The Russian constitutional crisis of 1993 occurred when a war erupted between the Russian President, Boris Yeltsin, and the Russian Parliament. The conflict that was spread over a period of 10 days gave rise to the deadliest street battle ever witnessed in Moscow. The issue was later resolved through the use of military force.

In 1998, Lennart Dahlgren (Dahlgren), a prominent IKEA employee, who was on the verge of retirement, was asked to oversee the setting up of IKEA's operations in Russia. Dahlgren stated that he, like many others in the West, had harbored several negative opinions about Russia, including the thought that the country was teeming with poor people. He quickly abandoned this view and came to realize that there was a large retail opportunity waiting to be tapped. In the early 2000s, a market report from A. T. Kearney, a global market consulting firm, stated that in terms of retail expansion, Russia was the top country in the world. The report further said, "With a growth rate of 30 percent for retail sales from 1999 to 2003 and a relatively sparse retail network to serve its growing market, Russia is full of promise."[9]

In time, Dahlgren also realized that Russia had a highly corrupt bureaucracy, which demanded bribes for getting anything done. However, in concurrence with IKEA's policy of zero tolerance of corruption, Dahlgren decided that he would not give in to the corrupt system. On the issue of companies dealing with corruption in Russia, Dahlgren said, "Companies interested in Russia should be absolutely up-front and honest in their dealings. When a foreign company pays bribes, there is no end to demands for bribes. In turn, foreign companies should feel an urgency to report corruption."[10]

Dahlgren entered into discussions with the Mayor of Moscow, Yuri Luzhkov (Luzhkov), with regard to the opening of the first IKEA store in that city. However, IKEA's endeavor to open a store in Moscow's prosperous Kutuzovsky Prospekt[11] fell through when it became a victim of vicious slander. Later, Luzhkov suggested that IKEA set up its store in a recently constructed building complex. But IKEA found the building impractical for setting up its store.

After some deliberation, IKEA came across a site it found suitable for setting up the store and approached Luzhkov to get a lease on the site. But the city authorities asked for sky high land lease rates that the company deemed to be economically unfeasible. Dahlgren said, "Buying land on these terms would make it impossible to keep low prices on products."[12]

Consequently, IKEA decided to move the project to a suburb 12 miles north of Moscow called Khimki, whose Mayor displayed a friendlier demeanor toward the setting up of the store. As soon as the construction of the Khimki store began, the 'Russian Financial Crisis' or the 'Ruble Crisis', broke out. The crisis was the result of the Russian Government's default on domestic debt and devaluation of the Ruble. The crisis period caused a jump in food prices and a break-out of mass protests. Millions lost their life savings. In spite of the setback it faced as a result of the crisis, the company continued with the construction of the store.

Opening of the Stores

In March 2000, IKEA's first store in Russia was opened at Khimki. The inaugural day drew a large crowd of 40,000 shoppers. People waited for an hour to get into the store and all the roads leading to it were backed up with traffic for miles around.

Analysts believed that by the time IKEA opened its first store there was a lot of pent up demand in Russia, especially from the middle class. It was a time of transition in the country, with the rising middle class looking to abandon the old world Soviet-era furniture in favor of the modern Scandinavian furniture showcased by IKEA.

At a time when furniture stores in Russia offered only two extreme choices, pricey furniture for the affluent and cheap stuff for the other classes, IKEA's offering of simple, sturdy furniture at affordable rates created quite a stir. Many of the shoppers expressed disbelief over the pricing of IKEA's items, with some of them even wondering whether they were priced in US dollars rather than Russian Rubles. Speaking on this issue, Dahlgren said, "We spent the first weekend writing the word 'ruble' on all the price tags."[13]

In contrast to other stores in Russia, IKEA laid emphasis on customer service. It had a highly selective process of recruitment, with its initial 440 employees picked from a total of 16,000 applicants. Moreover, the Store Supervisors, whom it termed the "Core Employees", were provided training at IKEA stores in other countries. Through its stores, IKEA also offered several other amenities such as free shuttle services from select places, a playroom for children and coffee to customers who came in early.

The store continued to be popular, with 100,000 visiting it even after a month. Within a year, IKEA opened another store in the Moscow region. The Russian IKEA stores were similar in size, structure, and style to their counterparts in other parts of the world. In the first year of operations, IKEA reported sales of more than US$ 100 million in Russia, three times more than what the company had expected. IKEA's Khimki store became one of its top 10 grossing stores in the whole world. The rousing response to the store's opening encouraged IKEA to formulate ambitious plans of expansion.

In addition, IKEA tested its new business model for the first time in Russia. The company observed that the land value of the areas surrounding its new stores greatly appreciated in value over a period of time. It decided to take advantage of this by trying to develop the areas around its stores into commercial complexes.

The company had a land lease for its store's sites extending for a period of 98 years, with the option to purchase it, if Russia ever allowed it. This gave it sufficient leeway to make use of the excess land to increase its business prospects. IKEA invited other stores selling electronics, hardware, and clothes, most of whom were leading international brands, to set up operations in its store sites. It also set up areas for leisure such as movie

[9]Curt Hazlett, "Russia is an alluring but sometimes scary place for Western retailers," www.icsc.org, May 2005.

[10]Lennart Dahlgren, "The Basics of Doing Business in Russia," http://blogs .hbr.org, October 25, 2010.

[11]Kutuzovsky Prospekt is one of the key streets in Moscow. It is flanked by expensive residential areas.

[12]Maria Antonova, "Ex-IKEA Boss Bares Russia's 'Chaotic Reality'," www .sptimes.ru, March 26, 2010.

[13]Colin McMahon, "Russians Flock to Ikea as Store Battles Moscow," http:// articles.chicagotribune.com, May 16, 2000.

theaters, ice rinks, and play areas in these complexes. Apart from that, the company created comfort zones which housed cafés, restaurants, childcare facilities, and baby care rooms.

This initiative enabled certain IKEA stores in Russia to be operated as enormous shopping and entertainment complexes, unlike in other countries where they were standalone furniture stores. Over the years, IKEA's new division called the 'Mega Mall', which was set up to manage these complexes, made more money than the standalone retail business.

However, the company did struggle to make profits in Russia until the mid-2000s. The main reasons for this were the high startup costs and the steep 25% tariff imposed on imported furniture. IKEA got only 13% of the furniture it sold at its stores locally made. Dahlgren was of the opinion that the company needed to produce 30% of its furniture locally in order to make its operations profitable.

Accordingly in April 2002, IKEA started production at its first Russian factory, in the vicinity of St. Petersburg. Built at a cost of US$ 15 million, the facility employed 250 people. Apart from opening a production facility, the company provided its local suppliers with credit of US$ 400 million to purchase equipment and arrange for credit. Russia had about 25% of the world's hardwood supply and the company's efforts to develop its production facilities there were expected to make Russia a major supplier for the company for its global operations.

A Growth Story Marred by Problems

However, it was not all smooth sailing for IKEA in its expansion plans. The business environment in Russia dictated that IKEA constantly faced problems with regard to its stores from government officials in the fire, health and safety, electricity, tax, customs, and other related departments. These officials reportedly discovered problems with IKEA stores, especially during critical times such as store openings. Analysts observed that IKEA would then be provided pointers by the same authorities to overcome these serious issues by way of some monetary payment or engaging a party recommended by them to rectify the problem.

A few weeks before the opening of its first store, IKEA was asked by the local utility department officials to pay a bribe to get an electricity connection for its stores. In order to counter this demand, IKEA decided to hire large diesel generators to power its stores. This became a standard practice for the company for most of its stores in Russia.

IKEA's earlier decision to move out of Moscow didn't go down well with the city authorities, causing them to hold a grudge against IKEA for a long time. When the company finally opened its first store, the Moscow City authorities did not give it permission to advertise the store in the Moscow metro. Dahlgren stated that the municipal authorities refused citing certain scientific studies which showed that people who used the underground had damaged psyches, thereby making IKEA's ads potentially harmful.

Later, when the company wanted to build an off-ramp over Leningrad Highway to ease traffic and enable customers to reach the Khimki store without hardship, Moscow put obstacles in its way. IKEA had not realized that the Leningrad Highway was controlled by Moscow City, rather than Khimki. Though IKEA had completed all formalities necessary to gain the necessary construction permits, once the construction began, the proceedings were halted by Luzhkov and his team. They refused to grant permission for construction of the off-ramp stating that it would thwart the view of a historic place called the Tank Trap monument, which depicted the place where the Red Army[14] obstructed the march of the German Nazi forces during World War II.[15]

The off-ramp stood half-constructed for about a year, causing hardship to customers and traffic snarls on the Leningrad Highway. Later, the company received permission to build the bridge after Kamprad appealed to Vladimir Putin[16] and the 200 other store owners in the complex protested against authorities on the issue.

However, IKEA did make certain compromises with regard to the construction. It agreed to get the off-ramp built by the company endorsed by the municipal authorities of Moscow. This cost the company in terms of cost and time, as it had to pay US$ 5 million more than the estimated cost. Besides, the off-ramp's construction took three times longer than necessary.

In 2003, the company planned to build a US$ 40 million warehouse in the Solnechnogorsky district of the Moscow region. Things worked out smoothly for the company as long as Deputy Governor Mikhail Men, who was well-disposed toward the company, was in office. Once he was discharged, the company began facing problems with authorities. Dahlgren accused Vladimir Popov, who was District Head at that time, of using the police to halt work at the warehouse. IKEA was given the go-ahead to continue work only after it donated US$ 30 million as aid to elderly people and hired a contractor endorsed by the regional government.

In December 2004, IKEA was all set to inaugurate its next store at Chimki, just outside of Moscow. The US$ 250 million store was one of the biggest in Europe with large boutiques, ice halls, children's play area, and cinema multiplex. The construction of the store began with the blessings of the Mayor of Khimki. However, when he was replaced with Vladimir Strelchenko (Strelchenko), an ex-military officer who showed marked indifference toward Western investors, the store's inauguration faced a major setback.

Officials stalled the store's opening saying that the road to the store ran over a gaspipe, making it dangerous. Therefore, the company was ordered to build a new roadway. It was another matter that the pipeline in question also passed

---

[14]Red Army or 'The Workers' and Peasants' Red Army' were the Soviet Union's communist war group, who were active during the time of the Russian Civil War (1918–22). Later, it became the national army of the USSR.

[15]World War II occurred during the period 1939–1945. Several major nations participated in it and it was considered to be the deadliest war in human history, due to the large number of human causalities and the use of nuclear weapons.

[16]Vladimir Putin has been the President of Russia since May 7, 2012. Previously, he had served as President from 2000 to 2008. He had also served as Prime Minister of Russia for the periods 1999–2000 and 2008–2012.

underneath a heavily used six-lane highway and a crucial railroad. Dahlgren stated that the company had agreed to construct a number of pressure reducers over the gas pipes, but the real reason the opening was stopped was because they had refused to pay bribes.

Dahlgren described the prevention of the store opening as "sabotage against Russia"[17] and raised his voice about the corruption dogging Russia, something which had never been done earlier by any official of a company doing business in Russia. He said, "Like all Western companies in Russia we're subject to blackmail, sabotage, and pressure for bribes. In many cases we're totally in the hands of local chieftains. IKEA is big in Russia and doesn't pay bribes."[18]

Dahlgren announced that the inauguration on December 10, 2004, would go ahead as scheduled. Though police forces blocked the store, Dahlgren and his team, along with the Swedish Ambassador to Russia held a grand opening ceremony. This incident drew the attention of the worldwide media and IKEA's plight gained it a lot of sympathy. At the same time, the Chimko municipal authorities drew harsh criticism. Strelchenko's superiors were worried about the incident and its possible ill-effects on Russia's reputation. They then put pressure on him to give the go-ahead for the mall's opening.

Even though Kamprad made several attempts to meet the political leadership of Russia, he was not able to meet either Putin or his successor Dmitry Medvedev.[19] In one such attempt in 2005 in which Dahlgren strove to arrange a meeting between Kamprad and Putin, he was told by a senior government official that it would cost US$ 5-10 million. Dahlgren said, "I sensed that it would be better not to get into that discussion any deeper."[20]

A Stop to Everything?

Fortunately for IKEA, it did not face only problems in Russia. There were instances when support from the authorities made things smoother. In 2005, IKEA opened another store called the 'Mega Kazan' in the Kazan region, 500 miles east of Moscow. The store was built in partnership with Ramstore hypermarket.[21] Mega Kazan went on to become the largest regional mall in Russia. Dahlgren said that the authorities in Kazan were very co-operative, which caused the store to be opened in record time. He said, "It took less than a year between the first meeting with Kazan's mayor and the store's opening — a record impossible to break anywhere in the world."[22]

Over a period of time, IKEA became the largest foreign retailer in Russia. The company invested US$ 4 billion in Russia over a period of 10 years, making it the country's sole largest foreign investor. It opened 14 stores and three manufacturing facilities, along with one distribution center. Company officials stated that IKEA's success was attracting other world retailers to set up their operations in Russia. The popularity of IKEA and its impact on the younger generation caused Russia's yuppies[23] to be named the 'IKEA Generation'. IKEA's Managing Director, Per Wendschlag said, "We are one of the top-selling IKEA countries in the world. The potential with 141 million people who are interested in consuming and furnishing their homes is big."[24]

However, despite its runaway success, IKEA put a freeze on its expansion in June 2009, after officials refused to give it permission to open two of its stores in the central cities of Samara and Ufa. According to Kirill Kabanov, Head of the NGO National Anti-Corruption Committee in Moscow, the reason for the non-opening of the stores was IKEA's refusal to give bribes to safety inspectors. Officials refused to give approval in Samara stating that the walls of the store were not in a condition to withstand hurricane-force winds, notwithstanding the fact that such weather conditions had never been experienced in that region.

A company official stated that the municipal authorities had recommended that IKEA use the services of a local construction company to "quickly help"[25] fix the construction deficiencies. Gigibulla Khasaev, Economic Development Minister for the Samara region, however, stated that the company's allegations were untrue and that IKEA was publicizing its complaints to divert attention from its substandard construction. He added, "To say the government is creating artificial barriers is an invention."[26]

IKEA stated that it was tired of being conned out of its money and was halting expansion. Kamprad claimed that the company had been swindled to the tune of US$ 190 million because of the failure of Russian authorities to provide electricity to its stores as promised. However, some incidents seemed to indicate that certain IKEA officials were bowing down to the all-encompassing corruption in Russia.

In 2009, IKEA discovered that the key executive responsible for renting the diesel generators had hyped up the rental charges in collaboration with the generator rental company, causing the company a loss of several million dollars.

In February 2010, IKEA fired two of its executives Per Kaufmann, a Director for IKEA in Eastern Europe, and Stefan Gross, a Director for IKEA's shopping mall business in Russia, for turning a blind eye to corruption.

Though they had not committed any personal indiscretion, their decision to overlook a corrupt transaction between a subcontractor of IKEA and an electricity company

[17]Curt Hazlett, "Russia is an alluring but sometimes scary place for Western retailers," www.icsc.org, May 2005.

[18]Andrew Osborn, "In Fear of His Life: Ikea's Man in Moscow Tells of Threats and Bribes," www.independent.co.uk, December 15, 2004.

[19]Dmitry Medvedev has been the Prime Minister of Russia since May 8, 2012. Previously, he had been President of Russia from 2008 to 2012.

[20]Maria Antonova, "Ex-IKEA Boss Bares Russia's 'Chaotic Reality'," www.sptimes.ru, March 26, 2010.

[21]Ramstore Hypermarkets are owned by Turkish retail giant, MigrosTürk Ticaret A.Ş. There are about a dozen Ramstore hypermarkets in Russia.

[22]Maria Antonova, "Ex-IKEA Boss Bares Russia's 'Chaotic Reality'," www.sptimes.ru, March 26, 2010.

[23]Yuppie stands for "young urban professional" or "young upwardly-mobile professional" and generally refers to the earning members of the upper middle class or upper class, in their 20s and 30s.

[24]"IKEA's Freeze Curtails Medvedev's Goal," www.themoscowtimes.com, March 15, 2011.

[25]"Why IKEA Is Fed Up with Russia," www.businessweek.com, July 2, 2009.

[26]"Why IKEA Is Fed Up with Russia," www.businessweek.com, July 2, 2009.

official in order to resolve a power-supply issue at IKEA's St. Petersburg mall, did somewhat dent IKEA's reputation for non-tolerance of corruption. Speaking on this issue, Kamprad said, "The documented mess in our Russian shopping center company is completely unacceptable. I have been too optimistic. It is shocking and deplorable that we have wandered off course."[27]

In April 2011, the Ministry of Economic Development of Russia got in touch with IKEA's senior leadership and persuaded them to carry on with their expansion plans in the country. Minister Elvira Nabiullina who met company executives claimed that IKEA had agreed not only to open new stores, but also to enhance its local manufacturing capability. Analysts felt that the company's meeting with the Russian senior ministry demonstrated a strategy of building relationships with authorities at the federal, rather than local level.

Apart from the rising cases of corruption being detected among its ranks, IKEA's image took a further beating when reports on its alleged unethical logging practices surfaced. In early 2012, a Swedish public service television came out with an investigative report that proclaimed that IKEA's subsidiary Swedwood cut down several hundred acres of old growth forests every year. This revelation caused various global conservation groups to condemn IKEA's logging practices. IKEA refuted the allegations and claimed that it was logging wood according to local guidelines.

However, analysts pointed out that IKEA was adhering to local guidelines that were highly questionable. Viktor Säfve, Chairman of Swedish NGO 'Protect the Forest', said, "This all comes down to a question of credibility and we believe that they are cheating their customers by claiming that the wood they use is sustainably sourced. The wood they are cutting down in Russia is from a high conservation area and we have the evidence to prove it. They are hiding behind flawed and criticized FSC accreditation."[28, 29] Analysts felt that IKEA should show greater responsibility in sourcing wood without taking advantage of defunct environmental guidelines in countries such as Russia and China, in which it mostly logged wood.

The Road Ahead

As of 2012, Russia was IKEA's primary target for expansion. Out of its three top globally performing stores, two were located in Russia. Apart from that, the country's extensive boreal or taiga forest belt was a source of high-quality timber. The company was also in the process of executing new business plans, such as the initiative to open a bank.

IKEA's journey reflected the fact that even though Russia was one of the fastest emerging markets of the world, and a part of the BRIC (Brazil, Russia, India and China), it was one of the toughest in which to do business.

Analysts said that the major stumbling block for business was the country's corrupt systems at both the regional and national levels. In Transparency International's[30] 2011 Corruption Perceptions Index, Russia was placed at 143rd position, on par with notorious nations such as Nigeria and Belarus. As per the cables published by Wikileaks,[31] it was estimated that bribery in Russia was worth US$ 300 billion per annum. Analysts opined that bribery was like another taxation system in the country, which benefited the political elite including the police and the Federal Security Service (FSB).[32]

Over the years, IKEA's clash with government officials across various store locations over corruption continued, prompting the Russian Government to come out with several promises that it would eradicate corruption. Speaking on this issue, Dahlgren said, "Officials regularly make public statements about increasing the war on corruption, bureaucracy, and abuse of office. But we did not notice any positive changes over all this time. While some legislation has changed for the better, the authorities have not."[33]

Political observers were of the opinion that unless Russia brought about major changes in its political system such as permitting the formation of a free press and allowing a genuine opposition to exist, which could then criticize government drafts, corruption and bribery would remain omnipresent. Speaking on this issue, Evgeny Kovrov, a Researcher at Retail Consultancy Magazin Magazinov, said, "Investors need dozens and dozens of approvals from an incredible number of agencies. That provides for unlimited corruption opportunities."[34]

On the other hand, analysts felt that corruption was an institutional problem and not a transactional issue. They agreed that multinationals took measures to ensure compliance of their conduct with their Code of Conduct, regulations prevalent in their home country, and internationally relevant rules and regulations. However, they felt that this was not enough to address a systemic problem like corruption, particularly in emerging nations. They were of the opinion that companies through 'Business Associations' and 'Chambers of Commerce' should develop a collective voice and strive for concrete steps to eradicate corruption.

As in Russia, IKEA passed through ethical minefields in certain other countries in which it had operations. In May 2012, it came to light that IKEA France had been spying on staff and disgruntled customers in that country over a long

---

[27]"Ikea Owner 'Distressed' Over Russian Expansion," www.thelocal.se, December 11, 2010.

[28]FSC (Forest Stewardship Council) includes some of the world's leading environmental NGOs who develop 'Principles and Criteria' - the highest standards of forest management which are environmentally appropriate, socially beneficial and economically viable.

[29]Annie Kelly, "Ikea to go 'Forest Positive'— But Serious Challenges Lie Ahead," www.guardian.co.uk, December 14, 2012.

[30]Transparency International is an international organization that measures corruption and publishes a comparative listing of corruption worldwide.

[31]Wikileaks is a non-profit organization which has been publishing secret and classified documents through its website launched in 2006.

[32]The Federal Security Service of the Russian Federation (FSB) is the successor to Soviet Committee of State Security (KGB). It is the primary domestic security agency of the Russian Federation whose responsibilities include ensuring security and gathering intelligence.

[33]Maria Antonova, "Ex-IKEA Boss Bares Russia's 'Chaotic Reality'," www.sptimes.ru, March 26, 2010.

[34]"Why IKEA Is Fed Up with Russia," www.businessweek.com, July 2, 2009.

period of time. The company had reportedly employed private detectives and gained access to police files illegally to gain information about them. To make amends, IKEA fired several key executives, including the country head.

In September 2012, a report released by research company, Ernst & Young claimed that East German political prisoners had been forced to manufacture products for an IKEA supplier for a period of 30 years. Speaking on this issue, Jeanette Skjelmose, IKEA's Sustainability Manager, said, "We deeply regret that this could happen. At the time, we did not yet have the well-organized control system we have today and clearly did not do enough to prevent this type of production method."[35]

It was obvious that IKEA's various global operations were floundering in their attempts to adhere to its own ethical standards. Speaking about the difficulty in maintaining the unique corporate culture and ethical stance across geographies, Christopher Bartlett, an emeritus professor at Harvard Business School said, "In any company that is as large and diverse as IKEA it does become a challenge [to maintain the culture]. There is often a tension between the corporate culture and a national culture."[36]

Case Questions

1. What are the various external factors which a company must take into account while devising a market entry strategy for a new country? Discuss these factors in the Russian context and in the actions taken by IKEA.

2. What is the impact of strong and co-operative political machinery on the business prospects of an emerging market? In this context, discuss IKEA's Russian sojourn. What should IKEA's business strategy be in the future?

3. What are the strategies that a company should use to grow its business in an emerging market? How do you establish a strong market presence in an underserved market? Discuss IKEA's strategy of establishing large shopping complexes instead of standalone shopping centers.

Suggested Readings and References

1. Anna Ringstrom, "One Size Doesn't Fit All: IKEA Goes Local for India, China," http://in.reuters.com, March 7, 2013.
2. "Ikea Announces Global Expansion Plans," www.oregonlive.com, January 23, 2013.
3. "IKEA Shopping Malls as Expansion Opportunity for Retailers," www.property-magazine.eu, November 22, 2012.
4. Mark Bergen, "IKEA in India: Heading into Untapped Retail Terrain," www.forbes.com, November 21, 2012.
5. Fiona Briggs, "IKEA's Mega Shopping Malls Are Gateway for Western Retailers to Enter Russia," http://retailtimes.co.uk, November 20, 2012.
6. Ben Quinn, "IKEA Apologizes over Removal of Women from Saudi Arabia Catalogue," www.guardian.co.uk, October 2, 2012.
7. Mark J. Miller, "IKEA Looks to Asia for Growth, as Russia's Old Growth (Trees) Cause Concerns," www.brandchannel.com, June 12, 2012.
8. Matt Hickman, "IKEA under Fire for Clearing Ancient Russian Forest," www.forbes.com, June 6, 2012.
9. "IKEA Sacks Four French Managers over Spying Scandal," www.telegraph.co.uk, May 18, 2012.
10. "IKEA to Open Bank in Russia," http://en.rian.ru, April 27, 2012.
11. Svetlana Smetanina, "Living in Russia as a Foreigner: The Memoirs of Former IKEA Boss Reveal an Unusual Truth," www.telegraph.co.uk, April 27, 2011.
12. Henry Meyer, "Corruption Halts IKEA in Russia," www.theage.com.au, March 7, 2011.
13. Henry Meyer, "Russia Repels Retailers as Ikea Halt Curtails Medvedev Goal," www.bloomberg.com, March 2, 2011.
14. "The Secret of IKEA's Success," www.economist.com, February 24, 2011.
15. Vivian Tse, "IKEA Owner 'Distressed' Over Russian Expansion," www.thelocal.se, December 11, 2010.
16. Jesse Heath, "IKEA in Russia: Now 'Everything Is Possible'…For A Price,"www.opendemocracy.net, February 22, 2010.
17. "Growing IKEA Russia Corruption Scandal – Two Execs Fired," http://therussiamonitor.com, February 15, 2010.
18. Andrew E. Kramer, "IKEA Tries to Build Public Case against Russian Corruption," www.nytimes.com, September 11, 2009.
19. "What IKEA's Decision to Halt Expansion in Russia Says about Corruption," www.goodhonestdollar.com, July 6, 2009.
20. Nataliya Vasilyeva, "Red Tape Stalls IKEA Russian Expansion," www.thestar.com, June 12, 2009.
21. www.ikea.com/ru/
22. eng.megamall.ru/company/Russia
23. www.ikea.com
24. www.retailbusinessrussia.com
25. www.pwc.com

---

[35]"Ikea 'regrets' forced labor use in East Germany," http://www.telegraph.co.uk, November 16, 2012.
[36]Richard Milne, "Ikea: Against the Grain," www.ft.com, November 13, 2012.

Glossary

achievement versus ascription   The source of power and status in society—one's achievement versus personal factors such as class, age, gender.

administrative distance   Lack of common trading bloc or currency, political hostility, nonmarket or closed economy.

affective appeals   Negotiation appeals based on emotions and subjective feelings.

appropriability of technology   The ability of an innovating firm to protect its technology from competitors and to obtain economic benefits from that technology.

appropriateness of monitoring (or control) systems   Systems that will not run counter to local practices, culture, and expectations.

appropriateness of technology   The use of technology in production or processes that is in line with local skills and level of development.

attribution   The process in which a person looks for an explanation of another person's behavior.

axiomatic appeals   Negotiation appeals based on the ideals generally accepted in a society.

B2B   Business-to-business electronic transactions.

B2C   Business-to-consumer electronic transactions.

balance-sheet approach   An approach to the compensation of expatriates that equalizes the standard of living between the host and home countries, plus compensation for inconvenience.

born global   Companies that start out with a global reach, typically by using their Internet capabilities.

CAFTA   The U.S.–Central America Free Trade Agreement.

chaebol   South Korea's large industrial conglomerates of financially linked, and often family-linked, companies that do business among themselves whenever possible—for example, Daewoo.

checklist approach   Measurement criteria to indicate changes in the creditworthiness of a country; ability to withstand economic volatility.

civil law   The comprehensive set of laws organized into a code; laws are interpreted based on codes and statutes; used in Europe and Japan.

clustering   Geographic concentrations of related, interdependent companies within an industry that use the same suppliers, labor, and distribution channels.

codetermination (mitbestimmung)   The participation of labor in the management of a firm.

collective bargaining   In the United States, for example, negotiations between a labor union local and management; in Sweden and Germany, for example, negotiations between the employer's organization and a trade union at the industry level.

collectivism   The tendency of a society toward tight social frameworks, emotional dependence on belonging to an organization, and a strong belief in group decisions.

common law   Law based on past court decisions and common custom (precedents); used in the United States and other countries of English origin.

communication   The process of sharing meaning by transmitting messages through media such as words, behavior, or material artifacts.

comparative advantage   A mutual benefit in the exchange of goods between countries in which each country exports products in which it is relatively more efficient in production than other countries.

competitive advantage of nations   The existence of conditions that give a country an advantage in a specific industry or in producing a particular good or service.

context in cultures (low to high)   Low-context cultures, such as Germany, tend to use explicit means of communication in words and readily available information; high-context cultures, such as those in the Middle East, use more implicit means of communication in which information is embedded in the nonverbal context and understanding of the people.

contract   An agreement by the parties concerned to establish a set of rules to govern a business transaction.

control system appropriateness   The use of control systems that are individually tailored to the practices and expectations of the host-country personnel.

convergence (of management styles, techniques, and so forth)   The phenomenon of increasing similarity of leadership styles resulting from a blending of cultures and business practices through international institutions, as opposed to the **divergence** of leadership styles necessary for different cultures and practices.

core competencies   Important corporate resources or skills that bring competitive advantages.

corporate social responsibility (CSR)   The belief that corporate activities should take into consideration the welfare of the various stakeholders affected by those activities.

CSV   Creating Shared Value (*see* shared value)

creeping expropriation   A government's gradual and subtle action against foreign firms.

creeping incrementalism   A process of increasing commitment of resources to one or more geographic regions.

creolization When countries fiercely protect their culture against outside influences and insist that immigrants assimilate into their society and respect their values.

cultural distance Differences in values, languages, religion, trust.

cultural diffusion When immigrants adopt some aspects of the local culture while keeping aspects of their culture of origin.

cultural noise Cultural variables that undermine the communications of intended meaning.

cultural savvy A working knowledge of the cultural variables affecting management decisions.

cultural sensitivity (cultural empathy) A sense of awareness and caring about the culture of other people.

culture The shared values, understandings, assumptions, and goals that over time are passed on and imposed by members of a group or society.

culture shock A state of disorientation and anxiety that results from not knowing how to behave in an unfamiliar culture.

culture-specific reward systems Motivational and compensation approaches that reflect different motivational patterns across cultures.

cybertheft Digital industrial espionage or interference (hacking); theft of financial or personal information through computers.

degree of enforcement The relative degree of enforcement, in a particular country, of the law regarding business behavior, which therefore determines the lower limit of permissible behavior.

dependency (in managing political risk) Keeping the subsidiary and the host nation dependent on the parent corporation.

differentiation Focusing on and specializing in specific markets.

direct control The control of foreign subsidiaries and operations through the use of appropriate international staffing and structure policies and meetings with home-country executives (as compared with **indirect control**).

distinctive competencies Strengths that allow companies to outperform rivals.

divergence *See* **convergence**.

domestic multiculturalism The diverse makeup of the workforce comprising people from several cultures in the home (domestic) company.

e-business The integration of systems, processes, organizations, value chains, and entire markets using Internet-based and related technologies and concepts.

e-commerce The sale of goods or services over the Internet.

e-commerce enablers Fulfillment specialists who provide other companies with services such as website translation.

economic distance Differences in level of development, natural or human resources, infrastructure, information, or knowledge.

economic risk The level of uncertainty about the ability of a country to meet its financial obligations.

environmental assessment The continuous process of gathering and evaluating information about variables and events around the world that may pose threats or opportunities to the firm.

environmental scanning The process of gathering information and forecasting relevant trends, competitive actions, and circumstances that will affect operations in geographic areas of potential interest.

ethical relativism An approach to social responsibility in which a country adopts the moral code of its host country.

ethnocentric approach An approach in which a company applies the morality used in its home country—regardless of the host country's system of ethics.

ethnocentric staffing approach An approach that fills key managerial positions abroad with persons from headquarters—that is, with parent-country nationals (PCNs).

ethnocentrism The belief that the management techniques used in one's own country are best no matter where or with whom they are applied.

expatriate One who works and lives in a foreign country but remains a citizen of the country where the employing organization is headquartered.

expressive-oriented conflict Conflict that is handled indirectly and implicitly, without clear delineation of the situation by the person handling it.

expropriation The seizure, with inadequate or no compensation, by a local government of the foreign-owned assets of an MNC.

Foreign Corrupt Practices Act A 1977 law that prohibits most questionable payments by U.S. companies to officials of foreign governments to gain business advantages.

foreign direct investment (FDI) A multinational firm's ownership, in part or in whole, of an operation in another country.

franchising An international entry strategy by which a firm (the franchiser) licenses its trademark, products, or services and operating principles to the franchisee in a host country for an initial fee and ongoing royalties.

fully owned subsidiary An overseas operation started or bought by a firm that has total ownership and control; starting or buying such an operation is often used as an entry strategy.

generalizability of leadership styles The ability (or lack of ability) to generalize leadership theory, research results, and effective leadership practices from one country to another.

geocentric staffing approach A staffing approach in which the best managers are recruited throughout the company or outside the company, regardless of nationality—often, third-country nationals (TCNs) are recruited.

geographical distance Remoteness, different time zones, weak transportation, or weak communication links.

global corporate culture An integration of the business environments in which firms currently operate, resulting from a dissolution of traditional boundaries and from increasing links among MNCs.

global functional structure Operations are integrated into the activities and responsibilities of each department to gain functional specialization and economies of scale.

globalism/globalization Global competition characterized by networks of international linkages that bind countries, institutions, and people in an interdependent global economy and a one-world market.

global geographic (area) structure Divisions are created to cover geographic regions; each regional manager is responsible for operations and performance of the countries within a given region.

globalization The global strategy of the integration of worldwide operations and the development of standardized products and marketing approaches.

global management The process of developing strategies, designing and operating systems, and working with people around the world to ensure sustained competitive advantage.

global management team Collection of managers in or from several countries who must rely on group collaboration if each member is to experience optimum success and goal achievement.

global product (divisional) structure A single product (or product line) represented by a separate division; each division is headed by its own general manager and is responsible for its own production and sales functions.

global staffing approach Staff recruited from within or outside of the company, regardless of nationality.

global strategic alliances Working partnerships that are formed around MNCs across national boundaries and often across industries.

governmentalism The tendency of a government to use its policy-setting role to favor national interests rather than relying on market forces.

guanxi The intricate, pervasive network of personal relations that every Chinese person carefully cultivates.

guanxihu A bond between specially connected firms, which generates preferential treatment to members of the network.

haptic Characterized by a predilection for the sense of touch.

hedging Companies' practice of taking out insurance or using local debt financing, for example, to reduce asset loss due to political risk.

high-contact culture A culture in which people prefer to stand close, touch a great deal, and experience a close sensory involvement.

high-context communication A type of communication in which people convey messages indirectly and implicitly.

high-context cultures Cultures where feelings and thoughts are not explicitly expressed; communication is implicit and as a function of the context and understanding of the person.

horizontal organization (dynamic network) A structural approach that enables the flexibility to be global and act local through horizontal coordination, shared power, and shared decision-making across international units and teams.

host-country national (HCN) A worker who is indigenous to the local country where the plant is located.

human capital Direct or subcontracted employees whose labor becomes part of the value-added assets of the firm's product or service. MNCs are increasingly offshoring (outsourcing) that asset around the world to lower the cost of human capital.

IJV control How a parent company ensures that the way a joint venture is managed conforms to its own interest.

indirect control The control of foreign operations through the use of reports, budgets, financial controls, and so forth. *See also* **direct control**.

individualism The tendency of people to look after themselves and their immediate families only and to value democracy, individual initiative, and personal achievement.

information privacy The right to control information about oneself.

information technology (IT) Electronic systems to convey information.

inpatriates Managers with global experience who are transferred to the organization's headquarters country.

instrumental-oriented conflict An approach to conflict in which parties tend to negotiate on the basis of factual information and logical analysis.

integration Coordination of markets.

intercultural communication Type of communication that occurs when a member of one culture sends a message to a receiver who is a member of another culture.

internal analysis A way to determine which areas of a firm's operations represent strengths or weaknesses (currently or potentially) compared to competitors.

internal versus external locus of control Beliefs regarding whether a person controls his own fate and events or are controlled by external forces.

international business The profit-related activities conducted across national boundaries.

international business ethics The business conduct or morals of MNCs in their relationships to all individuals and entities with whom they come in contact when conducting business overseas.

international codes of conduct The codes of conduct of four major international institutions that provide some consistent guidelines for multinational enterprises relative to their moral approach to business behavior around the world.

international competitor analysis The process of assessing the competitive positions, goals, strategies, strengths, and weaknesses of competitors relative to one's own firm.

internationalization The process by which a firm gradually changes in response to the imperatives of international competition, domestic market saturation, desire for expansion, new markets, and diversification.

international joint venture (IJV) An overseas business owned and controlled by two or more partners; starting such a venture is often used as an entry strategy.

international management The process of planning, organizing, leading, and controlling in a multicultural or cross-cultural environment.

international management teams Collections of managers from several countries who must rely on group collaboration if each member is to achieve success.

international social responsibility The expectation that MNCs should be concerned about the social and economic effects of their decisions regarding activities in other countries.

Islamic law The dominant legal system in Islamic countries; based on religious beliefs and followed in approximately 27 countries.

joint venture A new independent entity jointly created and owned by two or more parent companies.

keiretsu Large Japanese conglomerates of financially linked, and often family-linked, groups of companies, such as Mitsubishi, that do business among themselves whenever possible.

kibun Feelings and attitudes (Korean word).

kinesics Communication through body movements.

kinesic behavior Communication through posture, gestures, facial expressions, and eye contact.

knowledge management The process by which the firm integrates and benefits from the experiences and skills its employees learn, for example, when repatriating managers from the host country.

labor relations The process through which managers and workers determine their workplace relationships.

licensing An international entry strategy by which a firm grants the rights to a firm in the host country to produce or sell a product.

localization approach When firms focus on the local market needs for product or service characteristics, distribution, customer support, and so on.

low-context cultures Societies where people convey their thoughts and plans in a direct, straightforward communication style; communication and information is explicit.

locus of decision making The relative level of decentralization in an organization—that is, the level at which decisions of varying importance can be made—ranging from all decisions made at headquarters to all made at the local subsidiary.

love–hate relationship An expression describing a common attitude of host governments toward MNC investment in their country—they love the economic growth that the MNC brings but hate the incursions on their independence and sovereignty.

low-contact culture Cultures that prefer much less sensory involvement, standing farther apart and touching far less; a distant style of body language.

low-context communication One in which people convey messages directly and explicitly.

macropolitical risk event An event that affects all foreign firms doing business in a country or region.

managing environmental interdependence The process by which international managers accept and enact their role in the preservation of ecological balance on the earth.

managing interdependence The effective management of a long-term MNC subsidiary–host-country relationship through cooperation and consideration for host concerns.

maquiladoras U.S. manufacturing or assembly facilities operating just south of the U.S.–Mexico border under special tax considerations.

masculinity The degree to which traditionally masculine values—assertiveness, materialism, and the like—prevail in a society.

material culture *See* **object language**.

matrix structure A hybrid organization of overlapping responsibilities.

micropolitical risk event An event that affects one industry or company or only a few companies.

MIS adequacy The ability to gather timely and accurate information necessary for international management, especially in less-developed countries.

monochronic cultures Cultures in which time is experienced and used in a linear way; there is a past, present, and future, and time is treated as something to be spent, saved, wasted, and so on. *See also* **polychronic cultures**.

moral idealism The relative emphasis on long-term, ethical, and moral criteria for decisions versus short-term, cost–benefit criteria. *See also* **utilitarianism**.

moral universalism A moral standard toward social responsibility accepted by all cultures.

multicultural leader A person who is effective in inspiring and influencing the thinking, attitudes, and behavior of people from various cultural backgrounds.

multidomestic (or multi-local) strategy Emphasizing local markets, allowing more local responsiveness and specialization.

multinational corporation (MNC) A corporation that engages in production or service activities through its own affiliates in several countries, maintains control over the policies of those affiliates, and manages from a global perspective.

nationalism The practice by a country of rallying public opinion in favor of national goals and against foreign influences.

nationalization The forced sale of an MNC's assets to local buyers with some compensation to the firm, perhaps leaving a minority ownership with the MNC; often involves the takeover of an entire industry, such as the oil industry.

nearshoring Outsourcing jobs close to the domestic country of the firm or close to the firm's markets.

negotiation The process by which two or more parties meet to try to reach agreement regarding conflicting interests.

neutral versus affective Level of emotional orientation in relationships.

noise Anything that serves to undermine the communication of the intended meaning.

noncomparability of performance data across countries The control problem caused by the difficulty of comparing performance data across various countries because of the variables that make that information appear different.

nontask sounding (*nemawashi*) General, polite conversation and informal communication before meetings.

nonverbal communication (body language) The transfer of meaning through the use of body language, time, and space.

object language (material culture) How we communicate through material artifacts, whether architecture, office design and furniture, clothing, cars, or cosmetics.

objective–subjective decision-making approach The relative level of rationality and objectivity used in making decisions versus the level of subjective factors, such as emotions and ideals.

open systems model The view that all factors inside and outside a firm—environment, organization, and management—work together as a dynamic, interdependent system.

openness Traits such as open-mindedness, tolerance for ambiguity, and extrovertedness.

organizational culture (as different from societal culture) The norms and generally accepted ways of doing things within an organization.

outsourcing or offshoring The use of professional, skilled, or low-skilled workers located in countries other than that in which the firm is domiciled.

paralanguage How something is said rather than the content—the rate of speech, the tone and inflection of voice, other noises, laughing, or yawning.

parent-country national (PCN) An employee from the firm's home country sent to work in the firm's operations in another country (*see also* **expatriate**).

parochialism The expectation that foreigners should automatically fall into host-country patterns of behavior.

political risk The potential for governmental actions or politically motivated events to occur in a country that will adversely affect the long-run profitability or value of a firm.

polycentric staffing approach An MNC policy of using host-country nationals (HCNs) to fill key positions in the host country.

polychronic cultures Cultures that welcome the simultaneous occurrence of many things and emphasize involvement with people over specific time commitments or compartmentalized activities. *See also* **monochronic cultures**.

posturing General discussion that sets the tone for negotiation meetings.

power distance The extent to which subordinates accept unequal power and a hierarchical system in a company.

privatization The sale of government-owned operations to private investors.

projective cognitive similarity The assumption that others perceive, judge, think, and reason in the same way.

proxemics The distance between people (personal space) with which a person feels comfortable.

protectionism A country's use of tariff and nontariff barriers to close its borders partially or completely to various imported products that would compete with domestic products.

quantitative approach A means to develop a composite index used to monitor a country's creditworthiness and compare with other countries.

questionable payments Business payments that raise significant ethical issues about appropriate moral behavior in either a host nation or other nations.

regiocentric staffing approach An approach in which recruiting for international managers is done on a regional basis and may comprise a specific mix of PCNs, HCNs, and TCNs.

regionalization strategy The global corporate strategy that links markets within regions and allows managers in each region to formulate their own regional strategy and cooperate as quasi-independent subsidiaries.

regulatory environment The many laws and courts of the nation in which an international manager works.

relationship building The process of getting to know one's contacts in a host country and building mutual trust before embarking on business discussions and transactions.

repatriation The process of reintegration of expatriates into the headquarters organization and career ladder as well as into the social environment.

reshoring Bringing outsourced jobs back to the firm's domestic country.

resilience Traits such as having an internal locus of control, persistence, a tolerance of ambiguity, and resourcefulness.

reverse culture shock A state of disorientation and anxiety that results from returning to one's own culture.

ringi system Bottom-up decision-making process used in Japanese organizations.

self-reference criterion An unconscious reference to one's own cultural values; understanding and relating to others only from one's own cultural frame of reference.

separation The retention of distinct identities by minority groups unwilling or unable to adapt to the dominant culture.

shared value (CSV: Creating Shared Value) When the firm initiates internal and community plans to integrate with the community for mutual long-term benefits.

specific or diffuse Relative level of privacy in relationships.

stages model *See* **structural evolution**.

stereotyping The assumption that every member of a society or subculture has the same characteristics or traits, without regard to individual differences.

strategic alliances Partnerships between two or more firms that decide they can pursue their mutual goals better by combining their resources and competitive advantages.

strategic alliances (global) Working partnerships between MNCs across national boundaries and often across industries.

strategic business unit (SBU) A self-contained business within a company with its own functional departments and accounting systems.

strategic freedom of an IJV The relative amount of control that an international joint venture will have, compared with the parents, in choosing suppliers, product lines, customers, and so on.

strategic implementation The process by which strategic plans are realized through the establishment of a *system of fits* throughout an organization with the desired strategy—for example, in organizational structure, staffing, and operations.

strategic planning The process by which a firm's managers consider the future prospects for their company and evaluate and decide on strategy to achieve long-term objectives.

strategy The basic means by which a company competes: the choice of business or businesses in which it operates and how it differentiates itself from its competitors in those businesses.

structural evolution (stages model) The stages of change in an organizational structure that follow the evolution of the internationalization process.

subcultures Groups within a societal culture that differ in some degree from one another.

subculture shock A state of disorientation and anxiety that results from the unfamiliar circumstances and behaviors encountered when exposed to a different cultural group in a country than one the person is familiar with.

SWOT analysis An assessment of a firm's capabilities (strengths and weaknesses) relative to those of its competitors as pertinent to the opportunities and threats in the environment for those firms.

subsidiary A business incorporated in a foreign country in which the parent corporation holds an ownership position.

sustainability The ability for firms to operate on the principles of sustainable development.

sustainable development Business activities that meet the needs of the stakeholders in the present while also protecting and sustaining future needs for human and natural resources.

synergy The greater level of effectiveness that can result from combined group effort than from the total of each individual's efforts alone.

technoglobalism A phenomenon in which the rapid developments in information and communication technologies (ICTs) are propelling globalization and vice versa.

terrorism The use of, or threat to use, violence for ideological or political purposes.

third-country nationals (TCNs) Employees hired from a country other than the headquarters or the host country of a firm's activities.

transnational corporations (TNCs) Multinational corporations that are truly globalizing by viewing the world as one market and crossing boundaries for whatever functions or resources are most efficiently available; structural coordination reflects the ability to integrate globally while retaining local flexibility; typically owned and managed by nationals from different countries.

transpatriate A term similar to *expatriate* but referring to managers who may be from any country other than that in which the firm is domiciled and who tend to work in several countries over time—that is, a manager who has no true corporate home.

turnkey operation When a company designs and constructs a facility abroad, trains local personnel, and turns the key over to local management, for a fee.

uncertainty avoidance The extent to which people feel threatened by ambiguous situations; in a company, this results in formal rules and processes to provide more security.

universalism versus particularism The relative obligation toward an objective application of rules, versus a more personal and individual application.

utilitarianism The relative emphasis on short-term cost–benefit (utilitarian) criteria for decisions versus those of long-term, ethical, and moral concerns. *See also* **moral idealism**.

values A person or group's ideas and convictions about what is important, good or bad, right or wrong.

virtual global teams Employees in various locations around the world who coordinate their work and decisions through teleconferencing, email, and so on.

work centrality The degree of general importance that working has in the life of an individual at any given time.

workforce diversity The phenomenon of increasing ethnic diversity in the workforce in the United States and many other countries because of diverse populations and joint ventures; this results in intercultural working environments in domestic companies.

works council In Germany, an employee group that shares plant-level responsibility with managers.

World Trade Organization (WTO) A formal structure for continued negotiations to reduce trade barriers and settle trade disputes.

Index